ADVANCED INDUSTRIAL PSYCHOLOGY

Ram Nath Sharma
S.S. Chandra

Published by

ATLANTIC

PUBLISHERS & DISTRIBUTORS (P) LTD

7/22, Ansari Road, Darya Ganj, New Delhi-110002
Phones : +91-11-40775252, 23273880, 23275880, 23280451
Fax : +91-11-23285873
Web : www.atlanticbooks.com
E-mail : orders@atlanticbooks.com

Branch Office
5, Nallathambi Street, Wallajah Road, Chennai-600002
Phones : +91-44-64611085
E-mail : chennai@atlanticbooks.com

Printed in India at Nice Printing Press, A-33/3A, Site-IV, Industrial Area, Sahibabad, Ghaziabad, U.P.

PREFACE

Advanced Industrial Psychology is that branch of Psychology which examines human behaviour under modern industrial circumstances. The study of human behaviour covers both external behaviour and inner feelings in which research is carried out on the concerned behavioural problems that arise in an industrial environment. The Advanced Industrial Psychology plays an important role in industry in increasing production, promoting harmonious relationship among workers and in creating better understanding between labour and management.

This book covers the undergraduate and postgraduate syllabi of all the Indian Universities. Its subject matter has been planned and treated according to the weightage given to different topics in the University syllabi. Based upon standard books, it studies industrial psychology in the setting of Indian conditions. While data have been gathered from standard books and reputed research journals published in the West, an attempt has been made to give the reader an insight into the problems of Indian industrial conditions and Indian labourers. Causes of their problems have been explored and suggestions advanced for amelioration of their conditions. Thus, the book is equally useful for all those concerned with industry and labour. It includes a discussion of the problems of industrial management and their solutions, and illustrates psychological tests and methods of measurement along with vocational guidance to the reader so that he may develop an understanding for the choice of a career and achievement of job satisfaction.

The method of presentation in this landmark publication is lucidly analytic with central headings, side headings and sub-headings given in different types to facilitate understanding. Each point has been discussed in a separate paragraph. Illustrations have been given wherever required.

The book will be an indispensable source for all professionals, researchers and students in the field of Psychology and for anyone working in the related areas for acquiring an up-to-date overviews.

Although we have done our best to make this book an ideal textbook, yet suggestions are invited for improvement of the book in its next edition.

RAM NATH SHARMA
S.S. CHANDRA

CONTENTS

Volume II

1

IMPACT OF INDUSTRIALIZATION

The interweaving of human relations results in society. The human relations are determined by human attitudes. The pattern of human relations and the nature of human civilization and culture mutually determine each other. The pattern of human relations in an agricultural society is quite different from that of the industrial society. The measure of social relations in the primitive society is widely different. In short, the structure of society is determined by the trade and profession of the society and the attitudes of the members towards these. The social relations found in modern industrial society are very complex and intricate compared to the simple and straightforward social relations found in ancient societies. The industrialization has affected the society in every respect. The customs and traditions, the fashion and manners, the ways and modes of living all have been deeply influenced by industrialization. The processes of industrialization are intimately related with scientific processes. Therefore, the attitude of the members of industrial society becomes scientific. In an industrial society, the superstitions and blind faiths have no place. People expect and demand rational explanation of every phenomenon. The reason and not faith is the touchstone of every action and belief in the industrial society. The freedom of thought and individualism are the cornerstones of the industrial society. The methods and means of social control have changed. The ancient institutions of marriage and family have also changed. The old values and rules pertaining to religion and morals are undergoing radical changes. The new patterns of social stratification are being established. The caste system is being replaced by the class system. Even the means of recreation and entertainment are undergoing change in industrial urban society. Thus it is apparent that industrialization has influenced every aspect of society. It is not quite easy to judge if this impact is good or bad; but it is possible to study the consequences flowing from industrialization. The following discussion is an attempt to make an in-depth study of the impact of industrialization upon various aspects of society.

IMPACT UPON SOCIAL INSTITUTIONS

The institutions of marriage and family are to be found in every society. With the changes in the structure of society, these institutions also undergo changes. Traditionally the Indian society has recognized marriage to be a sacred and religious institution but in the modern industrial society, it has been reduced to a contract. In the past marriage was considered to be a permanent and inalienable bond which could not be terminated at will. But now, under the impact of industrialization, divorce and marriage go side by side. Now it is not considered an evil to terminate the contentious and miserable marriages. The following discussion will make explicit the impact of industrialization upon marriage :

(1) Marriage is a social contract Prior to heavy industrialization of India, marriage in this country was considered to be a religious and sacred institution. It was commonly believed by Hindus that marriage was necessary for emancipation or salvation and that anyone who did not marry could not find salvation in this life. Besides, marriage was regarded to be a permanent bond. Marriages were supposed to be made in heaven and only God could sever a marital bond. But with the advance of industrialization, these beliefs are considered superstitious and anyone holding them is frowned upon. Today marriage is regarded to be only a social contract between a man and a woman. The aim of marriage in modern times has ceased to be spiritual and now its aims are economic, social and biological only.

(2) Higher age of marriage In Indian society only a few decades back, parents used to marry their children at very early age. Child-marriages were quite common. But with the industrialization, the age of marriage is advancing; it is getting higher and higher. In metropolitan towns of India today, boys and girls are generally marrying at the ages of 25 to 35.

(3) Practice of non-marrying As we have referred to above the aim of marriage in India is no longer spiritual; the marital bond is no longer looked upon as sacred or inviolable. As a consequence of rejection of the traditional beliefs and attitudes, many young men and women in big towns prefer to live single. According to the thinking and beliefs of these young persons, the major need filled by marriage is biological and this can be easily satisfied out of wedlock.

(4) Practice of love marriages In industrial society men and women usually work together. In mills, factories, offices and other places men and women work together. Under these circumstances they get a chance of coming together, meeting and exchanging ideas and opinions. As a result of this human concourse, individuals become intimate and the intimacy becomes love which ultimately blossoms in marriage.

(5) Increase in divorce cases The industrial society is becoming more and more complex everyday. The philosophy of individualism is flourishing in society. Even husband and wife have different outlook and attitude. Both of them as a rule work in separate social spheres. As a result of this, marital bonds are from time to time rent by discord. The mental conflict increases and the situation of divorce develops. In all industrial societies today there is legal sanction for divorce.

The foregoing discussion makes plain the influence of industrialization upon marriage. Besides affecting the institution of marriage, the industrialization produces effects upon the institution of family. Following are some of the important effects of industrialization upon family.

(1) Difference regarding function of family As a result of industrialization the function of family has changed considerably. Compared to today the family had much more functions in the past. Now a number of functions which used to be performed by families in the past have been taken over by other institutions. Traditionally an Indian family used to be a centre of birth, rearing and education of children. The children used to get training in the ancestral profession. The function of socialization of children, too, used to be performed by the family. But in the industrialized society of today, the family is not required to fulfil these roles. Today children are born in hospital. Even for the nurture of the children, there are today a number of official and non-official institutions. In big towns we find today a number of Infant-Care Centres and Children Homes. The education of children today is done in schools and not in homes. The professional training also is no longer the obligation of the family. What is even more, even feeding is no longer the exclusive obligation of the family. Many people in metropolises eat out of homes. In almost all big cities, people rarely take lunch at home except on Sunday and holidays. In many families both husband and wife go out for work. In these circumstances the functions of a modern family are more formal than real.

(2) Breaking-up of joint family Traditionally most of the Indian families were joint families. As a result of industrialization, most of these joint families are breaking up and are being replaced by nuclear families. There are a number of reasons for this. Firstly, in industrial towns there is acute shortage of residential accommodation. Most of the people have to content themselves with a single- or two-room accommodation. In these circumstances it is physically exceedingly difficult if not impossible to retain the joint family system. Secondly, as a sequel to industrialization, family trades and profession have been eliminated. The sons of the same parents differ widely in respect of economic and social levels. This has given rise to individualism. As a result of all these conditions, joint family is all but finished in industrial towns.

(3) Small families As a result of industrialization, the cost of living has gone up. At the same time standard of living has also gone up considerably. Everybody wants good clothes, houses and other comforts of life. Obviously, it is not possible to maintain the standard with a big family. Therefore, people these days want to keep small families. The prevalence of contraceptives and abortion has made this goal easily attainable. Thus we find that there is a strong trend towards small families in industrialized towns.

(4) Change in the status of women In past the status enjoyed by women in Indian society was rather low. Women were shut up in the four walls of the home. From economic and social points of view, woman was subject to man. The woman enjoyed no independence. Without husband the condition of a woman was miserable. As a result of industrialization there has been much improvement in the status of women. Along with men, women today work in all walks of life. They are therefore becoming independent economically. Their status and respect in society have therefore improved considerably. Nowadays women consider themselves equal, even superior, to men. As a result of this feeling, many women today do not like to marry. They wish to assert their independence by defying the laws of the society.

(5) Disintegration of family As a result of industrialization, the outlook of intense individualism has grown. Everyone wants to have his own way; no one likes to be subject to anybody. Nobody these days appreciates the need for adjustment and give and take. Thus we find in modern society families cracking up under least strain. There is continuous tension and conflict in the minds of family members. As a consequence of this situation, it is small wonder that families are breaking up fast in urban society.

(6) Difference in family goals The goals and ideals which nourished the traditional Indian family were spiritual and religious. The housewife used to regard her husband as a god or divine being. They willingly subjected themselves to each and every whim of their husbands. Even children used to give unqualified respect to their parents. The father was regarded to be the head of the family and his command was rarely defied. In Indian homes Ram and Sita were ideals of paternal devotion and wife's dedication to husband respectively. In industrial society there is no room for such ideals. For a modern wife, the husband can be at best an honourable colleague and, under no circumstances, a god. The status of father in a family is being lowered as a result of industrialization. Compared to parents, children now have more say in the family affairs. In the past, the functions which were regarded sacred duty and ideals are now considered acceptable only from utilitarian point of view. The father no longer holds sway over family members.

Impact of Industrialization upon Social Stratification

From times immemorial human society has been riddled with inequalities and discriminations. From the very beginning of civilization we find some or other form of hierarchy in society. The society has always been divided into various classes having different rights and privileges and each enjoying a unique distinction and status in society. The classification and stratification in society have always been governed by some definite principles. As a matter of fact, neither all persons in a society are equal nor are the various functions in the society of equal value. Therefore, in order to maintain some system and order in society, it is necessary to establish a hierarchy of functions in society. In different societies the principle behind the hierarchical arrangement of functions is different. In some societies the distinction between classes is based on the relationship of master and slave while in others it is based upon the ideas of high, low and middle classes. Still in some other societies the governing principle of this distinction is caste system. In the modern industrial society, the classification and stratification of society are based upon the concept of economic classes. The society today is divided into the classes of capitalists and labour.

As referred to above, the basis of distinction between classes in society is different in different countries and at different times. This basis is sometimes biologic, sometimes historic and sometimes religious. As a matter of fact, in the stratification of any society, are reflected its values and ideals. In a religious society the gurus and godmen enjoy a place of pride. In a martial society warriors and conquerors occupy top positions. On the other hand, in a capitalist society, the wealthy persons are on top. In some industrialized societies like Japanese, the technocrats occupy privileged positions. Thus, it is apparent that in different societies, the basis of distinction among classes is different.

Basis of Stratification in Industrial Societies

In industrial societies there is a unique kind of social stratification. In industrial society the different strata of society are known as social classes. The basis of stratification in an industrial society is different from that of other societies. Generally social stratification in an industrial society occurs on the following fourfold bases :

(1) Occupation (2) Education

(3) Income (4) Birth

Now we shall study these in a little detail :

(1) Occupation In industrial societies the main basis of social stratification is occupation. In these societies the status and prestige of an individual are determined by the position and rank he occupies, the nature of his profession and his rank and status in that profession. What is meant is that rank and status are of crucial importance in industrial society. Indeed in an industrial society, rank and occupation are indicative of one's ability. The rank and status and occupation are not hereditary in industrial society; one has to strive and struggle for these. In a society where caste system is prevalent, the occupations and professions are hereditary. The son of a Brahmin does the job of a Brahmin and enjoys the same status and respect in society as were being enjoyed by his father. The son of a Brahmin becomes automatically entitled to respect and status of his father. On the contrary, in an industrial society, the son of a manager cannot claim the post of manager after the retirement of his father. He must possess all the necessary qualifications for it, that is, he must earn the managership. In order to gain status in an industrial society one has to strive hard. In an industrial society, there is no value for heredity but one has to strive for status.

(2) Education In an industrial society education is an important determinant of the status of a person. The better educated are regarded more highly than the less educated. Of course, in every society, the poets, writers and learned have got top rank and status. However in industrial society there is some difference in this regard from other societies. The industry has closer relation to science and technology than formal learning. This is why a person who is highly learned is not regarded so well as a person who is proficient in science and technology. In an industrial society it is not literary learning but the scientific learning that commands respect. As a consequence of industrialization the importance and value of subjects like philosophy and literature have gone down. The formal learning has been replaced by utilitarian subjects. The predominant outlook in education today is pragmatic. Naturally training in science and technology is conducive of industrial advance. It is applied science that is responsible for industrialization. On account of the utilitarian nature of science and technology, the scientists and technologists enjoy places of prestige in industrial society.

(3) Income Nowadays in industrial societies, the measuring rod of one's social status is one's income; the higher one's income, the higher one's social status. In materialistic societies, one's material possessions are indeed the exclusive determiner of one's worth in the society. The rich are worshipped and poor are hated. According to the materialistic outlook, the possession of material comforts and luxuries is the paramount aim of life and the more are one's material possessions nearer is one to the *summum bonum* of life. For acquisition of material comforts, money is needed. Therefore a person's income or salary determine his status in the society.

There is another reason also for regarding money and wealth as criterion of social status. In the industrial societies, the various types of qualifications are needed for earning money; without these qualifications it is not possible to earn wealth. A man must be laborious and hard-working in order to earn lots of money. It is natural in that background that one's wealth should be regarded as a measure of one's abilities and qualifications. It is but natural to accord high status to a man of ability. Thus, from both points of view, money and income are the determiner of one's social status.

(4) Birth In the determination of social status, one's birth and pedigree have always been kept in view. In different societies the family into which one is born has been regarded important in various ways. In the caste-based societies, the son of Brahmin was accorded the status of Brahmin without the slightest consideration of his actual merit. In feudal societies, the family had great importance in determining one's social status. In industrial society, too, the family has unique importance in determining the social status of a person. However, the reasons for the importance of family in social stratification in industrial society are not the same as in caste-based or feudal society. In an industrial society it is recognized that in order to develop or flower one's talents, the family plays an important role. A successful manager and technocrat needs especial opportunities of training, etc.; only those families which can provide such facilities produce successful persons in industrial societies. A man born in a high class family naturally gets more opportunities of development than a person who is less fortunate in this respect. In socialisation the family plays an important role. Thus from the above discussion, the role of family becomes apparent.

IMPACT ON CASTE SYSTEM

In Indian society the caste system has had a unique role and importance. The social status of a person was determined by his caste. The industrialization has diminished the role of caste. Following are the salient features of the impact of industrialization upon Indian caste system :

(1) Disintegration of caste system The industrialization in India has led to breakdown of caste system; under the impact of industrialization the traditional caste-based structure of society is collapsing. Traditionally, the social status of a person in Indian society was determined by the caste into which he was born. As a result of industrialization, the caste-based criterion of social classification has changed. In the industrial society it is the class and not the caste which fixes the social status of a person. Now the society is split into classes. Man gets social status according to his class. Thus the caste system is now disintegrating.

(2) Reduction in brahmins' influence and power In the traditional social structure the Brahmins enjoyed the highest status in the society. But as a result of industrialization, the influence of Brahmins is on wane; it is gradually losing its traditional hold on Indian society. Now there are other criteria of social stratification. It is no longer necessary that one should be a Brahmin in order to attain high social status. As a matter of fact, the traditional role of Brahmins in society is all but finished. Those who are unable to adapt themselves according to the changed circumstances have a parasitic existence in modern industrialized society. That is why a Brahmin today is looked down upon.

(3) Rise of shudra In the traditional Indian society, a shudra enjoyed the most inferior status in society. Indeed, his plight was miserable and he was treated no better than a slave. The shudras were subjected to all kinds of calumny and obliquity. They enjoyed little respect in society. As a result of industrialization there is some improvement in the condition of shudra. In the industrial society the criterion of social status is works and not birth. Anyone proficient in industrial know-how is bound to get a place of pride in society irrespective of the fact that he is a Brahmin or a shudra. Today a number of persons born into shudra family are occupying high-ranking positions in society.

(4) Abolition of caste-based functions In the traditional caste-based society each caste had some functions. Generally the entertainment was also caste-based. The Brahmin had the role of teacher, the Kshatriya that of warrior. Now all this has changed. It is no longer obligatory upon a shudra to do menial jobs for upper castes. Due to these changes the traditional functions of the castes stand abolished.

(5) Division of labour: Non-Proficiency-oriented Under the caste system the division of labour was based upon caste and upon the consideration of efficiency. A Brahmin was to perform the function of learned even if he was poor in learning. Under the influence of industrialization, the criterion of division of labour has changed. The industrialization has encouraged specialization. Nowadays a person is not given a task unless he is specially trained for it. In every department of society a specialized training is needed for the successful performance of a job. The shudras are today doing teaching jobs. On the other hand, Brahmins can be seen to be doing the menial jobs. A proficient shudra can now easily attain the position of an industrial manager and a number of Brahmins may be working under him.

(6) End of control of castes In traditional society the caste system was an effective instrument of social control. Each caste had its own code of conduct which was strictly adhered to, any violation thereof attracting strong social reprobation. The violation of caste-based code of conduct used to result in excommunication. In modern industrial society the control of caste has become loose and lax. The industrial society is highly intricate and complex. Nowadays persons of all castes work together and it is, therefore, well-nigh impossible to observe the separate caste-based codes of conduct. In modern industrial societies the instruments of effective social controls are provided by law and law enforcing agencies.

(7) Hold of untouchability loosening Under the caste system there used to be no inter-caste social mixing. The persons belonging to different castes did not get together and share a common board. As far as shudra was concerned, he could not even sit, stand or walk near the persons of upper castes. A shadow of shudra was scrupulously avoided. On the other hand, there are cases where shudras themselves did not welcome the opportunity of being in the company of Brahmins. They forbade Brahmins from entering their quarters. As a result of industrialization, the spectre of untouchability is relaxing its grip upon the thought and imagination of people. Today members of all castes work together in mills and factories and eat foodstuff from the same canteens and tuck-shops. Many a waiter in restaurants are shudra. Even Brahmins willingly partake of food prepared and served by these people. Besides in parks and public places there are no restrictions on the entry of shudra. Thus, industrialization can be said to have come as a boon for the low castes.

(8) Prevalence of inter-caste marriages Under the caste system, the inter-caste marriages were a strict taboo. Hardly anyone dared to defy this taboo and marry with a spouse of any other caste except one's own. The punishment for such marriages was nothing less than complete excommunication. In modern societies these taboos are giving way. Though inter-caste marriages are not very common, people do marry into other castes without much disapproval. In mills and factories persons belonging to different castes come together, develop common interests and form friendships. Some of these contacts bloom and flower into mutual love and attraction. The mutual attraction breaks the caste barriers and such persons marry. There is another reason for prevalence of inter-caste marriages. Due to frequent encounters with members of other communities, one comes to realize the fundamental oneness of all human beings. One begins to appreciate that stereo-typed thinking with regard to other castes is not valid. Thus, the factors like caste pride and hatred for other castes which help accentuate caste barriers become inoperative. Consequently there emerges a rational outlook. The factor of mutual regard and love comes to be considered as the only relevant consideration in regard to marriage.

IMPACT ON RELIGION

Some persons are of the view that religion prospers and flourishes only in ignorance. Even if this view is not altogether true, it does contain an element of truth. It is true that religion prospers most in societies where ignorance is rampant. On the contrary as the areas of science and knowledge spread, the hold of religion weakens. Generally science and religion are considered to be mutually opposed. In the absence of scientific explanation, small and insignificant things and events become pillars of religious faith and dogma. When the scientific explanation of any thing is wanting, it is replaced by dogmatic explanation. In pre-scientific days the phenomenon of rain, storm, etc., was linked with the religious phenomenon and it was imagined that there are gods of rain, thunder, etc. Thus, it is quite evident that the extension of scientific knowledge proves detrimental to religion. Industrialization is intimately related to science and technology and with the growth of industrialization there is spread of science and technology. The widespread use of science and technology engenders a scientific outlook. The scientific outlook is quite opposed to religious and dogmatic outlook. Therefore it is pretty clear that the growth of industrialization proves detrimental to religion. In Indian society religion and morals are intimately linked. The moral principles are grounded in religious faith and belief. Morality is based upon religion. This is the reason why with the decline in religion there is change in moral principles as well. The following discussion will make clear how industrialization has influenced our religious and moral thinking.

Industrialization has deeply influenced the course of religion. Following are some of the important features of influence :

1. Decline of orthodoxy and superstitions Under the garb of religion, orthodoxy and superstitions flourish. As a matter of fact the whole edifice of religion is built out of bricks of superstition and blind faith. Superstitions are due to ignorance. In practical life, belief in superstitions and orthodoxy proves harmful. For material and industrial progress it is very essential that men should be free from the clutches of superstitions. They must have rational and scientific outlook. The process of industrialization helps the spread and dissemination of science and practical knowledge. As a result of industrialization people learn the truth of physical reality. They begin to appreciate and value the practical results and are prepared to give up irrational beliefs. The knowledge disseminated and spread on account of industrialization subverts religious orthodoxy.

2. Development of religious tolerance As a result of industrialization, the outlook of general masses in respect of religion has become broad. Generally orthodox religious persons are of narrow and parochial outlook. On account of their parochial outlook, they regard their own religion as supreme and infallible. Their attitude towards other religions is that of contempt. As a consequence of industrialization, the persons of different faiths come together and get an opportunity of knowing and understanding the truth about each other. This results in dispelling of wrong notions about other faiths and an appreciation of basic unity of all faiths. Therefore as a result of industrialization, there is development of religious tolerance.

3. Founding of secular states Previously the states used to be theocratic; each state subscribed to some or other faith. Each nation had a national religion. The citizens professing faiths different from that of the state did not enjoy full rights and privileges; they were treated as second-rate citizens. But as a result of industrialization, the concept of theocratic states has become obsolete. Due to industrialization every state now has a sizeable number of minorities whose claims cannot be ignored. Therefore, nowadays it is a practice for almost all states not to consider any religion as special or state religion. The states today subscribe to the ideology of secularism, according to which state is neutral in matters of religion but accords equal status to all religions. This is secularism.

4. Social aspect of religion Religion and religious functions have dual aspect. The first is its spiritual aspect and the second is its social aspect. In an industrial society, the spiritual aspect of religion is not very important. Its social aspect, however, is quite important in industrial societies. Nowadays, festivals are celebrated not so much as religious affairs but as social functions. Even going on pilgrimage today is more of a social necessity than a spiritual need. A visit to temple or mosque even has come to assume social overtones.

IMPACT ON MORALS

Following are the ways in which industrialization has influenced morals :

1. Development of rational outlook The Indian society has been traditionally based upon morality and religion. In India there has been little critical thinking in regard to moral principles and beliefs. The moral principles were accepted as universal truths beyond the sphere of doubt and reason. As a result of industrialization, the outlook of common man has changed. Now people demand rational justification as to why a particular action is considered right or wrong. In industrial societies it is believed that the moral principles are man-made and that morality is for the sake of human life and society and not vice versa. The tendency to examine and evaluate every moral principle before acquiescing to it is graining around in modern society.

2. Development of materialist outlook On account of industrialization, the importance and value of physical progress and development have enhanced. An average citizen of to-day does not appear to be satisfied and contented. The maximum material acquisition seems to have become the aim of modern life. It is for this reason that common man of today is averse to religion and spirituality. Today there is a strong competition for acquiring as much wealth as possible.

3. Individualism The industrial societies are increasingly becoming complex and in all spheres of life there is reign of specialisation. Due to industrialization, large metropolises are coming up. In large communities there is decline in fellow-feeling. In such societies therefore the community feeling or the feeling of mutual belongingness is rather missing. Life becomes rapid and mechanical and people have little opportunity to look after the welfare of others. Life in industrial societies becomes self-centred. As a result of this, there is growth and development of individualism in these societies.

4. Permissiveness in sex morals As a result of industrialization, the sexual mores have become lax. There are numerous reasons for this laxity. Firstly, the opportunities for the mixing-up of sexes have increased. Nowadays boys and girls can meet without much difficulty and social opposition. In mills, factories and offices, men and women work together. As a result of this frequent encounter of sexes there is laxity in sexual morals. Moreover, industrialization has given rise to materialistic thinking and according to the materialist outlook of life, the traditional taboos on sex are harmful and that free sex is consistent with healthy and sane life. This is why that today premarital sex is not considered to be criminal or immoral. Indeed sex without marriage is coming to be considered quite normal, healthy and moral. In Western society all taboos on sex have broken down. A new highly permissive sex morality is the order of the day.

5. Increase in Crimes As a result of industrialization, there is an all-round rise in the incidence of crime. It is a common observation that the rate of crime is very high in industrial towns. In large metropolises family life is subject to many pressures. It is very difficult to have normal family life in those towns. On account of disintegration of family life, the control of family over individuals is becoming lax. Due to absence of this control, there is encouragement of crime. In every industrial town, prostitution and liquor consumption are rampant. Besides theft and dacoity also are commonplace in industrial towns. The incidence of violence and murder is also high in industrial towns.

6. Loosening of social control In industrial towns labourers and artisans from places far and wide come in search of jobs. Having found jobs, they settle in these towns. In industrial towns like Delhi, Kanpur, Bombay, Calcutta, etc. workers from all over India are settled. As most of these workers are outsiders, they are not subject to usual social controls. Moreover, caste and clan considerations are almost non-existent in big metropolises. On account of all these factors, the social control becomes loose and lax. In industrial towns it is neither the family nor caste and clan nor society in general that exercises social control. It is exercised by law and law enforcing agencies like police, courts, etc.

IMPACT ON ENTERTAINMENT

The entertainment and relaxation are essential to life. Relaxation is indispensable for the health of everyone. The means of relaxation and entertainment keep changing with time and circumstances. There is a big difference between the means of entertainment in pre-industrial and post-industrial societies. In India there has been significant change in means of entertainment as a result of industrialization. Following are the important influences upon entertainment due to industrialization :

1. Entertainment outside family Traditionally, in India family was the centre of entertainment. All entertainment was focussed upon family. Generally all families used to be joint and therefore were very large. A single family used to have about a dozen adult members and a dozen children. On account of large families it was possible to find all kinds of entertainment within the family itself. The adult male members used to beguile themselves by playing cards or chess and females used to gossip, swing or sing. As there were very many children in every family, the entertainment of children was easy. In the modern industrial societies, the situation is just the opposite of the old state of affairs. The families today are not joint. The size of families has shrunken. A family today consists of husband and wife and their two or three children. Besides, in many families both husband and wife are employed. Under these circumstances there is no scope of entertainment within the family. Today almost everyone goes out for entertainment. The entertainment today has become institutionalized.

2. Professional entertainment In industrial societies the entertainment has become a business and a profession. Today there are a number of institutions of entertainment. The cinemas, clubs, dance and gambling dens are all centres of entertainment. We buy entertainment today. Throw money and have fun is the situation today.

3. Artificial entertainment Due to industrialization entertainment has become a business and profession. A professional entertainment however lacks the true spirit of entertainment. It is artificial and usually debases the man instead of relaxing him.

Besides, entertainment in industrial societies is not only artificial but is base and low also. Today classical music and dance are little appreciated. Moreover these days entertainment by liquor and drugs is becoming common. In bigger towns prostitution is also a big source of entertainment. From all this it is apparent that the standard of entertainment has fallen steeply as a result of industrialization.

QUESTIONS FOR EXERCISE

1. Explain impact of industrialization on human behaviour.
2. Write short note on Impact of industrialization on entertainment.

2

INDUSTRIAL PSYCHOLOGY

WHAT IS INDUSTRIAL PSYCHOLOGY?

Industrial psychology, as the name indicates, is that branch of psychology which studies human behaviour under industrial circumstances. Psychology is a normative science of behaviour which can be observed in the social, economic, educational and other spheres. In the modern period, the different branches of psychology have developed during the study of human behaviour in these various fields. Educational psychology has been developed to study human behaviour in a social environment. This is an age of industrial progress, in which each progressive nation is expanding the scope of its industries. But industries cannot be made to function without human beings, because individuals are required in the capacity of managers, administrators, programmers, etc. And, wherever there are human beings, their behaviour will be influenced by their relationship. If, in the industrial field, human relations deteriorate, then the result is strikes and lockouts which have a widespread impact upon the economy of the nation. Since the future of every nation depends upon its industrial development and progress, this particular field of human behaviour becomes extremely important. It is the aim of industrial psychology to study the principles governing behaviour in the industrial field and to undertake research.

A Branch of Practical Psychology

Psychology is not merely a theoretical science for it not only enunciates general laws concerning human behaviour but also tries to improve human life by applying these principles. Like any other science, therefore, psychology also has two aspects — the theoretical and the practical.

Industrial psychology is naturally a branch of practical psychology because it is fundamentally a study evolved for the improvement of human relations in the industrial sphere. The knowledge provided by it is used to solve the problems of people who work in industry, as well as to solve those non-human problems which emerge from time to time in industries. Nowadays psychologists are appointed to study the problems which arise in the field of industrial psychology. A glance at the history of industrial psychology will show us that universities have been responsible for the research concerned with it, but even more important research has been carried on in big industries under actual conditions. It is, therefore, more appropriate to consider industrial psychology as a branch of practical psychology. It is the application of psychological facts and principles to the problems concerning human relations in business and industry. Psychological facts and principles are used in human relations in the field of business and industry and this constitutes industrial psychology. Industrial psychology provides practical solutions to the problems that arise in the industrial society and its economic organisation. The industrial psychologist makes a study of the behaviour of people working under conditions of business and industry. The subject matter of the industrial psychologist is always the human being, because it is the human being who is the object of a psychological study. Even in a business or industrial environment, this continues to be true. Just as social psychology studies the human being under social circumstances, industrial psychology studies the individual in a business environment. Whereas it has been called the study of conduct, but it would be better to substitute the word 'behaviour' for this term because conduct is more properly the concern of ethics, not of psychology.

Briefly, then, in defining industrial psychology, it can be said that it is that branch of psychology which studies human behaviour under business and industrial conditions, and in which research is carried on concerning the behavioural problems that arise in an industrial environment. It should be clearly kept in mind that the study of behaviour covers both external behaviour and inner feelings.

HISTORY OF DEVELOPMENT

The development of psychology as a science began particularly in the nineteenth century but by the twentieth century its scope had been extended so much that independent branches of it emerged soon after. Psychological studies in the sphere of industry became important enough to be constituted as an independent branch called industrial psychology.

Hence the development of industrial psychology should be said to begin in the twentieth century.

Even before the twentieth century, certain researches were carried out, which could be useful to industrial psychology. For example, during the sixteenth, seventeenth and eighteenth centuries, much important research was carried out on dynamics, the most noticeable being the work of Galileo, Borelli, Columb and Marey. In France in the nineteenth century, Mary and Mosso carried out research on muscular work and the problem of fatigue. In the beginning of the twentieth century, Ioteyko and Imbert did much research work on important methods in industrial psychology. Kraepelin did important work on the work curve, the training and selection of employees. Lahy located many important psychophysical factors which influenced the development of skill in typewriting.

Apart from these above researches, Lahy, Book,[1] Imbert and Scott[2] published valuable works on different aspects of industrial psychology.

Contribution of Munsterberg

Yet, the most important contribution to industrial psychology was the research work of Hugo Munsterberg, a German psychologist. He was the director of the psychological laboratory at Harvard University, from where he retired. Munsterberg was particularly interested in the study of individual differences. He established a correlation between individual differences and psychological tests. In his book *On the Witness Stand,* Munsterberg explained the role of psychological principles in finding out the causes of crime. In another book *Psychology and the Teacher,* Munsterberg elucidated the value of applying psychological principles to teaching. In 1910-11 he described some psychological discoveries in the field of industry. He had already started his work on industrial psychology when he was a lecturer in Berlin. In 1912 he published a book on this subject in German, which was later published in America in 1913 under the title *Psychology and Industrial Efficiency.* In 1914 Munsterberg published another book in German on the subject of the psychology of technical personnel.

In the sphere of industrial psychology, Munsterberg worked upon the possibility of improving adjustment and efficiency. He showed the great benefit of utilizing psychology in this field. He pointed out that psychology can help in three ways. In the first place, psychology can

1. Book, W.F., *The Psychology of Skill,* University of Montanna.
2. Scott, W.D., *Influencing Men in Business,* New York.

help in the selection of the best qualified individual for a particular job. In the second place, the psychologist can help in the creation of such psychological conditions in industry under which every employee can be encouraged to produce as much as he can. Thirdly, in industry the psychologist can give useful suggestions by which those employees who can make useful contributions to the work can be given special training. On the basis of these researches, Munsterberg gave many valuable suggestions about the use of psychology in the sphere of industry. He suggested that psychological tests should be employed in the recruitment of employees. He also showed that the process of learning can be speeded up by industrial training. He pointed out the importance of the conditions of work, the morale of the employees and the conditions of fatigue. Munsterberg's suggestions were not mere verbal jugglery because he demonstrated the value of recruiting motormen, telephone operators and naval officers by psychological teats. He thus made it clear that there is much advantage to be gained by using psychological principles and theories in the sphere of industry.

At the same time, great importance was attached to Taylor's plan for scientific organisation in the field of industrial organisation and administration. Munsterberg related his own theories with Taylor's plan and stressed the fact that in industries, manpower should be properly utilised for industrial and economic progress. He demonstrated that both industrialists and workers stand to benefit by the application of psychological theories to industry. By using psychological research it is possible to cut down the time consumed in industrial work, to increase the work done by labourers, to improve the standard of living of all concerned. Briefly, Munsterberg made it clear that the economic, cultural and social level of a country can be raised by using psychological principles in the sphere of industry because it becomes possible to provide every person with the kind of work in which he can take interest and do well. Munsterberg's books influenced much of the thinking in the industrial sector, and in the more advanced countries his ideas were soon put into practice. Not only in Germany but in all Europe and America there was almost a flood of research in the industrial sphere. For these reasons Munsterberg is believed to be the father of industrial psychology.

The First World War played an important role in emphasizing the work of Munsterberg because with the beginning of war it became necessary to make extensive use of psychological testing. Within a short period of the publication of Munsterberg's work, the war started leading to a very large scale recruitment of soldiers. Countries in which

Munsterberg's thinking had an influence quickly realised that by using psychological testing techniques, it would be possible to find the fittest individuals for the different branches of the armed forces. In England the psychologists were called in to help in the selection of army, navy and air force personnel. These psychologists devised techniques of testing adaptability of individuals for the armed forces. In Germany and France psychologists like Anderson,[1] Moede, Benary and Gamelli propagated the importance of psychological testing through the medium of their books. Later, psychological testing was adapted to the selection of people for different professions, and this helped the industry enormously.

Development of Industrial Psychology in America

In 1917 U.S.A. also entered the arena of war, and established a society for the purpose of administering psychological tests for people joining the armed forces. These tests were used on a very large scale in the recruitment to the armed forces. As a result, research in industrial psychology was encouraged and the literature connected with it started growing rapidly. Between 1916 and 1918 H.L. Hollingworth, A.T. Poffenberger and A.W. Kornhauser did valuable research work in industrial psychology. All of them were teachers in universities. In addition to their work, considerable research work was done by other people who were directly connected with industry. In 1919 H.C. Link wrote a book *Employment Psychology* on the psychology of employees. It included information on professional training, the prevention of accidents, analysis of work methods and means of removing indifference to work, and other industrial problems. The following are the more important works published during this period:

1. Hollingworth, H.L., *Vocational Psychology,* 1916.
2. Hollingworth and Poffenberger, *Applied Psychology,* 1917.
3. Kornhauser, A.W., and F.A. Kingsbury, *Psychological Tests in Business,* 1924.
4. Kitson, H.D., *The Psychology of Vocational Adjustment,* 1925.
5. Laird, D.A., *The Psychology of Selecting Men,* 1927.
6. Bingham, W.V., and M. Freyd, *Procedures in Employment Psychology,* 1926.
7. Moore, B.V., and G.W. Hartmann, *Readings in Industrial Psychology,* 1931.

---

1. Anderson, H.G., *The Selection of Candidates for the Air Service, Reports of the British Medical Society.*

In 1922 W.V. Bingham started the publication of *Journal of Personnel Research,* connected with the working class. He also published an important book on the psychological analysis of the various aspects of accidents, entitled *Personality and Public Accidents.*

In addition to the research work and the published work of different scientists, the American interest in industrial psychology went on to the establishment of many industrial associations which further encouraged research in the field of industry. In 1916 an association called the Bureau of Salesmanship Research was established to carry out research on the problems of distribution of goods. The year 1917 saw the establishment of a Research Bureau for Retail Training to study and analyse training in selling. The Psychological Corporation was established in 1921. In 1922 Bingham headed an association called the Personnel Research Corporation, which was later assisted by the National Research Council, the Engineering Foundation and the American Federation of London. From this brief account of the development of industrial psychology in America, it is clear that the Americans have made a very extensive and valuable contribution to its development.

Development of Industrial Psychology in Germany

Much has already been said about the contribution of Munsterberg to the development of industrial psychology. He was a German scientist who did his work in America, but many other German scientists also made valuable contributions to industrial psychology. In 1961W. Moede and Miorkowski conducted research on the use of psychological principles in the selection of motor drivers. Taking inspiration from their work, almost fourteen research centres were opened in Germany in the same year. Next year the Saxon Railway Company established a research centre in Dresden to conduct research on the use of psychological principles for the selection of locomotive engineers and other employees. The General Electric Company used psychological tests in the selection of individuals for mechanical work. The Greater Berlin Tramways Company established a research centre in Dresden to conduct research on the use of psychological principles for the selection of locomotive engineers and other employees. After the war Germany went through a period of industrial reorganisation, during which many psychological laboratories were also established to help in the work of most industrial complexes. By 1922 some twenty-two industrial complexes had their own psychological laboratories, and within four years the number went up to 100. The universities also helped in researches in industrial psychology. As a result

Germany produced much valuable literature on the subject of Industrial psychology, both in the form of books and journals.

Development of Industrial Psychology in England

Most of the important work in industrial psychology in England was done by two institutions, a brief description of which is given here :

1. Industrial Health Research Board The institution was established to find out means of increasing production, improving the efficiency of the workers, and overcoming fatigue, etc. In 1918 it was called the Industrial Fatigue Research Board, but it was later given its present name. The English scientific and industrial research department and the Medical Research Council provided valuable assistance to the development of this institution, while the government accorded it recognition. It conducted important and beneficial research on the psychological aspects of the health of workers, hours of work and physical conditions, wages, promotion and transfer, etc.

2. National Institute of Industrial Psychology This was established in 1921 with the help of industrial organisations. Its director was C.S. Myers, also the director of the psychological laboratory at Cambridge University. As a result this organisation got the assistance of industrial houses as well as universities and succeeded in doing considerable work in different spheres of industrial psychology.

Development of Industrial Psychology in Russia

Communist Russia, too, did not lag behind the other advanced nations in the development of industrial psychology because the Russian government paid great attention to all the developments in the field of industry. In 1920 Central Institute of Labour was established in Moscow under the direction of Gesteve. While in 1907 there were 60 research centres looking into the various problems of industry, their number rose to 100 within four years in Moscow alone. All of them were aligned to the central institute mentioned above. The chief objective of the institute was to carry out research on the use of tools and machines, the use of file, etc. Hence it did extensive studies in the defects and advantages of all kinds of machines and machine tools. In addition, it also did much work on the working conditions for the employees and on work methods. This institute employed the Taylor system for scientific organisation. In 1922 a laboratory for industrial psychology was established to conduct research on problems of workers. Even the Neurological Institute of Moscow University was conducting research into these problems to keep step with the progress of communism in all other spheres. Russia laid stress on research in ways of improving human relations in the industrial field because under the communist system, the differences between employer and employee were eliminated.

Development in other European Countries

Most of the other European countries also fell in step with the leaders and encouraged research in industrial psychology. Many institutes for this work were established in Holland, Belgium, Poland, Italy, Spain, Austria and other countries. The International Congress of Applied Psychology was established in Geneva, Switzerland. It conducted important research in vocational guidance and selection of personnel. At the same time, a research institute was established in Zurich, where research for training in industries and professions, in work method, etc., was done. In 1920, in these conferences, there was an exchange of opinion on the subjects of vocational guidance and the use of psychological principles in the field of industry. The third conference of this kind took place in Milan in 1922. In this conference, the interest centred on work analysis, the importance of psychology and physiology in the prevention of accidents, Taylor's plan, etc. In 1931 a conference was organised in Moscow in which different aspects of industrial progress and the economic progress of employees came under review.

It will be obvious from the above account that most of the European nations took a keen interest in research into various aspects of industrial psychology at the turn of this century, leading to the publication of numerous books and journals. At almost every place, universities, individual organisations, government and industrialists combined to work for the development of industrial psychology. On the other hand, the Asian countries developed interest in Industrial psychology at a much later stage. Japan is the sole exception because it went through a period of remarkable industrial progress which necessitated research in industrial psychology at about the same time as Europe. In 1921 Japan saw the establishment of an Institute of Industrial Efficiency.

Industrial Psychology in India

Interest was taken in industrial psychology in India only after Independence. Some research in industrial psychology began with the establishment of psychological laboratories in universities. Psychological research was then encouraged in industrial complexes because of the development of large scale industries and the increasing tempo of the labour welfare movement. Most of the big industries took the help of psychologists for the recruitment of personnel, but the most important and consistent work done was in the recruitment of armed forces personnel. Psychological testing by the psychologists became an essential part of recruitment to every branch of the armed forces. The government itself was responsible for the establishment of numerous psychological laboratories in which emphasis was laid on vocational guidance. At Allahabad, in Uttar Pradesh, considerable vocational guidance is provided to people after psychological testing at the State Bureau. There are approximately twenty-five school psychologists in various government schools whose task is to give vocational guidance along with other psychological help. Psychologists are consulted by big industrialists for their advertisement campaigns. The advice of the psychologists is sought by the industrialists not only in the recruitment of personnel but even in the sale of the goods produced by them. In this way, industrial psychology is steadily growing in this country but the progress here cannot be compared with the progress in Europe and America. In the last few years, many books on industrial psychology have been published in India, but they are textbooks, not concerned with any original research. No journal of industrial psychology is published in the country. Most of the university laboratories also conduct little, if any, research on industrial problems. And only in very few of the industrial organisations is the help of the psychologist sought. From this point of view, the country is far behind the Western nations but this backwardness is part of the lack of development in other spheres. Hence, there is hope of progress in this direction too. Most of the young educated industrialists are now trying to use psychological principles in such spheres as physical and psychological working conditions, the selection of employees, advertisement, sales, etc. Hence, there is reason to expect more development in industrial psychology in the near future.

INDUSTRIAL PSYCHOLOGY AND GENERAL PSYCHOLOGY

Psychology is a science of behaviour, the term behaviour being interpreted most liberally, for it comprehends not only both objective and subjective forms of human behaviour, but also the behaviour of the higher animals. Human behaviour includes man's behaviour under all kinds of conditions and circumstances, normal, abnormal, social, industrial, legal, in childhood, in adolescence, in old age. Psychology studies behaviour in all these conditions, but with reference to the environment and situations.

What is General Psychology?

Psychology is a positive science in which facts are studied. It tries to find out causal relations in behaviour by using the methodology of science. As a science, psychology finds out the principles of human behaviour and once it has established some causal relations, it makes predictions about behaviour. General psychology is the most extensive branch of psychology. Perhaps it is better called "Source" or "Ground" rather than a branch as aspect for it involves the study of all the general principles used in all its other branches. It studies all processes of human behaviour such as learning, thinking, memory, sensation, perception, emotion, feeling and personality. It also makes a study of the origins, the well-springs of human behaviour such as motivation, nervous system — the various levels of consciousness, etc. It even outlines the methodology of psychology. It differs from industrial psychology because its explanations are more concerned with the practical application of psychological principles.

Distinctions from General Psychology

From the above elucidation of general psychology, it is amply clear that industrial psychology differs from general psychology. The major differences are the following:

1. **Difference of nature** As has been pointed out, industrial psychology is a branch of practical psychology while, on the other hand, general psychology is more theoretical.

2. **Difference of scope** The scope of industrial psychology is more limited and, in, fact different. General psychology studies, in general, human behaviour under all kinds of situations. Industrial psychology, on the other hand, studies human behaviour only in industrial and business situations.

3. **Different Points of view** The point of view of general psychology is more theoretical but that of industrial psychology is chiefly practical.

Relation with General Psychology

Despite the above-mentioned differences between the two, there is an intimate relationship between general and industrial psychology. In industrial psychology, the psychologist makes use of those principles in an industrial situation which he has learnt from general psychology. For example, the conclusions of general psychology about such psychological processes as learning, perception, attention, memory and association, etc., are utilized under industrial conditions in order to improve the skills concerned with these processes. The psychology of interest and attention is much used in the field of advertisement. In this manner, the industrial psychologist must have extensive knowledge of general psychology, although the opposite is not true. The general psychologist does not need knowledge of industrial psychology.

NATURE OF INDUSTRIAL PSYCHOLOGY

It is easier to understand the nature and scope of industrial psychology by analysing its definition. Industrial psychology is a science, hence its nature is scientific. It employs scientific techniques to study the social aspect of human behaviour. It is a science in the same way in which general psychology and sociology are sciences. Along with the study of individual behaviour, industrial psychology also makes a study of group dynamics. The aim of this study also is to find facts and establish causal relations between them, to derive universal laws based on these causal relations and then to apply these laws to concrete situations and solve problems of a social nature.

What is a Science?

In order to test the validity of the statement that industrial psychology is a science, it is necessary to find out what science is. Science is the study of a limited field. If a study is to be called scientific, then its scope must be limited and also systematic. Yet a study cannot be called science only if its subject matter possesses both these traits, for the study must also make use of the scientific method. In fact, science differs from the arts and philosophy on account of its method, and its peculiar nature depends more upon the method than upon the subject matter.

Characteristics of the Scientific Method

It is, therefore, necessary to understand the scientific method if we are to understand the nature of science. In the scientific method, the subject matter of a limited sphere is studied systematically. It needs the use of great patience, courage, hard work, creative imagination and objectivity. In the absence of this scientific attitude or scientific spirit, no person can derive the full benefit of using the scientific method. Before starting his work, a person conducting research should make a detailed analysis of the problem which he wants to study, because if the analysis is detailed enough, the study itself becomes more facile. The scientific method is constituted by the following steps:

1. Observation The first step in the scientific method is a careful and detailed observation of the subject matter, often, by the use of apparatus. The apparatus itself must be accurate and dependable.

2. Recording The second step in the scientific method is the careful and systematic recording of all the observed facts. Objectivity is a necessary element in recording.

3. Classification Now the recorded information has to be classified and organised. This is an important and serious step. In Karl Pearson's words : "The classification of facts, the recognition of their sequence and relative significance is the function of science." Classification must be done in such a way that one can see some pattern and relationship between the scattered facts which have been observed. For this it is essential that the information is arranged on a logical and coherent basis.

4. Generalisation The next important step in the scientific method is the derivation of general laws on the basis of patterns observed in the organised matter. This general law, which is arrived at, is called a scientific law.

5. Verification Verification is the fifth stage because the scientific method does not conclude with the derivation of a universal law. It is necessary to test and verify the truth of this law. Validity is an essential condition of a scientific law, for without validity, the law cannot be called scientific.

Essential Elements of Science

We have now seen the elements that are necessary for any study to be classed as a science. Simply stated, a study must possess the following characteristics to be called scientific :

1. **Scientific method** As has been pointed out above, a study is called scientific not because the subject matter is of a particular kind but because it makes use of the scientific method.
2. **Factual** Science is the study of facts; it searches for facts. Its subject matter is constituted by facts, not ideals.
3. **Universal** Scientific principles are universal for they are found to be true everywhere if their basic conditions are fulfilled.
4. **Veridical** Scientific laws have a validity which can be put to test at any time. Whenever they are tested, they are proved correct.
5. **Discovery of cause-effect relationship** Science aims at the discovery of cause and effect relations between the various facts

of the subject. Having found the cause-effect relationship, it pronounces certain facts universal and valid laws.

6. **Prediction** Science can make predictions about the future on the strength of the universal laws enunciated by it, because these laws are based on cause-and-effect relationships, between facts-relationships, which are always true. Science itself is based on faith in causality. The scientist believes that what will happen in the future can be determined on the basis of what is, because the law of causality is incontrovertible and universal.

Industrial Psychology is Scientific

We will find all the above elements in industrial psychology, and hence we can conclude that industrial psychology has a claim to be considered as scientific.

1. Industrial psychology uses the scientific method All the methods of industrial psychology are scientific. It makes the greatest possible use of the experimental method. In the experimental method, the subject of study is placed in predetermined conditions and then studied. After careful observation, the industrial psychologist records all the facts observed, follows this up by a logical classification and the derivation of universal laws by generalization. It is these universal laws which make up the principles of industrial psychology. In this way, it is obvious that industrial psychology makes use of the scientific method. Although the other methods employed by industrial psychology are not as scientific as the experimental method, every effort has been made to invest them with a factual and scientific character, and much success has been achieved in this direction. Industrial psychologists may have many different opinions about the value and the utility of a particular method, but all of them agree that the method of study must be scientific.

2. Industrial psychology is factual Industrial psychology makes a factual study of behaviour, its conclusions are objective and impartial. Its conclusions about behaviour are not normative. It describes behaviour and tries to find out laws which govern it. Hence it is concerned with facts, not value.

3. The Laws of industrial psychology are universal The laws enunciated by industrial psychology produce the same results everywhere, under identical conditions. These rules prove to be the same at all times and places, irrespective of the differences in character of the persons involved. For example, the law that in industrial organisation, the conditions of work and wages will influence the quality and quantity of production, will prove to be true wherever it is tested.

4. The principles of industrial psychology are valid Upon verification and even reveriflcation, the principles of industrial psychology prove to be valid. Their validity can be tested by anyone and at any time. For example, the fact that there is always some dissatisfaction, repression or maladjustment at the root of all labour tensions can be tested anywhere.

5. Industrial psychology analyses cause-effect relationships Industrial psychology discovers the laws of behaviour and explains the causal relations existing between them. In industries, the psychologist tries to discover the causal relations underlying human relationship, advertisement and development, etc. He can thus discover very useful facts and laws. In this way, industrial psychology aims at finding out not only the 'what' of behaviour but also its 'how'.

6. Industrial psychology can make predictions Because industrial psychology can find out the causal relations that exist in human behaviour, it can make predictions about it, and these predictions also turn out to be true. For this reason, in all modern industrial nations, the predictions made by industrial psychologists are taken into account by the industrialists in solving industrial problems and disputes. These predictions have proved of much value.

It is clear from the above explanation that industrial psychology is an exact science, but one must not conclude from it that it is as exact as the physical sciences. In fact, it is a mistake to expect the same degree of precision and exactness from every science, because in every science the precision depends upon the nature of its subject matter. Obviously, a science which studies human behaviour in industrial conditions cannot be as exact as a science which studies physical things, because human behaviour is a complex, dynamic and changeable phenomenon. Hence, in calling industrial psychology an exact science, it is necessary to keep in mind its limitations, although these limitations cannot be fixed or determined with precision. And it is hoped that the precision of industrial psychology will improve with the development of more modern techniques of study.

INDUSTRIAL PSYCHOLOGY AND INDUSTRIAL SOCIOLOGY

Industrial psychology, as the name indicates, is that branch of psychology which studies human behaviour under industrial circumstances. Psychology is a normative science of behaviour which can be observed in the social, economic, educational and other spheres. In the modern period, the different branches of psychology have developed during the study of human behaviour in these various fields. This is an age of industrial progress, in which each progressive nation is expanding the scope of its industries. But industries cannot be made to function without human beings, because individuals are required in the capacity of managers, administrators, programmers, etc. And, wherever there are human beings, their behaviour will be influenced by their relationships. If, in the industrial field, human relations deteriorate, then the result is strikes and lockouts which have a widespread impact upon the economy of the nation. Since the future of every nation depends upon its industrial development and progress, this particular field of human behaviour becomes extremely important. It is the aim of industrial psychology to study the principles governing behaviour in the industrial field and to undertake research. According to M.L. Blum, "Industrial psychology is simply the application or extension of psychological facts and principles to the problems concerning human relations in business and industry."[1]

Industrial sociology also studies problems concerning human relations in business and industry though from the sociological point of view. This common subject matter naturally creates a close relationship between industrial sociology and industrial psychology. Even when working in an industry, the individual is never alone because he constantly comes into contact with other workers, supervisors, managers and industrialists. In business, the worker has to deal with all kinds of people. For this reason it also becomes necessary to study the social foundations of industrial psychology. Efforts are being made to bring industrial organisation to a scientific level. The more progressive countries try to improve the social life of the worker by organising various kinds of social programmes. The following points need to be considered in a study of the relationship of industrial sociology and industrial psychology :

1. Worker and social progress The progress of the industrial workers is a part of the general social progress. Hence the movements for social progress were accompanied by movements for an improvement in the conditions of industrial workers. It was accepted as a general principle that the work of social emancipation would remain incomplete so long as nothing was done to improve the conditions of industrial workers. For this reason social workers turned their attention in this direction. Bills were passed in parliament to this effect. Social workers directed the attention

1. Blum, M.L, *Industrial Psychology and Its Social Foundation,* Harper & Bros., New York, p. 3.

of industrialists towards the bad condition of the workers and insisted that they should be given human rights and their conditions changed so that the workers could improve their standards of living. Exploitation of workers was violently objected to and decried. Great stress was laid on providing social security to the workers. Political parties also began to pay attention to the amelioration of the lot of workers. In this manner the progressive nations linked the improvement of the industrial worker with the movements for general progress. This humanistic attitude is spreading rapidly in industry in all modern nations.

2. Workers' department and welfare schemes As a result of this humanistic approach, most modern nations have created workers' departments which undertake the task of safeguarding the rights of workers and working for their betterment. Labour welfare is now accepted as an important element in social welfare. Labour welfare includes the improvement in the social, economic and psychological conditions of the worker. In most large industries labour welfare officers are appointed to look after the workers and to help solve any disputes that may arise between them and the employers. The modern state is a welfare state the object of which is to enhance the welfare of the citizens in every sphere. The worker is an important part of the population and the government which does not undertake measures for labour welfare cannot hope to achieve its ideal of social welfare. After achieving Independence Indian Government, too, has begun to pay attention to the question of labour welfare. It has, from time to time, enacted laws to secure the rights of workers in various industries. Although even now many industrialists avoid the clutches of the law by various means, the pressure exerted by the trade unions is steadily changing the situation.

3. Industrial management Today efforts are being made to raise industrial management to the level of a science. The suggestions of Taylor and Thurston have been particularly valuable in this respect. A scientific industrial management implies the establishment of a management under which all the elements of production are most efficiently employed, thus eliminating the exploitation of any one element and the exhaustive use of any other. In a scientific industrial management system, a humanistic approach is adopted to deal with the workers and efforts are made to provide them with more facilities. The advanced countries are continuously making rapid strides in this direction.

Thus, both industrial sociology and industrial psychology are applied sciences engaged in study and research in the field of industry and the areas connected with it. The similarity between the two, however, ends here. They undoubtedly study common material but from a different viewpoint. In the words of R.M. MacIver, "It is a difference of attitude in regard to a common material."[1]

SCOPE OF INDUSTRIAL PSYCHOLOGY

Pointing out the scope of industrial psychology,[2] Harrell has laid stress on the following things :

1. Industrial psychology is concerned with the physical aspect of the environment of work, for example, the effect of light and temperature on work and safety.
2. It is primarily a study of the principles and behaviour of human relationships.
3. It is a study of the causes that lead to indifference and disinterest and the motives and attitudes that influence zeal and high morale.
4. It is a study of the methods by which neurotic people can be brought back to a level of normal mental health.
5. It is a study of the factors that create cooperation between labourers and the management, a study of the relations between the supervisor and his subordinates and of industrial conflicts.

It is clear from the above exposition that industrial psychology studies, apart from the physical environment, the principles of human relationships, the factors which lead to and maintain mental health, and bases of high morale. Briefly, then, the scope of industrial psychology is the following :

1. Economic, social and psychological aspects of industry Industrial psychology is concerned with human behaviour in the entire industrial environment. Consequently, it studies the economic, social and psychological aspects of human behaviour. In the modern age, most economic factors have some psychological influence. The various factors in the communal life of workers living in an industrial environment also influence the psychology of the worker. Industrial psychology studies this also.

2. Study of the physical aspect of work's environment In an industry the worker is greatly influenced by the conditions under which he works. If the conditions are to his liking, the worker feels satisfied and remains healthy while on the other hand if the conditions are not good the number of accidents goes up and workers become dissatisfied. Working

---

1. MacIver, R.M., *Community : A Sociological Study*, Macmillan and Co. Ltd., London, p. 65.
2. Harrell, T.W., *Industrial Psychology*, p. 1.

conditions include a number of factors such as clean air and water, arrangement for necessary rest, less noise, clean atmosphere, sufficient light, good relations between the worker and the management. In all these, guidance by the psychologist can prove of immense value. For example, it is better to consult the psychologist about the arrangement for lighting, about the quantity or intensity of the light and the angle from which it should come. Even the colour of the walls, floor and ceilings of the factory psychologically influence the worker. It has been seen in experiments that, if the colour scheme of the environment is good, there are fewer accidents and the atmosphere remains good. And it is for the psychologist to say what should be the colour of the machines, roofs, floors and ceilings. It can thus be said that industrial psychology studies the physical working conditions in industrial environment.

3. Principles of human relationships Irrespective of the automation introduced in any industry, the human element cannot be eliminated. Even the biggest and the most efficient machine needs an engineer to run it, and because the engineer is a human being, the importance of the psychological element in the running of the factory cannot be denied. The efficiency of the man will depend very much upon the nature of his relations with the management. In the last century most industrialists behaved like autocrats and considered the workers as nothing more than tools. But in that period the level of efficiency was never very high. It has been seen that an industrialist can achieve a higher rate of production if he behaves sympathetically with his employees. In the present age, the industrialist can no longer do as he wills, because of the existence of labour unions. An industrialist who cannot maintain good and cordial relations with his workers does not succeed for long. Being the science of behaviour, Industrial psychology tries to discover principles for improving human relationships in an industrial environment. At the root of most of the lockouts and strikes, two common forms of expressing discontent seen so frequently in most industries today, are distorted and injured human relationships. Industrial psychology helps to solve these problems.

4. Study of aptitudes and motives As in any other circumstance, human behaviour in the industrial environment is influenced and formed by attitudes and motives. Behaviour changes with the change in stimuli. Hence it is necessary to study the rules pertaining to correct attitudes and motives. Industrial psychology pursues this kind of study. One example of a study of this kind is the study conducted by the Hawthorne Works Western Electric Company into the effect of the attitudes of workers upon production. This study is known as the Hawthorne Studies.

5. Study of principles of mental health Today, all intelligent people realise the importance of maintaining the proper health of workers. The worker's mental health is profoundly influenced by the conditions under which he works and by the attitude of other people towards him. Industrial psychology studies the factors influencing the mental health of industrial workers and tries to discover principles for maintaining their mental health. Industrial psychology also gives suggestions for improving the mental health of those who are suffering from mental disease or are otherwise unbalanced.

6. Study of human relation Industrial psychology is the study of human behaviour in an industrial context. As has been pointed out earlier, the physical conditions of work have a direct and strong influence upon human behaviour. The manner in which the supervisor or the manager behaves towards the worker has a direct influence upon the efficiency, attitudes and motives of the worker. Some employees try to spread maladjustment among industrial workers for purely personal reasons. Even this is a problem of human relations. Being a branch of psychology, industrial psychology is particularly concerned with the observation and study of human relations about which it reaches conclusions through experiment and other study. On the basis of these conclusions it tries to discover general principles which can help in improving social relations between the workers and the management.

Briefly, all Industrial situations are within the scope of industrial psychology because every one of them influences human behaviour. The scope of industrial psychology expands with expansion of the sphere of industrial activity.

Problems of Industrial Psychology

In his book *Industrial Psychology and its Social Foundations,* the psychologist Blum has stated, "Industrial psychology offers a dynamic solution to the perplexing problems which confront an industrial society and economic system."[1] What are these problems concerned with industry or profession? These are the problems psychological in nature that arise in any sphere of industry. Briefly, the problems of industrial psychology are as follows :

1. Selection of the right man for the right job If success is to be achieved in any industry, it is essential that the right man should be found and appointed to the right job. This involves first an accurate work study

1. Blum, M.L., *Industrial Psychology and its Social Foundations,* New York, p.5.

and also the selection of the most qualified individual from among the applicants to suit that particular job. This is basically a problem for the psychologist because the selection involves many kinds of psychological tests to discover the various abilities of the individuals. It also happens sometimes that an individual working on a particular post cannot work efficiently for personal reasons, even though he is otherwise perfectly qualified to hold that post. In such a situation, the industrial psychologist is faced with the problem of giving suggestions which will once again render the individual fit for work.

2. Training of workers Although different individuals have varying degrees of ability to perform different kinds of functions, training can be useful in improving these abilities to such an extent that the individual becomes capable of doing work which he could not have done without training. The kind and length of training required to train a particular individual to bring him up to a certain level of efficiency can be determined by the psychologist. Hence, another problem for the industrial psychologist is the training of workers.

3. Morale in industry Despite the best possible working conditions in an industry, the highest efficiency cannot be achieved unless the workers also have a high morale. Morale can be seen on one hand in the enthusiasm and zeal with which work is tackled and on the other hand in the mutual cooperation extended to others in group activities. How a proper morale can be maintained in an industry and what steps are necessary to create it, is a problem of psychology, and it is the industrial psychologist who solves it.

4. Human relations in industry The problem of human relations in industry has assumed greater importance and complexity with the formation of trade unions, which have channelled the power of the workers into a single direction. Now, no industry can run successfully and smoothly for any length of time in the absence of good relations between the management and the workers' union. If the relations deteriorate, the level of production falls, accidents increase, and lockouts and strikes are the result. This problem of human relations is primarily the concern of social psychology and the person best equipped to solve it is the industrial psychologist.

5. Fatigue and boredom In industry, as in any other sphere of human activity, individuals become tired and bored after a long spell of mechanical work. Their psychological fatigue increases with this. Fatigue is both physiological and psychological. Scientifically viewed, the work and the instruments used in an industry should be so designed and planned as to result in the least possible amount of fatigue and the highest possible quantity of work. Specialists of engineering psychology have designed various kinds of machines and tools with this objective in view. They have also given many suggestions about the improvement of methods of work. Industrial psychologists also have conducted many experiments on mental fatigue and boredom, and given many valuable suggestions on the basis of their results. It has been observed, for example, that if there is arrangement for music and light entertainment in certain kinds of mechanical work, the extent of fatigue and boredom is greatly reduced.

6. Industrial accidents If we want a machine to function without any accident, two things are necessary. In the first place the machine itself should be in a good working order. In the second place, the worker manipulating it should be using it correctly, and his mental condition must be normal. For the first factor, engineering psychologists have given useful suggestions for keeping the machines functioning properly and without accidents. Regarding the second factor they have given some suggestions for the development of safety habits, proper maintenance and the maintenance of normal mental health. Hence, one important problem before industrial psychology is the prevention of accidents.

7. Responses towards physical environment It has already been pointed out that the physical conditions existing in an industry, conditions such as the quantity, quality and direction of light, arrangement for fresh and clean air, proper ventilation, hygiene, level of noise, the amount of humidity in the air, etc., have an important influence upon the efficiency of the worker. In order to find out the kind of conditions that should exist in a particular industry, it is necessary to find out the workers' response to their environment. Clearly, it is the industrial psychologist who can find out and determine the quantity and quality of these physical conditions which are desirable.

8. Problems of production Maximum production in any industry can only be achieved under certain circumstances. Even if the machines are the best, it is essential that the workers handling them must also be capable. How can this ability be tested? In every factory many machines are installed. How can one find the particular person best suited to operate each particular machine? And out of the many people who apply for a job in a factory how can one discover the few who may prove to be really capable? In order to achieve maximum production it is necessary that machines should be so designed as to induce the minimum fatigue and the lighting so arranged as to give the least possible strain to the workers. Besides, most people soon become bored with their work. How can their enthusiasm be reawakened? How should the factory work be designed so as to reduce the number of accidents? Psychology is needed to solve all these problems which beset every industry.

9. Problems of selling The work of an industry does not end with the production of things, but carries on till the produced goods are sold. If one does not get success in selling the final produce, its quality and quantity matter less than nothing. And in order to sell things, it is necessary that people should be acquainted with the product, its qualities, and should develop the need to buy them. Advertisement serves this purpose, and successful advertisement is based on appeal. Hence, the value of psychology in the field of advertisement can hardly be disputed.

10. Prevention and solution of industrial conflicts No industry is completely free from quarrels and conflicts of a minor or major kind. At times these conflicts get out of hand lead to strikes by the workers or lockouts by the management. There are extreme cases in which such conflicts lead to widespread arson, murder and wilful destruction of public and private property. Although some economic demands or political factors may be at the root of such industrial conflict, the most important factor influencing the actions of workers and management alike is the psychological element. That is why sometimes even great issues are overlooked so that no conflict occurs while relatively insignificant incidents like the impolite words of a manager to a worker may lead to strikes and violent conflicts. It is the psychological factor which results in strikes and conflicts becoming extremely violent. If, then, such conflicts are to be resolved, the mere satisfaction of economic demands is not enough. It is necessary also to remove those factors which, from the psychological standpoint, are responsible for the occurrence of such conflicts, If these psychological factors are kept in view from the beginning, it is possible to reduce the number of conflicts. And it is the task of industrial psychology to study these factors.

11. Problems of personal conduct While the majority of workers are inspired to revolt and conflict because of some defect in the environment, there are a few workers in whom the root cause of misconduct and conflict is some defect of personality and character. In such cases, it is necessary to consult the industrial psychologist who can trace the cause of the individual's maladjustment and offer a solution.

The importance and value of the industrial psychologist's advice in big industrial complex is evident from the above exposition of his role in solving various problems of industry. It is for this reason that in all progressive countries, industrial psychologist are employed in all large industries.

OBJECTIVES OF INDUSTRIAL PSYCHOLOGY

"The aim of Industrial psychology," according to Myers, "is not primarily to obtain greater output but to give the worker greater ease at his work. Ease does not mean mere physical ease but also mental ease."[1] As a branch of applied psychology, industrial psychology has the following objectives :

1. Personnel selection Industrial psychology tries to find out how a suitable individual can be selected to perform a particular task. If this can be done, then the work gets the correct worker while the worker himself gets the work he can do best.

2. Care of worker's health If the worker does not have good mental and physical health, the work of the industry cannot progress smoothly. His mental and physical health is profoundly influenced by the conditions under which he is required to work and by his relations with the management. The objective of industrial psychology is to discover the ideal conditions in which the best mental and physical health of the worker can be maintained.

3. Protection of worker's economic interests Mental health cannot be maintained unless a person's economic interests are secure. Besides, the worker cannot be encouraged to give of his best, if he is uncertain about his economic condition. Hence industrial psychology evaluates the efficiency of the worker and determines an adequate salary or suggests scientific principles on the basis of which an adequate salary can be determined.

4. Search of proper methods of work One important reason of accidents and mishaps in factories is the improper methods of work. Improper working also promotes fatigue and boredom. Hence, another objective of industrial psychology is to find out the proper methods of work so that accidents are prevented, and fatigue and boredom reduced to the minimum.

5. Removing maladjustment Another important factor which causes industrial conflicts is the lack of adjustment between the worker and his circumstances and the conditions in which he works. This maladjustment is primarily psychological in nature. It is the task of the industrial psychologist to locate the cause of maladjustment and to suggest means of rectifying it. This is another objective of industrial psychology.

6. Reform of working conditions It is the task of the industrial psychologist to find out the ideal conditions in which the highest

---

1. Myers, C.S., *Industrial Psychology,* pp. 14-15.

efficiency can be attained and the worker maintained at the peak of mental and physical health. The most important working conditions are — arrangement for adequate and proper lighting, proper ventilation, absence of noise, provision for periodical rest, normal conveniences for the male and female employees, etc.

7. Reform in machines The worker and the machine are equally responsible for the number of accidents and amount of fatigue induced in the worker. Prevention of accidents and reduction in fatigue can be achieved by the proper designing of machines. Industrial psychologists give useful suggestions for the improvement of machines and tools.

8. Reform in human relationships In order to maintain a proper atmosphere and a high degree of morale among the workers in an industry, it is necessary to have proper and cordial human relations between the workers and the management. One objective of the industrial psychologist is to suggest means of improving human relations.

9. Humanistic approach in industry Psychological studies have established that human relations in industry cannot be good unless a humanistic approach is adopted. Hence the relations existing between the management and the various levels of workers should be improved and the barriers between them removed. Industrial psychologists' help is spreading the humanistic approach in industry.

FUNCTION AND VALUE OF INDUSTRIAL PSYCHOLOGY

Progress in the field of industry depends not only on advances in technology but also upon the cordiality and pleasantness of human relations. In the field of industry, these human relations are also the industrial relations, and are fundamentally psychological in nature. They depend upon the interest, motives, sentiments and passions of individuals. If their nature is to be understood and they are to be made more profitable, it is necessary to undertake a study of interests, motives, sentiments and passions, which is the task of psychology. For this reason, psychological study in the sphere of industry is of great value. The following facts can be pointed out about the contribution of industrial psychology to industry:

1. Solution of labour problems Conflicts between management and workers is almost a normal feature of every industry and can be caused by almost any factor. Often they become so violent that they result in severe losses in terms of money and lives to both the management and the workers. At the root of all such conflicts are some psychological tensions.

It is the task of psychology to study these conflicts, and for that reason psychology can help in the solution of these problems. Most of the means adopted today to improve the relations between the management and the worker are in fact evolved from psychological observation and testing under actual industrial conditions over a long period. They cannot be changed by the wish of any one individual. The truth of the matter is that a conflict can be resolved only if the various factors inherent in it are separated and analysed. Even in the sphere of industrial conflicts, only the psychologist can do this. One major cause of conflict, for example, is the individual differences between individuals which are studied by psychology. Just as a doctor is consulted in the case of bodily disease, and the sociologist consulted about social problems, the industrial psychologist should be considered as a specialist on psychological problems in industry and his help should be sought.

2. Prevention of accidents Psychology has provided valuable suggestions not only in the solution of conflicts but also in the prevention of accidents. Psychologists have discovered the kinds of machines that should be designed, the manner in which they should be operated and the plan according to which they should be arranged in a factory. The purpose of this study is to find means of preventing accidents. The psychologist finds out how much accident-prone the workers are and suggests methods of getting rid of this propensity.

3. Study of aptitudes Irrespective of the quality and nature of the physical conditions prevailing in a factory, it depends upon the worker's aptitude to make the best use of them. If the worker has a favourable attitude towards the work it will be done but if his aptitude is not suitable then even the best conditions cannot persuade the worker to work. The study and measurement of aptitude is the subject of psychology and it is the psychologist who can help the industrialist here.

4. Maintaining morale In order to maintain a certain level of production and to improve the quality of production, it is necessary in every industry and profession to maintain a high level of morale among the workers. Morale is influenced by a large number of psychological factors such as affection and freedom, the desire to make sacrifices, availability of proper leadership, etc. By studying these, the psychologist can give suggestions for maintaining morale.

5. Creating proper leadership The study of leadership is the responsibility of social psychology. In the field of industry, the supervisor must not only be an official but also a capable leader because otherwise he cannot guide the workers properly and encourage them to work hard.

Social psychology can help in the field of industry by pointing out the qualities that are necessary for leadership and by explaining how such qualities can be developed. It can also tell the industrialist about the person who has such qualities or who is capable of developing them.

6. Measurement of individual differences Success in industry or a profession can be achieved only if the most capable workers are assigned jobs which they are best capable of performing. If this can be done, the workers perform their functions with greater interest and can thus increase production and improve its quality. And individual differences can only be discovered by a wide variety of psychological tests. Hence, the assistance of the psychologist can prove of great value in this sphere.

7. Study of efficiency In an industry all the workers do not have the same degree of efficiency. Nor is this required, because there are many different kinds of functions to be performed, for which varying levels of efficiency are needed. The psychologist finds out which person has the requisite efficiency to perform a particular job. In addition to this, the psychologist can also give suggestions for improving efficiency by removing those obstacles which hinder efficient working.

8. Use of psychological tests In the present day psychological tests are being extensively employed to select the most qualified individuals for particular jobs in industry. The chief tests are those of intelligence, interest, aptitude and personality. Sometimes several of these tests are included in a single test battery. Some of these tests are used on individuals while others are used to study the group qualities of workers. All of these tests have their own limitations but even then they are successfully used in the recruitment of employees in the industry.

9. Motion and time studies Different people take varying amounts of time to complete a specific job because they work at different speeds. Today time and motion studies are conducted to find out the efficiency of individuals and even of machines. These studies have also been used to find out means by which a specific work can be done better in a shorter time. Labour and time are saved by analysing motion studies so that the essential movements can be isolated and concentrated upon. Time studies help in economizing upon the time spent in a particular operation. In modern factories, the machines, the specific places at which particular workers sit and the positions in which they sit are so arranged as to save time and to improve efficiency. All this done to eliminate all unnecessary movement and duplication of work.

10. Aid in industrial training It is now accepted that the efficiency of a worker can be appreciably improved by the proper kind of training and that the expense involved in training is paid off double-fold. Training people can avoid accidents while the quality and quantity of their production are far higher than that of untrained people. Hence, different kinds of training programmes for different jobs are now called for. At the same time, training programmes for workers at all levels are now organised regularly. The industrialist stands to gain by all such training imparted to his employees. Such training programmes can be devised only by the psychologist, who can point out the basis of such training and methods employed in it.

11. Suggestions concerning motives An employee must be motivated if he is to progress in his job. This motivation can be supplied through increase in wages, promotion, praise or in many other ways. In the absence of motivation or on account of disappointment, the quality and the quantity of the workers' output both suffer. The special study of motivation is the task of psychology. Only a psychologist can point out how a worker can be motivated to improve the quality and quantity of his product, how the workers' motives can be prevented from leading them to strike, how motivation can be improved even without spending money, and how wages should be paid so as to constitute a permanent motive. All these suggestions tremendously help in the working of an industry.

12. Studies of fatigue and monotony The most important obstacle in the way of increasing production is fatigue and monotony. Psychologists have conducted extensive studies into the ways and means of eliminating them. These suggestions can be of great help in removing fatigue and monotony from industrial work.

13. Vocational guidance Vocational guidance involves the finding out of an individual's capabilities through psychological tests and suggesting the profession for which the individual is best suited. It is the suggestion given by a psychologist, which, if acted upon by the worker, will help him to his own talent to the great extent. In most of the progressive nations, an individual is given vocational guidance about the various professions he can enter profitably, even before he has completed his education. The chief benefit of this method is that the individual can then pursue a course of studies which will train him for the right profession.

14. Advertisement and selling In the sphere of industry, the psychologist's advice is not limited only to suggesting methods of improving production but is also concerned with suggesting methods of advertisement and selling. Advertisement is based upon the psychology of appeal. The psychologist studies those factors which are involved in appeal. It then gives suggestions about the subject matter and the layout of the advertisement so that it can attract the attention of the greatest possible number of people. One example of this is the use of neon signs for advertisement during the night. Apart from advertisement, modern industries try to make use of psychological ideas in selling so that they can convince the customer of the utility of the goods and persuade him to buy them. Psychologists have analysed the process of buying and selling things, and have given useful suggestions about selling. They not only explain how the salesmen should persuade the customer to buy his stock but also how the customer should avoid being trapped into unnecessary expenses by the salesman.

It is clear from the above explanation that psychology has great importance for industry and that this importance is increasing.

QUESTIONS FOR EXERCISE

1. What is industrial psychology? Explain its objectives.
2. What is the relationship of industrial psychology and industrial sociology.
3. Describe functions and value of industrial psychology.
4. Show the relationship of industrial psychology to general psychology.

3

METHODOLOGY

Industrial psychology, which is a branch of applied psychology, makes a study of human behaviour under industrial conditions. Hence, basically it makes use of the same methods as are used in applied psychology. In psychology, the most scientific technique is the experimental method because the conclusions gained from experiment under controlled circumstances are the most valid and reliable. Industrial psychology also makes use of the experimental method because it is the most scientific. But it also makes use of other psychological methods such as observation, interview, questionnaire, etc. A brief account of the methods used in industrial psychology are given below :

EXPERIMENT

An experiment is a question asked methodically. In this the experimenter is faced with a question which he tries to answer by conducting an experiment. This question is based on his hypothesis, which itself is based on his own experience. The results of the experiment either prove or disprove the hypothesis. If the hypothesis is proved to be valid, it is used as the basis for some scientific law which can be used as the basis for some other scientific law which can be used in other spheres. In every industry there are certain problems which are discovered through experience. Industrial psychology begins with certain hypotheses which are the various possible solutions to those problems. This can be better explained by an example. From his experience Taylor learnt of the difficulties of increasing production and in trying to overcome them he created the principle of scientific organisation, later called after him. He observed that every worker goes through certain motions in performing his functions. He came up with the hypothesis that if these motions are scientifically performed through the proper organisation of machines and training of the workers, then time can be saved and more production achieved in less time. In order to test the truth of this hypothesis, he made an experiment upon the labourers of the Bethlehem Iron Company which deal in iron. He studied their movements and conditions of work, and then explained his idea to the labourers and persuaded them to apply it. When the idea was put into practice, it was found that production increased three-to four fold. Hence, his principle of scientific organisation was proved correct. Gilbreth, a student of Taylor, made more experiments on the same principle in the brick industry and came up with the conclusions which supported Taylor's principle. Later on, many other psychologists applied Taylor's principle of scientific organisation to test its validity in many other industries. Finally, this principle was accepted as valid. It will be obvious from this example that in industrial psychology many hypotheses are tested through experiment. Those hypotheses which prove valid and correct are used as a base to make general scientific laws. These laws are valid because in an experiment, the scientist himself controls the circumstances under which the tests are conducted. For this reason, the experiment is being extensively used in industrial psychology.

SOCIAL SURVEY

Meaning of Social Survey

The term survey has two constituents : *sur* which means over and *veeir* which means to see. Accordingly the word survey means "to look over" or "to oversee" and this is precisely what we understand by survey in social context; observation is the main thing in survey. According to *Websters College Dictionary,* survey is "A critical inspection, often official, to provide exact information, often a study of an area with respect to a certain condition or its prevalence, such as a survey of the school." Social survey can be made only of a definite geographical area and that we cannot make survey if the area is unlimited. Moreover social survey deals with some definite social problems and conditions. It is a process by which quantitative facts are collected about social aspects of a community's composition and activities. It is an investigation of the structures and processes of a community, within well-defined geographical boundaries. It is a well-known fact that all social survey is undertaken with an implicit or explicit purpose of social progress and betterment. Keeping the progress and improvement of a community in view, an attempt is made to find out the conditions and causes suited to such a change. The social survey tells us both the reactionary and progressive elements in society, and this knowledge is the *sine qua non* of all social betterment. In brief, social survey is the investigation of social problems, conditions, structures, processes, etc., and the facts are collected through this means in order to bring about change for better in a social group or community occupying definite geographical limits.

The Aims of Social Survey

Following are the aims which motivate social surveys :

1. Data collection regarding social aspects of a community The primary aim of social survey is the collection of facts about certain definite aspects of a community in order to obtain scientific and well-ordered information. For this purpose, the social surveyor makes use of various techniques to gather information from a selected group of members of a community. The information data have both qualitative and quantitative aspects. Prior to undertaking investigation, the aim and purpose of investigation are well-defined and established. In as much as there are varieties of aspects about a community, their aims and purposes are different. The land-use survey, the political or the geographical surveys are about different aspects of a community. But social survey is called social in order to distinguish it from other types and also in order to stress the fact that in it only social aspects of a community are considered. The social survey is both descriptive and statistical; besides, it aims at social amelioration.

2. The Study of social problems and the conditions of working classes A glance at the history of social survey reveals that social survey is mainly, if not exclusively, concerned with the problems of society and the socio-economic conditions of the working classes and other depressed and underprivileged groups in the society.

The social survey aims at the study of the conditions and factors of social retardation or backwardness. It aims at the removal of reactionary forces from the society and thereby helps release of social energies into progressive channels. After making social survey and knowing the causes of backwardness, plans are formulated to remove these conditions. The socio-economic level of working classes is much lower than other groups in a society. All kinds of social problems and dysfunctions are found to abound in working classes. The problems of disease, epidemics, unemployment, juvenile delinquency, unhygienic conditions of living, moral depravity, sexual polymorphy, etc., are far more acute among industrial labour than in any other social class. Due to paucity of accommodation and low moral sense, children of workers are constantly exposed to immoral and drunken behaviour of their elders. As a consequence of this, sexual corruption and crime are rife among labour. Their moral sense is blunted. In order to improve their conditions, social surveys are a prerequisite. Most of the problems are inter-related. Unemployment and poverty, illiteracy and unhygienic conditions seem to be inter-related. Social survey studies social problems and tries to see relationship among them.

3. Practical and utilitarian viewpoint The motivation of social survey is practical and utilitarian. All surveys are undertaken with a practical end in view. Social research is born of natural curiosity and urge to know and it aims at pure theoretical knowledge; but social survey, on the contrary, is utilitarian. It is undertaken for the purpose of social welfare and betterment. In social survey, facts relevant to problem in hand are collected and upon their basis remedial measures are recommended or suggested. As a result of social surveys, government passes various laws to protect the underprivileged against exploitation. Many other measures are taken to help in a practical way the depressed and down-trodden. The special privileges granted to Scheduled Castes and Scheduled Tribes is a case in point.

Stages of Social Survey

Now we come to the study of various stages in social survey :

1. Selecting the problem As we have seen in the foregoing explanation of social survey, it deals with social problems. Accordingly, the first step of social survey is the selection of the problem. As long as the nature and character of the problem are not clear in the mind of the surveyors, they would not know how to make a start and will grope in dark; therefore clarity and definiteness about the problems is a *sine qua non* of any social survey. The social surveyor is not merely a spectator who can afford to dally with any and every problem he comes across in a community. His approach is practical and motivated by utilitarian considerations. Therefore, he must choose a problem which is significant and whose solution would make some practical difference to the life of the community. A social surveyor should choose his problem, keeping in view the importance of the problem for the community and the accrual of tangible benefits to the community consequent upon its removal.

2. Definition of aim Following the choice of the problem, the aim and purpose of social survey must be well-defined and made crystal clear. Social survey will lack direction in the absence of knowledge of goals. Moreover, the efficiency of a social surveyor can be measured only in relation with the achievement of goals and if we do not know a goal, we shall have no criterion to judge the success of survey. These goals may be specialized or generic. For example, collection of census data is for general purposes. The social survey of living conditions of labourers or the statistics regarding indebtedness of labour are surveys having specific aims. At time, the aim of survey is to bring out into general notice the facts which are known by some only. Whatever may be the aim of a social survey, it may be generic or specific, but it must be well-defined.

3. Definition of problem under study Now the nature of the problem selected should be defined. This will determine the scope of the problem and also its nature and character. For example, if we wish to study the problem of alcoholism among labour, then first of all we should define what we mean by the term alcoholism. We have to be clear in our mind as to what quantity of liquor consumed per day indicates alcoholism.

4. Analysis of problem by making a schedule After the problem is defined, we have to analyse the various elements, constituents or factors involved in the problem so that a detailed and systematic list of these may be formulated. It is only after this step that the relevant information can be systematically gathered.

5. Constitution of a Commission for survey The official surveys are always undertaken after constituting a commission to make survey and this commission is empowered to elicit various types of data and also has an access to classified material relevant to the study. Having constituted the commission, government defines its powers, terms, limit and scope of inquiry. It is also provided with both financial and personnel assistance. The commission also acts as processor of complaints received from surveyors or public and can redress grievances. It can and does from time to time issue instructions and determine code of conduct for surveyors. Having done fieldwork, the surveyors fill and send the data to the office of the commission where they are processed, classified and analyzed. The commission is headed by a director and has some members. The director and the members are responsible for all policy decisions. They determine the policy and oversee its execution. If need be, the commission splits itself into various committees and sub-committees to deal with specialised matters. In the event of controversy, commission members can give dissenting notes, though normally an attempt at consensus is made. In the event of dissenting notes, the majority report is considered to be the verdict of the commission.

6. Determination of scope The scientific study of a problem implies systematic investigation into a limited and well-defined subject matter. Without setting limits, no phenomenon can be studied. Accordingly, before the beginning of a survey, it is imperative to determine the scope of the problem. In determining the scope of a problem, the following techniques are made use of :

(a) Political and administrative division, such as nation, state, town, city, locality, etc.

(b) Professional classes, rich and poor people, labourer, etc. This means limiting the problem on the basis of economic levels or considerations.

(c) Child, youth, old, etc. This involves determination of the problem on biological basis.

(d) Married, unmarried, literate, illiterate, that is, determination on the basis of social status.

(e) Hilly areas, plains, deserts, etc., *i.e.*, determination of the scope of a problem upon geographical basis.

7. Determination of time limit Social survey requires the services of trained investigators and considerable amount of money. Accordingly, it is essential to set a time limit for it. Some problems are of topical importance and all problems undergo gradual change. In both cases, if the results of survey take too long period to be determined, the validity of results may be doubtful on account of change of conditions or the problems may no longer be quite relevant. For example, the special problems arising out of war conditions like displacement of population, etc., must be immediately tackled if the solution is to be effective. But if the government takes too long to come to conclusions about the nature and the extent of relief needed, the problem will be changed and the results of the survey will be inapplicable. Certain statistics cease to be relevant after lapse of some period. For example, if Census Commission submits its reports in 5 or 6 years, the census data collected by it will cease to be very relevant, because population of certain areas may have radically changed in number and character. While fixing the time limit, the time needed for each stage of social survey is determined and, therefore, delay in one stage will easily indicate that there would be delay in the completion of the survey. While fixing the time limit it has to be kept in mind that time and money consumed should not be excessive; it should not also, of course, be too short. In the first event, the character of problem may be changed during the period of survey and then much money and energy would be wasted. If the time is very short, the result may lack reliability on account of insufficient care, absence of check and cross-check. At times, the time limit has to be fixed to suit the convenience of persons giving information. For example, a survey conducted among students has to be so conducted that it can be completed prior to long leaves. To a large extent, time limit depends upon the technique employed. For instance, different amount of time is taken by questionnaire, interview, biographical records, observation techniques. The well-trained and competent surveyor will take less time than the ordinary surveyor. Therefore, while fixing time limit, the above considerations should be borne in mind.

8. Examination of the means of information After arranging survey, the next requirement is to decide about and examine the means of information. The sources of information must be accessible and free from duplicity and mischief. If the survey is being made for the first time, it is called primary survey and upon its basis there can be further advance. The data gathered through primary survey are called preliminary data. If the survey is being made a second time, it is called secondary survey and its data are called secondary data. In different types of surveys, different techniques of surveys are employed. Mostly the information is obtained through schedules, questionnaires and direct interviews of individuals. Secondary data are obtained through published or unpublished material of primary survey and also from official and non-official reports.

9. Determination of the unit of survey Before launching survey, its unit should be determined. On account of this determination field-workers are free from doubts and can easily gather the relevant information. The unit should be definite, unambiguous, stable, harmonized, simple and capable of being surveyed. In order to formulate a representative unit, it is necessary to define and well formulate the sample. If all units are to be surveyed, there is very little difficulty in the survey; but owing to unwieldiness and vastness of the area of survey, usually only representative units can be investigated. The units have to be determined keeping in view the time and money available for the survey. Their number and form depend upon the nature of the material. The sample technique can be employed only where there is no diversity of material or incoherence of time.

10. Determination of the amount of refinement of material Before undertaking the actual survey, it has to be made clear that to what extent refinement of the data is to be expected. In quantification, accuracy to the last percentile is considered a *sine qua non.* Accordingly, in quantitative survey, the surveyor has to obtain 100% accuracy; but in qualitative survey, the limit of accuracy and refinement is proportionate to the availability of time, funds and able personnel. However, it has to be borne in mind that in qualitative survey 100% accuracy is to use for the moon and should not be insisted upon.

11. The selection and training of researchers and data collectors Research requires a well-trained staff of researchers and field workers. The selection of researchers and field workers should be made keeping in view the nature and the scope of social survey. Having selected them they have to be trained for the job; they must become acquainted with their respective duties and manner of performing them. In selection not only the intellectual qualities should be emphasized but the personal qualities like amiability, good humour, pleasant appearance and tactfulness have to be particularly stressed, because the fieldworkers have to deal with various types of persons, and their personal qualities and resourcefulness will be much in demand.

12. Preparedness of informers In different types of survey, the individuals from different classes are used for collecting information. Before undertaking the survey it is essential to create responsiveness and preparedness for cooperation among individuals from whom the information is needed. For example, in the Census of 1917, government publicized through various media to make people aware of the need and importance of census, and the responsibility of public to give accurate information to fieldworkers without any fear, because all information of personal nature will be kept strictly confidential. Educated public can be informed by post or through newspaper advertisements. Uneducated persons can be approached through radio, television, cinema slides, and various leaders of the community can be entrusted to explain the uneducated persons orally the various aspects of a survey. Sometimes handbills are distributed, and, to approach uneducated, illustrated brochures are made available. If the individuals to be interviewed are persuaded to feel the importance of their cooperation, they will become responsive and give information easily.

13. Determination of survey techniques Before starting it should be made clear as to what techniques are to be used in survey. The choice of technique depends upon the scope and the nature of the survey. The determination of techniques facilitates survey. In questionnaire technique and the schedules to be sent by post, the list of questions is prepared beforehand.

14. Field work Having completed the above formalities, field workers go to respective individuals to gather information. In this they have to keep the convenience of persons to be interviewed in view. This work requires great resourcefulness and tact, because the cooperation of respondents can be had only if they are approached in the right manner. The fieldwork is done under the supervisor. After collecting information, the fieldworkers file it to their respective departments.

15. Organizations of material classification and statistical analysis The collected material is organised, classified and statistically analyzed.

16. Elucidation of conclusions, Having analyzed the data, competent and able researchers draw conclusions from them and elucidate these conclusions.

17. Presentation of graphs Lastly, the conclusions of a survey are graphically represented. Some schedules and charts are also given to aid the understanding of these conclusions.

When the conclusions of a social survey are made definite and have been well formulated, the recommendations are made to solve or relieve the problem. These recommendations are treated with respect as they have the backing of scientific inquiry. Upon the basis of these recommendations, official and non-official agencies take the necessary steps to implement them and since these recommendations are based on realistic scientific studies, their implementation usually yields desirable results. If there are repeated surveys in a particular field, the later surveys act as verifiers of earlier surveys.

Types of Surveys

Usually social surveys are of two types: general and specialized. In the general survey the entire community is studied in a general way. A specialized survey, on the contrary, seeks to study some particular aspects of the community such as hygienic attitude, child-welfare, unemployment, etc.; of these any one is studied at one time in a single survey.

Besides the above two types, there are some other kinds of social surveys. The important ones and their basic nature are treated below:

1. Direct or indirect survey In direct surveys quantification is possible whereas quantitative description is not possible in indirect surveys. For instance, the demographic surveys are direct; but, on the other hand, the surveys of health conditions and level of nutrition are indirect. Both types of social surveys have their own place in social study.

2. Census survey or sample survey In the census survey all units are counted separately and then the sum of all units is computed. On the other hand, in sample survey, some representative unit is studied. Compared to total or census survey, the representative surveys are less time and energy consuming, but they are valid only if the sample selected is really representative and the entire field is harmonious. If the units are heterogeneous, sample survey is not possible.

3. Primary or secondary survey In the primary survey, the task of survey is taken up afresh and the surveyor himself sets the goals and collects relevant facts; but if some facts are already available and there is no need to examine them afresh by a new survey, then the survey is called secondary. Primary survey is far more reliable than the secondary survey.

4. Initial or repetitive survey If in any area the survey is being made for the first time, it is called initial but if it is being made second or third time it is called repetitive.

5. Official, semi-official or private survey As is clear from the names, official surveys are conducted by the government, and the surveys conducted by quasi-government institutions like university, corporations, boards, etc., are semi-official. If the survey is conducted by some non-government person or agency, it is called the private Survey.

6. Widespread or limited survey The widespread survey takes a very large area or multiple aspects for survey purposes, while a limited survey is confined to a small area and usually deals with some specific question. Obviously, limited survey has greater reliability than the widespread survey.

7. Public or confidential survey Some surveys are of general types and their data are not of highly personal nature. Accordingly no secrecy is maintained in collection of data or publication of results. These surveys are, therefore, known as public survey. Against this if the nature of the survey is such that information collected is not to be revealed to public, the survey is confidential.

8. Postal or personal survey If the means of collecting data are mailed questionnaires, it is called postal survey; but if the information is collection by means of direct interview of respondents, it is called personal survey.

9. Regular or *ad hoc* survey Regular surveys are made periodically without fail. The State Bank of India makes such surveys, while *Ad hoc* surveys are conducted for a specific purpose and are not periodically revised.

Social survey in town and country areas Herman N. Morse has enumerated ten phases of survey which are being listed hereunder for the sake of comparison :

1. Definition of the purpose of object.
2. Definition of the problem to be studied.
3. The analysis of this problem in a schedule.
4. The delimitation of area or scope.
5. Examination of all documentary source.
6. Fieldwork.
7. The arrangement, tabulation and statistical analysis of data.
8. The interpretation of results.
9. Deduction.
10. Graphic expression.

The Value and Importance of Survey Method

The various types of survey and different techniques used in survey have their respective significance and value. In a general way it may be said that surveys throw useful light on the various aspects of the social problems and help in understanding the causes of the problems and the mutual interplay of the causes. On the strength of a survey practical remedies to solve and resolve problems can be put forward and these remedies will normally be efficacious because they are the outcome of scientific study and analysis. A general or widespread survey helps us to get an overall idea of the multiple aspects of the problem ranging over a very wide field, and, this, in turn, can indicate problems for specialised survey. A specialized survey may be called depth survey because it studies threadbare a particular problem in a limited range. The conclusions of a specialized survey are much more reliable than those of general or widespread survey. Accordingly, specialized survey is more important from scientific point of view. The postal survey is less expensive than personal survey; but postal survey can be conducted only where all the respondents are literate. Moreover, in case of doubt in respondent's mind, posted survey fails whereas personal survey can take care of all such contingencies. While personal survey is undoubtedly reliable and therefore desirable, its negative features are its expensiveness and various types of lures and temptations to which a fieldworker is exposed. There is a well-known case of an American who distorted information about a poor family because the mother offered him the sexual services of her comely daughter. Public survey can be made only in situation where the information is of general type and not of personal nature. But in survey of problems of disorganization, homosexuality, lesbianism, marital discord, smuggling, crime, etc., the survey has perforce to be confidential. In regular surveys, the reliability of conclusion increases.

The value of a primary survey is directly dependent upon the technique used. Here there is a lack of comparative material and this proves a stumbling block. However, primary surveys are highly important because through them a first attempt is made to gather well-organised information on a subject and these prove to be stepping stones for repetitive surveys. The census and income data can be kept reliable only through regular surveys.

In census survey, much money, time and staff are needed. The surveys of this type are countrywide and their conclusions are reliable and precise. But, on account of being less expensive, sample surveys are widely used in social sciences. Official surveys are initiated and conducted by government to gather accurate data on some problem confronting the government. As government have large funds and large brigade of trained personnel, official surveys are quite reliable and accurate. But government is liable to suppress information unpalatable and offensive to it and which may arouse people's resentment against it. Therefore private surveys, in spite of their obvious limitations, are very useful. The direct surveys, being quantitative in character, are more reliable than the qualitative indirect surveys.

The above discussion of variety of surveys and variety of methods bring into relief the fact that the utility and importance of survey cannot be determined in abstract. It is only in relation to the nature of the problem, its scope, the aim and object of survey, the availability of funds, staff and other facilities that one can know which type of survey will be useful under the given circumstances. Each type has its pros and cons, and the choice of type of survey is very crucial in order to derive full benefits from the survey.

OBSERVATION

In industrial psychology the observation methpd is used wherever it is impossible to control all the conditions. For example, the aptitude of workers can be controlled only within certain limits. In the same way one cannot deliberately create tension between the worker and the management to study tension. Tension can be observed only when it is actually found existing in a particular situation. Take the examples of strikes and lockouts. The psychologist does not try to create them. He only makes a careful observation of such phenomena as and when they occur. To begin with, he makes a careful examination of the behaviour of managers and workers in a situation of strike or lockout, and then makes a record of his observations. After similar examination and recorded observation at a number of different places, the psychologist analyses the information available to discover any general patterns of behaviour that may be common to all situations of strikes and lockouts. On the basis of these general patterns, he presents some general principles. In industrial psychology the observation method cannot claim as high a degree of validity as experimental method, because observation is influenced by individual prejudices. For example, the scientist with communist leanings will find traces of capitalistic exploitation of the labour class in all examples of strikes, and he will tend by and large, to favour the working class. Some scientists, on the other hand, may be completely opposed to the workers and thus may make partial observations. But prejudices of this kind can be eliminated to a great extent by training and practice. Actually, as has been pointed out earlier, the experimental method cannot replace the observation method, because many conditions which come under the purview of industrial psychology cannot be artificially created and hence cannot be completely observed and tested.

INTERVIEW

In many spheres of industry, industrial psychology makes use of the interview method. For example, in the selection of workers from among the many applicants, workers are interviewed. Besides, sometime individual workers are separately interviewed to find out their opinions on different matters concerned with the industry or on methods adopted for improving conditions. In an interview, the interviewer and the subject sit facing each other. Success in this method depends upon the ability of the interviewer to frame suitable questions which can elicit the information he requires. The chief advantage of this method is that a personal relation between the interviewer and his subject is established, by reason of which the interviewer learns many things which he would otherwise never find out. If the subject hesitates in answering certain questions, his hesitation can be removed. As far as industry is concerned, scientists can get valuable information on different problems of industry by separately interviewing the workers, the managers and the industrialists.

QUESTIONNAIRE

Another method now being used to find out the opinion of workers, managers and industrialists is the questionnaire. As is obvious from the name itself, the questionnaire method makes use of a list of selected questions which are intended to elicit the desired information. In the closed questionnaire every question is followed by a yes and a no, one of which has to be deleted by the person answering the questionnaire. In an open questionnaire the answers have to be stated in a few words or one or two sentences. But the questionnaire method suffers from the following defects:

(i) Very often the person answering gives the wrong answer and hides the truth.

(ii) Sometimes the questions carry one meaning for the scientist and another for the person answering them.

(iii) Fairly often the answers are put down without thought with the result that the conclusions arrived at are wrong.

Despite the above difficulties, the questionnaire method is less time consuming than the interview method because thousands of questionnaires can be printed and distributed by hand or by post and the answers received can be quickly analysed. But the chief difficulty is that, in the absence of any personal relationship between the research worker and the subject, the truth cannot be easily obtained.

THE SCHEDULE

The Meaning of Schedule

There are two ways in which the response to a questionnaire may be secured. In the first, it may be sent by post to various individuals; and, in the second, the researcher may himself present the questionnaire to the individuals whose responses are desired. The first method is called the mailed questionnaire, while the second method is called schedule. A schedule is a list of questions formulated and presented with the specific purpose of testing an assumption or hypothesis. For example, a social scientist believes on the basis of his general experience that women do not enjoy good status in a joint family; he will so formulate his questions that the actual state of affairs may come to surface in responses to those questions. According to W.J. Goode and P.K. Hatt, "Schedule is the name usually applied to a set of questions which are asked and filled by an interviewer in a face to face situation with another."[1] By a schedule we cannot, however, obtain information about many things at once. It is best suited to the study of a single item thoroughly.

From the foregoing discussion, it is quite clear that in the schedule method, interview occupies a central place and plays a vital role. As a matter of fact, success in the use of schedule is largely determined by the ability and tact of the interviewer rather than on the quality of the questions posed. Because the interviewer himself poses the questions and notes down the answer all by himself, the quality of questions has not any great significance. The list of questions is merely a formal document intended to maintain uniformity in the questions asked of different persons.

Important Features of Schedule

From the above-mentioned definitions, following salient points about schedule emerge :

1. The schedule is presented by the interviewer. The questions are asked and the answers are noted down by him.
2. The list of questions is a mere formal document; it need not be attractive.
3. The schedule can be used in a very narrow sphere of social research.

Aims of Schedule

P.V. Young has laid emphasis on the following aims of the schedule. According to her, a researcher makes the schedule a guide, a means of delimiting the sense of his enquiry, a memory tickler, a recording device. These may now be discussed pointwise :

1. Delimitation of the topic A schedule is always about a definite item of inquiry; its subject is a single and isolated subject-item rather than the subject in general. The interviewer presents questions about one item and notes down answers about it. Therefore, the schedule delimits and specifies the subject of inquiry.

2. Aide-memoire In an interview the choice of questions is left entirely to the interviewer; he may ask any question. In this there is always a chance of some important points being left. Therefore, in the schedule the

---

1. Gode, W.J. and P.K. Hatt, *Methods in Social Research,* p. 133.

list of questions is preplanned and noted down formally. The interviewer is always armed with the former document detailing the questions. Accordingly, in the schedule method, the interviewer is not dependent upon the memory.

3. Aid to classification and analysis When the interviewer obtains replies to the questions given in the schedule, these replies are classified and analyzed. Many different tables are used in the schedule; and the questions are also of many types. Some need only yes/no answer; others require choosing one of the alternatives given or arranging them in order of preference; still others require certain amount of thinking and can be answered in small sentences. Therefore, all varieties of replies are sifted and classified under various heads. This helps in analysis of the replies.

The above aims of schedule method have been condensed by Mrs. Young in the following words: "An observation usually serves several purposes. Simultaneously :

1. it is specific memory tickler;
2. it is an objective recording device which makes possible accurate accumulation of large quantities of data;
3. it is a standardizing device and
4. it aids to delimit the scope of the study and to concentrate on the circumscribed elements essential to the analysis."[1]

Types of Schedules

Scholars have described four types of schedules. These are to be discussed now :

1. Rating schedules In the fields of business guidance, psychological research and social research, the rating schedules are used to assess the attitudes, opinions, preferences, inhibitions and other like elements. As is evident from the term "rating," in these schedules, the value and trend of the above-mentioned qualities are measured.

2. Documents schedules The schedules of this type are used to obtain data regarding written evidence and case histories. In these schedules, those terms are included which occur frequently in documents and are to be generally found in case-histories. For example, in the field of criminology, rating schedules are used to gather data to be found in crime studies, the different kinds of crime, their incidence, the nature of earlier crimes and the personal data on criminals like school leaving age,

---

1. Young, P.V., *Methods of Social Survey and Research*, p. 181.

the age at the time of employment, the level of economic and social status and other sundry facts about crime and criminals.

3. Institutional survey forms of evaluational schedules The use of these schedules, as is evident from the name, is made to gather data about specialized institutions or agencies. The form and the size of evaluational schedules are determined by the nature and the complexity of the problems of an institution; more complex the problem, bigger the size of the schedule. To study the problems of American Public Organization for Health Services, a schedule running into as many as 38 pages, was used.

4. Observation schedules In these schedules, an observer records the activities and responses of an individual or a group under specific conditions. The observation schedules may need one or more research workers to be completed. The aim and purpose of an observation schedule are to verify some information.

5. Interview schedules A fifth form of schedules is sometimes treated independently and at other time considered included in the fourth type. In an interview schedule, an interviewer presents the questions of the schedule to the interviewees and records their responses in blank spaces.

Of all the above-mentioned types of schedules, the observation schedule is not most frequently used.

PSYCHOLOGICAL MEASUREMENT

In industrial psychology the most important problem is the selection of the right person for a particular job. Many kinds of psychological tests are used for this. These tests reveal the capabilities of the worker, and if he is found to be fit for the particular job in question, he can then be entrusted with the responsibility. Among the main kinds of psychological tests are the following:

(a) Intelligence tests The intelligence of an individual or a group of individuals is tested by getting answers to some questions or by making them perform certain tasks. Different intelligence tests are used for different age levels, and they may be verbal or non-verbal, individual or collective. They are chosen according to the situation in which they are to be used. In industry it is essential to know the intelligence quotient of the workers, as on the basis of intelligence quotient they can be graded and suitable work found for them.

(b) Tests of special abilities Certain jobs require a particular set of mental abilities. Special tests are used to discover these mental abilities in individuals. One example of tests of this kind is the test battery used by the Psychological Corporation of America which includes tests concerned with verbal arguments, numerical ability, abstract arguments, internal relationships, mechanical argument, writing speed and linguistic ability. Thurston's S.R.A. tests for primary mental abilities are well-known as tests of special abilities.

(c) Aptitude tests Among the aptitude tests, one of the most famous is the Minnesota mechanical adjustment test for measuring the mechanical aptitude of a person. Another famous test is the Bennet test for mechanical aptitude.

(d) Interest tests According to the principles of industrial psychology, every worker should be given work which he finds interesting. Hence, tests of interest are very common in the field of industry.

(e) Personality tests Certain traits of personality are essential for particular jobs in industry. Personality tests are administered to the candidate to find out whether he possesses such traits. The chief methods of testing personality are — case history method, interview method, questionnaire method, etc. By using these methods, one can find out the traits of each individual's personality.

MEASUREMENT OF APTITUDES

Studies have been conducted to find out the aptitudes of the workers, managerial staff and the industrialists — to find out their aptitudes towards the conditions of work, the conditions of wages and many kinds of reforms and improvements. Three kinds of standards are used to measure aptitudes :

(a) Opinion scale Examples of opinion scales are — Thurston's standard, Likert's standard and Gutmann's standard. By using these measures one can find out the opinions of people and then their aptitudes can be discovered indirectly. In these methods there are differences of construction and kinds.

(b) Rating scale In these, the evaluation of aptitudes does not depend upon the opinions or decisions of the workers themselves but upon the scientist's own decision. Rating is done on the basis of non-verbal behaviour, verbal behaviour, clinical interview, private essay, projection techniques and immediate experience, etc.

(c) Indirect scale In these, the workers are not aware that their aptitudes are being tested. In 1938 Ash, Block and Hurzmann studied changes of opinions among industrial groups through suggestions or hints.

TIME AND MOTION STUDIES

Apart from the above methods used in industrial psychology, there are certain other methods which are used in the solution of specific problems. One important method, for example, much used in industrial psychology, is the time and motion study in which all the movements made by the worker are studied and the time consumed by him is calculated. From this one can find out those movements which can be eliminated. It is also possible to find out those motions which can help in increasing production. Many time motion studies have been conducted in industrial spheres recently.

Briefly, the methods used in Industrial psychology are growing along with the number of new problems being brought up for research. In future too, one can hope for the evolution of new methods which can provide more valid results.

QUESTIONS FOR EXERCISE

1. Give a brief description of the chief methods of Industrial Psychology.
2. Write short note on Psychological Tests in Industry.
3. Write short note on Questionnaire Method.

4

FOUNDATIONS

Study of the development of modern Industrial psychology will reveal that its foundation is basically psychological, but this does not mean that the psychological basis is the only foundation of Industrial psychology. It also has economic and social foundations. But the psychological aspect should be considered more important since Industrial psychology is a branch of psychology in as much it studies human behaviour. A short description of the various bases of Industrial psychology is attempted in this chapter.

PSYCHOLOGICAL FOUNDATIONS OF INDUSTRIAL PSYCHOLOGY

In the beginning of the twentieth century, psychology came to be used in so many new branches that, based upon the practical uses to which it was put, sprang up. In the more progressive nations, as industry and the professions developed, the use of psychology in these spheres also increased. Thus a new branch of psychology called Industrial psychology came into being because it was being used to solve industrial problems. It primarily paid attention to industries and studied psychological facts which pertained directly to industry and commerce. Psychologists were appointed in many industries to give advice. In fact, these psychologists made valuable contributions in the various spheres of industry and business. It is possible to study the psychological foundations of Industrial psychology from three different angles which are as follows :

1. Psychology in industry There are many things in the industry where the assistance of a psychologist is particularly desirable. For example, it is necessary to conduct psychological tests for the selection of properly qualified personnel for particular jobs. Similarly, the psychologist can also give valuable advice about the conditions of work, both physical and psychological. The physical conditions of work include light, temperature, ventilation, music, hours of work and rest, and other similar conditions. Psychological conditions include the security of the workers, satisfaction of their needs, inspiration in their work, their relations with other workers and senior staff, etc. Psychological research is also valuable in the sphere of promotions and the principles upon which they should be based. Suggestions given by psychologists have proved to be of immense value in improving human relations in industry and in solving industrial disputes. The use of psychology has proved valuable in the field of industry and business.

2. Individual differences Recent psychological tests have definitely established that human beings differ from each other in respect of intelligence, interests, aptitudes, special abilities, personality, etc. These are called individual differences. If these individual differences are ignored then one cannot select the most able worker for a particular job. Industrial psychology is directly concerned with individual differences because they have to be kept in mind whenever some suggestion is given. An idea can be explained to one person in one particular way but a different method may have to be adopted to explain it to another person. Hence, from Wundt down to modern psychologists like Cattell,[1] Binet, Kraeplin and Munsterberg, all have made a special study of individual differences.

3. Personal adjustment It is necessary for each worker that he should make his adjustment with the environment surrounding him in the factory. Without this he cannot take interest in his work and will suffer from tension. If there is adjustment, the number of accidents and industrial conflicts is much less. Fatigue, monotony and boredom are also kept in control. In this connection industrial psychologists are continuously conducting research to find out how this adjustment can be achieved and then maintained.

SOCIAL FOUNDATIONS OF INDUSTRIAL PSYCHOLOGY

Even when working in an industry, the individual is never alone because he constantly comes into contact with other workers, supervisors, managers and industrialists. In business, the worker has to deal with all kinds of people. For this reason it also becomes necessary to study the

---

1. Cattell, J. Mick, *Mental Tests and Measurements,* pp. 373-80.

social foundations of Industrial psychology. Efforts are being made to bring industrial organisation to a scientific level. The more progressive countries try to improve the social life of the worker by organising various kinds of social programmes. The following points need to be considered in a study of the social foundations of Industrial psychology:

1. Worker and social progress The progress of the industrial workers is a part of the general social progress. Hence the movements for social progress were accompanied by movements for an improvement in the conditions of industrial workers. It was accepted as a general principle that the work of social emancipation would remain incomplete so long as nothing was done to improve the conditions of industrial workers. For this reason social workers turned their attention in this direction. Bills were passed in Parliament to this effect. Social workers directed the attention of industrialists towards the bad condition of the workers and insisted that they should be given human rights and their conditions changed so that the workers could improve their standards of living. Exploitation of workers was violently objected to and decried. Great stress was placed on providing social security to the workers. Political parties also began to pay attention to the amelioration of the lot of workers. In this manner the progressive nations linked the improvement of the industrial worker with the movements for general progress. This humanistic attitude is spreading rapidly in industry in all modern nations.

2. Workers' department and welfare schemes As a result of this humanistic approach, most modern nations have created workers' departments which undertake the task of safeguarding the rights of workers and working for their betterment. Labour welfare is now accepted as an important element in social welfare. Labour welfare, includes the improvement in the social, economic and psychological conditions of the worker. In most large industries labour welfare officers are appointed to look after the workers and to help solve any disputes that may arise between them and the employers. The modern state is a welfare state, the object of which is to enhance the welfare of the citizens in every sphere. The worker is an important part of the population and the government which does not undertake measures for labour welfare cannot hope to achieve its ideal of social welfare. After achieving independence, India, too, has begun to pay attention to the question of labour welfare. It has, from time to time, enacted laws to secure the rights of workers in various industries. Although even now many industrialists avoid the clutches of the law by various means, the pressure exerted by the trade unions is steadily changing the situation.

3. Industrial management Today efforts are being made to raise industrial management to the level of a science. The suggestions of Taylor and Thurston have been particularly valuable in this respect. A scientific industrial management implies the establishment of a management under which all elements of production are most efficiently employed, thus eliminating the exploitation of any one element and the exhaustive use of any other. In a scientific industrial management system, a humanistic approach is adopted to deal with the workers and efforts are made to provide them with more facilities. The advanced countries are continuously making rapid strides in this direction.

ECONOMIC FOUNDATIONS OF INDUSTRIAL PSYCHOLOGY

Studies conducted by Industrial psychology help not only in the personal problems and social problems of the workers but also in the solution of their economic problems. For this reason economic factors have also played an important part in the evolution of Industrial psychology. It has now been established that if an industrialist wants to progress rapidly he must pay great attention to the workers employed by him and create psychological conditions in which the morale and the efficiency of the workers can be maintained. With the introduction of sophisticated machinery, the importance of the worker was reduced for sometime, but scientists quickly pointed out that this was harmful. They emphasized the fact that industrial progress is impossible if the worker is neglected. As a result, efforts were made to provide industrial management with a scientific basis. F.W. Taylor,[1] an American engineer, did pioneering work in this direction and the principles enunciated by him came to be known by the name of Taylorism. His plan was given the name of scientific organisation.

Taylor's Principles of Scientific Management

Taylor first put forward the principles of scientific management in the field of industry and thus helped the progress of Industrial psychology. Taylor's method is based on two fundamental assumptions, the first that the worker wants to get the maximum amount of money he can from the industrialist, and the second that the industrialist wants to pay the least possible amount for the highest possible production. Besides, it was also believed that there is no organisation in industry in which the relations between the employer and employee remain cordial and both cooperate

---

[1] Taylor, F.W., *Shop Management*, New York, p. 21.

with each other for the purpose of achieving industrial progress. Taylor therefore presented a new programme of industrial management in order to achieve this objective. G.D. Babcock has explained this plan by the following four principles :[1]

1. The development of a science for every element of human work in order to remove the old fashioned methods.
2. The selection of the most capable individual for a specific job to be followed by a programme of training for that individual. This should take the place of the old practice in which the worker selected his own job and then trained himself to do it.
3. The development of a humanistic relationship between the management and the worker to promote progress, according to the principles given by the developed science.
4. Division of labour among the management and the worker in approximately equal proportions so that each department can undertake work it is best equipped to perform. This should replace the traditional conditions in which almost all the work and the responsibility fell on the shoulder of the worker.

It is evident from this that Taylor was in favour of replacing the old traditional methods by new scientific techniques. He wanted that the selection and the training should be conducted on a scientific basis. He stressed that the management and the worker should share the responsibility and the work, and cooperate in order to achieve industrial progress.

Taylor's Experiments[2]

Taylor's theory is based on certain experiments conducted by him. He used these principles first of all in solving the problems of the iron ore industry. He applied the principle of scientific management to the workers who transported iron ore, for the Bethleham Iron Company which employed nearly 75 labourers working in the traditional way. The majority of them were healthy and efficient, and were obeying the orders of the foreman. In carrying iron ore each worker bent down and lifted about 92 lbs of iron ore. He then carried it for a short distance and put it down at a particular place. In this manner he managed to transport about twelve and a half tons of iron ore in a day. The management of the

1. Babcock, G.D., *The Taylor System in Franklin Management, Application & Results,* New York, p. 17.
2. Taylor, F.W., *The Principles of Scientific Management,* New York, p. 42.

company was informed that if the workers worked according to Taylor's plan, they would be able to lift four times this weight, although the wages would not go up in the same proportion. Taylor explained that, if they worked according to his plan, each labourer would be able to lift 47 to 48 tons of iron. The management did not seem particularly enthusiastic but Taylor was not disappointed.

For his experiment Taylor selected a Dutch labourer from Pennsylvania who was well respected and had a good character. Taylor asked him whether he would like to be paid 1.85 shillings as daily wages or 1.15 shillings. The labourer naturally chose the higher rate of pay. Taylor told him that in that case he would have to work according to a new plan which would enable him to lift forty-seven and a half tons of iron. The worker had to work according to his new training and obey all the commands of the observer. This worker started to work when he was told and rested when he was instructed to rest. As a result he had lifted forty-seven and a half tons of iron by closing time and he received 1.85 shillings as wages. Using this Dutch labourer as an example Taylor tried to persuade the labourers to follow him but not everyone was prepared to work in this manner. Only one out of every eight workers was prepared to work in this way, with the result that only nine out of the original seventy-five employees of the factory were retained while the rest were turned out. The labourers unemployed as a result of this selection condemned Taylor but Taylor did not abandon his plan. Instead he tried to convince the unemployed workers that they could obtain higher wages elsewhere by following his plan of work. Actually, as a result of this plan, the workers and the management both profited. The company had to pay only a little more to obtain four times its original production because by paying 1.85 shillings instead of 1.15 shilling it got forty-seven and a half tons of iron instead of twelve and a half tons. On the other hand, the workers obtained about .70 shilling more than what they were getting. But although the labourers were working four times as much as they were working earlier they did not get a proportionate rise in wages. Consequently, the workers criticised Taylor and called him a tool of management and an enemy of the workers.

Thomson's Experiments

Another example is given to prove Taylor's principles. In this Thomson gave certain suggestions to improve the production and the quality of, the work done by ball bearing inspectors. Under this plan, provisions were made for rest within the period of work; besides, other conditions were also improved. Proper selection of workers according to the work was also introduced. Each worker was also given adequate and proper training, and allowed rest. As a result of these changes it was seen that the work previously done by 120 girls could now be done by only 35 girls. Their wages were also increased by 80 to 100 per cent. On the other hand, the hours of work were also reduced because each girl had now to work only eight and a half hours instead of ten and a half hours. On Saturdays the employees were allowed a half-holiday. Each girl began to feel that she occupied a position of some importance in the company, and as a result she began to work with greater concentration. Thus both the company and the workers were benefited by these scientific improvements.

Gilbreth's Experiments[1]

Gilbreth, a student of Taylor, also made use of Taylor's principles. He turned his attention to the mason's trade which, till then, was being followed on the traditional pattern in which no attention was paid to the location of the bricks, cement, plastering material, etc. The materials used by the mason were placed haphazardly with the result that the mason and his assistants had to make many unnecessary movements, thus wasting energy and time. Gilbreth made a study of these movements, located all the materials as near each other as possible, recruited talented masons and gave them proper training. All these reforms resulted in expected benefits. By the old method the mason could put together only 120 bricks in one hour but under the guidance of Gilbreth he began to put together 320 bricks per hour. In this way, the management was benefited by the increase in output while the mason gained through increase in his wages. Hence, both were benefited.

Elements of Scientific Management

It is evident from the above examples of the experiments conducted on Taylor's principles of scientific organisation that his main aim was to improve the conditions of work. Many means have to be adopted to improve working conditions. Taylor believed that the following methods are essential :

1. Study of the time taken in work and search for methods of increasing work in less time.
2. Division of work among foremen.
3. Use of more appropriate tools for a particular function.

---

1. Gilbreth, F.W., *Bricklaying System,* New York.

4. Establishment of a planning department.
5. Other rules in the organisation.
6. Using a time-sating plan and implementing simple rules and their improvements.
7. Arrangement for guidance of the worker.
8. Different scales of pay.
9. Division of work according to the construction.
10. Arrangement for guidance.
11. Determination of wages according to prevailing price levels.
12. Giving importance to outstanding work and giving incentives for it.

Taylor explained that a scientific organisation can he introduced in any industry by following these twelve principles. He also stressed that, apart from these twelve guidelines, constant efforts should be made to find new incentives and to use them to encourage the workers to increase production.

Social Aspect of Taylorism

Taylor supported the notion of social progress of the worker and made provisions for it in his system of scientific management. He pointed out that scientific management envisages the increase of wages corresponding to the increase in production and efficiency. Adoption of the scientific management system resulted in benefits for both the managers and the workers. Production and wages both increased. As a result, the conflicts between the worker and the manager decrease, both cooperate with each other and show respect to each other.

Criticism of Taylorism

Taylor's theory has been welcomed by many, but it has also come in for some severe criticism. As has been pointed out earlier, he was called the agent of the management by the workers because their salaries did not increase in proportion to the increase in production. The truth of the matter is that industrialists took advantage of Taylor's scientific plan to increase their production. In America, in particular, his plan for scientific management was enthusiastically accepted by industrialists because they benefited much more than the workers. And, there can be no denying that industrialists were chiefly responsible for propagating it. But if the worker's wages had increased in proportion to the increase in production, then Taylor's plan would have proved as godsend for the workers, although it is doubtful whether it would have been accepted by all industrialists in that case. In fact, Taylor paid more attention towards increasing production than to increasing the wages of the workers. Industrialists therefore found it a boon, and took full advantage of it. But from the scientific point of view, the importance of Taylor's plan cannot be doubted. Many of his students and followers adopted the plan to various conditions in many spheres. On the basis of his plan for scientific management, industrial psychologists conducted numerous experiments of his theories. Many industries adopted the method of selecting the most efficient workers for particular jobs, for which psychological tests were employed. In many industries attempts were made to reduce unnecessary movements and to prevent accidents and monotony. Attention was paid to the importance of periods of rest for the workers. Efforts were made to arouse the interest of the worker. Workers and foremen were given specialized training for their tasks. Studies of the necessary and proper physical conditions for health, rest and development were made. These conditions were then created in many industries. The laws concerning wages were also studied and the problems related to them were solved. In this manner Taylor's theories helped to organise the economic basis of Industrial psychology on a sound principle. Industrial psychology gained in importance because it gave suggestions for the increase of production as well as wages. The relations between the employer and the employee improved and direct exploitation was considerably reduced. Whatever exploitation remained was indirect. Industrial psychology thus helped to introduce extensive economic, social and psychological improvements in the field of industry.

QUESTIONS FOR EXERCISE

1. Give a brief introduction to the foundations of Industrial psychology.
2. Describe in detail the influence of the research of Taylor on Industrial psychology.

5

HUMAN RELATIONS IN INDUSTRY

In the older days, the workers in factories were regarded as objects no better than the machines and tools used in it. Behaviour towards them did not qualify humane. And in many cases, the workers were no better off than slaves. In the days of British India, in the margarine blue factories of the country, many national leaders had to raise their voices in protest against the cruelty meted out to workers by the owners of the factories. In the South, too, owners of factories and mines did not treat their employees at all well. The worker was daunted into submission, and in many occupations he was often turned out without prior notice or any compensation. In cases of accident, fatal or incapacitating, the worker and his family were reduced to object of misery and impecunious poverty. When machines were invented, women and children were also added to the labour force, no concessions being made to their delicate condition and ideally exalted position of life. Even when leave was absolutely necessary for women, it was not permitted, and pregnant women were often turned out of work. The system in the factory and working conditions were almost deplorable. The owner was concerned solely with his own profit, and the conditions in which work was carried on was not his concern. It was outside the sphere of his thinking to worry about air, light, sanitation, water, etc., that were not supplied in adequate quantities. There being no legal bar to the extent of work to be forced out of the labourer, the owners forced the poor workers to work long hours on very small remuneration. Promotion was a term unheard of, in that time. Incentives to workers were not given, and equally not tendered. In this way, exploitation was the rule of the time.

Propagation of socialist and democratic principles caused people to revolt against such conditions. Labour unions were formed at most of the places. Different professions made their own organisations. In progressive countries labourers and other workers in different professions combined together to voice their desire for better working conditions, and for workers in industries to be treated as human beings. Democratic and socialist governments also turned their attention to this problem. Besides this, thinkers and scientists came forward with the suggestion that because of absence of proper human relations in industry, workers were not the only losers; the government and the owners also suffered. This led to the propagation of the thought that efforts should be made to improve working conditions and human relations in industry.

PROBLEMS OF HUMAN RELATIONS IN INDUSTRY

In industry, human relations are in evidence in two spheres, in that of administration, and that of welfare. In the field of administration it is the relations between the authority and the worker which is important. A labourer is not a machine, nor a cog in a wheel. He is repleted with such human elements as motives, emotions, feelings, hopes, desires and needs. He wants as much as any other that his good work be praised and that his efforts should bring him additional gain. Love and respect are things for which he earns. Treated like a human being by those in authority above him, his work becomes very much easier and much more pleasurable for him. Various incidents of labour strikes and lockouts were mainly of administrative origin. Administration of a factory involves proper and systematic organisation of the factory, besides humane treatment of the workers. It is desirable that a feeling of security be induced in the workers by making precise and definite rules regarding appointment, promotion, etc., within the factory. The position entrusted that the worker should be made permanent. He should be made to know that the road to progress is straight and narrow, and that honesty is very much the best policy. Absence of these conditions is reason enough for the poor worker to feel dissatisfied and to lose his concentration in the work. A worker should be praised for any extraordinary effort that he may put in. He should also be made to benefit in some manner or the other if he does something unusually good. His salaries should be increased, so should his bonus, and he should be given a higher position. Conditions of work should be improved, and the workers of a high calibre be transferred to good places. Such factors being existent, the worker's inspiration in his work continues and so does his enthusiasm. Without these incentives, no industry can achieve much good results.

Misunderstandings and differences of opinion between workers and authority are nothing to cause much worry, as they are part and parcel of life, all of them being human and capable of harbouring various kinds of emotions regarding each other. Hence, occasions of conflict are only too natural. Such problems of human relations require careful and tactful handling. If those in authority show laxity of mood, unscrupulous individuals may take undue advantages and turn in bad performances. If, on the other hand, the authorities decide to make it rough for the workers, haul them up on every little thing, interfere constantly, offend their respect and threaten them every off and on, it would be difficult for the poor workers to maintain their equanimity of mind and work enthusiastically. Actually, the attitude and nature of every worker differs from one to another, but, nevertheless, efforts must be made to maintain cordial relations between them.

WELFARE IN INDUSTRY

At an earlier stage in the development of human thought, the responsibility of an owner was supposed to end once the worker had been remunerated for his efforts on behalf of the owner. Economics, as it stands today, is more interested in welfare than in financial disposal of obligations. Governments of today are haunted with dreams of the visionary welfare state. Consequently, it is now conceded that besides paying wages to the worker, it is essential to attend to his welfare also. Human services, conveniences and pleasures should be available to the worker as to any other individual. Atmosphere at home and in the office or factory should be congenial. They should get adequate opportunities of intellectual, material, moral and economic progress. Factors in their welfare would be the provision of such conveniences as convenient housing, educational and health service facilities, good food and adequate provision for rest and recreation. For female workers it is essential to provide more holidays and rest. Creches and maternity homes should be provided near the working premises for mothers. Special help should be forthcoming to workers when they are ill. Maternity benefit programmes are essential for women workers. Educational facilities should be provided for the children of workers. The future of the workers should also be made secure so that they should be able to concentrate upon their work wholeheartedly. Provident fund benefits, pensions and life insurance schemes are some of the ways in which this can be assured. In this way, it is now believed that the owners should do their best to provide for the integral development of the workers entrusted to their care by society.

In fact, the mill-owners and industrialists get a certain percentage of returns on the money that they spend on labour welfare, as this money improves the efficiency, skill and cooperation of the worker. And if in the process of working in a factory, a worker loses his life, or his capacity to earn money, it becomes the moral duty of the owner to arrange for the upkeep of his helpless family. Actually, money spent on labour welfare is more in the nature of investment than that of expenditure since whatever is spent ultimately influences the owner favourably. Increase in the labourer's skill means an economy in raw material and increase in production. Scientific selection of workers helps to eliminate the improper exploitation at the hands of middlemen, and this improves the peace and enthusiasm of the workers who work better. In the same manner, technical training of individuals involves an initial expenditure of huge sums of money, but finally it also means considerable additions to their income and profits because a trained individual works better than his untrained counterpart and reduces overall damage. He stands to gain because the trained labourer does better both in quantity and quality of work. An employer does not have to spend much in improving light, ventilation and other facilities on the factory premises, but they have a great influence upon the health and performance of the workers, with the result absenteeism falls, workers do not complain of fatigue, and they less often fall a prey to disease. Healthy conditions of work encourage the workers to attain a peaceful frame of mind and think more kindly and favourably of their employer as they are conscious of the latter's concern for them. This improves their mutual relations, and the workers do not tend to migrate to other jobs very often. Welfare work in respect of prevention of accidents has obviously a very direct advantage for the employer, since he stands to lose just as much as the worker does. He is compelled by the law to make some compensation in case of accident, besides which such occurrences lead to unrest among the other workers. If it is a trained worker who is involved in any serious accident, the employer is quite directly hit. Prevention of fire breaking out on the premises is a form of labour welfare that should be right after the employer's own heart, and should concur with his way of thinking. But it also leads to the welfare of workers' minds. Efficiency of workers can be increased by providing means and opportunity of rest and refreshment in the factory. Organisation of canteens helps them in getting food at the right time, and they can return to work shortly. It is in such ways as these that the employer stands to derive direct and indirect benefits from such schemes of labour welfare.

LABOUR WELFARE

Labour welfare pertains to all such works or schemes that lead to the benefit of labour, but such a general statement does not satisfy the scientific mind. It is a term whose meaning is relative to time and place; as a result it is capable of change. According to the report of the Royal Commission on Labour, "The term 'welfare', as applied to the industrial worker, is one which must necessarily be elastic, bearing a somewhat different interpretation in one country from another, according to the different social customs, the degree of industrialisation and the educational development of workers." In this manner, the meaning that the term 'labour welfare' will have in any specific country will depend upon the condition of the labourers there. Labour, in general, being uneducated in a country like India, the term will come to include their education also. As defined in the *Encyclopaedia of Social Sciences,* "Labour welfare implies the voluntary efforts of the employers to establish, within the existing industrial system, working and sometimes living conditions of the employees beyond what is required by law, the custom of the industry and the condition of the market." Hence, the term labour welfare does not comprehend those activities that are necessitated by the laws of the country, the traditions and customs of industry in that country, or by conditions of the market, instead, it means the voluntary actions on the part of the employer to improve the lot of his employees. The International Labour Organisation defines labour welfare in these words : "Workers welfare should be understood as meaning such services, facilities and amenities which may be established in, or in the vicinity of, undertaking to enable the persons employed in them to perform their work in healthy, congenial surroundings and provided with amenities conducive to good surroundings and provided with amenities conducive to good health and high morale." In this way, the term 'labour welfare' implies schemes and activities that produce conditions that improve the health of the workers as well as those circumstances that improve their morale. It may widely be taken to mean any voluntary action on the part of the employer that benefits the worker in any way. But it does not include any activity that the employer is compelled or coerced into performing, whatever be the benefit accruing to the labour class. Through the medium of labour welfare work, employers and industrialists try to achieve the integral or complete development of their employees.

LABOUR WELFARE ACTIVITY

Labour welfare work is believed to be of three kinds:

1. **Statutory** Legal compulsions regarding the safety and working conditions of workers, etc.
2. **Voluntary** Those works that the employer performs for the benefit of workers of his own volition, without any coercion being involved.
3. **Mutual** This kind includes the welfare work done by labour unions in cooperation with each other.

Dr. Broughton's View

Dr. Broughton has divided works of labour welfare into two classes: (1) Intra-mural, and (2) Extra-mural. The main ones among intra-mural works are :

1. **Scientific selection or appointment** The scientific selection of workers for the various jobs within the factory.
2. **Industrial training** Training in various factories for different jobs in the factory.
3. **Arrangement for light, fresh air and water** This classification comprehends arrangements in the factory for cleanliness, white washing, ventilation, drinking water, bathrooms, lavatories, urinals, light, air-conditioning, etc.
4. **Prevention of accidents** This includes arrangements for the protection from dangerous machines, extreme temperatures, fire fighting, etc.
5. **Other functions** Such as canteen, provision of rest rooms, refreshment, etc.

Major extra-mural labour welfare functions are the following :

1. **Provision of education** This includes adult education, social education, primary education, education of men, women and children, etc.
2. Arrangement of proper housing accommodation.
3. **Medical service** This includes rest, cure, paid leave, free treatment, subsidized medical aid, etc.
4. Provision of inexpensive and nourishing food.
5. **Facilities of recreation** Clubs, gymnasia, cinema, radio, reading-room, libraries, etc.

In addition to the above list, the following activities are also a part of labour welfare service :

(1) Social insurance scheme, (2) provident fund benefits, (3) pension, (4) sickness and maternity benefits, (5) arrangement of maternity homes

and creches, (6) provision of cooperative societies, (7) arrangement of cultural programmes, (8) schooling of children.

ADVANTAGES TO EMPLOYERS FROM INTRA-MURAL WELFARE WORK

In all modern countries, the employers do their best to introduce labour welfare programmes of various kinds because they have come to realise that the money spent upon labour welfare is not completely lost to them. A very definite percentage of the advantage accruing from it is diverted to them ultimately in the form of increased production or better quality of work rendered by the happy workers. Working in healthy and congenial surroundings, the workers feel contented and delighted in the concern that the employers evince in them. Cordial relations between employer and employee are thus precipitated, and the workers evince lesser desire to change employment at the least provocation. Prevention of an accident is a direct gain to the employer, even more so when the individual salvaged is a trained person whose training itself would have cost the establishment of a packet. Even otherwise, in case of accident, the employer owes it to his conscience to compensate the family of the sufferer in some measure. Other workers in the factory develop a feeling of insecurity if the rate of accidents is high in their establishment. Schemes and plans for prevention of fire or for fire-fighting are a direct gain to the employer, as he would not like to have his factory go up in flames. Skill and efficiency are changing things, and likely to remain in the best condition if the worker is occasionally allowed to rest and refresh himself, either by nourishing himself or by relaxing. Easy availability of good and wholesome food takes a load off the workers' minds, as it is very convenient to eat in a canteen near the premises. In this manner, the owner of a factory stands to gain directly from intra-mural efforts of the labour welfare.

Advantages to Owners from Extra-Mural Labour Welfare

An owner also gains finally from extra-mural labour welfare activity. Mainly, he is benefited in the following ways :

1. Improvement in workers' health Ordinary arrangements like healthy residences, inexpensive and nourishing food, proper relaxation and refreshment go a long way in maintaining the health of workers. Hence, absenteeism from the factory falls to a minimum, and the per capita output improves. Dissatisfaction is a thing of the past, cordiality and fidelity permeate the very atmosphere, to the delight of the owner.

2. Improvement in workers' efficiency When education is provided, the workers' efficiency and skill increases, and he can do better work in lesser time. His understanding improves and he is capable of avoiding the inflaming influence of vested interests.

3. Reduction in absenteeism Prevention of disease and arrangement of medical facilities help to reduce illness or to shorten its influence as a result of which the number of absentees in the factory decreases, disease being the main cause of it. Social welfare activity helps to induce a healthy outlook in the worker and to maintain a balance in his character which guides him to honest and responsible effort and conduct.

4. Good relations between employer and worker Provision of such facilities as social insurance, provident fund, pension, gratuity, etc., helps to remove a feeling of insecurity in the worker, as his future becomes secure, and he can rest satisfied with his employer. This improves the relations between the worker and the employer.

5. Reducing worker's dissatisfaction Healthy recreation facilities and welcome cultural activity help to sublimate the more destructive and undesirable tendencies in the worker's satisfaction. A worker's satisfaction is further increased if his female colleague has the benefit of such facilities as maternity benefits, maternity homes, creches for their children. Being satisfied he is not inclined to strike work, as a result of which the employer gains.

6. Improvement in quantity and quality of production When these benefits accrue to the workers in a factory, the quantity and quality of production in it improve, a direct benefit to the employer.

7. Employer's moral satisfaction But the greatest advantage of labour welfare that goes to the employer takes the form of moral satisfaction at having served the cause of humanity. No decent minded and right-thinking employer can be happy if his employees are poor, ill-fed, badly dressed, uneducated and unpresentable. Their labour does not bring them any pleasure. Economic improvement and benefit are not the sole basis of labour welfare, even though economic benefit does result from it. Behind it is the sense of humanity, a large heart and a moral or ethical consciousness. Absence of these things leads to the exploitation and ultimately to class-struggle.

From the above description it is evident that labour welfare activity benefits the employer no less than his employees, but such activity should be intelligently conceived and generously administered. Planning is a part of every scientific activity but generosity is an essential part of labour welfare because such plans are not based on material considerations but are instead guided by humanitarian principles and views. Finally, it can be said that intelligently conceived and generously administered labour welfare activity will ultimately benefit the employer.

VALUE OF LABOUR WELFARE IN INDIA

Compared to other countries, India has much greater need and importance for labour welfare work. Such a condition is caused by certain deficiencies in the Indian labour force, that are not to be found in its counterpart in other countries. It is these defects or deficiencies that increase the importance of labour welfare activity in the country. Briefly, then, the following are the reasons why labour welfare work in India assumes greater importance than in other countries:

1. Lack of labour unions In India, even today the workers are not united into a class. Keeping in view the numbers, labour union movements are still in its infancy. Even in the labour unions that do exists, there is a lack of enlightened leadership, and there is no unity between these unions themselves. Welfare of labourers is a secondary concern, the primary interest being the serving of a party and vested interests. In the absence of properly organised labour unions, the workers can neither place their demands effectively before the employer, nor can they think clearly and systematically of their own interests. In other modern progressive countries, workers are strongly organised into labour unions, but as their force is lacking in India, it is essential that the welfare of labourers in the country be efficiently looked after by the employers and the government. This should be treated as a sacred trust till the workers can evolve their own efficient and reliable organisation. This will help the workers stand on their own feet, develop strong union, think properly of their interests, to progress hand in hand, and to take a definite hand in the country's development.

2. Illiteracy As compared to other countries, the percentage of educated workers is very low, most of them being illiterate. Consequently, they are not in a position to receive advanced industrial training, understand the problems in industries, understand their own interests and those of the nation as a whole. This can prove a source of harm not only to the workers but also to the country. Hence labour welfare is required more in India than in other countries. It will help to make the workers secure, become industrially efficient, and become responsible citizens of the country.

3. Problems of absenteeism and migration Compared to workers in other countries the Indian labour is more restless and prone to frequent migration because life in the town does not provide for his needs, and the atmosphere in general does not suit him. Level of wages is far too low to adequately compensate for the high prices of most commodities. Hence, the labourer cannot comfortably settle down at one place. The worker's migratory tendency can be cured by providing him with adequate housing, improving the conditions in which he is required to work, and other welfare work of a similar nature. This will help the worker establish a home in the town, and he will not have to run frequently to the village for his family. Hence, the problem of absenteeism in factories will be reduced. Recreation and cultural facilities will prevent indulgence in drug addiction and alcoholism, crime and prostitution and other undesirable activity. Even more than this, the percentage of absenteeism in factories will fall.

4. Low Level of health and nutrition The Indian worker, as compared with his counterpart in most European countries, is unhealthy and ill-fed. This has reduced his production potential, as compared to the productive capacity of Western labourers. Hence he is in very great need of inexpensive nutritive food and facility in case of hospitalization.

5. Extreme poverty Another factor is the extreme poverty of the Indian worker. He is unable to provide a healthy living for his family and a good education for his children. Female labour in the country, as compared with female labour elsewhere, is in even a worse state of health, and adequate protection and assistance are not afforded to her in times of pregnancy and delivery. Hence labour welfare has much to do in this country. The Indian woman labourer will be as happy as other workers in the world when she is given the facilities of maternity benefits, maternity homes and creches for her children. It is essential that the education of boys and girls be provided for. Being poor, the Indian labourer is hardly in any condition to save something for the old age; hence he is in great need of provident fund, pensions and gratuity, etc.

6. Lack of training Percentage of trained workers in India is very low. As compared to other countries, trained personnel in India are hard to come by. Hence it is necessary to have training facilities for such a vast labour force. Possibility of accident increases when the worker is untrained. Hence, there should be adequate provisions for preventing accidents.

7. Lack of healthy recreation Healthy recreation is also at a premium in this country, with the result that the workers indulge in crime and activities of a reprehensible kind. Their efficiency is further diminished by energy being employed in all kinds of undesirable channels. Hence, it is essential that recreation and enjoyment of a healthy kind be provided.

8. Industrial backwardness of India From the Industrial standpoint, India is far behind other countries. Industrial progress is being aimed at through the medium of the five-year plans, but Industrial progress is dependent upon the efficiency of the labour force, and labour in India is in a pitiable state. Hence, the labourers are very much in need of all kinds of labour welfare work.

It would have become evident from the above description that labour welfare work in India assumes a much greater importance, as compared with other countries due to a variety of reasons. Labour welfare activities will save the labourer from moral degeneration, reduce the number of incidents of lockouts and strikes in industries, and help to achieve success in the country's plans.

INDUSTRIAL CONFLICTS

If, in some particular profession or occupation, the workers have faith in their employer who thinks considerately of them, their mutual relations remain cordial and occasions of conflict are rare. If workers do not revolt for some reason or the other against conditions of extreme exploitation and choose to bear their lot gracefully, then also conflict does not occur. On the other hand, if the employer is tactful and chooses to use his diplomacy, there is no reason for a lockout to take place. But these things do not occur very often. What does happen very often is that employers pay no heed to the plight of their employees, even forgetting that the poor chaps are human beings with certain basic needs, the fulfilment of which is essential, and that they may revolt against extreme exploitation. In the earlier stages when labourers were not united, the unscrupulous employers could keep them suppressed by tactfully causing dissension among their ranks. But in the present day conditions in almost every country, every big industry has its organised labour unions. Some labour unions are powerful enough to spread over countries, while certain unions have political parties to support them in their struggle against exploitation. Many of their leaders are powerful enough to become members of national councils and governments. Wherever any injustice to the labour class occurs, it is brought to their attention so that they can raise a hue and cry over it in the national assemblies and take the matter up with the government concerned; and this activity and representation at the highest level create a notion of power and security in the general rank of labourers. They are in a position to take the fight into the exploiter's half, and they can resist efforts at exploitation of their energies. They organise themselves into a single body, if they need to agitate for their demands and they resort to political propaganda, to meetings, processions and ultimately to strikes. Strike is one of the major problems of modern industry.

STRIKES

Strike is an announcement of non-cooperation with the employer, the first step in it being suspension of all activity, followed by meetings, organised processions, exhibitions in order to elicit the sympathy of the population in general, public representation of their demands carried to the employer through the senior representatives of the labour force. All these activities are adjuncts of a strike. Besides all this, strike nowadays, involves wide propagation of the aims of the strike in the public so that it can be persuaded to side with the labour force. Another aspect of the strike is in informing the government of its objectives and presenting it with a summary of its demands and their justifications.

Why do Strikes Occur?

Why do strikes occur at all? Basically, it stems from a distrust of the workers towards their employer. They do not strike, even when required to work in squalid surroundings, so long as they are convinced that the employer is conscious of their needs and is sincerely trying to improve their lot. But when the employer turns a deaf ear to their pleadings and entreaties, when their faith in his sincerity is undermined, they strike work. There is no necessary rule that the demands of striking workers are invariably just and proper. Some strikes take place because the workers are inflamed by some political groups that have some end of their own to achieve or are misled by some vested interests or are led to this extreme step as an expression of their disgust. They may choose this method of getting their revenge from the individual. Many workers form the idea that all that the employers possess, their magnificent mansions, their cars, their luxuries, are the outcome of exploiting workers. This leads to a feeling of jealousy which may find expression through strike even though the general behaviour of the specific employer may be good and the conditions of work normally above reproach. Occasionally, leaders of labour unions also inflame the workers and incite them to strike in order to achieve some personal objective. Most facts are twisted and distorted by the leaders and fed to the poor labourer who swallows them and prepares to strike.

Means of Ending the Strikes

In this manner, whether the strike is justified or not, whether its objectives are desirable or not, it originates in a feeling of mistrust between the labour force and the employer. This mistrust and lack of confidence are sometimes caused by the employer himself, but whoever is to blame, it is essential that conciliation should take place. Even if demands of the striking workers are unjust, they must be heard and attended to. In a strike, the workers conduct themselves in a manner similar to mob behaviour. They lose their power of reasoning. Their emotions are easily aroused and they become excited over the most insignificant thing. If in such events, the employers choose to behave in an irresponsible manner, the situation can worsen and may lead to setting fire to factories, arson and other destructive activity. But such events and damage can be averted if the workers' demands are given a patient hearing, the workers convinced of the sincerity of their employer, promises of prompt action upon them given, and the inflammatory sources disclosed.

Prevention of Strikes

But prevention is traditionally considered to be better than cure. It is for the employer to avert distrust or at least to prevent it from reaching such proportions that the worker feel to be justified in striking work. It is for him to try and win the confidence of his staff. Two things are essential for this. The first is that the behaviour towards the workers should be good and understanding, sincere and proper, and, secondly, attention should be paid to their well-being, improvements in working conditions made and their welfare considered carefully. If these things are done, the worker's trust in his employer becomes unshakable and strikes become an obsolete and an unknown activity.

LOCK OUTS

One aspect of the distrust between worker and employer is the strike, the other is lock outs. In this activity the office and working premises of the concern under conflict are locked, entry to Staff and workers is prohibited. Hundreds and thousands of workers lose their source of income, and are sometimes reduced to such abject poverty that they are on the verge of death because of hunger. The workers lose, but so do the employers. While the machines lie idle, they lose their income, raw material is destroyed in many cases, trade connections are broken because of lack of supply. Secondly, a lock out can incite the workers to violent activity which may cause them to destroy the factory as their daily bread has been snatched from them. This naturally is no small blow to the employer, or his insurance company. The employer has naturally to seek the assistance and protection of the police force, which may be compelled to fire on mobs of unruly workers indulging in destructive activity. If some of them happen to die, the employer is brought into disgrace. Lock outs harm the country's economy even more than they harm the individual owner of the factory. In the modern economic structure in most countries, every industry is dependent upon some other for one or the other thing. Lock outs in one industry can lead to very serious repercussions in other industries which may follow the bad example of the first and resort to lock outs. The worker is not the only class of people dependent upon the functioning of the industry, other classes of shopkeepers and middlemen are also deeply involved. Their earnings also are greatly depleted by such subversive activity. When production of a particular commodity is stopped, its supply drops with the result that this creates such an imbalance between the forces of demand and supply in the market that the prices go up, with much adverse influence upon the poor consumers. In this way, in the modern complex that is the nation's economy, lock out in any factory has wide influence. In this manner, it can turn into a problem of national magnitude.

Causes of Lock out

A certain concatenation of circumstances may make lock out an inevitable step, but usually it is not justified. It is sometimes used by the employer as an instrument with which to suppress the helpless worker. It may even be an expression of the employer's sadistic bent of mind, as it may give him pleasure to see the worker suffering. Lock outs are sometimes thought to be essential in cases where prestige and honour become involved. It may even be used to impress the worker with an employer's power over him. In all such cases lockouts are completely and beyond doubt unjustified and improper. Its lack of justification lies in the fact that the employer is led to sacrificing the interests of the nation and those of the working force in favour of his own. It should be considered obligatory on the part of the government to intervene, because it becomes a national question. In fact, all incidents of lock outs and strikes can be effectively prevented if the government enacts laws covering labour welfare activity, improvement in their condition of work, occasional incentives being given to them, security in cases of accidents and old age being provided, and if it ensures their efficient and strict observance.

As has been pointed out earlier, lock outs and strikes are two aspects of the same problem. They stem from mutual distrust between worker mid employer, prejudice, in-group feeling, selfish interests and unnecessary self assertion. All these are psychological in nature, but they do not arise without an antecedent cause. If they are present in weak conditions, they do not cause lock outs and strikes. These incidents occur only when these feelings flare up, an occurrence which can certainly be controlled and avoided. The most obvious way of doing so is by removing all causes of distrust, prejudice and assertiveness. For this, on the one hand, eye should be kept on individuals and groups that encourage them, and on the other hand, welfare work should be undertaken. But for this, cooperation between workers and employers is essential, in addition to governmental intervention. Hence, their solution should be cooperatively sought after by the government, labourers' representatives and their employers.

QUESTIONS FOR EXERCISE

1. Write a short note on industrial conflict.
2. Describe the various causes of conflict as well as areas of cooperation between labour and management.
3. Discuss some of the major labour-management problems in Indian industry. State some of the major psychological factors of conflict in Industry.

6

ORGANIZATIONAL PSYCHOLOGY

If two or more persons establish between them cooperative relations and make concerted efforts, the state of these cooperative relations and concerted effort is called as the organization. The organizations can perform simple or complex tasks. All individuals within an organization try to work for a common aim. The word organization is a derivative of the word organ. The word organ means a part or a limb of an animal or man. Thus brain, heart, liver, arms, legs, etc., are the various organs of man. The man or an animal as a whole is said to be a structure and organization. He is an organization because his various limbs, parts or organs are mutually and cooperatively related. A group of individuals working together for a definite common aim is called an organization. The mutuality and togetherness found in a group of persons engaged in industrial production is called industrial organization.

BASIC ELEMENTS OF ORGANIZATION

The organization may be industrial or formed for the attainment of some social or political aim. Every organization has some common basic elements. The basic elements constitute the structure of an organization. Generally three elements are considered basic for any organization. Firstly, an organization must have numerous components. As a living organism consists of numerous organs and millions of cells, in the same manner an industrial organization has many wings or components and hundreds of units. These components perform their respective roles. The second element basic to an organization is the adjustment also. Living organism provides best illustration. As an organism lives and functions only as long as its various organs function harmoniously, similarly an industrial organization retains its character only as long as its various components work in a complementary manner. It is true, of course, that there cannot be such ideal adjustment among the industrial components as in the case of human organism. Nonetheless without a minimum amount of adjustment there can be no industrial organization. It is not possible for workers to do any work if raw material is not supplied or supervisory staff is missing to supervise the work. The third basic element of an organization is that it should be suited to purposeful activity. This means that all elements of an industrial organization should be such as will contribute towards the aim specified for it. For the attainment of different aims, different types of organizations are required.

KINDS OF ORGANIZATIONS

Organizations are of two kinds : (i) spontaneous or informal organization and (ii) formal organization. The spontaneous organizations are natural and these are not formed for any particular purpose. The organizations in the man, animal and vegetable kingdom are the examples of spontaneous or informal organizations. A sudden voluntary get-together of human beings is an another example of informal organization.

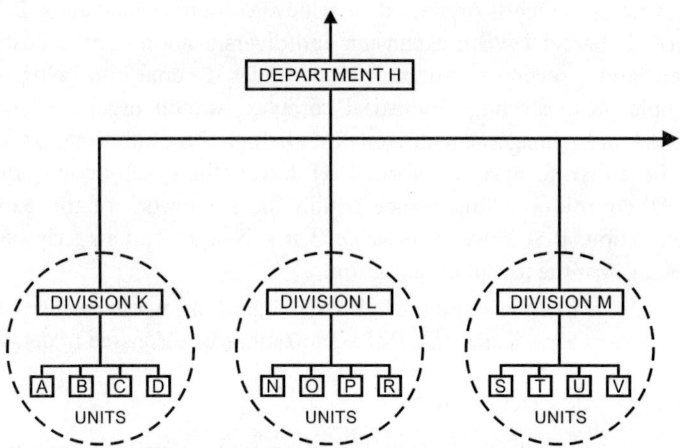

Fig. 6.1 Organizational Chart of a Typical Department

The relationship between departments, divisions, and units is indicated by the connecting solid lines, which indicate the lines of authority. Many companies have organizational charts drawn up so that positions at various levels are clearly defined. This chart is not a complete one but shows only a small department within a company. A complete organizational chart for a large company may have six or more levels. The broken lines, each enclosing a division and several units, represent potential discussion groups in which the division supervisor acts as the leader. Each unit supervisor would be the leader of groups of rank-and-file employees, not shown in the chart. All management personnel are potential participants in one grouping and leaders in another (The meanings of terms such as unit, division, and department vary from one company to another. A division may be a larger or a smaller unit than a department).

A formal organization is a result of deliberate efforts and is brought together for some specific purpose. Compared to informal organization, a formed organization is more systematic and works under specific rules. It is only within the framework of law and rules which brought it together that an organization remains an organization. In the event of violation of rules, it is liable to break down.

The industrial organizations are always the outcome of deliberate efforts and are established with a specific aim. In an industrial organization we find both kinds of organizations, that is, an industrial organization contains within it both formal and informal associations. In fact, wherever men get together both formal and informal organizations come into being. A deliberately organized structure brings together a lot of men. This togetherness, in turn, gives rise to certain formal organization which is organized to achieve certain specific aims. It has a formal character. With expansion and diversification of an industrial organization, several sub-organizations under it come into being. For example, in every huge industrial complex, several organizations of workers and managerial staff come into being. These sub-organizations can be either formal or informal. However, these sub-organizations have their role and importance within the framework of the parent organization. It is however possible that sub-organizations may be in revolt against the parent organization.

In order to understand the industrial organization, it is essential that the nature of formal and informal organizations be discussed in detail.

FORMAL ORGANIZATION

As it is clear from the above discussion, formal organization in industry is that human group which deliberately comes together for the achievement of a specific purpose or aim. Following are the chief features of a formal organization, according to C.L. Barnard :

The formal organizations are not concerned with nor do they revolve around a person or persons in particular. It is not the name or heredity or the person but his status and work that are important in a formal organization. An organization requires a man to perform according to his or her status. A formal organization has a hierarchy of status. On relinquishing of a post by one person, another person assumes his office and the work of the organization goes on. The members of a formal organization bear to each other impersonal and not personal relations. Their relations depend upon the plan of the organization. For example, if an industry X makes a component of a machinery and Y makes another component and Z fits them together, the relation between X, Y, Z is purely formal and is limited to certain processes in an industry. However, this does not mean that there are no personal relations among X, Y, Z. Indeed, in an organization, it is but natural that various members should spontaneously develop various types of relations, social, economic, religious, etc., among themselves. However, these relations are informal and are not strictly essential for the maintenance and sustenance of the industry. Within the framework of an industrial organization, the relations between members are formal but outside of its framework these are informal.

Another characteristic feature of formal industrial organization is that it is formal and functional, it is nonetheless in the background of vast social organization or system. The social atmosphere affects it much. The socio-economic-ethical conditions of a society affect the industrial organization directly or indirectly.

Another characteristic of the industrial organization is that it is scientific and systematic. Under the formal organization the role, status and importance of all the jobs is well determined. The structure of formal organization is quite explicit and this is tractable of easy investigation.

Departments of Formal Organization

Whenever an industrial organization develops and becomes vast it becomes complex and the functions within it becomes quite intricate. Under these conditions, the organization gets split up into various departments for its smooth functions. The departments are generally considered to be parts of the organization. Normally there are three such departments in an organization. These are :

1. Linear Organization.
2. Functional Organization.
3. Staff Organization.

1. Linear organization Once an industry assumes gigantic proportions, it requires a hierarchical system which can effectively control and manage the whole organization. This hierarchy directs the entire organization towards its predetermined end. This system is known as linear organization.

2. Functional organization The industrial organizations have variety of functions. For convenience each of these functions is entrusted to one department. This system of departmentalising of functions is known as 'Functional Organization'.

3. Staff organization In modern industry technological changes and inventions are taking place daily. New devices and sophisticated methods of work are being discovered daily in the fields of technology, economics, law and social sciences. The discoveries in all these fields have their direct or indirect application to industry. As a result of these there is a conceptual and practiced revolution in every aspect of business management, production, marketing, etc. It is not possible for everyone, to be fully posted with latest developments. Besides the scientific research is snowballing and requires special cadre to imbibe and absorb its impact. As industry requires successful application of various new techniques to maintain progress, every industry keeps a team of specialists to keep track of developments in science, technology, social research and law. Thus a successful industrial organization would have experts in engineering, sociology, science and legal studies, etc. This organization of experts is known as staff organization.

VARIOUS LEVELS OF INDUSTRIAL ORGANIZATION

Besides the classification described above, there are some other kinds of classification in an industrial organization. This classification is hierarchical and is according to status, and position. This is also known as vertical organization. According to this classification, there are different levels of posts and positions starting from labour and going up to the highest executive.

In any industrial organization, the top-wrung positions are occupied by those who are the founders of that organization. The capitalists themselves appoint the Board of Directors. The Board of Directors appointed by the capitalists elects the Chairman of the company. The chairman in turn entrusts to each director one department according to his ability and capability. There is some difference of opinion with regard to the number of top managerial posts. But generally top positions are as follows :

(1) Chairman; (2) Managing Director; (3) Executive Director; (4) General Managers; (5) Works Managers and (6) Regional Sales

Managers. For example, in India; Tata Oil Mills Co. Ltd. has the above described arrangement of posts.

Next to top-wrung officials are middle-wrung officials. This set of officials comes between the topmost and the low-wrung officers and workers. The middle-wrung officials are concerned with the implementation of the policies and directions laid down or given by the topmost officials. This set of officials must have plenty of practical knowledge. These officials are usually the specialists in the fields. The staff organization described above is the organization of these officials.

The third wrung of the industrial managers is occupied by supervisory staff. They occupy a position just above the clerical staff. Their job is to supervise work and report to the higher officials from time to time.

Thus in an industrial organization we find hierarchy of status. The persons occupying different places in this hierarchy have their respective privileges and obligations.

PRINCIPLES OF INDUSTRIAL ORGANIZATION

In regard to industrial organization and business management, new principles are being continuously established. However, certain principles laid down by relatively old experts still have their own significance. Some of these experts are : E.W. Taylor, H. Fayol, C.L. Barnard, L. Uriwick and P. Sargent. The laws and principles discovered and established by them have not only historic significance but have certain validity and practicability even to-day. These principles are based on actual experience of the industrial management. Henry Fayol has laid down fourteen principles for efficient industrial management. These are :

1. Division of work
2. Authority and responsibility
3. Discipline
4. Unity of command
5. Unity of Direction
6. Subordination of individual interests to general interests
7. Remuneration of personnel
8. Centralization
9. Scales chain
10. Order
11. Equity

12. Stability of tenure of personnel
13. Initiative
14. *Esprit de corps.*

The above-mentioned principles are crucial to every industry. By following these principles, one can conveniently obtain the desired goals.

INFORMAL ORGANIZATIONS

Besides formal organization, certain informal organizations spontaneously spring up in every industry. These informal organizations are generally complementary in nature and play a supporting role in respect of the main formal organization. The informal organizations are based upon personal as against the impersonal relations of formal organizations. Wherever some persons get together there is an exchange of social and personal human relations and this forms the basis of informal organizations. Many such informal organizations are found in industries. The informal organizations are neither deliberate nor do they possess neat well-defined structure. Yet there are certain preconditions for the formation of such organizations:

1. The first type of informal organization is the totality of members of the organization bearing with each other certain relations at personal level. In the terminology of sociology, this informal group is derivative or secondary group. In the secondary group, members have interpersonal relations remaining within the primary group.
2. The second type of informal organizations are those which spring upon on account of common tastes, interests or hobbies of some persons. The members of trade unions, for example, come together on account of commonness of interest or purpose. Certain clubs or societies develop. For example, we find dramatic clubs in many industries. This is a clear example of an informal organization. We also have in industries societies based on religion and language. There are also sports clubs which again are examples of informal organization.
3. The third type of informal organizations are represented by persons doing similar jobs in an industry.
4. The fourth type of informal organizations are of very few and limited persons. There may be half a dozen poets in an industrial organization and they may form a poetry club. Again, there may be more than two persons in an industry hailing from the same family. Their association will be an example of informal organization.

Besides family relations, such organizations may be based on friendship or intimacy.

It is imperative that there should be informal organizations within an industry. The informal organizations are generally complementary to formal organization. They are not contrary to it. If care is taken to nourish the informal organizations, they prove beneficial to the industry. If there is sufficient co-ordination and co-operation between industry and informal organizations within it, the chances of strikes and lock-outs are minimized. Any work connected with industry can be done easily through the heads of informal organizations. The efficient managers try to maintain rapport with these heads.

Now the questions is, why is an informal organization necessary and how it comes to be established. The answer lies in human nature. Basically, man is gregarious and has an instinct for establishing informal relations with his fellow beings. It is on account of this instinct that informal organizations come into being. Secondly, industrial workers are in the habit to avoid work. They need some or other thing to fill their empty hours. The informal organizations fill this void. The habits of gossiping, smoking, etc. are symbolic of this. Another reason for coming into being of informal organizations is that every worker knows well that he can be shunted from work, therefore he feels comparatively secure. Besides, informal organizations give emotional security.

INDUSTRIALIZATION IN INDIA

Though Industrialization in India is making rapid strides, it is still far behind the industrial growth in Western countries. After India became independent in 1947, the Government of India paid particular attention to industrial growth. It helped the local industry to grow rapidly. In order to put India on industrial map fast, the government decided to enter the field of heavy industry which demanded huge investments. The government setup many heavy industrial complexes all over India in order to promote a balanced growth and also to help the ancillary industry to expand fast.

As a result of fast industrialization, the process of urbanization too, is growing fast and this is having deep impact upon the society. The industrialization is not only pushing up the urban population but is also affecting the social conditions in nearby villages.

The Social Impact of Industrialization

The important consequences of industrialization, in India are as Follow :

1. Urbanization As a consequence of industrialization, the population in the cities has gone up. This will be clearly seen in the following table:

Year	*Urban Population (% of Total)*	*Increase*
1872	8.8	—
1881	9.3	0.6
1891	9.4	0.6
1901	10.0	0.3
1911	10.3	1.0
1921	11.3	1.9
1931	12.1	0.8
1941	13.9	1.8
1951	17.3	3.4
1961	18.0	0.7
1971	19.0	1.0
1981	23.0	4.0
1991	25.7	2.7
2001	27.8	—

2. Impact of Urbanization The process of industrialization increases the urban population. It is on account of industrialization that there is progressive rise in the population of cities in India. Whatever social impact is due to, the urbanization is indirectly due to industrialization. Therefore, the impact of industrialization and the impact of urbanization are in fact the facets of the same underlying process, namely, industrialization. The following are some of the important social influences of urbanization :

(i) ***Decline in the feeling of Sociality :*** The first and foremost impact of urbanization in India is the increase in the population of the cities, and this, in turn, has resulted in the progressive decline in the feeling of sociality. In villages, the feeling of sociality is stronger than in the cities. Therefore, the loss of village, population and increase of city population results in the decline of feeling of sociality.

In cities, the activities of almost everyone are self-centred and governed by the calculus of self-interest and personal gain.

Therefore, no one really bothers about other people except insofar as their association is helpful in promoting one's self-interest.

Thus people in cities prove to be calculating and display little altruism.

(ii) ***Decline in social control:*** With the decline in the feeling of sociality there is consequent decline in social control. Due to lack of community feeling and the fear of social disapproval, people are bound to become increasingly individualistic and even arbitrary in their conduct. Thus we find in towns to-day a glaring neglect of tradition and contempt for social approval. Everybody wants to do whatever pleases him.

(iii) ***Decline in family control*:** As the population of cities has grown, the cities have expanded. This has resulted in there being great distances between the places of work and places of residence, between educational institutions and homes. This has meant that people stay away from home environment for the best part of the day. Small wonder, then, that under these circumstances, there is progressive decline in the control of family over its members. The modern education, the excitement of cinema, fashion, clubs and societies have contributed greatly to this trend.

(iv) ***Decline in the influence of religion*** **:** The increase in the population of the cities leads not only to the decline of social and family control but also to decline in the influence of religion. In metropolitan towns, the life is highly materialistic and individualistic. This in turn promotes atheism. This means that people in cities are not guided by tradition and are indifferent to religious beliefs. Their conduct is governed by rational or personal considerations. Thus the life in cities is relatively devoid of the influence of religion.

(v) ***Change in the institution of marriage :*** The increase in urban population has resulted in certain changes in the institution of marriage. Generally, care is taken to take into confidence the spouses before marriage. Whereas, in villages, marriage is an affair between families rather than individuals, in cities to-day no marriage can be solemnized if any of the spouse is opposed to it. Even the incidence of love marriages is growing.

(vi) ***Changes in the institution of family :*** Another impact of urbanization is the gradual extinction of the joint family system and its replacement by nuclear family. Nowadays, most families consist of husband, wife and their progeny.

(vii) ***Changes in the condition of women***: With the changes in the institution of family, there are also changes in the position of women. Women are becoming increasingly independent and education among them is also spreading. They are becoming increasingly conscious of their rights and privileges but along with it there is also a tendency of arbitrary and wilful conduct. The incidences of illicit sexual relations, divorce, etc., are also on increase. The ostentation and intense fashion have also become the order of the day.

(viii) ***Increase of male ratio***: A significant impact of urbanization on the population is that the ratio of male population is increasing. The main reason for this phenomenon is that, due to shortage of housing, millions of people are forced to live single in cities. The evil of this phenomenon is that this gives rise to sexual corruption.

(ix) ***Commercialized entertainment*** : On account of industrialization there has been widespread growth of commercialized entertainment. The cinemas are becoming tremendously popular, prostitutes roaring business. Indeed there is a change on every kind of entertainment in the cities.

(x) ***Housing shortage***: The growth in population in cities is so fast that it is not possible to provide people with adequate residential accommodation. Indeed pressure on space in cities is so tremendous that most people are forced to live on roads or in shabby accommodation in cities like Bombay. The shortage of residential accommodation compels people to stay without families. The persons coming from villages are unable to bring their families with them. This phenomenon, as observed earlier, leads to inevitable sexual corruption.

(xi) ***Growth of slums***: Industrialization has resulted in shortage of accommodation and this, in turn, has given rise to slums, overcrowded shabby living quarters. These slums are populated by workers and other indigent people. The persons living in these slums are constantly exposed to all kinds of diseases, are liable to become social deviates and criminals; and loss of morals is an inevitable consequence of living in slums. The *ahatas* of Kanpur, *bastis* of Delhi, *chawls* of Bombay and *cheris* of Madras are stigmas on the face of India. These shabby quarters are worse than stables of horses and pens of cattle. There is no ventilation, no drainage, no drinking water. A besmirched, ragged piece of jute hanging in front of homes is an eloquent testimony of their pitiable condition. The glaring contrasts in the palatial lives of industrialists and the dirt-laden existence of workers testify to the hollowness of our socialism and democratic life J.L. Nehru was so moved emotionally on seeing slums that he wanted them to be burnt down and the persons responsible for them to be hanged. They symbolize extreme moral and physical decline — the nadir of all that is bad in life. According to Dr. Radhakamal Mukherjee, "In the thousand slums of India's industrial centres manhood is, unquestionably, brutalized, women dishonoured and childhood is poisoned at its very source."

THE ECONOMIC CONSEQUENCES OF INDUSTRIALIZATION

The following are the important consequences in the economic field of industrialization in India.

1. **Growth of capitalism** As a result of industrialization there is tremendous concentration of wealth in few hands. Due to industrialization, one man can control a business of crores of rupees and go on amassing wealth unabated. Thus like other countries, industrialization in India has also given tremendous fillip to the growth of capitalism.

2. **Vast production** As a result of industrialization, there is production on a large scale. In India steel, cement, sugar, jute, fertilizers, electrical equipments, rail material are being produced on massive scale. India with its vast population is near self-sufficient in these commodities and, today, it exports many of these.

3. **Growth of trade** On account of vast production there is unparalleled growth in trade and commerce. The development of fast means of communication has contributed a lot towards this end. The foreign trade has also shown tremendous rise.

4. **Division of labour and specialization** An economic impact of industrialization is the division of labour and specialization. Gradually, the number of technocrats and highly skilled personnel is growing.

5. **Rise in the standard of living** As a result of industrialization, there is a certain rise in the living standard. To-day electric fans, gas, radio and iron are common household goods.

6. **Economic crisis and unemployment** But whereas means of comfort and luxury are now easily available, there is, on the other hand, grave economic crisis. The mechanization of all production has thrown millions of people out of work. Due to industrialization there is a glut of many commodities. This leads to grave economic crisis.

7. **Industrial disputes and accidents** The industrial disputes and accidents are inevitable accompaniments of industrialization. Wherever

there is industry, there are thousands of workers. It is a natural tendency of workers to expect more and more out of their work; on the other hand, the industrialists want more production for less wages. Under these circumstances there are bound to be clashes of interests resulting in industrial disputes. The working conditions in Indian industry are not of high standard and accidents are very likely.

8. Problems of workers Besides strikes and lockouts, workers have some other problems. An important problem in this connection is that of rest and relaxation. Firstly, they have to work for long hours so that they get little rest. Secondly, whatever rest they get, there are not adequate sources of healthy entertainment available.

9. Spread of socialism and individualism The industrialization has promoted both socialism and individualism. As a result of it, capitalism grew and with it spread the ideas of individualism and *laissez-faire.* On the other hand, the ideology of socialism also spread as a result of industrialization. The industrial workers organized themselves into trade unions and political parties in order to gain their support to professed socialism.

10. Class conflict Like other countries industrialization in India has given rise to class conflicts and class war. There is a continuous tension among the poor and rich. However, the class war in India is as yet not very intense.

11. Decline of rural industry As a result of industrialization, the goods of daily use are produced on mass scale. The quality of machine-made goods is standardized and they are cheap. This results in larger inflow of goods into villages and has ruined the cottage industry of the villages.

INDUSTRIALIZATION AND SOCIAL DISORGANIZATION

Industrialization gives rise to many such processes which lead to social disorganization. The industrialization produces many problems at family, individual and community level. Industrialization induces individual and family disorganization. Industrialization gives rise to such facts as are responsible for social disorganization. Following are such facts :

1. Facts of individual disorganization The industrialization gives rise to facts which cause disorganization in the individual. Millions of workers migrate from villages to towns for jobs. As there is acute shortage of accommodation in towns and the life is otherwise costly too, they are unable to bring their families to cities. Therefore, after a day's hard work they can get neither any healthy entertainment nor the peace of home.

Lacking all suitable alternatives they take to drinking and prostitution, etc. This leads to their moral degeneration. The gaudy and exciting urban environment and materialistic outlook of life also contribute to moral degeneration. This produces disorganization not only among workers but in other persons, too.

2. Unemployment While industrialization has created employment opportunities for millions, it has also led to unemployment. The mechanization of production greatly reduced the need for workers. Whenever a new sophisticated machine is installed in any factory, hundreds of workers are thrown out of job. Many rural women come to cities in search for job, but, unable to find one, are forced into prostitution. The unemployment in turn leads to social disorganization.

3. Crime and immorality The process of industrialization has also led to rise in the incidence of crime and immorality. As referred to earlier, thousands of workers in the town are unable to find suitable accommodation or are unable to cope up with high expenses of urban life. They are forced to lead secluded existence. Being not highly morally trained, they succumb to the twin lure of wine and women. They drink country liquor and visit lowly prostitutes. The industrialization has also given rise to factionalism, materialism and mechanical character of life. All these things have encouraged crime. As a result of industrialization, small boys and girls take to work and they are easily spoiled.

4. Factionalism and heterogeneity The industrialization has contributed to factionalism and given rise to economic disparities. This is proving highly subversive of social cohesion and unity. The difference between rich and poor keeps growing and both classes tend to develop anti-social tendencies. Whereas industrialists live in fully air-conditioned palatial mansions, the poor are constrained to sleep on footpath and whereas the former live a luxurious life, the latter are unable to make their both ends meet. This economic disparity is productive of social disorganization.

5. Cultural lag The process of industrialization resulted in cultural lag. This is due to the fact that industrialization leads to fast progress in materialistic things. The manner and mode of life outwardly changes very rapidly but there is little progress of inward culture. Thus inward change does not keep pace with outward changes and this contradiction results in cultural lag.

6. Changes in values Industrialization has resulted in changes in values. On account of industrializations jobs are now available to women and children. This has resulted in changes in relations of husband and wife and children. Women are no longer chattel pieces of men. They enjoy now relative economic independence and their outlook on life has changed. The relations between various people are no longer based on tradition but are guided by the calculus of self-interest.

7. Family disorganization Industrialization has resulted in disorganization of family life also. The husband and wife go to their respective places of work and there is no one back at home to take care and look after the children. Where children also do jobs there can be no proper provision of education. Due to changes in values and consequent change in the attitudes, the cohesion of family life is severely disturbed. If husband and wife both stay out of home, chances of disharmony among them increase. If women and girls go out of home for job, the chances of illicit sexual relations increase. On account of all these factors, family disorganization results.

8. Urbanization An inevitable consequence of industrialization is the increase in urbanization. Due to urbanization, big cities spring up with population far in excess of their capacity. As a result a large number of persons have to live in one or two-room quarters. In this situation there is disaffection among married couples and unmarried persons get frequent opportunities to peep upon sexual activities of married persons. This has evil effect on impressionable young persons and they indulge in premature sex. Many a time queer sexual intimacy among family members is the outcome of this hopeless and helpless situation. The relations among individuals in cities are of impersonal character. The urbanization results in loosening of social control. The community life is disrupted. The gaudy and exciting life of cities produces imbalance in social and personal relations. The freedom of contact between sexes also disturbs family life. The life in clubs and society is a life of rebellion against social traditions and restrictions. The slums, the epidemics, immoral outlook have all combined to knock the bottom out of harmonious and peaceful life in cities.

Steps to Check Effects of Industrialization

From the above discussion of social and economic effects of industrialization, it is quite clear that industrialization has been rising due to a number of evil effects. These include housing shortage, labour problems, unnatural life, increase in crime and exploitation, ruin of rural industry, etc.

Following measures should be taken to counteract the evil influences of industrialization:

1. Town planning The industries should be at a reasonable distance from the residential colonies and the main centres of the city. The slums should be cleared and replaced by good hygienic houses.

2. Planning of factories The factories should be well planned. They must be well-ventilated and must have all amenities. They should be so structured and equipped that the chances of accidents are minimal.

3. Enactment of labour laws There must be well laid down rules for the workers. Their wages, bonus, working hours, gratuity, pensions, leaves, etc., should be governed by laws enacted by the government and these should be strictly enforced.

4. Promotion of rural industries The government should encourage rural industries. It must give liberal loans for their development.

5. Decentralization Many an evil effect of industrialization is due to the fact that there is usually concentration of industry at one place. This should be avoided and there should be diversification of industries.

6. Development of cottage industry A number of evil effects of industrialization are due to mechanization and specialization. This lop-sided development can be greatly averted by promotion and encouragement of cottage industries.

7. Housing As a result of industrialization there is acute housing shortage in industrial towns. Numerous evil effects flow from the shortage of housing. These can be avoided by giving building of houses top priority.

8. Healthy entertainment The increase in the incidence of crime, juvenile delinquency and prostitution in industrial towns is due to lack of healthy entertainment. If we know the cause of a phenomenon, it is easy to control it. Thus by providing healthy entertainment we can counteract the above-mentioned evils.

All the above-mentioned suggestions for the improvement of urban areas and for counteracting the ills of industrialization have been in one form or the other accepted, at least in principle by the Government of India. Fortunately, industrialization in India is still not so intense and concentrated as to produce alarming problems. If some advance steps can be taken at this stage, it is possible to mitigate the more severe types of ills consequent upon industrialization. The acute problems of industrialization are in India confined to few metropolises like Calcutta, Bombay, Kanpur, etc. Of course, the efforts being made at these centres to mitigate the evil effects of industrialization leave much to be desired. The existence of slums is a glaring fact of all industrial centres. It is an indelible blot on our society. The working conditions of labour are neither healthy nor hygienic. There is no provision of wholesome entertainment. The government needs to pay special attention to this aspect. The closing down of red-light areas is no solution of the problem. The government alone does not have resources to solve the monumental problems posed by industrialization. It needs the cooperation of local-self government and also the efforts of the industrialists.

QUESTIONS OF EXERCISE

1. Describe formal organization in an industry.
2. Explain informal organization in an industry.
3. Describe the relationship of industrialization and social disorganization.

7

INDUSTRIAL BUREAUCRACY

In the industrial system the most important factor is that of industrial bureaucracy. The industrial bureaucracy is a hierarchical arrangement of authority in the industry. The first systematic study of industrial bureaucracy was made by the eminent sociologist Max Weber. In the times of Max Weber bureaucracy was establishing itself as a result of great strides being made in the field of industrialization. According to Weber bureaucracy is a hierarchical arrangement which helps to control and regulate the industrial management.

MEANING OF INDUSTRIAL BUREAUCRACY

The literal meaning of the term bureaucracy is hierarchical arrangement of authority in the field of industry. The term bureaucracy is derived from the French word "Bureau" which means desk. Therefore, quite appropriately, Finer has termed bureaucracy as Desk Government. The word bureau also means tier or step and therefore it signifies hierarchical arrangement of officialdom or management in the field of industry. In modern world the states are so big in size that it is not possible to run their administration; it has to be done indirectly through a large paraphernalia of officers and subordinates. The modern scientific technology has transformed the entire complexion of industry. The industries of the world today are nothing but king-sized. Some of them are indeed big giants and empires. No single person or even a set of persons can afford to control them directly. We shall now examine some of the definitions of industrial bureaucracy given by eminent authorities :

1. According to Max Weber, "Bureaucracy is a system of administration characterized by expertness, impartiality and absence of humanity." In

this definition industrialized systems are taken to be akin to a type of administrative system whose chief characteristics are efficiency in work performance, an objective and impartial outlook and most important of all lack of human touch, that is, it operates mechanically. The absence of human touch and sensibility in the bureaucracy is due to the fact that bureaucracy functions under the framework of rules and regulations though this may militate against human sensibility. Bureaucracy as a rule, is riddled with formalism and red-tapism. Bureaucracy has come under trenchant criticism on account of these features. Besides above features, there are some other characteristics of bureaucracy, according to Max Weber. These include tier-wise arrangement of officialdom, predominance of files and written work and dependence upon written formalized rules and regulations. Bureaucratic functioning requires technical training.

2. According to Professor Laski, "A system, the control of which is so completely in the hands of officials that their power jeopardizes the liberties of ordinary citizens." Professor Laski's definition of bureaucracy is more in the nature of critique than an explanation of the bureaucracy. Laski considers the freedom of citizen to be crucially important and is opposed to any restriction of their essential freedom. However, this cannot be said to be the chief characteristic of bureaucracy, Admittedly, there is a constant threat to freedom from bureaucracy.

3. According to Robert K. Merton, "Bureaucracy is a secondary group structure designed to carry on certain activities which cannot be performed on the basis of primary group criteria." This definition emphasizes the fact that bureaucracy is based on secondary group structure. The characteristic features of secondary group structure, namely formalism, social differentiation and indirect relations are based upon its sociologic peculiarity and the same are found duplicated in the realm of bureaucracy. The dependence of bureaucracy upon secondary group structure implies, Merton clearly emphasizes, that the tasks assigned to bureaucracy are such as cannot be performed by the primary group. As it has been stressed earlier as long as the industries were on the level of cottage or small scale, the need for bureaucracy was not felt. The need for bureaucratic set-up is felt only when the number of persons engaged in a particular unit exceeds the limit in which direct and face-to-face relations are not feasible.

4. According to Louis Coser and Rosenberg, "Bureaucracy may be defined as that type of hierarchical organization which is designed rationally to co-ordinate the work of many individuals in the pursuit of large scale administrative tasks." In this definition the bureaucratic set-

up is likened to hierarchical structure which is used to co-ordinate the works in large scale organizations. Thus as a matter of fact, bureaucracy is indispensable in large scale organizations and there is indeed nothing wrong as long as it is free from corruption and other malpractices. In conclusion we must admit that for running the modern large-scale industries, the bureaucratic set-up is unavoidable.

CHARACTERISTICS OF THE INDUSTRIAL BUREAUCRACY

The bureaucracy displays the following characteristics :

1. Particular system The bureaucracy is a special type of system needed to run the organized industry.

2. Hierarchy The bureaucracy is arranged in a system of lower to higher order. In a hierarchical arrangement, papers move from below to top and the policies are laid down at top and implemented by the lower cadres. There are various levels or rungs in a hierarchical system and it is the peculiarity of this system that under it no level can be side-tracked or circumvented. The papers must move through all the levels intervening between the level initiating them and the apex.

3. Definition of duties of officers In bureaucracy the rights and duties of all the concerned officers are well-defined. Anyone acting beyond his jurisdiction is taken to task. It is violative of the code of conduct to attempt a task which does not explicitly belong to the person concerned.

4. Specialization In bureaucracy the officers at different levels possess various types of qualities and have specialized in different areas. When an industry needs officers at a particular level, it advertises for the post and also mentions the minimum requirements, special qualifications and abilities needed for the proper performance of jobs.

5. System of fulfilment of duties In as much as the various officers at different levels have particular qualifications and possess specific specializations, each man in the bureaucratic set-up has specialized duties. As long as each man performs functions and duties proper to him, there is harmony and smooth working in bureaucracy and the bureaucratic system proves fruitful.

6. Based on documents and files The majority of bureaucratic functions are performed through the medium of files and documents. A detailed record of the appointment of workers, their grade, cadre, salary, increment and promotion is kept by all industrial organizations. Besides a written balance sheet of expenditures and receipts is also maintained. The record of old files is also maintained for certain specified periods.

The files are maintained in a serial order and subject-wise. The efficiency of bureaucracy rests in the quick disposal of files. A clumsy and inefficient handling of files is known as red-tapism.

7. Promotion on seniority and ability In an industrial organization there are two bases for promotion : seniority and ability. The dual criterion of promotion is essential for the healthy functioning of bureaucratic set-up. Both seniority and ability must be given weightage in deciding upon promotions. This is so because if seniority alone is adopted as criterion of promotion, the able will suffer because persons of lower abilities will occupy senior positions. Moreover, the men of ability may leave the organization to join some other industrial organization which gives more consideration to ability.

8. Service for career In bureaucracy every person tries to do his job earnestly and honestly in order to gain a better place in the organization. The able, efficient and hard-working individuals are rewarded by better situations and successes in career. Thus, ability and efficiency of a person in bureaucracy can be safely gauged from his career. But when people take to corrupt practices in order to advance their careers, the results are deleterious.

9. Difference in theory and practice Generally we find a gap between theory and practice in bureaucracy. This has given rise to the view that bureaucracy is an inhuman system. But inhumanity is not an invariable concomitant of bureaucracy. It can be removed.

10. Secrecy of functions In bureaucracy each official maintains secrecy of his functions.

11. Training As a matter of fact, in bureaucracy each official gets intensive training prior to his joining the post. But, in order to increase proficiency, these officials are allowed to undertake special training.

12. Bureaucrat personality An important feature of bureaucracy is that there is usually a gap or chasm between the official and non-official personalities of the bureaucrats. At times there is conflict and tension between the two. Though such instances are common, yet this cannot be considered to be an essential feature of bureaucracy. Indeed a successful bureaucrat is one who can keep his personal and official interests separated. If he completely identifies with his official work himself there is no conflict But an ambivalence between official and personal interests is dangerous.

TYPES OF BUREAUCRACY

The types of bureaucracy are determined by the criteria adopted for the recruitment of bureaucrats. For example, if officers are recruited on the basis of merit, the resultant hierarchy of officers will be called Merit Bureaucracy. And if this recruitment is made on the basis of caste, the Caste Bureaucracy results. Besides the classification of bureaucracy is made on the basis of the conduct of officers. For examples, if the conduct of officers is guided by the principles of justice and fair play and is directed to general welfare of the masses, the system is know as Guardian Bureaucracy. And if the conduct of officers displays favouritism and is directed to protect the interests of a particular section, this system is called Patronage Bureaucracy. It must, of course, be obvious that compared to Caste Bureaucracy, the Merit Bureaucracy is to be preferred and that compared to Patronage Bureaucracy, the Guardian Bureaucracy is to be preferred.

ADVANTAGES OF BUREAUCRACY

The foregoing description of the features and types of bureaucracy brings to relief the following advantages of bureaucracy:

1. Systematic administration As is evident from the various definitions of bureaucracy, its system is devised to make administration systematic and scientific.

2. Administration by able persons In a bureaucratic set-up the work of industry is divided into various levels and departments and the persons having suitable qualifications for each type of work are recruited. This ensures that only capable persons are allowed to handle each type of work.

3. Effective control The bureaucracy functions on principles, and, under it no room is allowed for personal likes and dislikes. At times this feature may render it seemingly inhuman, but this ensures effective control and minimizes arbitrariness.

4. Possibility of large scale industry Above all, the greatest advantage of bureaucracy is that with the help of this system, huge industrial empires can be built up and run efficiently. Whatever may be the defects of bureaucracy all these are overruled and set aside by the fact that, without bureaucracy, no big industry can be conceived of.

DISADVANTAGES OF BUREAUCRACY

The above advantages of bureaucracy notwithstanding, various eminent thinkers have bitterly criticized bureaucracy. According to Laski, it is an attack on the freedom of common man. Bernard Shaw calls it the feudalism of high dignitaries lusting for power. Ramsay Muir has likened bureaucracy to fire, which, as a servant, is indifferent to humanitarian considerations. Briefly, following are the demerits of bureaucracy:

1. Red-tapism Red-tapism is the biggest defect of bureaucracy. In a bureaucratic set-up, the files and papers move at a snail's pace and it takes inordinately long time to reach any decision on any matter. Usually, so much time is consumed in the disposal of files that by the time a decision is taken it loses relevance. Of course, the red-tapism is more serious in public and government-run industries, whereas in private managements the defect of red-tapism is not so serious.

2. Authoritative tendency In a bureaucratic set-up the officers occupying top ranks are liable to make an arbitrary use of their authority. They tend to act with scant consideration for the harmful effects of their decision upon the persons concerned. Therefore, bureaucracy tends to become non-human.

3. Superiority complex In bureaucracy the top ranking officers are afflicted to egoism; they bluff and bluster. Drunk with power, they treat their subordinates with little respect. Therefore, the subordinates feel slighted and demoralized.

4. Emphasis on impersonal relation It is a common observation that even those personnel who are very polite and courteous in their behaviour turn rude and indifferent upon assuming the position of authority. As a rule, impersonality of relations is an essential characteristic of bureaucracy and within limits this is rather good, but, when this tendency is carried to extreme, it becomes an evil and creates an unbridgeable gulf between the officers and subordinates.

5. Circumlocution In bureaucracy the officers tend to abide by a too literal interpretation of rules and give credence to statistics available in their books even when a reasonable doubt can occur in this matter. All this leads to unrealistic solution of problems.

6. Conservative Bureaucracy is conservative and is opposed to any idea of equality. The officers wish to have strict control over their subordinates, and, in the name of discipline, determinedly crush any innovative thinking among the subordinates.

7. Class consciousness In bureaucracy, the officers consider themselves as an upper caste and look down upon the subordinates.

8. Emphasis on routine In bureaucracy, innovativeness is sacrificed and routine encouraged.

SUGGESTIONS FOR REFORMS

As we have had an occasion to refer to earlier, the above-mentioned defects of bureaucracy are characteristic more of giant industrial houses or public companies than of small industries. In giant complexes, bureaucratic structure itself becomes so vast, that it gets out of control. As a matter of fact, if strict control is maintained on bureaucracy as is done in private managements, many of the above-mentioned defects can be removed. Following constructive suggestions can be offered :

1. The bureaucracy should be kept under strict supervision of the industrialists or governmental authority. As and when the actions of the bureaucrats are inimical to general welfare, they should be suitably reprimanded.
2. The bureaucrats should not act as patrons but guardians of their subordinates. They should not overlord them but try to work for their welfare.
3. A number of defects in bureaucracy creep in due to faulty recruitment. If ability alone is kept as the criterion of recruitment, most of the defects are avoided, but when patronage or caste is the criterion of recruitment, the above-mentioned defects are bound to creep in.
4. There should be an independent tribunal to adjudicate the complaints of subordinates against the officers high-handedness.
5. A research should be made into ways and means of improving the bureaucratic set-up.

QUESTIONS FOR EXERCISE

1. What is Industrial Bureaucracy? Describe its characteristics.
2. Give types of Bureaucracy. What are their disadvantages? Suggest reforms.

8

INDUSTRIAL LEADERSHIP

At various levels or stages of work in industry, the senior officers supervise, guide and control the functioning of their subordinates. The supervisory function is not merely one of overseeing but also involves guidance and control. In one word, the supervisory function includes the function of leadership. The supervisor is not a mere observer who passively watches what others are doing; but, on the other hand, it is his business to guide and control the overall direction of work. He is therefore required to co-ordinate the work of subordinates under him. Thus supervision is a complex activity and includes co-ordination, guidance and direction. In the words of M.S. Viteles, "Supervision refers to the direct, immediate guidance and control of subordinates in the performance of their tasks." While guidance is a positive aspect of supervision, control is its negative aspect. In industrial supervision both aspects are of equal importance. The value of supervision in industry cannot be exaggerated. Its importance is realized by all and is clear from the fact that everywhere in industry we have supervisors. The supervisors perform various kinds of functions. They not only supervise but also critically evaluate and redirect the works of their subordinates. They also try to remove chances of friction and conflict in the course of work. Besides they train the workers as how to do the task efficiently and well. Above all, the supervisor has in him the quality of leadership which inspires the men under him.

LEADERSHIP IN INDUSTRY

The study of leadership comes into the province of Social Psychology. In all walks of life there are leaders. The leaders coordinate, direct and guide the behaviour of their followers. The industrial psychology dwells on the psychological aspects in industry. The field of psychology is the field of human behaviour and conduct. The terms behaviour and conduct include both personal and social behaviour. The leadership in human affairs plays the role of setting standards and guidelines of human behaviour and conduct. Thus in modern industry there is great value and importance of leadership. In some industries certain persons are specifically appointed leaders; but even in those establishments where there are no such specific appointments, certain individuals automatically emerge as leaders. We can thus see leaders anywhere. Wherever there is a group of human beings working together, the emergence of leadership is automatic and natural. However, the leaders who are superimposed, that is those who have been appointed by the management, do not enjoy an unqualified support from the workers and are unable to play as effective and salutary a role as those who are elected by the workers themselves. The reason for this state of affairs is obvious. Only on the basis of personal qualities can one be a true leader. These qualities can by no means be endowed on any one by the management or government. Besides one can voluntarily follow only that person whom he has elected or willingly accepted. On the contrary, a person externally imposed, no matter how hard he may try, cannot evoke and receive voluntarily allegiance of workers. This is the reason why labour leaders are far more powerful than the leaders appointed by the management. The management can ill afford to ignore the labour leader. The popularity of a worker can be gauged from the sociogram of the group of which the worker is a member.

LEVELS OF LEADERSHIP

In accordance with the object of leadership we find three levels of leadership. These are :

1. **Senior managerial level** At this apex level are those senior executives by whose order a mill or a factory runs. If this top executive maintains a rapport with the workers, the workers carry out his orders. But, however, in the absence of such a rapport, the labour leaders may prove to be more powerful than senior executive.
2. **Intermediate managerial level** At this level we find middle range executives like foremen, supervisors, etc. They have intimate contact with the workers and are capable of providing effective leadership.
3. **Labour leaders** These leaders, as is apparent from the name, are the representatives of workers and are usually elected by the workers. Each group of workers selects a leader. There may be conflict among

the leaders of the workers. However, if there is a single trade union in a mill or a factory, then there is one leader in the whole of the factory. The labour leaders are quite powerful.

They can organize strikes at a short notice. They act as go-between among management and workers. Sometimes labour leaders are more anxious to find out their own political interests than to work for the real welfare of the workers. As a result of this duplicity of labour leaders, no real benefit accrues from strikes, etc. It is essential that workers should beware of these leaders and keep them at a distance.

TYPES OF LEADERSHIP

Psychologists have classified the types of leadership and supervision in identical terms. In other words, the types of leadership and supervision are similar or parallel or that the supervisory role in industry is the same as that of leadership. The present study of leadership, however, has nothing to do with the problem of political leadership. The industrial leadership and political leadership are quite distinct affairs. The study of leadership in this chapter concerns only the first two types of leadership described above. It is not concerned with labour leaders, who, according to psychologists, are not industrial leaders. An industrial leader *ex hypothesi* must be a supervisor, too. Thus we find the following types of industrial leaders :

(I) Authoritative supervisor An authoritative supervisor exercises control and direction over his subordinates by virtue of the authority vested in him. In authoritative leadership we have the two following types of supervisors:

1. The hard-boiled autocrat An autocrat, as is explicit from the term, believes in unflagging discipline and firm control over the workers. He would rarely appreciate the role or work of his subordinates. Rather he looks upon them with slight and mild contempt. He keeps himself aloof from the workers and does not give them a chance to get near him. An autocrat wants automatic obedience of his orders and can brook no criticism of his directions and orders. Though workers obey such autocrats, but, from the core of their heart, they oppose him. Whenever possible they ruin the work and shift the responsibility to someone else. Such autocrats are apt to give credence to backbiting and this leads to tension and conflicts in industry. In as much as autocrats show no respect for the feelings of their subordinates, the subordinates also harbour a spirit of vindictiveness against such persons. At times this flares up and finds expression in violence against supervisors. As a matter of fact, a hard-boiled autocrat does not deserve to be called a leader. He lacks all the qualities of leadership. The obedience of

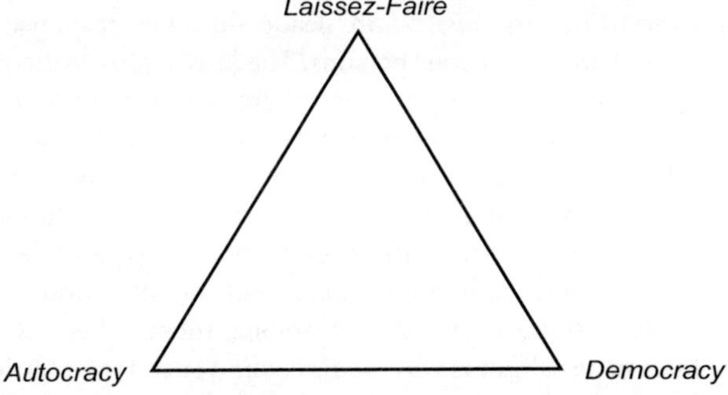

Fig. 8.1. Relations among Autocracy, Democracy and *Laissez-faire*

Democracy is not the opposite of autocracy; rather, both are deviations from individual freedom or *laissez-faire*. In group effort, complete individual freedom leads to chaos. Both autocracy and democracy limit freedom, but, in one case, the limitation is imposed on the group while, in the other, it is assumed by the group.

which he is able to claim is not due to any personal quality in him but is due purely to the authority vested in him.

2. The benevolent autocrat The benevolent autocrat gives guidance and direction in all matters. He wants to maintain discipline and is annoyed by any infringement of the discipline. But unlike the hard-boiled autocrat, the benevolent autocrat is not averse to saying a word of praise to the workers who perform their duties well. The workers carry out the orders of such supervisors though they do not really feel inspired by them.

In modern times an extensive research has been done to evaluate the authoritative leadership, to discover its *pros and cons.* It is true that authoritative leaders are capable of giving express orders and have them carried out. In certain cases these leaders come to symbolize the father and this helps to bring forth easy and free allegiance of workers. This helps smooth functioning of the factory or a mill. The authoritative leader is impressed by the quality of his decision but his decision cannot become an effective instrument, unless and until it is accepted by all workers, and they feel agreeable to it. There is a little difficulty in its successful implementation.

(II) *Laissez-faire* leadership In *laissez-faire* leadership the freedom of workers is of greatest value. This type of leadership is exact reverse of the autocratic leadership. While in autocratic leadership there is no place for the personal freedom of workers, in *laissez-faire* leadership the personal freedom of workers is respected. Whereas in autocratic leadership, the leader is considered responsible for everything, in *laissez-faire* leadership the responsibility is distributed among various persons. The *laissez-faire* leaders do not try to impose any decision upon others nor do they coerce them to any type of action. These leaders act democratically. They try to seek the voluntary cooperation of workers. These leaders do not project any fixed goals. Obviously, there are some undesirable consequences of *laissez-faire* leadership. This type of leadership gives rise to indiscipline and discontent among workers. It also promotes a sense of insecurity among them. There is loss in production also. That is why we rarely find such type of leadership in industry.

(III) Democratic supervision Today the most prevalent form of leadership and supervision in industry is democratic supervision. According to Bradford, democratic leader believes in the following things:

1. Problems should not be allowed to crop up.
2. For the sake of collective action and thinking, assemblies and conferences are a must.
3. There should be fixed collective ideals.
4. The criteria of action should be fixed.
5. The reasons for decisions should be known.
6. With progress, freedom and responsibility increase.

As we have referred earlier, the above-mentioned characteristics of democratic supervision are corresponding to and congruent with modern democratic ideals. In democracies this is the most appropriate form of supervision. However, everyone cannot be led democratically. Some workers misunderstand the democratic attitude of the supervisor and take it to be a symptom of weakness. They try to exploit this weakness and shirk work. This results in loss of production.

Democratic leadership is not opposed to autocratic leadership. Indeed both are deviant forms of *laissez-faire* leadership.

The complete and unfettered freedom degenerates into license. The licentious freedom is obviously fraught with great dangers. It easily results into anarchical conditions. The licentious freedom is possible only in *laissez-faire* leadership. Under democratic leadership everyone gets a chance to participate in supervision. This increases the mutual confidence among workers. The workers feel that whatever they are doing is a result of their own free will. The supervisor merely proffers technical advice and he is accepted by workers as one of them. Briefly, democratic leadership or supervision is a collective leadership and it is best suited to industry.

THE CONDITIONS OF EFFECTIVE LEADERSHIP

The quality of leadership determines the nature of relationship between senior officers and his subordinates. Thus by effective leadership we mean an effective control and deep impression of the leader upon his followers. Following are conditions essential for effective leadership:

1. Favourable social environs An essential condition of an effective leadership is the creation of an atmosphere of mutual trust and confidence. It must be able to associate workers in decision making and feeling of responsibility. Under such an atmosphere, the directives of the leader are easily accepted and carried out by the workers.

2. Knowledge of company's policy Another condition of effective leadership is the knowledge of policy and philosophy of the company. The

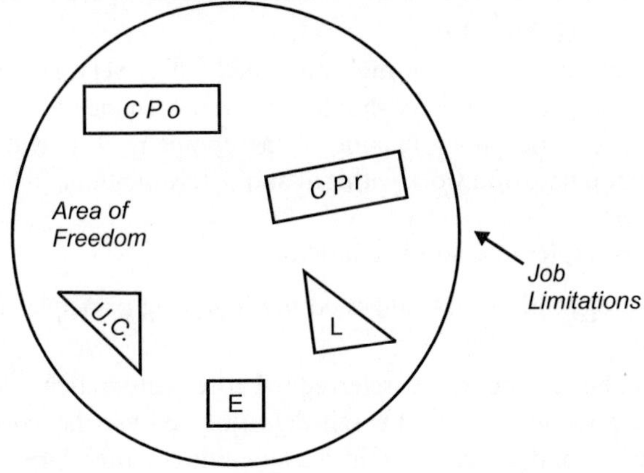

Fig. 8.2. The Area of Freedom for the Practice of Democratic leadership.

The circle represents the limitations which the job situation imposes upon activity; C. Po and C. Pr. represent the limitations imposed by company policies and company practices, respectively; represent activity areas removed by union contracts and legislation; U.C. and L represent activity areas removed by union contracts and legislation, respectively; and E represents problem areas solved by experts. The remaining area falls within the authority of a given level of supervision, an problems in this area may be solved by group techniques. (From N.R.F. Maier, "A Human Realtions program for Supervision," *In dust and Labour* Rel., Rev., 1948, 1, 442-64).

leader must know the fundamental tenets which govern the functioning of the company. Without possessing such knowledge, no leader can be successful. The leader must acquaint the workers with the policy and the rules of the company. He must further explain in clear and frank terms his status and role in the company. This would enable him to feel secure because he knows what he has to do and what he must avoid doing.

3. Gaining confidence of workers A good leader should win the confidence of workers. Before effecting any change in the technique of production, a good leader will consult the workers even if the change has been finally decided upon. This will help to induce a sense of well-being and confidence among the workers and they will highly appreciate the fact that workers are considered worthy for consultation by authorities.

4. Strict discipline Whatever rules and regulations are framed once, these should be strictly adhered to. If a worker violates them and deserves to be penalized, he should be penalized without fail and without any let or hindrance; similarly the good works must be rewarded. Therefore, if the performance of a worker is noteworthy and deserves reward, he must be rewarded ungrudgingly.

5. Participation in decision-making Finally, it is very necessary for good leadership that workers should be given a chance to participate in the decision and policy making of the company. This will enthuse workers to toil hard and work with grit and determination.

General Principles of Good Leadership

The psychologist Blum has suggested the following principles for good leadership:

1. **Don't be an autocrat** As referred to earlier, autocratic leadership is not a good leadership. It is self-defeating because the workers feel alienated and do not obey the leader willingly. Therefore autocracy in leadership should be eschewed.
2. **Listen carefully** It is very essential that the leader should be a good listener. The supervisor must listen carefully to everything told to him by his subordinates. He must accord full opportunity to the worker to present his case. Only when the worker has presented his case should the leader express his opinion.
3. **Don't decide hurriedly** It is rash to form an opinion about some person hurriedly after a casual glance or brief hearing. Some persons deny their subordinates the opportunity to speak out of their mind and pay no attention to their complaints. While it is true

that most of the complaints are not genuine, some are certainly so and if these are not removed, the morale in the company would suffer.

4. **Don't argue with subordinates** A supervisor should under no circumstances indulge in arguments with his subordinate, because if he fails to be persuaded or convinced by his subordinate, or his arguments, he is liable to issue orders to vindicate his point of view. This creates frustration and sense of insecurity among the workers. The good leader does not argue but listens carefully. Only after careful listening he issues orders.
5. **Don't criticize publicly** Nobody likes to be told off or reprimanded in the presence of others. If a worker is rebuked publicly he feels insulted. The workers are usually rash and they tend to retaliate if they are Wounded emotionally. Therefore, a good leader avoids discussing the faults of workers in public. He points them out in private and in a direct manner.

Some more facts can be pointed out with regard to successful supervision. However, it is not possible to describe and classify all laws about supervision. The supervision is an art rather than a science; and it is not possible to describe all facts about art. Some persons are very persuasive in their reasoning. They have the gift of leadership and they are easily accepted by others as leaders. The persons who have the natural qualities of leadership are the best supervisors.

QUALITIES OF LEADERSHIP

1. **Physical qualities** (i) Sound health, (ii) Vitality, (iii) Endurance.
2. **Psychological qualities** (i) Personal Magnetism, (ii) Enthusiasm, (iii) Co-operation, (iv) Ability to inspire, (v) Forcefulness, (vi) Tact.
3. **Intellectual Traits** (i) A high degree of intelligence, (ii) An open mind, (iii) A capacity for sound judgement, (iv) An ability to teach, (v) Scientific Approach.
4. **Qualities of Character** (i) Integrity, (ii) Self-discipline, (iii) Fair play, (iv) Willingness to accept responsibility, (v) Physical and moral courage, (vi) Humanism.

TRAITS COMMON TO ALL LEADERS

The traits approach to leadership study was especially popular during 1930-50. As traits have no direct relation with the leadership, therefore, common traits are hardly found in two leaders. Each leader has different traits. Therefore, analysis of traits in different leaders made the list of traits longer and longer but there was very little consensus over common traits among researchers. Though very significant in determining a successful leader but personal traits and leadership have no relations. The studies of past leaders' life indicate that certain useful traits which they had really made them leaders such as 'strength of character' or 'power' or 'dominance' but it was the environment which made the traits active.

IMPORTANCE OF LEADERSHIP

1. Directing group activities In an organization leadership is mainly concerned with the group. Its main responsibility is to get the work done effectively by fruitfully engaging the workers or subordinates. For this purpose, the leader promotes the sincerity of purpose among the workers and directs them rightly towards the accomplishment of organisational goals. By his personal conduct and behaviour, the leader-infuses confidence in his subordinates and induces them to work hard. To quote George R. Terry, "A leader shows the way by his example. He is not a pusher, he pulls rather than pushes."

A group cannot work efficiently without leadership because a leader alone can consolidate the efforts of the group and divert those efforts towards the goal. He interprets the goal and plans of the group to the followers and takes the lead in all activities. So, directing the group activities towards a common goal is the main function of the leadership.

2. Better utilisation of manpower The leader is important as he makes plans, policies and programmes and carries them out. As plans, policies and programmes cannot work themselves, he mobilises the workforce to engage them to get higher performance. He co-ordinates their efforts to utilise the available manpower effectively so as to get highest production with minimum human cost. Achieving best performance from workers is the key to successful and effective leadership.

3. Source of motivation Leadership is a source of motivation to the subordinates. It does not mean simply the existence of leadership traits in a person. It is to utilise those traits in motivating the people at work towards the desired goal by applying a leadership style most suited to the situation. Motivation is an element of dynamic leadership in whose absence the success is doubtful.

4. Developing good human relations Human relations represent the relations between the leader and the subordinates. An efficient leadership develops the talents of the individuals, promotes self-confidence in them and provides them an opportunity to demonstrate their ability apart from the motivation towards the accomplishment of goal. Thus, the leader emphasises the cooperative attitude of workers. It creates an environment of good human relationship which increases the productivity of the organisation.

5. Promoting the spirit of co-ordination The activities of members of a group and those of different groups must be co-ordinated in order to achieve the desired goal. A leader promotes the spirit of co-ordination among workers.

6. Fulfilling social responsibilities Only an effective leadership may get the work done effectively. A well satisfied worker will help serving the organisation's interest under a good leadership. Good leadership is always concerned with the need and satisfaction of its workforce which provides higher standard of living to workers, higher productivity and production to the organisation, lower price to consumers, increased revenue to the nation, and a fair return to the investors. Thus, only under the guidance of dynamic leadership, an organisation can fulfil its social responsibilities towards different sections of the society: consumers, workers, investors, government, etc.

FUNCTIONS OF LEADERSHIP

1. Integration Leadership integrates the efforts of its followers and directs them towards organising goals. The leader integrates the efforts of the group. Common objectives cannot be achieved and co-ordination is not possible without that. In this age of specialisation, each individual does a part of the whole work. The integration of the parts of the whole is the leadership function.

2. Communication Communication of organisational policies, procedures and programmes is necessary in order to integrate the efforts of the members of the group. A leader communicates authority and responsibility to each individual so that he may come to know what he is to do and what not. He knows the way as to how he can attain the goals and discharge his responsibilities.

3. Production A leader should follow the production-oriented supervisory style of leadership; he should do utmost to increase the production and productivity of the organisation though not at the cost of human relations.

4. Representation A leader represents the organisation and its objectives before those who work for it and those who are outsiders. He represents workers before the higher management and outsiders. He represents management before the workers. Thus, he provides link between his management and subordinates.

5. Fraternity Leadership should promote fraternity among the subordinates. Its approach and style play an important role in developing industrial harmony. He should develop a climate of co-operation among workers in the organisation to achieve the success.

6. Organisation Organising capacity of a leader is an important trait. He is to decide who will do what and how? He provides necessary inputs to get the work done effectively. Failing in organising functions, he loses his confidence among the workers and also the organisation.

7. Evaluation of Performance A leader evaluates the performance of his subordinates. If a worker does well, he is adequately rewarded and if he fails in discharging his responsibility, he is punished. Both reward and punishment aim at motivating people to improve the situation. In the words of Stogdill, "Leadership is concerned with problems of human performance and interaction."

8. Initiation A leader must lead. He should take initiative to introduce changes in the organisation and the group's efforts wherever necessary. He should communicate the changes and reasons behind them to convince the workers about their rationality.

9. Domination A leader dominates his followers. He holds authority and some organisational power to use his power constructively or destructively. He may ignore his follower's wishes but he should not do that. He should be participator. He must use his power in the interest of group of which he is a leader.

DIFFERENT APPROACHES TO LEADERSHIP

Broadly, there are five main theories of leadership: (1) Traitist theory, (2) Situationalist theory, (3) Behavioural theory, (4) Followers theory, (5) System theory or Path-Goal Theory.

1. Traitist Approach or Theory

According to this classical theory, leadership behaviour is produced by certain traits (qualities) inherent in a person. In other words, leadership behaviour is sum total of the traits. A leader behaves according to his traits. Studies have focused the traits of past and present leaders in terms of their family background, education, career, events, character, etc. They have made a list of traits or attributes which a leader should possess. A number of traits have been identified by various researchers to distinguish successful leaders from unsuccessful ones or followers. The one way to identify the traits is to enquire from the leader himself, how he considers himself different from others.

A successful leader is supposed to have the following traits:

(i) Good personality, (ii) Tirelessness, (iii) Ability to quick decision, (iv) Courage, (v) Persuasion (vi) Intelligence, (vii) Reliability, (viii) Imagination, (ix) Physically fit, (x) Intellectually sound, etc. Psychologists have grouped these traits of a leader into four categories: (a) Physical, (b) Psychological (c) Intellectual and (d) Qualities of character.

Earlier, traits theories maintained that leadership qualities are inherited. Later theorists conceded that many of these traits could be acquired and developed by experience and training. Thus, traits are not only inborn but acquired as well. It has now been well established that leader is not only born but also made.

Weaknesses of Traits Theory

Though widely accepted for a pretty long time during 1930s-1950s, trait theory suffers from the following weaknesses:

1. No exhaustive list Various thinkers have supplied different list of qualities of a successful leadership. No two lists agree on the essential characteristics of the effective leader. None of the thinkers have listed the traits; in order of importance, lists of traits sometimes confuse the readers.

2. No common or universal traits Neither leadership traits are common nor universal. Therefore it is very difficult to indicate what traits are necessary to make an effective leader. Measurement of traits is problematic.

3. No room for future leaders Traits theory stresses the inborn qualities of an individual which cannot be developed or acquired. Earlier it was assumed that leaders are born and, therefore, it left no scope for development of future leaders. It was later accepted that such inborn traits can be developed or acquired through experience or training.

4. No Consideration of situational factors Trait theorists do not consider the situational factor for leadership which influence the leaders more than their inner traits. Traits come to light when a situation arises. They are helpful in facing a particular situation but traits are useless without a situation.

5. Different roles require different traits This is so even in the same organisation. At lower managerial level, where there is a direct contact between a worker and the supervisor, technical knowledge is of paramount importance. Human relations and skills are of prime importance at middle management level, where policies are elaborated and interpreted. Conceptual skill gains prominent position at higher management level, where policies are framed and planning is undertaken. In a larger organisation, leadership has a limited role. In a small organisation it demands multiplicity of roles. Thus different combinations of traits are required in different organisations or at different organisational levels.

6. Negligence of other variables of leadership These include acts of leader, followers and their acts, situation and their effects on the leader.

7. Traits of an individual cannot be known unless situation arises When an individual faces a problem, then only the presence or absence of the traits is known otherwise traits remain unknown.

2. Behavioural Approach or Theory

When it was apparent from the critical evaluation of traitist theory that traits fail to explain the leadership phenomenon, the theorists diverted their attention to the study of leadership behaviour.

Under classical management approach, a man or worker was regarded as a commodity or just an appendage to a machine. Hence the management coerced, directed and motivated workers through the offer of economic rewards. It attempted to increase efficiency or productivity by reducing waste of time and material. No consideration was given to men as an asset. The basic assumption under classical theory was that the people, by nature, were lazy, uncreative and irresponsible and therefore the leader should be directive. However, scientific management approach in management by Taylor and Hawthorne experiments by Elton Mayo and his associates discovered that human behaviour of workers is the sole concern for the leadership.

This approach demarcated various leadership styles such as autocratic, democratic or supervisory style which produce different and conflicting results, since the behaviours of leader and followers differ in different situations. Behaviour theory explained the leadership phenomenon in terms of behaviour of the leader. What the leader does was the main concern. Hence the investigators examined the styles followed by the leader, *i.e.,* authoritarian or democratic. It may be a mix of the two.

The main limitation of behavioural approach is the questionnaire which has its own limitations. Scientific tests cannot be applied in studies which are likely to be affected by perceptual differences and a variety of interpretations of questions. As no measurement methodology, *i.e.*, questionnaire, observation or interviews has been universally accepted by behavioural researchers, this is an unavoidable limitation.

3. Situationalist Approach or Theory

While the trait approach explained some of the desirable characteristics that a leader should have, it could not suggest that one who possesses particular set traits shall be a leader. On the other hand, the behavioural approach explained the various practices or styles available to a leader to discharge his leadership function but failed to indicate the best style of leadership which may be universally appropriate. Both these theories — Traits and Behavioural Theories — initiated further researches. During 1970s it was established that it were not the traits or behaviour of a leader that mattered but it was particular situation in which a particular trait or behaviour (style) was effective or ineffective. Thus both Trait and Behavioural approaches accepted the situation as an important element.

Situationalist theory advocates that a leader is strongly affected by the situation in which he works. It is a situation that helps developing leadership and from which leaders emerge, while traits or behaviour may be supportive elements. A person may be a good leader in a particular situation or set of circumstances, but he may be quite ineffective in a different situation. Situationalist theory further believes that there exists an interaction between a group of workers and its leader. The people tend to follow the leader who is capable of fulfilling their aspirations. The leader is to recognize the needs of situation and the aspirations of the followers and to act accordingly. Thus, it is a situation that produces the leadership.

Situational theory suffers from the following weaknesses:

(i) ***Overemphasis on the situational aspect of leadership:*** Situations may affect the decision of a leader in a particular time but it is not everything. Hence it should not be overemphasized.

(ii) ***Neglect of the traits and behaviour:*** The theory neglects the traits and behaviour of a leader which play an important role in the emergence of a particular leader. The head and heart of a leader play a decisive role in every situation.

4. Followers Theory or Acceptance Theory

Followers theory asserts that the followers are important in deciding whether a person is a leader or not. If they accept a person as their leader, he is a leader irrespective of his traits or behaviour. This theory cannot be applied without a group of followers. It is based on the assumption that groups have certain basic needs which they want to be fulfilled through their leader. A person is assumed to be their leader who is successful in satisfying their basic needs. If he does not succeed in getting their needs satisfied, he may neither be said to be a good leader nor will he be allowed to function as such. Thus need of the followers is the most crucial and guiding factor in the leadership event.

Followers theory ignores the quality aspect of leadership. However, modern managers are of the opinion that it is the followers theory that is now playing a significant role in managing the people today. This theory is playing a dominant role in business, industrial and political leadership in India.

5. System Approach or Path-Goal Theory

According to this theory, leadership is governed by a person's acts rather than by his traits. Leadership co-ordinates the efforts of the people and stimulates them towards the achievement of their goal in a particular situation. This approach is called system approach because it considers all the variables present at the same time, *i.e.*, leader, followers, situation, goals, leadership traits, environment, and group's nature, characteristics and needs, role, behaviour of the leader and his co-ordinating efforts. This theory is recognised as the modern theory of leadership.

LEADERSHIP STYLES

Styles describe how a leader behaves with his group or how leadership is applied in practice.

1. Motivational Styles: Positive and Negative Leadership

Motivation of followers or workers in a business enterprise is the main function of a leader. Motivational styles cover two main approaches, which are generally followed by a leader: (i) Positive approach and (ii) Negative approach.

- **(i)** ***Positive approach to leadership*****:** Leadership is said to be positive when a leader motivates the people to work hard by offering them various rewards, monetary or otherwise. The more is the reward, the higher is the efficiency. Positive leadership promotes industrial peace. For example, encashment of leave will certainly reduce the absenteeism in the organisation because it increases 'workers' real wages.

(ii) *Negative approach to leadership:* It is said to be a negative approach or negative leadership where the leader induces the followers to work hard and threatens them to penalise if work is not up to the mark. Thus, in a negative leadership, emphasis is laid on penalties for the shortcomings. The stronger is the penalty, then more negative it is. For example, if a manager imposes a salary cut for the absence from duty it is a negative approach to improve absenteeism.

Though negative leadership gets acceptable performance in many situations, it has high human costs. Negative leaders are domineering. They impose the penalties like loss of job, reprimand before others, leave without pay, etc. In order to get the work done, they display their authority with the false assumption that it frightens everyone into productivity. They are more bosses than leaders.

In negative leadership, followers work only to protect themselves. They always try to shift their responsibility to others.

Almost every manager uses both the styles off and on but the predominant style sets the tone within the group. It depends on the situation of the case, and the organisation behaviour model as to which of the two styles is the best. A manager may follow the positive approach but he may be a supporter of negative approach next time in similar case due to a situation. Thus a modern manager uses both styles according to the circumstances of the case.

The organisational behaviour model also sets the tone. The autocratic model tends to cause a negative style. The custodial model follows somewhat positive or somewhat negative or a mix of both the styles and the supportive model is clearly positive. Positive leadership achieves higher productivity to the organisation and higher job satisfaction to subordinates.

2. Power Styles — Autocratic, Democratic and Free-rein Leaders

Style of use of power also establishes a type of style. Power styles may be of three types: (a) Autocratic Leadership, (b) Democratic Participative Leadership and (c) Free-reign Leadership.

***(a) Autocratic or authoritarian leadership*:** Under this style, power or authority and decision making are centralized to the leaders. They create work-situations and environment for their subordinates. The subordinates, in turn, do whatever they are told, nothing less and nothing more. The leaders enjoy full authority and assume full responsibility. They are power-loving and never like to be devoid of power. Subordinates or followers are not aware of the organisational goals; they feel insecure and afraid of the leader's authority. This leadership is negative. However, leadership may be positive under this style if the leader uses his power in the best interest of the group and disburses rewards to motivate them. Autocratic leader having positive motivational style is known as benevolent autocrat. The benevolent autocrat gets productivity and full satisfaction as followers are habituated to culture of authorities in the society such as teachers, parents, government bureaucrats, etc. They feel satisfied and secure under autocratic leader. They respond well to action. Sometimes, benevolent autocrat leaders are more successful than the democrat leaders.

Advantages of Autocratic leadership

(i) It provides strong motivation and reward for the leader.

(ii) As a single person decides for the whole group, quick decision-making is guaranteed.

(iii) Less competent sub-managers are not involved in decision-making process. They may be used to carry out the orders of the boss.

(iv) Decision making, planning or organising need no initiative.

Disadvantages of Autocratic Leadership

(i) It is disliked if it is extreme and the motivational style is negative.

(ii) Frustration, low morale and conflict develop easily because subordinates dislike the work they have to do. They work half-heartedly due to lack of any motivation.

(iii) Managers are poor motivators.

(iv) Full potential of subordinates and their creative ideas is not used for the benefit of the organisation.

(v) In the absence of the leader, organisational continuity is threatened because subordinates gets no opportunity for the development.

If subordinates are uneducated, unskilled and submissive, autocratic leadership is appropriate, because subordinates in such cases cannot take decisions. It may also be desirable when the organisation endorses fear and punishment as accepted disciplinary techniques.

(b) Participative or democratic leadership: As opposed to autocratic leadership, under this style, power and authority are decentralised and thus decisions are not unilateral. Subordinates are consulted before taking any decision, and thus they are fully aware of the path and goal of the organisation. The leader and group work together as a social unit. While autocratic leaders control through authority vested in themselves, participative leaders exercise control mostly by using force within the group.

Democratic leader delegates his authority to his subordinates to get the work accomplished towards goals of the organisation. The present trend is towards wider use of the participative practices. Workers' participation in management is gradually getting popular.

Advantages of Participative Leadership

(i) Workers or subordinates are consulted. They participate in the decision-making process and hence they feel satisfied.

(ii) Workers are aware of what is happening in the organisation. Hence they take interest in producing more and more.

(iii) Subordinates get full opportunity to utilise their capabilities because it cultivates decision-making ability of subordinates.

(iv) The leader adds to his abilities through the contribution of his followers.

Disadvantages of Participative Leadership

(i) Power is not centralised to the leader. He may use it only in consultation with his subordinates.

(ii) Decision-making and implementation are delayed as compared to autocratic leadership because under this style, more than one person is involved in decision-making process.

(iii) As authority is decentralised, less competent executives cannot be used.

(iv) It cannot yield positive results when subordinates prefer minimum interaction with the leader.

(v) It may be used as a means of passing the buck to others and of abdicating responsibility.

(vi) It requires considerable persuasive and communicating skill on the part of the leader.

(c) Free-rein leadership: Under free-rein style, leaders enjoy no power. They delegate their authority to the subordinates themselves who take decision. The leadership is employee-centred. The group of employees is free to establish its own goals and work-out its own problems. The members of the group train themselves and provide their own motivation.

The leader keeps contact with outsiders to bring to the group the information and resources, the group needs to fulfil its job. Leadership ignores the leader's contribution in the same way as autocratic leadership ignores the group. It fails to provide the benefits of leader's inspired motivation to the group. Sometimes it creates chaos.

Advantages

(i) Job satisfaction and morale of subordinates increases.

(ii) There is a maximum possible scope for the development of subordinates.

(iii) Potential of subordinates is fully utilised.

Disadvantages

(i) Subordinates do not get the guidance and

(ii) Leader's contribution is ignored.

3. Orientation Style or Supervisory Style

(i) Employee-oriented leadership: Employee-oriented leaders are concerned about the needs of their employees and pay attention to their subordinates' attitudes, interests and necessities, etc. They try to get increased productivity by improving the working conditions and environment and solving the problems, if any, faced by them during the course of their action at the job.

(ii) Production or task-oriented leadership: Production or task-oriented leaders believe that they are concerned mainly with the production while employees are not of much concern. They believe that they can attain results by planning better methods, keeping people constantly busy and using them to produce. They do not consider human aspect of the workers.

Employee-oriented and production-oriented leadership styles are both related and independent They are not opposed to each other. A manager who is more employee-oriented, is not necessarily against production-oriented or *vice-versa.* Each orientation is somewhat independent. A manager must combine these two orientations. He must think in terms of higher production and not at the cost of human values. He must honour the initiative and abilities of employees and try to satisfy their needs.

Suitability of the Different Styles

Modern research findings about leadership style suggest that a universally accepted 'best' style is very difficult rather impossible due to the complexities of the modern organisation. Those who consider a single style of leadership to be best for every kind of organisation at every level and with any kind of subordinates, ignore important influences of factors like subordinate characteristics, level of education, and standard of living. As a leader's style does not operate in vacuum and influences the others' behaviour, these situational factors cannot be ignored. It is highly unrealistic to talk of a single best or normative style of leadership. A leader should not be rigid to any one style of leadership. He should get the work done as the situation warrants. He may be autocratic at one time and democratic at the other. Sometimes he motivates people through positive rewards and sometimes he is forced to get results through democratic methods involving the people at large in the decision-making process, satisfy human needs not at the cost of human values, by following positive motivational measures. But he cannot always abstain from attempting negative autocratic style, if a situation so warrants.

FIEDER'S CONTINGENCY MODEL

Application of Contingency Model

Fieder and his associates have classified the relationship between consideration and structure, and presented 'Contingency Model of Leadership'.

This theory specifies that the effectiveness of a group is contingent upon the motivational system of a leader and the degree to which the leader has control and influence in a particular situation. The leader's effectiveness may be measured with the leader-member relations, task structure and leader's position and power. The situation is regarded to be highly favourable to leadership effectiveness. If leader-member relations are good, task is structured and leader position power gets strong. On the contrary, if leader- member relations are not good, task is unstructured and leader's position and power get weak, and the situation may be regarded as highly unfavourable to the leader's effectiveness. Favourableness or unfavourableness determines the effectiveness of the leadership. As a leader operates in a particular situation, it is an important question to decide what type of leadership style is needed in a particular type of a situation. Contingency theory suggests that a particular leadership style is effective only in a particular situation. In other words, the effectiveness of a leader is contingent upon the relationship among all these variables.

Types of Variables

1. Leader-member relations The leader-member relations are determined by the manner in which the leader is accepted or rejected by the group. For example, if in an organisation there is a group friction, orders are generally flouted, the leader-member relations are said to be poor. If there is co-operation between leader and members, orders are carried out in proper manner and according to leader's desire, and the relations may be regarded as good.

2. Task structure A task is said to be highly structured. It is highly specific, if it can be done only in one way and rules and procedures are well defined, and there is no scope for different interpretations. The task is regarded as highly unstructured if it is completely non-routine, there are many routes to reach the goal or rules and procedures are not clear. In a highly structured task, leader's ability to influence the group is restricted because the task dilutes the leader's potential influence. In case of unstructured task, the leader has great potential for influencing the group as he has more knowledge than his followers.

3. Leader position power Leader's positional power indicates the power provided to him by the position in an organisation such as power to hire and fire, status symbols, power to give promotion and pay raise, punishment, rewards, etc. In most business organisations, the leaders possess high position power while in social organisations, leaders have very low positional power.

In addition to leader's employee-orientation ranging from a highly favourable position to a highly unfavourable position for a leader, Fieldler has considered eight combinations of three variables. In the middle of these two extremes is the intermediate position of favourableness for the leader.

(i) ***In highly favourable situation:*** The task-oriented leader performs better. The least preferred worker is also motivated by task accomplishment.

(ii) ***In favourable situation:*** The workers support him when task is structured and leader-member relations are good, even if the task-oriented behaviour of the leader may be considered friendly.

(iii) ***In unfavourable situations :*** When task is unstructured, the relations between the two are not good, and the power position of the leader is poor. He is more concerned with the performance and his efforts are to remove the ambiguity and anxiety. If the leader possesses more knowledge than his subordinates, the followers are willing to accept the task-oriented structure.

(iv) ***Intermediate favourableness:*** A leader obtains better group performance in moderate conditions. (i) The task is structured and leader is disliked, therefore, he demonstrates that he cares for the emotions of the subordinates, or (ii) the leader is liked and the task is unstructured and the leader depends upon the willingness and creativity of the group's members to accomplish the goals.

Leader Match Training

On the basis of his contingency model of leadership, Fielder developed the 'leader match' training programme to improve leadership's effectiveness. The programme was based on the assumption that as it is much easier to change the situation rather than to change the fundamental style, therefore, the job should be fitted to the manager.

Thus, the contingency model of Fiedler has helped to resolve confusion about optimum conditions for a considerate, people-oriented leader, compared with a more structured, task-oriented leader.

Criticism of Contingency Model

1. Undimensional While the model suggests that the leader can be either task-oriented or relationship-oriented, in reality, leader is multidimensional. It is not necessary that a leader, who is high on one side may be low on the other side. He is rather a combination of the two.

2. Confusion of combinations and style Fiedler suggested a measuring rod of style, putting eight possible combinations on the LPC (Least Preferred Co-owners) which is quite confusing and unreliable. Different researchers reveal that there is no direct relationship between the combinations and style.

3. Changing appropriateness Fiedler's model fails to explain why the same style is appropriate in both — most favourable and most unfavourable situations.

4. Negligence of many variables The model does not consider many situational variables such as subordinates' expectations of leader's behaviour, ability of the leader to influence his superior and the congruence of leadership styles among organisational levels.

5. Complex The model is very complex and based on small samples. It does not explain how the situational variables affect the leadership style.

Advantages

In spite of the above limitations, Fiedler's model of leadership has proved advantageous because it operationalises the set of actions that may be used to improve leadership effectiveness. It considers both personal and situational variables. It has intuitive appeal. It is based on commonsense reasoning. A leader can enforce accountability, if his power is strong, but when his power is weak he has to cultivate relationship to get things done.

QUESTIONS FOR EXERCISE

1. What is industrial leadership? Explain condition of effective leadership.
2. Explain the themes industrial leadership.
3. Describe styles of industrial leadership.

9

INDUSTRIAL AND PERSONNEL MANAGEMENT

MEANING OF MANAGEMENT

A review of the following definitions of management will help to make clear the meaning of the term management:

1. Encyclopaedia of Social Sciences "Management may be defined as the process by which the execution of a given purpose is put into operation and supervised. The combined output of various types and grades of human effort by which the process is effected is known as management in the human sense."

2. F.C. Hooper "Management is the driving force that inspires an undertaking to knit itself into an entity and creates the conditions and relationships which bring about a full use of all its powers and resources."

3. J.L. Lundy "Management is principally a task of planning, co-ordinating, motivating and controlling the efforts of others towards a specific objective."

4. F.F.L. Brech "Management is the responsibility for the effective planning and regulation of the operation of an enterprise; such responsibility involving (i) the installation and maintenance of proper procedure to ensure adherence to plans; and (ii) the guidance, integration and supervision of the personnel comprising and carrying out operations."

5. Kimbal and Kimbal "Management may be broadly defined as the art of applying the economic principles that underlie the control of men and materials in the enterprise under consideration."

6. Wilson "Management is the development of people and not the direction of things."

7. E.H. Peterson "Management is the ordering and co-ordinating of functions and of the men fulfilling their functions in order to achieve a given purpose."

CHARACTERISTICS OF MANAGEMENT

From the above definitions, the characteristics of management become quite plain. These are:

1. Science As management is based upon certain scientific principles, it can be considered to be a science.

2. Art There are quite a few aspects of managerial skill for which no scientific principles can be laid. These depend upon sound judgement and fact. Hence, management can be said to be an art.

3. Procedure The management in an industry or a factory is based upon certain procedures. A manager tries to achieve his objective of working within the limits laid down by the procedures.

4. Definite aim Management is always goal-directed and has a definite aim in view.

5. Direction of efforts If the workers are allowed arbitrary choice of action, this will lead to chaos. It is necessary, therefore, that actions of various workers should be properly concatenated so as to give definite results.

6. Co-ordination In an industry work is divided into many sections. This needs co-ordination.

7. Control Besides direction, instruction and issuing guidelines, it is also essential to exercise control on the activity of workers.

8. Standard The work in the industry must conform to a specified standard.

9. Co-operation Above all, co-operation between managers and workers is necessary for successful management.

CONCEPT OF INDUSTRIAL MANAGEMENT

According to *Encyclopaedia of Social Sciences,* a group of persons who cooperate to work for some project are engaged in the industrial management. Thus industrial management involves direction, planning, adjustment, control and co-operation for realizing industrial projects. In an industrial project, a number of elements are involved such as materials for production, workers, managers, capital investment, etc. The materials for production include land, raw material and machinery. According to J.R. Tarry, industrial management consists of realizing the industrial aim with the help of wherewithal of industrial production. There are various types of management. The important ones are as follows :

1. **Production management** In the production management are included the following elements, (i) job analysis; (ii) determination of the system or production; (iii) standardization; and (iv) study of time, speed and fatigue.

2. **Development management** In this we study the kind and quality of raw material, techniques of production and also the consumer needs.

3. **Financial management** Under this, budgeting is done and also data regarding market conditions are collected.

4. **Distribution management** Under this are included advertising, market research, export and sale, etc.

5. **Sales management** Under this are included inviting tenders, organizing sales and making provisions for stock and storage.

6. **Maintenance management** Under this are included maintenance of building, etc.

7. **Transport management** Under this are included arrangement for packing, transportation, warehousing, etc.

8. **Office management** Under this, data regarding production and distribution are collected and their record maintained.

9. **Personnel management** Under this are included the recruitment and training of workers and managers. Also the pay scales are determined and rules for promotion arid increment laid down.

FUNCTIONS OF INDUSTRIAL MANAGEMENT

The industrial management is a complex process and it involves a number of functions. In brief, following are the main functions of the industrial management:

1. **Forecasting** First and foremost function of the industrial management is to make industrial projection, that is, to assess before hand the demand for goods. Besides, when a new venture is undertaken, forecasting consists of making assessment of the needs for labour and equipment.

2. **Planning** By dividing the complex industrial processes into their constituents, planning is done. In words of L. Urwik, planning is a mental process, a decision to do the work in a proper manner.

3. Organization According to Brech organization is to divide the responsibility and entrust it to various departments. To organize means to entrust each worker in an industry with jobs for which he is suited.

4. Direction According to G.R. Terry, direction consists of the following steps to speed up the work, to inspire the group and to create in each worker an aptitude and liking for the work.

5. Leadership The business of leadership is to guide and inspire the workers in such a way that optimum production is achieved.

6. Staffing The most important element of any industry is workers. The quality of workers makes or mars the industry. Therefore, appointment of workers is the most important factor in the industry. The appointment, training, etc. of workers come under this head.

7. Motivation In an industry production is done by various machines but these machines are operated by men. Men need to be motivated if satisfactory results have to be achieved.

8. Co-ordination Defining co-ordination, Brech writes that coordination in an industry means distribution of work in such a way that cordiality of relations is maintained. Mary Parker Follet has enumerated four principles of co-ordination. These are:

(i) To effect co-ordination in various processes from very beginning.

(ii) In order to remove the defects of bureaucracy to maintain direct contact with the workers.

(iii) Co-ordination of production, sale and labour.

(iv) To maintain and sustain co-ordination.

9. Control Defining control, Brech calls it to achieve maximum production by determined effort. The control is of four types: budgetary control, control over cost of production, control over management and lastly financial control.

10. Communication To maintain contact and rapport between workers, consumers, shareholders and suppliers is called communication.

PERSONNEL MANAGEMENT

By personnel management we mean the recruitment, supervision and control of the labour force. Personnel management also deals with the efficiency of labour force and increase of production and general welfare of the workers. It is the aim of personnel management to maximize the utility of workers for industrial production.

Definition

The following definitions of personnel management will help to make clear the meaning of this term:

1. E.F.L. Brech "Personnel management may be conveniently described as part of the management process which is primarily concerned with the human constituents of an organization. Its object is the maintenance of human relationships on a basis which by consideration of the well-being of the individual enables all those engaged in the undertaking to make their maximum personal contribution to the effective working of the undertaking."

2. T.G. Spates "Personnel administration is a code of the ways of organising and treating individuals at work so that they will get the greatest possible realisation of their intrinsic abilities, thus attaining a maximum efficiency for themselves and their group and thereby giving to the enterprise which they are a part, its determining competitive advantage and its optimum results."

3. M.W. Comeng "Personnel management is concerned with obtaining the best possible staff for an organization, and having got them, looking after them so that they want to stay and give their best to their respective jobs."

Characteristics

From the above definitions of personnel management we learn its following characteristics:

1. Branch of industrial management P.G. Hastings has aptly observed that the personnel management is the aspect of management having it's goal to the effective utilization of the labour resources of an organization.

2. Art of maintaining workforce According to American Society for Personnel Administration, "Personnel administration is the art of acquiring, developing and maintaining a competent workforce in such a manner as to accomplish with maximum efficiency and economy, the functions and objectives of the organisation."

3. Cultivation of workers' qualities From the definitions given above it becomes plain that personnel management helps to cultivate among the workers qualities like zest, education, responsibility and *esprit de corps.*

4. Job satisfaction In personnel management, the work is so organised as to afford maximum satisfaction to the workers. According to G.P. Fillipo, "Personnel management is the planning, organizing, directing and controlling of the performance of those operative functions."

5. Good relations among workers and managers It is the paramount task of the personnel management that cordial relations are obtained between the workers and managers.

6. Reform management In personnel management adequate attention is paid to the conditions of work, pay-scales, technical education and recreation of the workers.

7. Maximum worker capacity Lastly, it is the endeavour of the personnel management to maximize the efficiency and the work capacity of the worker. For this purpose there should be a unanimity of objectives among the labour, management and employers. Only co-operation and mutual understanding between the three can bring about maximization in production.

Aims

The aims of personnel management are divided into two sections: general and specific.

(A) General Aims According to learned authorities L.P. Alfred and H.R. Britt, the general aim of personnel management is the reform and improvement of the services with the help of technical advisors and to inspire confidence in workers. Briefly, following are the general aims of personnel management:

1. Maximum use of human resources.
2. To promote active co-operation among workers.
3. Maximum utilization of the services of each worker.

(B) Specific Aims Besides general aims there are certain specific aims of personnel management. These are:

1. Recruitment of workers.
2. Training and guidance of workers.
3. Effective means for the adequate remuneration of workers.
4. Promotion of the morale of workers.
5. To secure adequate allowances and other economic benefits besides adequate wages. Included among the facilities are medical aid, provident fund, paid holidays, technical training, recreation, etc. Above all, the retirement benefits like pensions, etc. must be ensured.
6. Another specific aim of the personnel management is to sort out the complaints of workers and to ensure adequate promotion facilities.

7. To ensure cordial relations between workers and management.
8. To promote research.

Principles

1. Learned authorities The specialists have enumerated following principles of personnel management:

(i) ***Justice***: In an industrial management, the most important principle is that of justice. In securing justice, six things must be taken care of. First of all there must be adequate wages and remuneration of work. For this purpose minimum wages for each kind of job should be fixed. The payment of wages must be done on fixed days. The skilled workers must be paid according to their proficiencies and workers must also get adequate share out of gains on the capital. Secondly, there must be proper avenues for promotion, increment, etc. Thirdly, workers should be inspired to make progress and for this purpose it is necessary that the promotion should be non-partisan. Fourthly, workers should be allowed to determine the conditions of their work. Fifthly, deficiency of management must be removed and the conditions for full employment must be created. Sixthly, penalties for faults and misconduct must be just and opportunity of appeals must be there.

(ii) ***Personality***: It is an important principle of personnel management that all-round development of the personality of workers should be encouraged.

(iii) ***Co-operation***: The third principle is that there should be cordial relations and cooperation among the workers and management.

(iv) ***Democratic basis***: The management must be democratic. Each person should have the right to put across his viewpoint and he must get the opportunity.

2. George D. Helse has enumerated following principles necessary for successful personnel management:

(i) Proper and intelligent selection of workers.
(ii) Providing suitable jobs to workers.
(iii) Ridding the workers of the feeling of uncertainty and insecurity.
(iv) To inculcate a feeling of pride and glory for the company in which a worker works.
(v) To ensure healthy and congenial work environs.
(vi) To create an organisation in which the duties and obligations are clearly understood.

(vii) Objective assessment of the work performance.

(viii) Participation of workers in management.

(ix) Upright conduct and appropriate policy.

3. Institute of Labour Management of Great Britain has enumerated the following principles of personnel management:

(i) Determination of appropriate principles of personnel management.

(ii) All workers should have a right to approach the management overtly or covertly.

(iii) The job should be secure; there should be open policy of recruitment; ability should get precedence over all other considerations; the recruitment should be made on scientific principles; there should be realistic assessment of work performance; there must exist adequate facilities for training and nobody should be dismissed without adequate grounds.

(iv) The policy of adequate wages should be followed.

(v) To create an atmosphere and conditions congenial to discipline.

(vi) To raise the standards of work.

(vii) Promotion of harmonious relationships between labour and management.

(viii) Freedom to become members of the trade unions for the workers.

(ix) To provide for the recreation and other facilities for overall development of the personalities of the workers.

Functions

The personnel management functions are of four kinds: (1) Advisory Functions; (2) Managerial Functions; (3) Administrative Functions and (4) Workers' Welfare Functions. Each of these will be discussed below:

1. Advisory Functions Under this function an attempt is made to establish a rapport between the workers and managers. This is done to establish a rapport between the workers and managers. This is also done to establish a cordial and congenial atmosphere so as to boost production and avoid friction in industry.

2. Managerial Functions Indeed these are the main functions of personnel management. These include:

(i) ***Recruitment and employment:*** Under the recruitment and employment are included finding suitable means of filling up the vacancies; to scrutinize the background, antecedents and other particulars of the employees; to acquaint the new entrants with the policy of management and to collect data about wages, etc.

(ii) ***Training:*** Training is an important constituent of the managerial function. The method and rules for training are laid down and arrangement for the training is made.

(iii) ***Promotion, transfer and retirement:*** Under this, rules and guidelines are determined regarding promotion, transfer and retirement.

(iv) ***Functions concerning service:*** In this, schemes for labour welfare, education and recreation of workers are made.

(v) ***Remuneration and incentives:*** Under this, rules regarding pension, bonus, insurance, loan etc., are made.

(vi) ***Collective bargaining of workers' representation:*** Under this, attempts are made to associate workers with management.

(vii) ***Remuneration scheme:*** As is clear from the heading under this an effort is made to evolve a pragmatic management.

(viii) ***Unification of organizational and worker's interest:*** In this an attempt is made to boost the morale of the workers.

3. Administrative functions Lastly, in personnel management the management of the welfare of workers is of crucial importance. By welfare is meant the promotion of physical and mental health of the workers and an improvement in their social and economic status. Much thought is being accorded these days to this aspect and new ways and means to improve the welfare of workers are being suggested.

DEPARTMENTS OF PERSONNEL MANAGEMENT

The work of personnel management has become so intricate and complex as to require it's division into various departments. These are:

1. Employment department The function of this department is to provide the necessary labour force. It keeps statistics of vacancies and also maintains contact with sources from where workers might be available. Besides it also determines the pay-scales and lays down guidelines for transfer etc.

2. Training and education department In order to increase the efficiency of the workers, there is need to give them training and education in the suitable skills. These functions are looked after by the training and education department.

3. Welfare department This department looks after the physical, mental and cultural welfare of the workers. It sets up clubs where workers can play, read and amuse themselves.

4. Security department For the protection of men and materials and goods in the industry, a posse of security force is employed.

5. Medical and health department. This department takes care of the health of the workers and gives them medical aid when a worker is ill or hurt.

6. Industrial relations department This department determines the policy regarding relations between workers and management.

7. Wages and salary department This department is concerned with the assessment of the work performance and determines the wages and salary of the workers.

8. Research and data department This department collects statistics and carries on scientific research.

9. Women labourers' department An industry employing a sizable portion of women labour force maintains this department.

PERSONNEL POLICY

The personnel policy should specifically take care of the following points:

1. Clear The policy should be brief, lucid and clear.

2. Just The policy should be just toward workers.

3. Personal Policy should be such as to give workers a sense of belonging.

4. Security The policy should increase security among the workers.

5. Cordiality The policy should be such as to promote cordial relations among the workers.

6. Recognition of work The policy should allow adequate room for the recognition of the work done by the workers.

7. Flexibility The policy should be such as to adjust itself with the changing circumstances.

QUESTIONS FOR EXERCISE

1. Explain the concept of individual management.
2. What is Personnel Management? How is it carried on?

10

PROFESSIONAL INDUSTRIAL MANAGEMENT IN INDIA

India experienced industrialization in 19th century under British rule. In the initial stages enterprise was owned and managed by a single individual owner or along with his kinship members. Later on Britishers introduced joint stock companies. This paved the way for the emergence of large scale industries. These industries needed huge capital investments. Therefore, a group of persons with their joint capital started big industries. The increasing complex organization of these large scale industries led to the need of a specialized person, other than proprietor or director, to manage. With this need, management has passed from family hands to outside personnel, the managers.

Earlier manager was considered responsible to carry out only the daily routine jobs. He was concerned with the implementation of the decisions and policies stated by the managing directors. After Independence, India stepped on planned industrialization. Now the importance of managerial role increased further. Some of the factors which provided for the take-off stage of management in India are: increasing size of industries, huge capital investments, keener competition within the country and outside, wide scientific researches, mechanization of production operations, need for better quality, scarcity of resources and energy, increasing number of labourers and their unionization, bureaucratization of industrial organizations, complex legislations, the governing idea of business as public service, etc.

More and more calculation, market research, technical know-how, planning, budgeting, costing, etc., require formally trained personnel to perform these tasks effectively. Obviously, owners on their own could not afford to acquire all these managerial skills. Hence, the importance of management, training and trained managers in the industries of 20th century. Today managers hold the key position in the industrial organization. Management has developed as a new profession. Professional managerial class is emerging as a new social stratum. Managerial role is not limited to the industry. Manager is expected to play a constructive role in the overall development of the nation. This increasing importance of the role of managers has led to many unresolved issues.

REVIEW OF LITERATURE

Due to the stronghold of a few families over the industries, there was little scope for professional management. Sen (1974) called this situation as 'the jagirdari system among Indian managers'. After independence India exhibited a slight movement towards managerial revolution. In a survey of 1958 (Myers, 1959) 24 managers per one thousand employees were calculated in the factory sector. It was expected that industry will need 3,084 managers additionally per year. The Once 'closed shop' family-owned industries are now admitting qualified non-family members who are receiving managerial education. Managers are developing as a distinct class of professionals (Agrawala, A.N., 1970; Sethi, 1978).

Few studies have analysed the factors contributing to the development of professional management in India (Dutt, 1965; Basu, 1967). Increasing size of industries, operation, development of industries for social welfare have led to the development of management. The factors impeding the emergence of management as a profession have also been identified (Trivedi, 1969). Concentration of economic power in few hands, tendency of employers to give jobs to their own kith and kin, are the two factors which inhibited the development of professional management. Regionalism, religion and casteism also played a negative role.

One of the most debated issues which the divorce of owner and manager has led is that who is the main decision-maker between the two? Scholars have responded differently. While some argue that now manager is the main decision-maker than owner, the others argue that he is only the implementer and the decisions are made by the owner. The votaries of managerial revolution (Sengupta, 1974) argue that even though managers have very small or no shareholding in the capital, they enjoy the power to control due to increasing technical complexities of business operations. The diffusion of ownership and management led to the emergence of the latter as a free floating centre of power. The old picture of a ruthless and self-oriented company director has given place to the picture of a modern, non-propertied manager responsible to society at large. They call managers as 'The New Maharajas'.

The advocates of pluralist model (Subramaniam, 1971; Poulantsas, 1975; Kumar, M., 1982) strongly disagree with the proponents of managerial revolution approach. In the bureaucratic organization, the real economic power lies in the hands of owners and the managerial class is more in a sense of faithful servants of ruling class of owners. Managers in this sense become magnified clerks. Only those managers have powers who have large shareholdings. Further, managers at the middle and lower levels have least powers and only the managers at the top enjoy certain amount of power.

After the separation of owners from management, it was expected that the industrial organization has democratised, and the exploitation of workers has reduced. But scholars like Karl Marx (1959) and C. Wright Mills (1959) disagree with this. Managers belong to the elite class and serve the purpose of the owners. They are tools for extracting the surplus value in a much systematic way. Managers are loyal to the owners and to the community.

The increasing need of trained managers and the increasing specialization in the knowledge of management have paved the way for the professionalization of management. It has been assumed that the management training makes the manager professional. But the management training alone does not make a manager professional. The trained managers do give emphasis to the careerism (Rudrabasavaraj, 1978; Rao, 1978). K.L. Sharma (1982) maintains that the number of managers holding degrees in management is not the only requirement but conformity to the professional techniques and values is the index of professionalization of management. He further explains that this conformity may depend upon the extent of authority and autonomy enjoyed by managers. The empirical studies on Indian managers' ethic conclude that managers are more influenced by egoistic concerns like prestige, honour, dignity, power. In administration they practise bureaucratic and not professional authoritarianism. They are more concerned with high profit, high production, efficiency and stable growth of organisation (Aggrawal, K. C., 1978; Rao, 1978; Dhingra and Pathak, 1982). For managers, what is good for business is good ethic. Therefore, they exploit by bribes, personal, favours, gifts, etc. (Monappa, 1977). These studies show that Indian managers do not have professional values. There is a need to frame managerial philosophy according to Indian values. Keeping in view the changing scene of industries, the managerial ethic is to be redefined. Every manager should have a set of professional values necessary for effective functioning (Mehta, 1961; Dayar, 1964). Indian manager is still in search of style (Roy, 1967; Vatsal, 1970). Hence, managers have no style, no specific professional ethic. Sharma (1980) concluded: "The Indian manager is anything but professional as his ethical values are not clearly defined, the young managers made no contribution to the profession; their ethical standards are more identified with organizations rather than the profession. Managers do not have a client or community orientation which they must have as professionals. They do not have collective authority, autonomy and monopoly."

The change-over from hereditary to professional management is a challenge to management organizations in India. Management has to develop a professional ethic, a unique style, a philosophy of its own. This is not an impossible task but only needs a systematic attempt (Mafat Lal, 1964; Saraogi, 1976; Dias, 1976).

Professionally trained managers are perceived as more efficient for industrial organization than those who are not (Haga, 1976). The need of a trained manager is felt with the increasing mechanization of industries. At the same time it has been noticed that it makes no difference whether a manager is professionally trained or not (Lorant, 1980). In industrial organization many situations come where common sense, guess-work and dynamism are required and not only training. It has been noticed that the professionally trained managers expand the organization size beyond expectations thus leading to the increasing consumption of organizational resources.

Numerous roles, other than organizational are expected to be played by the professional manager. On the one hand he has one responsibility that is to contribute to the economic performance of the industry. On the other hand, management is supposed to perform major social responsibilities in addition to economic ones. Manager is responsible towards the employees and towards the public. He should not restrict himself to micro issues. He needs to extend his vision beyond the problems of his daily routine job. He is a social worker and, therefore, has to look after the interests of the community. He is a responsible citizen and should contribute constructively in solving the problems of the nation. Private sector managers should observe the interest of the people as the public sector managers do (Randeria, 1963; Wood, 1964; Aggarwal, S.C., 1976).

Scholars have compared Indian managers with their counterparts in other countries (Haire and Porter, 1963 and 1964; Sethi, 1969). In such studies it has been stated that the style of working of the former is different from that of latter due to the socio-cultural and industrial environment of the country.

Professional manager has to function in a bureaucratic organization. The relationship between the professions and bureaucratic organizations has been debated a lot. One finds two streams of thought on this issue: firstly, professionalization is positively associated with bureaucracy (Wilensky, 1964; Weber, 1966; Ritzer, 1972; Montagna, 1977). Secondly, from the point of view of free profession, a professional will always face unavoidable conflict situations in bureaucratic organisation (Etzioni, 1959; Scott, 1966; Gouldner and Ritt, 1967; Richard Hall, 1967 and 1968).

The proponents of inherent conflict approach argue that the conflict between the two is necessary and unavoidable. Professional autonomy is one of the basic characteristics of the professions which provide the support to this argument. Professionals require a kind of autonomy, that is antithetical to Weber's model of rational legal bureaucracy. The ideology of professionalism implies a trade-off between professional's autonomy and power in the organization. In a bureaucratic industrial organization, manager will come in conflict with the bureaucratic hierarchy, between the service to the organization and the service to the community, between loyalty to the professional community and to the organization, between the ethics of the organization and of the profession, etc.

Scott (1966) while summing up professionals' position in a bureaucratic organization argues that on the one hand, professionals will be able to operate in organizations more effectively by applying greater expertise with respect to task knowledge. On the other hand, professionals are increasingly likely to resist or reject various bureaucratic rules, standards and supervision. They may reflect only conditional loyalty to the bureaucracy. He maintains that the professionals are likely to reject bureaucratic rules because they perceive themselves as capable of establishing a more functional set of rules. Their expertise entitles them to operate professionally without the constraining regulations or interference from others. They resist standards of bureaucratic organizations, because they adhere to the standards of the profession. They are increasingly discontented with bureaucratic supervision in many instances, as the authorities over them are not qualified in their own field of specialization. However, the loyalty of professionals towards their employing organizations cannot be predicted absolutely. Professionals follow the norms and behavioural expectations of their profession rather than those of the employing organization.

These arguments, given in reference to professionals' functioning in a bureaucratic organization are fully applicable in regard to manager's position in industrial bureaucratic organization. Professional manager is a salaried employee, performing his activities within the structural framework of bureaucratic organization of an industry. Jenkin's (1970) while summing up the position of the professional manager in a bureaucratic organization, maintains that he participates in two distinct irreconcilable systems. The professional manager is a member of two institutions — the profession and the organization. Each of these attempts to control his occupational activities, and the manner in which the former establishes standards and norms for the conduct of professional activities, contrasts with the way in which the latter specifies task objectives.

This assumption of an inherent conflict has been questioned by many scholars. Bureaucracy is not a necessary bar to professional commitments. It has been argued that all the components of Weberian ideal typical of bureaucracy are not negatively related to the professions *e.g.*, rationality is the common characteristic of the two. Further, there are different types of bureaucratic organisations far and near to the ideal of typical construct and with this it depends on the nature of the organization concerned. No generalization in this case is possible. Professionalization and bureaucratization are interdependent. Weber (1966) himself has noticed a two-way relationship between the two that is each contributing to the other.

Management is not a full-fledged free profession. It has to function in a bureaucratic industrial organization. Etzioni (1969) mentions that there is a continuum of professionalism upon which the fully-fledged and semi-professions can be identified. Semi-professions are employed largely in bureaucratic organizations. They have a shorter period of training than the fully-fledged professions, a less legitimated status, a less specialized body of knowledge. Thus, management is a semi-profession. The arguments made by the advocates of inherent conflict approach become of less importance as they perceive management from the viewpoint of a free profession which it is not.

The role of professional managers has been compared with the role played by the dynamic entrepreneur-owner. It is argued that the success of an industry depends more on entrepreneur rather than on the professional management. Aiyar (1983) argues that the professional manager is an invaluable instrument for preventing industries from being spoiled by incompetent generation of owners. If we look at the big industries of the world we will notice that the credit of success goes to the entrepreneur and not to professional manager. However, there are a number of cases where professional management has failed. In Indian public sector, professional management has failed to give any good results. Multinational subsidiaries in India have always been run by professionals. These industries used to look down with contempt at the Indian business families trying to compete with them. He gives the example of Firestone which was one of the best known multinationals in the world. When Modi group wanted to enter the tyre business, Firestone, Dunlop and Goodyear, the three multinational firms with professional managements were already there. Today Modi group has defeated all the tyre companies in competition. Firestone has been sold out to Modis. After the Modi family took charge from the professional management, the production of this went up by 50 per cent. The success of Tata and Birla is due to dynamic entrepreneurship and not due to professional managers.

Aiyar has not been justified in neglecting the role of professional management. He maintains that the professional management only helps in maintaining an industry established by the entrepreneur. There are examples where professional management is successful *viz.,* Hindustan Lever Limited, Brook Bond, Lipton, Bata, etc., multinationals. On the other hand, there are examples where family managed industries are decaying viz., Modi Industries, Swadeshi Cotton Mills, Dalmia Cement etc. However, one cannot neglect the role of professional management in the success of an industry. Flory (1983) maintains that if a new industry is to be successful, its management must complement and enhance the personality of entrepreneur. Thus, managers are the vehicles for entrepreneurial excursions.

One may find many reasons for the poor performance of professional managers, One reason may be the conflict between the owner's ethic of self-interest and the professional manager's ethic centred on the community interest (Sharma, K.L., 1975). The other reasons may be the limited autonomy, and the structural constraints. Further studies in this area are required.

The managers have been studied in both the sectors public and private. Banik (1965) and Hanson (1962) both studied the role of managers in public enterprises. They have also discussed the managerial control and autonomy subsequently. On the other hand, Murthy (1964) has discussed the functions performed by managers in a private sector industrial organization. Little attention has been given to the comparative studies of public and private sectors. Some of the studies indicate that as far as the functions performed by the managers are concerned, no significant difference has been noticed between the managers of two sectors (Mathai, 1965; Lau and Pavett, 1980). The main difference lies in terms of the emphasis given to the profit orientation, which is of less importance in public sector management in the two sectors. It has been, therefore, suggested that the managers of both the sectors should look into a total perspective, that is, managers in public sector giving due importance to profit orientation and vice versa the managers in private sector should take into consideration the community interest.

The young generation of professional managers is perceived as more mobile. The mobility depends on two factors, *i.e.,* manager's own motivations and the opportunities available to him. The first may be perceived as subjective and the second as objective. Manager's educational qualifications play an important role in his movement. If he has technical qualification or professional training in management, he will get more chances for movement. Manager's career also counts for his movement. Laggatta, T. (1978) has identified the following factors influencing manager's mobility, *i.e.,* age, level of education, nature of education, organizational size, career and length of service.

Manager's mobility is perceived in two ways. Firstly, intra-organizational movement and secondly, inter-organizational movement. In big industrial organizations, the chances for intra-organizational movement are more than in small or medium size organizations. Srinivas (1965) studied managerial mobility in an organizational perspective. In his view managers should be exposed to the new situations in order to make them more dynamic and functional for organizational effectiveness.

Few studies are focused on manager-workers relations probing into the workers' expectations from managers (Singh, 1962; Desai, 1969). Few scholars have studied managers from the leadership perspective identifying the leadership characteristics of managers as ability to undertake the challenging tasks, ability to organize, ability to inspire confidence among the subordinates (Kapur, 1963; Singh; 1963). Managers are yet to be studied adequately from the perspective of a profession.

STATEMENT OF THE PROBLEM

It is argued that after the separation of ownership and management, it is the manager who holds the key position in the industrial organization. Now the question arises what authority has been given to managers and how much autonomy do they enjoy in a bureaucratic industrial organization. It is argued that professionals will certainly face unavoidable conflicts in a bureaucratic organization, since there is a conflict between the ideology of business and profession. Business is centred on the pursuit of self-interest in contrast to the profession which is concerned with service to the community regardless of one's own interests. Business is based on egoistic motives while profession maintains altruistic motives. All these arguments indicate the structural constraints a manager will face in a bureaucratic industrial organization.

From the review of literature it is noticed that managers have not been adequately studied from the perspective of professional authority and autonomy. The structural constraints managers face in the areas of authority and autonomy, are yet to be studied systematically.

Objectives of the Study

In view of the above discussion, the research objectives for the present study may be specified as below:

1. To identify the nature and extent of manager's authority.
2. To examine the amount of autonomy managers enjoy in the area of their authority.
3. To elucidate the structural constraints that managers face in the area of authority and autonomy.
4. To explicate the sources of these structural constraints.
5. To analyse the reactions of managers to these structural constraints.

UNIVERSE AND SAMPLE

The rationale for selecting Meerut city for the present study was the fact that the industries of this city have not been studied, since industries emerged here much later than in other cities of Uttar Pradesh such as Kanpur and Ghaziabad. No statistical principle was applied for drawing specific sample. Since it is an exploratory study and no list of managers in the industries of Meerut was available, no statistical method could be followed in drawing the sample. Fifty managers were interviewed, *i.e.*, 26 from public limited industries and 24 from private limited industries. The size of sample was arbitrary.

METHOD OF DATA COLLECTION AND ANALYSIS

An interview schedule was constructed in order to obtain the data. Data thus collected were codified and classified into meaningful categories.

Some questions received multiple answers which were minimized into meaningful categories without losing the objectivity of the data.

CHARACTERISTICS OF MANAGERS

Managers have been portrayed as a new class in a loose sense of the term. The professional managerial class comprises salaried mental workers, not owning the means of production, who tackle the common problems and situations (Enrenreich and Enrenreich, 1977). It has been argued that a growing centralized surplus and increased struggle between the bourgeoisie and the proletariat were the necessary conditions fostering the expansion of managerial class. Pal (1966) maintains that this growing managerial class is emerging as an elite social group. They are the main decision-makers in the industries of today.

Laggatt (1978) does not agree with the advocates of professional managerial class. On the basis of his study of the British managers, he submits that the managers do not make a homogenous group. They are heterogeneous and do not form a class. There are disparities in their economic statuses. This criticism of Leggatt, however, does not seem to be logical one. The advocates of professional managerial class do not have an economic perspective in defining it. They define it from the perspective of profession. The professional managerial class is a social category. They belong to the same profession, sharing common values and ethical standards, thus forming a class.

The entry in the professional managerial class is open. There is no restriction as we find in the entry in other professions. Managers are coming from different educational spheres, *viz.,* law, social sciences, natural sciences, engineering besides management courses. Professional management training is not a necessary prerequisite for becoming a manager. Professionally trained managers are considered to be more efficient, but untrained managers are also recruited because of their managerial qualities, *viz.,* dynamism, achievement motivation, enterprising aptitude, etc. On the other hand in other professions *viz.,* legal and medical, entry is restricted. Minimum educational qualification for entering the profession is clearly stated. Without having that minimum education one cannot become a member of that profession. For entering in legal and medical professions, one must have a graduate degree in the respective disciplines. Thus professional managerial class is an open class. This is one reason why there is educational heterogeneity in managerial class. This heterogenous educational background subsequently leads to other heterogeneities *viz.,* in ethical values, aptitudes, motivations, etc.

For analysing the class backgrounds of professional managers in India, an attempt has been made in the study of S.C. Jain (1971). He maintains that managers generally come from families with high educational and occupational background. They are mainly urbanities and belong to enterprising communities *viz.*, Jain, Marwari, etc. They come largely from families engaged in elite occupations. Their fathers are business executives, government officials and professional men. The majority of managers have come from the most industrialized or urbanised states. Managers are found to be a highly educated group, nine out of ten managers having had a college degree or professional diploma. He studied the influence of the social background factors on the mobility of managers. He maintains that at the initial stages, regional origin does not have a significant influence on the career of a manager. But at an advanced level, it does *i.e.* managers coming from the native state of their employers, move faster than others. Subramaniam (1983) has also found more or less similar background characteristics. According to him, the large majority comes from the professional middle class and more than half from the upper middle class. Majority attended a public or convent school. They are heavily drawn from urban areas. Majority is drawn from states such as Maharashtra, Gujarat, Tamil Nadu, Kerala and Punjab. In most of the cases they are domiciled in states other than their states of birth. Caste-wise, majority comes from the literate Brahmin and high caste non-Brahmin communities. Marginally they are from the commercial castes. B.R. Sharma (1976) studied the social background of candidates who applied for admission in management courses. He found that candidates from higher income groups had a much better chance of getting admitted. Those who had their early education in English-medium public or missionary schools and colleges had an edge over those who came from a non-English school. Further, urban domiciled had a better chance of selection than rural domiciled. These findings reflect on the managers' social background.

Significant changes have taken place in the Indian management scene in the past two decades, says a study made by Director of Foundation of Organizational Research, Mr. N.K. Singh (1984). He does not find any notable change in the religion and caste profiles of managers. He maintains that a large majority of managers continue to be drawn from amongst Hindus. One-third of the total managers are drawn from among Brahmins. However, there has been considerable change in the rural-urban distribution of managers. While in 1971 people of urban origin dominated (80 per cent), in 1983 only 60 per cent were drawn from urban areas. The study says, elitism seems to be on the downward trend if family occupation is the criterion. In 1971 one-third of the manager's jobs were held by occupation groups such as business, profession and management. In 1983 majority (60 per cent) of the managers were from salaried people. The educational level of Indian managers seems to be on the increase as the study revealed that 84 per cent of managerial jobs in 1983 were occupied by graduates and post-graduates against 65 per cent in 1971. The managerial world is becoming more broad-based in terms of regional distribution. While in 1971 the majority of managers came from Gujarat, Punjab, Maharashtra, Tamil Nadu and Kerala, in 1983 Delhi, Andhra Pradesh and Uttar Pradesh also started making significant contribution, Findings of the study on the personal background of managers show that 60 per cent of managers belong to cities or large towns and only 13.4 per cent are from villages. In terms of income groups, 76.8 per cent have come from upper middle income families.

There are very few studies comparing the background characteristics of Indian managers with the managers of other countries. Every country has its own peculiar social structure which plays a significant role in the supply of managers, *e.g.*, in India caste and religion play an important role. Kassem (1971) did an attempt in this direction. He compared the background characteristics of managers in India, Egypt and the U.S.A. He maintains that the socio-cultural milieu of a country has a unique influence on the native managers.

PROFESSIONAL AUTHORITY

Professional authority has been considered as one of the most important characteristics of professionals (Carr Saunders, 1933; Goode, 1957; Ritmer, 1975). The professions and occupations form a continuum. For an occupation to move towards the professional end of the continuum, the attainment of professional authority through formalised education and technical competence is a basic prerequisite (Hughes, 1971). It is expected that the specialised knowledge will be used for safeguarding the interests of the clients. This belief became the basis for providing the professional authority to the professionals.

Authority is an institutionally recognized right to influence the actions of others, regardless of their immediate personal attitudes to the direction of influence. It is exercised by the incumbent of an office or other socially defined status (Parsons, 1949). Authority in this sense is an institutionalized power which has the legitimation of coercive sanctions. Professional authority gets its legitimacy from the community sanction which is based on the technical competence of the professional. Parsons maintains that the professional authority is based on the superior 'technical competence' of the professional man. The area of professional authority is limited to a particular technically defined sphere. It is characterized by specification of functions. The technical competence is always limited to a specific field of knowledge and skill. A professional has authority only in his own field of knowledge. Other scholars have also accepted that the specialised and technical competence is the basis for legitimacy to the professional authority (Millorson, 1964; Wilensky, 1964; Halsey, 1970). The professional can decide what is good or bad for his client who accepts his authority with the belief that his knowledge will benefit him. The client's ignorance in the field of the profession's competence reinforces the authority. The community gives the professional a right to make decisions in the area of his specialised knowledge.

Managers are perceived as forming an elite class on the basis of the high amount of authority they enjoy in an industrial set-up. It is argued that the managerial revolution consisted of a drive for the attainment of power and the position of a ruling class. The fusion of knowledge and authority has created a new kind of professional technocrat occupying the elite position (Burnham, 1945; Mills, 1956).

In the present study it is noted that the managers claim professional authority on the basis of their managerial skills. Specialized knowledge and technical competence do not provide the basis of authority. One of the reasons for this may be the slow space of the professionalization of management in India. In the present sample, only very few managers (6 per cent) were having specialized knowledge or training in management. The managers who are professionally trained in management are perceived as professional managers. In view of this fact it can be stated that the managers do not have professional authority based on specialized knowledge and technical competence. The legitimacy of their authority is based on the rules and regulations of industrial organization which are usually stated by the managing directors. Thus, the source of manager's authority is the managing director, who has the final decision-making authority in an industry. Despite the high claims of democratic functioning, most organizations have rigid authoritarian structures and scant scope for participation of managers in decision-making. This sometimes reduces the managers to nullity. Managing directors can withdraw, increase or decrease their authority.

Manager's authority can be perceived in two forms, *i.e.*, ascribed and achieved authority. Ascribed authority is inherent in the job itself by virtue of its responsibilities. The sphere of this authority has been clearly specified in the rules of the industry. This authority is conferred to the office of the manager irrespective of the person who occupies it. In Weberian paradigm it is called legitimate authority, legitimacy of which is drawn from the rules laid down by the managing directors. On the other hand, achieved authority is one which the manager, due to his personality traits, skills, etc., acquires from his subordinate incumbents and managing directors. This is the traditional type of authority, legitimacy of which lies in the obedience to the particular person concerned.

Manager's authority is often limited. The job description, the union involvement, revision of authority, special executive orders, etc., constrain his authority. Moreover, authority can also be resisted by subordinates through group inaction and informal organization. Subordinates may function in direct confrontation by subtle or other means when the authority is felt to be unwarned, excessive or threatening. The limitations on authority are sometimes formalized by providing different degrees of authority which may be pending, subject to review, shared with other departments, exercised only as granted, delegated and granted for a limited duration and for a particular purpose.

PROFESSIONAL AUTONOMY IN THE AREA OF PROFESSIONAL AUTHORITY

Professional autonomy signifies the freedom from control by an outside agency, *i.e.,* a profession is self-controlled. Professional autonomy has two aspects, *i.e.,* structural and attitudinal. Structural autonomy is maintained with the help of professional associations. These associations control the entry into the profession and provide the right to practise profession with autonomy and control the member of professionals. A professional can make judgement with relative confidence which can be questioned only by the professional peers. Attitudinal autonomy is the feeling in the professional that he is free to make decisions in the area of his specialised knowledge. He is free from the external pressures of clients and of those who are not the members of the profession.

The degree of autonomy enjoyed by a profession depends on the extent to which professional practice is based upon theoretical knowledge and the degree of observation of the ideal of altruistic service (Carr Saunders, 1933). Goode (1960) maintains that the profession is a powerful force in the society and over the individual. Most of the legislations concerning the profession are generated by the professional peers. Society's legal control is weaker because public and legislators do not know much about the work of professionals. This mechanism allows the profession to maintain its autonomy.

The autonomy of the professional in the work setting is the freedom from the control over one's work. To maintain the autonomy of a profession, its body of knowledge must remain secret, a mystique must be built around its practices. To ensure autonomy, professionals will often attempt to strengthen the mysticism of the profession by introducing new and complex ideas and practices (Hughes, 1971; Johnson, 1972). Freidson and Rhea (1965) have provided a more exclusive definition of professional autonomy. They perceive it as control over the technical content of work. They call it 'autonomy of technique'. The professionals have the special privilege of freedom from the control of outsiders. This privilege is justified by three claims: first, their work requires such a high degree of skill and knowledge that only fellow professionals can make accurate assessment of professional's performance. Secondly, a high degree of selflessness and responsibility characterises professionals, so they can be trusted to work conscientiously. Thirdly, in those rare instances in which industrial professionals do not perform with skill, their colleagues may be trusted to take the proper regulator action. A similar definition has been given by Larson (1977). She maintains that professional autonomy signifies the self-control, *i.e.,* they can become almost immune to external regulations. It allows the professionals to select, according to their will, the inputs which they will receive from the laity. They live within ideologies of their own creation.

Professional autonomy is based on the monopoly over the specialized knowledge. The professional is able to attain and maintain his position because the masses do not have the prerequisite knowledge to replace him. Further, professional autonomy has the sanction of the community. It is believed that the professional will use his knowledge in the interest of the society. He is expected to give first preference to community interest sacrificing his own interests.

The client needs the services of the professionals since he is unable to solve his problems himself. The professional is expected to have that knowledge with the help of which the client's problems can be solved. It is expected that the professional uses this knowledge in the best interest of the client. In this client — professional relationship lies the autonomy of the professional. Professional is given full autonomy in the sphere of his specialized knowledge because the client has a trust over him.

Professional autonomy is determined by the amount of authority a profession has been able to attain. Authority is an institutionally recognized right to influence the actions of others. On the other hand, autonomy signifies the freedom from external influences. To explain it further, it can be stated that on the basis of the professional authority, a professional can influence the actions of his clients while on the basis of his autonomy he cannot be influenced by anyone who is not the member of his profession. Those professions which have more authority are comparatively more autonomous. Further, if the profession is well organized and has its own controlling body or association, it attains more autonomy. Hence, the more organized the professions, the more the autonomy.

Management is not a free profession. The managers have to function in the bureaucratic organization of the industry. Thus, managers' autonomy cannot be thought of in terms of the autonomy enjoyed by the professions like law, medicine, etc. The goals, policies and rules of an industrial organization limit managers' autonomy. Though his autonomy is defined by the rules of the industry yet on the basis of his personality traits and expertise, he may be able to extract more autonomy. The conflict between manager's professional ethic based on the primacy to community interests and in the business ethic based on primacy to self-interest, may limit his professional autonomy. Manager's autonomy also depends on his position in the management hierarchy. Those at the top may have more autonomy than those who are at comparatively low positions. Further, there are so many other organizations within the industry which may limit manager's autonomy *viz.,* the labour union, union of white-collar employees, etc.

STRUCTURAL CONSTRAINTS IN THE AREA OF PROFESSIONAL AUTHORITY AND AUTONOMY

Management is not a free profession. Managers perform their activities in a bureaucratic industrial organization where they are to face unavoidable conflict situations. On the one hand it is argued that the bureaucratic organization enhances the efficiency of a manager. On the other hand, a difference between the ethics, goals of professional managers and industrial bureaucratic organization is noticed, which reduces the efficiency of the managers.

Scholars have identified various sources of these strains. Seller (1963) has classified these various sources into two categories *viz.*, traditional and modern. Traditional causes of conflict include personality differences, personal ambitions and whims, competition with the colleagues for more power, etc. Modern causes are hidden in the industrial organization itself viz., distribution of authority in various departments and shifting of responsibilities when the task is shared by two or more departments.

Various causes of strains which are observed in the field situations can be classified into two broad categories *viz.,* subjective and objective. Subjective causes include personal values, ambitions and way of thinking. Objective causes include communication gap, union involvement, misunderstanding with subordinates, colleagues, senior personnel, etc.

Parsons (1949), contrasting the business and profession, maintains that the former is based on self-interest and the latter on disinterestedness. The businessman was thought of as pursuing egoistically his own self-interest, while the professional was altruistically serving the interests of others. He further maintains that in spite of the differences in the nature and interests, the two have three features in common *viz.,* rationality, specificity of function and universalistic value orientation. MacIver (1955) has also differentiated the business from profession on the basis of ethics. The business has not attained a specific code of ethic, resting on considerations broader than the sense of self-interest. Hans Nagpal (1971) also, just like Parsons and MacIver, found a contrast between the unselfish preoccupation of the professional who serves his fellow-men without much consideration of monetary rewards and the selfish preoccupation of business, *i.e.,* to accumulate personal profit at the expense of others. Thus, a fundamental contradiction of the ethics of business and professionals has been considered as the major cause of strains between the two.

There are very few studies focused on conflict analyses in an industrial bureaucratic organization (Choudhary, 1969; Dayal and Adhikari, 1969; Prabhakar, 1979; Sheth and Patel, 1979). Choudhary in his study found a generational conflict between the younger and senior managers created by the differences in their ideas. Dayal and Adhikari noticed that the stresses and strains are caused by the authority relationships among the managers. Sheth and Patel maintain that the differences between the goals and aspirations of an organization and of managers cause strains in their relationships. Prabhakar in his empirical study studied the conflict between the production and purchase departments of selected industries. It was pointed out that the cause of conflict was the clash of authority. This may be due to the diffused distribution or overlapping of authority. The difference in personal values was also a cause for such conflict. Thus, various causes, subjective as well as objective, have been identified by different scholars.

While discussing conception of bureaucracy, Sharma (1983) maintains that in Weber's view bureaucratic organization is characterised by harmonious relations and absence of extraneous pressures which generate higher efficiency among the members. But he argues that this conclusion is based on invalid assumptions. The incoherence of the interests of the members causes tension, conflict and minimizes the harmony of relations. This argument holds true in reference to industrial bureaucratic organizations also. It is noticed that many times the interests of the owners and managers do not coincide which leads to strains. Not only this, the managers at many occasions come in conflict with colleagues and subordinates as well.

Thus, in view of the above discussion it can be said that the main source of conflict between the manager and managing directors or owners is the difference of their ethic. Here two specific issues crop up. First, will the manager be completely dominated by the organization, *i.e.,* will be rationalized and ignore his personal values when these come in conflict with the impersonal, efficiency-dominated and profit-oriented values of organization? Second, will he maintain his altruistic values when these come in conflict with the profit oriented values of the organization? These two propositions are yet to be tested.

In a family controlled industry, the main source of strain lies in manager's relations With the managing director. Manager is dependent on him for his job, salary, promotion, career and thus, becomes obedient. But the obedience to the owner may sometimes hurt his professional sentiments. In order to maintain his professional ethics, sometimes, the manager will have to deviate from this obedience. It cannot be expected from a professional manager to be a blind follower to the authority of the managing director. However, this deviance will lead to the strains in their relations. Secondly, unnecessary interference of the managing director, in the day-to-day functions of managers, may lead to strains in their relations. Thirdly, managers have to get their major decisions sanctioned by the managing director, who can modify these decisions and can also completely change these. This undue interference in managers' decisions leads to strains in their relations. Fourthly, the manager recommends for the appointment, transfer, promotion, demotion, reward and penalization of his subordinates. Managing director may or may not accept these recommendations. His negative response to manager's recommendations leads to strains in their relations. Fifthly, in big industries the manager's career within the organization depends on managing director. Sometimes, a manager's promotion is made on the basis of his relations with the managing director and not on his skills. Thus, the more deserving manager may suffer if he does not have very cordial relations with the managing director. Lastly, managing director's way of dealing with the managers determines the nature of relations between them. Sometimes managing director is not well behaved. He may scold or even abuse the manager. This misbehaviour leads to the strains in their relations. These are some of the basic factors causing strains in manager's relations with the managing director.

Every manager has his own network of relations within the organization. This network of relations can be classified in three categories *viz.,* relationship network with seniors, colleagues and subordinates. A manager may have strains in all the three categories of networks. In big industries where the number of senior managers is large, he may have strains with them which may be due to various reasons *viz.,* misunderstandings, communication gap, etc. Sometimes senior managers exploit junior managers by virtue of their seniority, which leads to strains. Manager may have strains in his relations with his colleagues due to many reasons *viz.,* diffused distribution and overlapping of authority. Every manager has to maintain harmonious relations within his department. He has to resolve all the conflicts emerging among his subordinates. In doing so he may have strains in his relations with them because in such situations he cannot always satisfy both the parties equally. Thus, it will lead to strains in his relations with the dissatisfied party.

INDUSTRIAL MANAGEMENT IN INDIA

After Independence India exhibited a slow movement towards professionalization of management. Some of the factors which provided for the take-off stage of management in India are : increasing size of industries, huge capital investments, competition within the country and abroad, mechanization of production operations, scarcity of resources and energy, increasing number of labourers and their unionization, bureaucratization of industrial organizations, the governing idea of business as public service, etc. To tackle these problems efficiently, a need for trained manager with the specialized knowledge of management has paved the way for the professionalization of management.

From the review of literature it is found that managers have not been studied adequately from the perspective of a profession. The professionalization of management has led to many unresolved issues. Two of the most debated issues are: first, what authority managers have been given after their separation from owners? Second, while functioning in a bureaucratic organization a professional has to face many unavoidable conflict situations. Thus, the amount of autonomy managers enjoy while functioning in the bureaucratic organization of an industry is significant.

The present endeavour has been made to study five inter-related research objectives: first, to identify the nature and extent of managers' authority. Second, to examine the amount of autonomy managers enjoy in the area of their authority. Third, to elucidate the structural constraints that managers face in the area of authority and autonomy. Fourth, to explicate the sources of these structural constraints. Fifth, to analyse the reaction of managers to these structural constraints.

This study has been conducted in the Meerut city of Uttar Pradesh. The rationale for selecting this city was the fact that the industries of this city have not been studied. The industries emerged here much later than in other cities of Uttar Pradesh. Fifty managers were interviewed from both the sectors — public limited and private limited. Data were obtained with the help of an interview schedule.

By the study of the background characteristics of managers, it is found that the majority of the managers are below forty years. Religion-wise, most of the managers are Hindu and few others are Jain, Sikh, Parsi and Muslim. In terms of the level of education, the majority is highly educated. So far as the nature of education is concerned, the majority has general education. The role of engineer-managers and professionally trained managers in management is increasing. Most of the managers are from Uttar Pradesh with few from Punjab, Maharashtra and Delhi. All the managers are married and the majority have planned family *i.e.,* three or less than three children. Highly educated young managers perceive planned family as an ideal. Service; class families dominate the supply of managers. The remaining few are from business families, professionals' families and the farming families. Majority of the managers are drawing a salary of less than Rs. thirty-five hundred per month. Age-wise senior managers are drawing high salary. Level of education has no significant association with salary. More or less similar background characteristics have been found by Jain (1971), Subramaniam (1983) and Singh (1984).

Majority of the non-Hindus and immigrants are in public industries. This can be explained by the fact that such industries are large size and in most of the cases are multinationals. The criteria for the selection of managers are more universalistic specified by the rules which are strictly maintained. The salary scale of managers is high in public limited industries than in private limited industries. This may be due to their large size and huge capital investments. In private limited industries, engineer-managers are in great number. Such industries cannot afford to have engineers and managers separately due to their small size and small capital investment. The engineer-manager is more economical.

The first objective of this study was to identify the nature and extent of authority managers have been given in the industrial bureaucratic organization. Managers do not have professional authority in the true sense of the term. Professional authority gets its legitimacy from the community sanction which is based on the technical competence of the professional. Managers' authority lies in their office. The legitimacy of their authority is based on the rules and regulations of the industrial organization which are usually stated by the managing director who may withdraw, increase or decrease it. Authority in this sense is an institutionalized power which has the legitimation of coercive sanction.

Managers' authority is scored in two ways. First, their overall authority and secondly in different areas of their functioning, *i.e.* decision-making, directing, coordination, staffing, planning, reporting and budgeting. The mean score is calculated, and it is perceived that those scoring below it, have low authority and those above, high. Most of the managers perceive that they have sufficient amount of authority. Very few managers were not satisfied. While scoring overall authority of managers it is found that 50 per cent of the managers have high authority and the remaining have low authority. Their authority in decision-making is very limited. All the major decisions taken by them are to be sanctioned by the top management which may change them, reject them or accept them. To carry out these decisions, the managers give general and specific instructions to their subordinates directly or indirectly depending on the person for whom they are made. Majority of the managers have low authority in the sphere of directing. Now the question emerges: how much flexibility managers give to their subordinates in carrying out these instructions? Majority of the managers want their instructions to be followed strictly. Few sometimes allow flexibility and few give sufficient flexibility to the subordinates. Further, it is reported that before giving instructions, every manager seeks the opinion of the concerned person.

Managers recommend for the awards and punishments for their subordinates. Further, appointments, terminations, promotions, demotions and transfers of the subordinates excluding senior personnel, like assistant manager, engineers, etc., are recommended by the manager. All these recommendations are to be approved by the top management. Managers have low authority in such matters.

Managers have very little authority in the area of planning. Their plans are put before the managing directors for approval. In most of the cases they are changed. Further, every manager sends the progress report of his department, sometimes weekly, monthly, biannually or annually depending on the rules of the concerned industry. The top management may call for explanation on this report. Managers do not have much authority in budgeting. One-third of the managers do not have any participation in budgeting. Very few managers participate directly and about 50 per cent participate indirectly. All the final decisions in such matters are to be taken by the top management.

Senior and high salaried managers have more authority. Level of education has no significant association with the amount of authority. Those who are at high positions in the organizational hierarchy have more authority.

In all the areas of their functioning, managers in the private limited industries have more authority than their counterparts in public limited industries. Various reasons may be adduced to explain this variation. First, managers in such industries are more committed due to their personal involvement in the interests of the organization on account of which they are given more authority. Secondly, managers in such industries have a direct and frequent access to the managing director due to which they are able to extract more authority by way of influencing him. Thus, it seems that the size of the organization has a bearing on managers' authority. The small size of private limited industries is the basic factor which facilitates the managers to have high authority. In public limited industries, due to their large size and more division of labour, authority is shared, and it also overlaps. Further, due to a distance in the relations with managing directors, they do not get much opportunity to manipulate more authority. Hence, less authority to managers in public limited industries.

The second objective of this study was to examine the amount of autonomy managers enjoy in the area of their authority. This objective has been examined in view of the obtained empirical data. While professional authority signifies the institutionalized power to act in a certain way, the professional autonomy is the freedom of action and the absence of external interference. On the basis of his professional authority, a manager can influence the actions of his clients while on the basis of his professional autonomy he cannot be influenced by anyone who is not the member of his profession. Professional autonomy is based on the monopoly over the specialized knowledge. Managers' autonomy is not much based on this monopoly over the specialized knowledge in the true sense of the term. Their autonomy has two sources, first, from the rules of the industrial organization and secondly, their own personality traits and to a very little extent the specialized knowledge they have.

Managers' autonomy is scored in two ways. First, their overall autonomy and secondly in different areas of their functioning similar to those of authority. The mean score is calculated and those below it are perceived having low autonomy and those above it high autonomy. It is found that the majority of the managers have low overall autonomy. In decision-making they do not have much autonomy but in giving instructions to carry out these they are quite autonomous. The recommendations they make for the awards and penalization for their subordinates are normally accepted. Managers do not have much autonomy in recommending for the appointments, terminations, promotions, demotions and transfers of their subordinates. In planning, majority of the managers have high autonomy particularly those who have high authority in planning. In budgeting all the final decisions are taken by the top management and managers do not have much autonomy. Those managers who have direct active participation in budgeting have high autonomy.

Senior, highly educated and high salaried managers have comparatively more autonomy. The managers who have high overall authority have high overall autonomy. The managers who are at the higher position in the organizational hierarchy have high autonomy.

Most of the managers have moderate autonomy and they are satisfied with it. Few, who have little autonomy are just satisfied or dissatisfied. On being asked how much autonomy managers should be given, majority favoured moderate autonomy.

Managers in the private limited industries have more autonomy than their counterparts in public limited industries. This variation may be explained in various ways. First, in private limited industries, the number of senior and peer managers is less. Therefore, the check over managers' autonomy is very limited. Secondly, in such industries managers make every decision after consulting the colleagues, senior managers and managing directors and thus are able to extract more autonomy. Thirdly, managers in such industries are more autonomous. On the other hand, in public limited industries, due to their large organizational hierarchy, managers have little autonomy particularly those who are at the middle and low positions. Further, involvement of the unions also limit their autonomy particularly in dealing with subordinates.

Structural constraints managers face in the area of their professional authority and autonomy, their sources and managers' reaction to these have been analysed in this study. Managers face strains in all directions of their network of relations, *i.e.,* with managing directors, seniors and peer managers and subordinates. The main source of strains lies in their relations with the managing directors particularly in a family-controlled industry. The main reason being the difference in their ethics *i.e.,* egoistic ethics of the managing directors and altruistic ethics of professional managers. Other sources of strains are unnecessary interference in managers' authority and autonomy, undue response to his recommendations, etc. At many occasions senior managers exploit juniors on the basis of their authority. The overlapping and diffuse distribution of authority among peer managers leads to strains in their relations. Communication gap and involvement of the union lead to strains in managers'relations with subordinates.

The various problems which the managers face in the industrial organization become the sources of strains. Managers were asked to point out some of the most common problems causing strains. Most of the managers reported communication gap as a major problem leading to strains. The other problems causing strains are misunderstanding, misbehaviour, involvement of the union, laziness of workers, low morality, no sincerity, etc. Managers try their best to tackle these problems. Sometimes they feel helpless in spite of their urge to tackle them, may be due to their limited authority.

The strains become very severe when any decision is imposed on managers or they are stopped from doing according to their own will. Managers may respond to such situations in many ways. Majority of the managers discuss with the top management before following the imposed decision. Few keep quiet and follow such decisions while others show reluctance. Senior, high salaried managers respond more boldly in such situations. Level of education has no significant association with managers' response.

The size of the organization has a bearing on the extent of strains faced by the managers. In large size organizations of public limited industries, the strains are from varied sources and are more severe. Such industries, have a large hierarchy of managers who have competition with each other which becomes a cause of strains. Further, there are more chances of communication gap, overlapping and diffuse distribution of authority leading to strains. In private limited industries due to their small size, these problems remain within control. Managers in such industries work with more mutual understanding and cooperation with managing directors, senior and peer managers and subordinates. Such industries almost do not have the problems caused by the unions which is very severe in case of public limited industries.

In a nutshell it can be maintained that the majority of the managers are satisfied with the amount of authority and autonomy they have been given. On the other hand, few are not satisfied or just satisfied and they want more authority and autonomy. A good number of managers are not satisfied with the amount of autonomy. Managers favoured for moderate autonomy. In private limited industries, managers have more authority and autonomy than in public limited industries. Various reasons have been adduced for this variation. The strains managers face are part of the game. They try their best to overcome these and usually get success. The strains in large size organizations of public limited industries are more severe and from varied sources. Two issues crop up here which need further probing. First, how much authority and autonomy managers should be given so that they may function efficiently? Secondly, in what ways the strains managers face can be minimized and a conducive, healthy industrial environment developed?

QUESTIONS FOR EXERCISE

1. Write an essay on professionalism in Industrial management.
2. Explain the problem of industrial management in India.

11

INDUSTRIAL SUPERVISION

MEANING OF SUPERVISION

1. Literal meaning Supervision is a Latin word in which 'super' denotes 'from the above' and 'vision' 'to see'. In ordinary sense, the term supervision is called 'overseeing activity'. But 'overseeing' alone does not convey anything worth taking note of. In management supervision means 'overseeing the subordinates at work with authority and with an aim to correct the employee if he is going to be wrong.' The real purpose of supervision is to oversee the employees at work.

2. Vitales "Supervision refers to the direct and immediate guidance and control of subordinates in performance to their task."

3. Davis "Supervision is the function of assuring that the work is being done in accordance with the plan and instruction."

4. G.R. Terry "Supervision is the task of achieving the desired results by means of intelligent utilisation of human talents and utilising resources in a manner that provides a challenge to human talent. It is concerned with initiating action, putting into effect the plan and decisions by stimulation of the human resources of the enterprise."

To conclude, supervision is the direction, guidance and control of working force with a view:

(i) to see that they are working according to the plan, policy, programme, instruction and keeping up the time schedule and

(ii) to help them in their working if they are in need of help of any kind to accomplish their assigned tasks.

Who is a Supervisor?

America's Fort Hartley Labour Act of 1947 defines supervisors as "those having authority to exercise independent judgment in hiring, discharging, disciplining, recording and taking other actions of a similar nature with respect to employees." Therefore, supervisors are those persons in authority who have direct control over their working force. According to Allen, a supervisor is an authority who is responsible to get the work done. He is to see that directions are being followed, instructions and orders are being carried out, the plans, policies and programmes are being executed and deviations, if any, are being corrected and reported to the authority to whom one is answerable.

ESSENTIAL QUALITIES OF A SUPERVISOR

1. Knowledge of techniques of supervision A supervisor should have knowledge of different techniques of supervision. This will enable him to know his men and he can make use of them according to the requirements.

Supervisory techniques are usually divided into the following three categories:

(i) ***Autocratic technique:*** In it there is a concentration of power in the hands of the supervisor. He uses 'rules of thumb' as weapon discriminately. He is a hard taskmaster. He imposes his will upon the workers who are to carry it out without 'if's and but's'. Workers have nothing to say about in the management decisions. The, supervisor commands fear and has full control over his men.

(ii) ***Democratic technique:*** In it the democratic principles are followed. Workers have full say in the management decisions. They are taken into confidence by the management. They are allowed to participate in the decision-making process. Debates precede the decision. Supervisor is also responsible for getting the work done. He is not allowed to function by rule of thumb; he has to rule by consent. He seeks co-operation. He motivates their skill, knowledge, training, working capacity and wisdom and helps them in increasing their abilities and efficiency.

(iii) ***Free-reign technique***: In it the policies, programmes, the time schedule and objectives, etc. are fully explained to the workers. The workers are left free to work as satisfactorily as possible for them within the framework of the instructions, methodology and other allied things already explained to them. They have to follow the explained path and procedure and are responsible and answerable for deviations. The supervisor only guides the workers. He leaves the supervision part of his functions to the sound judgement of the workers themselves.

It is the individual trait, the working force, the work and the requirement which decide as to which of the three techniques are best for an organisation or in a given situation. It may differ from one situation to another, one individual to another, one group to another and one organisation to another.

2. Leadership qualities The supervisor leads a group of personnel who look at him for guidance and direction. Unless he possesses the leader's qualities he will lack the rhythm of supervision and thus desired discipline, loyalty and efficiency in the group cannot be expected.

3. Managerial skill The supervisor is a part of the management. He must therefore possess the knowledge of managerial skill. The management functions require him to encourage team spirit in his men and solicit all types of co-operation. He must command respect and unquestioned loyalty to him by the use of managerial skill and technique.

4. Unbiased and fair The supervisor should behave in an unbiased manner. He should be fair to all. He should not be prejudiced to any-one of his men. Bias leads to troubles and vitiates the atmosphere. Therefore, it should be avoided at all costs.

5. Know and let know The supervisor's duty is to know all his men, their work, conduct, skill, training, knowledge, wisdom, success, failures, habits, temperament, likings and dislikings, social status, domestic problems, and all which that could possibly be known. He should understand the spirit of his men. And his behaviour should be adjusted accordingly. On the other hand, he should let his men know about him. This will remove suspicion, develop friendly attitude and create oneness.

Thus, a supervisor is required to play a very significant role in an industrial organisation. He is in constant and direct touch with the operating staff, that is, the real working force. He is responsible for getting the work done from the work force of which he is the supervisor, and, who, are under his direct control. Because of his peculiar but significant position in the organisational structure the supervisor :

(i) influences the work environment,

(ii) influences the support of workers and

(iii) influences (a) the attitude, (b) the behaviour, (c) the conduct and even (d) co-operative efforts of the workers under his charge.

He is a morale booster. He influences the wholesome attitude of the whole lot. To quote Peter F. Drucker, "Even the best supervisor is not a substitute for poor principles and practices in managing workers."

TYPES OF SUPERVISION

Scholars have classified the types of leadership and supervision in identical terms. The types of leadership and supervision are similar or parallel. The supervisory role in industry is the same as that of leadership. The industrial leadership and political leadership are quite distinct affairs. An industrial leader *ex hypothesis* must be a supervisor. There are the following types of industrial leaders:

1. Authoritative supervisor An authoritative supervisor exercises control and direction over his subordinates by virtue of the authority vested in him. In authoritative leadership there are the two following types of supervisors :

(i) ***The hard-boiled autocrat:*** An autocrat believes in unflagging discipline and firm control over the workers. He rarely appreciates the role of work of his subordinates. Rather he looks upon them with slight and mild contempt. He keeps himself aloof from the workers and does not give them a chance to get near to him. He wants automatic obedience of his orders and can brook no criticism of his directions and orders. Such autocrats are apt to give credence to backbiting and this leads to tension and conflicts in an industry. As the autocrats show no respect for the feelings of their subordinates, the subordinates also harbour a spirit of vindictiveness against such persons. At times this flares up and finds expression in violence against supervisors. In fact, a hard-boiled autocrat does not deserve to be called as a leader. He lacks all the qualities of leadership. The obedience which he is able to claim is due purely to the authority vested in him.

(ii) ***The benevolent autocrat:*** The benevolent autocrat gives guidance and direction in all matters. He seeks to maintain discipline. He is annoyed by any infringement of discipline. But unlike the hard-boiled autocrat, he is not averse to saying a word of praise to the workers who perform their duties well. The workers carry out the orders of such supervisors, though they do not really feel inspired by them. In certain cases, such a leader comes to symbolize smooth functioning of the factory or mill. The authoritarian leader is impressed by the qualify of his decision but his decision cannot become an effective instrument, unless it is accepted by the whole group.

2. *Laissez-faire* supervisorship The *laissez-faire* is exact reverse of the autocratic supervisorship :

(i) ***Freedom of workers***: While in autocratic leadership there is no place for the personal freedom of workers, in *laissez-faire* leadership the personal freedom of workers is respected.

(ii) ***Responsibility***: Whereas in autocratic supervisorship, the leader is considered responsible for everything, in *laissez-faire* supervisorship the responsibility is distributed among various persons.

(iii) ***Autocracy of democracy***: The *laissez-faire* supervisors do not try to impose any decision nor do they coerce the workers to any type of action. These supervisors act democratically. They try to seek the voluntary co-operation of workers. These supervisors do not project any fixed goals. The *laissez-faire* supervisorship gives rise to indiscipline and discontent among the workers. It also promotes a sense of insecurity among them. There is a loss in production also. That is why one rarely finds such type of supervisorship countenanced in an industry.

3. Democratic supervision The most prevalent form of leadership and supervision in an industry is democratic supervision. According to Bradford, a democratic leader believes in the following things:

1. Problems should not be allowed to crop up.
2. For the sake of collective action and thinking, assemblies and conferences are a must.
3. There should be fixed collective ideals.
4. The criteria of action should be fixed.
5. The reasons for decisions should be known.
6. With progress, freedom and responsibility increase.

The above-mentioned characteristics of democratic supervision are corresponding to and congruent with modern democratic ideals. However, everyone cannot be led democratically. Some workers misunderstand the democratic attitude of the supervisor and take it to be a symptom of weakness. They try to exploit this weakness and shirk work. This results in the loss of production.

CONDITIONS OF EFFECTIVE SUPERVISION

1. Favourable social environs Creation of an atmosphere of mutual trust and confidence is an essential condition of an effective leadership. It must be able to associate workers in decision making and feeling of responsibility. The directives of the leader are easily accepted and carried out by the workers under such an atmosphere.

2. Knowledge of company's policy The leader must know the fundamental tenets which govern the functioning of the company. He must acquaint the workers with the policy and the rules of the company. He must explain his status and role in the company in clear and frank terms. This would enable him to feel secure because he knows what he has to do and what he must avoid doing.

3. Gaining confidence of workers A good leader should win the confidence of workers. Before effecting any change in the technique of production, he should consult the workers even if the change has been finally decided upon. This helps to induce a sense of well-being and confidence among the workers and they highly appreciate the fact that workers have been considered worthy for consultation by respective authorities.

4. Strict Discipline Whatever rules and regulations are framed once, these should be strictly adhered to. If a worker violates them he should be penalized without let or hindrance. Similarly, if the performance of a worker is noteworthy and deserves reward, he must be rewarded ungrudgingly.

5. Participation in decision-making Finally, it is very necessary for good supervisorship that workers should be given a chance to participate in the decision-and policy-making of the company. This will enthuse them to toil hard and work with grit and determination.

PRINCIPLES OF EFFECTIVE SUPERVISION

The psychologist Blum has suggested the following principles for good supervisorship :

1. **Don't be an autocrat** Autocratic supervisor is self-defeating because the workers feel alienated and do not obey the supervisor willingly.
2. **Listen carefully** The supervisor should be a good listener. He must listen carefully to everything told to him by his subordinates. He must accord full opportunity to the worker to present his case; only after it should the supervisor express his opinion.
3. **Don't decide hurriedly** It is rash to form an opinion about some person hurriedly after a casual glance or brief hearing, as most of the complaints are not genuine. But some are certainly so and if these are not removed, the morale of the company would suffer.

4. **Don't argue with subordinates** Under no circumstances supervisor should indulge in an argument with his subordinate, because if he fails to persuade or be convinced by his arguments, he is liable to issue orders to vindicate his point of view. This creates frustration and sense of insecurity among the workers. A good supervisor should not argue, but, listen carefully, and issue orders only after careful listening.
5. **Don't criticize publicly** If a worker is rebuked publicly he feels insulted. The workers are usually rash and they tend to retaliate if they are wounded emotionally. Therefore a good leader avoids discussing the faults of workers in public. He points them out to him in private and in a direct manner.

SUPERVISION TECHNIQUES

The following are the important supervision techniques :

1. Autocratic technique.
2. Democratic technique.
3. Free-reign technique. Success of this technique depends on :

(i) Unrestricted supervision,
(ii) Free delegation of authority, and
(iii) Efficient and effective communication.

According to R. Lickert, "There is no one best way to supervise. Supervisory practices that are effective in some situations yield unsatisfactory results in the other." Indeed supervision is an individual trait and wisdom. Techniques are being developed by the supervisor himself in a given situation. His techniques differ from situation to situation, from work to work, from individual to individual, from group to group and from organisation to organisation. Under these circumstances, it is difficult to adjudge any one of the three as 'best'.

FACTORS AFFECTING SUPERVISION

1. Human relations skills Supervision assimilates in itself the following functions:

(i) Guiding the working force,
(ii) Instructing them and
(iii) Inspiring them for better performance.

The supervisor has to depend on the decisions of top and middle-order management for the following:

(i) Leadership
(ii) Counselling
(iii) Communication
(iv) Determinants of human relations

Without their guidelines, the supervisor remains handicapped. In modern set-up, he can take routine decisions within the framework provided for the purpose. But he cannot take a major decision without consulting his superiors in middle order and top management. He is the person who has to toe the lines as suggested by his superior though he is directly responsible to get the work done. But he is the person who is in direct touch with his men. He watches them to work. He knows their emotions, feelings and sentiments, notes them and shares them. He is on the spot. Therefore in these matters he is left with no alternative but to take quick decisions before any sparking situation arises. He is the best judge of human relations. He has to apply his skill, use his training, draw lessons from his experiences and handle the situation accordingly. So far as human relations are concerned it is a matter of skill.

2. Technical and managerial knowledge The guidance and instructions are largely based on the technical knowledge and the managerial acumen. These helps the supervisor in serving his organisation well. His supervisory capabilities are increased by adequate training and sufficient technical and managerial skill.

3. Leadership position The supervisor's ability of supervising his workmen depends on his position and status in the organisation. This position may either be delegated or may be acquired. The supervisor can improve his position provided a status worth of his responsibilities is given to him. This is fundamentally important and no organisation can afford to ignore it.

4. Improved upward relations A supervisor is well heard and respected by his superiors at all levels of the management. His adverse reports as well as appreciations are equally respected to and action taken accordingly. He must have good relations with his superiors by way of encouragement. Thus helps him in establishing good relations with his workmen.

5. Relief from non-supervisory duties A supervisor must be free from all duties except supervision and its related functions. Submission of reports, returns, etc. is not his job. If he is free from all these then he may devote more time with his workmen. Job training too is not his duty. Instead it should be given to instructional staff. The supervisor should be allowed to concentrate on directing functions for which he should be given sufficient authority under the basic norm of management — 'power with people'. This would ensure the maximum supervision from which results can be generally expected.

QUESTIONS FOR EXERCISE

1. What is supervision? Describe qualities of a supervisor.
2. Describe kinds of supervision. How can supervision be made effective?
3. What are the factors affecting supervision?

12

IMPACT OF INDIVIDUAL DIFFERENCES

Meaning of Individual Differences

According to Skinner, "Today we think of individual differences as including any measurable aspect of the total personality." From this definition of individual differences, it is evident that it comprehends every aspect of the human personality, albeit all aspects that are in some manner measurable. Aspects of this nature can be many such as variability, conformity, difference in the rate of learning and development, mutual relationship between the various characteristics of the personality, etc. In this manner, various individuals exhibit differences of physical and mental development, nature, rate of learning, ability, specific abilities, interest and personality, etc.

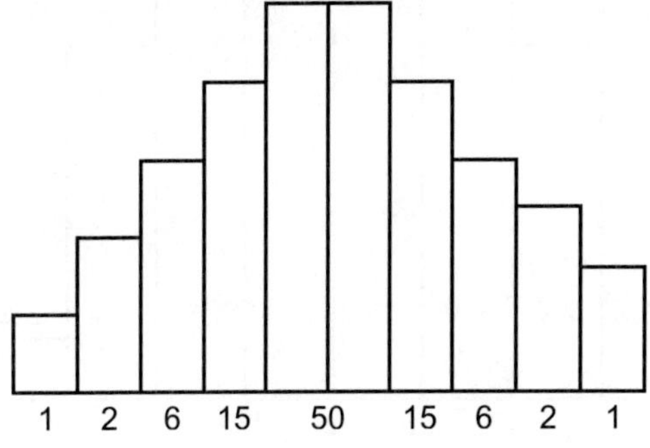

Fig. 12.1. Normal Probability Curve of Individual Differences

TYPES OF INDIVIDUAL DIFFERENCES

The following brief description may serve to make individual differences a simple concept that can easily be grasped:

1. Average intelligence Individuals are seen differing in considerable measure in respect of their general intelligence. It is not possible to send children with a higher intelligence quotient to go to school. Children with intelligence quotients between 50 and 70 can learn only the simplest tasks. Even the small schools trouble children whose intelligence quotient varies between 70 and 80. Children between 75 and 90 I.Q. are considered morons and they have considerable difficulty in progressing, along with the other children, in their learning. Generally, 40 to 60 per cent of the children in school have I.Q.s varying between 95 and 105, being the children with average intelligence who form the basis for the formulation of the syllabus and curriculum as well as the method of teaching.

Children who are either above or below this level of intelligence require special educational methods and conditions. Children with intelligence quotient varying between 115 and 120 are considered brilliant or intelligent. The following facts have come to light concerning individual differences of intelligence in children:

(a) However good and beneficial the environmental and the method of education, the moron invariably reaches his highest level of learning much later than an average or the intelligent child.

(b) In favourable circumstances, the average child generally gives a good account of himself in his academic pursuits.

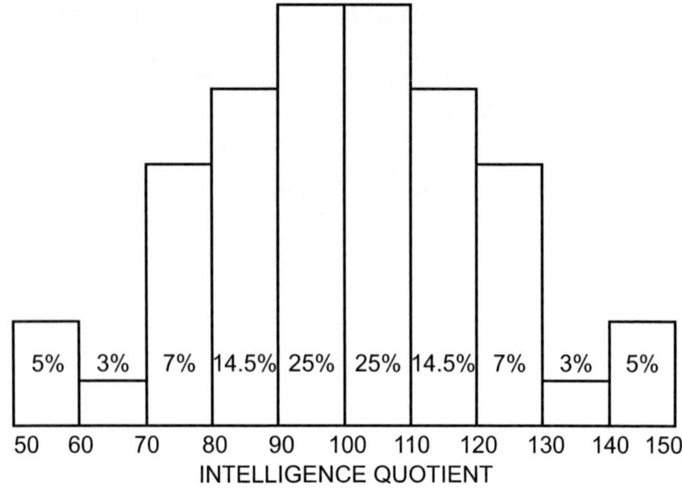

Fig. 12.2. Distribution of Intelligence in 3,184 Children

The height of the columns over each of the scores on the base-line indicates the number of children making a given score. (After J.P. Guilford, *General Psychology*, New York: D. Van Nostrand, 1939, p. 506; based on data from L.M. Terman and M.A. Merrill, *Measuring Human Intelligence*, Boston: Houghton Miffin, 1937.)

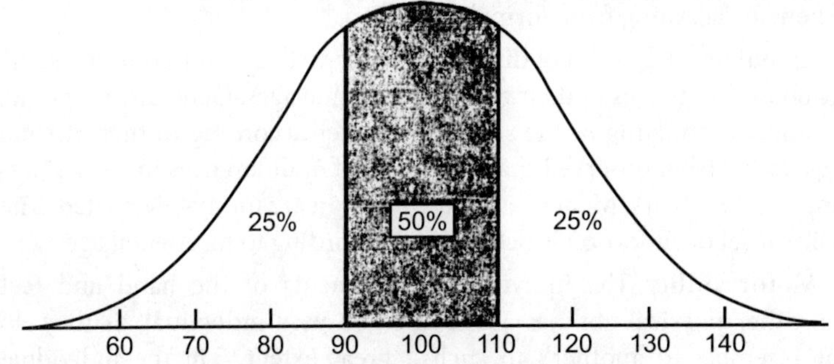

Fig. 12.3. Normal Distribution Curve

The height of the curve indicates the frequency with which the various scores shown on the base-line appear in population. Half of the people make scores which fall in a narrow band in the middle. The other two quarters make scores which are spread over a wider range, both above and below the middle band. If the middle half is divided into two quarters, the population is thereby divided into four groups of equal size.

(c) If the circumstances are favourable, the intelligent child shows great alacrity in the process of learning.

(d) Adverse circumstances have the worst effect on all children, and their learning activities are hindered.

2. Special abilities During the junior and senior high school as well as at the college stage, the individual differences in respect of special abilities, in addition to the general intelligence, are also important, since special professions and specialized fields of vocation all need certain specific abilities. Abilities of this kind are concerned with mental, artistic or motor ability.

3. Differences of background In school, the, differences that children exhibit are the outcome of their different families and their communities. Attitudes towards education and authority differ in each family, culture and class. Some of these attitudes are favourable while others are unfavourable to education. In either condition, the difference of attitudes results in differences among the children. Besides these attitudes, the child's emotional, social, aesthetic and moral development is influenced by his family and neighbourhood. Hence, differences of background are also manifested in individual differences.

4. Alacrity in learning Difference in the quickness or alacrity in learning is visible, not only in children of different ages, but also among children in the same age group. This difference is dependent upon their maturity and educational background. Differences in the alacrity of learning result in benefits accruing from formal education.

5. Mental age Children of different ages as well as children of the same age show differences in their respective mental ages. Generally speaking, all students studying in the same class differ according to their mental ages. It has been observed that at the age of 6, differences in mental age range up to 5 years. Mental age and education are intimately related. The child's level of education is determined according to his mental age.

6. Motor ability The individual's movements of the hand and feet and other physical abilities are seen to be very individual, as they do not resemble to another's to such a great extent. Till the individual attains adulthbod, his manual dexterity, rate of muscular movement and resistance to fatigue develop continually. In this manner, the same individual in different ages and different individuals in the same age group manifest considerable differences in manual dexterity.

7. Sex differences Makneimer and Terman discovered the following differences between men and women, on the basis of some studies :

(a) Women have greater skill in memory while men have greater motor ability.

(b) Female handwriting is superior while men excel in mathematical logic.

(c) Women show greater skill in making sensory distinctions of tastes, touch, smell, etc., while men show greater reaction and consciousness of size-weight illusion.

(d) Possessing greater linguistic ability, women are superior to men in languages, etc. On the other hand, men are superior in physics and chemistry.

(e) Women are better than men in mirror drawing. Faults of speech, etc., in men were found to be three times of such faults in women.

(f) Women are more susceptible to suggestion, while the colour-blind men are more than women.

(g) Young girls take interest in stories of love, fairy-tales, stories of the school and home and day dreaming, and show various levels in their play. On the other hand, boys take interest in stories of bravery, science, war and scouting, stories of games and sports, scouts stories and games of occupation and skill.

8. Racial differences Many scientific studies have indicated the presence of various kinds of differences between individuals of different races, although differences of environment are a normal factor in causing these differences. Karl Brigham has composed a list on the basis of differences in levels of intelligence among people who have migrated to United States from other countries.

On the basis of these average differences between the races, the mental age of a particular individual of a definite race cannot be calculated since this difference is based on the environment.

9. Nationality Many studies have led to the conclusion that individuals of different nations differ in respect of nature, physical and mental differences, interest and personality, etc. Such a difference is only natural since their culture and geographic environment are distinctive.

10. Economic situation Economic differences are seen causing differences in the children's interests, tendencies and character, etc.

11. Differences relating to learning In respect of learning, children manifest such differences as past experience and learning, ability in the use of various kinds of apparatus, rate of learning, interest in learning, etc.

12. Difference in respect of development Difference in development is in evidence not only in individuals of different age groups but also between individuals of the same age.

13. Difference of interests As has been pointed out, the difference in sex leads to a difference in interests. Similarly, factors such as family background, levels of development, differences of nationality and race, etc., cause differences of interests.

14. Personality Differences in respects of personality have led psychologists to make in-depth study, and on the basis of this study, individuals have been classified into many groups. Jung, for example, has divided individuals into three groups: (a) Introvert, (b) Extrovert, and (c) Ambivert. This is the psychological classification of people. Stephenson has divided human beings into two categories — preservator and non-preservator. In this division, people of the first group are very sensitive and susceptible to experience while people of the second group are not influenced by it quite to that extent. Cattell has put people into the Surgent and the Surgeless or Non-surgent classes. The former is similar to Jung's extrovert while the surgeless resembles his introvert individual. Terman has put people into nine classes according to their level of intelligence:

(a) Genius, (b) Near genius, (c) Very superior intelligence, (d) Superior, (e) Average, (f) Backward, (g) Feeble-minded, (h) Dull, (i) Idiot.

Thorndike has divided people into four categories on the basis of thinking: (a) Abstract thinkers, (b) Ideational thinkers, (c) Object thinkers, (d) Thinkers in whom sensory experience is predominant. These names indicate the peculiarities of thinking in these individuals.

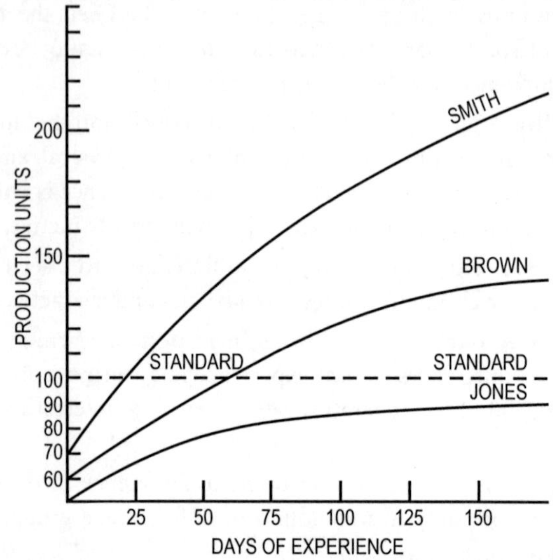

Fig. 12.4. Carves Showing Rates of Improvement with Experience

Although all people get profited by the job experience or training, some get profited more than others. The hypothetical curves of Jones, Brown and Smith differ in: (a) the points at which they begin, (b) the steepness of the progress, (c) the height at which the curve levels off to indicate the Ceiling of their progress and (d) the length of time over which improvement will occur. Smith is superior on all counts, but Jones will never reach 100 units. Since 100 is the production standard, this means that Jones will never be satisfactory.

Concerning these classifications of human personality, it should be remembered that although one specific person may exhibit the main broad characteristics of one class of personality, but the differences between various personalities are so subtle and minute that it is not scientifically feasible to divide them into classes.

CAUSES OF INDIVIDUAL DIFFERENCES

It is not even within the realm of possibility to describe all the causes of individual differences among the children, yet the main ones are the following:

1. Age It is a matter of common knowledge that age creates differences of intelligence, abilities, physical capacity and maturity, etc., in different children.

2 Physical development Differences in height, weight, physical structure, and the rate and quantity of development of the various parts of body lead to differences between the individuals.

3. Heredity It has now been established that hereditary differences result in the quantity arid rate of physical as well as mental development being different, in different individuals. Many physical as well as mental diseases are the result of heredity in persons. According to many scientists, a person inherits many mental peculiarities and abilities from his parents.

4. Environment or atmosphere Modern psychologists do not believe heredity to be the only cause of individual differences. Personality is the outcome of mutual interaction between heredity and environment. Hence the influence of heredity and gradual changes in a child's environment can be seen reflected by the changes in his personality. An individual exhibits good and bad qualities as accruing from a good or bad environment. Generally speaking, environment comprehends family, school, neighbourhood, society and culture. The child is open to a very wide range of influences such as the social and economic level, standard of living, education, profession of parents, their mutual relationships, their relations with their children, and their personalities, nature of other people's character, personality and attitudes, etc.

5. Effect of race and nation Although, modern psychologists believe that race does not lead to differences in the mental structure of individuals, yet it cannot be denied that individuals of different races exhibit very pronounced differences, even though, it may be induced by the environment. Similarly, individuals of different nations show differences in respect of their personality, character and mental abilities. These are the outcome of their geographical, social and cultural environment. Many scientific tests have established the existence of differences between Eastern and Western, Negro and American, Chinese and Japanese, English and Indian individuals.

6. Sex differences Although modern psychologists are not prepared to accept sex differences as the basis of differentiation between boys and girls, yet sex does lead to differences between individuals, even though the family, social and cultural environment may play a major part in it. Development of boys and girls exhibits difference in sex.

7. Intelligence and mental Age Many studies have indicated that many individuals differ because the differences of intelligence and mental age, and environment cannot be accepted to account for majority of such differences. Individuals who are well below the average of intelligence and mental age find much difficulty in learning and picking up easily.

8. Emotional stability Due to many physical, mental and environmental factors, the emotional stability of individuals is differently affected, and this leads to differences in their respective natures.

9. Temperament Medical men, and in particular Indians, believe that individuals have different temperaments. Some people are by temperament quick and short-tempered, while others are secretive, some active and others inactive.

10. Difference relating to learning Individuals differ from each other because of their attitude to learning, their zeal, rate of progress and transfer of training, etc.

11. Other causes In addition to the above causes, many other causes lead to differences among the individuals, *e.g.*, interest, attitudes, various sentiments of personality, communal circumstances, etc.

Value of Individual Differences in Industry

Individual differences have great importance in the field of industry. In an industry, different individuals with different qualities and abilities are required to perform various functions. If the work is to be of the best in quality and quantity, it is essential that each operation should be performed by the individuals best qualified to perform it. And the best person for a particular job can be located by testing individual differences through special tests. Any individual can be superior to others only when he is compared to them. How is such a comparison to be made? By studying the general distribution curve the superior can discover the kind of performance that can be expected from the average worker for a particular job. If, now, a particular individual gives a better performance than can be expected from the average worker for a particular job, he can be taken to be superior to average. On the other hand, an individual who shows result below the average can be classified as inferior. It is generally seen that the better qualified or able individuals do not put in all their time at work while the less able individuals continue to work for long hours without completing their assignments. And this can only be found by turning out the irresponsible worker and then finding out how many people are required to perform the same function that he was performing. Only then one can discover individual's level of efficiency. A job which can be performed only after many hours of labour by the inefficient worker, can be performed by the more able in a much shorter time, which is why he is seen roaming around and wasting his time. In fact, some people are so capable that the supervisor gets a headache in trying to keep them occupied. Such people become even more problematic when the work is measured in terms of time and not in quantity because then they are not inclined to produce more than the average, which takes them much less time than the average worker. Consequently, they loaf about, wasting their own time and that of the others.

Just as the exceptionally able proves to be a problem in industry, the less able worker is also a source of constant anxiety. When doing more work than they are capable of, they lower the quality of work. It is difficult to save them from accidents. Besides, they turn against the managers very often. Sometimes such inefficient individuals have an adverse influence upon the work of more efficient workers because then even the better worker reduces his own quality to suit theirs.

The importance of taking account of individual differences is evident from the above account. Many of the problems in industry have their origin in this difference between the individuals. The more efficient workers complete their task assignments within a short time and then roam around wasting the time of others. In offices, in particular, individuals of this kind can be seen sitting around at others' tables, taking tea or smoking cigarettes in the canteens, despite the fact that their daily assignments are invariably completed. Such behaviour hinders the working of the less efficient workers because the latter cannot achieve the same level of work despite complete application and dedication. Hence, the supervisor is forced to create work for efficient workers in order to keep them occupied but more often than not this work is also rapidly finished by them, after which they can again be seen roaming around. In such a situation, the able administrator must pay attention to the individual differences and divide the work according to the individual abilities. In the first place, he should conduct tests and find out the more appropriate function for each worker in the distribution cycle. This will help him to assign tasks according to the capacities of each worker and lead him to expect normal quality and quantity of production from each of them.

The importance of individual differences in the field of industry can be illustrated even better by the example given by Norman Meyer.

When a foreman in the telephone industry was asked about the production efficiency of the workers under him, he pointed out that six were above average and six below it. None of them was average. The above average individuals were installing four telephones a day while the below average workers were installing three. This report was obviously defective because half the workers cannot be above average. Besides, even among the six above average workers there might have been one or two who would be capable of installing more than four telephones a day. In the same way, one or two below average individuals must also have been installing less than three telephones a day. But this never occurred because whenever a worker failed to install three telephones he was either transferred or relieved of his job. But the most prominent fact was that, there was no individual who was installing between three and four telephones a day, implying the installation of 3-5 telephones per day. Hence, it became necessary to find out why all of them installed telephones only in round figures. Secondly, why were some of the individuals not taking interest in putting in more work? Thirdly, what was the foreman's behaviour towards those who failed to install three telephones? If the better workers were not giving optimum production merely in order to allow the less efficient workers to keep up with them, this fact was important and should have been noticed. It was also necessary to see the level of production below which a worker stood in danger of being thrown out of his job. This minimum level of acceptable production should never be of a kind so as to destroy the morale of other workers. To continue the above example, the installation of four telephones a day was essential because otherwise the workers were fired. Consequently, all the workers must necessarily have been worried about their security and many must have had to leave the job. In fact, industrial psychologists believe that it is improper, in any industry, to expect that all workers will provide the same level of production. Such a demand is in direct contradiction to facts. Since workers exhibit individual differences it is only natural to expect some to produce more than the average and others less than it. The sensible organiser is one who is not unnecessarily strict with the less efficient nor unnecessarily preoccupied with the more efficient. Actually, the average production does not suffer because the less efficient work of one is balanced by the more efficient work of another.

VALUE OF INDIVIDUAL DIFFERENCES IN VOCATIONAL GUIDANCE

Vocational guidance is the name given to the process of guiding an individual in his selection of a profession which will suit him. It is commonly accepted that every individual cannot perform every kind of task. Besides, different professions and different kinds of jobs require individuals with different aptitudes, qualities, personality, levels of intelligences, etc. Hence, the process of vocational guidance starts with the application of various tests for the measurement of the individual's intelligence, mental abilities, interests, aptitudes, physical development, qualities of personality, etc. Some jobs require mechanical ability while others require sociability or educational qualifications. Hence, to find the right man for the right job and right job for the right man, it is essential to test an individual to find out the qualities he possesses and the level of such qualities. For example, such professions as teaching, authorship, scientific research, legal practice, require a high degree of education, creative ability, power of reasoning and a high level of development. Only when a person possesses all these qualities that he can hope to find success in such professions. This happens because professions are categorised as mechanical, quantitative, scientific, creative, literary, social service oriented, etc., according to interests.

TESTS FOR MEASUREMENT

Now the most important question arises concerning the measurement of these individual differences. In recent times psychologists have constructed various kinds of psychological tests to measure these individual differences. Intelligence tests are used to discover differences in levels of intelligence. Differences in the subtle qualities of the personality are brought out into the open through personality tests. Specific tests have been devised to discover special abilities which may be latent. Mechanical tests are applied to test the mechanical aptitude of the individual. Interests are discovered through interest lists and scales. Various kinds of scales, such as rating scales, etc., are used to evaluate aptitudes.

In addition to the information being provided by the above-mentioned tests, individual differences are also exhibited through the diplomas and degrees that the individual acquires during the time he spends in colleges and universities. One of the best method of

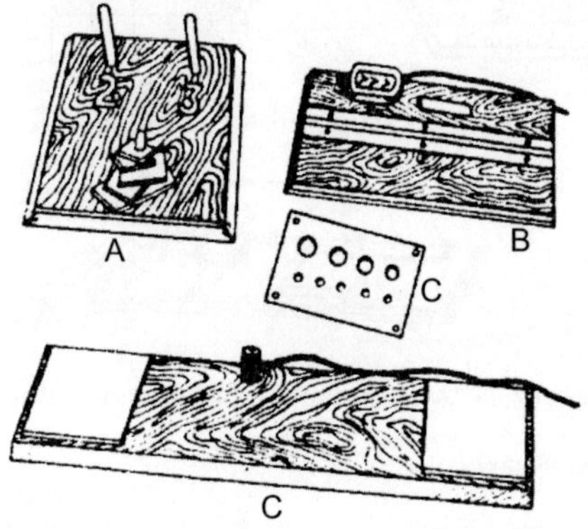

Fig. 12.5. Example of Aptitude Tests

understanding individual differences is to interview the individual because in an interview it is possible to come to important conclusions about the individual's personality, interests, aptitudes, intelligence and many other personal factors. For this reason, almost all industrial organisations insist on an interview despite the written applications which provide a complete bio-data of the applicant. But, if the interview is to be successfully used to discover individual differences, the person conducting it must have psychological insight. It is only if he has this insight, that he can expect to find out the desired facts from the answers he has obtained. Only a person with psychological insight can correctly interpret the implication of the other person's behaviour at the time of interview.

A. Pyramid puzzle The pyramid problem involves moving the blocks to a designated post without placing a larger block on a smaller one. Demonstrates problem-solving.

B. Steadiness tester Groove type. Calibrated. Sides are electrified to activate buzzer of the electric counter.

C. Steadines tester hole type. Conventional hole type with terminals for completing electric circuit to activate buzzer of counter.

D. Tapping board Stainless steel metal plates at each end; completes circuit when stylus contacts each successive plate.

(From equipment made by Lafayette Instrument Co.)

			2	A				
			3	B	7			
	3	1	2	C	1		2	
		2		D	2		3	
	2		1	E		1	7	
	3		7	F	1	3		2
		2		G	2	3	2	
	3		3	H		2		3

Fig. 12.6. Munsterbeg's Test of Motorman

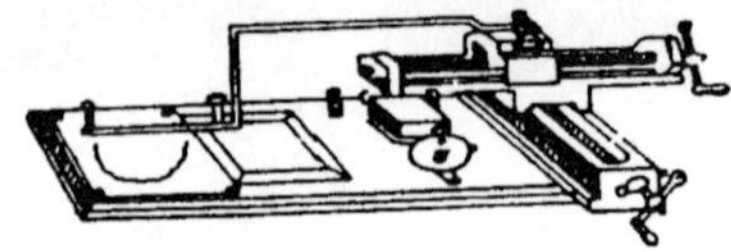

Fig. 12.7. Wiscounsin Tes of Engine-lathe Aptitude

Questions for Exercise

1. What are individual differences? Describe their kinds.
2. Give two tests for measurment of individual differences.

13

PSYCHOLOGICAL TESTING AND MEASUREMENT IN PERSONNEL SELECTION

Psychological tests have proved to possess great utility in many spheres. Briefly, the utility and importance of mental tests can be observed in the following spheres:

1. Guidance As has been indicated earlier, psychological tests are indispensable in all forms of guidance.

2. Appointments Psychological tests are nowadays resorted to for the appointment of appropriate individuals to posts in offices, factories and government service. It has the doubly beneficial effect of securing proper and desirable jobs for individuals according to their interests, inclinations, intelligence and abilities, as well as ensuring that the highest level of efficiency is achieved by the right man being in the right job. In this way, both the employed as well as the employer are benefited.

3. Selection for training An individual can be benefited from training for some particular job only if he is in possession of the requisite intelligence, abilities and qualities, besides the necessary interest in the work involved. It is evident that the individual should be tested in respect of these qualities before any training is imparted to him. Hence, in all advanced nations of the world, all kinds of training institutes make use of psychological tests for selecting the required candidates. In India, for example, the recruitment to the Police Training Colleges, the Government Teacher's Training Colleges, and other technical institutions is done only on the basis of psychological tests. In public schools, the students who receive scholarships are selected on the basis of psychological tests in order to ensure that the scholarships are not wasted, as they might be if they are provided to the wrong individuals. Psychological tests are further used for selection of candidates for the National Defence Academy in the country. Such use of psychological tests for the selection of personnel in training schools is constantly on the increase.

4. Classification according to the level of intelligence Nowadays, all educationists agree that the success of education depends upon the student being provided education of a kind that accords with his level of intelligence. Hence, individual students are classified and stratified according to their level of intelligence, and different curricular and extracurricular programmes devised for the three categories of students, the brilliant, the average and the retarded. The classification is based on intelligence tests. It is not only in the field of education but also in various vocations, armed forces and industries that intelligence tests are used to classify individuals so that they can be given the proper kind of work that is within their capacity to perform with reasonable success.

5. Prediction The term indicates the forecasting of success in the case of an individual. While guiding the individual, a psychologist can normally make fairly accurate predictions as to the degree of success that one is likely to achieve. The prediction is based upon psychological tests; the greater the capacity of a psychological test to assist in prediction, the greater is validity and its reliability.

6. Diagnosis Before giving any guidance, the directing psychologist makes a diagnosis of the problem present before him. He gives suggestions for alleviating a certain condition only after he has decided upon diagnosis, since it is only upon diagnosing some problem that he reaches the root causes. And psychological tests are essential for diagnosis; without them, a proper diagnosis cannot be achieved.

7. Research Psychological tests are of use even in the field of psychological research. Intelligence tests, inventories, personality tests, tests of mental abilities and personal qualities, help in research in these specific directions.

WHAT ARE MENTAL TESTS?

Importance of psychological tests is fairly evident from the preceding exposition of the subject. Before proceeding to a study of the various kinds of tests, it is essential to know the kinds of psychological tests that are in use, and the principal elements active in them. Defining psychological tests, Mursell writes, "A psychological test, then, is a pattern of stimuli selected and organised to elicit responses which will reveal certain psychological characteristics of the person who takes them."[1] In this way psychological tests are an organisation of some stimuli. These stimuli are selected with some special objectives in view. The object is to discover some psychological characteristics of the person being tested. Stimuli present in psychological tests are called test items, and they can be of several kinds — pictures, figures, wooden blocks, word groups, sentences and figures, etc. And the way in which these stimuli cover psychological characteristics will be evident from a description of each of them.

Psychological Tests and Experimentation

What should here be kept well in mind is that psychological tests differ from psychological experimentation although in both cases some stimuli are given, and it is the reaction to them that is examined. As has been pointed out, the object of psychological tests is to ascertain the psychological characteristics of the subject, while in the case of psychological experimentation, the object is more purely academic as they aim at discovering a mental process concerned with the particular experiment. In this manner, it is evident that while psychological tests lead to the discovery of abilities or capabilities, the psychological experiments discover and confirm various mental processes. Nevertheless, the difference between the two is very subtle, since nowadays, psychological tests are also being used for discovering and identifying mental processes.

CHARACTERISTICS OF A GOOD TEST

Good tests of psychological nature bear the following features:

1. Reliability The higher the degree of reliability that results of a test have, the greater is considered the reliability of the test itself. And the reliability of its conclusion means that if the same test is performed upon the same individual more than once, results obtained in each case should be the same or commensurate with the first one, if it is modified by changed circumstances.

2. Validity The validity of a test lies in the fact that it succeeds in testing the particular quality which it is designed to test. For example, intelligence tests can be valid only if they, in fact, test correctly the intelligence level of the individual.

3. Objectivity A test can achieve a high level of objectivity only if the answer to each of its various questions is distinct and precise and if there no difference of opinion regarding it among the various examiners. Its

---

1. Mursel, J.L, *Psychological Testing*, New York, p. 1.

efficacy lies in the fact that the conclusion or result is in no way influenced by the examiner's individual thoughts or opinions, so that the conclusions or results are obtained no matter what the number of examiners who examine the same subject.

4. Comprehensiveness Another feature of good test is its comprehensive nature. This feature is inclusive of all features or qualities allied to the one in question. It will provide information of qualities concerned with the one quality actually being tested. In this manner, in a comprehensive test, questions cover the quality in question as well as allied qualities so that no aspect to be measured or tested ability escapes attention.

5. Discriminating Power This applies to the ability which helps to distinguish between persons with greater or less ability so that they score more or less points or marks.

6. Utility This feature concerns the extent to which a particular test can be used with facility. And for this, it is essential that the questions asked should be simple, the method easy, the time involved less and the expenses negligible.

Of the above, mentioned characteristics, the most important are validity and reliability. Hence, both these qualities will be described in detail here.

CLASSIFICATION OF PSYCHOLOGICAL TESTS

Mental tests are of various kinds. They have been classified from various different standpoints. Classifications are as follows:

1. Classification according to method of testing Tests have been divided into two classes; in this case classification is based on the method involved.

(a) Individual tests These tests are administered to one individual at one time, as indicated by the term denoting them. They include performance tests. In addition to these, they also include tests that require linguistic ability. Some examples of these are Stanford-Binet intelligence test, Wechsler-Bellevue intelligence tests, Kohez's block design test. These are particularly appropriate for testing of individuals, but they are not financially suitable as they are expensive, in addition to requiring more expert training than in many other cases. Secondly, they are less objective than group tests.

(b) Group tests In this category, the tests included are performed upon a large number of people simultaneously. Some examples are the group intelligence tests of the Psychological Bureau of Uttar Pradesh, interest lists, vocational lists, etc. They are more objective and less expensive, requiring very little, if any, specialised training that may prove expensive. But in these tests, no real rapport between the subject and the examiner is established. Hence, they are less useful for solving problems of individuals, than are the individual tests. Nevertheless, they have proved really useful in the case of education and vocational guidance requirements.

2. Classification according to the medium of instruction In these tests, classification is based upon the medium of leaching of the subjects. The psychological tests, from this viewpoint, are divided into following two classes:

(a) Verbal tests This classification comprehends tests in which questions are orally asked, linguistic and concerned abilities being essentially required. One of the best examples of verbal tests is, Dr. Sohan Lal's intelligence test utilised at Uttar Pradesh Bureau of Psychology. These tests are not intended for and cannot be used in the case of illiterates, only slightly educated persons and small children, since such people lack linguistic ability.

(b) Non-verbal tests This classification substitutes figures, which do not require the use of language, but substitutes figures, pictures, blocks and, other implements for it. Examples of it are Pidgon's non-verbal tests and Raven's progressive matrices. Their particular felicity lies in the fact that they can be applied to the testing of illiterates, very slightly educated individuals and very young children. This category includes all non-verbal tests.

(c) Interest tests These tests help to discover the interest of the individual, some examples of which are Strong's Vocational Interest Blank, and Cudor's Vocational Inventory. Both of them are described in detail at a later stage. Besides these, the vocational interest list devised by the Bureau of Psychology, Uttar Pradesh, is also an effective test.

(d) Aptitude tests These tests are devised by combining the different tests of mental abilities.

(e) Personality tests These help to find out the individual's personality traits or characteristics. The main methods of personality testing are Rorschach's Ink Blot Test and T.A.T.

INTELLIGENCE TESTS

Historical Outline

As the new individual dissimilarities came to light, psychologists tried to measure the various individual differences, and to this end, different tests were evolved. Among these tests, those devised to measure intelligence achieved a lot of fame. Near the close of the 19th century, Galton developed some tests to measure the functions of the different organs. By these, Galton measured sensory discrimination, sensory perception and sensory acuity. Though, these measures are not directly related to intelligence, they may be accepted as the forerunners of intelligence tests.

In 1880, Ebbinghaus prepared several tests to measure the differences of intelligence in various individuals. In 1890, a famous American psychologist, Cattell, evolved some mental tests. On the basis of these, Cattell measured individual differences between some students of Columbia University, in respect of speed reactions, sensory acuity, memory and some other simple mental activities.

But, in fact, the first concrete step in the direction of intelligence tests was taken by a famous French psychologist Alfred Binet. Alfred Binet was conducting some research in the mental activities of school-going children. In the course of his research, he observed that, in order to give any useful education to the feeble-minded children, it is essential to put them in special classes. In order to investigate this subject, a committee headed by Binet was formed in 1904. The first difficulty concerning the study of feeble-minded children was need of a scale with which to measure the intelligence of children.

With Simon's assistance Binet developed and published a scale in 1905, what we know as the Binet-Simon Scale. In this scale, some 30 tasks, from the simplest to the most complex, were prescribed in a serial order. On the basis of experiments with the average and feeble-minded children carried out with the help of this scale, Binet and Simon determined norms by various age levels. According to the Binet-Simon intelligence tests, if a five-year old child is capable of performing tasks which an average child of three can perform, his mental age will be rated as three years and if that child fails to perform more than the first five among the thirty tasks he will be classed as idiot.

Binet and Simon made revisions in this scale from time to time. The first revised scale was published in 1980. From the success of this revision, psychologists of other countries developed intelligence tests suitable to the environment of their own countries. Among them, Hurt's London Revision and Terman's Standford Revision are well known. The modern revised edition was published in 1937 under the name of Terman-Merrill Scale.

In the Terman-Merrill Scale which was a revision of the Standford-Binet Scale, some more subjects, related to intelligence tests, were included. It now became useful for the age range of 2 to 18 years. In this scale, there were provisions for two types of two to four years. Many other subjects were included for the adult people. For every age group there were six to eight subjects. In this scale there are tests which enable the examiner to examine the intelligence of an individual in a very short span of time.

In Indian conditions, Binet's test was adopted for the first time by Dr. C. Herbert Rice. But its revised form is almost completely different from the Binet tests. These tests were compiled in Urdu and Punjabi. There are two types of scales in it, one having 10 tasks, the other 35 tasks, and it was the smaller scale of tests which proved dependable. In 1927, Dr. J. Munry of Christian College started verbal group tests in Urdu, English and Hindi. In 1933, Mr. Lajja Shankar developed group tests for children from 10 to 18, which adopted a revised and studied form of Terman's group tests. Besides these, the group tests started by Dr. Jalota of Lahore, in Hindi, Urdu and English proved to very valuable. In Bihar, under the direction of Dr. S.M. Mohsin, a test battery was constructed to measure mental abilities and intelligence of participants in many group tests. In the non-verbal group tests for college students, important contributions have come from Dr. Lalit Kumar Shah, C.T. Philip, H.C. Banerjee, D.H. Roy, T.P. Bhowimck and H.P. Maiti. The above description makes it quite clear that not much work has been done in the direction of non-verbal tests. There is a hope of development in this direction in future.

Types of Intelligence Tests

Intelligence tests are classified as follows according to the activities prescribed in them:

1. Verbal Tests.
2. Non-verbal Tests.

As the name itself suggests, verbal tests make use of language while the non-verbal include such activities which do not necessitate use of language. Both these types are suitable for individual as well as group tests. Consequently, verbal and non-verbal tests are further subdivided into two classes — individual and group. Thus, finally, there are four types of intelligence tests:

1. Verbal Individual Intelligence Tests
2. Non-verbal Individual Intelligence Tests
3. Verbal Group Intelligence Tests
4. Non-verbal Group Intelligence Tests

Verbal Individual Intelligence Tests

The very name of verbal individual intelligence tests suggests that these are intelligence tests given to individuals or in other words they are meant to test the intelligence of the individuals. Language finds adequate use in them. Binet-Simon tests and the various revisions are all included in this classification.

The State Bureau of Psychology of Uttar Pradesh has adopted a Hindi version of the Terman-Merrill Scale. This revision includes a variety of materials, from solid objects to difficult questions. The activity in the beginning is simple, like constructing a bridge or a tower of blocks or fitting an irregular wooden blocks in their proper places supplied to them. At the same time, at the end of the tests there are difficult questions which need considerable thinking. These tests are divided into several age groups. The higher groups use language and its use gradually declines with the age group. For example, the two years' group includes the following activities:

1. The form panel with three holes
2. Recognition of objects by name
3. Recognizing the organs of the body
4. Making a tower of blocks
5. Naming an object from its picture
6. Word-building

Non-verbal Individual Intelligence Tests

It is quite apparent from the above example that in verbal tests, the child's knowledge of language is more in demand, and therefore, the use of these tests is limited to students and literate persons. But these verbal tests cannot be used in the case of illiterate individuals as these tests involve an extensive use of language which fails as a medium to measure the individual differences between the illiterates. Consequently, illiterate individuals are tested with the help of non-verbal individual intelligence tests. The name itself indicates the nature of these tests. These tests involve the least possible use of the linguistic ability and are similarly almost unaffected by knowledge derived from books. An example of these non-verbal tests is the Performance Intelligence Tests.

Merrill-Palmer Block Building Test

One of the most important of performance tests for children is Merrill-Palmer Block Building Test. Besides Seguin Form Board, it includes block building test as well. In the figure given, a four-year old girl is making structure by means of blocks as demonstrated by the tester.

Fig. 13.1. Merrill-Palmer Block Building Test

Pintner-Paterson Performance Scale

An example of the performance intelligence tests is the Pintner-Paterson Performance Scale. It was evolved by Pintner and Paterson in 1917. In this scale there are 15 types of tests, of which 4 are form boards, 6 picture completion, memory span and the rest picture puzzles and imitations, etc.

Porteus Maze Test

Another example of the performance intelligence test is the Porteus Maze Test. In it, paper and pencil mazes are used. For his tests, Porteus created mazes for children from 3 to 14 years. It gets difficult, corresponding to the increase in age. The subject is allowed two chances and if he fails in

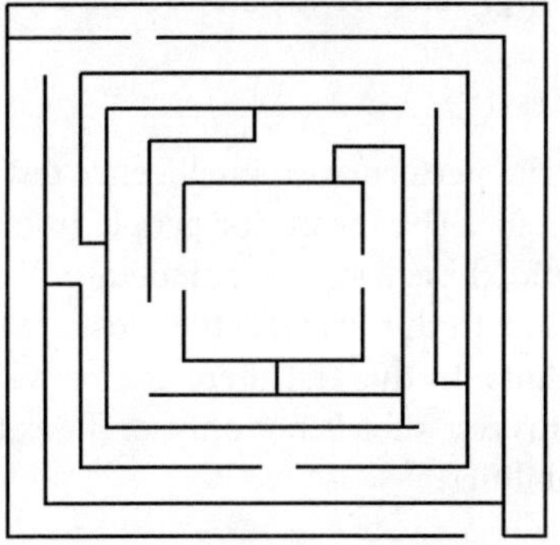

Fig. 13.2. Porteus Maze Test

the attempts then the conclusion is that his intelligence is not of that age level. Children of 12 to 14 years are given four opportunities. These tests designed by Porteus not only measure intelligence, but they also reflect the temperament of the individuals. It is distinguished from other tests as the Stanford-Binet test.

Form Board Test

A comparatively simple of the performance intelligence tests is the form board tests; among them the test of Seguin and Goddard deserve special mention. In the form board test, there are numerous blocks and a board in which there are holes corresponding to this block. The subject as shown has to fit the blocks in these corresponding holes in the board, the time taken and mistakes committed being noted from which the score of the test is calculated.

Fig. 13.3. Seguin Form Board

Wechsler-Bellevue Test

Another example of the performance intelligence tests is the Wechsler-Bellevue test, evolved in 1939, meant for people from 10 to 60 years of age. In a modern clinic, these tests are included in Binet class, as one of the most important one. In this way it is the most apt test for measuring the intelligence of adults. In this test there are five verbal tests and five performance tests. This test affords not only an index to mental abilities but also a profile of abilities.

Bhatia's Battery of Performance Tests

The description of performance intelligence tests is incomplete without reference to Bhatia's Battery of Performance Tests. It is the battery created by the former director of Uttar Pradesh State Bureau of Psychology,

Dr. Chandra Mohan Bhatia. It has the following five sub-tests :

1. Kohez block design test Ten items of test out of the Kohez block design test have been included in the battery. There is one card on every subject upon which is depicted a colour design. The subject or the examinee sees this design and makes a similar one out of the blocks. These designs become correspondingly more and more complex, having been simple at the start.

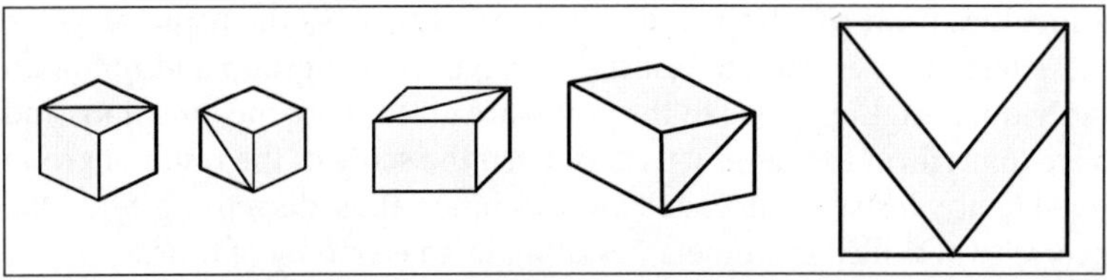

Fig. 13.4. Kohez Block Design Test

2. Alexander pass along test The Bhatia's battery also includes Alexander pass along test, in which, too, there are some designs. The subject shifts coloured pieces in an open box and places them into a similar design.

3. Pattern drawing test This test has been developed by Dr. Bhatia himself. In this there are eight cards on each of which there is a particular form. The subject draws a particular figure or pattern after seeing this form.

4. Immediate memory test Some digits are recited, which are immediately repeated by the subject; this activity throws some light on the immediate memory of the subject.

5. Picture construction test In this sub-test there are five subjects in which pictures relating to the rural life are fragmented into 2, 4, 6, 8 and 12 pieces respectively. At one time, piece of picture is placed before the subject, who puts them in order and constructs the picture.

Difficulties in the Individual Intelligence Tests

Some difficulties are faced in both the verbal and non-verbal types of individual intelligence tests. They are roughly as follows :

1. The difficulty of time The individual intelligence test takes an hour usually and only one person can be tested at one time. Obviously, at this rate it would be essential to have a very big number of trained examiners and in spite of that it would be difficult to test all the people.

2. Need for experienced examiners The second obstacle in the individual intelligence tests is the need of experienced examiners because the correct result cannot be arrived at if the examiners are inexperienced. At the same time, availability of such a large number of trained personnel is almost impossible.

Notwithstanding these difficulties, in some circumstances, the individual intelligence tests become unavoidable. This is because the level of accuracy reached by the individual intelligence tests, in the assessment of a person's intelligence, is beyond the reach of the group intelligence tests.

VERBAL GROUP INTELLIGENCE TESTS

The group intelligence tests owe their origin and development to the difficulties from which the individual tests suffer. As the name suggests, these tests are designed to test the intelligence of a group and not of an individual. All the people in the group are given the same directions and have to perform the same activities. Even the score of the result of group intelligence tests is calculated by machines thus dispensing with the necessity of skilled examiners, resulting in an economy of time.

Army Alpha and Beta Tests

An excellent example of group intelligence tests is afforded by the Army alpha and beta tests, which were evolved during the World War I in order to test the American soldiers. For example, it revealed separately the feeble-minded, men capable of becoming skilled specialists, men capable of becoming officers, men needing some training, etc.

Naval and Army General Classification Tests

Due to the success which attended these tests, some group tests for classification of naval or army soldiers were evolved during the World War II. Of these, two particular forms deserve mention. These two are: (1) Naval general classification tests and (2) Army general classification tests.

With the type of calculations made by Cruze, some one billion people were tested by the military general classification tests during the years 1941 to 1946. In these tests there are three subjects, *viz.*, those relating to vocabulary of counting blocks.

From the above example, it is quite clear that these verbal group intelligence tests examine the reasoning ability, ability of comparing and contrasting sense of directions, ability in numerals and language of the individuals who constitute the group. It is essential that the examiner should be fully acquainted with the test and he should also understand the corresponding directions. Thus, often the examiner examines himself to start with. At the same time, it is necessary for the examiner to have some knowledge of the mechanical aspects of the conditions of examination such as the proper seating arrangement of the examinees, the distribution of test blanks and the preparation of material related to the tests, like paper and pencil, etc.

Difficults in the Verbal Group Intelligence Tests

Even after taking in all the precautions, some difficulties are discernible in the verbal group intelligence tests which can be eliminated only by reverting to the individual intelligence tests. The difficulties of the verbal group tests are fundamentally as follows:

1. Difficulties related to co-operation in tests In these tests it is difficult to judge whether the examinee is extending his full co-operation or not.

2. Difficulties related to the balance of the subject In these tests it is difficult to determine whether file physical and emotioned balance of the examinee is even or disturbed.

3. Difficulty related to the ease of the subject In the verbal group intelligence tests, it is difficult to ascertain if the examinee is feeling at ease and free or restrained.

4. Possibility of cheating by the subject Another difficulty is to ensure if the examinee has written the answer himself or copied it from his neighbour.

In spite of the difficulties which arise in the verbal group intelligence tests, they have their own advantages due to which they are used comprehensively. As has been said before, these advantages are the same as the difficulties, of the individual intelligence tests.

NON-VERBAL GROUP INTELLIGENCE TESTS

As has been mentioned earlier, the verbal intelligence tests are meant only for the literates because of the requirement of linguistic ability. It is for this reason that the non-verbal group intelligence tests have been developed, the examinee making a minimum use of language but performing, instead, many activities. One example of the non-verbal intelligence tests is Cattell's Culture Free test, Raven's Progressive Matrices and the N.I.I.P. test. In these non-verbal group intelligence tests, the examiners have to explain to the examinees even the simplest directions which are also demonstrated as far as possible. All this is done to make the least possible use of language. There are some performance tests in these group intelligence tests, in which the examinee draws some simple figures, or performs some simple activities. Some psychologists do not give credence to these non-verbal tests in their role of measuring intelligence of the subjects, while, on the other hand, some psychologists consider them to be better than verbal tests. For example, in Alexander's opinion, "A complete performance battery will be a better measure than a complete verbal battery."

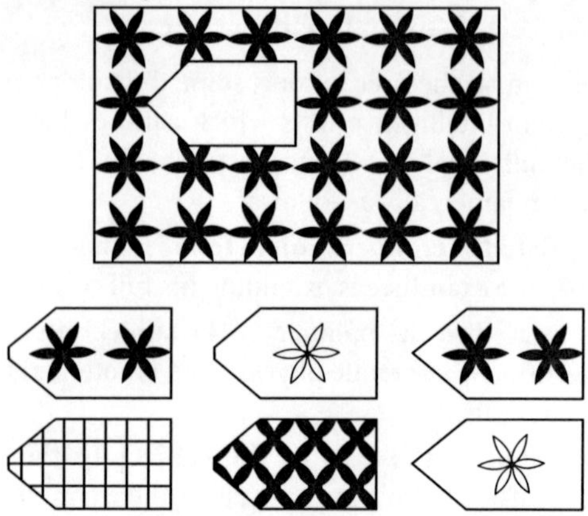

Fig. 13.5. Raven's Progressive Matrices

Characteristics of the Non-verbal Group Intelligence Tests

The truth is that even if non-verbal group intelligence tests are not more important than verbal tests, they are certainly not less important. Some of their characteristics are as follows:

1. Comparison of various human groups The first obstacle in the comparison of human groups of various languages and cultures is the difference in their language. This obstacle can be overcome by the non-verbal group intelligence tests and a comparison between different human groups is rendered possible.

2. The testing of illiterate workers The verbal group intelligence tests are manifestly inapplicable to illiterate workers for the testing of their intelligence. Consequently, the abilities of illiterate workers are assessed by employing the non-verbal group intelligence tests and the possibilities of learning are known.

3. Intelligence testing in children The linguistic ability is very low in the case of children and consequently the verbal group intelligence tests cannot be given to them.

MEASUREMENT OF PERSONALITY

Psychologists employ a number of methods to measure personality, *e.g.*, situation test, psychoanalytic tests and projective method, etc. Besides these, case history method, interview and questionnaire and rating methods have their own importance. Briefly, the methods of measuring personality are:

1. Case History Method
2. Interview Method
3. Questionnaire Method
4. Performance Method
5. Rating Method
6. Situation Test
7. Psycho-analytical Tests
8. Projection Techniques

Among the above-mentioned methods, the projection techniques are most popular. A brief description of other methods, before we make a detailed description of this specific one, would be quite in keeping with the context:

1. Case history method In the case history method, as the name obviously indicates, the facts concerning the life of the subject are collected. This case history supplies all the facts related to man's environment and heredity. This method can be employed to study both normal and abnormal personalities but it needs experienced testers.

2. Interview method The interview method is the most common of all the methods for the study of personality. It is the method widely used in the selection of people for government, semi-government and private services. In this, the subject and the tester sit facing each other and the former answers questions asked by the latter. Besides the answer which the subject offers, his personality is indicated by his expression. The method, like the case history method, needs very experienced testers, who ask questions which may probe the correct thing, and enable the subject to express himself without any apprehension. Thus the interview method depends as much on the tester as it does on the subject.

3. Questionnaire method Questionnaires have been used extensively in the investigation of personality. The name suggests that it is a list of selected questions, the answers to which throw light upon different traits of personality. 'Yes' and 'No' are written in front of these questions. The subject either strikes out the wrong answer or indicates the correct one. Questionnaires are used to gain knowledge of traits like self-confidence, sociability, introversion or extroversion, tendency to dominate or be dominated, etc.

There are some difficulties in the questionnaire method. It has the following limitations:

(a) Often the subjects conceal the fact and give wrong answers.
(b) Sometimes the framing of the questions is such that the tester takes them to mean one thing and the subject another.
(c) Usually the subjects write the answer without an adequate amount of thinking thus leaving possibility of mistakes.

Fig. 13.6. Minnesota Multiphasic Personality Inventory

In spite of these difficulties, the questionnaire method has proved to be of tremendous value. All port and Minnesota, etc., have formed questionnaires which help in the study of some subtle traits of personality. It affords a lot of assistance to comparative study because of various answers of the subjects to the same questions. The conclusions based on these questionnaires are comparative as well as numerical. They also facilitate wide study because a number of people can be studied simultaneously.

4. Performance method The performance method was developed by May and Hartshorne. In this method the subject is given a variety of specific jobs to be performed and the particular trait of his personality is examined. For example, in order to test the honesty of children, some weights with little difference between them, were presented to them. The exact weight of each was written under it and the children were told to place them in the correct order. The honest children were told to place them in the correct order. The honest children experienced great difficulty while the dishonest read the weights under them and placed them in order promptly. A very simple method of judging the honesty of the students in the class could be something like this. Some piece should be dictated and the copies collected and examined. The mistakes of each should be secretly noted without any markings on the copy, following which the copies should be returned with the direction that the mistakes are to be noted and marks allocated. The dictation should be written on the blackboard. The honest will mark their mistakes while the dishonest will quietly correct them. The honesty of the students can be judged by comparing these with the mistakes previously noted.

5. Rating method Another method of measuring personality is the rating method, in which the procedure is of two types: one, the subject is asked to answer questions related to traits of personality. The answers which the subject offers or selects exhibit his personality. Another way of applying the rating method is to place the subject in real situations and then study his behaviour and reactions. For example, in order to judge personality traits, a person is given a variety of jobs to perform.

The rating method is very simple. But it needs more skilful testers. Roughly speaking, it presents the following difficulties:

(a) Much skill and capability are essential in the tester.
(b) The possibility of prejudice is very great.
(c) It is very difficult to enumerate or evaluate the subtle traits. Mistakes are often made in this.

In spite of the above-mentioned difficulties, both social and industrial psychologists make much use of this method. As has been pointed out previously too, it can be made useful to a large extent if the tester is very skilful.

6. Situation test As usual, the name suggests the nature of the method. In it, the subject is placed in some specific situations and the traits of his personality are ascertained. Actually, it resembles the performance method, the difference lying in the fact that in this case the person is placed in a situation while in the performance method he is given some work to do.

7. Psychoanalytic method In the psychoanalytic method of measurement of personality, two types of tests are more popular — Free Association and Dream Analysis. Both these tests show the traits of the personality in its unconscious aspect. In dream analysis, the subject describes his dream and without using reasoning, associates freely the dream objects and activities. Because of the absence of reasoning, the truth of the unconscious mind is expressed by this association by which the psychoanalyst discovers many characteristics of personality. The psychoanalytic method is mostly used in discovering the personality traits and mental ailments of abnormal people. Its main condition lies in the need for a skilled and experienced psycho-analyst. Often, the psychoanalyst has to analyse his own mind in order to remove the possibility of any prejudice.

8. Projective techniques The most popular of all the methods for the investigation of personality is the projective method. Its name suggests the fact that it is founded upon the element of projection. The Taj Mahal, to take an example, is a marble building many people go to see. Different people find in it different things, in keeping with the peculiarities of their personalities. An emotional person sees it in the form of a formal symbol of emotions while to the person who gives importance to political and economic questions, it may be a symbol of exploitation. This is an example of a material object but it does make clear the fact that a human being does not see an object as it is but also projects the traits of his own personality upon it. Many peculiarities of the personality are investigated by an analysis of this projection and a comparison of it with the projections effected by others.

Two tests in the projective techniques are more widely used:

1. Rorschach Ink-blot Test.

2. Murray's Thematic Apperception Test, known in brief as T.A.T. They are extensively used in the investigation of personality. These will, therefore, be described briefly here.

1. Rorschach Ink-blot test This test was developed by the Swiss scientist Hermann Rorschach. He used ten original ink-blot cards which are still in use today. There is no picture made in these blots. Five of these are black, two black and red and the other three multicoloured. To investigate personality, they are exhibited before the subject one after the other and he is asked to describe everything he sees in the blot. These are shown for a definite interval of time. Then they are shown to the subject for a second time and he is asked to point out the location, of whatever he has seen, on the blot. In order to establish the meaning of the subject's reaction to the blots, the psychologist analyses the location, determining factors and the object. The analysis of the location serves to indicate whether the subject reacted to some particular spot on the blot or towards the blot as a whole. As a general rule, it is believed that the person who reacts more completely is more principled.

Fig. 13.7. Rorschach's Ink-Blot

The analysis of the determining factors is an attempt to find out whether the reaction of the subject is towards the shape of the blot or to the colour or motion in the blot. As to the object, the analysis shows whether the subject sees in it the figure of a man or an animal or anything else.

Besides the above analysis, facts like the time taken by the subject to react to the whole blot, the number of activities which he did and whether he did them normally or not, are also noted and observed. All these things tend to help in the analysis and investigation of the unconscious peculiarities of the subject.

The difficulty in the ink-blot test is that the description of the subject's reaction becomes quite subjective, which conceals to some extent the correct personality traits of the subject. But efforts are being made to make this test more objective.

2. Murray's Thematic Apperception test The founder of this test, Murray investigated the personality traits with the help of some pictures. These pictures are still considered to be standard. Observing these pictures, the subject, by projection, identifies himself with the characters in the picture. The pictures are presented one by one to the subject who has to compose a story on each of them within some fixed time period, say five minutes. He does not get time to think. Therefore the story expresses his natural desires, emotions, sentiments, etc. On the basis of these stories, the psychologist analyses the personality of the subject and uncovers his traits.

As in the Rorschach ink-blot test, there is some difficulty in Murray's thematic apperception test also, since the personality investigation done by it is not numerical but qualitative with possibility of mistakes. But there is no doubt that an experienced and skilful psychologist can use this method to uncover many hidden traits of the personality of the subject. This test helps in the discovery of many abnormalities of personality as well.

MEASUREMENT OF SPECIAL ABILITIES

Such problems as the profession an individual may adopt or the course of study a student may profitably pursue are ones that need guidance and for this guidance it is essential that in addition to measuring the individual's level of intelligence, his special abilities are investigated. Hence, efforts have been made to devise tests to discover special mental abilities and they are being extensively used.

Before going on to the testing of special mental abilities, it is necessary to know the age in which these tests can be suitably administered. This question arises for the simple reason that in childhood, these special abilities are not distinctly present and psychologists are not unanimous in their opinions regarding the age in which these abilities become distinct and separate. According to some, man's special mental abilities can be separately distinguished at the age of 11, while in the opinion of Cyril Burt, it is at 13 that these abilities become distinct. Generally, it is the former opinion that is accepted. Accordingly, all educational guidance is rendered at the age of 11 or thereabouts.

Number of Special Mental Abilities

Having determined the age at which the special mental abilities become distinct, it is now essential that their number also be determined. In feet, it is very difficult to determine the exact number of special abilities, and there is no unanimity of opinion on this question. In 1938 Thurston and his associates fixed the number of special fundamental abilities at seven, calling them Primary Mental Abilities — verbal abilities or V, numerical ability or N, reasoning or R, memory or M, word fluency or W, and spatial ability or S, and perceptual speed based on these mental abilities. Another test battery formed on the same principle is used in the American Psychological Corporation. It contains the following seven tests:

1. Verbal reasoning,
2. Numerical ability,
3. Abstract reasoning,
4. Space relation,
5. Mechanical reasoning,
6. Clerical speed and accuracy,
7. Language uses.

Now, we can go on to a slightly detailed account of some special abilities tests.

Thurston's S.R.A. Tests of Primary Mental Abilities

To repeat, Thurston has discovered the presence of seven fundamental mental abilities through his study. This conception of primary mental abilities wrought a great change in the field of guidance and counselling. Following this discovery, in the field of guidance even more importance began to be attached to these abilities, than to intelligence, since mental abilities of different individuals with similar levels of intelligence were found to differ at the extreme. On the other hand, people with the same mental abilities were found to have different levels of intelligence. In fact, the choice of a course of study to be taken up by a student or the choice of a profession by a person requires a test since success in these fields depends more upon innate as well as acquired ability than upon intelligence. Hence in England and America, many tests of mental abilities were evolved, and they were combined to from test batteries. Then, these test batteries were used extensively in the field of education and professions.

Thurston constructed three batteries of tests for special abilities for various children in the following three age divisions and used different test items in each of them:

(a) For children between 5 and 7 In the test battery for this division, he included, tests of verbal reasoning, spatial ability, speed of perceptual knowledge and tests of motor ability.

(b) For children between 7 and 11 Test battery for this classification includes tests of verbal ability, numerical ability, speed of logic and perceptual knowledge.

(c) For children between 11 and 17 Test battery for this division includes tests of verbal ability, numerical ability, word fluency, spatial ability and power of abstract reasoning.

TESTS FOR INDIVIDUAL ABILITIES

Test batteries devised by Thurston reveal the main mental abilities of children of different ages, but in addition to this, there are individual tests for separate mental abilities. It would be in keeping with the context to describe them also.

1. Spatial ability tests This reveals the person's spatial or form ability. One example of this is the N.I.I.P, form relation test devised by the National Institute of Industrial Psychology, London. It has been described earlier. The Psychological Bureau of Uttar Pradesh has been making use of it for quite some time; besides the Bureau has also formulated its own test for measuring spatial ability. Another example of such a test is the Minnesota Paper Form Board which includes 64 test items in which one has to combine various incomplete geometrical forms to complete the figures. In the Minnesota Spatial Relation Test, there are four tests of the form board. Both these tests have proved to be of immense value.

2. Mechanical ability tests Through these tests, the person's ability of handling mechanical devices is measured. For this, some laboratories use paper and pencil while others use mechanical took and objects.

One example of this is the Minnesota Mechanical Assembly test. In this there are three boxes that contain the various parts of some common mechanical device. In the test, these parts have to be put together to form the complete object. Other tests of mechanical ability that are famous are the Bennett Test of Mechanical Comprehension, and MacQuarrie Test for mechanical ability.

3. Motor dexterity tests In these tests, the motor ability of the hands and figures is measured. Examples of such tests are Bennett Hand Tool Dexterity Test, Purdue Peg Board, Steadiness Tester and O'Conor Tweezer Dexterity Test. Only the first two will be described here:

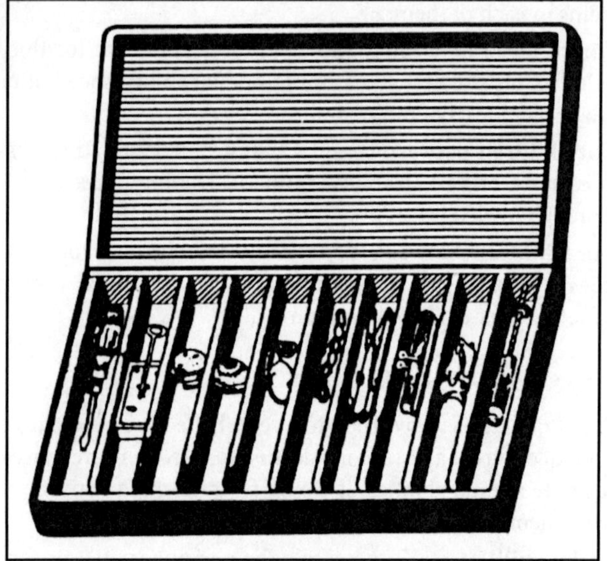

Fig. 13.8. Minnesota Mechanical Assembly Box

(a) ***Steadiness tester*:** This device examines the steadiness of the hand and the fingers. In this, there is a box on one side of which there are numerous holes arranged systematically so that they proceed from the widest to the smallest. The subject takes an instrument called the stylus into his hand and inserts it completely and draws it out, of these holes successively. If in doing so the stylus touches any of the walls of the hole, a bell rings. The test consists in the ability to prevent the stylus touching the wall while inserting it into the hole and drawing it out. The hole in which the bell rings is tried thrice by the subject. This test helps to discover the individual's dexterity with his hands and fingers and the extent to which he can handle minute instruments.

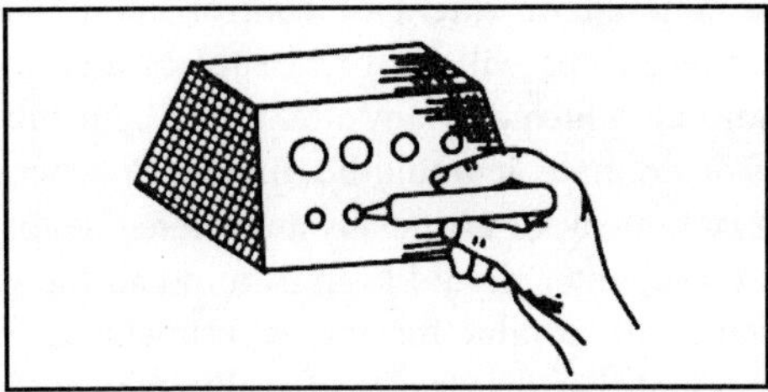

Fig. 13.9. Steadiness Tester

(b) ***O'Conor's Tweezer Dexterity test*****:** In this test, there are 100 small holes on a board, in rows of ten each. There are 100 pins placed by the side. The subject has to use a tweezer to place each of these pins in this board, one in each hole. He scores according to the time he takes to complete this task.

4. Clerical tests These tests measure the individual's ability concerning writing and composition. It is composed of tests in arithmetic, word groups, distinct reading and good writing, tests in direct knowledge, etc. One example of the clerical test is the Minnesota Clerical test which has two parts. In one part there are pairs of numbers, the correct pair having to be marked in which both numbers are given. In the other part, one has to point out pairs of names that are similar.

5. Artistic or aesthetic ability test In these, the individual's ability concerning art is tested. One example of this is the McAdory Art Test. Sea Shore Measure of Musical Talent measures the individual's ability in respect of music. Meier Art Judgement Test is another test of artistic and aesthetic ability. In this test there are 100 pairs of pictures. In every pair there is one original and the other copy, and the student has to select the original and its copy in respect of every pair. Success in this depends upon his aesthetic ability and acuity since the original has more beauty than the copy.

MEASUREMENT OF ATTITUDES

Difficulties in Measuring Attitudes

Attitudes contain many elements which are very difficult to measure. To take but one, the emotions and feelings involved in attitudes cannot be measured and hence attitudes can be measured only by internal systems. In this form, they do not admit of any measurement, but the individual's external behaviour is generated by inner tendencies. Hence, attitudes can be measured from the external behaviour. For the measurement of attitudes, it is necessary that the immediate circumstances be controlled.

The greater the amount or extent of control upon these immediate circumstances, the greater will be their success and their reliability. Hence, the conditions which defy any attempts at controlling them must be eliminated. For example, it would be difficult to generate communal attitudes in the laboratory, or artificially anywhere else. In a situation of this kind, the experimenter should keep in mind all these details of the actual circumstances in conducting the experiment upon the attitude. It is therefore evident that the degree of reality which can be obtained in the measurement of external behaviour cannot be expected in the measurement of attitudes, which in addition, do not offer the same degree of reliability. Yet it is too precipitate to conclude from this that no reliability at all can be expected in the measurement of attitudes. The accuracy of the measurement of attitudes can be tested by the capacity of prediction. The extent to which any measurement can forecast and predict the future conduct of any individual is accurate.

Limit to measurement of attitudes The following conclusions are to be drawn from the preceding discussion on the measurement of attitudes:

1. Attitudes can be measured only indirectly.
2. The greatest possible degree and extent of control should be levied upon the immediate circumstances in the measurement of attitudes.
3. In studying attitudes, the uncontrolled circumstances should be carefully studied.
4. The measurement of attitudes cannot be as reliable or accurate as the measurement of external behaviour.
5. The accuracy of the measurement of attitude can be judged from the accuracy of prediction of the individual's subsequent behaviour.

METHODS OF MEASURING ATTITUDES

Hence, the social psychologist has evolved various methods for the measurement of attitudes. The major ones are:

(a) Opinion Scales
(b) Rating Scales
(c) Indirect Scales.

(a) Option Scales

Opinion scales are methods of measuring attitude through the medium of opinions. That accounts for the name. Our attitudes towards some specific person or subject can be known by analysing our opinions concerning them. Hence psychologists evolve scales for discovering the opinions of individuals concerning different objects, problems and persons. These standards differ in respect of the method of their construction and kind. But the aim of every standard is to locate and determine the position of an individual upon a measure extending from one limit of acceptance to the other limit of refusal. We have had an occasion to point out before that it is not possible to measure attitude directly by means of any available standard. The opinion scales reveal the reactions of the individual towards some particular things, and from the reactions his attitude can be deduced. Obviously, the scale should be so devised as to throw the maximum possible light upon the attitudes of the individual. For this there should be, in the scales, a selection of statements which can efficiently give expression to the concurrence or otherwise of the attitude of the person.

Characteristics of an Adequate Scale

A scale which has any claims to adequacy in serving the purpose for which it is intended must possess the following characteristics:

1. **Reliability** The most prominent characteristic of the scale is its reliability. Reliability means that the scores obtained under two distinct but similar circumstances should not be too different. The more this quality is present in a scale, the greater will be its reliability.

2. **Exactness** Besides being reliable, the scale should also be accurate and exact. For this the scale should possess elements which can indicate the actual mental tendency of the person.

3. **Objectivity** The construction of the scale should be objective and relative to the subject matter. The choice of its various questions should not reflect and should not be influenced by the mental tendencies of the subjects or testers.

4. **Psychological quality** The scale can be a success only when the questions contained in it and the answers which are forthcoming to them have a psychological relation with the attitudes of the individual. The choice and selection of questions of this nature depend upon the capability of the person constructing the scale.

5. **Distinction in different items** In order to be exact, the questions, items, statements, etc., should be mutually distinct. If this is not so, the answers will also not be clear. This can lead to mistakes in the result.

Various scales Many forms of opinion scales are prevalent in social psychology, but the main among them are the following:

1. Thurston Scale Construction Method
2. Likert Scale Construction Method
3. Guttman Scale Construction Method

In addition to these methods, the Borgardus Scale, Rank Order Scale and Paired Comparison Scale are also important, but they are not described here due to lack of space.

1. Thurston Scale

Thurston and his colleagues constructed scales for the measurement of opinions and beliefs of human groups concerning such varied questions as war, the church, Negroes, capital punishment, birth control, etc., in 1929 and 1931.

Construction method The Thurston Scale Construction Method was constituted of the following items:

1. Collection of numerous simple opinions related to the question or object presented.
2. To determine the value of the scale for these opinions by some definite determinant. This evaluation leads to the elimination of controversial statements, leaving only statements concerning which all specialists are unanimous. Opinions extend between a negative and a positive limit.
3. To determine the median point for every statement according to the opinions of the specialist judges.
4. Finally, it is necessary to see whether the questions contained in the scale are in a definite order or not. The order of statements should be such that they proceed from maximum to minimum acceptance. For this, in the beginning of the scale, those questions are arranged concerning which all specialists are agreed while at the end questions concerning which all specialists are disagreed are arranged.

Precautions The following precautions are observed in the construction of the Thurston Scale Construction Method:

1. Every statement of the scale should be clearly worded.
2. The number of determining specialists should be large enough to indicate clearly the position which should be given to the opinion professed by the subject. For this, the number of judges is usually above hundred.
3. The scale should comprised only those statements concerning which the judges are unanimous. For this, every specialist places

all statements of maximum and minimum acceptability in eleven classes. If a particular statement is placed in the same class by each of the specialists, it should be definitely chosen. But if the statement is placed in a different class by each of the specialists, it should be rejected because it is controversial.

Examples One example of the Thurston Scale Construction Method is the scale constructed by Droba. It has 22 statements, and was constructed in 1930. This printed scale is given to an individual in order to find his attitude score. The statements which the individual finds correct, he marks them right. The median of the scale score of these statements shows the attitude of the person.

Some of the statements of Droba's scale are the following :

1. No country can gain prestige without national respect, and war is the only means by which national respect can be defended.
2. If war is declared we also should enlist.
3. It is right to start a war only if the weaker nation is protected.
4. War and peace are necessary for progress.
5. The most that we can expect is that war be partially destroyed.
6. Lack of respect for life on the part of people engaged in war results in a wave of crime.
7. Every nation should immediately disarm itself.

2. Likert Scale

In 1932, Likert constructed a scale which differed from the one given by Thurston. This scale aimed at discovering the attitudes of various human groups concerning imperialism, internationalism and Negroes.

Construction method. The following are the items in the Likert Scale Construction Method:

1. To construct many statements related to the object or a problem, the attitudes towards which are to be studied.
2. To show these statements to the subject and to get them classified into the following groups:

(Strongly approve)	(Undecided)	(Disapprove)	(Strongly disapprove)	(Approve)
5	4	3	2	1

3. To award points to the above classifications in the following manner:

(a) To find the correlation between the total score of the subject and the score of the statements individually.
(b) To exclude those statements which bear a negligible correlation to the total score.

3. Guttman Scale

In 1941, Guttman constructed a scale to measure and study the level of morale in American soldiers. Guttman's scale possesses the following main elements:

1. To determine whether any statement can be shown upon by the scale or not.
2. To prepare scalogram to test the consistency of any statements.
3. To vary the questions concerning the same problem in such a manner as to determine that the opinion of the subject is consistent.

Fastigner bitterly criticised Guttman's scale in 1947.

(b) Rating Scales

As was stated at the outset, the second method of measuring attitude, after the opinion scales, is that of rating scales. The special feature of the rating scale is that the attitudes are evaluated not on the basis of the opinions of the subjects but on the basis of the opinion and judgements of the experimenter himself.

Means of collecting data In the rating scale, the experimenter collects the data by following means:

1. Non-verbal behaviour, such as accepting or rejecting customs.
2. Verbal behaviour, such as expressing concurrence or objection.
3. Secondary expressive cues such as facial expression, etc.
4. Conical type interview.
5. Personal documents, such as autobiography, letters, diary, etc.
6. Projective techniques — such as ink-blot test.
7. Immediate experience, such as the emotions, thought, perception, imagination of the individual, etc.

From the above source, the experimenter gets enough data concerning the attitude. The speechless behaviour of the individual also provides a lot of information though of course precautions must be taken while interpreting it. Compared to speechless behaviour, the easier method of understanding attitude is that of conversation. In addition to conversation, various facial expressions and the fluctuations in the volume of sound are also good indicators of attitude. "It is a commonplace belief that what a man says may be less revealing than how he says it," say Krech and Crutchfield, with a happier choice of phrase. In this way, the manner of expressing an opinion may be more informative than the verbal expression itself. In a clinical interview, the subject can be made to respond to questions from which he would normally hesitate, but does so now under the belief that the answers are necessary for his treatment. Diary, essays, letters, poetry, story and other kinds of individual writings manifest the attitude of the individual. Among them, diary is of the greatest importance since it is the most personal. An autobiography also reveals the attitudes of the author. Projective techniques have also proved very useful in revealing attitudes. Two among them are: (a) Rorschach's Ink-blot Test, and (b) Murray's Thematic Apperception Test or T.A.T. In Rorschach's Ink-blot, the subject is given ten original cards with ink-blots on them and he is asked to describe what he sees on them. In Murrary's Thematic Apperception Test, the individual is presented ten original picture cards one after the another and is asked to write a story on each of them in short but indefinite period of time. In the projective techniques, the subjects, thoughts, perceptions, etc., of the individual also help in revealing his attitude to the experimenter.

Types of Rating Scales

Roughly, rating scales are of two kinds — relative and absolute. One example of the relative method is the Rank Order Scale, while one example of the absolute type is the Percentage of Population. It would be opportune to describe both of these scales briefly:

Rank order scale In this scale the experimenter gives to the individual's attitude, a position in the scale extending from the highest quality to the lowest quality. In examining the individual in the circumstances of the human group, his position, relatively to the position of others, is kept in view. In this way, in the Rank Order method, the individual is given a relative position in the population. In this method, a definite population is put to the test and then the opinions of one individual are examined. Now the examiner places the opinions of the individual on the scale, which shows the percentage of the population concurring with his opinions as well as the percentage differing from him. This also reveals the percentage of his opinions in which he leads the population and the percentage in which he is behind the population.

(c) Indirect Scales

The third method for the measurement of attitudes is that of the indirect scales. All the methods so far mentioned for the measurement of attitude suffer from the defect that the subject generally realizes that he is being examined and he therefore tries to conceal his real attitudes. Hence, psychologists have favoured the indirect scales for the measurement of attitudes, in which it cannot be guessed that tendencies are being examined. In 1938 Asch, Hertzman, and other scientists attempted to study attitudes by means of the indirect scales. With the help of signs they studied changes in opinions in industrial groups. Nowadays, many social psychologists are making efforts to study attitudes by indirect methods.

Importance of Measuring Interests

Knowledge of interests is important for the task of guidance. The task that an individual can perform with success and efficiency depends upon his interests, besides his intelligence and general abilities. In suggesting any particular course of study or subject, that an individual student should pursue, one must keep in mind his intelligence, his ability and also his interests. In this respect, whether the guidance be educational or vocational, it is essential for the guide to be aware of the interests of the individual whom he has undertaken to advise. Normally, most novices to the intricacies of psychology think that the only way of knowing a person's interests is to enquire them from him. People are normally seen asking each other as to their respective interests and inclinations or the task that suits them best. But science cannot rest satisfied with such inane and cursory enquiry. It requires that every element, with which it is required to deal, should be as objectively determined as possible. Hence, psychology has invented many tests whereby it discovers and measures interests.

Lists of Interests

The simplest and most prevalent test of interests is asking the individual himself. The subject is equipped with a long list of interests and he is required to pick out the vocations that interest him, the psychologist thereby coming to know what interests the subject, or at least, what the subject thinks is of interest to him. Of the many such lists that are in use, Margaret E. Hoppock's check-list of occupations is of particular importance and deserves mention.

Limitations of Interest Inventories

The above described inventories of interests do, to a certain extent, help in guiding an individual regarding his occupation, but these lists have some limitations that are natural to them, and which must be kept in mind in making use of them. Roughly speaking, they are subject to the following limitations:

1. Difficulty in collecting description of vocation As has been pointed out, vocational inventories or lists provide description of vocations. But it is manifestly difficult to collect a complete description of any vocation, that is a description of all activities undertaken in it, the natural abilities required for those functions and the interests required, and other equally nebulous details. Let alone any psychologist, probably even the people engaged in these professions themselves could not provide a detailed account of them.

2. Suspect responses The subject to be guided is not examined as to the various occupations, interests area and functions, but his reactions are enquired from him. Evidently, such material as yielded by him is not sufficiently scientific since the individual's responses are questionable, being always 'open to doubt. In addition to this problem, there is no way of ascertaining the accuracy and validity of the answers provided.

3. Variability of interests Interest inventories provide information concerning interests, but interest is no permanent part or trait of the individual's nature. Interests keep on varying. To maintain the individual's interests creates a problem since it is not reasonable to determine from his interests of the check-list the profession into which he should put himself. It is quite possible that his abilities may fit him for a particular profession in which he shows no interest at present but he may develop affection for it when he actually gets into it. It may grow on him, as they say. Of vocations, it is usually observed that one which did not interest the individual in the beginning later on interested him if he had persevered with it for some time. On the contrary, there are other vacillating individuals who profess the deepest interest in some profession so long as they have nothing to do with it, but once they have been in it, they change their minds and decide not to like it. Hence, these vocational lists or inventories are no foolproof or even provisionally reliable methods of determining a person's interest in a particular profession.

4. No relation of invariable concomitance between Interest and Success To forecast success on the basis of interest shown in the vocational preference lists is not scientific. That an individual is definitely interested in a particular profession is no guarantee that he will also succeed in it.

5. Classification of occupations is not scientific Another major fault in these inventories of occupations is that the classification by which the professions have been divided is not scientific. Truly speaking, no two occupations included in them are the same. Every profession has its own specific functions, its responsibilities and its specific qualities that lead to success, and such independent occupations number in hundreds if not thousands. To prepare a list of all these occupations, and then to include a detailed description of each, is a difficult task.

It is improper to conclude from the above description of the shortcomings of vocational preference list that they are completely worthless. In fact, interest itself is a subject in which the decisions reached cannot be expected to contain a high degree of objectivity. As a makeshift method, these interest inventories are important, but when putting them to use, it is essential that the above shortcomings be kept well in mind.

QUESTIONS FOR EXERCISE

1. Describe in brief the role of psychological testing in personnel selection.
2. Evaluate the significance of psychological testing in measuring fitness for work.
3. "The need for evaluating the potentialities of men is as great in business and industry as in any field of human activities." Discuss and evaluate the part played by psychological tests in solving the problem in industry.
4. What kinds of tests are needed for measuring individual differences in the field of industry?
5. Discuss and evaluate the part played by psychological tests in solving the problem of selection of personnel in industry.
6. What kinds of tests are needed for measuring individual differences in the field of industry?

14

PERSONNEL SELECTION TESTS AND INTERVIEWS

Testing is the most vital technique of selection gaining significance in recent years. As it is difficult for the organisations to evaluate the candidate's performance only on the basis of application blank and/or interviews, selection tests help the management in evaluating the candidate's suitability to the job. According to Dale S. Beach these tests are also called psychological tests because psychologists have contributed a lot in developing these tests. Edwin B. Flippo defines selection test as an instrument designed to measure the nature and degree of one's psychological potentialities, based on psychological factors, essential to perform a given job efficiently. Their purpose is to help in judging the ability of a candidate in a given job-situation. According to Daniel Golman, the tests are useful in selection, placement, promotions, performance appraisal and potential appraisal, help in ranking candidates and are valuable in determining subsequent success on the job. Monappa and Saiyadain write, "Psychological tests are an objective and standardised measure of a sample of behaviour".

GUIDELINES TO TESTING

Dale S. Beach has suggested the following guidelines for the employment tests:

1. Tests should be in addition to other selection techniques as entire tests can only provide information about a part of total behaviour of candidate.
2. Test information should be taken into consideration to find out candidate's weaknesses rather than strength (as tests are more accurate at predicting failures than success).

3. Tests are helpful in picking a most likely successful group from a larger group rather than successful individuals.
4. A test should be conducted in one's own organisation as "a valid test is one that measures what it is supposed to measure".
5. Tests can be held only in case of failure of other selection devices in providing satisfactory information.
6. Test administrators should not heavily depend upon test score in making-decisions regarding selection of a candidate.
7. As relationship between test score and job success is not always linear, decision-makers should use the test score judiciously.

STEPS IN TESTING

1. Job analysis It provides basic information about the type of the candidate needed by the organisation. Job analysis includes job specialisation and employee specification. Job specification and job requirements provide information about the demands made by a job on the incumbent. Employees specification provides the information about the characteristics, qualities, behaviour of the employee needed to perform a job successfully. It is the basis to decide upon a particular test or tests. It provides minimum acceptable score required to test whether the candidate possesses the required amount and degree of behaviour and qualities like intelligence, aptitude to perform the job successfully.

2. Reliability After identifying the test(s), the administrator should ensure the reliability of test/instrument. It refers to the level of consistency of score or results obtained throughout a series of measurements. The test is reliable if a person obtains same or similar score in the tests conducted in first, second and third time, under the same conditions. The reliability of any selection technique/test means its freedom from systematic errors of measurement or its consistency under different conditions. If the score differs considerably in first, second and third measurements, a test is unreliable. The causes of low reliability are: conducting the test under non-standardised conditions, administering the test by different persons and under different psychological states of candidate, existence of factor of luck and ill-luck, etc.

As suggested by Beach, the reliability coefficient should be between +0.85 and +1.00. Higher reliability can be obtained from written tests.

3. Validity A selection device aims at finding out whether a candidate possesses the skills or talents required by a particular job. Each selection test aims at finding out whether a candidate possesses that particular skill/

talent. For example, intelligence test aims at testing whether a particular candidate possesses the nature and level of intelligence essential to perform a job. An intelligence test effective in measuring the level of intelligence is a valid one. According to Dale S. Beach, "The validity of a test is the degree to which it measures what it is intended to measure". A valid test accurately predicts the level of success or failure of a candidate on the job. According to Dale S. Beach, there are five kinds of validity *viz.,* concurrent validity, predictive validity, content validity, construct validity and face validity.

4. Personnel Programme Now the personnel manager has to develop a testing programme with the following steps:

(i) Formulation of the objectives of testing programme.
(ii) Analysis of jobs to identify those characteristics that appear necessary for job success.
(iii) Making of a tentative choice of tests for a try-out.
(iv) Administering of those tests to an experimental group of people.
(v) Establishing of criteria for job success.
(vi) Analysis of results and making of decisions regarding test application.

TYPES OF SELECTION TESTS

1. Aptitude Tests

(a) Intelligence test
(b) Mechanical aptitude
(c) Clerical aptitude tests

2. Achievement Tests

(a) Job knowledge test
(b) Work sample test

3. Situational Tests

(a) Group discussion
(b) In-basket

4. Interest Test

5. Personality Tests

(a) Objective tests
(b) Projective tests

1. Aptitude test Aptitude tests measure whether an individual has the capacity or latent ability to learn a given job. Aptitudes can be divided into general and mental ability or intelligence and specific aptitudes, such as mechanical, clerical, manipulative capacity, etc.

(i) ***Intelligence test:*** Intelligence tests measure intelligence quotient (IQ) of a candidate. IQ is the capacity for comprehension, reasoning, word fluency, verbal comprehension, numbers, memory and space, etc. Other factors such as both forward and backward digit spans, information known, comprehension, vocabulary, picture-arrangement and object assembly are also included in intelligence.

Intelligence tests are verbal and non-verbal meant for literate and illiterate employees respectively.

(ii) ***Mechanical aptitude test:*** Measuring the capacities of spatial visualisation, perceptual speed and knowledge of mechanical matter, these tests are useful for selecting apprentices, skilled, mechanical employees, technicians, etc.

(iii) ***Psychomotor test:*** Measuring abilities like manual dexterity, motor ability and eye-hand coordination of candidates, these tests are useful to select semi-skilled workers and workers for repetitive operations like packing, watch assembly, etc.

(iv) ***Clerical aptitude test:*** Measuring specific capacities involved in office work, items of these tests include spelling, computation, comprehension, copying, word measuring, etc.

2. Achievement test Conducted when applicants claim to know something, these tests are more useful to measure the value of specific achievement, when an organisation wishes to employ experienced candidates. These tests are classified into:

(i) ***Job knowledge test*****:** It tests a candidate in the knowledge of a particular job. For example, if a junior foreman applies for the job of a senior foreman, he may be tested in job knowledge, where he is asked questions about the job for which he has applied.

(ii) ***Work sample test*****:** In this test, a portion of the actual work is given to the candidate, and the candidate is asked to do it. If candidate applies for a post of mechanic, he may be asked to operate specific machine as a work sample test. Thus the candidate's achievement is tested regarding his knowledge about the job and actual work experience.

3. Situational test It evaluates a candidate in a similar real life situation. The candidate is asked either to cope with the situation or solve critical situations of the job. Situation tests are of two types:

(i) ***Group discussion:*** It is administered through group discussion. This test needs to solve a problem under which candidates are observed in the areas of initiating, leading, proposing valuable ideas, conciliating skills, oral communicating skills, coordinating and concluding skills.

(ii) In-basket: In situational test administered through in-basket, the candidate is supplied with actual letters, telephone and telegraphic message, reports and requirements by various officers of the organisation along with adequate information about the job and organisation. The candidate is asked to take decisions on various items based on the in-basket information regarding requirements in the memoranda.

4. Interest test Consisting of inventories of the likes and dislikes of candidates in relation to work, job, occupations, hobbies and recreational activities, this test seeks to find out whether a candidate is interested or disinterested in the job for which he/she is a candidate and in which area of the job range/occupation is he/she interested. The assumption of this test is that there is a high correlation between the interest of a candidate in a job and job success. Interest inventories may not fluctuate after the age of 30.

5. Personality test To discover clues to an individual's value system, his emotional reactions and maturity and characteristic mood, these tests probe deeply traits like self-confidence, tact, emotional control, optimism, decisiveness, sociability, conformity, objectivity, patience, fear, distrust, initiative, judgement, dominance or submission, impulsiveness, sympathy, integrity and stability.

- **(i)** ***Objective test:*** Most personality tests are objective tests suitable for group testing and can be scored objectively.
- **(ii)** ***Projective test:*** Under these tests candidates are asked to project their own interpretation of certain standard stimulus situations, basing on ambiguous pictures, figures, etc.

Personality tests can be faked by sophisticated candidates. Most candidates give socially acceptable answers.

DEVELOPING A TESTING PROGRAMME

As the most valid test for a particular job may be quite unreliable for another job, the suitability of a candidate for a job cannot be judged on the basis of a single test. A group or battery of tests alone can give useful results to judge the suitability of a candidate. Rather than an individual specialist, a team of specialists like technical specialist, industrial psychologist, personnel psychologist, etc. can develop and administer a test more successfully.

PRECAUTIONS IN USING TESTS

Certain precautions should be taken in using tests in different areas. These areas are: human relations aspects, operational suggestions and uses of test scores.

1. Preserving privacy Some people, particularly deprived people, do not want to reveal all about themselves. This is more so because of their caste, community, economic background etc. This category of people may feel that tests discriminate them against forward classes. Such people fear and suspect the test secrecy and validity. It affects privacy. The test administrator should take steps to reduce the fear and to maintain fair human relations so as to infuse confidence into the applicants.

2. Operational precaution Without pre-testing, same tests should not be used even for the same job in the same organisation again and again. Tests should be pre-tested on experimental basis. Sufficient time and resources should be provided for designing, developing, testing for validity and reliability, and administering a test or a battery of tests.

3. Care in use Much care should be taken in deciding upon cut-off score which would be the lowest score beyond which a candidate is totally misfit. Correlation figures should be properly interpreted and used with much care. A team of specialists should design, develop and administer the tests. Tests should be used to find solutions to the problems of selection, placement, performance and potential appraisals, training, development, accidents, operational problems, etc.

WHAT IS SELECTION INTERVIEW?

According to William L. Donoghy, studies indicates that over 90 per cent of selection decisions involve interviews. Though they may not resort to any one or all other selection techniques, almost all the organisations, big or small, in organised and unorganised sectors, managed on traditional or modern lines, adopt interview technique. Interview measures all relevant traits and factors. It integrates all necessary information about the candidates, collected through various means. Its scope is wider than any other selection technique. Dale S. Beach has defined interview as "a conversation or verbal interaction, normally between two people, for a particular purpose". It is an open exchange between persons of unequal status for a mutually agreed upon position. It may also take place between a person and group of people and between two groups of people.

Objectives of Selection Interview

1. To collect accurate and essential information about the candidates;
2. To provide the candidates with the facts of the job and the organisation;
3. To establish a rapport with the prospective employees;
4. To sell the company at a premium to the candidates;
5. To judge and evaluate the suitability of the candidate to the job, based on job and organisational requirements;
6. To see the inner view and feeling of the candidates.

Types of Interviews

1. **Selection interviews** These are for selecting the most suitable candidate for a job;
2. **Appraisal interviews** These are for appraising the performance of a subordinate by superior;
3. **Sales interviews** These are for convincing a customer by a salesman.
4. **Counselling interviews** These are for counselling the employees regarding their family, personal and career problems by the Personnel Manager.
5. **Grievance interview/disciplinary interviews** These are interviews discussing and enquiring about the grievance or a disciplinary case.
6. **Data collection interviews** These interviews seek collection of data and information for a research study.

Types of Selection Interview

Various types of selection interviews are adopted to solicit different kinds of information and to measure the candidates, skills, knowledge, etc., at different planes. Selection interviews can be divided into preliminary interview, core interview and decision-making interview:

1. Preliminary interview An exchange of basic information between the candidate and the Personnel Manager about the job and organisation. Like job nature, salary, working conditions, benefits, etc., it is helpful to the organisation to weed out unwanted hands and to the candidate to select or reject the job. When the exchange of information between the candidate and the organisation is not true, it may prove to be unsatisfactory. This interview may generally be informal and unstructured:

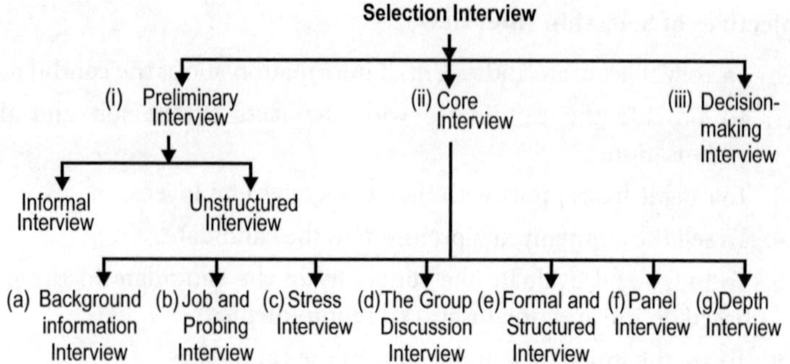

Chart 14.1 Types of Selection Interview

(i) Informal interview: Informal interview can be conducted at any place by any person to secure the basic and non-job related information. It is the interaction between the candidate and the Personnel Manager when the former meets the latter to enquire about the vacancies or additional particulars in connection with the employment advertisement.

(ii) Unstructured interview: In unstructured interview the candidate is given the freedom to tell about himself by revealing his knowledge on various items/areas, his background, expectations, interests, etc. On the other hand, the interviewer provides information on various items required by the candidate.

2. Core interview An interaction between the candidate and the line executive or experts on various areas of job knowledge, skill, talent, etc. This interview may take the following forms:

(i) Background information interview: This interview is intended to collect the information which is not available in the application blank and to check information provided in the application blank, it is regarding education, place of domicile, family, health, interests, hobbies, likes, dislikes, extracurricular activities of the applicant.

(ii) Job and probing interview: It aims at testing the candidate's job knowledge about duties, activities, methods of doing the job, critical/problematic areas, methods of handling those areas, etc.

(iii) Stress interview: It seeks to test the candidate's job behaviour and level of withstanding during the period of stress and strain. It puts the candidate under stress and strain by interrupting him from answering, criticising his opinions, asking questions pertaining to unrelated areas, keeping silent for unduly long period after he has finished speaking, etc. Stress during the middle portion of the interview gives effective results.

Stress interview should be handled with utmost care and skill. It is often invalid, as the interviewee's need for a job, his previous experience in such type of interviews may inhibit his actual behaviour under such situations.

(iv) *Group discussion interview:* Group interview method and discussion interview method are two methods of conducting group discussion interviews.

(a) *Group interview:* Under group interview, all the candidates are brought into interview room and are interviewed one by one. It helps busy executives to save valuable time. It gives a fair account of the objectivity of the interview to the candidates.

(b) *Discussion interview:* Under the discussion interview, a simple topic is given for discussion to the candidates who assemble in a room and are asked to discuss the topic in detail. Discussion interview helps the interviewer in appraising, certain skills of the candidates like initiative, interpersonal skills, dynamism, presentation, leading, comprehension, collaboration, etc.

Because of its informality and flexibility interviewees are at ease in this category of interview However, it may fail to cover some significant portions of the candidates' background and skills.

(v) *Formal and structured interview*: In formal interview, all the formalities and procedures like fixing the value, time, panel of interviewers, opening and closing, intimating the candidates officially, etc., are strictly followed. Depending on job requirements, the course of the interview is preplanned and structured in advance. The questions/ items for discussion are structured. Experts are allotted different areas and questions to be asked. There is very little room for the interviewers to deviate from the questions prepared in advanced.

(vi) *Panel interview:* Owing to lack of knowledge and competence in multiple disciplines and areas, one person may not be effective in judging the candidates in different areas/skills. Therefore, most organisations invite a panel of experts, specialised in different areas, fields and disciplines, to interview candidates. The panel interviews each candidate, judges his performance individually and prepares a consolidated judgement based on each expert's judgement and weightage of each factor. Known as panel interview, this type of interview is more effective as each candidate is appraised by an expert in relevant areas. Experts should not try to achieve over accuracy, excessive weightage to a particular factor and domination of other experts, etc.

(vii) *Depth interview*: In depth interview, the candidates are examined by experts in that particular field in core areas of knowledge and skills of the job by posing relevant questions in order to extract critical answers initiating discussions regarding critical areas of the job and asking the candidates to explain even minute operations of the job performance.

3. Decision-making interview Now the head of the department/ section concerned interviews the candidates once again, mostly through informal discussion. He examines the interest of the candidate in the job and organisation, his reaction and adaptability to the working conditions and his career planning, promotional opportunities, work adjustment and allotment, etc. The Personnel Manager interviews the candidates to find out his expectations acceptance of salary, allowances, benefits, promotions, opportunities, etc. After exchanging their views, the head of the department and the Personnel Manager jointly inform their decision to the chairman of the interview board, who finally takes the decision about the candidates performance and their ranks in the

INTERVIEW PROCESS

Interview is a process consisting of several steps. The major steps are grouped into four categories shown in Chart 14.2.

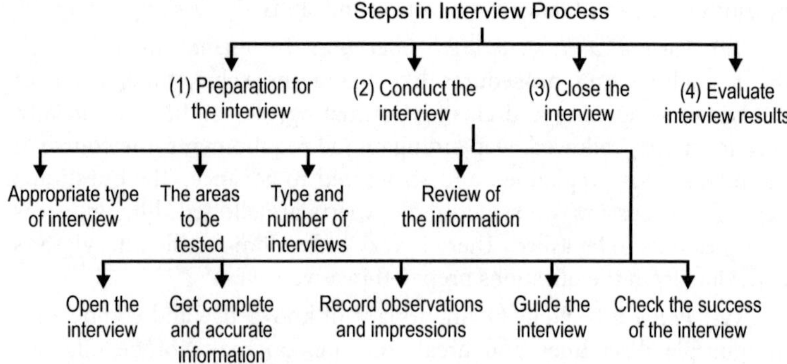

Chart 14.2. Steps in Interview

1. Preparation for the interview Advance preparation for interview focuses its coverage on the vital aspects and helps the interviewer to remember and absorb many impressions and facts. Before starting an interview the following preparations have to be made by the organisation:

(i) ***Appropriate type:*** Choose the appropriate types of interviews based on job requirements and the nature of the interviews discussed earlier.

(ii) ***Areas to be tested*:** Identify the knowledge, skill areas to be examined through interviews based on job requirements.

(iii) ***Types and number of interviewers:*** Interviewers should be selected on the basis of personal characteristics, technical competence, initiative, common sense, general smartness, ability to inspire confidence, capacity to work in a team and potential for growth.

Interviewers may be drawn from personnel specialists, line managers, experts in the discipline concerned, academicians, practitioners and psychologists.

Research studies and observations by Milton M. Mandell regarding the effectiveness of psychologist conclude that:

(a) As in case of other specialists, there is a wide variation in the abilities of psychologists;

(b) If he has got knowledge of job requirements and organisational interests, the psychologist would be a competent interviewer;

(c) If he is qualified, experienced and trained, psychologist's ability as an interviewer is higher than non-psychologists;

(d) Rather than a deciding factor, psychologists would act as an additional source of information.

Therefore, psychologists may also be included among interviewers.

Interviewers may interview the candidates either jointly or separately, but a panel interview is preferable to individual interview. The number of interviewers should be decided on the basis of number and nature of areas to be covered by the interview, number of candidates to be interviewed and the time available for interviewing.

(iv) Review of the information: Collected in advance through other selection methods, finding out the validity of those methods, the scores obtained etc., thc information available in the application blank is thoroughly checked. It is as follows:

(a) Accuracy and validity.

(b) Acquainting about the applicant.

(c) Finding out stability, reviewing the number of positions and length of time held in each of the past jobs.

(d) Comparing the nature of positions in the previous employment with that of proposed employment.

(e) Checking the employee growth with the organisational progression in the past employment.

(f) Finding out discharges, etc., through unexplained breaks.

This helps in avoiding further evaluation of those areas appraised effectively by other means through interviews.

(v) *Decision:* Decide upon the administrative arrangements,

(vi) *Finalisation*: Finalise the physical setting including time convenient to interviewees and interviewers.

(vii) *Determining the coverage of the interview*: Generally the interview should cover the areas like relevance of qualifications and experience to job requirements, gaps in employment history and causes, reasons for choosing course, school, occupation, etc., likes and dislikes, sense of humour, quickness of reaction, ability to recognise thoughts, manner and poise, cultural level, etc.

(viii) Finding out the conditions under which the interview technique is effective. This includes:

(a) Consistency in the results of various selection techniques.

(b) Using the interview technique to test the candidate in those areas where other techniques are ineffective.

(c) The purpose of the interview is to find out the most suitable position to the applicant.

2. Conduct the interview The next major step in the interview process is conducting the interview. As it is difficult, most of the line managers avoid this task. In the process of conducting interview, the interviewers should take much care because there is much scope for committing mistake at various levels. Adequate information can be obtained from the candidate by listening to and observing rather than talking too much. Interviewers very often commit the following mistakes:

(a) Indulging in discourtesy and rudeness.

(b) Arriving at conclusions before the interview is over.

(c) Asking questions mechanically.

(d) Feeling shyness in asking questions.

(e) Failing to observe the behaviour and tap the unexplored areas.

Mistakes by interviewer can be avoided by selecting competent interviewers, training and developing them.

SUBDIVISION OF INTERVIEW

(i) *Open the interview*: During the first few minutes of the interview, the interviewer has to open the interview with a conscious effort and with Conducive voice, speech and appearance. This helps the interviewer to establish a rapport with and gain the confidence of the interviewee.

(ii) *Get complete and accurate information:* The interviewer should get full information by structured interview relating to skill, knowledge, aptitude, attitude and traits of the candidate. In order to get complete and accurate information, the interviewer must do the following:

(a) Be alert for pauses, omissions and diversion of discussion.
(b) Use the language which is clear to the interviewee.
(c) Ask direct and straight questions in order to avoid ambiguous answers.
(d) Make unjustifiably favourable remarks or unfavourable comments about the applicant's motives or actions with a view to obtain truthful information.
(e) Frame the questions in such a way that the candidate's answers should be elaborate.

(iii) *Record observations and impressions*: In order to manage the information system for evaluating the candidate's suitability at the later stage, the interviewer should record his observations and impressions in the course of interview.

(iv) *Guide the interview*: Guiding the interview is essential to have just sufficient (neither too much nor too less) discussion on a topic. It should lead the applicant tactfully and surely towards the interview goals while some applicants are talkative and others are intelligent in giving information which they know and in avoiding other areas. The applicant is sometimes reticent.

While aiming at getting complete and reliable information, the interviewer has to guide the interview tactfully without causing much psychological inconvenience to the interviewee.

(v) *Check the success of the interviewer*: The next major step of the interview is to check the success of the interviewer in conducting the interview. The success of the interviewer in conducting the interview can be checked through the following items:

(a) Making favourable impression on the candidate at the beginning of the interview;
(b) Refraining from making judgement at the beginning;
(c) Putting the candidate at ease;
(d) Giving chance for further discussion;
(e) Asking questions at right time, clearly and in appropriate language;
(f) Avoiding unnecessary interference;
(g) Avoiding expression of approval or disapproval of any attitude;
(h) Talking to a minimum;
(i) Guiding the interview;

(j) Obtaining relevant and adequate information;
(k) Following up leads;
(l) Taking notes;
(m) Giving opportunity to the candidates to ask questions;
(n) Creating and keeping good impression throughout the interview;
(o) Giving the candidate a feeling of fair and just in conducting the interview.

3. Close the interview Closing of interview should end pleasantly. It is as important as its commencement. The interviewer may show some signs of the close of the interview at an appropriate time. After closing the interview, interview results should be evaluated.

4. Evaluate interview results The interviewer or the board of interviewers evaluate the candidates, strengths and weaknesses against the job and organisational requirements. Their evaluation is based on the observations, impressions and information collected during the course of interview. The final decision about the suitability of candidate is made on the basis of the results of all selection techniques. Much more than any other technique, the interview results influence the selection decision. The evaluation may be in descriptive grading or rating form. The interviewer has to strike a fine balance between the job requirements and employees, values, skills, knowledge, etc. He should give explanation of rating on each factor. This clarifies his thinking and enables discussion among the interviewers. To minimise errors in evaluation and to evaluate the candidate effectively, in general, the interviewer should also take into consideration the equational record, physical attributes, attitudes, sociability and social intelligence, flexibility in behaviour, tact, manners, temperament, dependability, self-confidence of the candidate.

LIMITATIONS OF THE INTERVIEW METHOD

1. Validity and reliability Research has indicated the questionable nature of the validity and reliability of interviews.

2. Impression Often the interviewer gets impressed favourably or unfavourably with the job applicant for wrong reasons. For example, a qualified male applicant should not be rejected merely because the interviewer dislikes his long hair.

3. Bias Like all people, interviewers have personal biases. They react, positively or negatively, to fluency of speech, correctness of grammar and punctuation, poise and other characteristics.

4. Inbred notion There are probably several inbred notions the interviewer holds that will colour the company's selection of a candidate.

5. Non-verbal behaviour According to Dale and H.G. Heneman, interviewers often use non-verbal behaviour patterns as a basis of reaching a decision. These are, how the person looks, sits in the chair, and maintains eye contact.

6. Halo effect The problem of the halo effect occurs when the interviewer allows a single prominent characteristic to dominate judgement of all other traits. For example, it is easy to discount other characteristics when a person has a pleasing personality, though having a pleasant personality does not necessarily ensure that the person would fit in the organisation. Sometimes the halo error can work in the opposite direction. According to Richard Arvey and James Champion, an interviewer may assume that a poorly groomed individual is stupid and dishonest.

7. Contrast errors According to Jack Hallovan, these errors take place when an interviewer is overly influenced, in favour or against, by the interviews of previous applicants. For instance, if a qualified applicant follows a brilliant applicant, his qualifications tend to pale in comparison. This is unfortunate, since the qualified candidate may be rejected because of the contrast error.

The above limitations can be minimised by appointing trained and qualified interviewers. A trained interviewer is likely to make fewer errors because he understands potential errors, has learned how to ask questions effectively, is able to establish a positive relationship with applicants, and has systematically organised the interview.

QUALITIES OF A SUCCESSFUL INTERVIEWER

To be successful, the interviewer should possess the following qualities:

1. Elderly outlook, social detachment, intelligent, emotionally matured, interest in understanding human behaviour, sociability, active interaction, judgement, expressing of genuine feelings, etc.
2. He should be well-educated and trained. He should show interest in reading latest literature, equipping himself with latest knowledge and should have thirst for knowledge.
3. He should have thorough understanding of jobs, organisation, human behaviour, human qualities, etc.

MEANS TO MAKE THE INTERVIEW EFFECTIVE

According to Michael Jucius, the interview technique can be effectively used through the following means:

1. Selecting the interviewers with higher status, calibre, skill and knowledge.

2. Resorting to right type of interview depending upon the situation.
3. Studying the background information data, facts about the candidates before the interview.
4. Assessing and evaluating the characteristics and traits of the candidates accurately.
5. Basing interview coverage on job and organisational requirements.
6. Following time management techniques, to collect as much important information as possible within the available time.
7. Checking before hand the reliability and validity of the interview and method.
8. Respecting interviewee's interest and individuality.
9. Clearly informing the interviewee the purpose of the interview.
10. Making interviewee feel ease throughout the interview.
11. Encouraging interviewee to speak freely.
12. Interviewer should try to understand the words used by the interviewees.
13. Interviewer should not have personal views and opinions.

QUESTIONS FOR EXERCISE

1. Define Selection Test and give guidelines to testing. Outline various steps in testing.
2. Describe important types of Selection Tests. How are they developed? What precautions should be taken in using them?
3. What is Selection Interview? Explain its objectives and types.
4. Explain various types of selection interviews.
5. Describe the steps in interview process for selection of jobs.
6. What are the limitations of the Interview Method? Describe qualities of a successful interviewer and point out means to make interview effective.

15

VOCATIONAL GUIDANCE

WHAT IS GUIDANCE?

Guidance may be defined as the process of helping the individual in selecting, preparing, entering and progressing in the behaviour patterns which comprise human activities in the educational, vocational, recreational fields as well as in connection with community service group. This help takes the form of personal help on the psychologist's part. It is, again, in the form of advice. This does not solve problems but only helps the individual in solving his problems. In this way, guidance prepares the individual for his adjustment. It informs the individual of the kind of education that he requires, the subjects that he would be advised to choose in his study, the vocation to which he should employ when faced with problems that he must solve. In society every individual has a specific status and certain roles that are concomitnant with it. For example, a male member is the head of his family, and from this position is derived his responsibility of providing for the needs of the family and keeping in mind the proper development of every member. But an individual does not maintain the same status throughout his life. At one and the same or at different times, he passes through stages where he occupies the status of son, father, husband, teacher or advocate, a citizen of the nation, etc. In each of these different statuses, he has distinct and definite roles to play. The person who has ability or sense enough to work as benefits his status in society is the one who wins the acclaim of society and its approval as well. It is in the performance of these various roles and duties, which conform to his differing statuses, that he needs guidance. In this way, the psychologist's guidance helps the individual fit into his role and status in society. Every individual is not fit to take up any and every position in society. Teaching, doctoring, advocacy and a variety of other professions are not jobs that require the same individual qualities from the person occupied in doing them. Introducing fitness in an individual to occupy some position is a matter that has two aspects. The first is that his ability should be commensurate with the requirement of the job and the second that he should try to become qualified to occupy that position. The second of these aspects has some limitations. Whatever the effort expended, every person cannot become an artist or author, because every individual does not have the ability or quality to adopt any and every profession. Even every individual cannot become a successful trader as that requires a definite shrewd and calculating mentality that is not possessed by everyone. Hence, in order to prove able for some particular position, a person should choice the position that concurs with his capabilities and qualities. Educational psychology helps the individual in his choice. In this way, guidance helps the individual to settle down into the positions that are, or are not, of his own choose. As has been said in the preceding definition, guidance helps to prepare the individual for his future life. Preparation for the future life implies creating abilities in the individual to bear responsibilities and this can take a variety of forms. Normally, for example, every boy and girl gets married when he and she grow up, creates a family and indulges in prolific procreation. In this manner, every individual is to face in the future responsibilities concerning his children, responsibilities concerning the partner he has chosen for life as well as future responsibilities of the family in general. And in the normal circumstances, again, most young men and some young women have also to adopt some or the other profession, whether to their liking or not. A child grows up to be not only a man but also a citizen of his country and in this position certain rights develop upon him that bring with them some additional responsibilities. Consequently, when we talk of preparing an individual for the future, we mean to prepare him for bearing his responsibilities ably and sufficiently whether he be called upon to do so in the field of family relations, the economic sphere, the political field or any other situation of life. For this every individual boy or a girl should turn to a profession that conforms to the education they have had so that they may be in positions for which they have been prepared and act with skill and confidence. They should decide upon the profession that they would like to adopt. They should have the capacity to face and solve their own problems as well as the problems that are likely to arise in their relations with the others. Guidance helps the individual in all these kinds of efforts.

It should be quite apparent from the above detailed discussion on the meaning of the term that guidance helps in determining the objective of life, in establishing a synthesis in life and in solving various kinds of problems. In the words of Jones, "Guidance is the personal help that is given by one person to another in developing life goals, in making adjustment and in solving problems that confront him in the attainment of goals."[1] In this manner guidance is the personal assistance. Although guidance is sometimes offered at the group level, yet even in these matters, every member of the group is also individually given advice. Applied psychology is based on the conception of individual differences. General experience and scientific research have both established that every single individual has certain abilities, problems and difficulties that are distinctly his own, as distinct from those of others. Evidently, if any advice or guidance is to be rendered, it must be rendered individually and personally. This personal help is forthcoming from one individual to another. One of these two individuals is a psychologist, or one who knows psychology and the other a person who is in need of psychological guidance. Guidance, then, is the help rendered to an individual by the psychologist. In its more extensive sense, the term may be taken to comprehend the advice rendered by any individual who is in the know concerning psychology to another who is in need of it. For example, if a father guides his son in solving a problem, this, too, amounts to guidance, irrespective of the fact that it may or may not be based on the most correct notion of psychological principles. But this extensive meaning of the term has its general meaning and implication. In a scientific analysis it is not taken in its general meaning but reduced to more definite and precise terms whereby its meaning becomes limited. That is why it is first defined. Guidance, in psychology, means a particular thing. It is the personal advice or service rendered by a psychologist, and not by any Tom, Dick or Harry, to another person. This guidance takes the form of advice which helps the guided individual to adjust to various conditions and circumstances. If one would only look at it that way, it would become evident that adjustment is the basic problem of human life. The person who fails to adjust to his circumstances becomes a failure, suffers pain himself and inflicts it upon others, and is branded as an abnormal being. In this way, educational psychology, through its helping the individual in adjusting himself, helps to spread happiness, peace and organisation in the society. Problems in human life do not come to an end, because new ones keep on arising. There is no end to trouble. A child, for example, is

---

1. Jones, A.J., *Principles of Guidance*, McGrew Hill Book Co., New York, p. 85.

faced by very few problems, much of his anxiety being centred around the work forced upon him by the teacher, or the means of dealing with more recalcitrant of his friends and such minor things. He has not to worry about keeping the home fires burning. But these are problems that gradually engulf every individual as he grows older. As a general rule most people marry and have children who go to school and with equal inevitability fall ill and be treated for it, only to grow up and get married themselves and keep the almost eternal circle moving forward. Thus, one trouble grows out of the other, and never lets the individual being sit back contented and unharried. Human psychology is much like this. One's desire arises and destroys the being's peace till it is satisfied. Hence he immediately busies himself in searching for the means to satisfy this desire and achieves this after more or less trouble. But the story does not end here; it is followed by the arising of another desire, and the inevitable circle of objective, search for objective, obstacles in search for means of solving the desire, overcoming of the desire, and the arising of another desire. It is evident that every individual is continually faced with new objectives, achievement of which entails the facing of many other difficulties. As Jones has stated in his definition, guidance helps in overcoming these difficulties that beset the achievement of an objective.

KINDS OF GUIDANCE

As has been pointed out, an individual has to turn to the psychologist, in the latter's role as a specialist, for personal advice when he fails to solve the problems that confront him. This personal advice is guidance. How this guidance can take effect depends on the fact that it is given in the context of some problem the solution of which is being sought. As a matter of fact, it is no easy matter to recount all the possible problems that arise in various spheres of human life, but some psychologists have attempted a classification of them. For example, Jones has divided the problems of life into eight spheres on the basis of their nature: (1) Related to health and psychological development, (2) Related to house and family, (3) Related to time for recreation, (4) Concerned with personality, (5) Religious, (6) Education, (7) Social and (8) Vocational or occupational. Having achieved the classification of problems, it becomes possible to classify the kinds or forms of guidance that is to be given correspondingly. For example, vocational guidance is required in connection with profession and educational guidance in the field of education. Psychologists have professed many and various kinds of guidance. For example, Myers has mentioned the following eight kinds of guidance:

1. Vocational Guidance,
2. Educational Guidance,
3. Recreational Guidance,
4. Civic Guidance,
5. Community Service Guidance,
6. Social and Moral Guidance,
7. Health Guidance,
8. Leadership Guidance.

The present discussion makes a study of three kinds of guidance. The Bureau of Psychology, Uttar Pradesh, has also put guidance in these three categories, and much the same classification of guidance kinds has been followed in the other Indian states as well. These three kinds are: (1) Educational guidance, (2) Vocational guidance and (3) Personal guidance.

If the matter is looked at closely it will be seen that the above three classes in fact include all kinds of classification. If child guidance is considered, for example, and this guidance requires the opening of clinics in various places, it will be found that problems concerning the children are either concerned with education or are of the personal nature. Hence, child guidance is jointly comprehended under education and personal guidance. Similarly, the various forms of guidance, such as health guidance, recreational guidance, civic guidance, social and moral guidance, community service guidance and leadership guidance are all comprehended in personal guidance.

Dividing of the various spheres of guidance does not imply that these spheres are completely separated and unconnected. In fact, guidance is a dynamic and progressive concept in which advice given on every aspect of human life is comprehended, but, nevertheless, with a view to convenience in discussion, its aspects and spheres have been differentiated. Educational guidance and vocational guidance are closely related, and both of them are very intimately concerned with personal guidance. The basis of this correlation between the various spheres is that all problems of human beings are connected with each other. For example, when a person experiences difficulty in selecting a particular curriculum or a definite profession, his indecision may stem from certain personal difficulties. It happens quite often that young men become so engrossed in their careers and future. Death of a close and loved relative may be another reason why he may be at a loss and groping in dark. The fundamental problem here is of a personal nature, with the result that all education or vocational guidance to such an individual will be modified by the personal guidance given to him. On the other hand, many personal problems may be the consequence of certain deficiencies of education and the lack of educational guidance. If a child runs away from school and becomes vagrant, finds no interest in study but chooses to pursue a life of crime or one of anti-social conduct, then it is evident that there is something wrong somewhere and as likely as not it may be that his choice of curriculum may have been undesirable. In much the same manner, certain individual and personal problems may be the outcome of an absence of vocational guidance. A young man, for example, in his school days may have been a very fine sportman, and by its virtue he would naturally not appreciate a job that ties him down, offers no opportunity of leadership, and does not allow the development of any of his sportman-like qualities like motivation, patience, adventure and courage. If he is forced to take on such a job for a variety of reasons, it would be natural for him to become irritable and lose his mental balance and calm to some extent. This may lead to further complications in the form of personal problems. Here the personal problems have been caused by lack of proper vocational guidance. Similarly, educational, vocational and personal guidance is mutually related.

CLASSIFICATION ACCORDING TO THE MODE OF GUIDANCE

The above classification that we have been viewing is made on the basis of problems for which guidance is required. If the mode of guidance is taken into consideration, guidance can be classified in the following manner:

1. Individual Guidance,
2. Group Guidance.

Before going on to a detailed description of educational, vocational and personal guidance, it would be advisable to comprehend this classification of guidance made on the basis of its modes:

1. Individual guidance method In the individual guidance method, the person to be guided and his guide, the psychologist are in direct and personal contact with each other. He invades the ill person's house and makes a study of his family conditions, and for this purpose he interviews the various members of the individual's family. His social, financial and cultural background is also investigated so that no possible source of information is left untapped. And for this it becomes essential to study his neighbourhood and to collect as many facts of his life as are possible so as to build up a fairly complete case history. The schools and colleges that he has attended are contacted in scholastic attainments there. His teachers, too, are consulted on the matter.

Study of this type and the collection of all possible information concerning the individual is followed by testing of the individual himself. He is made to take tests of intelligence, specific mental abilities, interests, attitudes, and personality. Interview is another weapon that is used to uncover much information and, incidentally, to learn the person opinion about himself. Accordingly, then, in an individual guidance, the following information concerning the individual is gathered:

1. Information concerning his intelligence, mental abilities, interests, attitudes and personality.
2. Information concerning family conditions.
3. Information concerning the social, financial and cultural background.
4. Other relevant information.

Having gathered all this information, it is subjected to close and intelligent scrutiny, and then curative measures are introduced to remove the problems which have made this guidance necessary. Among these efforts are logical arguments, suggestions, psychoanalysis, etc.

The individual guidance method has the following qualities:

1. It renders almost complete information concerning the individual. Hence a proper cure can be effected.

2. Cures in this method are simpler and more effective.

Despite these advantages, the method suffers from the following drawbacks:

1. It consumes much time, with the result that a very large number of psychologists are required if there is a big number of patients.

2. Accordingly, this method is extremely expensive also.

3. It needs highly trained and specialist psychologists.

2. Group guidance method These shortcomings of the individual guidance method are not found in group method because in this, a number of people are guided simultaneously. Group guidance should not be interpreted to imply that it involves guiding the group. Actually, the guidance is aimed at the individual because it consists of the personal assistance rendered by a psychologist. In the group guidance technique, a complete group is guided. But this guidance is intended to help the individual member of the group to solve his own problems, the sole difference being that the group comprises individuals facing more or less the same problems. Evidently, then, there is no need to waste money and time in giving individual guidance to individuals who are facing similar problems and the advice given is likely to be similar. Hence, there can be no questioning of the importance of the group guidance technique. It economises upon time and money.

Nevertheless, group guidance technique lacks all the advantages that accrue from an application of the individual guidance method. Due to the smaller degree of personal contact between the psychologist and his subjects, the cures are not quite so effective as in the case of individual guidance. When group guidance is administered it is also not possible to gather the same amount of authentic information concerning the subject as is feasible in the individual guidance method. Hence, it may be tentatively concluded that group guidance method can be of value only in circumstances in which the problems faced are similar to a degree without wide individual differences and are also not particularly complex.

VOCATIONAL GUIDANCE: ITS HISTORY

Vocational guidance was defined by the 1954 Committee of the International Labour Organisation in its suggestions concerning vocational guidance, as assistance rendered by an individual to another in the latter's solving of problems related to his progress and vocational selection, keeping in mind the individual's peculiarities or special abilities and their relations with their occupational opportunities. In this manner, the objective of vocational guidance is the proper and complete utilization of a nation's manpower through helping the individual to achieve his development and satisfaction in his profession. An individual should choose a profession that suits his abilities in order that both he and the nation may profit. It is not possible for any one individual to be capable of doing every job. Special kinds of job require particular kinds of skills and special know-how. It is possible that it may be asked why guidance thereby becomes necessary since every individual can tell the kind of skill he has and choose a profession accordingly. But if the situation is objectively viewed, it will be found that it is not precisely of this nature, as only few people are able to gauge their own abilities and capabilities. A large majority of persons are wrong in their estimate, of their own capabilities, many of them overestimating while a fair number denigrating themselves. It is not possible for the proverbial human eye to see the very grit, that is, that the human eye rarely lights upon the individual's own defects. If one were to go to any student doing post-graduate work in the university and ask him as to what he proposes to do after obtaining the degree, the most likely reply would be that he would take one of the competitive examinations, preferably the administrative service, and if not fortunate enough to be selected, carry on to do research and finally become a teacher. The audacity and overweening self-confidence of the students is stupendous. If you were to ask him as to what he will do if neither of these contingencies comes about, then it will only be a regard for your social standing that will prevent him from denouncing you on the spot. The implication is that very few of the students who fail in these and other competitive examinations realise that they do not possess the requisite qualities. When they fail, they turn their wrath upon the examiner while the more charitable abuse only their bad luck. There will hardly be one student who will acquiesce in the knowledge that it was he himself who was lacking in the qualities required for the job. Again, to prevent unnecessary meanings being read into these statements it must be pointed out that the competitive examinations held in the present era can hardly be considered sufficient to gauge an individual's inherent merit. The sole intention of introducing this example is to point out the fact that young men and women do not think rationally and scientifically when faced with the choice of a profession. Vocational guidance helps in the solution of this problem. Scientific testing reveals all that there is to know of the individual and then advise the former as to the profession most suitable for him. Experiments have succeeded in pointing out roughly the qualities that a particular kind of profession requires in the individual. For example, efforts were made to establish the intelligence level required for various kinds of jobs.

The following table states the intelligence quotient that a person should possess in order to go in for one or the other profession:

S.No.	*Professional Class*	*I.Q.*
1.	Administrative work and high level professional work	150 or more
2.	Low level professional and technical work	130 to 150
3.	Clerical or high level skilled labour	115 to 130
4.	Skilled work	100 to 115
5.	Semi-skilled work	85 to 100
6.	Work not requiring intelligence	70 to 85
7.	Labour work	50 to 70

Similarly, other tests and experiments have been conducted to establish some relationship between vocational and other mental abilities. For example, engineering and other industrial work requires mechanical skill in the individual, with the result that persons who possess it in a slight degree cannot in the normal course be expected to become successful engineers or skilled technicians. Some kinds of work, for example, the repair of chronometers and surgery, require the ability to do minute work skilfully. Lacking this quality, no individual can become a good surgeon, watch-repairer or experimenter or research worker. In much the same manner, other industries and professions require different kinds of expertise and skill.

The above description makes evident the importance inherent in vocational guidance. But this hardly means that the guide pays no attention to the person's aptitude. Aptitude is one of the basis of guidance, but one thing that is beyond question is that no individual can attain much success on the sole basis of aptitude. Accordingly, the guide has to collect elaborate and detailed information concerning the individual's aptitudes and capabilities, and give guidance on the basis of such information. Vocational guidance does not involve categorical declaration that one shall be a professional while such another shall be a clerk or an engineer. It is only a hypothesis and a suggestion that has its own limitations. What the guide says is simply that such and such person should choose a particular profession, and there is much greater possibility of success in that profession than in any other for that individual.

Personnel Selection

It was the National Institute of Industrial Psychology that commenced research on matters concerning vocational guidance, and its results have been used much by all big industries. Every productive unit has a large variety of functions which can best be performed by individuals having different kinds of ability and training. Now, the selection of separate individuals for each of these jobs is called personnel selection. And this personnel selection is based upon vocational guidance. Hence, it is essential that the distinction between personnel selection and vocational guidance be well marked and known. In both it is essential that the qualities fit for different jobs be present in the person being considered for selection or guidance, as the case may be. But, in personnel selection, the quality required for some particular function is remarked, and one person out of many applicants is selected to perform that function, of course care being taken that the best of the applicants is thereby selected. In vocational guidance, the qualities of a person are gauged and he is accordingly advised to take up some vocational training or adopt a particular profession that suits him and is likely to bring him satisfaction. Vocational guidance and personnel selection are two branches of vocational psychology. Both these branches are interdependent since the provision of the right man for the right job and right job for the right man requires, on the one hand, analysis of the individual, and an analysis of the job on the other.

The Western nations have done much work concerning vocational guidance, particularly in the United States of America, personnel selection is itself a specialised job now. Considerable modernisation and improvement are being carried on to improve and the method of selection. A Directory of Occupational Titles has been prepared to search for thereby providing information concerning vocations that are open to individuals. Then, an Occupational Code has been prepared by classifying the vocations according to the qualities that they require in the man according to their different levels. Detailed information regarding every profession is collected. Job description, which is an important organ of the information concerning every profession, provides a detailed and exhaustive account of the various factors such as conditions of work, wages, responsibility, etc., that are operative in the industry or vocation. The first dictionary included details of 75 per cent vocations and occupations, and it comprehended some 90 per cent of working population of that country. This directory went through additional and improved editions in 1942, 1944 and 1945 while in its 1959 revised version some thousands of professions were detailed, and job analysis in 1942 was confined to 16 professions.

Vocational Guidance in India

In India, vocational guidance is not easily available, as there are few other technical and specialised services. In 1945, the Training and Employment Service Organisation Committee headed by Shri B. Shivarao suggested that occupational information be selected and published. As a result, during the Second Five Year Plan period a project was prepared to set up 50 vocational guidance centres to supplement the efforts of the employment exchanges in their personnel selection. There have been certain appointments in this connection but the actual achievement is not very noticeable. And the books on occupations that have been published are not scientific research material but merely constitute a description. Besides with the efforts of the Government of India, the state governments have also opened some centres, while this in turn has been supplemented by certain non-governmental agencies. Among them the

Y.M.C.A. and the Rotary Club have achieved things that deserve mention. As is apparent from the above rather short account, the progress in the direction of vocational guidance for a large country like India, is not worthy of praise. It need hardly be pointed out that much of this failure is to be attributed to the lack of organisation.

List of Abilities and Traits

Much important research and modification work has been carried on in connection with finding out the qualities and traits required for different professions. The National Institute of Industrial Psychology of England has prepared a list of approximately 20 psychological abilities and traits. On the basis of this list, an industrial survey was undertaken. In this survey, the specialists and senior officers working in the different occupations were requested to supply information as to the qualities and traits required for their respective functions. Specialists of different occupations effected a rating from three standpoints — average, high level, and a very high level. Now the specialists of the National Institute took the average of the ratings made available from some 80 occupations. This average was categorised in the form of a table. And on the basis of this table, it is possible to determine whether a particular individual is suitable for a specific profession or not. For example, this table, clarifies the qualities that are requisite for the medical and the legal professions and the qualities that are quite desirable.

Another bit of important research work in connection with various professions and mental abilities was carried on by R.B. Cattell. Cattell tested some, 1000 adult persons and found out their average intelligence level. This average indicates the approximate level of intelligence required by a person wishing to join some particular profession. This is made apparent in the following table:

S.No.	*Profession*	*No. of Trained People*	*Average I.Q.*
1.	Teachers of universities and intermediate colleges	30	151
2.	Doctors and surgeons	25	146.5
3.	Teachers of government schools	50	145
4.	Civil engineers	20	142
5.	Mechanical engineers	18	140
6.	Teachers of primary schools	90	137
7.	Managers of industry	20	137

Continue.....

S.No.	*Profession*	*No. of Trained People*	*Average I.Q.*
8.	Stenographers	57	129
9.	Clerks	54	127
10.	Travelling representatives	24	123
11.	Nurses	250	122
12.	Telephone department employees	52	115
13.	Workers doing minute work	19	114
14.	Workers doing gross work	—	106 to 78

Test by Devorak and Dodge

Devorak and Dodge also conducted tests upon employees of different professions, on persons successful and unsuccessful within one profession, of people working in the same profession but in different capacities. This testing was based upon a wide variety of authentic psychological testing techniques. These tests revealed considerable differences between the abilities of motor mechanics, successful or unsuccessful clerks, and other people. But these tests were neither extensive and comprehensive to be applied to a majority of professions nor concentrated enough to have completely distinguished one profession from another. In this manner, it is essential to exercise the greatest care in applying the conclusions in these tests. Dodge himself has acknowledged this fact.

Minnesota Occupational Rating Scales

In Minnesota University six mental abilities and their extent was determined for 430 professions and occupations. And even in this, the ability was individually divided into four categories — *a, b, c, d.* These six mental abilities were Verbal, Mechanical, Sociability, Clerical, Musical and Artistic. And these six abilities were divided into four classes each for different professions. For example, the Minnesota Occupational Rating Scale concerning the ability of verbal efficiency can be understood from the following table:

Class Level of Intelligence	*Necessary Ability*	*Example*
(a) High level	Highest university education, creative ability and power of argument.	Professors, authors, scientists, advocates, etc.
(b) Higher than average.	High school and college level of education	Clerks, photographers, foremen, etc.
(c) Average level.	High School level of education	Typists, mechanic, etc.
(d) Below average.	Junior high school or eighth grade education.	Labourers, porters, etc.

PROCESS OF VOCATIONAL GUIDANCE

The preceding description of vocational guidance must have made it apparent that it requires two kinds of information or subject matter to be collected, the first concerning indispensable information about the individual, and the second pertaining to knowledge of the industrial or occupational aspect. In this manner, vocational guidance has two aspects:

1. Study of the individual.
2. Study of the occupational or professional sphere.

Study of the Individual

Before any vocational guidance can be rendered to an individual, it is essential that adequate information concerning his education, level of intelligence, mental abilities, aptitudes, interests, physical development, health, nature, personality characteristics and economic status be gathered, because variations in any of them will necessarily require change in guidance.

1. Education Individuals need differing levels of education in order to enter into and succeed in different professions, as for example, the highest education is required for advocates, professors, engineers, doctors, and other such professions whereas a general and lower level of education can serve the purpose if the profession is of clerk, overseer, mechanic, compounder, teacher, etc. Besides these there are certain other occupations in which the medium level of education suffices, *e.g.*, business salesmanship. In such professions, only the basic necessities of literacy must be fulfilled, as much else depends upon practice. It is only because of this importance of various levels of education being relative and relevant to different professions that most advertisement for applications for jobs contain specific instructions regarding the educational qualifications. For example, a person teaching students at the high school and intermediate level need only be a graduate while no mere graduate can teach the college or graduate level. Doctors require medical degrees while in order to qualify as an engineer, it is essential that one passes an engineering examination.

2. Training Education does not merely imply the degree obtained at the end of a session by passing a prescribed examination. Nowadays, most occupation units make it obligatory on all new entrants to be trained in addition to be educated, and this is being carried to the extent that only a trained individual is allowed to fill the post of a high school teacher. Certain occupations need training inevitably, for example the occupation of an electrician, stenographer, chemist, compounder, etc. In certain professions, the individual after having entered it, the training is oriented for a period of few weeks, and only then he is allowed to handle work on his own responsibility.

3. Level of intelligence Besides differences in education, different professions require differing levels of intelligence. For example, the medical, technical, legal, teaching and administrative professions require the highest intelligence level, while, on the other hand, the peon and the domestic worker can be selected from people with a much more lower level of intelligence. Other professions require only the average level of intelligence, so that, evidently, before a person can be told of the profession that suits his natural endowments, it is essential to now the level of intelligence to which he belongs.

4. Special mental abilities Individuals differ not only in respect of their intelligence but also in respect of their special mental abilities. For example, all people do not possess mechanical ability to the same degree and neither is verbal felicity shared by all in equal degree. Different professions require differing mental abilities, verbal ability being required by advocates and teachers, etc., mechanical ability by doctors and engineers, etc. Hence prior to the selection of a profession, it is essential for the individual to be aware of his mental abilities.

5. Aptitudes Success in a particular profession seems to depend to some extent upon one's aptitude for it. If a person lacks artistic and creative aptitude, there is not much likelihood of his succeeding in the role of an artist, and one need not expect of it. As a general rule, it is advisable for every person to join the profession for which he has any natural aptitude. Hence, knowledge of a person's aptitude is also essential before he can be given any vocational guidance.

6. Interests Interest helps to increase the possibility of success in a profession. Interesting work is done enthusiastically and patiently while uninteresting work tends to fall upon most men, and requires very conscious application to be carried through. Success in work requires that serious interest be taken in the work, or that interest in that kind of work be created, and this is possible. Interests are mutable, and it is possible to create interest in work that was once repugnant. But, hardly be repeated as a slogan is, that a knowledge of the person's interest is essential before any vocational guidance can be rendered.

7. Health and physical development As a general rule, proper health and physical development are necessarily taken into consideration in every profession, but in certain other occupations, success depends almost solely upon these factors. For success in the armed forces or in the police department, health and good physical development are quite indispensable. In the absence of these factors, the presence of no other qualities of ability will bring success to the individual. Hence, physical development, constitution and health are additional factors that must be taken into consideration when the question of vocational guidance comes up for consideration.

8. Nature Different people show very pertinent and obvious differences in their nature, some being introverted while others more extroverted. And, different kinds of people can successfully settle down only in some specific professions that suit their nature. An extroverted personality, for example, is essential if one wants to succeed as a salesman, agent, administrator or even as a leader, while on the other hand, gifted introverts make great artists, authors, scholars, scientists, specialists, etc. If choice of a profession is contrary to one's natural grain then one is not happy and enthusiastic in his work, and these conditions are not conducive to progress and success. Hence, before vocational guidance can be ventured upon, it is necessary to judge a person's nature also.

9. Personality characteristics It is a fact generally known that different qualities of the personality are required in such widely separated professions as teaching, artistic creation, selling, labour work, etc. Hence, choice of profession should also be made with due regard for the qualities of the person's personality.

10. Financial status As a general rule, it is improper and unnecessary to take into consideration a person's financial status before making a choice of profession, but in a country like India where scholarships are hard to come by, the economic status of the student also plays an important part in his choice of the future that he wants to shape for himself. Now, a person with middle-class status is in no position to afford a technical or medical education for his child because either of these two special courses involves the expenditure of a considerable amount of money. And it is unnecessary and improper to advise a poor and needy person to go in for higher education when he cannot afford it. It is equally useless to advise such a person to choose a profession in which high education and specialised qualification are desired. Hence a person should be recommended only to that profession for which he can afford to gain education and any training that may be essential. He must have the means to gain such training. It must also be remembered that economic or financial status can be a bar to entering some professions only under certain circumstances. There are many examples of people who came from poor families having gained very high education and improved their lot in life. The truth or crux of the matter is that instead of discouraging a student from entertaining thoughts of a profession for which he apparently has not the economic means, the psychologist should expend his effort in arranging scholarships or other facilities whereby he may be able to attain the goal for which the former is striving, as he stands great chances of success. In India, these things are still unexplored, and many individuals fail to gain satisfying and rewarding positions in life that conform to their abilities, interests and aptitudes, for no reason other than that they were born in poor families.

11. Other important factors In addition to all the elements pointed out above, it is necessary to keep in mind certain other factors concerning the individual before giving vocational guidance. Age of the person, for example, is another factor that must be taken into account since many jobs and occupations set the maximum and minimum age limits on all applications so that people not qualifying for them in this respect cannot enter these services. Hence, there is hardly any point in advising them to take up such a profession. Sex of the person is another consideration in vocational guidance upon which much depends because occupations are more suitable to the male individual while others are within the capacities of the female, and for these she is eminently suitable. Nursing and caring for the diseased in hospitals is one function that can safely and even desirably be allocated to women, while in the armed forces and the police, most of the jobs, with very few exceptions, are suitable only for the male.

Study of the Professional World

Having collected all the necessary and desired information regarding the individual under consideration, it is necessary to be true to another aspect of vocational guidance, that is of studying the professional world. While the psychologist must necessarily have enough information concerning the person to whom he is imparting vocational guidance, it is equally important that he be well informed on its professional and occupational aspect. Only then can he provide proper and effective assistance. It is not enough for the psychologist to be knowing the number and kinds of professions but also the kind of education, training, intelligence, mental abilities, interests, aptitudes, personality, etc., that are desired as well as the conditions of work that prevail therein.

Occupations have been classified in different ways, according to the viewpoint adopted in trying to know all the professions from one point of view and can be selected from among them. This has the two-fold advantage of narrowing down the range from which the selection is to be made while at the same it provides a number of alternatives. It will be advantageous now to glance at these various professions.

1. Classification according to interest Professions have been divided into the following classes on the basis of interest:

(a) Occupations concerned with child life,
(b) Mechanical occupations,
(c) Computational occupations,
(d) Scientific occupations,
(e) Occupations concerned with change,
(f) Artistic occupations,
(g) Literary occupations,
(h) Musical occupations,
(i) Occupations concerned with sociality,
(j) Clerical occupations.

In each of these classes, there are professions belonging to five levels, depicted in the following classification.

2. Classification on the basis of education level, mental ability, or skill, training, age and social respect This classification of the professions is the work of Beckman, which is as follows :[1]

(a) *Executive, managerial and professional*: This class includes the following three kinds of occupations:

(i) Verbal such as advocate, judge, educator, auditor, professor,
(ii) Scientific, such as doctor, engineer, scientist, accountant, etc.
(iii) Executive or managerial, such as the various kinds of managers and executives, etc.

(b) *Business and sub-professional*: This class includes the following two kinds:

(i) Business such as trader, salesman, agent, etc.
(ii) Sub-professional, such as actor, photographer, designer, etc.

(c) *Skilled occupation:* This class includes the following two kinds of occupations:

(i) Physical labour, such as an electrician, dyer, machineman, and press mechanic, etc.

---

1. Beckman, R.O., "A New Scale for Gauging Occupational Rank".

(ii) Intellectual such as clerk, supervisor, stenographer, cashier, etc.

(d) ***Semi-skilled occupation:*** Such as policeman, bus conductor, driver, guard, etc.

(e) ***Unskilled occupation:*** Such as labour, peon, night-watchman, etc.

3. Classification according to the form of work Professions have been divided into the following four classes according to the nature of work done by them:

(a) ***Social occupations:*** These professions require that the person be possessed of social qualities and a high degree of sociability because he comes into contact with many individuals. Examples of such professions are advocate, leader, trader, salesman, agent, administrator, manager, teacher, etc.

(b) ***Occupations of manual skill*:** In these professions tools are used for work that requires a high-degree of manual skill, examples being carpenter, mechanic, mason, binder, overseer, engineer, etc.

(c) ***Occupation concerned with offices*:** This class includes all people concerned with office organisations such as clerks, cashiers, peons, etc.

(d) ***Intellectual and scholarly occupations:*** In this class comes the professions that require acumen and love of academic work of the individual, examples of which are philosopher, author, inventor, poet, scientist, etc.

Job Families

From the above classification of occupations, it becomes evident that there are many professions that are similar in respect of their nature of work done, conditions of work, desired skills, interests, mental abilities, and personal qualities, etc. When such similar families are put together, a job family is constituted. In one job family the work can be carried out on different levels such as high, medium or low. Evidently, then, the individual will first have to select a job family, and then the level of that family on which he is capable of functioning.

Sources of Information regarding Occupations

The question that may be justifiable intriguing the beginner is the source of all this comprehensive information regarding a profession. The following are the sources from which such information is forthcoming and can be gathered:

(a) Through Papers and magazines.

(b) Through information published by government organisations.

(c) Through radio discussions.
(d) From employment exchanges.
(e) From information broadcast by industrial and commercial institutions.
(f) Through lectures delivered by specialists.
(g) Through examination of factories and people working in them.
(h) By working in any particular profession.
(i) From guidance psychologist and vocational adviser.

Significant Facts in Vocational Selection

After gathering information regarding the professions from one or more of the above-mentioned source, it is possible to select one's profession but before committing oneself finally, as has been pointed out before, the following things must be taken into consideration and made note of:

1. Nature of work which includes the kind of work, charge, responsibility, duty, interest, etc.
2. Working conditions, which include both psychological and physical needs.
3. Necessary personality traits such as nature, adeptness in behaviour, power of leadership, etc.
4. Level of intelligence.
5. Mental abilities.
6. Interest and aptitudes.
7. Necessary education and training.
8. Income, chances of promotion and permanency of work.
9. Procedure of entrance.
10. Necessary physical development and health.
11. Social prestige.
12. Demand of the job.

In this manner, a profession is chosen after analysing the individual on one hand, and the various occupations on the other. Analysis of the individual reveals the abilities and qualities present in him while analysis of the job or profession reveals the desired qualities and abilities. Now, all that remains to be done is that the person who possesses abilities and qualities requisite for a particular profession should be prompted to join it.

Steps of the Vocational Guidance Method

Vocational guidance, as in the case of all other forms of guidance, can be given by two methods — the individual method and the collective method. And, in these methods, the steps are the same as were described in the case of educational guidance. In this manner, vocational guidance will involve the following steps:

1. Orientation talks.
2. Psychological testing.
3. Collection of data from the school.
4. Collection of data from the family.
5. Interview.
6. Formation of profile.
7. Achievement, besides the above important steps in vocational guidance, which means that the psychologist, along with providing vocational guidance, also helps the individual to attain to the desired profession. For this, he keeps in contact with employment exchange offices and social workers.
8. Follow up studies.

QUESTIONS FOR EXERCISE

1. Discuss the scope and purpose of guidance, keeping in view the limitations of group instructional method.
2. What are the main objectives of guidance? Distinguish between vocational guidance and vocational selection?
3. Write short note on Personal guidance.
4. Distinguish between educational and vocational guidance.
5. Explain the concept and kinds of guidance. What is guidance?

16

PERSONNEL SELECTION: JOB ANALYSIS AND WORKERS ANALYSIS

PSYCHOLOGY IN INDUSTRY

Psychology is seen to be present in whatever sphere of human life that boasts of human relationships or human endeavour. In the sphere of industry, the relations between the labourers and the proprietor present a large variety, and one comes across many specimens of behaviour. Industry has many problems, including those of human conduct. For example, cases of labour unrest and dissatisfaction are not uncommon. Many causes culminate in unwillingness on their part to cooperate with the management, and in the desire to coerce the management into paying wages out of all proportions to the work achieved. They indulge in such inflammatory practices as occasional or frequent strikes that lead to factories being closed, ultimately causing loss to the management, and equally to the nation. On the other hand, bosses and factory owners are reputedly callous of their unconcern for the welfare of their employees. The least disturbance finds them indulging in lockouts, a process that has disastrous results as the piece-wage employee knows to his detriment. The country loses at the same time. Basically, all these problems are problems of human behaviour, and hence psychology is required to solve them.

Difficulties in Production

Greater and better quality of machinery is an undeniable requirement, but it is no less important that it be operated by skilful and, moreover, willing hands. How can this skill be gauged? There being a vast variety of functions and occupations in a factory, how can one discover the most adequate person for a particular job? Of the many hundreds of individuals who apply for jobs in factories, how is one to select the people who will prove to be the most efficient? For high levels of production, it is essential that the machines should be designed so as to avoid fatigue to the operator as much as is practicable. Lighting should be adequate to avoid inconvenience, accidents and unnecessary strain upon the eyes of the workers. Often, individuals lose their enthusiasm very soon for a routine kind of work. How is their interest and attention to be sustained and recreated? What should be the proper plan of a factory so that accidents are avoided? Psychology can help in the solution of all these problems that face the industry.

Problems of Distribution

With production, the work of industry does not come to an end. What is equally important is that these produced goods be sold, and sold at profitable rates. If the industry does not meet with success in this direction, all production is worthless, whatever its inherent quality. And for goods to be sold in the market, it is essential that the common buyer be acquainted with the commodity, with its quality. But for anything to happen it is necessary that there should be the necessity for a demand for the commodity, and that the consumer be aware of this need. Here, advertisement pays good dividends. And successful advertising is based upon psychological appeal. Evidently, psychology is no less important for the purposes of distribution.

Conditions of Work

In industry, the conditions under which work is undertaken has an important influence upon the labourer. In healthy conditions, the labourers are healthy, and a general atmosphere of well-being and satisfaction pervades the community. If, on the other hand, labourers are required to work in bad conditions, the number of casualties through accidents increases and this leads to dissatisfaction among the labourers. Conditions of work include many tangible and intangible factors such as proper sanitary conditions, arrangements for good air and water, provision of adequate resting places, peaceful atmosphere, good climate, proper lighting, and cordial relations between the workers and the bosses with smooth liaison between the two. Guidance from the hands of the psychologist brings about the best results in each case. The psychologist must cooperate with the opthalmic surgeon to decide the best angle of lighting. Colour combinations within the factory premises are known to affect the efficiency of the worker, experiments having revealed that a smoothing combination of colour effects improves general efficiency and also reduces the accident rate. And it is for the psychologist to pronounce judgement as to when the machines and general factory premises should be painted.

Human Involvement

Having chosen the right man for the right job in the factory is not the end of the problem, as it is necessary, for high levels of production, that the efficiency of the worker be maintained and even improved if his optimum has not been achieved. Labourer is a human being, and not a cog in the wheel. If his talent is to be exploited, it is necessary to keep in view human motives and human psychology. Psychology can easily help to solve all the human problems that crop up in an industry.

Field of Industrial Psychology

The foregoing description should have convinced the reader that psychology pervades every aspect of industry, and can do good. Its actual importance for the modern era can be gauged by the knowledge that application of psychology to the field of industry has led to the emergence and development of a separate branch of psychology, known as Industrial psychology. In the words of Blum, "Industrial psychology is simply the application or extension of psychological facts and principles to the problems concerning human relations in business and industry." Human relations in industry came into the limelight. Under extensive investigation after the Industrial Revolution in Europe. Realisation of the magnitude of the problem led to the development of Industrial psychology in the twentieth century, a science which tells of the capability and interest of an individual for a particular function. It helps to select the correct person for specialised Jobs. It defines the principle whereby proper conditions can be created to achieve the maximum efficiency with the least possible amount of exertion and fatigue. One important aspect of Industrial psychology is Job Analysis. Every factory and mill provides various kinds of work, all of which are analysed by the psychologist who then lays down the qualities that are required of the individual who is to perform it. In a factory, there must be constant supervision of the labourers' work. And Industrial psychology effects improvements in the methods of supervision and observation. It helps to maintain an atmosphere in the workhouse which promotes cordial relations between the workers and the boss. It puts forward constructive suggestions for improving the efficiency in order to provide a check on his progress or failure. It has been pointed out earlier, and is fairly evident, that industry today has much need for effective and strong advertisements and propaganda. Nowadays, Industrial psychology has extended its function to include advice on the manufacture of machinery that can help to minimise fatigue and improve production.

Humanist Thought in An Industry

In the present era, there are many factors promoting the development and increase of humanist thought in the field of industry, reputedly a mechanised giant not amenable to human approaches. No longer is the labourer looked upon in the light of a small cog in the wheel of progress, a mere tool in the massive production machinery. Realization that industry is benefited by the happiness and satisfaction of the labour class has dawned, and industrial progress has been allied to labour welfare. This humanization of industry is a state of human thought for which psychology must be praised. It is due to the prevalence of such enlightened thinking that the capitalist class can be persuaded to think of the welfare of their workers. Stress on the alliance between the physical and mental aspects of human labour is the contribution of psychology. It contends that efficient physical endeavour is not possible in the absence of mental satisfaction. This fact must be kept in mind while improving the methods of work in the factory.

In this manner, an industrial is rendering valuable assistance in the entire field of industry. As knowledge of the human individual increases in the domain of psychology, the importance of psychology in the sphere of industry will grow.

Difficulty in the Selection of Workers

Modern psychology has by now undoubtedly established that individuals differ from each other in respect of their abilities, qualities of the personality, capabilities and interests. On the other hand, different functions within various industries require particular qualities and abilities in the individuals obliged to perform them. Hence, for this, it becomes essential that for a particular function only that person should be retained who possesses the requisite qualities and abilities, a requirement that leads to the problem of selection. This problem has a positive as well as a negative aspect. In its negative aspect, the activity of selection consists in sorting out the undesirable individuals from among all those who have applied for the appointment to a particular post, while in its positive aspect it consists in selecting one individual from all those who, *prima facie,* seems to qualify for the job. Such selection must take into account the interests, requirements, abilities and attitudes of the applicants.

Why is Personnel Selection Essential?

The main cause of the necessity of personnel selection is the fact of individual differences. Many experiments have led to the establishment of the fact that abilities in individual beings differ considerably as a consequence of hereditary differences. Certain qualities are innate and cannot be improved upon much through training. An individual's attitudes, mental tendency, etc., become fairly evident even in his infancy, and in greater or lesser degree they remain the same throughout his life. These attitudes have considerable importance for an individual's life. Generally speaking, any work that one can perform best is the one in the direction of which one has a mental tendency. It is not in the mental make-up of every individual to be a successful and skilful engineer, and neither is every man made to be a giant tycoon of a business. Some children evince great interest in manual work of a skilled nature and in science, and it is these children who usually develop into good engineers or scientists. All these psychological facts go to prove that any individual can be fitted into any job and that training can prepare an individual for any function are wrong. Hence, personnel selection is very much in vogue in every industry in the modern world.

Two Aspects of Personnel Selection

Personnel selection has two aspects: one, which is the analysis of each and every particular independent function in an industry in order to establish the qualities required for the individual performing it. The second function of this selection is to examine all candidates and determine the qualities and abilities that each of them possesses. The first function is called job analysis while the second aspect is called worker's analysis.

JOB ANALYSIS

Aims of Job Analysis

It has been pointed out before that the main objective of job analysis is the selection of personnel. But it can also have other objectives such as improvements in the methods of working, training of employees, promotion of employees, obviating accidents and protection of health, etc.

What is Job Analysis?

Defining job analysis, Blum has remarked, "A job analysis is an accurate study of the various components of a job. It is concerned not only with an analysis of the duties and conditions of work, but also with the individual qualifications of the worker." It is evident that job analysis will reveal the duties of individuals in a particular job or profession, as also the conditions in which they will be required to work. It will also bring out the qualities required of an individual aspiring to perform some definite function or a piece of work. According to J.D. Hackett, in the process of job analysis, the fundamental elements of a job are established and clarified, while simultaneously the abilities desirable out of the worker are known, the abilities that will help him to perform his function skilfully. Thus, job analysis has two aspects, one analysis of duties and conditions of work, and the other, the analysis of qualities desired in the worker or an employee.

Advantages of Job Analysis

Job analysis confers many advantages. On the basis of 401 essays concerned with job analysis, Zerga pointed out twenty advantages and utilities of job analysis. One is the increase in efficiency, as well as increase in the mutual feelings of the workers since everyone is happy to be employed in the job he cherishes. Job analysis can help to determine the salary or wages accruing to the employee for a particular function performed by him. Job analysis helps in the classification of professions and occupations; it thereby becomes possible to determine the qualities required for them. Through job analysis it also becomes possible to determine the extent of training necessary for a specific individual to be given a particular job. Job analysis determines the duty of everyone in his own job by determining the responsibility inherent in any kind of work.

Various Components of Job

Now, the first thing to be mentioned in connection with job analysis is the presence of various components in a job. Headings of information collected in this connection are as follows:

1. Identification of the Job.
2. Number Employed.

3. Statement of Duties.
4. Machines Used.
5. Analysis of Operations.
6. Conditions of Work.
7. Pay and Incentives.
8. Relation to Other Allied Jobs.
9. Opportunities for Transfer and Promotion.
10. Time and Nature of Training.
11. Personal Requirements:
    (a) General — Age, Sex, Nationality, Marital Status.
    (b) Physical.
    (c) Educational.
    (d) Previous Experience.
    (e) General and Special Abilities.
    (f) Temperamental and Character Requirements.

As is evident from the above list, there is an extensive collection of data regarding job analysis.

Methods of Job Analysis

Of the many methods employed in job analysis, the main are as follows:

1. Individual Psychographic Method.
2. Questionnaire Method.
3. Job Psychographic Method.
4. Job Analysis by Text.
5. Motion Study Method.

These methods will now be described in brief.

1. Individual psychographic method In this method, the mental peculiarities of an individual, successful in a particular kind of job, are examined, a list of these peculiarities prepared and this list is transcribed in figure form on graph. This provides some standard of judgement in future recruitments for the same job.

2. Questionnaire method A list of questions is prepared on the basis of the different qualities of personality concerned with the job. This list is then provided to the individuals doing that job, and they are asked to answer these questions. An analysis of the answers received helps to reveal the special qualities necessary for the job, a list of which can now be prepared. This, too, helps in the future selection of candidates for the job in question.

3. Job psychographic method According to Viteles, there are three things essential for job psychographic method:

(a) Accurate classification of mental qualities.

(b) Valid methods of evaluation.

(c) Direct examination or analysis by trained examiners.

In this manner, in this method, some specialist analysts study the work, and they evolve a valid and standard method of evaluation. They prepare a very accurate list in which the various mental qualities required for the job are properly and reliably classified. A graph of these qualities is prepared so that selection of candidates for the job may become easier.

4. Job analysis by test In the test method, some reliable and valid tests are performed on the basis of essential qualities and abilities. The candidates are tested for selection and suitability by these tests.

5. Motion study method Under this method, the speed of individual worker in performing some job and the time consumed therein are both noted. Similar examinations are performed on the other individuals doing the same work, and the results obtained are compared. Such a study of speed and time helps in job analysis and classification of the workers.

Job analysis can be done by any one or more of these methods, the choice of method being governed by the situation or circumstances.

WORKER'S ANALYSIS

Essential Elements in Worker's Analysis

The second step in personnel selection is that of worker's analysis. In worker's analysis, as is apparent from the term used to denote it, detailed information regarding the applicant's qualities, abilities, experience and other factors is obtained. Roughly speaking, worker's analysis requires information under the following heads:

1. Age,
2. Caste,
3. Sex,
4. Nationality,
5. Physical health and characteristics,
6. Education and training,
7. Experience,

8. Level of intelligence,
9. Mental abilities and their level,
10. Interests and aptitudes,
11. Personality traits.

Having gathered the above information regarding a particular applicant, it becomes possible to determine the kind of a job he is likely to prove proficient in, and the kind of job in which he tends to be a failure. Worker's analysis also reveals the extent and nature of training that a particular individual will require; before he can successfully enter a particular profession. Worker's analysis can also help to make a rough estimate of the remuneration that can justifiably be paid to the worker, for the job in which he is expected to excel. Worker's analysis prepares a picture of an individual's personal excellence, by virtue of which it is also called as an individual's analysis.

METHODS OF WORKER'S ANALYSIS

Worker's analysis is now a matter of science, so that it has come to use certain specific methods. Broadly speaking, the following are the various methods used in worker's analysis:

1. Application Blank,
2. Letters of Recommendation,
3. Academic Record,
4. Psychological Tests,
5. Group Tests,
6. Rating,
7. Interview.

It is not essential that all the above methods be used to analyse the abilities of any individual worker, a selection of any one of them being required to meet the need in a particular case. It will be in keeping with the context to glance briefly on these methods.

1. Application blank Nowadays, the first step in the worker's analysis is the filling in of a blank by the applicant. This application blank can be designed to reveal much information of a varied kind, sometimes being so successful as to reveal the individual's entire background. In the application blank, the individual provides information regarding his age, sex, caste, nationality, earlier or past level of education, training, personal experience, history, etc. What kind of information should be provided in the application blanks is determined differently in different professions.

Professions that are likely to be influenced by the worker's attitudes, mental inclinations, interests, etc., require that information regarding them should also be provided in the application blank. Many advertisers do not make a detailed report of what the applicant is expected to include in his application; they make a brief mention of a very few things. Application blanks of this kind do not qualify for scientific consideration. An application blank should preferably contain detailed inquiries regarding all important facts and details. Research in this direction can help to form outlines of application blanks for various professions, and according to that outline, blanks can be provided to the various applicants and aspirants. Often, evidence is required to substantiate the acts detailed in the application.

2. Letters of recommendation. Letters of recommendation also help in worker's analysis. In this method, the aspirant produces various recommendations, recommendations from his previous employer, the Principal of his school or college, or from some respected stalwarts of society, etc. In these letters, in addition to the natural commendation, some degree of ability is also evidenced, but often these letters are seen to contain many confusing and incorrect pieces of information regarding the individual. One of the simplest ways of misleading the intended employer is to include many qualities that the aspirant does not possess, or to overemphasize the qualities that he is fortunate enough to possess. As a general rule, such letters of recommendation usually prove to be hindrances rather than helps to the process of job analysis, but if they are valid and reliable, they can definitely promote job analysis or worker's analysis.

3. Academic records Different professions require different levels of education as an essential qualification. Academic records are evidences of the individual's educational progress and proficiency. These sometimes include cumulative records of the universities.

4. Psychological tests But the most important and valid method of worker's analysis is that of psychological testing in which the applicant's mental ability, interest, personality and particularly attitude are tested. Results of these tests should be employed with exemplary caution since they can also lead to very serious mistakes,

5. Physical tests There are some jobs that require physical fitness of various kinds as an essential pre-requisite, for example, the eye-sight of a railway guard should be normal and not impaired. And for satisfaction on this point, different physical tests have been devised to suit various professions and their requirements. Nowadays, physical or medical tests have become an essential part of examinations for governmental jobs.

6. Group tests There are some professions in which many workers have to work collectively but even if they work individually they are constantly thrown together in the process of their work. Hence in their case, it is essential for them to possess certain group qualities which are otherwise not taken into consideration. And it is with the intention of evaluating such qualities of collective behaviour in the individual that the employees or applicants are tested in the group. In other words, their conduct in the group is judged.

7. Rating One of the many aspects of worker's analysis is the rating given to the individual by his Principal in school or college or by psychologists. This rating is sometimes taken into consideration by the worker analyst.

8. Interview Finally, in most of the industries today, the applicant is personally interviewed by the employer and some other specialists, during which he is questioned by them on various topics so that they can form some estimate of him as an individual. Every examiner or individual of the board of interviewers asks some or the other question, but even while the applicant is engaged in answering it, the rest of the board is very minutely observing his reactions and conduct. Interview as a method of judging personality has advantages over other methods in that it reveals certain aspects of the individual that cannot be brought to light otherwise. It helps to form an estimate of the individual in respect of his self-confidence, self-control, response to discipline, presence of mind, dynamicity, interests, manner of dressing, conduct, behaviour, manners, attraction of personality, if any, etc., besides many other intangible things that make an impression on the mind of a viewer. But for this method to yield valid and desirable results, it is essential that the interviewers themselves be educated, trained arid unbiased since, otherwise, such an interview can lead to many misunderstandings and misjudgements.

The method of personnel selection is fairly evident from the detailed description of its two aspects, job analysis and worker's analysis. Following job analysis and worker's analysis, all that remains to be done in the way of personnel selection is to provide the individual with work for which he has been found and pronounced to be most able.

QUESTIONS FOR EXERCISE

1. What are the important methods of personnel selection? Explain any two methods.

2. Distinguish between job analysis and worker's analysis and describe briefly how either is carried out.
3. Estimate the value of vocational guidance and selection in industry.
4. Discuss briefly the methods of personnel selection and give the merits and demerits of each.
5. What is job analysis? Illustrate it and discuss its importance.
6. Discuss the social and economic importance of vocational selection.
7. Discuss the importance of scientific methods of personnel selection in industry.

17

INDUSTRIAL WORKING ENVIRONMENT

In different factories, offices and other professional premises, the worker is compelled to work under certain conditions, examples of which are innumerable. He may be required to continue his effort, of a definite kind, in some specific place. His health stands to be influenced greatly by virtue of the fact whether his place of work is adequately and properly ventilated or not. Provision of adequate lighting is an essential condition, and one which justifiably occupies the worker's mind, since it will influence his eye sight, thereby his fatigue and consequently his efficiency and the quality of his output. It is well known that noise can be a disturbing element, and may put one off one's work. One of the conditions of work is that there be little, if any, noise; hence this must be taken into consideration. Temperature or the climate is another factor that influences the potential of a worker as it is known that in certain temperatures, a worker cannot work well, while in a more moderate or suitable temperature, his work takes a turn for the better. Temperature, also, must be taken into consideration while looking out for the place of work. In addition to these physical conditions, there are many other psychological conditions that also influence the worker and consequently his work. Of these, some are the behaviour of those in authority, mutual relationships among the workers, their respective family lives, incentives to work, etc.

In this manner, the conditions of work can be divided into two classes :

1. Physical conditions,
2. Psychological conditions.

PHYSICAL CONDITIONS OF WORK

Of the physical conditions, the main ones are :

1. Intensity, location, distribution and colour of light,
2. Temperature,
3. Ventilation,
4. Noise,
5. Working hours,
6. Rest pauses,
7. Music,
8. Other physical conditions.

Of the psychological conditions that affect work, the main are:

1. Behaviour of the Authorities,
2. Mutual Relations of the Employees,
3. Security,
4. Satisfaction of Needs,
5. Incentives.

1. Intensity, location, distribution and colour of light. The kind and intensity of light differ with the occupation that employees have adopted. As a normal rule, individuals over 35 require light of a greater intensity than their younger counterpart. If the objects handled are minute, then, naturally, the light must be fairly bright, while in work where objects handled are of a large size, and the workers are fairly young, intense light is not necessary. Light provided should never be so intense as to cause glare, and never so dim as to cause strain in concentrating upon an object to be worked. Work that requires light of high intensity also requires the use of special protective glasses, as is the case with welding, where the light of a very high intensity is produced by the welding flame. Protection from its harmful effects is achieved by the use of coloured glasses.

The source of light should be so located as to avoid falling directly upon the eyes; instead, it should fall on the instrument that is to be manipulated and then also in a manner as to avoid all reflection into the eyes of the person handling it. Hence, light should be evenly distributed and for this, tube-lighting has been found to be superior to bulb lamps, which are now considered obsolete.

Daylight is naturally uniform in its distribution; it is only when the work is done at night that the problem of uniform and even lighting arises, and it is a problem that requires expert handling and planning.

Besides the intensity and location of light, it is necessary to pay attention to its colour. It has been uniformly experienced in a large number of cases that, light that resembles daylight is very nearly the best and most beneficial. Hence, white light has been considered the most superior. And in coloured light, the best is yellow but a healthy yellow and not a sickly pale yellow. All other coloured lights harm the eyes in some measure.

2. Temperature Temperature of the working premises has considerable and direct influence on the worker's health. It has been found that working in too high or too low temperatures leads to disease and accidents. Proper temperature maintains good health in the workers, and reduces the number of accidents as external conditions do not divert the attention of the worker and thus reduce his efficiency. H.M. Vernon found that in the British mines, where the temperatures are above 750 Fahrenheit, there were greater number of accidents while the perception and sensitivity of workers were also adversely affected. Extreme temperatures in working areas cause discomfort to the worker, so much so that the quality as well as quantity of his output are reduced. Temperature further influences the ventilation in a room, as it is essential for proper ventilation and flow of air to have only an adequate temperature.

3. Ventilation Inflow of fresh air is essential in a place of work, as its absence tends to increase the fatigue and laziness or drowsiness of the workers. Air easily becomes contaminated in places where a large number of individuals work together, such as mines, factories and offices. For this, the use of exhaust fans is particularly desirable. Transport should be freely and easily available in places of work. Health is adversely affected if the percentage of oxygen in air is varied even within very narrow limits. According to Poffenberger, when the percentage of oxygen in air tends to fall below 14, the workers show signs of adverse effect. Ventilation also influences the body temperature of the workers, and if the body temperature varies it leads to fatigue and drowsiness. Another important factor is the presence as well as the percentage of humidity in the air. Excessive humidity is undeniably very harmful.

4. Noise Excessive noise normally distracts attention and obstructs smooth working. It is for this reason that in every industry now attention is paid to the noise produced, and efforts are made to curb noises that distract attention. But noise of a continuous nature is often to be more soothing than disturbing, and when it is discontinued it disturbs the attention of people used to it. The truth of the matter is that only excessive noise is harmful and has the worst effect on the auditory system. Keeping in mind these observations, efforts should be made to regulate noise.

5. Hours of work Professions in which the hours of work are so long and so badly planned that the worker is completely fatigued by the time he stops working, find themselves confronted with the problem of continuously decreasing efficiency among their staff. In addition to this, these professions become prey to all kinds of very serious problems of human relationships. When a worker is compelled to work for long hours beyond his physical endurance limits, he becomes diseased and loses his efficiency. Besides, his irritability increases. For this reason, in most progressive nations, the government promulgates certain orders whereby the hours of work for different occupations, for individuals of different ages and of different sexes, are determined. If need for more work arises, the employer is faced either with the alternative of indulging in illegal activity or remunerating the worker for his extra labour. But if he chooses to evade these laws, he incurs the displeasure of the law, and this is never to his advantage.

6. Rest pauses Whatever the ability and endurance of an individual, even if he be abnormal in this respect, he cannot work continuously for long periods of time. After a certain period of time he feels the need for a rest, and his need has been found to have psychological justification, as it has been found that better results can be obtained by working in shifts and periods than by working continuously. Increases of between 10 and 20 per cent in production have been found to occur as a result of provision of rest in between work. The length and frequency of rest that are required depend upon the nature of work, the endurance and age of the worker and the general conditions of work. Hard work requires relatively longer and greater number of rest pauses. Similarly women, young children and old people require longer and greater number of rest pauses than young men. Nowadays, in practically every profession and occupation, rests of 15 minutes to an hour, are provided once or more so that the worker may be able to take refreshments and restore his vitality. Rest in between hours of work not only removes fatigue, it also eliminates the elements of monotony and boredom, thereby regenerating enthusiasm and vitality.

7. Music One of the conditions of work taken into consideration is music. From their experiments W.A. Keir and H.C. Smith concluded that music has a beneficial and desirable influence upon the mental condition of workers, and thus it helps to induce some increase in their productive capacity. And one often sees people singing at their work, a phenomenon particularly obvious in the case of Indian women working at the grinder or in the fields or even when at their domestic chores. The rhythm in music has a beneficial effect on the rate of working. Tatas in India provide music in their various factories. In Western countries, particularly in the United States, the use of music in factories and other working places is steadily on the increase. Through a questionnaire H.C. Smith collected the views of one thousand workers regarding the provision of music in working places, and found that as many as 98 per cent of them were in favour of it, as they found considerable pleasure in it. The influence of music on routine work is as yet under extensive study.

8. Other physical conditions In addition to these conditions, there are other physical and material considerations which influence the worker and his work. For example, if there is good provision of clean urinals, latrines, bathrooms, refreshments rooms, canteen, etc., the worker's time in the office becomes more pleasant, and many of his difficulties are removed. A place of work should not be foul smelling, neither should it be dirty or dusty, as any of these conditions disgust the worker.

PSYCHOLOGICAL CONDITIONS OF WORK

Of the psychological conditions of work, the more important have the following influence:

1. Behaviour of those in authority A worker's mind is very susceptible to the behaviour of his boss. If the behaviour of authorities is desirable and good, the worker's enthusiasm and interest in his work are maintained, but if their behaviour is bad and inconsiderate, it is potentially a dangerous state as it can lead to conflict and unnecessary tension that has the worst effect upon production. Good behaviour does not imply laxity in administration and in dealing with the workers, as in such circumstances it is inevitable that the lazy and designing individuals in the organization will have a field day and do no work at all. It is essential that constant attention be paid to the worker's performance, but tact and diplomacy should be employed if it becomes necessary to point out his shortcomings. Senior officials and employers who are in the habit of constantly haranguing and bickering with their staff, are very often faced with continuous conflict and non-cooperation. Employees are not inclined to respect and work for people who are irritable, highly inflammable and ingratiating types. Working under a considerate individual not only keeps the worker happy but also inspires him to work more and work better.

2. Mutual relations of workers One of the psychological conditions of working is the nature of relations that exist between the workers themselves. Where the number of workers is fairly large, and the nature of work demands their constant co-operation, better results are obtained if the workers have happy relations. If the relations are not happy, work suffers. And particularly the work that requires comparative effort suffers too much if there is no co-operation.

3. Security in profession If the worker is confident that he is secure in his job, then his work shows definite improvements. If a profession that offers no security of employment, or in a position in which one can never be confident of remaining safe, a worker cannot work with enthusiasm or with his mind on the work. Hence, a profession must offer security of future employment. After a certain predetermined period of service has been completed, the worker should be made permanent in his position, as is now done in all government jobs and many private firms. Even most governments in many countries have made laws regarding such employment procedure. Besides this minimal security of profession, other inducements are insurance during unemployment, old age insurance, and security of insurance in the event of accidents that render the individual incapable of further work. Nowadays, in all progressive states, government and other general employers make provision for these benefits, as in their absence it is only natural for the worker to spend time in wondering about his future and making efforts to secure it, efforts that enfeeble him for his regular work.

4. Satisfaction of life's needs Every individual has some personal and other family requirements, such as adequate food and housing for his family, and purchasing power to the extent of his other reasonable needs. Besides this, there are certain needs that foster self-respect, and these, too, cannot be neglected. Progress has made it necessary for employers to pay attention to these aspects of the human personality also. Consequently they have to initiate and finance certain schemes of labour welfare that involve some expenditure, which provide many direct and indirect benefits to the worker that place him in a very favourable state of mind. Their needs being fulfilled, they are inclined to respect and obey their employers, to work for their better prospects in turn. They have confidence in their employers, and thus they are never inclined to work contrary to the interests of their employers.

5. Incentives in industry Motives have an important place in the life of a man. In the absence of a motive, no individual can either work hard or do anything better in his life or improve his work in any way. Inspiration of this kind is available to the individual in his trade in the form of various kinds of incentives such as increase in wages, praise by authorities, promotion, bonus, etc. Incentives are now an important part of any well geared up industry. In most progressive nations, the workers stand to benefit through bonus if the production rises, and thus improve their earning, their morale goes up. In most professions, an individual is promoted to a senior position if he shows satisfactory work. If the people in authority are sensible, they will always praise the extra efforts of their subordinates. Their wages can also be increased so as to provide an extra inducement.

All the aforementioned physical and psychological conditions have considerable importance for commerce and industry. And psychologists have now seriously drawn the attention of the industrialists to this aspect. It is necessary not only with regard to economic or fiscal gain, but also with regard to humanity that the workers should have the opportunity to work in beneficial conditions, both physical and psychological. Workers, being part and parcel of the fibre of the nation, the government also should take steps to have such conditions created. When such a system is in existence in industry, the conflicts are reduced and the production increased, with the result that the employer, the employee and the state all benefit.

CHANCES OF PROMOTION

Every employee wishes that at various stages of his service he be given chances of promotion and progress. Promotion involves change in status or position of authority within the official structure. In every profession and occupation, the services are graded in one definite order. In administrative service, for example, the deputy collector supersedes the tehsildar while he in his turn is superseded by the collector. Above the collector is the commissioner. Similarly, in the army, there are various posts, such as second-lieutenant, lieutenant, captain, major, lieutenant, colonel, etc. In every profession, the higher post or status carries better salary as well as greater authority with a correspondingly greater responsibility. Hence, it is only natural that every individual should wish to occupy as high a post as is within his grasp.

Kinds of Promotion

But promotion should not be taken to imply the gaining of a higher post. Although that precisely is the sense in which it is usually interpreted, yet the term should be more properly used to include all increases in pay, increase in leave, improved conditions of work, increase in respect and honour, etc. Walters has described the following eight kinds of promotion:[1]

1. Walters, J.E., *Applied Personnel Administration,* Wiley.

1. Increase in wages, salary or remuneration,
2. increase in position, authority or responsibility,
3. increase in leave or decrease in hours of work,
4. transfer to a better place or department,
5. improvement in place of residence or of working,
6. opportunities of gaining training and experience becoming available,
7. greater security of position of benefit,
8. increase in the period of service.

In this manner, then, if the worker's salary or remuneration is increased, he will be deemed to have been promoted. He will equally be deemed to have benefited in the same manner if he is given a higher position, greater authority or responsibility. He may be allowed to work for fewer hours. Or, in other words, time available for recreation will have been increased, whereby he stands promoted. As an indication of promotion, individual may be transferred to a better place or to another department considered better. Services or employments that involve transfer of employees from one place to another make use of this device to promote their personnel. Seeing that a particular person is good at his work, he can be shown signs of favour by improving his working conditions or by improving his place of residence. Employees who work well are given chances of gaining further training and obtaining additional experience. In almost all services, if the employee continues to show improvement after his appointment thereto, his post is made permanent and secure. Security of employment is another form in which promotion may be indicated. When individuals show a consistently good record of work, their period of service is increased. In many cases, people are re-employed after having been officially retired from service.

From among the various forms or kinds of promotion described above, different individuals favour different kinds, relative to the various professions. Some people place the highest premium upon economic gain while others find more value in increased respect and honour. Improvement in the conditions of work is another mode of promotion that is dear to some individuals. And it is equally inessential that in some specific context only one form of promotion may be awarded. In very many cases, promotion leads to increased wages, authority and responsibility as well as better conditions of working. In this manner, often the employee gets his promotion in more forms than one.

Bases of Promotion

In every profession there are some definite laws governing promotion, just as there are definite ways of selection and appointment. One of the commonest methods of promotion is that of seniority in which every employee is promoted after he has put in a definite period of work in one situation. But, equally, in almost all services, attention is paid to the individual's ability when he is being considered for promotion, over and above the extent of his service. It sometimes occurs that an individual's ability and efficiency are so great that he is given promotion by superseding other senior officials. Private business lays much stress on work as well as on ability. The employer stands to gain something if his employees work better and more, so that he is easily enabled to enhance their wages or to give them a greater share in the profits. But in certain occupations, inside and outside the government structure, where the employer himself does not superintend the work, or where there is no objective or concrete employer himself, or where the employer is of the ingratiating type, promotion depends more on pleasing authority than upon seniority, ability or results obtained. In professions in which there are no definite laws and rules governing promotion of the workers, promotion takes place through the whim of those in authority.

From the above description, it is evident that promotion depends upon the following factors:

1. Seniority,
2. Ability,
3. Better and more work,
4. Kindness of the authorities.

Promotion on the Basis of Seniority

In most occupations and services, wages of the employees increase somewhat every year, and thus seniority is a basis of promotion common to almost all occupations. Seniority as a basis of promotion has psychological sanction, as every worker wishes that in view of the greater period of service rendered, he should be given a post above the newcomers. Absence of any definite rules regarding promotion on the grounds of seniority leads to discontent and people lose interest in work. At the same time, they show no inclination to stick to any one profession. Naturally, the profession as a whole tends to suffer through such vagrancy as every new entrant takes his time in learning the ropes and if the old ones keep running away, much efficiency and effort are lost.

It is for this reason that in every service, wages improve with seniority, and in most cases promotion also takes place on the same basis. But it is incorrect to consider seniority the sole basis of promotion. Just as the senior individual desires promotion, the more able and efficient also desires promotion and better prospects. If his talent is allowed to lie dormant, and if he has to wait a number of years before he comes into authority, or if he is required to constantly serve under a less efficient man, he is inclined to lose patience and become dissatisfied. His mind wanders out of the periphery of his work, and he feels imposed upon if asked to obey the less able individual who is in authority. And this insubordination leads to defective administration. Hence, ability should be taken into consideration along with seniority when the question of promotion comes up.

Promotion on the Basis of Ability

The second major basis of promotion is the individual's ability that takes very young people to the tops of their professions in very short periods of time. And if seniority be the sole basis, then an individual starting at the lowest rung can never reach the top. For this, ability, and consideration of ability, are very essential. Yet, for this reason alone, it is not safe to completely discount seniority, as many occupations place the premium upon experience. Secondly, having put in years of hard and honest service, the employee desires that he be given some token of appreciation for his selfless service, because if he is not promoted he becomes dissatisfied. And, there can be no general rule regarding the alternate propriety of seniority or ability as the basis of promotion in any individual case, or any single profession. Generally speaking wages or salary should be commensurate with the years of service put in. But before a key post, or a position that wields very wide authority can be handed to a person, it is essential to inquire into his antecedents and evaluate his abilities.

Promotion on the Basis of Results

Those in authority everywhere, whatever the profession, whatever the service, desire subordinates should give off their best. Where private business is concerned, the employer is interested in one thing exclusively, that is, results in terms of work, both as regards quantity and quality. Hence, in such cases, promotion is also dispensed on the basis of results obtained by the individual under review. This particular method of promotion gives very good results in a large majority of cases since it not only satisfies the instincts and interests of those interested in efficiency and ability, but also appears inducement to those not so inclined. It leads most people to emulate others, and very good results are achieved all round.

Promotion on the Basis of Kindness or Recommendation

Recommendation or kindness of authorities is perhaps the worst method of promotion. Yet, it is very much in vogue in this enlightened age. In government and semi-government organisations, it is the ingratiating type of individual who figures the highest on lists of promotions as he makes his presence felt by grovelling to the authorities, by entertaining officers, by making judicious presents to them and to members of their families or by benefiting them in other respects. Lacking this effusive sociability, even the most efficient, honest and hard-working individual with a good seniority remains in position without any hope of progress. Cases of this nature also present very bad examples to other workers, with the result that the best part of their energies are wasted in pleasing the authorities rather than in working.

Modes of Promotion

The above description of the bases of promotions also reveals the mode of promotion. In fact, an individual has to be selected for promotion in much the same manner in which he is to be selected for appointment. In both cases, much care and understanding should be used in making the selection. What more usually happens is that the care taken in selecting an individual for appointment is far greater than the attention paid to his promotion. And in most cases promotion is done on the basis of seniority, one of the most prevalent methods. Promoting an individual on the basis of his ability is none the worse. Another good, and fairly reliable, method of promotion is the one based upon efficiency and results obtained in previous position. But to promote an individual on one's whim, on recommendation, on one's pleasure, is not at all a good method, but a thoroughly undesirable one. It is unscientific, unethical and harmful also.

Importance of Promotion

Promotion is an important aspect of every profession. Its propriety is based on the psychological fact that every employee wants promotion and improvement on the basis of efficiency, ability or years of service. Promotion is also an important inducement to the employee to work better and to work more. Promotion gives the worker enthusiasm and confidence, encourages him to produce even better results. Existence of definite rules of promotion induces a sense of security in the employee, as then he can decide on the method he has to follow in order to benefit and gain promotion. Under these conditions, they are not only discouraged, but are even inclined to try even harder. For this reason, it is essential that in every establishment the rules of promotion be definite and precisely laid down, so that there be no cause for complaint. Seniority, ability and the quantum of work done form the propriety of promotions. Promotion based on recommendations or personal likes or dislikes, or because of considerations of personal gains is completely improper and unjustified. Such behaviour kills the initiative of other workers, and their efficiency falls. Evidently, promotion in any service is as important for the employer as it is for the employee. The employer can use that as a basis for selecting good workers, and thus his work benefits. The worker's incentive to continue his effort is maintained. He is even inclined to improve the quality of his work. But promotion is actually beneficial only when its rules are observed, and are so known to every employee. Its best use can be made only if its basis is correct, proper and scientific.

QUESTIONS FOR EXERCISE

1. Citing relevant studies, discuss the influence of noise on industrial output.
2. Citing relevant studies, show how physical conditions of work affect the worker and production.
3. Describe the effect of noise and music on industrial efficiency.
4. Distinguish between the physical and psychological environments of the worker and state the importance of latter.
5. What are the organizational and psychological climates in the many and varied industrial environments? Discuss the importance of psychological climates in industry.
6. Attempt an analysis of the basic criteria that should be taken into account in evaluating working conditions in industry.
7. Distinguish between the physiological and psychological factors of working environment and discuss their interrelationship.
8. List the physical aspects of industrial environment that affect efficiency of work and discuss any two of them fully.
9. Show how rest pauses and noise affect the efficiency of work.

18

EFFICIENCY, TIME-MOTION STUDY AND THERBLIGS

Quality and quantity of work, in any factory, industry or office do not depend upon the machines alone. Whatever the quality of mechanical equipment existing in the factory, for a very high level of production, it is essential that the individuals operating the machines be experts, and highly qualified. Hence, Industrial psychology makes a detailed study of the factors and problems influencing efficiency. Psychologists have also suggested various measures for improving and maintaining the efficiency of working personnel.

WHAT IS EFFICIENCY?

What is this efficiency? How can it be discovered or determined? Efficiency is the individual's skill in any specific job, by virtue of which he can perform that function well. Efficiency is not a general quality because no individual can do everything efficiently. He can be highly skilled in only a couple of functions. Different individuals have skill in different kinds of jobs while people who are skilful in the same work differ in the degree of skill. His efficiency, or a statement of it, must be qualified by the function in respect of which he is acknowledged to be successful. A skilful person can perform some definite function better and quicker than the average worker. Hence, efficiency is measured or reckoned by the quantity of work done, and the time taken in doing it. If mere saving of time is effected, the person cannot be said to be skilful because he must also maintain the quality and quantity of work in that reduced time. Similarly, skill as a quality cannot be attributed to any individual who merely does a lot of work. Evidently, efficiency requires more and better work to be done in less time. If a person possesses all these three qualities, in connection with some definite form of work, more than other individuals doing the same work, he will be said to be more efficient. Evidently, then efficiency is a relative term. Individuals are efficient as compared to one another. But this efficiency is not affected at all times and between all individuals. Normally, when an individual is said to be efficient, it is implied that he does more work than the average worker in the same unit and does it better in the same time.

DETERMINANTS OF EFFICIENCY

In order to maintain and improve upon the efficiency of individuals, psychologists made a detailed study of the conditions or determinants of efficiency. Efficiency is a psycho-physical state in which both mind and body are directly involved. Hence, its determinants can also be roughly divided into the internal and external. External conditions are the following:

1. Rest,
2. Work period,
3. Health,
4. Climate.

Now these various external conditions will be described in some length:

1. Rest In the foregoing chapter of fatigue it was mentioned that a person becomes tired if he works without rest, and his skill decreases proportionately: hence it is evident that rest is one essential factor of efficiency. In an experiment Sheppard put twelve college students on the chest-waist machine for eight hours, the work to them being repeated but with intervening periods of rest. This experiment illustrated that uninterrupted work reduced the worker's efficiency. Watt's experiments showed that work done with adequate provisions for rest led to an increase in efficiency of up to 9.3 per cent. Vernon and Bedford studied workers in an electricity plant or power house who worked both with rest and then without rest. They came to the conclusion that work done without rest does not produce very good results. Other experiments have proved that where the work is of a purely mental nature it is best to relax for a period of five minutes after every hour of work, while a ten-minute break is better. Of the entire hours of work in a day, the workers should be given 16.6 per cent as rest.

It must also be kept in mind that providing unnecessary periods of rest has no real benefit, but is instead prone to cause loss. Too long a period of rest leads the worker's mind away from his work completely. Ten minutes are enough under normal conditions. But it is wrong to imagine that lunch time is a period of rest. During the period of rest, the worker must not be give n any physical or mental work. Another important thing in this connection is that the time of rest should be predetermined as its uncertainty is harmful because of the tension created by it. As it is, the existing tension is not reduced. The time required for rest in a particular form of work is something that cannot be laid down with any severity. There can be no general rule. As a general rule, some rest is required in every form of work, but normally more tough or difficult work requires longer periods of rest.

Rest creates mainly the following benefits:

(a) Production increases in quality and quantity.

(b) Accidents in the industry decreases.

(c) Boredom and disinterest are eliminated.

(d) Relaxation reduces tension and provides comfort.

2. Time of work Another important determining factor of efficiency is the time of work. If the period of work required from the employee is unnecessarily long, it will be natural for the worker to feel exhausted with the result that his efficiency will fall. Many experiments have proved that the labourer should not be compelled to work for more than eight hours. Forty hours in the week is quite sufficient and adequate. As the hours of work increase beyond this, the worker's enthusiasm, efficiency, health, strength and capability, etc., steadily fall, the ultimate outcome of which is harmful for the employer. Hence, the salvation of the employer as well as employed lies in the fact that the hours of work should not be increased beyond well-defined limits.

3. Health A good health is another requirement for high efficiency. If the worker does not enjoy good health, he will be prone to fatigue and low quality of work done. The importance of health in industry is evident from the development of a new branch of science, the Industrial Hygiene. It makes a study of all conditions and circumstances that influence the worker's health, and helps in the creation of conditions that will favourably influence it. The advent of industrial hygiene led to the improvement in the health of workers as well as in the quality and quantity of work produced by them. According to industrial hygiene, in order to maintain a good standard of health among workers in industrial centres, the following facts should be attended to:

(a) Every industrial centre should be equipped with a good doctor who can immediately attend to a worker falling ill.

(b) Special attention must be paid to the prevention of contagious diseases from spreading among the workers. Immediately as some worker contracts any such disease, he should be quarantined, and put under expert medical care.

(c) As far as possible, alcoholic and other stimulants should not be available to the workers, and even the ones addicted to it should be helped to get rid of their addiction.

(d) Workers should be given essential information on matters of health, and on the prevention of some common diseases.

(e) Special attention should be paid to workers physically, mentally or financially backward, and special facilities provided to reduce the degree of backwardness.

4. Climate Climatic conditions of the place of work also influence efficiency. Many of the important things in this connection have been mentioned in a previous chapter entitled Psychology in Industry. Modern factories that are scientifically designed have special arrangements for controlled lighting, ventilation, running water, cleanliness, temperature, sound, etc. If this is not done, the health and ultimately the efficiency of the worker suffer.

In addition to the external conditions, efficiency is also affected by some internal conditions, which are as follows:

1. Motivation,
2. Monotony,
3. Application,
4. Emotional adjustment,
5. Aptitude and personality differences.

1. Motivation Motivation is intimately concerned with efficiency. If it is lacking, the presence of all physical comforts cannot induce any efficiency. But if is present, and most other comforts lacking, efficiency is maintained to a fairly large extent. And ways of providing motivation in industry have been studied in a previous chapter. For motivated working in industry, it is essential that the needs of worker be fulfilled, his health be maintained, his future be fairly secure, and that he be promoted and otherwise rewarded adequately for efficient and skilful work. If promotions come as a result of ingratiating behaviours towards the authorities, even the most efficient worker loses motivation. If the people in authority do not behave properly, the worker loses his-motivation. All these things have been studied.

2. Boredom Boredom is another factor that has an adverse effect upon the efficiency because in it the mind and body both lose their vigour. Hence, psychologists have conducted many experiments towards discovering the nature of this phenomenon of boredom, and have tried to analyse its causes. The following means can be employed to reduce or prevent boredom in work:

(a) *Variety in work:* According to Poffenberger, one cause of boredom is the repetition of same kind of work. It is a matter of common experience that one tires of the same work if persisted in, and this fact does not need the endorsement of a psychologist. Hence, if interest in the work is to be maintained it is necessary that the work presents some variety to the worker. This variety can be used to reduce or even prevent boredom.

(b) *Rest along with work*: If there is no adequate arrangement for rest along with work, an individual becomes exhausted and tends to become bored. Hence, it is desirable to have some definite arrangement for rest along with work, if boredom is to be avoided.

(c) *Short hours of work*: If the hours of work are very long, the worker becomes bored and tends to remain fatigued most of the time. Hence, it is essential that the hours of work be not long.

(d) *Arrangement of recreation*: Recreation refreshes the individual, hence it is most essential for removing boredom. Therefore, it is now a common practice to provide the workers with all kinds of equipment with which they can amuse, and refresh themselves. It creates novelty as well as a diversion that helps to recreate interest in the worker.

(e) *Motivation*: To keep boredom away, motivation in the work of the worker should be maintained by various means. He should not be allowed to work under heavy pressure of any kind. He should be encouraged to develop his own motivation for the work he does.

(f) *Selection of work according to intelligence, personality and abilities*: If any work that the individual does, does not conform to his level of intelligence, qualities of his personality, his capacity and special abilities, then he will gradually become increasingly bored. Hence, it is essential that the person chooses his occupation with due regard to his own personality and its complication.

3. Application Another important and essential internal condition of efficiency is the undisturbed and undivided application of the employee to his work. For this, it is necessary to remove noise and other obstacles or interferences. Sometimes the absence of motivation is another cause of indifference to work. For efficiency it is essential that all internal as well as external diverting factors be removed from the sphere of activity, and the worker encouraged to pursue his work undisturbed and with the fullest application.

4. Emotional adjustment A study of most accidents reveals that they are caused by inattention, lack of interest, laxity or mental conflict. And all of these factors have emotional maladjustment at their root. Hence, another important condition of efficiency is emotional adjustment. In order to maintain it, generally the conditions of work of the employee should be good. In addition to this, individual guidance should be available to them in order to help them to solve some of their personality problems.

5. Characteristic interests and personality traits Finally, efficiency also depends to a large extent upon the individual's own characteristic interests and personality traits. If his occupation conforms to them, his efficiency is maintained but in case of an adverse choice of trade, his efficiency lies unexploited. Secondly, there is a certain class of individuals in the case of whom it is very difficult to maintain any definite level of efficiency, though efforts can achieve some degree of success in this direction.

From the above account of the various conditions and determining factors of efficiency, it would be apparent that industrial psychology has made considerable headway in its research on this aspect, and that continuous efforts are being made to discover systematic law. Such an effort can only have the most desirable results for both employer as well as employed.

TIME-MOTION STUDY

Taylor's Studies

Study of time and motion in industrial psychology has revealed many important things regarding efficiency. In 1910 Taylor carried out certain experiments concerning motion. In this study he divided a single function into numerous component parts, and noted the time taken in the performance of each part. After this, he increased their wages, and, reducing the time taken in the performance of each component task, he studied the results. Following motion study there was time study.

Gilbreth's Studies

But the most important study on this aspect was by Gilbreth. Through a study of time-motion Gilbreth tried to discover the method by means of which a worker can do the greatest amount of work

Symbol	Name of Symbol	Symbol	Name of Symbol
	Search	#	Disassemble
	Find	0	Inspect
→	Find		Pre-Position
∩	Grasp		Release Load
	Transport Loaded		Transport Empty
			Rest for overcoming Fatigue
9	Position		Unavoidable Delay
#	Assemble		Avoidable Delay
U	Use	8	Plan

Fig. 18.1 Therbligs Chart

possible in less time than normal. For this, he observed that maximum economy in this could be effected only if all unnecessary activities were eliminated from the function, and only the absolutely essential or inevitable activities were allowed to remain. Conducting experiments of this nature on labourers who haul bricks, Gilbreth concluded that, if all unnecessary movements were excluded, the work normally done in twelve hours could be completed in five, while, instead of moving 120 bricks in an hour it is possible to displace some 350 bricks in the same time. In his study Gilbreth made use of the cyclegraph for studying movements. Stop-watches were used to record time. In a time-motion study, all the movements required in any function are divided into the smallest invisible units. Then, analysis reveals the unnecessary and the necessary activities, the unnecessary or superfluous being eliminated. At a later stage, motion came to be studied with automatic cameras, and with tri-dimensional cameras even later. Nowadays, besides noting the length, breadth and height, it also records the time. This complete picture is known as the stereo-crono-cyclegraph. With its help it is possible to study all the motions of any one piece of work at the same time.

THERBLIGS

In addition to studying motion, Gilbreth also tried to validate them, and for doing so he determined the symbols of various movements, and he started using those symbols to describe those particular kinds of movements. Gilbreth formed seventeen such symbols of various movements.

These symbols are called therbligs. This work contains all letters that Gilbreth's name includes, only their order is reversed. A simochart prepared with the help of these therbligs. In the simochart, using the diagrammatic or plotting method, the motions of the various parts of the body are filled in, keeping a definite scale and the due proportion between themselves, and their relative therbligs indicated thereon. The simochart reveals the activity that the specific part of the body has to do for a specific time in performing a specific function.

Advantages of Time-Motion Studies

Time-motion study has proved of immense value to the industry. On one hand, it helps in job analysis, while on the other it helps to discover the method by which a maximum work can be obtained in the shortest period of time by eliminating all unnecessary movements. Thirdly, studies of this nature also indicate the nature of training to be imparted to trainees intended for certain specific functions. Another benefit deriving from this study is that it helps to fix the value of a particular function, and thereby the salary payable to its performer.

QUESTIONS FOR EXERCISE

1. What is efficiency? Describe its determinants.
2. Explain Time and Motion Studies.
3. Write short note on Therbligs.

19

MORALE IN INDUSTRY

WHAT IS MORALE?

Whatever the industry, production does not depend exclusively upon the machines. Machines are driven by labourers. In addition to labourers, the factory has clerks, managers and other workers. If the factory is to be run efficiently and profitably, it is essential that all the human elements in the factory should co-operate and work in co-ordination. It should be in an organised affair. And this can be achieved only when all the workers are in a position to be enthusiastic and happy about their work. The attitude that the workers have towards their work in the factory makes a very great difference. It is this individual approach or viewpoint that constitutes their morale.

High Morale and Low Morale

Morale can be high as well as low. The successful industrialists make constant endeavours to maintain a high morale among their working staff because only if this is done, can the work in factory proceed smoothly and efficiently. Production is maintained at a high level and the quality of work done is admirable. On the other hand, once the morale of the factory workers has fallen, the organisation as a whole is constantly faced with problems of all kinds. Sometimes production falls while at others it is the accident rate that goes up alarmingly. Sometimes the workers do not see eye to eye and strikes are the result. Today, the importance of human relationships has come to be recognised in all industries. A high morale is evidence for the desirable condition of human relations.

Aspects of Morale

It is evident that morale has a very potent influence upon the social behaviour and conduct. It has, therefore, the two aspects—the psychological and the social. In its psychological aspect, morale is constituted by the organisation of industry, and the behaviour or mental tendency of workers towards those in authority above them. In its social aspect, morale is evidenced in the social behaviour of the workers. Accordingly, then if morale among the workers is high, they exhibit discipline, obedience and communal unity. The lower the tone of this feeling of unity, the lower will be the level of morale.

Influence of Morale upon Attitude towards the Authority

Hence, morale has a very explicit influence upon the worker's attitude towards authority. In this connection, Jenkens conducted a very interesting experiment. In it, he took up two groups in one of which the morale was very high and in other very low. In each group, besides one commander and one officiating officer, there were 17 workers. In order to measure their attitude towards those in authority, each worker was individually and secretly asked to name the officer with whom he would prefer to undertake air travel, and also the name of the officer with whom he would prefer not to undertake any such project. The results of this experiment led to the conclusion that in the case of high morale, the attitude towards authority was positive and favourable, while in the case of low morale it was negative and unfavourable. In the group which had a high morale, eight workers or soldiers chose the commander as a travelling companion while six of them selected the officiating person as more suitable. On the other hand, in the group with the low morale, no soldier chose to undertake or even prefer an air journey in the company of the commander. Contrary to this, nine soldiers gave evidence of a positive distaste for flying with the officiating individual.

Morale and Mental Condition

One characteristic of a high morale, in addition to the favourable attitude towards those in authority, is that it shuns disappointment or negation. In other words, when the morale is high, disappointment or hopelessness do not exist, and a high level of enthusiasm is maintained. If any problem does rear its head, immediate efforts are made to arrive at the solution. On the other hand, if morale in a particular group of individuals is low, frustration and disappointments increase. People lose faith in future. They are prone to find darkness all around them in which they find themselves groping, to no apparent advantage. Solutions of problems is a far cry, people being more prone to shutting their eyes and looking in the other direction. They exhibit such tendencies as fear.

Morale and Adjustment

In this manner, in conditions of high morale, organisation of the workers is strong, and they can easily adjust to changing circumstances. Usually, they are not conscious of any differences and distinctions among themselves. On the other hand, in the case of low morale, adjustability decreases.

Difference in the Morale of Individual Workers

Here, it should be kept in mind that if due to some reason, the circumstances in a factory deteriorate temporarily, there is no necessity for the morale of every worker falling. On the other hand, while the general level of morale is high in a unit, it is possible that certain individuals are influenced differently by changes and variations. On the other hand, even among the workers working in the same factory, positions and situations are different. For example, a particular worker may be in the good books of his boss, and this may give him a high

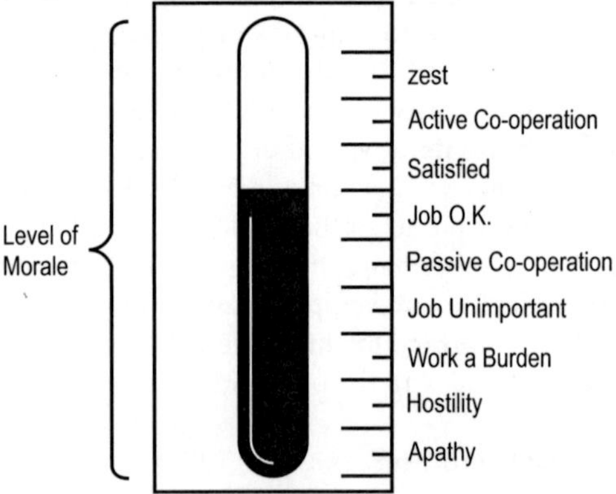

Fig. 19.1. Groups may be Compared on the Basis of Level of Morale

On the basis of scores made on questionnaires, values could be assigned to groups. The descriptive words used suggest meanings that different scale values might communicate. If these values are carefully studied, it is often possible to predict certain group behaviours, such as striked, riots, demonstrations, formations of cliques and internal revolts.

morale, while other people may be suffering from low morale as they may not be in the good books of authority. Similarly, the same single occurrence or situation may have the result of improving morale of some people while it may depress others completely. For example, if, in a factory, special benefits are being made available to the individuals of a particular group, caste, tribe, or religion, this may positively affect their morale while it may have a negative influence on their less fortunate colleagues. It may even be so deep-rooted that they may turn antagonistic towards those in authority and this may cause a farther fall in their morale.

Characteristics of a High Morale

From the above description it becomes evident that the following characteristics are evident in the case of a high morale:

1. Positive or favourable attitude towards those in authority.
2. Self-induced obedience.
3. Positive feeling of respect and confidence for authorities.
4. Collective administration, unity and adjustability.
5. Rejection of frustrations and a sense of enthusiasm.
6. Mental peace and satisfaction.
7. Productivity and system in work.

Requirement for a High Level of Morale

Norman Meyer has laid much stress on team spirit in morale. Morale is maintained intact if there is a team spirit, and following things are required for maintaining a high level of team spirit:

1. **Application to work** This assimilates the essence of enthusiasm and powerful motives, as a result of which the person moves consistently in the direction of pre-determined objectives.
2. **Avoid diversion from work** This is a quality of existent morale. In a state of this kind, people are not easily diverted from their tasks even when faced with failure.
3. **Sense of co-operation** If a sense of co-operation within a community is present, people do not think in individual terms but in collective terms, and co-operate with each other as they identify personal success with the success of community.

Characteristics of Low Morale

Contrary to high morale, the following characteristics are in evidence in case of low morale:

1. Antagonistic attitude towards those in authority.
2. Lack of obedience or forced obedience.
3. Feelings of hatred, jealousy, doubt, disrespect, lack of confidence towards those in authority.
4. Disappointment, unenthusiastic insipidity.
5. Lack of collective administration and unity, belief in lone effort.
6. Mental turmoil and unhappiness.
7. Lack of system and productivity in work.
8. Tendency to circulate all kinds of rumours.
9. Poisoning minds of others towards authority behind its back.
10. Lack of application to work.
11. Mutual conflicts and non-co-operation.

Methods of Measuring Morale

In order to discover the level of morale in a worker in any industry, it is necessary to observe the above-mentioned characteristics in him. Nowadays, morale is measured by the use of many scientific methods that reveal not only the level of morale that exists, but also the causes whereby it has come into existence. They can then be remedied and a high morale restored. The main methods are following:

1. Common worker's opinion analysis One very popularly used method of measuring the morale is the common worker's opinion analysis method in which the opinions of the average worker are collected and analysed. For this, certain scientific questionnaires are prepared that reveal the workers' opinions regarding the various aspects of industry as well as towards the authorities. The worker does not have to reveal his name in answering these questionnaires. This has the initial advantage of assuring the worker of secrecy regarding his views. When questioned by the workers, it becomes possible to see the various scores on which the workers have complained. If some particular object or subject is a matter of complaint in a large majority of cases, efforts can be made to rectify it. Success in this method depends upon the degree to which the questionnaire is scientific, and upon the degree of truth in the workers' responses.

2. Interview of departed workers In this method, those individuals are directly interviewed who have departed from the unit in question for various reasons. One main advantage of this method is that it reveals the reasons whereby the workers feel compelled to seek jobs elsewhere, so that future desertion on the part of present employees can be discouraged. Another feature of this method is that having left the employment of a particular concern or unit he feels free to give expression to his frank views on any and every aspect of the business. Another advantage of this method is that the views of departed employees cannot result in any harm to the administration or to those in authority. There can be no doubt that some workers may have grievances against the administration or their job that has no relation whatsoever with actual and real conditions. But if many workers leave their jobs on the same pretext, then, evidently, it is necessary to put an end to the source of complaint in order to maintain a high level of morale. In this manner, this method has proved extraordinarily useful in measuring the existing level of morale, and suggesting methods for improvements. It also locates the causes of falling morale. If, however, most of the departed employees speak well and favourably of the work and the administration of the factory or business house, then there is every reason to believe that morale is at a high level.

3. Attitude measurement As has been pointed out earlier, morale is an expression of the workers' attitude towards their work, the authorities and general administration or organisation. Hence, the workers' attitudes can be known in order to evaluate their morale. For example, if the answers to the following queries were supplied by the workers, their attitudes in these respects could be known:

1. I work in the company under compulsion.
2. The authorities in the company believe in the policy of paying as little wages as can practicably be paid.
3. If I can get the same salary in a different company, I am prepared to resign from my present position.
4. I have no respect for or faith in those in authority above me.
5. The conditions under which I work cannot be said to be good by any standards.
6. I find no freedom, pleasure or satisfaction in my work.

The worker's attitudes can be discovered by requiring him to mark the above queries right or wrong.

If most of the workers mark the above observations as correct, then obviously, the level of morale is notoriously low. Other statements of a similar nature can be distributed among the workers in the form of a printed form or brochure and they can be required to mark them right or wrong according to their own inclination, so that the level of morale can be discovered as well as their attitudes towards various aspects of their occupation. Much importance in this method is attached to the choice of statements, which should be selected scientifically, as this makes the whole process much easier. The statements should be precise and exact so that the workers Should be able to express their opinions clearly and categorically; vagueness must be avoided on both sides. This method is especially efficacious in the case of workers of clerical class. Even uneducated and illiterate workers can make a mark on the statements. As this method also does not require the worker to reveal his name, he can fearlessly and without fear of bias or prejudice give expression to his frank opinion. Various statements are evaluated previously, and the scoring can be done accordingly. This gives the whole method a certain air of validity and accuracy. Once the answers have been received, the median of the various scores can be taken to gauge the attitude of the individual worker. If most of the answers are adverse, it is concluded that morale is low, following which efforts are made to discover the causes that made it to be low, and remedies are suggested and in some cases actually applied. Generally speaking, every industry can formulate its own list of statements, but among the most important of the kind is that prepared by Arbauk and Bergon. Thurston and Kiev have made a detailed analysis of these statements.

4. Sociological method Nowadays, particularly in the case of group studies, the sociological method is very prevalent. Moreover, a method for measuring the morale can be used to discover the characteristics of a workers' group organisation whereby the level of morale can be discovered. In the Jenkens' experiment he described characteristics of the workers' group organisation. Accordingly, the worker is given a questionnaire containing certain questions intended to throw light on the characteristics of group organisation. For example, the workers are asked to name and enumerate the individuals with whom they would like to work, or under whom they would prefer to work, in which sort of company they would prefer to work, or have anything to do. If the answers of many individuals to these questions seem to speak favourably of any one individual, and, the answers seem to show respect, love and confidence for the individual, it is fairly evident that he is capable of becoming a good administrator. If he is already in the administrative cadre, then it evidences a high level of morale in the workers, for respect and confidence in authority is a sign of high morale. But if he is not so situated, then the answers seem to show lack of confidence in the existing administration a lack of confidence that can be rectified by promoting the desired individual into the administrative, block, or otherwise by advising the existing administrative group to mend its ways and adopt others, more calculated to win the confidence and respect of their subordinates. In this manner, it is evident that Moreno method can help in realising the conditions of morale in any unit, and in discovering the means of improving the existing morale.

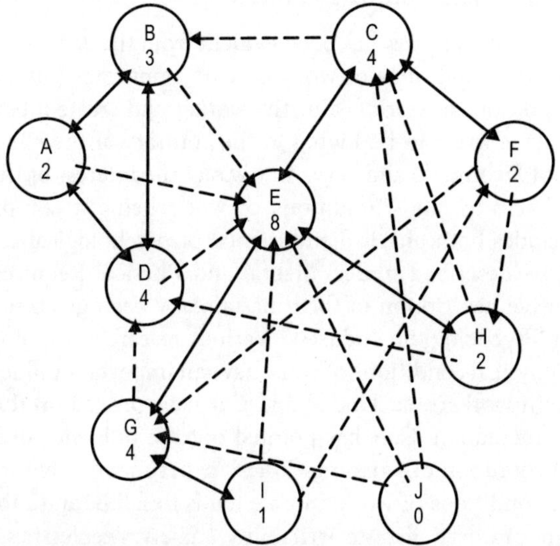

Fig. 19.2. Sociogram of a Group of Ten Workmen

Each workman is represented by a circle, the letters of the alphabet being substituted by names. Each member of the group was asked to vote for three men most desired as working companions. The numerals in the circles show the number of votes that each man received. The arrows indicate the direction of choices, whereas solid and broken lines designate mutual choices and one-way preferences, respectively. Individuals A, B and D form a triangle, E is a star, and J is an isolate.

ESSENTIAL REQUIREMENTS FOR HIGH MORALE

Having studied the methods by which morale can be measured and evaluated, it is better to make a study of the elements that determine it. These elements are roughly divided into the following three classes:

1. Physical requirements This classification includes those physical conditions that influence morale, such as conditions of work, post, pay increase, methods of salary payment, conduct of inspector or authority, etc.

2. Mental requirements These include such elements as praise, knowledge of success, fulfilment of co-operative needs, patience, forbearance, freedom, unity, feeling of equality, motivation, self-confidence and other psychological elements.

Physical Requirements for High Morale

1. Conditions of work As has been evident from the account of morale all through, the conditions of work have an important influence upon it. If the conditions of work favour the worker and create interest in the work, morale is likely to be high. On the contrary, if the conditions of work are not favourable and serve to distract the interest of the worker, morale is likely to fall. 'Conditions of work' being a comprehensive term, it includes both physical and mental or psychological conditions. These will be described under 'Mental and Physical Requirements'. A fairly extensive description of them has already been given in previous chapter on 'Psychology in Industry'. Various researches have led to the belief that physical conditions of work have an important influence upon the morale in workers, as Tindall and Car have proved on the basis of their experimentation. Cair has pointed out the influence of music on the mental condition of workers. Culier's experiments seem to indicate that in bad conditions of work, morale tends to fall because the worker evinces signs of worry, distaste, irritability, anxiety, sleeplessness, laxness, lethargy, etc.

2. Position and promotion Studying the morale of various individuals in various positions of different companies, Arbrock came to the conclusion that the attitude of foremen is better than that of clerks while that of clerks is more favourable than is the case with other classes of workers. This study reveals that the morale of individuals is also susceptible to such influences as the post that one is holding. The main psychological fact at the root of this phenomenon is that if the individual in question does not get a position that concurs with his psychological bent of mind, his enthusiasm begins to wane, and he loses confidence in those who are in authority above him. Hence if morale is to be kept high in any industry, it is essential that posts be allotted in accordance with the ability and labour of the individuals, and that these posts be improved from time to time. Much the same phenomenon came to light in a study of promotion in a previous chapter.

3. Increase in salary It is a psychological fact that workers are primarily concerned with their salary or wages. Sheppard has stressed the fact that if the worker's wages are reassessed from time to time and appropriate changes are made, the morale tends to occupy a high level. On the contrary, if the wages remain stationary for a long time, and there is no advancement, the workers' enthusiasm is dampened, and they tend to heap blame on their officers. Increase in pay should be made dependent upon hard work and other qualities. If increase in pay depends upon the personal idiosyncrasy of the individual in power, most people become cynical as they do not like to cringe before such a person. Secondly, even the ingratiating types who win increase in pay and promotions through subservience rarely have a high morale. Hence, for pay increase to have a favourable influence upon morale, it is essential that the basis of increase be proper, and the same for everyone.

4. Method of distributing salaries Morale is also influenced by the method of distributing salary no less than by increase in it. All studies to date on the subject have not led to any conclusive idea as to which method is definitely the best. Some methods are of course, better than certain others. Various methods will be examined briefly here:

(a) *Share of profits:* Under this method, the workers in companies and factories are given bonuses and share of profits from time to time. The following facts need to be mentioned in connection with this method:

(i) This method engenders dissatisfaction in the better and more efficient workers because they find that others less efficient and skilful than themselves are deriving the same benefits without actually deserving them.

(ii) In this method, the worker is never sure of his actual income in the near future because neither the quantity of profit is shared nor the time of its distribution is certain.

Despite the above clear difficulties and drawbacks, this method has been found to meet with the approval of approximately one-third of the workers. Besides, this method is also rather simple, as a consequence of which it is one of the most widely used today.

(b) *Remuneration according to work:* In this method, the worker is reimbursed according to the quantity of material he produces. The research made by Mathewson on this subject has made it abundantly clear that the method call succeed only if the worker Is confident that the range of payment will not fall, because he usually expects that if he works more he will earn more but also thereby create a reason for the company reducing the rate of payment. Fear of this kind guides them to reduce their rate of working.

It is evident that if the worker can be convinced of the stability of payment rates, the piece wages method is superior to the bonus method, but it requires that the following facts be kept in mind:

(i) Attention should be concentrated not only on quantity but also on quality.

(ii) In paying the worker, it should be made abundantly clear to him that he is being paid according to a certain definite rate for a specific kind of work so that no doubt lingers in his mind that compels him to work slower.

(iii) In connection with remuneration, the rate should be constant and there should be no fear of the rate of payment being reduced.

If the above facts are kept in mind, and the appropriate arrangements made, the morale of the worker can be kept high through the piece wages method, because it is by this method that the worker is constantly inspired to work more and to produce better results. It is also very good from the point of view of creating good incentives.

5. Ability to profit Among the physical requirements, other is the possibility and opportunity of progress in any concern. If the workers in a company are being paid dividends out of its profits, then it should be equally distributed. In other words, all workers should be given the opportunity to progress and earn high wages, without any discrimination. If this is not done, most of them tend to turn against the authorities in their company, while at the same time a feeling of jealousy for those who have progressed is engendered in the unfortunate ones. This destroys not only collective organisation and administrative efficiency, but also faith and belief in the authorities. Hence, the rules governing promotion and increase in salary should be equally applicable to all, and they should be clearly understood by all of them. No one should be given a chance to complain on these grounds.

Psychological Requirement for High Morale

Having completed a cursory study of the physical requirements of the morale, a detailed study of its psychological requirements will now be made:

1. Praise It is a matter of general psychological knowledge that praise of good work and effort helps to infuse further enthusiasm and energy in the worker.

Studies conducted by such eminent psychologists as Thorndike and Hurlock, evinced that praise of a worker's effort helps to increase his motivation. In fact, the influence of the reward and punishment scheme on work is fairly evident and widely known. Any work that derives punishment for the perpetrator is shunned by reward. Praise is a psychological reward. Praise by individuals for whom we have respect and in whose judgement we have faith, matters a lot to us. If the authorities in the factory or office praise all good effort, then morale becomes high among the workers. On the other hand, if good work and hard labour go unpraised or unnoticed, enthusiasm wanes in the worker, as he feels that he is not being valued according to his merits. This fact is one of the important reasons why work in an impersonal psychological organisation like government office is rarely of a high order of efficiency. Direct praise or blame is rarely forth-coming, except from very conscientious individuals in authority.

2. Knowledge of success Some other experiments have brought to light the fact that if the worker is aware of the degree of success he is achieving in his work, his interest and enthusiasm in it are maintained, and so is the high level of morale. In very big factories where the individual work does no more than make only a very small cog in a very big wheel, and is not aware of the effect of his own effort towards the completed wheel, boredom and disinterest are likely to set in very early. Result of work can be bad as well as good. Knowledge of failure can only serve to lower the morale, but if the worker is again encouraged to think in terms of success, morale can be regained. As a general rule, success ensures a high morale. Success is the reward of effort. And reward is a favourable element in the creation and maintenance of morale. Colstaad's studies showed that the morale of workers in shops that have a very big turnover with large profits is much higher and better than that of workers employed in smaller organisations with a smaller turnover and lesser profits. This evidence is rooted in the psychological fact that success increases an individual's confidence in himself, and he comes to realise the need to maintain all these privileges intact. He is driven to work with even greater energy and resolve.

3. Fulfilment of collective needs Man works not only to meet the needs of his body, such needs as food and clothing, but also to satisfy certain other collective psychological requirements. He is also desirous of meeting others, giving vent to his feelings and emotions, thoughts and beliefs, exhibiting himself, knowing himself, and winning social prestige and recognition. Any kind of work that affords all these advantages to the worker is almost certain to create a very high morale in him, but if all these things are not made available to him, morale is likely to fall, if it was ever high. Hence, for maintaining the morale of their workers, the organisers and authorities should keep in mind the fact that the worker's collective needs be also fulfilled and satisfied.

4. Forbearance and good behaviour of authorities Workers attach much importance to the behaviour of inspectors, managers and other in authority, towards them. If their conduct towards them is not all that can be desired, general morale is likely to suffer. If the worker is constantly interrupted and scolded over his work, he loses all respect for the officer. Actually, the only course of keeping workers contented that is open to the officers and authorities is that of good and considerate behaviour towards them. In such circumstances, the workers are inclined to pay little attention to other conditions around them, and are enthusiastic enough to do anything that is likely to benefit their factory or organisation. This is due to an identify of interests that is felt by the worker. A sense of possession invades him. On the contrary, the worker's self-respect is injured if the authority above him behaves in an irresponsible manner towards him. In fact, a position of authority does not require occupational skill so much as it requires the qualities of leadership and organisation, a skill in diplomacy. A leader plays an important part in maintaining the morale of a group of people. In company offices and factories, it is good for them to have a fair knowledge of human psychology. Their behaviour towards the workers should be such that it should easily adjust in the collective organisation. Tolerance is an important quality for leaders. Tolerance not only adds to the respect that is forthcoming, it does not detract from it. But tolerance does not imply that the officer or leader should calmly overlook the mistakes of his subordinates. What is important is that due importance be given to all things brought to notice. It is hardly proper to be constantly wrangling over small and inconsequential matters. But to overlook a thing of great magnitude is again a serious fault that should be avoided. Studies conducted in the Iowa University of the United States of America have revealed that a group working under a democratic leader is more organised. In such a group, the workers continue with their duties even during the leader's absence. They have favourable mental attitudes towards the leader and other fellow-workers. Contrary to this, morale in the group and work under an authoritarian or autocratic leader is usually low, work being continued in his presence because of fear but suspended in his absence. They entertain feelings of jealousy and hatred for such a leader. In this manner, it is evident that for maintaining a high level of morale among workers, there is a great importance attached to tolerant and considerate behaviour on the part of officers.

5. Freedom of workers In whichever company or factory a worker loses his identity to the extent of being reduced to the level of a small cog in the huge wheel, he is dissatisfied with his work because it appears heavy and insipid to him. Hence, in order to maintain the worker's morale at a high level, it is essential that he be given the maximum degree of freedom that his function and position allow. He should also not be prevented from meeting other fellow-workers, in particular those individuals who are in authority. It helps in creating a more intimate and knowledgeable atmosphere, in which he can tell his troubles to the proverbial daddy. But giving freedom does not imply that discipline should be done away with. Freedom within the framework of laws is the most desirable state of affairs.

6. Sense of organization and identity or equality It has been pointed out earlier that collective or group organisation is indicative of high morale. Hence, it is essential that a sense of organisation and unity should circulate freely among the workers. Psychologists, May and Wright, concluded from their examinations and study that in order to maintain a high morale among the workers in industries, it is essential that the workers must have in themselves a feeling of being organised and united or equal. The workers should be able to identify themselves with their factory or office or organisation, and think of its interests as if they were their own. If this is achieved, even the most difficult times can be successfully seen through by making a collective effort by many things such as a definite name of the company or organisation, a definite dress and a common badge. Besides these, certain group objectives can be set up, the achievement of which involves organised and collective effort on the part of workers. Exerting oneself along with many others, straining for the same objectives serves to lessen tension, increase mutual goodwill and help the organisation. Workers should be made to realise that they are an important and responsible part of industry. They should also be equipped with knowledge of various parts of industry, so that they can come to look upon it as their own industry. Some millowners are under the impression that their interest lies in keeping the workers quarrelling among themselves. As a policy, this may have some immediate benefits but in the long run this is a very harmful policy because lack of collective organisation in workers lowers their morale, and this finally has an adverse influence upon the quality and quantity of work done by the workers.

Other Requirements

Apart from the above-mentioned physical and psychological determinants of morale, there are some other factors that influence it. For example, through his experiments and research, Super has established a relationship between age and morale. Similarly, the research of Arbrock has shown that the level of morale is higher in case of women workers than in the case of male workers. Actually, maintaining a very high level of morale requires careful attention to all aspects of the worker's personality and to all aspects of his work. In this connection research work is continuing that is expected to yield harvest of interesting facts.

QUESTIONS FOR EXERCISE

1. What do you mean by Industrial morale? What are its determinants?
2. What is morale? Explain the value of morale in increasing production.
3. What is industrial morale? State the main factors of the declination.
4. Write short note on industrial morale.
5. How will you define industrial morale? What are its indicators of good morale?
6. Explain the concept and the importance of industrial morale and discuss its main determinants.
7. What do you mean by dimension of morale? Discuss the various factors which are conducive to industrial morale. Cite some important studies conducted in this field.
8. What psychological factors are basic to good morale among workers?
9. What is worker's morale? How is it measured? State the determinants of morale in industry.
10. What is worker morale? How is it measured? Evaluate the methods of its measurement.
11. How is industrial morale measured?

20

JOB SATISFACTION

WHAT IS JOB SATISFACTION?

The term job relates to the total relationship between an individual and the employer for which he is paid. Satisfaction means the simple feeling-stage accompanying the attainment of any goal. It is feeling accompanying the attainment by an impulse of its objectives. Thus, job satisfaction refers to a person's feeling of satisfaction on the job, which acts as a motivation to work. It is not the self-satisfaction, happiness or self-contentment but the satisfaction on the job. Job dissatisfaction means absence of motivation at work.

Human resource is sum-total of inherent abilities, acquired knowledge and skills represented by the talents and aptitudes of the employed persons comprising executives, supervisors, and the rank and file employees. Human resources should be utilised to the maximum possible extent, in order to achieve individual and organisational goals. The employee's performance ultimately decides the attainment of goals. The employee performance in its turn is influenced by motivation and job satisfaction.

Definition of Job Satisfaction

1. R. Hoppoch "Any combination of psychological, physiological and environmental circumstances that cause a person truthfully to say I am satisfied with my job."

2. E.A. Locke Job satisfaction is defined as the "pleasurable emotional state resulting from the appraisal of one's job as achieving or facilitating the achievement of one's job values". In contrast, job dissatisfaction is defined as "the unpleasurable emotional state resulting from the appraisal of one's job as frustrating or blocking the attainment of one's job values or as entailing disvalues." Satisfaction and dissatisfaction were seen as, "a function of the perceived relationship between what one perceives it as offering or entailing".

THEORIES OF JOB SATISFACTION

Basically, there are five approaches/theories of job satisfaction. They are: (1) Fulfilment theory, (2) Discrepancy theory, (3) Equity theory, (4) Two-factor theory and (5) Social Reference Group theory.

1. Fulfilment theory The advocates of this theory measure satisfaction in terms of rewards which a person receives or the extent to which his needs are satisfied. There is a direct/positive relationship between job satisfaction and the actual satisfaction of the expected needs.

(i) ***Limitations:*** Job satisfaction' as observed by willing, is not only a function of what a person receives but also what he feels he should receive as there would be considerable difference in the actuals and expectations of persons. Thus job satisfaction cannot be regarded as merely a function of how much a person receives from his job.

(ii) The strength of the individual's desire of his level of aspiration in a particular area should be included to predict job satisfaction accurately. This led to the development of the discrepancy theory of job satisfaction.

2. Discrepancy theory The proponents of this theory argue that Satisfaction is the function of what a person actually receives from his job situation and what he thinks he should receive or what he expects to receive. When the actual satisfaction derived is less than expected satisfaction, it results in dissatisfaction. As E.A. Loche puts it, "Job satisfaction and dissatisfaction are functions of the perceived relationship between what one wants from one's job and what one perceives it is offering."

Limitations This approach does not make it clear whether or not over satisfaction is a part of dissatisfaction and if so, how does it differ from dissatisfaction. This led to the development of equity theory of job satisfaction.

3. Equity theory The proponents of this theory are of the view that a person's satisfaction is determined by his perceived equity, which in turn is determined by his input-output balance compared to his comparison of others' input-output balance. Input-output balance is the perceived ratio of what a person receives from his job relative to what he contributes to the job. Equity theory is of the view that both under-and over-rewards lead to dissatisfaction. While the under-reward causes feelings of unfair treatment, over-reward leads to feelings of guilt and discomfort.

4. Two-factor theory This theory was developed by Herzberg, Mausner, Peterson and Capwell who identified certain factors as satisfies and dissatisfied. Factors such as achievement, recognition, responsibility, etc. are satisfied. Their presence causes satisfaction but their absence does not result in dissatisfaction. Factors such as supervision, salary, working conditions, etc., are dissatisfiers, the absence of which causes dissatisfaction. Their presence, however, does not result in job satisfaction. As the studies designed to test this theory failed to give any support to it, it seems that a person can get both satisfaction and dissatisfaction at the same time, which is not valid.

5. Social reference-group theory The social reference-group theory is similar to need-fulfilment theory except that it takes into account not the desires, needs and interests of the individual, but rather the point of view and opinions of the group to whom the individual looks for guidance. The "reference-group" defines the way in which the individual should look at the world and evaluate various phenomena in the environment including himself. According to this theory, if a job meets the interests, desires and requirements of a person's reference group, he will like it and if it does not, he will not like it. A good example of this theory has been given by C.L. Hulin who measured the effects of community characteristics on job satisfaction of female clerical workers employed in 300 different catalogue order offices. He found that with job conditions held constant job satisfaction was less among persons living in a well-to-do neighbourhood than among those whose neighbourhood was poor. Hulin provided strong evidence that frames of reference for evaluation may be provided by one's social groups and general social environment. However this theory gives an incomplete explanation since while some people may go along with group opinions and group evaluation of organisational phenomena, many people are independent of these pressures.

FACTORS OF JOB SATISFACTION

Job satisfaction refers to a general attitude which an employee retains on account of many specific attitudes in the following areas: (1) Job satisfaction, (2) Individual characteristics and (3) Relationships outside the job. Job satisfaction depends on the following different factors:

1. Personal factors These include workers' sex, education, age, marital status and their personal characteristics, family background, socio-economic background and the like.

2. Factors inherent in the job These factors include die work itself, conditions, influence of internal and external environment on the job which are uncontrolled by the management, etc. These factors have been found to be important in the selection of employees. Instead of being guided by their co-workers and supervisors, the skilled workers would rather like to be guided by their own inclination to choose jobs in consideration of 'what they have to do'.

3. Factors controlled by the management These include the nature of supervision, job security, kind of work group, wage rate, promotional opportunities, transfer policy, duration of work and sense of responsibilities. All these factors greatly influence the workers. Their presence in the organisation motivates the workers and provides a sense of job satisfaction.

DETERMINANTS OF JOB SATISFACTION

According to Abraham A. Korman, two types of variables determine the job satisfaction of an individual: (1) Organisational variables and (2) Personal variables.

[A] Organisational Variables

(1) Occupational level The higher the level of the job, the greater the satisfaction of the individual, because higher level jobs carry greater prestige and self-control. Relationship between occupational level and job satisfaction stems from social reference group theory in that our society values some jobs more than others. Hence people in valued jobs will like them more than those who are in non-valued jobs. The relationship may also stem from the need-fulfilment theory. People in higher level jobs find most of their needs satisfied than when they are in lower level ones.

(2) Job content As job content in terms of variety and nature of tasks called for is a function of occupational level, the theoretical arguments given above apply here also. Greater the variation in job content and the less the repetitiveness with which the tasks must be performed, the greater the satisfaction of the individuals involved.

(3) Considerate leadership As people like to be treated with consideration, considerate leadership results in higher job satisfaction than inconsiderate leadership.

(4) Pay and promotional opportunities Other things being equal, these two variables are positively related to job satisfaction.

(5) Interaction in the work group Interaction is most satisfying when it results:

(i) in the cognition that other person's attitudes are similar to one's own, since this permits the ready calculability of the other's behaviour and constitutes a validation of one's self;

(ii) in being accepted by others and

(iii) it facilitates the achievement of goals.

[B] Personal Variables

For some people, most jobs are dissatisfying irrespective of the organisational conditions involved, whereas for others, most jobs are satisfying. Personal variables like age, educational level, sex, etc., are responsible for this difference.

DETERMINANTS OF JOB SATISFACTION

	Author	*Name of the Study*	*Determinants of job satisfaction*
1.	Stagner, Flebbe and Wood (1952)	Working on the rail-road; a study of job satisfaction (*Personnel Psychology*, 1952, 5, 293-306). This is a study of 715 male unionised rail-road workers.	1. General working conditions 2. Union-management relations 3. General quality of supervision 4. Grievance handling procedures.
2.	Gadel (1953)	Productivity and satisfaction of full and part-time female employees (*Personnel Psychology*, 1953, 6. 327-42). This is a study of 301 women doing typing and routine clerical work. Sixty per cent of this number were at least 40 years old and more were married.	For younger group: 1. Type of work 2. Working conditions 3. Pay 4. Co-workers 5. Ease of commuting to workplace 6. Advancement opportunities For older group: 1. Security 2. Supervision 3. Company prestige 4. Working hours
3.	Ross and Zander (1957)	Need satisfaction and employee turnover (*Personnel Psychology*, 1957, 10,327-38). This is a study of skilled women in a large company.	1. Recognition 2. Autonomy 3. Doing important work 4. Fair evaluation of work done.
4.	Durganand Sinha (1958)	Job satisfaction in office and manual workers (*Indian Journal of Social Work*), 1958, 19, 39-46).	1. Job status 2. Type of work 3. Supervisory 4. Work group.

(1) Age Holding such factors as occupational level constant, most of the evidence on the relation between age and job satisfaction, seems to indicate that there is a positive relationship between the two variables up to the pre-retirement years and then there is a sharp decrease in satisfaction. An individual aspires for better and more prestigious jobs in later years of his life. Finding his channels for advancement blocked, his satisfaction declines.

(2) Educational level With occupational level held constant, there is a negative relationship between the educational level and job satisfaction. The higher the education, the higher the reference group which the individual looks to for guidance to evaluate his job rewards.

(3) Role perception Different individuals hold different perceptions about their role, *i.e.,* the kind of activities and behaviours they should engage in, to perform their job successfully. Job satisfaction is determined by this factor. The more accurate the role perception of an individual, the greater his satisfaction.

(4) Sex Holding such factors as job and occupational level constant there is as no consistent evidence as to whether women are more satisfied with their jobs than men. Considering the generally lower occupational aspiration of women, one might predict this to be the case.

CREATING JOB SATISFACTION

The importance of job satisfaction is fairly evident from a description of the importance of maintaining morale in any industry. If a worker is not satisfied with his work, then both the quantity and quality of his output will suffer. If his job satisfaction increases then there is an improvement in both the quality and quantity of production. Factories in which the workers are satisfied with their work are also characterised by a high morale. The following things are generally important for creating the job satisfaction:

1. Attending to and solving problems It is desirable that the complaints of the workers be heard patiently and the problems solved as far as possible. Factories in which the worker' demands are not heeded, suffer because the workers lose confidence in the management and become frustrated.

2. Satisfactory future Every worker is definitely concerned about his future prospects. If the factory rules clearly lay down the conditions of promotions and advancement, and if the worker gets the expected promotion and improvement in pay scales at the right time, he feels satisfied and becomes confident of his future. If, on the other hand, the worker feels that even good work will not be rewarded, he becomes frustrated and slack in his work.

3. Testing the worker's ability and progress Every worker, whether in a factory or an office, desires that he should be paid according to his ability. If he has undergone some new training or has increased his ability to work in some way, he should be compensated for his better ability through a raise in salary. Organisations in which the management keeps an eye on the ability and progress of its workers normally have a high degree of job satisfaction among their workers. It is necessary that the management should give the worker some opportunity of progressing higher and higher. If, on the other hand, the organisation does not pay any attention to the abilities and increased efficiency of its staff, it suffers in the long run because the workers lose interest in their job and do not often try to improve their level of efficiency. This happens because they feel that an increase in qualifications or efficiency is not related to progress or promotion.

4. Respect for creative suggestions Generally speaking, the worker working under a particular set of conditions is best qualified to say how and where improvements can be made. If workers are encouraged to suggest ways and means of improving the conditions of work, they often come up with very valuable ideas. This helps in increasing the job satisfaction because when the worker is praised for giving a good practical idea, he tends to pay more attention to his work in order to win more praise. If such suggestions are neglected then the worker feels dissatisfied since apparently there can be no improvement in the conditions in which he works.

5. Cordial analysis or evaluation of the work In every organisation, the manager or the supervisor has to offer criticism of the work performed by the worker because he must point out the worker's mistakes and try to eliminate them. If this criticism is offered in a cordial and friendly way more as suggestion than as criticism, then the worker feels gratified and pays attention to it. His job satisfaction is also thereby maintained. But if the worker is abused or bitterly criticised for his mistakes, he loses his peace of mind.

6. Increase in wages Rules governing increase in salary should be clear and explicit and should be acted upon impartially and regularly. If the worker gets the anticipated increase in salary at the right time, he feels satisfied with his job. If this does not happen, dissatisfaction is the result. Increase in wages is, in fact, the most important factor in job satisfaction.

7. Praise for good performance If workers are not praised for exceptional performances in their work, they lose interest in it and as a result, the organisation suffers. Even if they do good work, they still remain dissatisfied and disgruntled. Generally, the worker prefers to work well and remain occupied than merely to pass the time allotted to him. If he is also encouraged in his work by an occasional word of praise and respect, he is further motivated to maintain a high level of efficiency and in fact to improve it. If he is not praised for his work, his enthusiasm and zeal immediately fall.

8. Promotion according to ability In every organisation some people are always being retired after completion of their tenure while younger people are promoted to take their places. If promotion is based upon the ability of the worker then the worker's mental satisfaction is maintained. If, on the other hand, promotion depends upon other factors such as casteism, personal favour, etc., then the worker's interest in his work declines.

9. Proper quantum of work If job satisfaction is to be maintained, it is essential that the quantity of work does not exceed the individual's ability to complete it. If he has to work more than he comfortably can or for a long time, the worker is bound to become disgusted, depressed and tired.

10. Equal Wages for Equal Work Labour unions in almost every industry are now demanding that there should be equal pay for equal work. In any factory or office, a worker must be paid as much as other workers are being paid in other organisations for similar work. The worker feels satisfied if this equality is maintained. If it is not, then the worker loses his satisfaction.

11. Freedom to seek help in solving problems Very often the worker is faced by problems in his work that he cannot solve alone. In such a case he should be free to seek help and guidance from other workers or even from the managers.

12. Absence of unnecessary intervention and criticism No individual wants to sacrifice his self-respect. If the worker is unnecessarily shown disrespect or abused, he quickly becomes dissatisfied. Hence he should be protected from useless interruptions and criticism.

13. Satisfactory hours of work The hours of work in any factory or office should be convenient and so arranged as to offer the least possible inconvenience to the largest number of employees. If this is not looked into, the workers become dissatisfied.

14. Availability of leave and rest In every industrial organisation, the workers should be given the proper amount of rest and holidays on festivals and other occasions of social celebrations. Nowadays it is thought necessary to give a half holiday every fifteen days in addition to the weekly holiday. Rest given on festivals and on occasions of general celebration is in addition to this. Besides, the worker is also permitted to take leave for medical or other private reasons. Female workers are allowed fairly long leave during pregnancy. It is generally seen that workers feel satisfied if the management in any organisation follows a liberal policy towards leave for workers.

It is evident from the above description of factors influencing job satisfaction that it necessitates the creation of certain conditions of work. Different factors may be of importance in different situations. Increase in wages is a common factor which is important everywhere. Promotion is another factor which plays an important role in maintaining or destroying the job satisfaction. Apart from this, the other factors may be more or less important depending upon the situation. For example, an organisation in which the worker's educational degrees have great importance should also see to it that the worker is promoted when he adds to his qualifications. On the other hand, in an organisation in which training or academic qualifications have no value, this question will not arise at all. Finally, it can be said that job satisfaction depends on all those factors which influence morale.

QUESTIONS FOR EXERCISE

1. What is job satisfaction? Describe the various facts affecting job satisfaction.
2. Discuss the importance of job satisfaction for job performance.
3. What are the main factors leading to satisfaction in work? How do measures of labour welfare affect satisfaction of labour?
4. Write a short note on job satisfaction.
5. What do you understand by job satisfaction? Discuss the factors that influence it.
6. Explain what you understand by job satisfaction, and discuss the factors that operate as its determinants in industrial setting.
7. What do you understand by Vocational Fitness? Explain in detail.

21

THE WORK CURVE

WORK AND PLAY

Some people say that play should be treated as work and work as play. What they mean is that one should play with the same interest with which one works and work should be made to yield the same pleasure that play does. Play as you work, and work as you play, certainly, but do not forget that the two are distinct. Such proverbs are characteristically misleading as they seem to suggest that work and play are the same. Such a notion is psychologically wrong and indefensible. Work and play differ mainly in the following respects:

1. Difference of objectives When you see a child playing, you may be inclined to enquire of him as to what he is doing and why, and normally the answer would be that he is playing, and that he is playing for the sake of playing. In this way, play is a normal and common tendency, an objective and aim in itself. Play is indulged in, of its own accord, rather than from any external motivation. Usually it is seen as the contradiction of work, with the result that all children more interested in games are considered lazy. Many young students run away from the school and spend their entire time in playing and roaming about. If one enquires the reason of things from a card player, the almost inevitable response is that one may play and see for oneself. The pleasure resulting from it constitutes the reason why it is played. Now to take up the cudgels on behalf of work, one immediately perceives that no work is done without any motive and definite objective. All the hundreds and thousands of vocations peculiar to the human animal, including study and labour, are pursued with some objective in view. The actual aim may be accumulation of wealth or the achievement of fame, or any other conceivable aim, but no work can be aimless. Work is not its own objective; one does not work for the sake of working. It is the thought that it is a fruit to come in the future that infuses courage and enthusiasm in the worker labouring in the present. But while playing a game, every movement brings its own fresh pleasures and amusements; there are no future fruits to be considered. Its pleasure is in the moment. Of course, one may astutely object that one ever present motive in the play is the desire to defeat and overcome the opponent. Then how can objective or aim be used to distinguish between the games and work? But if in answer to this question, one were asked what the winner gains in defeating his adversary and what the latter loses in being defeated, then it would have to be admitted that there is nothing concrete involved. In fact, as Drever has pointed out, the objectives and aims of play belong to the world of imagination while the aim in working belongs to the essential reality and concreteness of the world and everyday life. One often finds that work carries with it the fetters of compulsion while no such feeling accompanies the play.

2. The meaning of play is within the act of playing while that of work lies outside According to Drever, "In play the value and significance of the activity is found in the activity itself, whereas in work, the value and significance of activity are found an end beyond the activity". In this way, every moment spent in play brings its own rewards in terms of pleasure and amusement, whereas work is accompanied by no such pleasure. Usually, it is the opposite, as work is attended by pain and effort. It attains fruition a long time after it, itself has been completed.

3. Play Gives Immediate and Work Remote Pleasure Man is by nature an epicurean who turns towards things that bring him pleasure and instinctively turns away from the objects that bring him pain and misery. Hence, in both work and play, the aim and object of the child are obtaining pleasure but while play yields its pleasures immediately and in the present, the pleasures to be had of work, are slower in their coming, It sometimes never comes at all even in the future, and sometimes even brings pain and suffering.

4. Play creates energy while work consumes it All work and no play makes the proverbial Jack a dull boy. Play is a kind of recreation. It takes away the individual's fatigue and brings him balmy rest. It is for this reason that young and old, none are averse to playing. But this does not mean that play does not result in physical exhaustion. But the fatigue that results out of playing differs in nature from the fatigue that originates in hard work. The fatigue of play is health giving. Of course, excessive practice in competitive games may harm physical progress of the individual and stunt his growth. Playing acts as a tonic both for the body and the mind, provided games are not played in excess of the body's energy. Such a condition can be easily recognised if one observes the physical condition after play. The individual should be refreshed and be enthusiastic about the work before him, and should have the energy to perform it. In physical games, the blood circulates rapidly through the body so that many undesirable elements present in the body are eliminated and the individual feels lighter and more energetic. After the day's tiring routine, most people feel the need for some form of recreation and enjoyment. Play is one form of it. On the other hand, work reduces the efficiency of the individual. Hence games and work should be rationally synthesized.

5. Difference in mental attitudes Play and work differ in respect of their accompanying mental attitudes. Play is independently indulged in without any hint of compulsion whereas work is associated with the feeling of necessity and inevitability. The necessity may be due to some external compulsion such as the order of a superior or it may be imposed on the self from within. Man naturally engages in and concentrates upon the play, but whereas work concentration is a matter of conscious effort rather than one of effortless ease. The feeling of responsibility is conspicuously absent when one is playing; he is not answerable to anyone and he has nothing much to lose if he makes a mistake as nothing is valuable at stake. But on the other hand, in work, the individual is conscious of a certain burden, and he is answerable to certain other individuals if he fails to perform his functions efficiently. He is responsible for the work he is allotted, and he is very likely to become a prey to boredom easily. It is for these reasons that the child, in his infancy and childhood, is allowed little work and more play. Even the things that he is taught are presented in such a manner that he treats them as a child's play. But when he attains adolescence and adulthood, he is entrusted with work of greater and greater responsibility. He even comes to perform such responsible functions avidly and enthusiastically.

Relationship between Work and Play

Despite the above superficial points of difference between the work and play, there is little if any fundamental dissimilarity between them. There can be no sharp and precise dividing line that demarcates the two and divides them into water tight compartments. The child learns both from play and work; in both he finds material that helps to develop his character, and both are essential and beneficial to him. Then, every individual can obtain some pleasure from the work he is engaged in, by orientation and conscious effort. And in the case of very efficient and capable individuals, it is said that work is a child's play for them. The ease and comfort with which famous authors compose voluminous works appears play to their readers and sometimes even to themselves. In fact, the ability with which an individual introduces the pleasure of play into his work depends upon the efficiency with which he can perform that work. To quote: Sir T.P. Nunn, "An agent thinks of his activity as play if he can take it up or lay it down at choice or vary at will the condition of its exercise; he thinks of it as work if it is imposed on him by unavoidable necessity, or if he is held to it by a sense of duty or a vocation." The person who looks upon it as play and accepts it willingly and freely excels in it both quantitatively and qualitatively. To take a simple example, the gardener engaged in the gardening can choose to look upon his job as play or as a vocation. In the first instance, the work will afford him much pleasure whereas if he chooses to treat it as a vocation he will be depriving himself of considerable pleasure.

What is Work?

Work can be defined as an action performed with the object of achieving some particular objective. Hence work is an action with a particular aim which is fulfilled by the action. Human beings do various kinds of work to earn their livelihood. Apart from the earning of livelihood, actions may have some other objectives such as study, earning prestige, etc. Here it may be objected that play also has an objective and for that reason it would be difficult to distinguish play from work. But two things must be kept in mind. In the first place, the player does get some satisfaction of his physical and psychological needs, but he does not start by considering this satisfaction as his goal. In the second place, it is not possible to draw a dividing line between play and work. The same activity may be a game for one individual and work for another, depending upon the attitude. For example, just as the player devotes his entire attention to playing the game without being overtly conscious of the results, the determined worker may perform some activity with complete concentration and be oblivious to the actual results. On the other hand, every player does think in terms of winning and losing, irrespective of how much sporting spirit he has. Hence, while the definition of work given above shows its relative difference from work, it does not indicate that there is a complete difference between the two. As far as the pleasurable and interesting aspect of play is concerned, the success of many great people lies in the fact that they found as great pleasure in doing work as they did in play.

KINDS OF WORK

Work is broadly divided into two categories — muscular work and mental work. Before going on to a detailed description of these two kinds, it is necessary to remember that the two are so intimately connected with each other that the distinction between the two is merely verbal and a matter of practical expediency. Muscular work requires physical energy. On the other hand, mental work requires the expenditure of nervous energy. But there is no physical work which does not require some mental participation just as much as there is no mental work which does not consume some physical energy. Hence both kinds of work are mutually dependent, not mutually exclusive.

Muscular Work

Every human being performs a multitude of muscular actions everyday in his life. Muscular work, depending upon the difficulty involved, results in more or less fatigue, sooner or later, and one arrives at a stage when one stops work due to the fatigue. This limit differs from individual to individual and from work to work.

Measurement of Fatigue in Muscular Work

The fatigue which is consequent upon all muscular work is measured by the ergograph, an instrument which measures the contraction of the muscles. Although many kinds of ergographs are in use, the most commonly used are Mosso's and Kraeplin's ergographs. In using the ergographing, the right or the left arm of the subject is tied in such a way that he can move only the middle finger. Before starting the experiment, the instrument for measuring rhythm is fixed at 60°. Then the subject pulls the thread fixed to the ergograph at the first beat of the metronome and relaxes it at the second beat. The contraction and expansion of the muscles in the middle finger are recorded on a sheet of a smoking paper through a needle. Since this work of pulling and relaxing the string is continued over a long period and since the relaxing is loaded with some weight, the subject's finger becomes fatigued until a stage is reached when the finger cannot pull the thread at all. As fatigue increases, the height of the markings on the smoked paper begins to fall and at the time of total fatigue, the markings take the from the straight line. In this manner the ergograph helps in the study of effects of fatigue on muscular work.

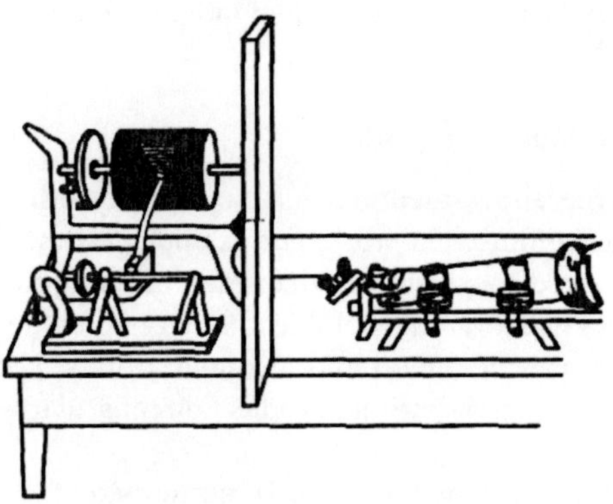

Fig. 21.1 Mosso's Ergograph

Effect of Rest on Muscular Fatigue

Muscular work also reads to the exhaustion of muscles and if the muscles are allowed to rest for sometime, the fatigue is reduced. It may even be completely eliminated. Many experiments have been conducted to observe the effect of rest on muscular fatigue. Many important facts as regards the length and the frequency of the rest period have thus been discovered. For example, in one experiment, the subject was given a six-kilogram weight to lift. Having lifted the weight caused fatigue in muscles. The subject was given a ten-second test after every lifting. As a result, the subject continued to lift the weight at ten-second intervals for an indefinite period. After sometime, in a second experiment, the rest interval was reduced from ten seconds to only two seconds and it was found that within one minute the subject became so tired that he could not lift the weight at all. Besides, he had to rest for two hours to get rid of the fatigue accumulated in that one minute of work. It is, therefore, evident from this that it is not only the rest given which is effective in removing fatigue, the rest interval must be given with the right frequency and it must be in proportion to the time spent in work.

Influence of Mental Factors on Muscular Work

The extent of fatigue and time in which it occurs also depends to a great extent upon mental factors. It has been seen that if the individual takes interest in his work, he can produce more work for longer time and still do not complain of fatigue. Generally, mental fatigue has an adverse effect on muscular activity, although there are many exceptions to this. Sometimes individuals are seen performing muscular work with great skill and application despite mental fatigue. Yet, mental factors do undoubtedly influence muscular work.

Other Factors in Muscular Work

In addition to the above-mentioned factors, many other factors also effectively influence muscular work. For example, it has been observed that women get tired more quickly than men in doing muscular work. Lombard's studies had a very favourable influence upon the introduction of rest as well as practice, food and alcoholic drinks. Harley's studies showed that tobacco has a detrimental effect on muscular work.

Study of Muscular Work by the Hand Dynamometer

All the above examples of muscular study were made by the ergography. But it is also measured and studied by the use of hand dynamometer. In this instrument, the subject fits his finger into the dynamometer and pulls it with his entire strength and then relaxes it. The meter is fixed at 60°. An interval of four seconds is allowed between the two successive acts of pulling the handle. The subject performs this function for one minute and in every case the force exerted by the subject is measured in terms of kilograms. If the subject does not take rest but performs this action continuously he tires rapidly and a diminution in his energy is soon apparent. But if he takes rest at regular intervals then he can continue to do this work for a much longer time since he does not become fatigued so quickly.

Value of the Study of Muscular Work

As has been pointed out earlier, the study of muscular work is valuable from the psychological point of view. It is a matter of common experience that output can be increased if muscular fatigue can be prevented. Therefore, many measures are adopted to reduce muscular fatigue in most factories and offices. Generally, the workers are allowed to have one or two rest intervals during the working hours, and the period of rest varies from half an hour to one hour. Arrangements are also made for refreshments. Efforts are also made to make the work interesting. In some organisations, music is played for the workers while they are working. Then, normally only men are employed to do only muscular work while children and women are allowed to do only light muscular work because they become tired much quicker. Studies are still being conducted to discover ways and means of reducing fatigue. In addition to this, bonuses are offered to improve the motivation of workers. It need hardly be pointed out that the worker's efficiency and skill can be vastly improved by these studies of muscular work.

MENTAL WORK

What is Mental Work?

Mental work involves the use of mental energy. All individuals are not endowed with the same amount of mental energy and therefore, all people cannot be expected to perform the same kind of mental work. One common example of mental work is the work of study. In this kind of work, too, some functions are difficult and hard while others are simple and easy. It is, for example, easier to take notes than to write a book. Hence individuals with varying amounts of mental energy are required to perform these simple and complex tasks. Individual differences in respect of mental energy are seen just as they are present in the case of muscular energy. Besides this, some individuals have exceptional capacity for certain specific kind of tasks and takes but negligible capacity for these. For example, the good teacher is rarely a good writer while the good writer may or may not be a good teacher.

Study of Mental Work

Among the many methods adopted in the study of mental work, the more commonly used are:

1. Letter elimination method As is evident from the name itself, in this method the subject has to eliminate certain words from the list provided. He is made to sit comfortably and then given a list and a pencil with which to eliminate letters. This work can be done for any fixed period, from half an hour to an hour. The subject is informed of the completion of the work a minute or two before it actually ends. At the end of the test, the subject's personal examination is also recorded. Now the letters cancelled by him, the letters left untouched and the letters cancelled incorrectly are counted and an evaluation of his work is made. From this, one can evaluate the mental efficiency of the subject.

2. By addition or subtraction In this, the subject is required to do some addition and subtraction and his work and its quality are evaluated on the basis of the right and wrong answers given by him.

WORK CURVE

Work curve, as is evident from the term itself, is that line on a graph which indicates the work done by an individual. Work curves can be prepared both for mental work and muscular work. The work curve of an individual's performance possesses the following three features:

1 **Initial spurt.** Whenever an individual begins to do some work, he sits down to it fresh and, for that reason, his production progresses rapidly in the initial stages of the work. Hence, the work curve progresses quickly in the beginning.

2 **Plateau.** This initial spurt, or rapidity is not maintained for a long time because the individual invariably, begins to get exhausted as he continues to work. For this reason, his progress begins to fall and then stops increasing.

3 **Final spur near to the end** Whenever the individual learns that his work is coming to an end, he puts in a special effort near the end. This also leads to a rise in the work curve although this spurt lasts for only a short time. In this stage, the individual works enthusiastically although he is exhausted.

The above sketch of the nature of the work curve does not indicate the extent and variety of factors that influence the production. But it does suggest that the work curve declines due to fatigue. Fatigue is delayed if the worker has practice in his work. On the other hand, fatigue also has a detrimental effect on the habits formed by practice. Sometimes, the worker produces as much in a fatigue condition as otherwise but, in that case, the quality of the work is definitely inferior to his normal production. All these factors are known as the factors which influence the production of work.

FACTORS INFLUENCING THE PRODUCTION

The factors influencing the production have been discovered after many experiments. Some of these factors help production and increase it while others hinder and retard it. Basically, these factors can be divided into the personal and environmental categories. Personal factors are again of two kinds — the mental and the physical.

(a) Personal Factors

These are the factors which are inherent in the worker himself. Every kind of work is a consequence of the worker's mental and physical application and it needs the use of mental and physical energy. For that reason, the personal factors influencing production are psychological as well as physical.

1. Psychological factors This category includes all those factors which are part of the worker's psychology and have some influence upon the work produced by him. The main ones are as follows:

(i) *Motivation*: Motivation is the most important factor in production because production increases when motivation increases and falls when motivation is reduced to a lower level. Although motivation alone is not enough, it does influence production under more normal circumstances. It is of even greater importance when the work is difficult and complex. The truth of the matter is that motivation will have great influence upon production when the work is more difficult.

(ii) *Incitement*: Many experiments have established that production can be increased by incitement. It is difficult to be skilled in one's work if this is lacking. Its influence is not very apparent in work which is done continuously, but it can be seen that all work is done at intervals. This fact has been reasoned. The workers are given incentives in different professions so that they may produce more.

(iii) *Interest*: It is a commonly accepted fact that production increases if there is an interest and decreases if there is none. Interest helps to delay fatigue and also to reduce it. Many experiments have shown that interest is the cause of application and dedication to a task and this increases production.

(iv) *Reward and punishment*: The consequences of an individual's work influence his production. If the result is reward, he tends to return to his work with even greater enthusiasm. The reward may be material, as in the case of money, or verbal, as in the case of praise, etc. Different individuals react differently to various kinds of rewards but it has some effect, more or less. But the more effective reward is one which is neither too easily available nor impossible to attain. It also should not be so cheap as to have no real value and neither should it be so valuable that the worker may show greed for it. The effect of reward and punishment can be seen clearly in the case of students. It has a very great importance for games.

(v) *Coordination*: In any industry, the production achieved by a worker depends upon his coordination with the work. It has been seen in the experiments of Kraeplin that in the absence of coordinations there is much greater distraction of attention. When the coordination improves the loss of attention is considerably less with the result that he can concentrate on he work and produce more.

(vi) *Established rapport among the workers*: If many workers are to work simultaneously to complete some work then rapport must be established between them. Besides, production is also better when the relations between the workers are friendly and cordial. On the other hand, absence of such relations leads to loss of production in terms of quantity as well as quality.

(vii) *Blocking:* The effect of blocking of production can be seen in the experiments conducted by Bills. According to him, no person can perform some mental work continuously. In certain cases, the frequency of blocking is as high as four or five times within one minute. Sometimes the period of blocking itself may last for one minute. In the duration of blocking, the worker's mental condition is more or less stunned. Although it is impossible to say why blocking occurs at all, it cannot be denied that it does occur and that the frequency and the actual length of blocking vary from one person to another and even from one kind of task to another in the case of the same person.

2. Physiological factors The physiological factors which influence the production are those which depend upon the bodily condition of the worker. The main factors are:

(i) *Health and capacity of physical organs:* Different bodily organs such as hands, feet, eyes, etc., are employed during different kinds of tasks. If these organs are defective or weak then production is very adversely affected. On the other hand, more production can be done if these physical organs are healthy and strong. Hence the total quantity of work done by a worker depends upon the condition of his bodily organs.

(ii) *Fasting*: Fasting also influences production. The experiments conducted by Glaze indicate that fasting for more than one day has a distinct influence upon production although fasting for a day or less may have no apparent effect. Glaze experimented upon three subjects and observed that production went down in each case due to fasting. Later on, the skill was regained when the fasting was stopped.

(iii) *Sleep*: Sleep has an important influence upon production because lack of adequate sleep leads to a fall in the quantity and quality of production. Adequate sleep has a beneficial effect on production.

(iv) *Drug addiction*: Almost all experiments in this connection have proved that drug addiction is bad. Hollingworth has substantiated this view after conducting an experiment on six subjects.

(v) *Use of tobacco*: The experiments conducted upon the effect of tobacco chewing on production have not yielded uniform results. In the case of middle-aged people addicted to smoking, it was found that tobacco has a beneficial effect. On the other hand, if tobacco is taken by people not accustomed to it, their production registers a sudden and sharp fall because tobacco renders their mental and physical condition abnormal.

(b) Environmental Factors

The environmental factors influencing production include all those circumstances and conditions which alter production in any way. The more important ones are as follows:

1. Light In every kind of industry, some degree of light is necessary. But if the intensity of light is more or less than required, then, the production suffers. The quality of light, in addition to its quantity, also affects production. The best light is the natural light of sun. It not only helps vision but also has a good effect on health but in its absence white light is believed to be the best substitute. In addition to the quantity and quality, the distribution of light available is another effective factor. The light should be so distributed over the working area that it should light up and illuminate the machines and other instruments being used by the workers. But it should not fall directly upon the eyes of any worker because this may dazzle him and lead to accidents. If the light is adequate, it will avoid straining the eyes and in this manner contribute to the skill of the worker.

2. Ventilation If many people work together in the same premises, it becomes necessary to make provision for the flow of clean air into the place and of stale air out of the place. Besides, in many kinds of work, many harmful gases are generated in production. All kinds of experiments have indicated that proper ventilation has a positive effect on production and the absence of such arrangements leads to the ill-health of the workers and a subsequent fall in production.

3. Temperature In many offices and factories, it becomes necessary to control the room temperature in the premises in order to maintain the efficiency of the workers because excessive heat or excessive cold have an adverse effect on production. The proper temperature can be determined only by the nature of the work, the local climate, the location of the factory and also by the average health of the workers. But it can be said definitely that it is necessary to maintain proper temperature for good production. For this reason, many laboratories are air-conditioned nowadays.

4. Noise Some experiments conducted upon the effect that noise has upon the production indicated definitely that when noise rises above a certain pitch, it is definitely harmful. The pitch of the noise that can be tolerated depends upon the habits of the worker, his skill and the nature of work. Many experiments have been conducted in this connection and many means devised to reduce the volume of noise in factories. Many modern laboratories are sound-proofed to external noise so that the workers within are not disturbed.

On this account of factors, only the more prominent personal and environmental factors have been taken into account. In actual fact, it is not possible to list the total number of factors. Besides, psychologists attached to different industries continue to study these factors and make experiments. They help in revealing many new facts.

5. Rest pause It has been found that adequately timed rest pauses of proper duration have a positive influence upon the production. It is possible to determine by experiment the length and frequency of rest pause which will be adequate for a particular individual. Vernon and Bedford conducted an experiment on 17 young girls in which the girls were given a rest of ten minutes after every hour of work. A 20 per cent increase in production was observed. In another experiment in which seven girls were involved, a 13 per cent increase in production was noticed when they were allowed to rest after every hour. In an experiment by Ermaski, it was seen that when a five-minute interval was introduced after every hour of work and a fifteen minute interval after every hour and quarter of work, 25 per cent improvement in production was noticed. Graff conducted some experiments and concluded that production is increased if a rest of two minutes is given after forty minutes of mental work. On the basis of experiments it was found that a rest pause of 6 to 10 minutes after every two hours of work proves useful and beneficial in the case of middle-aged workers. Some other experiments have shown that if the rest pause is more or less than a particular limit then it will hinder production instead of helping it. If the rest pause is too long, it is harmful because the worker's enthusiasm cools down and it amounts to beginning afresh. Besides, it also leads to boredom and disgust. In an experiment by Amberg, a rest pause of 5 minutes was found useful while a rest pause of 15 minutes proved definitely detrimental. In the same way, different length and varying frequencies of rest pauses can be determined for different persons. The basic fact is that the rest pause should be long enough to eliminate fatigue and make the worker fresh but it should not be so long that it may induce boredom, lethargy and disinterest. It is only natural that different rest intervals will be required for individuals with varying personal interests, capabilities, abilities, etc. Hence it is the worker who himself can tell how much rest he requires and after what interval of time. The basic principle governing the timing of the rest pause is that it should be introduced after the period of maximum production because soon after this, production begins to fall. If rest is provided at this time, this inevitable fall in production can be eliminated.

6. Group situation Psychologists have conducted many experiments to find out whether production improves while working in a group or if it is better when the individual is working alone. Modi induced a group of youngsters to do muscular work on the hand dynamometer first individually and then in pairs, and came to the conclusion that production was 2 percent more in the group situation than while it was done alone. In his experiments on college students, Whitmore saw that production was 26 per cent more when work was performed in a group situation. The main reason for this increase in production in the group situation is that a definite competitive spirit comes into play while working together. As a result, the individual worker is induced to bring into work his entire energies. But this kind of increase in production is mainly quantitative because in terms of quality, the work generally deteriorates. The reason for this phenomenon is that the worker is constantly interested in the total work done by others and in trying to do better than them, fails to consider the quality of his own work. Although, generally the more skilful individuals retain their quality while working collectively, some individuals are found to perform better while working alone. This fact depends on one side upon the individual nature and working habits of the persons, and on the other side upon the nature of work. For example, mental work in which quality counts, the creation of art or literature is better done alone because in a group situation there is too much distraction of attention. But this fact cannot be said to be true for all writers and artists, because much depends upon the working habits of each individuals. On the other hand, mechanical and physical work in which quantity alone is important, is normally better performed collectively.

QUESTIONS FOR EXERCISE

1. Write a short note on Work Curve.
2. Explain the characteristics of a work curve. Prove that the introduction of the rest pauses enhances the efficiency and output of the work.
3. What is work? Explain muscular work and mental work.
4. State, how rest affects work. Illustrate your answer with examples from everyday life.

22

PERFORMANCE APPRAISAL

WHAT IS PERFORMANCE APPRAISAL?

1. Shubin "Performance appraisal is a systematic appraisal of the employee's personality traits and performance on the job and is designed to determine his contribution and relative worth to the firm."

2. Dale Yoder "All formal procedures used in working organisations to evaluate personalities and contributions and potentials of group members."

OBJECTIVES OF APPRAISAL

1. To serve as a basis for job change or promotion By establishing whether the worker can contribute still more in a different or a higher job performance appraisal helps in his suitable promotion and placement.

2. To guide training and development programme By identifying the strengths and weaknesses of an employee it serves as a guide for formulating a suitable *training and development programme* to improve his quality of performance in his present work.

3. To serve as a feedback to the employee By letting the employee know how well he is doing or where he stands with his superior performance appraisal tells him what he can do to improve his present performance and go up in the management hierarchy. It thus facilitates self-development and makes the employee aware of his key performance areas.

4. To serve as incentive Performance appraised serves as an important incentive to all the employees who are assured of the management's continued interest in them and of their continuous possibility to develop.

They realise that they being continuously observed and have not been forgotten.

5. To increase observation The existence of a regular appraisal system tends to make the supervisors and executives *more observant* of their subordinates as they know that they will be expected to fill out rating forms periodically and would be called upon to justify their estimates. This knowledge results in improved supervision.

6. To provide rational foundation for wages Performance appraisal provides a rational foundation for the payment of piece-work wages, bonus, etc. It estimates of the relative contributions of employees help to determine the rewards and privileges rationally.

7. To evaluate effectiveness of selection devices Performance appraisal serves as means for evaluating the effectiveness of devices used for the selection and classification of workers. Its knowledge of the characteristics of superior and inferior workers can be helpful in selection and placement of workers.

8. To help planning Permanent performance appraisal records of employees help management to do planning such as fixing targets, responsibilities, etc. without relying upon personal knowledge of supervisors who may be shifted.

FACTORS AFFECTING PERFORMANCE APPRAISAL

According to Prof. S.K. Chakraborty,[1] before doing performance appraisal it is always advisable to make a preliminary survey of the following factors within which the employees of an organisation are working:

1. Environmental constraints There are several environmental constraints outside the control of a worker. It would be unjust to ignore this fact in judging his performance. For example, the quality of raw material in an organisation may deteriorate over a period or the machinery may break down unexpectedly. Hence both productivity and quality may suffer. But the performance appraisal of the worker should not be affected if selection of materials and maintenance of machinery are done at higher levels in the organisation.

2. Style of organisational leadership The style of the leadership of an organisation to a large extent determines the loyalty and commitment of employees to the goals of an organisation. Effective top leadership orients and motivates the entire organisation for better performance. Employees at every level become highly performance conscious. Under such

1. S.K. Chakraborty, *Managerial Development and Appraisal.* Macmillan: India (1978).

condition performance appraisal is liked by everybody. It is considered an imposition or stricture in the opposite conditions.

3. Interdependence of sub-systems A big organisation is composed of a number of interdependent sub-systems, the success or failure of which must be interpreted in the context of all other sub-systems to which it is related. For example, the sub-standard output of the production department may be due to the poor quality of purchases made by the Purchasing Department. It may be at some higher level sub-system where planning for the production and purchase departments has been done.

Because of this interdependence of sub-systems suggestion is often made to start performance appraisal from the apex. This leads to more systematic and logical cause-and-effect tracing of performance at all levels within the organisation.

4. Organisational structure Burns and Stalker[1] classify organisational structure into: "organistic" and "mechanistic". Organistic structures have quite flexible organisational structure. Elaborate organisation chart or manuals are usually non-existent. In rapidly changing environments such structures can quickly manoeuvre themselves into vantage position to confront new situations. This makes such structures responsive to innovations of all kinds. On the other hand, mechanistic structures tend to be rigid, with clearly defined relationships and responsibilities. As shown by readily available organisation blueprints and the like a formal awareness of the structural pattern pervades such organisations. By implication, these structures tend to be static and are designed to carry out a nearly fixed strategy in a relatively environment. In a mechanistic structure initiative, drive and imagination do not receive encouragement.

CRITERIA OF PERFORMANCE APPRAISAL

1. Job Analysis

It identifies the components of a particular job which helps in distinguishing one job from the other. In performance appraisal the goal is not to make distinctions among jobs, but rather to make distinction among people, especially among people in the same job. Criterion development is the critical intermediary process. In it the important job components identified in job analysis are transformed into a number of performance criteria which may be used to measure the proficiency of an employee. These criteria may be classified into two main categories: objective criteria and subjective criteria.

---

1. Burns, T. and Stalker, G.M., *The Management of Innovation*. Tavistock: London, 1961.

(i) *Objective criteria:* Amount and quality of production, work sample tests, length of service, amount of training necessary, absenteeism, accidents, etc. are all examples of objective criteria.

Although objective measures of performance are intuitively attractive, they suffer from the following weaknesses:

(a) ***Contamination:*** These measures sometimes become contaminated by several situational factors, which give a wrong picture of employee's performance. Thus employees who are equal in performance may be rated differently on the basis of difference in their outputs which may be the result of differences in the quality of materials handled, the condition of machines, working conditions, supervisory pressure, experience, age, sex, time at which measurements are made and so on. The difference in the rupee volume of sales of two sales persons may be due to the difference in the sales potential of their territories.

(b) *Neglect of behavioural aspect:* Objective measures sometimes fail to take into account the behavioural aspect of performance, *e.g.*, a worker's ability to get along with his fellows.

(c) *Difficult to specify:* Objective measures are difficult to be specified for higher level jobs which are complex and vague.

The weaknesses of objective measures have led organisations to rely heavily on subjective measures of job performance.

(ii) *Subjective criteria :* Rating of employee's job proficiency by their superiors, peers and subordinates, extent of upward communication of ideas, degree of knowledge about corporate goals, contribution to socio-cultural values, etc., are all examples of subjective criteria.

However, since subjective measures are prone to certain kinds of errors associated with the rating process as they are dependent upon human judgement.

TYPES OF PERFORMANCE CRITERIA

1. Performance Criteria for classes of employees in an organisation

(i) Quantity and quality of output in a given period
(ii) Work sample tests
(iii) Length of service
(iv) Amount of training necessary
(v) Ratings by supervisors
(vi) Number of accidents in a given period
(vii) Number of absent in a given period

2. Performance Criteria for Frontline Supervisors

(i) Quantity and quality of output in a given period
(ii) Labour cost per unit of output in a given period
(iii) Material cost per unit of output in a given period
(iv) Total cost per unit of output in a given period
(v) Absenteeism rate for a given period
(vi) Turnover rate for a given period
(vii) Manshifts lost due to stoppage of work in a given period
(viii) Number of accidents in a given period

3. Performance Criteria for Middle-level Managers

(i) Quantity and quality of output in a given period
(ii) Labour cost per unit of output in a given period
(iii) Material cost per unit of output in a given period
(iv) Total cost per uhit of output in a given period
(v) Rational use of overhead facilities
(vi) Coordination among supervisors
(vii) Degree of knowledge among supervisors about corporate goals and policies
(viii) Extent to which frontline supervisors regard themselves as managers and behave likewise
(ix) Extent of upward communication of ideas, information and queries from frontline supervisors

4. Performance Criteria for Managers

(i) Return on capital employed
(ii) Labour productivity indices (improvements in labour productivity arise from capital investment, better work methods, better personnel policies, etc., all of which originate at the top echelons of management)
(iii) Capacity utilization
(iv) Gain or loss in market share
(v) Degree of knowledge among middle level managers about corporate goals and policies
(vi) Extent to which middle level managers regard themselves as managers and behave likewise
(vii) Extent of upward communication of ideas, information and queries from middle level managers

(viii) Contribution to the socio-cultural values of the environment (a consideration of this aspect is essential to determine whether the organisation has secured a niche for itself as a worth-while institute in society)

Criterion Development

(i) ***Production:*** For a worker engaged on a production job the number of units produced in a given time would accurately represent his proficiency. To make it directly comparable with the output of other workers amount of output should be adjusted for variation in quality, if any. But if the units of measurement differ for different sub-groups of workers or if production in different sub-groups is done under different conditions, direct comparisons of outputs between workers in the two sub-groups are not possible. Hence each worker's output may be expressed as a percentage of the average for his department or sub-group and then the productivity of workers in different groups can be compared.

(ii) ***Work sample tests*****:** When accurate output records of workers cannot be obtained, work sample tests can serve as a measure of proficiency. Here the employee performs exactly the same work as that involved on the job. The typing proficiency tests are the most commonly employed work sample tests.

(iii) ***Length of service*****:** In many situations the longer a worker has remained on a job the more successful he is considered. His long stay on the job reflects his ability to adjust to the working conditions, get along with his fellow workers, satisfaction with the job and similar factors.

(iv) ***Amount of training necessary*****:** Training time can be used as a measure of worker's proficiency when the training period is expensive to the organisation. The worker needing a longer time to learn is considered inferior to one who learns in a relatively short time.

(v) ***Ratings of supervisors*****:** Ratings are quantitative statements of opinion of foremen, managers and others in supervisory authority. Ratings are about such characteristics of a worker as job knowledge, about tools and equipment, coordination and speed of body movements, ability to read drawings correctly, interest in work, attendance, attitude toward suggestions, work place set-up and regard for safety, cooperativeness and so on.

(vi) ***Weighing*** **:** A weight must be assigned to each of the component measures of efficiency in the following ways:

(a) *Equal weighing:* Cattell objects to equal weighing thus: 'Ten men and two bottles of beer cannot be added to give the same total as two men and ten bottles of beer. Two men with the same composite score may have very different patterns of scores on the criterion elements. The driver whose number of collisions with vehicles and pedestrians is small may achieve the same composite criterion score as another driver whose number of collisions is big but whose number of traffic violations is small. Since these two patterns of work behaviour are so different in nature it makes no sense to assign them the same composite score which would possibly result if the components were equally weighed.

(b) *Weighing according to the judgement by experts:* Here a satisfactory agreement in their ratings is seldom attainable.

(c) *Weighing according to the reliability of the criterion measures:* Here a given measure may be highly reliable and consequently would be given a high weight though it may be relatively unimportant because it is not highly representative of the job requirements. If the measures available are equally representative of the job, then weighing them in terms of their reliability is a very effective procedure.

(d) *Multiple cutoffs:* A minimum standard is set for each measure of proficiency. A worker who is above the standard on every measure of proficiency is deemed successful, whereas a worker who falls below on any one of the measure is considered unsuccessful. Thus workers are classified into two groups —the successful and unsuccessful. Every single aspect is considered essential. For example, no matter how good an aeroplane pilot is on take-offs, navigation, cross-country flying, etc., if he is poor in making landings he must be considered unsuccessful.

(e) *Net contribution:* The contribution that a worker makes to an organisation in terms of output and the costs that result from his activities through wastage, accidents, errors, etc., can be expressed in rupees. The net contribution in terms of rupees made or lost to the company can be determined. As all measures of performance are expressed in the common terms of rupees they are readily combined.

METHODS OF PERFORMANCE APPRAISAL

1. Ranking method
2. Rating-scale method
3. Check-list method
4. Forced-choice method
5. Field review
6. Critical incident technique
7. Confidential report

8. Essay appraisal
9. Assessment centre

1. Ranking method To compare one man with all other men and place him in a simple rank order is the oldest and simplest method of performance appraisal. In it ordering is done from best to worst of all individuals comprising the group. Though this method is both simple and natural, it has following disadvantages:

(i) It is highly subjective.

(ii) People are compared as a whole. Comparison of the various components of a person's performance is not done.

(iii) The magnitude of differences in ability between ranks is not equal at different positions. For instance, the difference in ability between the first and second individuals may be much greater in absolute terms than the difference between the second and third. In terms of ranks, however, the differences between these individuals are the same.

(iv) Its use is difficult in large groups as the rater cannot compare several people simultaneously. The paired comparison method of ranking has been evolved as an answer to this problem. In it the rater compares each man with every other man in his group, with the final ranking of each worker determined by the number of times he was judged better than the others. The number of comparisons involved in this method is very large. It can be determined by the following formula:

Number of comparisons $= \frac{N(N-1)}{2}$ where N stands for the number of men to be rated. For a 50-man group, for example, there would be 1,225 separate comparisons which is obviously far too great to permit expedient use of the method.

2. Rating-scale method Ranking methods are unsuitable where the number of persons to be appraised is large and where it is desired to gain information about the size of absolute differences between the rated individuals. Rating-scale methods may be used in such cases. These methods provide some kind of a scale for measuring absolute differences between individuals. The scales used are generally of two types:

(i) *Discrete:* Where two or more categories are provided, representing discrete amounts of ability or degrees of the characteristics, the rater can tick mark the category which he feels best describes the person being rated. The characteristic 'Job Knowledge' may be divided into 4 categories on a discrete scale: 'Exceptionally Good', 'Good', 'Average', and 'Poor'.

(ii) ***Continuous (or graphic)*** Where an uninterrupted line is provided just above the category notations the rater can tick at any point along its length as shown below :

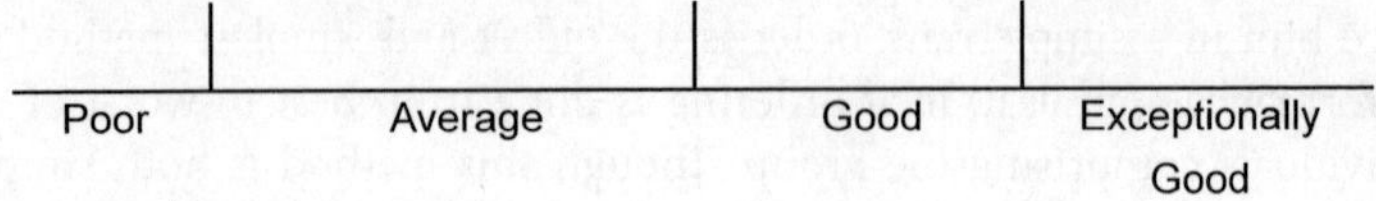

Standards Used in Rating Scales

Four kinds of standards are used in both discrete and continuous types of rating scalesss:

(i) Numerical standards: In these a series of numbers is provided. It is supposed to indicate varying amounts of the characteristic being rated. If a person were judged as the best possible workers on a scale ranging from 0 to 10, he would be rated 10. Sometimes 0 is the value assigned to average ability, with a series of positive numbers indicating superior degrees of the characteristic and a series of negative numbers indicating inferior degrees. Sometimes letters are used as standards. In a five-step scale the highest category might be *A* and the lowest *E*.

(ii) ***Descriptive-adjective Standards:*** This is a series of descriptive adjectives such as exceptional, excellent, superior, good, competent, satisfactory, adequate, average, ordinary, fair, weak, poor, etc. These are used to indicate varying amounts of the characteristic being rated.

In both the above types of scales the numbers or alphabets or adjectives used to describe the various categories of a characteristic do not convey the same meaning to all raters.

(iii) ***Man to man standards*:** These standards are very concrete because there are neither numbers nor alphabets nor descriptive adjectives but persons of varying ability whom the rater has selected and ranked in the ability under consideration. Thus a scale of men is created for each trait. In rating other persons the rater simply looks over this scale and compares them with the persons on the scale. Following are the objections to this scale:

(a) Its construction involves difficult and laborious procedure pre-scaling a group of present employees.

(b) As there is also the very touchy problem of using the names of models without any embarrassment, one must be very careful that the scale is not made public.

(c) The intervals between the men on the scale are often not of equal magnitude.

(iv) *Behaviour-sample standards:* There are a series of actual descriptions of behaviour which is supposed to indicate varying amounts of the characteristic being rated. Its use reduces some of the differences in interpretation usually found among different raters. For example, on a rating scale measuring the trait 'job knowledge', it is highly probable that the agreement among different raters on the descriptions 'unfamiliar with the work', 'works with reasonable accuracy and turns out satisfactory work', 'noticeably better than the ordinary run of men', and 'thoroughly familiar with his work' will be greater than the agreement on the meaning of the adjectives 'poor', 'average', 'good' and 'exceptionally good'.

3. Check-list method It is a list consisting of a number of statements about the worker and his behaviour. Depending upon its importance each statement on this list is assigned a value. Both statements and their values are derived from preliminary research in which are used the pooled judgements of persons familiar with the job. In rating a person, the rater is asked to place a plus sign, minus sign, or a question mark in front of each statement, depending on whether he feels the description applies, does not apply, or there is doubt, respectively. No restrictions are put on rater about the number of statements he should mark. The worker's final rating is the average of the scale values of all statements that his superior has checked with a plus sign. This method requires only a reporting of facts from the rater. As the values assigned to different statements do not appear on the list, the rater does not know how highly he has rated a given individual. He does not to distinguish among various categories for each of the several traits considered for each of the several employees working under him.

Limitations

(i) It is difficult to construct a good check-list.

(ii) A separate check-list is required for each job because statements used in one check-list to evaluate one category of workers cannot be used in another check-list to evaluate other category of workers.

(iii) As the rater does not know the values given to different statements, he may resent the system as a whole and not give it his whole-hearted support.

4. Forced-choice method It consists of a number of statements describing an individual being rated. Groups in twos, threes or fours, all groups on the rating form are made of, sometimes favourable statements only, sometimes unfavourable statements only and sometimes both favourable and unfavourable statements. The rater makes two checks in each group one for the statement which best described the individual and one for the statement which is least descriptive.

Advantages

(i) Impartial This method has built-in safeguards against partiality. The rater does not know which of the statements in a given group has been considered to be critical or relevant for effective job performance and what value it carries.

(ii) Easy rating The relevance of a statement and its value are determined by extensive preliminary research. Statements which have more discriminative power to distinguish between good and poor workers are given more value. Statements which have no discriminative power are given zero value. A worker's final rating is arrived at by adding together the values of all the statements that have been checked as describing him.

Limitations

(i) Expensive It is expensive because the statements must be custom-tailored to the demands of the particular job and company.

(ii) Lack of trust Because the implicit assumption behind it is that the rater cannot be trusted to make impartial evaluation, it is resented by the rater.

5. Field review Graphic ratings are often combined with a systematic review process if there is reason to suspect rater bias or when some raters appear to be using higher standards than others. In the field review, the personnel officer meets small groups of raters from each supervisory unit and goes over each employee's rating with them to (a) identify areas of inter-rater disagreement, (b) help the group arrive at a consensus, and (c) determine that each rater conceives of the standards similarly.

As supervisors generally resent what they consider the staff interferences, this method is not widely used. It is also very time-consuming.

6. Critical incident technique In this method one draws up for each job a list of critical job requirements which are vital for success or failure on the job. For example, the following critical factors may be identified in the job of a salesman :

(i) Following up: complaints, requests, orders.
(ii) Planning ahead.
(iii) Communicating true information to managers and customers.
(iv) Carrying out promises.

(v) Persisting on tough accounts.
(vi) Pointing out uses for other company products besides the salesman's own line.
(vii) Using new sales techniques and methods.
(viii) Preventing price-cutting by dealers and customers.
(ix) Knowing customer requirements.
(x) Initiating new selling ideas.

Limitations

(i) It is difficult to identify critical factors.
(ii) It requires the supervisor to jot down incidents regularly.
(iii) It is hardly desirable to confront an employee with a misdeed or mistake which he committed six months or a year ago.

7. **Confidential Report** In this method each employee is rated confidentially by one or more senior officers for his performance. Important disadvantages of this method are:

SAMPLE

Confidential Report

Name .... Division ....
Designation and present duties ....
Service with the company......................... Years .... Months ....
Age...................................... Qualification ....
Present scale and salary ....
Next increment date...

REPORT ON YEAR'S WORK AND GENERAL OPINION

Describe your estimate of his/her personal qualities and capabilities:

(a) taking particular note on his/her reliability, judgement, adaptability and ability to organise, supervise and co-operate with others.

(b) mentioning any work of an outstanding character carried out by him/her during the year or any failure on his/her part to achieve the standard expected.

Do you consider that he/she is capable of rising to a higher position:

(a) In his/her present sphere.
(b) In another direction, if so, suggest which one.
(c) Whether at an early date after further experience.

(d) What is needed for his/her development.

Date	Manager
Date	Director
Final Review	
Date	Committee of Management

Limitations

(i) ***Not data-based*****:** The method is impressionistic. The appraisal is done on the basis of impressions, only minimal data are used.

(ii) ***No feedback*****:** The method does not give feedback to the appraisee on his performance, who never comes to know about his strengths and weaknesses. When one of his junior colleagues supersedes him in promotion, he keeps wondering what he lacks. He loses enthusiasm and motivation.

(iii) ***Closed method*****:** A few companies give negative feedback to the appraisal. But these companies do very little to openly discuss the employee why his performance is considered poor.

(iv) ***Evaluation not development:*** The method lays greater stress on evaluating the employee rather than developing him. For getting over his weaknesses the employee never comes to know what opportunities are available to him.

(v) ***Loss of credibility*****:** Personnel department lose its credibility.

8. Essay appraisal It is very common for appraising individuals for professional positions. In it the rater, who may be the former employer, teacher or associate of the candidate, is requested to give in writing an informed and honest account of the candidate's strengths, weaknesses, potentials, and so on. The biggest drawback of this technique is the account's variability in length and content, due to which it is difficult to compare two essay appraisals.

9. Assessment centre Many organisations use assessment centres to predict future performance more accurately. An assessment centre is a multiple assessment of severed individuals performed simultaneously by a group of trained evaluators using a variety of group and individual exercises. Individuals from different departments are brought together to spend two or three days working on individual or group assignment similar to the ones they will be handling if they are promoted. The pooled judgement of observers leads to an order of merit ranking for each participant.

Advantages

(i) All assessees have an equal opportunity to display their talents.

(ii) All are seen under similar conditions in relevant situations designed to bring out the particular skills and abilities needed for the position or positions for which they are being considered.

(iii) All are evaluated by a team of trained assessors, unbiased by past association, who are intimately familiar with the position requirements and the institutional climate.

(iv) People chosen by this method prove better than those chosen by other methods.

(v) The centre makes it possible for unknown people to compete with people from more well-known departments. This equalises opportunity, improves morale and enlarges the pool of possible promotion candidates.

REQUIREMENTS OF ASSESSMENT CENTRE

(i) Multiple assessment techniques at least one of which must be a simulation.

(ii) Multiple trained assessors.

(ii) Judgements based on pooled information from all assessors.

(iv) Evaluation made at a time separate from the observation of behaviour.

(v) Simulation exercises should first be tested for their reliability, validity and objectivity.

(vi) The dimensions, attributes, characteristics or qualities evaluated by this programme must be determined by an analysis of relevant job behaviour.

From the foregoing analysis of various performance appraisal techniques, it is clear that no single technique can achieve all the goals of performance appraisal. The choice of a technique should always be made in the light of goals. Separate methods may be used for separate purposes.

PERFORMANCE APPRAISAL OF MANAGERS BY MBO

Meaning of MBO

MBO is a popular technique of performance appraisal of managers. The first original work on it can be found in Peter Drucker's book *The Practice of Management,* published in 1954. In 1965 George Odiorne made a major contribution to MBO.

MBO is a process whereby performance goals and objectives are set by each subordinate in collaboration with his superior at the start of the appraisal period. Progress is now tracked and results are evaluated periodically. According to Prof. Reddin "MBO is the establishment of effectiveness areas and effectiveness standards for managerial positions and the periodic conversion of these into measurable time-bound objectives linked vertically and horizontally and with future planning".

Elements of MBO Programme

1. **Areas** Each manager identifies his key effectiveness areas where he should show results.
2. **Objectives** Each manager establishes his long term as well as short term objectives in such effective areas. The objectives should be:

(i) Qualified and time-bound.

(ii) Horizontally linked up with the objectives of the peers in the department, and vertically aligned with the objectives of the boss and the subordinates.

(iii) Related to and be part of the total organisational plan.

(iv) Established by the job-holder and the boss together. In other words, goal-setting should be participative. Unilateral imposition of goals by the boss is totally alien to the spirit of MBO.

3. **Evaluation** Mutually agreed objectives are used for evaluating performance. Periodic review and updating of these objectives is made by the boss and the subordinate together. Data-led objective consideration reveals whether the target was carelessly fixed or whether other reasons are responsible for inadequate performance.

The Elements of MBO in Actual Practice

(i) The document A document called the 'Management Guide' or 'Management Job Description' is usually prepared to facilitate the administration of MBO programme. It consists of 3 parts. The first part is the Title Page in which there is a concise statement of the purpose of the job, the job-holder's position in the organisation, as well as his responsibilities.

(ii) Key results analysis This part consists of 4 different columns. The first column names the key result areas of the job. In the second column the agreed objectives or performance standards are mentioned against each identified key result area. In the third column, the job-holder mentions the source and frequency of the control information which he proposes to use in checking his progress against standards. In the fourth column suggestions are made for improving results.

(iii) Job improvement plan This is a check-list agreed on by the manager and his boss covering the tasks which the manager is going to carry out in the next few months. It is usually drawn up at the performance review, but it can be amended at any time. It is important that each item in this list is given a date by which the manager undertakes to complete the assignment.

Advantages of MBO

1. More effective planning and control It sparks more effective planning and more effective controls. It forces managers to think of planning for results rather than merely planning activities of work. It also requires the manager to think of the way he may accomplish given results, the organisation and personnel he will need to do it, and the resources and assistance he will require. There is no better incentive for control and no better way to know the standard for control than a set of clear goals.

2. Reveals deficiency It reveals organisational deficiencies such as overlapping of authority, ineffective delegation and communication, etc.

3. Commitment It elicits people's commitment for performance.

4. Objectivity It furnishes objectivity and reduces the element of pure judgement.

5. Positive It is a more positive technique because in it the emphasis is shifted from the appraisal of an employee's weaknesses to the analysis of his strengths. In this technique, the employee is helped to improve his performance by developing his strengths and by overcoming his weaknesses.

Limitations of MBO

1. Fixing individual goals It presupposes fixing of individual goals and responsibilities, though all work in an organisation is a group effort where activities are so closely interrelated that no single individual can be blamed or rewarded for any end-result.

2. No comparative ratings It is difficult to make comparative ratings of individuals because each individual's goals are different from those of others in terms of complexity, etc.

3. No identification of potential It is difficult to appraise and identify potential as MBO only deals with performance on the present job.

4. Time consuming The method is extraordinarily time-consuming.

5. Inhibits honesty MBO presumes a certain level of trust throughout the hierarchy. But the organisational life teaches people to be cautious which inhibits honest dialogue and appropriate goal setting.

6. Narrow applicability It is especially suitable for managerial, professional and sales people in whose case performance is variable and it is possible to set flexible goals. MBO is less applicable to routine worker-level jobs, such as an assembly line, where performance levels are relatively fixed.

LIMITATIONS OF APPRAISAL METHODS

1. Emphasis on human performance without regard for human values George S. Odiorne has denounced all appraisal methods for their single inherent weakness that they lay emphasis on alikeness and conformity if human performance ignoring measurement of human values. All appraisal methods, are like quality control systems which force subordinates to conform to certain standards of physical performance without caring for human values. Thus, the appraisal methods rank both the benevolent and despotic managers equal if they are found equal in their physical achievements, though their value systems are widely different.

2. Halo effect The superior allows his good impressions of one or two important work characteristics of an individual to carry over the total evaluation. He rates all the characteristics of a person much higher than they should be. For example, if he is very fond of punctuality, a punctual worker may get a high rating on practically every factor though many factors have little to do with punctuality.

3. Hypercritical or "Horns" effect A superior rates people lower than their performances justify. Following are some examples of this effect:

(i) The superior is a perfectionist. As his expectation level is very high, he is more often disappointed and rates his people lower than he should.

(ii) The maverick or the non-conformist gets a low rating simply because he is "different".

(iii) One who has failed may wipe out the effect of years of good work on his appraisal and be rated low on his recent behaviour.

(iv) One who is too meek, too passive or who lacks some trait we attach to good men may suffer in his rating.

(v) One who does not do the job as well as we remember we did it when we held that job may suffer more than those who do work unfamiliar to us.

4. Central tendency and leniency. The superior is guilty of awarding average or more than average ratings to all his workers, on the ground that it will not injure the rate and that it will not expose his lack of more definitive information. Leniency reflects a desire to err on the generous side to avoid controversy by giving each rate the benefit of the doubt. To meet this situation the 'forced distribution system' is used where the rater is instructed about the percentages of cases which should fall in each category on the rating scale. For example, on a scale of 'job knowledge' the following percentages might be used:

Poor 10%, Below average 20%, Average 40%; Above average 20% and Exceptionally good 10%.

5. Reluctance to "play God" Managers are unwilling to "play God" by judging others as accepting the responsibility for being a judge for the future of another person causes severe anxiety in them. The tendency to complete the appraisal form at the last moment when they are due and to treat the entire process casually is necessary to relieve the anxiety of the evaluator in the role of "judge". The aggrieved employee is invariably left with the feeling that the superior is arbitrary in his judgement. This is a very frustrating experience for an honest and impartial superior.

6. Defensiveness of employees The appraisal process frequently creates defensiveness among employees as the supervisor's appraisal influences the employee's most vital job concerns — promotions, transfers and dismissal — During an appraisal interview the employee's defensiveness often 'makes the procedure unproductive for both the supervisor and the subordinate.

OVERCOMING OBSTACLES TO EFFECTIVE APPRAISAL

Companies generally take a two-pronged approach to overcome the obstacles to effective appraisal: they try to design the kind of system that will counteract tendencies to human errors and biases, and they train managers in the correct use of appraisal procedures. A training programme for managers generally covers:

1. The nature of the halo effect and of central tendency errors, and how to guard against them.
2. The desirability of placing emphasis on observable behaviour, where possible, as opposed to emphasis on personal traits of the rates.

POST-APPRAISAL INTERVIEW

According to Normal Maier, there are three types of appraisal interview 'Tell and Sell', Tell and Listen', and 'Problem Solving'.

1. "Tell and Sell" In this type of interview the interviewer is cast in the role of a judge who comes with the diagnosis and the remedy. But the subordinate who is being judged tries to conceal his weaknesses and if he feels the criticism is severe or the praise faint, he either protests or gives defensive responses. Its objectives are (i) to let the employee know how he is doing, (ii) to gain the employe's acceptance of the evaluation, and finally (iii) to get the employee to follow the plan that is outlined for his improvement.

The skills required for success in this type of interview include the ability to persuade the person to change in the prescribed manner. This may require the development of new needs in the person, as well as a knowledge of how to make use of the kinds of incentives that motivate each particular individual. This type has its greatest potential with young and new employees who are inexperienced and insecure and want the advice and assurance of an authority figure. The superior is respected not only because of position but also because his knowledge and experience are greater than theirs.

2. "Tell and Listen". Its objective is not only to communicate the evaluation to the employee but also to drain off his feelings aroused by the evaluation. Dividing the interview into two parts, the superior covers the strong part of the interview and avoids interruption and controversy by postponing any points of disagreement for later consideration. The second part of the interview is devoted to exploring the subordinate's feelings about the evaluation.

Initially, the reactions to the Tell and Listen method differ radically from Tell and Sell method with respect to the way disagreement and resistance are handled. Instead of the interviewer dominating the discussion to clarify his views, he always listens to disagreements. Actually he sits back and encourages the employee not only to disagree with the evaluation but also to relate his feelings. Thus during the second part of the interview the interviewer becomes a non-directive counsellor.

The skills of the Tell and Listen approach are (i) careful listening, (ii) making effective use of pauses, and (iii) responding to feelings in order to show that one understands them.

Advantages

(i) It creates a good relationship between superior and subordinate during the interview. The subordinate is likely to leave the interview with a favourable attitude toward the superior.

(ii) It tends to encourage upward communication and make management personnel employee-minded rather than production-minded. Listening and learning about the employee needs and aspirations during the interview the superior transmits his knowledge upward to grow a suitable organisational philosophy.

3. "Problem-solving Interview" Technically known as counselling, the objective of this approach is employee development. Here the appraisal of the subordinate is not directly communicated to him because an awareness of a weakness is not essential to development. The "telling" part of the interview is relevant only if this knowledge is a first step in the development process. If, however, the development of an employee can proceed without going through the step of locating and correcting weaknesses or faults, there is no need to communicate the appraisal to him.

This interview takes the interviewer out of the role of a judge and makes him a helper. He sacrifices his right to determine the direction of improvement of his subordinate. He does not specify the area in which this development should take place because this would constitute diagnosis and judgement. He limits his influence to that of stimulating thinking rather than supplying remedies or solutions. He is willing to consider all ideas on job improvement that the employee brings up. Forgetting his own viewpoint he tries to see the job as the employee sees it asking the employee to review the year's progress and discuss the problems, needs, innovations, satisfactions, and dissatisfactions he has encountered. This provides the employee an opportunity to get the boss's ear.

Steps in Problem-Solving Interview

1. Establishing rapport or prepare a case for communication It generates the necessary confidence in the subordinate. It assures him of his superior 's genuine interest in helping him. The counsellor should *carefully listen* to what the subordinate says and *display warmth and responsiveness* from his behaviour.

2. Exploring information about performance During this stage the counsellor puts to the subordinate various questions which may elicit elaborate information on the latter's achievements, strengths, failures and shortcomings to make the subordinate himself introspect and define his strengths and weaknesses.

3. Helping define the future goal and internalise the problem After the counsellor has succeeded in making the subordinate reflect on his strengths and weaknesses he can easily make him realise his problems.

There is generally a tendency to attribute one's failures, weaknesses or shortcomings to external reasons. The counsellor has to help the subordinate to internalinse the problem and its causes and in setting his future goals.

4. Drawing action plan Both the counsellor and the subordinate jointly consider all possible alternative solutions to the problem. Their pros and cons are weighed. The best alternative is selected. A step-wise action plan is prepared along with a time table. The subordinate is allowed to monitor the plan himself. The plan is reviewed by the two parties at regular intervals.

Requisites of Problem-Solving Interview or Counselling

1. Individual's desire to improve The individual given counsel should be interested in developing himself while superiors usually hold the view that subordinates do not take sufficient interest in their growth and development, subordinates allege that they do not feel free to participate in the process of review and feedback.

2. Continuous dialogue Not a one-way process of communicating to the employee what he should or should not do. Counselling is a process of continuous dialogue directed toward better understanding of the situation. It presupposes the existence of a general climate of openness, mutuality and trust.

3. Genuine interest of the superior in his subordinates' development The counsellor should have empathic attitude towards his subordinates. Counselling should not be considered as a burden or an unpleasant task and to be practised half-heartedly or as a compulsion.

4. Mutual participation Both the superior and the subordinate should whole-heartedly participate in the goal setting and reviewing of goals and performance. Counselling would be a futile exercise without such collaboration.

5. Focus on work-related behaviour Counselling should focus only on work-related goals and behaviour. Discussion about personal issues and personality problems should be done only in so far it is helpful in understanding the subordinate's difficulties in performing his organisational role more effectively. The feedback given by the superior should be objective and not just impressionistic.

ESSENTIALS OF A GOOD APPRAISAL SYSTEM

1. Understandable If the system is too complex or too time consuming, it may be anchored to the ground by its own dead-weight of complicated forms which nobody but the experts understand.

2. Support of all line people who administer it If the line people think it is too theoretical, too ambitious, too unrealistic, or that it has been foisted on them by ivory-tower staff consultants who have no comprehension of the demands on the time of the line operators, they will resent it. A similar goodwill and understanding must exist between the rater and the rates.

3. Open and participative Not only should it provide feedback to the employees on their performance it should also involve them in the goal setting process. This helps in planning performance better.

4. Both valid and reliable The validity of ratings is the degree to which they are truly indicative of the intrinsic merit of employees. The reliability of ratings is the consistency with which the ratings are made, either by different raters, or by one rater at different times. Both validity and reliability result from objective data-base.

5. Built-in-incentive A reward should follow satisfactory performance.

6. Follow up The system should have genuine follow-up mechanism to identify employee's growth needs. Otherwise, every employee would view the post-appraisal interview as a mere eyewash or as an exercise by management to force its views on him.

7. Supportive The system should make the employee feel that he has been treated in a supportive manner.

8. Periodical evaluation The system should be periodically evaluated to ensure that it is continuing to meet its goals. There is a danger that subjective criteria may become more salient than the objective standards originally established. There is the further danger that the system may become rigid in a tangle of rules and procedures, many of which are no longer useful.

QUESTIONS FOR EXERCISE

1. Define performance appraisal and explain its objects.
2. Describe the factors affecting performance appraisal and explain its criteria.
3. What are the methods of performance Appraisal? Which of these would you recommend for appraising managerial personnel in India?
4. Describe the process of establishing a forced choice system of rating. What are its advantages and disadvantages?
5. Compare any two methods of performance appraisal according to their relative simplicity. Specify the conditions necessary to make effective of a result oriented appraisal system.

6. Explain the meaning, elements, advantages and limitations of performance appraisal of managers by MBO.
7. Describe the Limitations of Appraisal Methods.
8. Explain the types of post-appraisal interview and point out the essentials of a good appraisal system.

23

FATIGUE AND BOREDOM

Fatigue can be both mental and physical, but to understand their difference, it is necessary first to understand their nature.

1. Physical fatigue In physical fatigue, as is evident from the name itself, one finds physical characteristics of fatigue. Physical efficiency and capacity fall down and physical co-ordination becomes difficult. A poisonous fluid known as lactic acid is produced in the muscles and the nervous system, and when this increases beyond a certain level, the entire body becomes lax. If it is confined to any one part of the body, then that particular part becomes tired but when exhaustion increases, it is introduced into the bloodstream and steadily spreads over the entire body. In addition to lactic acid, the body also produces ammonia and carbon dioxide during fatigue. Both these elements are poisonous and by their influence, the energizing elements in the body steadily decrease while the poisonous matter increases. Many psychologists have examined the condition of fatigue, the most valuable work having been done by Miller, Helmholtz and Wundt. Miller confined his study to the state of the nerves in a condition of fatigue. Later on, Helmholtz made a study of the function of the sensory nerves and motor nerves and discovered that, in a condition of fatigue, the experience of anything is conveyed to the brain in greater time while the motor nerves take a longer time to react than under normal conditions. Helmholtz invented the Myograph, an instrument used to measure the contraction of muscles. It was later used in 1858 by Wundt in his experiments. This instrument is now used to measure fatigue.

2. Mental fatigue Fatigue is not merely physical because it is sometimes manifested even when one has no physical work. This is mental fatigue.

Mental fatigue is normally apparent after excessive physical fatigue. The symptoms of mental fatigue are an absence of desire to work, emotional condition, lack of interest and concentration, lack of normal efficiency in work of interest and concentration, desire to rest, etc. At times one's efficiency does not suffer despite some mental fatigue. It is boredom in which one experiences mental fatigue. One important cause of mental fatigue is the absence of motivation and of a proper aptitude. In such a case, an individual loses interest in his work even though he is not physically exhausted. People complain of fatigue despite good working conditions if their attitude is not correct and if there is absence of sufficient motivation.

Difference between Physical and Mental Fatigue

The difference between physical and mental fatigue is evident from the foregoing description of their respective natures. When a person complains that he is fatigued, in fact he is suffering from both mental and physical fatigue. The symptoms of the two conditions are different. Physical fatigue is recognised by the condition of the muscles, chemical changes, nervous fatigue, changes in the blood chemistry and in the mental condition. On the other hand, mental fatigue is diagnosed from the absence of exhaustion yet one is averse to work. The removal of fatigue needs the creation of elements which provide the correct motivation and the correct attitude.

Relation between Physical and Mental Fatigue

Despite the differences between physical and mental fatigue mentioned above, the two should not be taken to be entirely different, for they are intimately related to each other. A person who complains of fatigue is, in fact, suffering both from mental as well as physical fatigue. Sometimes a persons does not notice physical fatigue if a strong motivation is coupled with absence of mental fatigue. In most forms of fatigue, one finds both physical and mental symptoms. According to Watson, mental fatigue is caused by the contraction of the vocal cord. It is also caused by damage to the nerve centres in a condition of physical fatigue. Physical work cannot be done well in a condition of mental fatigue. For this reason, it is better to define fatigue as a psychosomatic or psychophysical condition rather than a physical or mental condition. In fact, it is a physical and psychological condition in which the individual's mental and physical efficiency is reduced. The truth of the matter is that the physical and mental aspects of fatigue can be distinguished only superficially, because in actual fact they are dependent on each other.

Occupational Conditions of Fatigue

In different professions, there are different conditions which lead to fatigue which itself leads to a deterioration in the mental and physical health of the workers and ultimately to a fall in production. Such conditions can be briefly summarised as under:

1. Long hours of work In some industries, the hours of work are so long that the worker becomes exhausted while, in fact, these longer hours of work do not result in a proportionate increase in production. Many researches have thrown light on this fact. Muscio has mentioned the case of one lady worker who worked six hours instead of the conventional twelve-hour day observed by the other workers and still showed a higher level of production than any other worker. In this factory, the working hours were from 6 to 8 in the morning, 8-30 to 12-30, 1.30 to 5.00 and from 8.30 to 12.30. This particular lady refused to work before breakfast and late at night, explaining that by working for such a long time she could not maintain her efficiency. Over a period of one month it was seen that she worked for 237 hours, despite which she showed more output than the others. It is evident from the research conducted in various countries on the methods of work that production is higher in shorter working weeks than in longer working weeks. In the second world war the working hours were increased in England. In the first week of Dunkirk, the work done each week was 36 hours but after Dunkirk, in all factories connected with war production, the time was increased to 69.5 hours. In the beginning, the production increased by about 10 per cent but later on the production in the factories began to fall and the number of accidents and absenteeism began to increase. In a few months it was noticed that the actual working hours fell to 51 hours although the stated working time was 68.5 hours. Before the change, the number of working hours averaged 53 out of a stipulated 56 hours. And in fact, although the working time was increased, the actual production fell by 12 per cent. After six months, the working hours were again reduced, and it was noticed that production again increased. One explanation of this is that fatigue caused a fall in production when the working hours were increased. It is obvious that long hours of fatigue resulted in ex-haustion.

Myers made a study of ladies working in a London factory. Their job was to reverse fuses. When their working hours were reduced from 66 hours to 48.5, the production went up by 15 per cent.

2. Absence of rest periods If a person works for a longer time continuously then he feels fatigued. If he does not, take rest and continues to work, then his fatigue increases even more rapidly because he is working in an exhausted condition. If he is allowed to rest as soon as he begins to feel exhausted, then he returns to his work refreshed and his fatigue does not increase. Hence, it is seen that fatigue is eliminated in all working methods where the workers are allowed to rest for shorter periods during their work. Absence of rest period is an occupational condition that promotes fatigue. Even if some workers steal a few minutes of rest where it is not officially provided for, they do not feel relaxed and rested because during that period their aptitude is not correct. In fact, relaxation of this kind results in greater fatigue. Gilbreth's[1] experiments successfully established that production can be increased by providing periods of rest for the workers instead of keeping them at work continuously.

3. Incorrect temperature Incorrect room temperature is another occupational condition which results in fatigue because in such cases, the room is either too hot or too cold. In both cases, the mental and physical condition of the worker deteriorates and he soon feels exhausted.

4. Absence of proper ventilation If a person does not get clean air while he is working, he soon gets tired. In an office or a factory in which the air is polluted, the incidence of fatigue will be far greater than in any other factory where there is adequate ventilation.

5. Improper illumination Fatigue also increases if the illumination in the working area is not adequate and proper because the eyes begin to feel exhausted and dry if the light is not enough or too bright. Hence, it is desirable that there should be proper arrangements for illumination in factories and offices, proper light coming from the right direction. For example, in reading or writing, it is desirable that the light source should be placed behind and to the left of the worker. If this is not done, then the eyes suffer great strain. In working on a machine, it is desirable that those instruments should be lighted up which are to be seen constantly by the operator. Hence, the light provided should neither be too little nor too much, for in both these conditions, the strain on the eyes leads to fatigue.

6. Design of the machinery Certain machines are so designed that they too exhaust and tire the operator working on them. Hence modern

---

1. Gilbreth, L.M., *Fatigue Study,* New York (1965), p. 297.

psychologists give suggestions even in the construction of machines so that they should be designed to minimise fatigue and increase production. This branch of industrial psychology is called engineering psychology. Today, the aim is to design machinery which involves the least possible amount of movement while maintaining the highest level of production. When the workers become used to operating such machines, their fatigue is reduced and their work improves.

7. Absence of an adequate seat It is a well known fact that a person feels exhausted much earlier if he has to operate a machine while standing. That is why the absence of an adequate seat is one occupational condition which causes fatigue. Another important feature of the seat is that it should not offer too much comfort because in that case, the operator feels sleepy. On the other hand, it should not be so hard that the operator may feel discomfort. Arrangement for a proper seat can help in reducing fatigue.

8. Excessive noise Another occupational condition which increases fatigue is the presence of excessive noise at the place of work. An individual can work for a long time in an atmosphere which is peaceful and free of noise. Some degree of noise can be tolerated, for it has no appreciable effect on work but when noise rises above a certain level, it creates fatigue. Now experiments are made to find out if the noise produced by the machinery is of high enough a pitch to induce fatigue. If this happens, then efforts are made to reduce the pitch of the sound produced and so reduce the level of noise. Kornhauser[1] conducted an experiment on four typists who worked in a noisy environment for four days. The psychologist came to the conclusion that the work went down by 3.2 per cent while the incidence of errors went up by 23 per cent. In an experiment conducted by Weston workers engaged in peaceful surroundings than when working in a noisy environment produced better results.

9. Unhealthy conditions Fatigue is intimately connected with health. If the occupational conditions are such that they do not promote good health then they are conducive to fatigue. Unhealthy conditions include such factors as incorrect room temperature, improper ventilation, excessive noise, etc. In addition to these, certain other occupational conditions like excessive humidity, absence of rest, presence of some disturbing smell, inadequate arrangements for medicine and medical attendance or the total lack of such facilities also have a bad influence upon the health of the workers with the result that they soon become tired.

1. Komhauser, A.W., The Effect of Noise on Office Output Ind. Psycho. 2 (1927), pp. 62-72.

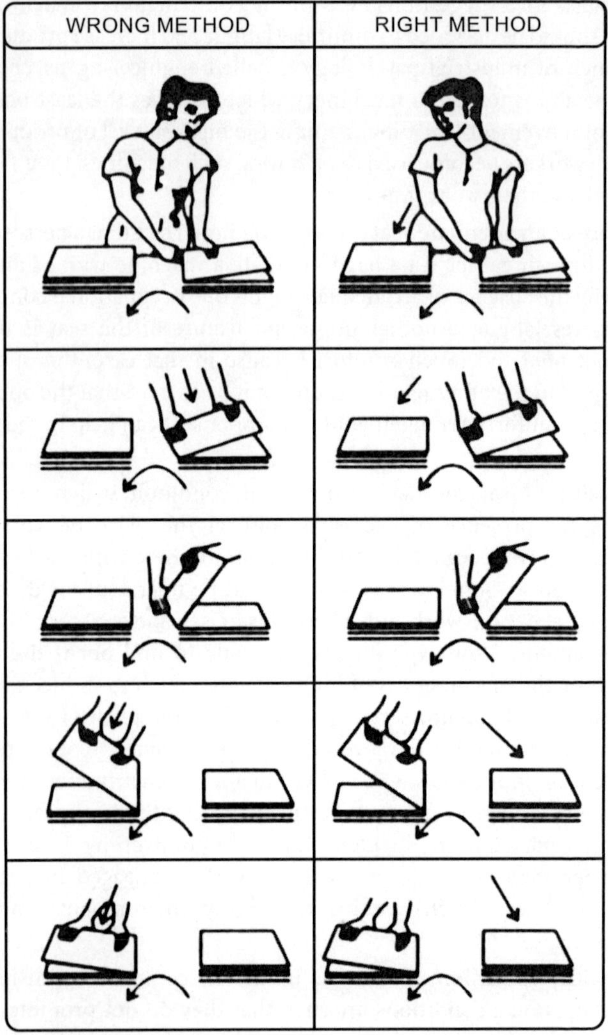

Fig. 23.1 Wrong and Right methods of inspecting the plates from J. Tiffin, *Industrial Psychology,* Prentice Hall, New York, 1952.

10. Absence of proper training In every profession there are certain functions which require some training before they can be properly performed. If such functions are entrusted to untrained employees then these workers become exhausted very rapidly. Hence the employees should be trained by the best methods about the easiest and least tiring way of handling certain instruments. They should also be guided in adjusting the hours of work and the periods of rest according to their individual differences. Hence, the absence of proper training is also an occupational condition which results in fatigue.

11. Lack of sleep In factories in which the workers have to work at night and cannot get adequate rest during the day, lack of sleep forms another factor which results in fatigue. To eliminate this, facilities for sleep should be provided for the workers so that they can sleep during their periods of rest. Absence of sleep is invariably an exhausting factor, irrespective of the condition which leads to it.

12. Low morale Conditions which are conducive to low morale are also conducive to fatigue. Condition which result in low moral are harmful attitudes towards the management, hatred, suspicion and jealousy, dissatisfaction with work and absence of any hope, mental unrest and dissatisfaction, uninteresting work, improper rules governing promotions, absence of a proper wage increase, improper methods of distribution of wages, lack of adjustment; on the part of management, etc. In all such conditions, fatigue also increases rapidly and leads to physical fatigue. Conditions in which high morale can be generated also lead to energetic work.

13. Defects in the social environment The defects in the social environment of an occupation in which many people work also leads, to fatigue. A worker cannot maintain high morale in a condition in which the relations between the employers and employees are not good or in which the atmosphere is one of hate or suspicion. The result is that in such conditions, the workers feels exhausted very quickly. Since people have now understood the significance of social environment, efforts are made to make the social atmosphere in the place of work, cooperative and refreshing or encouraging. This must be done so that the worker can work for a longer time without feeling exhausted.

In fact, all occupational conditions which have an adverse influence upon the worker's mental and physical condition are conducive to fatigue because in such conditions, mental and physical fatigue is very rapid. Hence all such conditions should be corrected if fatigue is to be avoided. But for this all the workers, the managers and the government will have to work co-operatively.

MEANS FOR REDUCING FATIGUE

Roughly speaking, the chief method of reducing fatigue is to eliminate all occupational conditions which increase it. Hence, mention will here be made of those means by which fatigue can be reduced. It should always be kept in mind that work invariably results in some degree of exhaustion and that there can be no ways of eliminating fatigue completely. One can only hope to devise means by which fatigue can be reduced or controlled before it becomes excessive. Briefly, this can be done in the following ways:

1. Reducing the hours of work One way of reducing the fatigue is to reduce the hours of work. It has been seen in many experiments that fatigue is reduced when working hours are reduced, whereas the production does not fall proportionately but in many cases actually increases. In 1928, Sheppard pointed out that for the previous thirty years, workers were made to work ten hours a day for six days a week in all American industries. On the other hand, the workers are now made to work eight hours, besides which, on Saturdays they are required to work only for four hours, while Sunday is a day of rest. But actually production has increased as a result of this decrease in the hours of work. Many other experiments have substantiated Sheppard's conclusions. Hence, one way of reducing fatigue is to reduce the hours of work. But at the same time, care should be taken to avoid reducing working hours to such an extent that the worker's energy is not fully utilized. The most appropriate method is to have sufficient working hours in which the worker can continue to work without feeling totally exhausted. Evidently, the working hours will differ from industry to industry, according to the nature of work.

2. Provision of rest periods Another way of reducing fatigue is to introduce appropriate and properly timed periods of rest. An appropriate period of rest involves calculation of the total rest period allowed in proportion to the work expected from the worker. And a properly timed rest period implies the time at which this rest should be allowed and the frequency with which it should be allowed. After every hour, according to Sheppard, the worker who works for eight hours a day should be allowed to rest for 16.6 per cent of the total working time. It is evident that in providing rest periods, one must consider the total rest period in proportion to the working hours as well as the frequency and duration for which it should be given.

3. Arrangements for maintaining the correct temperature In order to reduce fatigue, it is necessary to maintain the correct room temperature in the place of work. Arrangements should be made to raise the temperature in winters and to lower it in summers. If the temperature is adequate then the workers can work for longer hours without experiencing the fatigue.

For this reason, many modern factories have air-conditioned rooms or other means of reducing the heat during summers while heaters and other contrivances are used to increase the temperature in winter months.

4. Proper ventilation Fatigue can also be reduced by improving the ventilation so that the polluted air is eliminated and fresh air admitted into the factory. Most factories make use of exhaust fans designed to push out such a polluted air out of a room or a hall.

5. Arrangement for proper lighting Fatigue can also be reduced to some extent if proper provision is made for lighting up the area in which the workers work. For this, it is necessary that the light should come from the right direction and it should be of a particular intensity. The advantage in this is that the eyes do not suffer strain and hence the workers do not become tired quickly.

6. Improvements in the design of machines The shape and the size of a machine operated by the worker also influences fatigue. If the machine is so designed that it can run efficiently by making the minimum possible movements the worker will not feel exhausted.

7. Proper seating arrangement A proper seating arrangement for the worker also helps to reduce fatigue. As far as possible, the workers should be allowed to work while sitting. The seat should provide normal comfort to avoid fatigue but it should not be too comfortable, for in that case it will induce sleep. But it should also not be too hard.

8. Control over noise Since excessive noise also induces fatigue, it is desirable to have some control over the amount of noise in or near the working place, if fatigue is to be avoided. This can be done in many ways. It is more difficult to reduce the noise made by the machines installed in the factories but efforts should be made to control the noise produced. If the noise in the factory or a office is less, the workers' fatigue will also be less.

9. Healthy working conditions If the working conditions are conducive to health then fatigue always remains at a low level because the worker's health and his fatigue are directly related to each other. In order to create healthy conditions, it is necessary to pay attention to ventilation, sufficient light, absence of noise, proper room temperature, control over humidity, medical facilities, adequate arrangement for rest and food, etc. All these things help to refresh the worker.

10. Arrangements for industrial or professional training The worker feels less fatigued in manipulating a machine for which he has been trained because he does not make any unnecessary movements. Hence professional training can also help to reduce the fatigue.

11. Proper arrangements for sleep In many kinds of work, it is necessary to provide some arrangement for sleep. Even if the worker is given a chance to sleep or comfort for only half an hour out of the total working time, much of his fatigue disappears. Such an arrangement is particularly useful for the workers working in shifts.

12. High morale High morale can also help to reduce the fatigue among the workers. Maintenance of high morale requires an attitude favourable to the management, self-generated discipline, group administration, enthusiasm, mental satisfaction and peace, respect for and confidence in the management, etc. If these factors are present, the incidence of fatigue is much lower.

13. Proper social atmosphere Even the social atmosphere plays an important role in reducing the worker's fatigue. The worker's enthusiasm can be easily maintained and fatigue kept at a low level if good relations with the management can be created and if the general atmosphere is one of the co-operation.

14. Special means of reducing fatigue In addition to the factors explained above, many other means are now being adopted to reduce the worker's fatigue. For example, in many factories, arrangements have been made to play music to the workers while they are engaged in their work because the workers feel less tired if they sing as they work. Many new experiments are being conducted on this aspect these days. Besides, change in the nature of work also helps to keep the workers' interest alive. Efforts are made to make the work interesting in many different ways. As industrial psychology progresses, many new ways of reducing fatigue will definitely be discovered.

CRITERIA OF FATIGUE

The criteria of fatigue implies the symptoms by which its presence can be diagnosed and recognised. In order to understand this it is essential to keep in mind the various aspects of fatigue. Since fatigue is a psychophysical condition its symptoms are both mental and physical. It can be recognised by the following factors:

1. Feeling of exhaustion The chief symptom of fatigue is the feeling of fatigue even if the individual is not feeling physically exhausted. In a state of exhaustion, the desire to work is noticeably reduced and the desire to rest is clearly heightened. Generally, it also leads to a fall in the individual's production, though this is not universally true. In the state of exhaustion, the individual's feelings about work changes and he evinces no desire to do any kind of work.

2. Muscular condition In a state of fatigue, the muscles lose their power to contract and expand. Hence, physiologically, fatigue is a muscular condition and the failure of the muscles to contract and expand is one criterion of fatigue.

3. Chemical changes As a person works, the proportion of acetic acid and other poisonous chemicals in his body increases. In a healthy body, the oxygen is properly distributed through the blood stream with the result that poisonous matter is eliminated from the body. When the muscles become tired, this process of elimination does not work efficiently. This leads to a fall in the quantity of glycogen in the body along with an increase in the quantity of poisonous matter. In this manner, many chemical changes occur in the body during fatigue, and it can be recognised by these chemical changes.

4. Nervous slackness. One criterion of mental exhaustion is nervous slackness. Sometimes it is caused by muscular fatigue but it also has many other causes. In a state of nervous exhaustion, the nerves lose their power to react with the result that the individual cannot work efficiently. Many experiments have established that, in a condition of exhaustion, the nerves and muscles do not have the power to react properly or to achieve the normal state of excitation. As a result of this slackness, the sense organs do not react properly. The sense of smell is particularly influenced while the powers of seeing, hearing and touching are also adversely influenced.

5. Changes in the blood chemistry Some symptoms of exhaustion can also be found in the tired person's blood. If some of this blood is introduced into the blood of some healthy person, one will find the symptoms there too. The same is true for muscles too. On one hand, the blood stream helps to eliminate poisonous matter from the body, but on the other hand, it also helps to distribute the fatigue all over the body. For this reason, the whole body shows symptoms of exhaustion even when only one part of the body is bearing all the strain. If any one part of the body is put to excessive use then that part shows signs of fatigue early but soon these symptoms can be seen all over the body because exhaustion is communicated by the blood.

6. Changes in the mental condition One criterion of fatigue is the change in the mental conditions because in an exhausted condition, the individual experiences deterioration of his mental powers and a loss of interest. He cannot concentrate upon anything for a long time and becomes bored with work. Because of this influence upon the mind, fatigue is considered a psychophysical phenomenon.

7. Increase in the number of accidents An analysis of accidents in industry has revealed that majority of accidents occur either in the morning or late in the evening. This fact has been generally substantiated by studies in Germany, England and America. A study of fatigue has also shown that it is greatest early in the morning and late in the evening. Hence one can estimate the extent of industrial fatigue from the number of accidents. For this reason now provisions are made for introducing rest periods in the early hours and in the late evenings. This pattern of accidents can be seen in almost any industry. While the morning accidents are uniformly present, the late evening accidents follow various patterns in different industries. Accidents in the late evening take place more rapidly but the total number is not much more than that of the accidents in the morning. One can see a difference in the number of accidents that take place during the morning and the night shifts. Hence, the relationship between fatigue and accidents is obvious.

It should be kept in mind that despite the clear relationship between fatigue and accidents, fatigue is not the sole cause of accidents and for this reason an increase in accidents is not a criterion of increasing the fatigue. Many other factors apart from fatigue often prove far more important in causing the accidents. For example, women are more accident prone than men because women tend to tire easily and more rapidly. It cannot be denied that in a state of exhaustion, the individual becomes restless, he cannot control his movements properly, he may even go to sleep, he lacks concentration. Despite this, fatigue cannot be accepted as the sole cause of accidents.

8. Fall in production Sometimes fatigue is defined in terms of the fall in production. As has already been mentioned in connection with accidents, the early morning shift and the late evening shift result in accidents and also in a fall in production. The cause of this fall in production is believed to be fatigue. During the first hour in the morning, the production rate rises steeply because this is the warming up period. This warming up can be due to numerous mental and physical causes. And the period consumed in warming is up to the individual differences between one worker and another. Two factors which are responsible for the rate of worker's output are health and the nature of the conditions under which he has to work. It is normally seen that production reaches its highest peak in the third hour, after which production again begins to fall due to fatigue. It is for this reason that a rest period is provided after the third quarter of the day. The phenomenon of warming up is not seen at all for the work starts at a high speed. But this rate of work declines steadily till it reaches the lowest level of production in the last hour of the day. Apart from fatigue, many other factors may also account for this. Sometimes the workers begin to put away their tools quite just before the closing hour, which is one reason why the production during the last hour is much lower. It is evident from the above explanation that the fall in production after the first two hours and again in the afternoon can be accepted as a criterion of fatigue.

In addition to the above factors, all other symptoms of physical and mental fatigue can be accepted as the criteria of fatigue. Fatigue can be recognised by such mental and physical conditions as changes in the respiration, blood circulation, blood pressure, disinterest, lack of concentration, slackness, etc. Nowadays many scientific instruments are employed to measure the fatigue.

DIFFERENT ASPECTS OF FATIGUE

In order to fully understand the nature of fatigue, it is important to consider its objective, physical and mental aspects:

1. Objective aspect In its objective aspect, fatigue can be defined as a fall in the efficiency to perform some function. This occurs when some work has been done for a long time. Fatigue does not occur if the worker interups his working periods with short rest periods. In the laboratory, the decline in the ability to work is measured by the ergograph while the decline in the mental ability to work is measured by the word elimination method. Fall in efficiency is evinced not only through the fall in production but also through the deterioration in the quality of the work because the worker begins to make more mistakes when he is exhausted.

2. Physical aspect The physiological aspect of fatigue is concerned with its influence upon the body. Many experiments in this connection have revealed that in a state of fatigue, the poisonous substances in the body increase in quantity while the energizing elements fall in number. From the physiological point of view, in a condition of fatigue, one can observe an increase in the rate of respiration, blood circulation, blood pressure, etc. Many other chemical changes also occur within the body.

3. Mental aspect The mental symptoms of fatigue are exhaustion, lack of desire to work, emotional instability, lack of concentration, slackness, etc. All of these are expressed through lack of interest in work and a desire to rest.

A complete definition of fatigue cannot be produced by placing stress on any one of the above aspects of fatigue. The objective aspect is not the best method of recognising fatigue because fairly often people do not show any deterioration in the performance of work despite some mental fatigue. Despite fatigue the production does not fall nor do the number of mistakes go up. Poffenberger conducted an experiment on twelve college students. In this experiment, the students were required to make sentences, and the scientist showed that over a period of five and a half hours, the ability to make sentences did not deteriorate despite increasing the fatigue. On the other hand, Robers' subjects showed a decline in the quality of work despite an absence of any feeling of fatigue. Hence, the objective definition of fatigue is incomplete.

Separate explanations of the mental and physical symptoms of fatigue may lead one to the conclusion that they are completely disconnected, but this is not true. Hence it is incorrect to believe that fatigue can be exclusively mental or exclusively physical. Fatigue of all kinds is manifested by physical as well as mental symptoms, a fact which has been established by experiments. Watson has proved that the contraction of the vocal muscles leads to mental fatigue. In the same way, any damage to the nerve cells in the higher parts of the brain leads to mental fatigue. It is a matter of common experience that one cannot efficiently perform physical work in a condition of mental fatigue, or mental work in a state of physical exhaustion.

Briefly stated, fatigue can be defined as a psychophysical condition in which the individual's mental and physical ability to work deteriorates. It is apparent from this definition that the mental and physical symptoms or aspects of fatigue are verbally differentiated only for convenience because in actual fact they are not independent of each other. And while on the subject of ways and means of removing fatigue, it is necessary to remember that only unnecessary fatigue can be eliminated by these means. There is some necessary fatigue which accompanies every kind of work, and this cannot be eliminated completely. To put it differently, it is not possible to create conditions in which fatigue can be eliminated completely. It is, on the other hand, possible to reduce it.

MEASUREMENT OF FATIGUE

As far as the measurement of fatigue is concerned, it is essential to remember that the measurement can be definite only if all the other factors and their influence are shown. For example, fall in the production curve is an incontrovertible proof of exhaustion because it can also be caused by changes in aptitude, excitement or interest, etc. At present, we have no means of knowing whether fatigue is the cause of the fall in production or whether it is caused by any of these other factors. For this reason, the psychologist Muscio believed that the measurement of fatigue is unscientific. Dhers said. "Fatigue can neither be scientifically isolated nor measured." Despite this, fatigue has been measured with varying degrees of accuracy, and most of the methods employed have proved of some practical value. Mosso, Greff, Kraeplin and other psychologists have discovered some valuable scientific facts by the measurement of fatigue. Hence, it would be in keeping with the context to give a brief account of the methods of measuring fatigue. Generally, the methods of measuring fatigue are divided into three parts according to the three aspects of fatigue. They are objective methods, physical methods and mental methods:

1. Objective methods These include mainly those methods which measure variation in the quality and quantity of production. Such tests as word elimination method may be included in this category. But it should be kept in mind that these tests do not determine whether fatigue is present or not because the fall in production may even be caused by such other factors as opposite motivation, lack of enthusiasm or excitement. On the other hand, the normal level of production may be maintained through habit, despite the presence of fatigue.

2. Physical methods These include the methods which measure the physical symptoms of fatigue. Methods involving the chemical analysis of urine and saliva, the measurement of pulse, heart-beat and blood pressure are included in this category. The ergograph, hand dynamometer and Martin's spring balance can also be included in this group. But the symptoms measured by them may have some source other than fatigue.

3. Mental methods This group includes the methods which measure the mental symptoms of exhaustion. Such symptoms are the deterioration in attention, memory, imagination, mental decision, emotional analysis and power of reasoning. As in all the other methods, these methods too cannot determine the true source of the change, because it may be caused by something other than fatigue.

Fig. 23.2. Instrument for Measuring Value of the Work in Terms of Fatigue

It is evident from the above brief account of the methods of measuring fatigue that the results arrived at may not be valid. Even eminent scientists have their doubts about the validity of such experiments. But it cannot be denied that these methods have helped in practical situations and it is possible that the future may bring more accurate methods of determining the fatigue.

ERGOGRAPHIC STUDIES

The ergograph is used in the measurement of fatigue. The instrument was invented by Angelo Mosso, a famous Italian psychologist. With the help of ergograph, he studied the relation between fatigue and the functioning of any particular part of the body. He studied the working of a particular part of the body. He studied the working of a particular muscle and induced fatigue in it. In this manner he eliminated the influence of such complex psychological phenomena as boredom and monotony, and studied fatigue in its more simple manifestation.

Ergograph is a simple instrument in which the hand is placed on a frame in such a way that it is not exerted or pressed in any way, but it cannot move. All the fingers except the middle one are tied in such a way that they cannot be used. Then a string with some weight on the other end of it is tied to the middle finger. This weight is lifted by the middle finger. In the ergograph, this string passes over a pulley and has a weight attached to it. In the more modern adaptation of this instrument, arrangement is made to expand and contract the finger without lifting the weight. The finger is made to perform various functions according to the pattern determined by Metronome, and then these movements are studied. The most important thing to be noted is the frequency of contraction and expansion of the muscles. For this reason, only this contraction and expansion are controlled. The graph of the fatigue is prepared by a moving string attached to a needle which moves on a revolving drum and draws straight lines. The frequency of contraction and expansion in the muscle is shown by the irregularity in these lines drawn by the needle.

Conclusions Reached through Ergographic Studies

Ergographic studies provided many results which have proved useful for application in industries. Mosso reached the following nine conclusions about fatigue on the basis of ergographic studies:

1. If the frequency of muscular contraction, in lifting any weight, is once every two seconds, then the rate of contraction gradually falls, till at the end there is no contraction. With a weight of six kilos, this state is reached in approximately one minute. If the weight is then reduced, the contraction of the muscle can be started again but even then fatigue will be induced soon.

2. If the muscular contraction is induced after a long time period, such as ten seconds, for the same weight, then there is no external manifestation of exhaustion. In such conditions even the weight of six kilograms can be lifted for an infinite number of times.

3. If work done is measured in terms of quantity of weight, then the work done for smaller weights is definitely much more than for heavier weights. Hence, a weight of three kilograms can be lifted more than twice the number of times than that a weight of six kilograms can be raised.

4. If the given weight is raised rapidly a number of times, then the fatigue induced is greater than in lifting it once. But if the weight is lifted slowly, then fatigue is less.

5. Time taken to regain energy increases with an increase in the intervals between periods of work. For example, if the time required to regain energy for sixty contractions is two hours, then the time required to regain energy for 30 contractions may even be 30 minutes. When a situation is reached that the finger cannot be moved at all, then the fatigue

which has been induced by the attempts to lift weight cannot be easily eliminated. It requires a very great time to regain energy, and this cannot be done by providing the normal intervals of rest. Putting it another way, as fatigue accumulates the effect of fatigue in contracting the muscle also increases rapidly and cannot be overcome easily.

6. If other muscles of the body also function at the same time as the finger, then the finger loses its ability to lift weight to some extent. If the individual has performed some strenuous exercise before the ergograph experiments, than the state of total inactivity is arrived at much sooner than under normal circumstances. In this way, the ergograph exercises indicate that fatigue is communicated to those parts of body, through the blood stream, which are not being used at that time.

7. Such factors as lack of sleep, mental causes, hunger and the shortage of blood in the muscle reduce the efficiency of the muscle. In fact, any factor which is an obstacle to nourishment or tends to reduce it, will also tend to increase the fatigue.

8. The efficiency of the muscle can be increased by massaging it, by increasing the quantity of sugar in the blood, by giving nourishment to the body and by improving the general health.

9. Different people get exhausted at different rates but the principles governing fatigue which have been mentioned above hold true despite all individual differences.

Industrial Applications of Ergographic Studies

Psychologists applied the findings of the ergographic studies to industrial situations, although some objected that this should not be done because the conditions prevailing in an industry and in the psychological laboratory differ to a very great extent. Besides, in ergographic studies, only the finger is made to work, while in a factory the worker has to exert his entire body. For this reason, the laws governing fatigue in the two cases may not be the same. But these objections against the conclusions obtained through ergographic studies were not found to be valid because the conditions in the psychological laboratory and in an industry have some common features, although there are many differences. The application of these conclusions to industry has provided many beneficial results. Despite this, it should be kept in mind that ergographic studies that have been conducted in the laboratory and the results obtained should not be applied exactly as they are without testing their validity in the industrial situation, because in a factory the worker has to exert his whole body, not only his finger. Besides, the production of some workers may suffer or change not only because of the work done or the number of hours of work but also as result of his attitudes and motives. If the worker wants an interval in his work, it is not only because he wants rest but also because he may wish to have a chat with his colleagues over a cup of coffee. Sometimes workers ask for an interval soon after arriving in the factory, or soon after the lunch interval. It also happens that some workers utilise the lunch interval to do some personal work and then use the rest interval to take lunch, in which case the purpose of the rest interval is defeated.

One difficulty in applying the results of ergographic studies to industry is created by the attitudes of the industrial trade unions. It has been seen that once the working hours are reduced and the rest periods increased, the workers do not easily agree to an increase in working hours and a reduction in the rest periods. Many industrial organisations are not prepared to increase the rest intervals for the simple reason that despite all such increase, the workers always demand for a further reduction in the working time and an extension of the rest hours. If some company reduces the working hours from nine to eight, the workers immediately demand that they should be reduced to seven. Even if the company accedes this, the workers do not stop but go further and demand that the working hours should be further reduced to six. For this reason, an industrialist prefers to control the workers from the very beginning. In addition to this, it is a generally known fact that, according to their individual qualities, each worker becomes tired after different time and he requires a different time to recoup his energies. Hence, it is apparently unscientific to give the same time of rest to each worker and also to provide it at the same fixed time. On the other hand, if differing periods of rest are given to the workers according to their individual differences, then the workers immediately voice protest against the apparent injustice and inequality in treatment. No trade union is prepared to accept the fact that the worker doing the same work and obtaining the same wages should be allowed to have varying amounts of working time and rest time. All these factors greatly hinder the application of ergographic conclusions in industries, but this does not imply that it is impossible to be benefited by their application. At many places, the workers and the management have co-operated with each other and thus introduced many reforms in the conditions of work and rest.

Now, we must turn our attention to the extent to which ergographic conclusions can be applied to the industries.

One general fact which can be derived from the first five conclusions of the ergographic studies is that more work can be done if the limited energy of the muscle is consumed slowly, rather than rapidly. In fact, the principle governing the expenditure of muscular energy can be applied to the use of energy in any form. If, for example, a car is run at high speed, it consumes more fuel than when it is runs at low speed. Hence, if one wants to travel the greatest possible distance by using the least possible fuel, then one must run the car at a low and steady speed. Another example of this kind is the long distance runner, because such an athlete must learn to control his energy. If he runs fast in the earlier stages of the race, then he consumes most of his energy very early and fails to complete the race. The long distance runner must begin the race at low speed, increasing it gradually, till he attains the highest speed near the end of the race. He can run fastest near the end of the race because he then loses nothing by becoming exhausted at this stage. But, if he becomes fatigued in the beginning, he cannot hope to complete the race, let alone to win it. Here one must keep it in mind that the general tendency is against such a careful utilization of one's energy. Generally, a person likes to work quickly when he is fresh, without realizing that although he is working faster, he is, in, fact wasting a good amount of energy. If a person has to complete some big project, he must learn how to husband his strength and to expend his energy gradually because if he finishes his stock of energy in finishing half the work, he will never be able to complete it. Another difficulty in keeping one's work at a steady pace is the human tendency to retire for rest only when one has become tired and restless, although actually the period of rest should come much earlier. As has been pointed out earlier, a person can do much more work by interspersing the working hours with short periods of rest in which he can recoup his energies. This happens because once a man is completely exhausted, he needs much more time to regain his energy. For this reason it is believed that the worker should be allowed a shorter period of rest after some period of work, if one is to put the worker's energy to the best use.

Muscio has proved the validity of the above ergographic principle by giving another example of its application to industrial conditions. In this experiment, one individual was made to lift six kilograms of weight three times on the ergograph under different conditions. In the first condition, he was made to contract his muscles every two seconds till he could not lift the weight at all. Then, he was allowed to rest till he could regain all his energy. In working by this method, the individual contracted his muscle thirty times and then rested for two hours. In this way he could sit for the experiment four times in an eight-hour period and in each session he contracted his muscles thirty times, a total of 120 times in the entire period.

In the second condition, the individual was allowed to rest for half an hour after every fifteen muscular convulsions. The result was that he could put in 16 sessions of muscular exercise, in each of which he lifted the weight 15 times. Consequently, he convulsed his muscles a total of 240 times. It is, therefore, evident that the individual doubled the quantity of his work because he was given rest at more frequent intervals.

In the third condition, the individual was allowed a rest of ten seconds before each muscular exertion. This speed of working was so slow that he did not experience fatigue at all. He took two seconds to convulse his muscle and ten seconds to rest it, with the result that he performed one unit of work in twelve seconds. Consequently, he could contract his muscles three hundred times in one hour and twenty-four hundred times in eight hours. The quantity of work thus achieved was twenty times the work done in the first condition.

By comparing the first and second conditions of work, we come to the conclusion that in the first condition, the individual took half an hour to regain the energy he had spent in contracting his muscles fifteen times, an average of two minutes to each muscular contraction. But, it took 90 minutes to regain the energy spent in the other fifteen contractions, an average of six minutes for each contraction. Under the third condition, it only took ten seconds to regain the energy spent in each contraction. It is evident from this that more time is taken to regain energy after work if the periods of rest are far apart. And, the most expensive movement is that in which the individual tries to lift some weight when he is almost completely exhausted.

An experiment of this kind cannot be applied to industrial conditions in precisely the same way because in this experiment only some particular muscles were called into play and were used till they were completely exhausted. In an industrial situation, neither of these two conditions holds good because, neither is it necessary to use any one particular muscle nor it is used to such an extent that it becomes completely exhausted. Despite this, the experiment provides a guideline that the intervals of rest should be distributed in such a manner among the working hours that the energy spent can be regained as rapidly as possible. And if the intervals of rest can be increased and they do lead to even a 15 per cent increase in production, the change should be considered significant. As is evident from the other ergographic principles explained earlier, if the intervals of rest are distributed between small units of work, it is possible to work for longer periods without becoming exhausted. This fact has also been substantiated by the experiments of Gilbreth. He made a study of time and motion, and concluded that fatigue can be reduced by reducing the load, increasing the intervals of rest and balancing the movement in the work. But it depends upon the nature of the work as to which load should be reduced, where the interval of rest should be increased and which movement should be controlled. Concerning the use of a spade, the experiments of F.W. Taylor revealed that more work can be done by using of the spade will depend upon the nature of the work and the individual using it. A larger spade is needed to lift a light weight and a smaller spade to lift a heavier weight. Yet, it is possible to decide the size of the implements to be used by workers in some particular industry. Large spades induce fatigue, while smaller spades do not. But less weight can be transported by a smaller spade, and if the weight transported is less than the weight of the spade itself, then the amount of work done declines sharply. And since the quantity of work done is measured by the total weight carried by the spade, not by the weight of the spade itself, it is perfectly possible to have a spade so small that the work done by it is negligible. Still, between the extreme limits of a very big and a very small spade, it is possible to decide upon some practicable size of spade which can be used efficiently in some particular industry. By making experiments of this kind, it is possible to decide the best possible size and weight of the tools used by different artisans.

Certain functions can be performed by two people working together, and in all such work it is seen that the result of the combined effort is always better than the sum total of the work done by each individual separately. Whenever it is impossible to reduce the load to be lifted or to allow them to work together, efforts should be made to reduce their fatigue by giving them more periods of rest. In certain industries, instead of lifting heavy loads, the workers have to make some movements rapidly. In such industries, the speed of movement should be regulated or the work should be divided into small units so that intervals of rest can be given between each unit of work. Although it is difficult to determine the speed of work in any kind of performance, it can generally be said that the speed of work should be slow in the first half hour of work, normal in the later hour and the fastest near the end. Maintaining slow speed in the beginning is necessary because it gives the worker time to warm up, after which the speed of work can be increased to the normal level. This normal level should be maintained. The purpose behind increasing the working speed near to the end is to finish the work which has been leftover and thus avoid the adverse effects of fatigue on production. Certain people begin the day by working as hard as they can with the result that their speed falls as time passes. This method is supported by the argument that the worker tries to achieve as much as he can while he feels fresh. But, in fact, the worker tires very rapidly if he begins working fast too early in the day, and then he continues to work in a state of exhaustion with the result that the working speed declines steadily. This always results in lower production.

Fatigue covers the entire body Among all the conclusions drawn from the ergographic studies, the sixth is that fatigue is general although only one part of the body is employed. Fatigue is communicated from one part of the body to all the body by the blood stream. It is evident from this that fatigue can be eliminated by giving rest to the whole body, not only to one part. Hence, it is not enough only to stop work, if one wants to rest. The worker must get complete rest during his interval for rest. Arrangements should be made to provide comfortable beds and easy chairs for the workers' use during the lunch and rest intervals. It is essential to have proper arrangements for drinking water. Briefly, fatigue cannot be eliminated merely by stopping work. Arrangement for complete rest should be made.

Importance of Health and Nourishment

The seventh and eighth conclusions drawn from the ergographic studies of work fatigue indicate the value and importance of bodily health and proper nourishment for reducing fatigue and increasing output. Hence it is desirable that the conditions even outside the factory should be such that they promote healthy living and proper nourishment. In this connection, H. Gartner, a German scientist, has suggested that attention should also be paid to the distance a worker has to travel from his house to the place of work. If this distance is so great that the worker becomes exhausted in travelling, then the quality and quantity of his production will be below normal because he will be worldng for the entire day in a condition of exhaustion. It has been suggested that the residential districts of the workers should be within the vicinity of the working place. Nowadays there is a great demand that factories should be located outside the city to avoid pollution of air. It therefore becomes even more necessary to pay attention to the aspect of distance from home to factory. Visualizing the problem one can see that the worker should be provided a house near the factory, and in addition arrangements should be made for the schooling of his children and for purchases which he requires from day to day. The importance of this factor has been realized by many industrialists, and consequently they recruit only such people who live within a reasonable distance from the factory. In Gartner's opinion, the worker should live at such a distance from his place of work that he can reach it within thirty minutes.

Arrangements for the worker's rest should be made within the factory so that his health can be maintained. But the time that should be given for rest is a controversial subject. Two factors that should be kept in mind are that the period of rest should not be so long as to induce lethargy and not so short as not to provide adequate rest. Gartner has suggested that the worker should sleep for thirty minutes in order to get adequate rest. If the workers are allowed to sleep for more than thirty minutes, it is possible that their sleep at night may be disturbed.

Food plays an important part in removing fatigue, and hence arrangements should be made to provide cheap, wholesome and appetizing food for the workers. Even if the organisation has to spend some money to provide this facility, it stands to lose nothing and to gain much by maintaining the health of its employees. It has been seen that the food brought by the workers themselves for their lunch is more often than not neither nutritious nor adequate. The place provided for lunch, should not be too far from the place of work, because if the worker becomes tired in travelling to the place reserved for eating, the organisation will lose because the production will fall. If, on the other hand, canteens are attached to the factory premises, the workers enjoy taking their food, with the result that their health does not suffer. Their fatigue is reduced both by the nourishment and by the pleasure they derive in taking good food. The organisation benefits by the consequent increase in production. Food can be provided both in the morning and in the afternoon.

The health and nourishment of the worker depends not only upon the rest and the food which are provided to him. Certain other factors also play an important role in it. For example, economic worries have a detrimental effect on health. For this reason, it is desirable that the employer should provide facilities for small short term loan so that the workers can tide over a difficult period. Medical facilities provided at low cost also help the worker to great extent.

Healthy recreation is another factor that helps to build up the mental and physical health of the worker. For this reason, most modern industrial organisations provide healthy recreation by opening clubs, cinema halls and other forms of entertainment near to the industrial complex.

Importance of Individual Differences

The last conclusion drawn from the ergographic studies places stress upon the importance of individual differences insofar as they have some influence upon fatigue. It is generally known that some people become tired quicker than other people and also take a longer time in recovering their strength and energy. Other people tire less easily and also regain their energy more quickly. This fact of individual differences has special importance with respect to work in which more than one person work together. If, for example, all the people are deputed to perform a single task, they tire easily, and the task will be completed only with great difficulty. For this reason, the fact of individual differences should be kept in mind while selecting people to perform different functions in a factory. Difficult work should be assigned to people who do not tire easily. Certain kinds of work require a lot of hard work in the beginning, but at the end they can be performed without too much effort. For such work, it is better that it should be started by a person who is capable of greater effort. It can then be completed by another person who is weaker.

The importance of ergographic studies has been made clear by the application of their conclusions to actual industrial conditions, an account of which has given above. Many industrial organisations have benefited by introducing lunch and rest intervals. Wherever some difficulty has been experienced as a result of introducing these intervals, it has been caused by those workers who return late to their work, or collect in great numbers in the coffee shops, factories and offices or even in the elevators. As a result, organisations do experience some difficulty, but nobody complains that the introduction of such intervals is harmful or that it is not beneficial. Some of the important researches and studies conducted on these subjects are outlined here.

1. Haggard's research.[1] According to W.S. Haggard, a 10 per cent increase in production resulted when the workers were provided two additional lunches. The workers also reported that they are helped in recovering their energy and that despite the increased work they experience less fatigue. The provision of comfortable chairs and beds in some other industrial organisations also resulted in an increase in production. The truth of the matter is that if the management does not make provision for rest, the workers themselves take time out for rest, unauthorisedly or without permission. In some offices the clerks are seen sleeping on their chairs while in others, the workers leave their desks by inventing some or

1. Haggard, W.S., *Work and Fatigue, Mech. Engin.* (1936), 58, pp. 298-301.

the other excuse. Sometimes the worker seeks relief only in reducing the tempo of his work. If the worker can think of no other excuse, he gees and stands in the queue outside the lavatory. It is therefore better that the management should itself provide a rest interval for the workers. Not every worker can think up excuse to get rest and neither can one actually feel relaxed by stealing rest in this way.

2. Mezerik's research.[1] On the basis of his studies Mezerik has written that in one particular rase, a 32 per cent increase in production was seen merely by providing sitting stools for women workers. Women are employed in many modern industries to perform the lighter functions. The management's attention has been drawn towards providing rest to the female workers because it is realized that the feminine body is naturally softer. Wherever female workers are employed in modern industries, provisions are made for rest intervals, beautiful and comfortably furnished rooms for resting, reasonably comfortable working seats, etc. If this is not done, the workers experience a feeling of dissatisfaction which, in the long run, harms the employer. The expense incurred in providing such basic amenities is recovered manifold through the increased production.

3. Bonmann's studies The researches of E. Bonmann, a German scientist, have thrown light on the ergographic conclusion that the effect of fatigue continues to increase if the individual continues to work. For this reason, he has suggested that the lunch intervals should be provided after one-third of the total working time has been consumed. By doing this, the persistent increase in fatigue can be avoided.

It is evident from the above discussion that the application of ergographic principles to industries has benefited most of the people, but the extent to which intervals of rest should be introduced can be determined only through further experimentation. The kind of arrangements for maintaining the health of the worker, the extent of rest, the kind of food, will depend upon the nature of the work done in a particular industry, upon the age and sex of the worker, and upon numerous other factors. The maximum advantage can be derived only after sufficient thought has been devoted to these factors.

REST PAUSES

1. Studies by Viteles.[2] M.S. Viteles proved by his studies that increase of 10 to 20 per cent in production can be seen by the introduction of rest pauses. For example, in one industry employing female workers, a 20 per

1. Mezerik, A.G., *The Factory Manager Learns the Fact of Life,* Harper's (1943), pp. 288-97.
2. Viteles, M.S., *Industrial Psychology,* pp. 470-82.

cent increase of production was noticed when they were provided a ten minute rest pause in their morning work. These girls pasted labels. This example has been cited by H.M. Vernon and T. Bedford[1] in their essay on rest pauses.

2. Studies by Farmer and Bevington.[2] Explaining the conclusions arrived at as a result of one experiment, Farmer and Bevington have pointed out in their essay that an appreciable rise in the production curve was seen when seven-minute rest pauses were introduced in the morning and afternoon working schedules.

In addition to the above experiments and studies, the benefits of rest pauses have been noted in many other industries. It has been seen that it is advantageous to give a five-minute rest after every hour of work.

Experiments can be conducted to determine the length of rest pauses which will suit different industries and different kinds of work. This is so because the rest pause will depend upon the nature of work, the length of the working time, the length of the working week, the age and sex of the workers, the level of nutrition and the individual differences between the workers. For example, women workers require a longer rest interval than male workers. Similarly, workers who do not enjoy good health require more frequent and longer rest periods. While some people require many and long rest intervals, other people can continue to work for a long time without experiencing fatigue and can also recover their energy in a comparatively short time. Motivation also influences the rest pause because in cases of strong motivation, individuals continue to work for a long time without fatigue. Some laboratory experiments have brought useful facts to light in this connection. G. Shepherd[3] conducted an experiment on educated university students to determine the influence of light and heavy work on the muscles. These students were studying at the Purdur University and were given wages for the work performed by them. They were required to spend eight hours a week under working conditions. They were also given a bonus so that the working conditions should resemble actual industrial conditions. The nature of the work was such that they were required to go towards a machine, to stretch away from it and lift and drop some heavy weight. In order to avoid, the accumulation of fatigue, they were given a 19-hour rest on the previous

1. Vernon, H.M. and T. Bedford, *The Influence of Rest Pauses on Light Industrial Work* (1924).
2. Farmer, E. and S.M. Bevington, *An Experiment in the Introduction of Rest Pauses,* Nat. Institute, *Indus. Psychol.* (1922) 1, pp. 89-92.
3. Shepherd, G., "Effects of Rest Pauses on Production," *Person. Jour.* (1928), 7, pp. 186-202.

day, besides which they were provided with comfortable cots to be used during the rest intervals. The work varied between 25 and 60 minutes while the rest pauses varied between 7 and 16 minutes. In other tests, the rest pause of this changed while the work was kept constant. As a result of this experiment, it was discovered that the best results were achieved when the rest interval extended over 16.7 to 20 per cent of the total working time. It was also discovered that it is better to provide a short rest pause after less work than to provide a long period of rest after continuous work over long periods. The maximum distribution of the rest pause was tested with two students. While experimenting with a rest pause of 18.2 per cent, it was observed that the greatest benefit of the rest pause was derived when rest pauses of one-minute were given in the working schedule. Under these conditions, it was also seen that there was no deterioration even near the end of the work schedule, although falling off of production near the end of a working day is normal. Here it should be kept in mind that such frequent rest pauses can be introduced only in that work in which there is no system or organisation. In this experiment, another fact observed was that whenever the distribution of rest period was left to the students themselves, they could not use it properly but when they were trained in the underlying principles of the distribution of rest pauses, they could place them more beneficial in the work schedule.

As has been pointed out earlier, the existence of the rest pause does not depend upon the sweet will of the employer. Even if no such rest interval is officially provided by the management, most of the workers do manage to take sometime off for rest. Many workers work at such slow speed that they take some rest at regular intervals. For example, most workers engaged in house building in India sit down for a smoke after few minutes, a kind of rest interval in addition to the normal time taken off for lunch. This fact is true of almost all kinds of workers. Some labourers and office clerks make a habit of leaving their place of work or desk every few minutes. Some leave the work in order to drink water or to urinate, and very often they do not even trouble to switch off the machines on which they are working. Hence the only way in which the management can prevent such unofficial intervals is to introduce an official rest pause because when the worker resorts to such actions, it does not imply that he does not want to work. In fact, he is only trying to avoid fatigue and get some rest. People who have to work for a long time normally work at a slower rate than those who have to work only for a short time. Some important experiments have been conducted in this connection. In one of the studies H.M. Vernon[1], made a study of the working methods of workers who worked for six hours. When the working day was eight hours, an average rest period of 12.50 minutes per hour was observed by the workers. Hence in the six-hour working day, the rest period was 17 per cent of the total working time, but when the working day had eight hours, the rest pause was 20.8 per cent of the working time. But it should also be remembered that this rest pause was not taken after every hour. In fact, the average is obtained by dividing the total working time with the total rest period taken by the workers. The managers of industry should try to find out the length of a rest pause required after a particular stretch of work so that maximum production can be achieved while the motivation of the workers is maintained at a high level. When such rest pauses are provided by the management, the number of unofficial rest intervals will decrease.

Numerous studies were conducted to solve these industrial problems. These studies have revealed a vast fund of interesting and useful facts. For example, ergographic studies have indicated that the rest pause should be given at a time before the production begins to fall due to fatigue. If the rest interval is given before production falls then the worker can regain his energy and continue to work at the same rate. Sometimes rest pauses can also lead to obstruction in the work. For this reason, the workers should be consulted while determining the rest interval. Besides, it should not be rigorously imposed. For example, it is foolish to force a person to rest when he is working at high speed with complete concentration because in that case production will fall while the individual Will not get any real rest also. Hence the working pattern of the workers should be carefully studied before the rest interval is introduced. The work and rest should be divided only on the basis of this pattern of work. The best way, of course, is that the workers should be trained to distribute the work and rest themselves so that they can make this distribution on the basis of their own individual capacities and abilities.

Another beneficial effect of officially providing a period of rest is that the workers gain confidence in the management since they feel that the management is conscious of their welfare. This helps to develop a positive attitude to the work, and this attitude helps to increase production. Hence, the total effect of giving a rest period depends upon the rest and also upon the positive attitude generated by it. This benefit cannot be derived when the workers take unofficial rest because the attitude of the work does not favour the management since he has stolen the rest. It has

1. Vernon, H.M., *Industrial Fatigue and Efficiency*, pp. 107-10.

not been provided to him. Besides, some of the workers are not capable of such disloyalty with the result that they have to bear the maximum burden of the work. Hawthorne's experiments have also yielded useful results concerning the rest pauses. It has been seen that a fifteen-minute rest pause during the morning, a lunch interval and a ten-minute rest pause during the afternoon have great advantages.

Many experiments have been conducted to find out the maximum work that a worker should be forced to do so that he gives the maximum production. In one organisation, the workers worked ten hours a day at packing apples while in another organisation, the workers put in eight hours a day at similar work. By comparing the total amount of work done, it was seen that the workers who worked for eight hours a day packed on an average five cases more every day. Evidently, production had fallen with an increase in the working time. Hence, in most of the modern industries, the management takes care not to increase the working schedule to such an extent that it should prove harmful.

EQUIPMENT DESIGN

After making a study of fatigue, boredom and accidents in industry, it has been concluded that in addition to the environmental and personal factors which influence industrial loss, the design of the equipment also plays an important part. In fact, it would not be wrong to say that equipment design is a comparatively more important factor than environmental and individual factors in causing industrial production. It is natural that industrial efficiency should be influenced by equipment design, if the equipment is so designed that the worker becomes tired rapidly, out of all proportion to work, or if he cannot work without some interruption or if he can achieve only a very low level of production. As far as automatic machines are concerned, they are usually designed to avoid accidents. It is necessary to see in such a case how the worker will sit, the amount of light he will get and the direction from which it will come, and the movement he will have to make in order to control such a machine. It is essential that the light should fall on the instrument panel and not on the eyes of the worker. If the light disturbs his vision, he will not be able to see the instrument panel, thus increasing the chances of an accident. He may even be dazzled by the light and thus operate the machine incorrectly.

While operating different kinds of machines, workers have to make different kinds of movements with their hands and feet. Fatigue is directly related to the kinds and extent of such movements. If some specific muscles are brought into play in operating some machines, then it is only natural that the muscle will suffer extreme fatigue. That is why psychologists have assisted in designing of equipment which will result in maximum production while inducing the least possible amount of fatigue. Motion studies are of great value in the designing of this kind of equipment. In recent years, psychology has been able to help machine designing to such an extent that a branch of psychology known as engineering psychology has come into existence.

Equipment design is concerned not only with the shape and size of machines and tools but also with the order in which they are placed within the factory premises. It is common knowledge that the tools and machines required by a particular worker should be placed within easy reach so that he can pick them up by extending his hand. In addition to this, the tools should be placed in the order in which they will be required. Even this arrangement of the tools is the work of the psychologist.

If a worker has to stand and work, he will naturally become tired more quickly and thus his industrial efficiency and output will both suffer. For this reason, psychologists have suggested the construction of machines which the worker can operate while sitting. A study of physical fatigue has revealed the various positions of the body in which the individual tires rapidly. On the basis of this knowledge, the psychologists have given suggestions for the construction of machines in which the worker's body is placed in such a position that he does not tire easily. When machines are designed in this way, the worker can increase his production without becoming extremely exhausted.

The importance of equipment design for industrial efficiency is evident from the above exposition. Psychologically considered, if the machine design is adequate, the accident rate falls, fatigue declines, enthusiasm is maintained and industrial efficiency increases.

MUSIC IN INDUSTRY

Effect of Music on Production

Today music is provided for the workers while they work so that their boredom and monotony can be kept at a low level. B.E. Benson believes that music is of great importance in industry. The first experiments on this aspect were conducted in England. Music was provided to reduce boredom. When music was played to the workers while they were doing normal mechanical work, a 6 per cent increase in production was observed. A marked difference between production on ordinary days and production on days in which music was provided was thus seen. It was also seen that the duration of music was not very important. More benefit can be derived by providing music in the morning than in the afternoon. In explaining the importance of music for industry J.F. Humes[1] has mentioned one particular study. A study of fast, slow and mixed music programmes was conducted in a factory making radio tubes. It was noticed that when the music was either fast or slow, the loss of tittle was much less. But the loss was much greater either when there was no music or when fast and slow music programmes were broadcast alternately.

Influence upon Mental Condition

Music programmes influence the worker's mental condition and also the production. W.A.W. Kerr made a study of the effect of music on industrial workers and concluded that it has a positive and useful effect on the mental condition of the workers. H.C. Smith saw in his research that music has a good influence upon the attitudes of the workers, upon the production and upon the prevention of accidents. Smith has given a detailed account of the varying influence of music on various kinds of work and the different work shifts. He indicated that the provision of music resulted in a 7 per cent rise in production in the day shift and a 17 per cent increase during the night shift. It was also observed that music has the greatest influence in those operations in which memory of recall plays an important part and conversation is possible. Mcghee and J.E. Gardner[2] showed by their experiments that music did not result in any increase in production but in this case music was provided for workers engaged in some complicated operations. These operations necessitated the use of decision making, constant attention and thought and determination. But even though the production did not increase, the workers were under the impression that they had produced more while music was played.

Influence upon Boredom

Music has the most beneficial effect upon boredom. Although it takes the attention of the worker away from his work for a short time, it does not force him to use his mind. Besides, the provision of music helps to maintain the interest of the worker in functions needing recall.

---

1. Humes, J.F., "The effect of occupational music on scarppage in the manufacturing of Radio Tubes", *Journal Applied Psychology,* 25, pp. 573-87.
2. Mcghee, W., and J.E. Gardner, "Music in a Complex Industrial Job", *Person. Psychology.* (1949), 2, pp. 405-17.

Effect on Accidents

Many valuable studies have been conducted to study the effect of music on accidents. It was generally taken for granted that music would cause more accidents because it would distract the attention of the worker. And this would hold true in the case of operations in which constant attention to the work is essential but in many functions, such constant attention is not necessary. In all such operations, music has a beneficial influence. Music helps the mind to wander a bit thus reducing boredom and monotony. By allowing the mind to wander, music does not let the mind become lethargic. Distraction caused by music is not the same as lack of attention which results from fatigue. The latter kind of disinterest normally leads to accidents but the distraction of music does not. For example, the car driver can allow his mind to wander a bit, but as soon as any obstacle presents itself or another vehicle comes within range, his mind immediately snaps back to car driving and despite the distraction accidents do not take place. This wandering of the mind helps the driver because it reduces the monotony of car driving, which becomes mechanical after long practice. Wherever industrial operations are of a similar nature, functions in which the worker can afford to let his mind wander a bit without leading to accidents, music has a positive influence because it maintains the interest of the worker and avoids monotony.

Positive Effects of Music in Industry

Briefly, it can be said that music has a beneficial effect on an industrial situation. Most workers also testify to the fact that music gives them pleasure. Although 1 or 2 per cent of the workers oppose the introduction of music, they do so because of some individual attitudes or difficulties. Almost 75 per cent of the workers are in favour of music. The kind of music and pitch of the sound at which it should be played can be determined by experiment and study, and it can be made to suit different kinds of functions. Some of the major facts in this connection are the following:

1. Music at low pitch is more useful than music played very loudly.
2. The music should also be changed after sometime.
3. Instrumental music distracts attention less than vocal music. It is also more satisfying.
4. Music should not be provided all through the working hours. It should be provided at a time when fatigue is maximum.

5. Music provided during the night shift has proved more advantageous than music given during the day shift.

BOREDOM AND MONOTONY

Meaning of Boredom and Monotony

In the context of psychological fatigue, insofar as it pertains to industry, the words boredom and monotony are used in addition to fatigue. Monotony is a mental condition which is produced by the constant repetition of some function over a long period of time. On the other hand, boredom is a mental condition in which the individual evinces negative attitudes and aptitude for a particular work. In other words, he does not want to do that work. Both boredom and monotony contribute to fatigue but neither is the result of physical fatigue. Both of them are caused by mental attitudes. Boredom is caused more by the personality of the worker, his aptitude, his emotional condition and the apparent importance of the function he is performing. When these factors are varied, one person will feel no boredom in some particular function which bores another person. Some people become bored rapidly with some work requiring repetition but many other people adapt themselves very quickly to such work. For these reasons, the workers have completely divergent opinions about work which is boring and other work which is not. Some important facts connected with this subject were revealed in the study of S. Wyatt, J.H. Langdon and F.G.L. Stock.[1] This study was conducted on ten individuals and five kinds of work. Each individual was required to do each kind of work for one month, and at the end of the period each individual was required to point out the extent of boredom experienced in each kind of work. The worker was to award zero points to the work which contained no boredom and five points the work in which he felt consistently bored. When this evaluation was analysed, it was seen that all the workers considered two kinds of work consistently boring, although some awarded five points to one work and some awarded them to the other. Apart from this, the ten individuals showed no unanimity of opinion. The average evaluation for the five kinds of work was 4.2, 2.4, 2.3, 1.7 and 1.7. It is evident that different individuals made a separate evaluation of boredom according to their individual differences. The scientists conducting the study pointed out that boredom was evinced by workers with a higher intelligence quotient and an extrovert tendency, put this fact has not been substantiated by other studies.

---

1. Wyatt, S., Langdon, J.H. and F.G.L. Stock. "Fatigue and Boredom in Repetitive Work".

Fig. 23.3. Instrument for Measuring Boredom

Causes of Boredom and Monotony

Factors which cause boredom and monotony have been revealed through many studies. Some of the factors leading to boredom and monotony, briefly stated, are:

1. Individuality of the worker As has already been demonstrated above, boredom and monotony are closely connected with the individual traits of the individual workers. It is commonly seen that one particular kind of work will strike some people as boring while others will find no boredom in doing it. In an experiment on 400 students of Munsterberg's college, it was seen that boredom depends upon the individual's particular personality traits, not upon the nature of the work. Different individuals take interest in different kinds of work, and that is why the pattern of boredom in each case is different.

2. Intelligence of the worker Among the different qualities that make up individual differences, intelligence is important and it has a close relation with boredom and monotony. As has been pointed out earlier, the more intelligent individual is inclined to be bored by mechanical repetition of some activity. On the other hand, the less intelligent individual makes a better adjustment with his work. But in this connection it would be better to give a brief review of some of the studies conducted on this subject. The more important studies are the following:

(i) *Thomson's study*: Thomson experimented upon 32 people and came to the conclusion that boredom has nothing to do with intelligence.

(ii) *Viteles' study*: Viteles conducted an experiment on girls working in the salary section and concluded that the more intelligent girls experience more boredom with the result that majority of such girls are among those who leave this kind of job.

(iii) *Kornhauser's research:* A.W. Kornhauser conducted an experiment on office workers and supported the contention of Viteles. He also found that the more intelligent people soon become bored with the work and run away. The less intelligent continue to retain their interest in their work.

(iv) *Burnett's study:* Burnett came to the same conclusion when he conducted an experiment on four girls. He also concluded that the less intelligent girls achieved higher production than the more intelligent girls.

(v) *Studies by Wyatt, Frazer and Stock:* These psychologists also came to the same conclusion. It was observed by them that the less intelligent girls take more interest in their work than the average or exceptionally intelligent girls.

In his book *The Iron Man in Industry,* A. Pound has remarked, "A morone trained in habits of doing regularly and obedience; is, for many practical purposes, more valuable to his boss for good production than one in higher mental state."

3. Attitude to the work Many studies have established that workers with a negative attitude to their work experience boredom and monotony much sooner than those with a positive attitude. People with a positive attitude can maintain their concentration in their work for a much longer time.

4. Satiation Some people soon become fed up with doing work that needs recall, and they do not want to continue doing it. Their attention in the work gradually decreases as their mind becomes more and more satiated. As a result, the quantity and quality of the production also decline. Satiation is a psychological condition in which physical fatigue is at a very low level. A. Karsten conducted an experiment in this connection with some college students. When they had become completely bored with the work of writing they were asked to write names on a sheet of paper, in which they experienced no difficulty at all. In an experiment with poetry, it was seen that some individuals who did not want to utter one more line of poetry were willing to continue talking for a long time when the subject was changed. They, too, did not experience any fatigue. It is evident from both of these experiments that only those muscles were being exercised which already appeared to be fatigued. But this apparent fatigue was due to boredom and when the subject was changed they again began to function normally because the boredom was removed. Obviously, the difficulty in working was not due to muscular fatigue but due to satiation, a psychological condition. Satiation is caused by doing the same kind of work. It does not imply fatigue. This was also proved by the fact that some workers complaining of fatigue resumed their work when they were allowed to change their position.

5. Feeling of progress Many experiments have also yielded the fact that if the worker is aware of the progress he has made in his work, he does not experience boredom or monotony. In fact, as the work progresses, the worker becomes excited at the prospect of achieving his target and works with renewed energy. An individual becomes bored very quickly with some work, the end of which he cannot see or which leads to no tangible result. For this reason, it is always better to have recognisable targets at shorter intervals in any work. The desire to finish the day's work can itself be an aim. In such a case, one can observe the increase in the speed of working. But the feeling of having achieved some target or of being near to the end also depends upon the individual's attitude. If the attitude is negative, this feeling of achievement is weak. Fairly often, the boredom of the individual can be reduced if he can be convinced of the value and importance of his work for others.

6. Other qualities In addition to above, individual qualities of the worker also influence boredom. The more important ones are leaning of attention, emotional condition, peculiarities of nature. If these are in favour of the work, the work will produce less boredom. But if these are negative, the individual will soon become bored with his work.

7. Feeling of leaving something uncompleted One particular worker was lying on his death-bed. He was asked to mention the last wish he would like to have fulfilled. He said that he would like to have a board on which the screws were only half tightened. He wanted to complete the work of tightening those screws. This individual had spent all his life fixing screws on a board and half-tightening them. But he was always filled with the desire to tighten these screws fully. Similar phenomena have been observed in many studies. A worker feels dissatisfied and deprived if he is not allowed to complete his task. In another example, it was seen that one foreman ordered a worker to leave the work in hand and go on to something else. The worker did not want to leave his work incomplete, so he refused to obey the foreman. Using his position, the foreman ordered him to leave it. This led to an exchange of words and a scuffle in which the worker pushed the foreman who fell against a machine and was killed. The only thing at the root of this incident was that the foreman wanted to take the worker away from his work, which the worker wanted to complete. It is also seen that many workers do not want to start some fresh assignment near the end of the day. They know that they will not be able to complete it, and it is against human psychology to leave the work incomplete. A refusal in such conditions does not amount to disobedience, disrespect or obstinacy, and should not be interpreted as such. Man has a natural desire to finish anything that he has begun, and if he is prevented from doing so, he loses his balance, a fact which has been established by many psychological experiments. Many experiments have shown that man first of all shows the desire to complete any work which has been left incomplete. When the worker enters the factory, he first of all wants to complete the previous day's work before going on to something fresh. While working, an individual enters a psychological state in which he wants to leave some work only after he has completed it. This motivation can differ in degree from person to person and from work to work. And providing an opportunity to complete the work is an important element in job satisfaction. This tendency of completing unfinished work is seen more particularly in those kinds of work which influence the emotions, irrespective of their inherent interest or the lack of it. If the worker is indifferent towards his work, he will show no desire to complete it. A worker is seen working rapidly only because he is pressed by the desire to finish it. For this reason the desire to finish some work has an important influence upon boredom or monotony. If this desire is present, the individual does not become bored. In this way, this tendency is directed against boredom because it creates motivation. In industrial conditions, it is desirable that the work should be divided in such a way among the workers that they get an opportunity to complete their part of the work. This increases motivation and reduces boredom.

8. Conditions of work From the above account of causes of boredom and monotony, it should not be taken for granted that only individual and personal factors are responsible while the external environment plays no part at all. In fact, the truth of the matter is that the manager or the employer can do more to remove boredom and monotony by changing the external conditions of work than he can by trying to condition the worker's mind or to control his attitudes. Monotony can be reduced and production increased by making adequate changes in the working conditions. This can be done by making the following changes:

(a) ***Provision for rest***: Boredom or monotony increase in the absence of any rest period. In a study conducted by Mayo, it was seen that the workers in a cloth-mill suffered from boredom because they did not have any rest interval in their working hours. When provision was made for rest, an immediate decline in the level of boredom was noticed. This has also been substantiated by the research of other psychologists.

(b) ***Arrangement for wages:*** The salary system plays an important part in creating interest among the workers. They feel dissatisfied and bored if the wages are not paid at the correct time or at the correct rates. Shaaz saw in his studies that the worker experiences less boredom and achieves a higher level of production if he gets proper wages.

(c) ***Working method***: Wyatt Frazer and Stock studied the work technique of three girls working in a factory making cigarette boxes. One of these girls had to work three times as much as the third girl, with the result that they regularly exchanged their positions. The scientist, instead of allowing one girl to work at one position for the whole day, made the girls interchange their respective positions six times a single day. It was noticed that their boredom grew less and they produced an extra 10 per cent of work.

9. Nature of work One cause of boredom is the nature of work because if a particular function does not vary at all, the worker becomes bored very soon and experiences monotony. If the work is varied and changed frequently, the worker's interest in it is maintained. Many experimental results have confirmed this view. Wyatt and Frazer conducted experiments in which six girls were asked to pack soap, fold handkerchiefs, gather cycle chains and to do a variety of other kinds of work. It was noticed that production went up and monotony declined.

10. Social factors Boredom and monotony also depend to a large extent upon some social factors because the worker works in a social environment which has a decided influence upon his mental condition. If the mutual exchange between the management and the worker is entertaining and cooperative then the boredom is quickly done away with. Then the worker takes an interest in his work. As long as conversation and laughter do not interfere with the performance of work, the workers should be allowed to indulge in conversation. This helps to maintain the worker's interest in his work. It has also been noticed that less boredom occurs if men and women work together. On the contrary, if the atmosphere is one of mutual suspicion and distrust in which the management goes out of the way to scold the worker, the worker soon loses his interest in work, thus adversely affecting production.

MEANS OF ELIMINATING BOREDOM AND MONOTONY

Many psychological means have now been evolved in industrial psychology to relieve boredom and monotony. Since monotony depends upon the nature of the work and upon the individual differences of each worker, different means are adopted to remove monotony from different kinds of work. But even then the following general measures can be useful in eliminating boredom:

1. Exchanging job The most important single measure in removing boredom is to exchange the jobs of the workers among them. Since different kinds of work exhaust different muscles of the body, a change of position often helps to give rest also. Besides, a change of job helps to maintain the novelty of the work and thus monotony is avoided. Again, the worker also gets an opportunity to gain experience about different kinds of work, while repetition of the same work does not provide any variety of experience. In addition to an exchange of jobs, the worker should be allowed to do the same job in many different ways since this helps to reduce mental and physical fatigue and maintains interest in work. In case of girls working in a telephone exchange, it was seen that they took more interest in their work and complained of boredom less frequently when they were allowed to exchange their jobs. By his studies, J.R.P. French has shown that job exchange has a positive and beneficial influence upon morale. In his study, the working girls were allowed to change the rate and method of working.

2. Relating the job to the large picture Some people become bored with their jobs only because their function is not connected with a comprehensive picture of the job. If a woman who cleans dishes treats each dish as nothing more than another dish, she will soon become bored and will experience monotony. Norman R.F. and Maier[1] has described the case of a subnormal boy who cleaned all the dishes in the house, irrespective of the number of guests. And as there were already fifteen members in the household, he should ordinarily have become bored and tired very soon. But he never required any help in his task because, for him, each dish had individual characteristics and he could identify each dish by some mark on it. He treated each dish as a friend and found pleasure in cleaning the face of each friend. Some of them he liked more than others and therefore he had reserved special places for them. He found interest in his work because he experienced the feeling that he was rapidly meeting one friend after another.

---

1. Maier, Norman R.F., *Psychology in Industry,* George G. Harrap & Co., London (1955), p. 477.

It has been seen that working girls soon become bored in their office work if they do not have interest in it. On the other hand, a typist will not experience monotony if he finds the official correspondence interesting or if the office's functions interest him. For this reason, it is desirable that all the workers should have sufficient knowledge of the work of their organisation. As long as they are ignorant of this, they cannot gauge the importance of their own contribution to it. Once they realise this importance, their own job can be seen in the right perspective as part of the larger picture. Then the sense of responsibility increases and better work is done. Sometimes the worker is told to mind his own business and to carry out orders as they are given to him, without taking interest in the working of the organisation. The consequence of this kind of management is that the worker is not interested in the quality of his own work and neither does he make any effort to improve his method of working.

3. Use of sub-goals In order to reduce monotony, it is desirable to create sub-goals within the work which can be achieved quickly. One such goal is the completion of the day's work with the result that the worker feels he is making progress as the day wears on. If the goal is too far away or can be achieved only after a long time, it does not serve to inspire the worker in this way. In addition to this goal of completing the day's work, his rest intervals can also be made sub-goals. The worker is inspired to complete his work because he feels that soon he will get the chance to rest. It is often seen that the speed of working increases as the time of rest comes nearer. In this way, the rest period provides relaxation and removes monotony.

Another way of creating goals is to divide the work into larger units. For example, if we start reading a book with the intention of finishing it chapter by chapter, then the book can be completed without loss of interest or creation of boredom. Besides, the reader experiences a feeling of progress as he moves from one chapter to the next.

In order to enhance this sense of achievement in industry, the various units of production should be distributed among the workers and each one should be encouraged to complete his own unit. Production can thus be increased by making production itself a goal. The unit of production is between two periods of rest, and the desire and enthusiasm to complete the unit tend to reduce monotony.

4. Use of pacing method and automatic work habits Psychological analyses have revealed that monotony is a repeated activity. It is not caused by recall but by repeating the work. Nowadays efforts are made to turn all repetitive functions into automatic activities, as far as is possible. When this is done, the work becomes natural and continues to be done without any attention being paid to it so that the worker can allow his mind to wander here and there. Work of this kind does not cause monotony. For example, people do not notice the distance they have walked if they are talking to another person at the same time. But if the individual concentrates his attention on the activity of working, he will soon find it monotonous. Hence, if the work is of the same nature as walking, then the worker should have the liberty to talk to others or to daydream, if he so desires. Many studies have shown that, given the liberty to daydream, monotony can be kept at a low level.

Improvement in performance can be seen when some repeated activity is made rhythmic. It has been seen that when many workers are performing the same function, they tend to follow a rhythm. Men who carry heavy loads can be seen working in this way. Similarly, less boredom is experienced when walking in step rather than in walking without any rhythm.

5. Provision of industrial music Another means of reducing boredom is to provide music to the workers in industry. This measure has proved of great value in all work situations which do not require the constant attention of worker. And it should be noted that instrumental music proves more useful than vocal music.

6. Increase of experience of completion The awareness of having completed some work provides natural motivation and stimulation. For this reason, boredom can be reduced by allowing the worker to have a greater sense of having completed his work. The managers should try to avoid interruption of the worker at his work and in particular not to interfere with him before he has completed his task. The consciousness of completion is created when the worker is aware of the progress he has made. Leaving the work in hand as soon as ordered is not a sign of effective administration or obedience in industry. No intelligent manager will stress that the worker should suspend his work as soon as he is ordered. The manager will allow the worker to complete the work in hand and then ask him to report. By doing this, the manager can help to maintain the motivation of the worker and avoid boredom. In addition to this, the work can be divided into small units so that it gives more frequent experience of completion and achievement. These smaller units themselves become the goals for the worker and he gets a feeling of completion and the satisfaction when he achieves even this smaller goal. The total work and the working hours should be divided in such a manner that there should be the satisfying experience of completing each unit. The job of preparing records and maintaining accounts can be made more satisfying by dividing the work into separate files so that the worker can feel relieved after finishing work on one file. Job satisfaction increases as the work is seen coming to an end.

7. Attending to individual differences In dividing the work among the workers attention should be paid to their individual differences. If this is done the incidence of disinterest and boredom will be less. As far as possible a worker should be given a task which suits his intelligence, attitudes, spheres of attention, nature and emotional conditions.

8. Improvement of working conditions Generally, boredom and monotony can be kept in control by providing a properly timed and sufficiently long period of rest, payment of wages at the correct time, by introducing the proper methods of working, permitting freedom to laugh and enjoy, and generally improving he working conditions.

9. Proper social environment Finally, the most important method of reducing boredom is to maintain an atmosphere of love and confidence, cooperation and faith among the workers and the management. If the social environment is encouraging and pleasant, boredom normally does not occur.

QUESTIONS FOR EXERCISE

1. Distinguish between physical and mental fatigue. How can fatigue be eliminated?
2. Describe the causes of mental fatigue in an industry. Suggest ways and means to remove mental fatigue.
3. Explain the physiological and psychological aspects of fatigue in detail.
4. Distinguish between different types of fatigue in industry and show how these are assessed.
5. What are the industrial circumstances in which fatigue is produced? What measures should be adopted to minimise fatigue?
6. What are the industrial circumstances in which fatigue is produced? Distinguish between physical and mental fatigue and point out the relation between them.
7. Examine the general concept of fatigue, and discuss the factors that underlie its causation in industry.
8. What is the nature of fatigue in industry? What measures would you recommend for the elimination of fatigue?

9. Explain the concept of industrial fatigue and discuss the factors that underlie its causation.
10. Critically examine the concept of fatigue in different aspects.
11. Examine the concept of fatigue, and comment on the statement that in testing fatigue we "tend to measure that of which we have only the adequate knowledge by procedures which are not altogether valid".
12. Describe the different types of measurement of fatigue. Is fatigue curve in any way related to accident frequencies?
13. Briefly describe the various tests of fatigue and explain their importance in industry.
14. Write a short note on Ergograph.
15. Indicate the industrial application of the ergographic studies of work and fatigue.
16. What are the main findings of ergographic studies of work and fatigue? Consider their implication for industry.
17. Write short note on Industrial music.
18. Write critical note on Importance of music during work.
19. Write critical note on Music and job performance.

24

INDUSTRIAL ACCIDENTS

ARE ACCIDENTS ACCIDENTAL?

When the scientific attitude had not been adopted by the industry, it was believed that accidents were accidental. But when scientific research began in the sphere of industry, it was soon learnt that if there were provisions for safety, the number of accidents fell. Where safety methods were introduced, a downward trend in the number of accidents was soon noticed. When people were trained to avoid accidents, a marked improvement was observed. Hence, it is no, longer believed that accidents are accidental. The Workmen's Compensation Laws have played an important role in this change because once this legislation was introduced, the industrialists in England and America had to pay very heavy compensation to any worker injured or incapacitated in an accident. The consequence was that accidents became very undesirable as far as the management was concerned and they tried to prevent them as far as possible. With the passing of time it was noticed that the sum spent on introducing safety devices proved to be far less than the total compensation paid out in case of the accident. Hence safety devices proved to be more economic, and the industrialists stood to gain by introducing them and increasing them. Finding these safety measures a paying proposition, the industrialists in every sphere sought to introduce them and also trained their employees to avoid accidents and become more safety-conscious. Another advantage of introducing safety measures was that the loss of working hours through accidents decreased and led to a further increase in production. Besides, the workers now developed a more trusting and confident attitude towards their employers and thus worked harder, again benefiting the industrialist. Many subsequent researches and studies have established beyond doubt that the introduction of safety measures led to the saving of millions of dollars. And the production everywhere went up in proportion to the safety measures introduced, besides the improvement in human relations between the workers and the management. For this reason, great attention is now paid in all industries to the prevention of accidents. This proves that accidents are not really accidental.

Causes of Accidents

If accidents are not accidental, it is obvious that they must have some cause. What, then, is the cause of accidents? Psychologists have undertaken numerous studies of the working conditions, the methods of working, the mental condition of workers, to locate the causes of accidents. They can be briefly enumerated as follows:

1. Improper working conditions Factors such as the improper temperature in the factory, the intensity and the quality of illumination, the working hours, the extent of humidity, the arrangement of machines, the work shift, are responsible for accidents. Factors which are directly responsible for increasing accidents are following:

(a) ***Absence of proper temperature*****:** Many studies have established that the number of accidents goes up if the temperature rises or falls far above or below the normal. This fact proves to be most truthful about the labourers working in mines. It was seen that the number of accidents in the hottest mines was three times as much as the number of accidents in the coldest mines. The frequency of accidents increases with any extreme variation in temperature. Even when the temperature falls below the normal, the number of accidents increases. Women can adapt to higher temperatures better than men. One cause of this can be the different kinds of clothing used by men and women. Yet, it is necessary to determine the normal, the highest and the lowest temperatures differently for every country because of the different climate. The normal temperature in a very cold country may still be sufficiently cold to cause accidents in an otherwise hot country because for people of hot and temperate climates that temperature may still be too low to be tolerated easily. Hence it is necessary to make experiments to determine the normal temperature in a factory in a particular location. Then efforts can be made to maintain that level of temperature so that accidents are avoided and the highest possible production maintained. Osborne and Vernon conducted an experiment in a shoe factory, and they came to the conclusion that the least number of accidents occurred when the temperature was between

55° and 59° Fahrenheit. This conclusion was further substantiated by the studies of Bedford and Vernon.

(b) ***Amount of humidity*****:** If the humidity in a particular factory is far above normal, then the bodily health of the worker is adversely affected with the result that the possibilities of accidents increase. This has been proved to hold true of mines. Hence it is now considered necessary to control the amount of humidity in working areas.

(c) ***Absence of proper light:*** The absence of proper illumination is another cause of accidents because excessive or too little light strains the eyes and leads to fatigue. Natural light is always better than artificial light. It has been seen that accidents increase by about 25 per cent when natural light is replaced by artificial light. The relationship between accidents and lighting is further proved by comparing the number of accidents in the day and night shifts. By making this comparison, Osborne and Vernon[1] have shown that there are fewer accidents during the night shift than in the day shift. More railway accidents take place at night than during the day because at night, the light is far less than it is during the day. But it should be remembered that the quantity of light is not the sole cause of accidents because fewer road accidents occur, at night, despite less illumination. This happens because during the day roads are more frequented than during the night.

(d) ***Work shift*****:** Vernon[2] has shown by his studies that fewer accidents take place during the night shift than during the day shift. This is explained by the fact that during the day shift, the worker arrives at his work after a night's rest and is also well fed at time. What happens is that after working for sometime he becomes careless. This leads to accidents. On the other hand, the workers in the night shift have already been awake for a number of hours before coming to work, with the result that they pay more attention to their work and thus accidents are avoided. Some studies have given results which contradict the findings of Vernon because it was then seen that more accidents took place during night shift than during day shift. Some workers were involved in accidents during night shift either because they could not get adequate sleep during the day or because they came to work in an intoxicated condition. Railway workers have more accidents during the night because they become inattentive due to sleep. In view of the contradictory findings, most scientists do not agree about the number of accidents during the night and day shifts. While during the day there is more light and the workers

---

1. Obsborne, E.E. and H.M. Vernon, "The Influence of Temperature and Other Conditions on the Frequency of Industrial Accidents".
2. Vernon, H.M., *Industrial Fatigue and Efficiency*, London, p. 264.

are better rested, they have accidents because they become careless. But the workers in night shift tend to be more careful and attentive.

2. Work methods Work methods are also sometimes responsible for accidents. It has been seen that factors, such as lengthy period of work, severity of work, the rapidity of production, fatiguing work methods, play an important role in causing accidents. Among the more important factors relating to work methods responsible for accidents are the following:

(a) ***Length of work periods***: Long working periods have more accidents because fatigue tends to increase and to accumulate over a long period of work. In one of the studies conducted by Osborne and Vernon, the number of accidents in a day shift fell by 10 per cent when the working time were reduced from 59 hours to 56 hours. A decrease of 25 per cent in the number of accidents was observed when the working time of one particular night shift were reduced from 63 hours to 48 hours. It has also been seen that more accidents take place when the worker works in overtime in addition to his normal working hours. Hence, it can be said that when the working period extends beyond a definite limit, the number of accidents increases.

(b) ***Severity of work:*** Any work which needs extreme physical endurance and leads to physical exhaustion can be called a severe work. Severe work of this kind is more prone to accidents than other kinds of work. Goldmark made a comparative study of severe work and other kinds of work and also of accidents taking place in the morning and evening. He came to the conclusion that severity of work is one cause of accidents, and as fatigue increases, so does the possibility of accidents.

(c) ***Speed of work*** : Vernon's studies have shown that the possibility of accidents increases with an increase in the speed of work. One main cause of this is that fatigue increases when the speed of work increases. Miles proved the truth of this statement with the help of the pendulum test. He demonstrated that the frequency of accidents increases with the speed of work. But, on the other hand, many studies have not led to similar conclusions. For example, the American Engineering Council conducted a survey of safety measures and production on an estimated ten lakh employees and came to the conclusion that accidents fall as the speed of work increases. In actual fact, much depends on what is considered as the most appropriate speed of working in a particular industry. And this speed may even vary from one individual worker to another. Some people have the capacity to always work faster than others, and such people may in fact have more accidents if their speed is reduced.

In the same way, the speed of working will also depend upon the tools and instruments being used. Then again a tired worker cannot work at top speed for a long time while a healthy and fresh worker may be able to work much faster without being involved in any accident. What has been established is that if the speed of work increases beyond the appropriate level, then the possibility of accidents becomes greater, but the appropriate speed of work can only be determined by many factors such as the nature of work, the construction of machinery, the health and motivation of the worker, etc.

(d) ***Methods which increase fatigue*****:** Any method which increases fatigue will also increase accidents because increasing fatigue leads to accidents. It has been seen in motor car accidents that they occur most often when the driver of the vehicle is exhausted. The same has been found to be true in the case of railway accidents.

Absence of safety devices Conditions of work which do not make provision for safety devices also contribute to accidents. In some factories, the machines used have no safety devices attached to them, while in some other cases, the machines are provided with safety devices but the workers ignore them because they want to show that the devices are superfluous and that they can work without them. In order to forestall all such tactics, it is better to have the safety devices integrated with the machinery so that the workers cannot avoid using them. As the safety devices increase, the accidents become fewer while the absence of safety devices leads to an increase in the accidents.

3. Factors concerning the worker In addition to the conditions and the methods of work, there are certain factors concerned with the worker which lead to accidents. Such factors are mainly:

(a) ***Immature age:*** Many studies have indicated that as compared to mature workers, immature worker; are involved in a greater number of accidents. In this connection, Lippman, Gates and Schmitt have conducted valuable studies. Now, most modern industries do not encourage immature people to become workers.

(b) ***Inexperience:*** Among all those who operate machines, the experienced worker is less inclined to cause or become involved in an accident than the inexperienced worker. For this reason, inexperience is an important contributing factor for accidents.

B. Fisher[1] conducted a study on this aspect with the Carnegie Steel Company, Youngstown Steel Company and some other similar organisations and came to the conclusion that workers having experience

---

1. Fisher, B., *Mental Causes of Accidents*, New York, p. 34.

of one month have six times as many accidents as more experienced workers. From this, it is obvious that inexperience is an important factor.

(c) ***Bad state of health*****:** If the worker's health is not good, if he constantly complains of head aches or stomach aches or back aches or generally suffers from one complaint or the other, then he is more accident prone than a healthy worker. In the course of a study, Farmer and Chambers observed that there was a direct correlation between the number of accidents and the presence of workers in the hospital. E.M. Newbold established a relationship between accidents and the less important disease. By conducting a study of 135 workers of the Philadelphia Electric Company, Viteles[1] came to the conclusion that the suffering workers had a record of three times as many accidents as the healthy workers. Bingham[2] made a study of workers suffering from blood pressure and came to the conclusion that this disease was one cause of accidents. In this way, ill-health has been established as a cause of accidents.

(d) ***Physical defects*****:** Different kinds of work require different kinds of efficiency and capacity from the different physical organs. For example, if a worker has to work efficiently on some machines, it is desirable that his eyesight should be normal. If it is not, he may cause some accidents. For this reason, the eyesight of a person is especially checked before he is allowed to take up a job with the railways. The nature of the work determines the most important part of the body and the necessary level of the efficiency it must possess. A worker using a heavy hammer with his hands must necessarily have strong muscles in his arms. Otherwise he will cause some or the other accident. On the other hand, if a particular part of the body is not used in any particular function, then it does not matter if that particular part is damaged or otherwise handicapped. If a person is to work as a script writer, it matters little if his feet are deformed.

(e) ***Influence of sex differences*****:** It has been seen that because of sex differences, both men and women are better fitted for some particular kinds of work. Generally, women cannot perform dangerous and very severe work as efficiently as men, and for this reason if they try to do so they soon meet with accidents. The number of female car drivers involved in accidents is normally larger than the number of male car drivers. In severe work, women workers normally have three times as many accidents as male workers.

---

1. Vitals, M.S., *Industrial Psychology*, p. 352.
2. Bingham, W.V., *Prone to Accident Driver, Proceedings 17th Annual Conference on Highway Engineering*, p. 4.

(f) ***Unfavourable mental and emotional conditions*** **:** The possibility of accidents also increases if the worker's mental and emotional condition is unfavourable when he is working. It is for this reason that mentally unhealthy and emotionally unbalanced individuals are involved in more accidents than the more normal workers. That is why, in most factories no workers are, allowed to enter the premises in a drunk condition. Alcoholic drinks tend to disturb the mental balance and thus make work impossible. Hersey's studies indicate that almost 50 per cent of all accidents are caused by the mental imbalance of the workers.

In addition to the above, mentioned causes of accidents, there are certain momentary factors which lead to accidents. For example, such conditions as failure of the safety devices, inattention of the workers, ignorance, being intoxicated or exhausted, arguments between the worker and the manager, etc., can also cause the accidents. For this reason, it is always considered necessary to go into the causes of an accident so that the responsibility for it may be placed. It is best to pay attention to the conditions of work, the method of working, the individual qualities of the workers involved in the accident, but even more to the social conditions, the relationship between the management and the worker and the conditions existing at the time of accident.

MEANS OF PREVENTING ACCIDENTS

The only means of preventing accidents is to remove all the causes of accidents that have been mentioned earlier. Generally speaking, accidents can be avoided or prevented if the following measures are adopted:

1. Reform of the working conditions If accidents are to be prevented, then the conditions of work should be improved. The temperature in the working premises should not be such that it may lead to discomfort. This helps to improve the health of the worker and thus prevents accidents. The illumination provided should also be only strong enough and not too intense. Besides, the light source should be installed at the correct angle. Only those parts of a machine should be well lit which are to be constantly in the eyes of the worker. The light should not fall directly on the eyes of the operator. Besides, the machines in the factory should be so arranged that the workers should be able to get maximum production by making the minimum possible movements, so that there is not waste of effort. If some particular machine is likely to cause accidents or if it is dangerous to go near some particular machine, then safety devices should be installed to keep the workers away from it.

2. Provision of safety methods Nowadays engineers and psychologists cooperate to design safety methods by which even dangerous machines lead to fewer accidents. Engineers have been responsible for designing safety devices, special kinds of gloves, special kinds of spectacles which shield the eyes, and other gadgets by which machine can be operated from a safe distance, without ever being touched by the human hand. Methods of keeping the operator away from the machine while working have also been adopted but sometimes operators wish to show that they are not afraid of the machines and they deliberately avoid using these devices. In such cases, devices have been developed to ensure that the worker cannot operate the machine efficiently. If it is not possible to install such devices on some particular machines, the workers should be trained and encouraged to use these devices.

WHICH IS BETTER?

Fig. 24.1. Two Approaches to Safety

And if it is not possible to make provisions for training the workers, then they should be paid some compensation in lieu of this training. In short, the workers should be encouraged in every possible way to adopt these safety devices.

The left-hand figure shows the foreman instructing his man to work safely. If the man learn his lesson well, he will not fall over the pipe. This is a way of preventing accidents by changing the obstruction. The right-hand figure shows a runway built over the pipe. In this instance, the hazard is reduced by a change in the obstruction.

One basic condition of safety device is that it must be 100 per cent safe. If it is not completely safe then accidents will increase because the workers depend on it and in their own way become careless. If the device offers only 50 per cent safety factors, it proves actually harmful because accidents increase. On the other hand, if there are no safety devices, the worker naturally pays more attention and tends to be cautious with the result that fewer accidents occur. Actually, the worker makes his own adjustment with every kind of condition. If he is asked to operate a dangerous machine on which there are no safety devices, he operates it with extreme caution. Workers working in the night shift tend to be more cautious than workers in the day shift because they realize that lack of caution will lead to accidents. The result of this is that while more accidents should occur during the night under artificial light, in actual fact more accidents take place during the day. But if the machine is fitted with safety devices, the worker himself does not take so many precautions and if the device fails, an accident occurs immediately. This fact can be seen in the case of car accidents caused by speed. Fewer accidents take place at slow speed because no driver has the opportunity to speed up, and besides die presence of other cars makes it dangerous. But when the driver finds an empty and clear road he tends to drive much faster, with the result that many accidents take place on rural roads, and only 5 per cent on the urban roads in America, although the rural roads are generally deserted while the urban roads are far more crowded and carry much more traffic. Similar examples can be found in diffeffht industrial conditions.

In addition to the adoption of the above measure, every new worker in a factory should be carefully warned about the dangerous machines. In many modern factories, such machines have a danger sign printed on them so that the workers may be constantly warned. Sometimes a device installed for safety in one particular direction becomes the cause of an accident in some other. For this reason, engineers and psychologists should design safety devices in such a way that they do not disturb the normal pattern of working. In fact, even safety devices should help the worker in his work. If such machines are designed, then production increases along with safety, while fatigue is reduced. The worker tends to become tired if he is aware of danger because then he is always tense. But if safety devices are provided, this mental tension is avoided and fatigue is reduced.

3. Pay attention to individual differences Many accidents take place because the worker is required to perform some work which is beyond his physical capacity. Women, for example, cannot do heavy work, and if they are asked to do it, accidents become inevitable. Hence it is desirable that before allocating a particular task to a particular worker, information about his age, experience, mental health, emotional condition, sex, nature, intelligence, physical qualities and defects should be collected. If, after all this information has been collected, he proves to be capable of performing the particular task, he should be entrusted with it. Besides, if one worker has proved a failure at a particular task and is involved in many accidents in doing it, he should immediately be taken away from it and put to some other work. And before putting a man on some dangerous machines, it is better to test his accident proneness.

4. Training in right work methods. Many accidents occur because the operators using machines have not been trained in the correct use of them. It is always better, therefore, to train a person in the use of a machine, in its maintenance, before allowing him to handle it. Another reason why accidents occur due to wrong methods of work is that in such a case, the worker becomes tired very rapidly. And once a person is exhausted, his tendency to commit mistakes and cause accidents increases rapidly.

5. Means of removing fatigue It has already been pointed out that one important cause of accidents is fatigue. Hence one important measure of avoiding accidents is to remove fatigue. The most important method in this connection is to provide properly timed rest at frequent intervals so that the worker can regain his energy and avoid reaching a stage of complete exhaustion. Besides, the hours of work should not be too long so that complete exhaustion should not occur at all. Fatigue can also be prevented by providing a worker with a job which suits his mental and physical capacity. Fatigue can also be reduced by allowing the worker to have a sense of satisfaction by completing his job, by creating an atmosphere of cooperation and happiness, by creating cordial relations between worker and management, by making arrangements for timely payment of salary, etc. In addition arrangements should also be made for providing drinking water, wholesome and cheap food, and comfortable furniture for resting during the working hours.

6. Proper speed of work Accidents frequently occur when the work is performed at a speed much greater than that which is desirable. Drivers who often drive at high speeds are very frequently involved in accidents. Therefore, the speed of the worker in an office or a factory should be controlled. Accidents can also occur if the workers make a habit of putting in overtime, in addition to their normal working hours. If the worker tries to work rapidly as soon as he starts working, he becomes tired very quickly with the result that he works for the rest of the day in an exhausted condition, thus increasing the chances of accidents. Hence the workers should be encouraged to work at such a speed that they can maintain their efficiency and work throughout the day without unnecessary fatigue.

7. Organisation of safety committees Another measure for preventing accidents suggested by psychologists is the formation of safety committees. There should be one such committee in each factory, or even in each department of the factory, should the factory be exceptionally large in size. In addition to the workers, even safety officers and psychologists may be asked to function in this committee. In this committee, the suggestions and complaints of the workers are recorded and considered so that the possible areas of accidents can be known and measures for preventing them instituted. At the same time, such an organisation helps to interest every worker in preventing accidents. Such safety committees can also be organised on a national scale, so that representatives from different industries can take part in them. Such committees help to train the worker, make him more safety conscious, and also help to develop or invent new safety techniques. Another benefit which can be derived here is that the worker who is negligent of safety measures or who habitually pays no attention to the possibility of accidents can be criticised and even socially ostracised.

8. Safety campaign and posters Safety can also be promoted in another way, by organizing a campaign, in factories and offices. Posters and slogans can also be used in such a campaign, but normally the slogans should not be negative. For example, a slogan like 'The careless worker is a fool', is not a proper slogan. Instead one can have more positive slogans such as 'Beware of danger', 'Keep the hat on the head', 'There is a danger of poisonous gases here', Cross the road here', 'Smoke, if you must, but in the next room'. These slogans will help the worker to control his actions. Such slogans can be printed and hung up in various places within the factory premises. They will help to drive away the worker's fear, awaken his sense of safety, and direct him to act in the correct way. Any poster concerned with accidents should not contain only a mention of the accidents possible because this will serve only to frighten the worker. Posters should tell him not only that accidents are possible but also how he can avoid them.

9. Habits of safety Despite all the safety measures adopted, by far the best and the most successful method is the creation of habits of safety. If some worker has made a habit of operating his instruments improperly and of not using the safety devices, he may have an accident despite his efforts to prevent it. Different kinds of safety devices are built into different machines, and it is necessary that the worker should be trained in the use of them. But he must also be in the habit of using them. At times, the workers resist the installation of some new safety device. In such a case, they should never be forced to use the new device. They should be psychologically convinced that it is to their own advantage to make use of the safety devices. Once they are convinced they rarely have any hesitation in using it. If such habits have been formed, it is no longer necessary to remind the worker to be careful of accidents because caution becomes part of his thinking. This is why training is considered to be so important in all industries. Experience also has importance precisely for the same reason.

10. Motivating safety Unless the worker is motivated to exercise caution and to make use of the safety devices installed for his benefit, accidents cannot be prevented. Therefore, nowadays workers are motivated and encouraged to work cautiously. One way of doing it is to increase the salary of those workers who follow the safety regulations. Another way of doing it is to counteract opposite kinds of motivation. For example, if a worker is encouraged to adopt safety measures on the one hand and is also forced to increase production on the other hand, then the work will defeat its purpose. Sometimes safety devices are not adopted by the workers because they cause discomfort. In that case, efforts have to be made to make these devices more comfortable and endurable. Sometimes workers are even punished by fines if they do not make use of the safety devices but this method is harmful in as much as it does not encourage the worker to make use of the safety device but only forces him to find ways of concealing his practice. To put it briefly, the best way of encouraging the use of safety devices is to make use of the psychology of motivation. In the first place, contradictory motivations should be removed and then useful safety devices should be sought out. Workers should also be rewarded for making use of them. Even safety committees encourage the use of safety devices.

It is evident from the above description of the means of preventing accidents that the goal can be achieved only by the willing cooperation of the management, the workers and the psychologists. The government too can make a valuable contribution in this effort. Nowadays great efforts are being made to avoid industrial accidents in all progressive countries.

ACCIDENT PRONENESS

What is Accident Proneness?

Generally more accidents take place in some industrial circumstances as compared with the others. Most psychologists feel that a particular pattern can be seen in accidents. For example, once a person has been involved in one accident, he is inclined to get involved in another because the first accident makes him lose his self-confidence. In other words, his accident proneness increases. Another proneness is that tendency due to which some particular person gets involved in more accidents than some other person. Accident proneness is found is industrial circumstances which lead to more accidents, while there are certain individuals who, because of their psychological and physiological structure, are inclined to be involved in more accidents.

Laws of Accident Proneness

Psychologists have made a study of accidents in order to discover the laws governing accident proneness, and in this connection it is possible to make the following remarks:

1. If the accidents are accidental then some people are only rarely involved in them. While some are involved very frequently, the majority of people are at a stage somewhere between the two extremes.
2. If the accidents are due to circumstances then it will be seen that people who suffer from many accidents in a particular period, will be comparatively free of accidents in the following period.
3. If accident proneness increases because of accidents, then the particular individuals found involved in accidents in a particular test will also be found to be involved in accidents at any later test.
4. If the accidents are due to some particular qualities of the individuals then people obtaining a particular grade in a particular accident will obtain the same grade in future accidents also.

Psychologists have been able to come to some conclusion about the causes of accidents. Most studies have indicated that some individuals are so constructed that they are involved in more accidents than others, and are also the cause of involving other people into the accidents. Individuals of this kind are called accident prone. Normally there is always some scope for more or less accident proneness in every sphere where human beings work. It has, therefore, come to be believed that instead of throwing out the accident prone worker, it is better to analyse his accident proneness. This phenomenon can have many causes, and it may be possible to remove some of them. It has been found, for example, that accident proneness is definitely reduced if the individual is imparted training in some specific job. Then there are certain kinds of work which naturally lead to a greater number of accidents than other kinds of work.

Experience also takes care of accident proneness because the individual becomes less prone to accidents once he gets experience. Besides, the basic cause of accident proneness is some fault in the working conditions, such as improper illumination, lighting which is either too strong or too dim, or lighting which is directed from the wrong angle, or improper arrangement of machinery, etc.

Tests of Accident Proneness

Psychologists have succeeded in evolving certain tests by which it is possible to discover accident proneness. These tests have been developed after extensive study of accident proneness. It is sometimes noticed that the more skilled workers are more accident prone than the less skilled ones. One cause of this is that they work with such speed that the probability of accident increases rapidly, and for this reason accident proneness cannot be taken as an indication of lack of skill. In the second place, identical characteristics are not found in all individuals who are accident prone. Despite this, it has been possible to identify certain characteristic qualities which tend to promote accident proneness. The tests for determining these qualities are as follows:

1. Sensory motor tests. Accident proneness and muscular coordination are intimately related. Individuals whose muscular coordination is not good suffer from more accidents. It has been observed that the relation between accidents and results obtained in sensorymotor tests increases with experience. In the second place, skill and accident proneness have been found to have a definite relationship. If the individuals who achieve the lowest scores in tests for accident proneness are selected, there are fewer accidents and the standard of the workers rises. It is a commonly accepted fact that lack of skill, slackness of motor reaction cannot escape from a situation with an accident potential without sustaining some injury and in certain situations they cannot escape accidents. They may just be accident prone without being careless or irresponsible. Hence, it is evident that accidents take place due to lack of proper muscular coordination.

2. Emotional stability tests Emotionality and accident proneness are also intimately related and it has been found that highly emotional taxi drivers are involved in more accidents than other drivers while people with more stable emotionality have a lower accident proneness. Lower accident proneness is found in those individuals who are capable of controlling their reactions even in situations which distract attention or which disturb the individual. Briefly said, individuals obtaining high test scores in emotional stability tests have four times the probability of avoiding tests as compared that with accident proneness. It has been seen that depression was the cause of almost two hundred minor accidents out of four hundred such accidents.[1] On the other hand, production went up by 8 per cent in a mood of happiness which proved that this mood not only prevents accidents but actually promotes production. Himler[2] made a list of 28 personality traits which were the causes of accidents and more than half of them were connected with emotional coordination or stability.

3. Intelligence tests Tests which indicated a relationship between accidents and muscular coordination or emotional stability did not indicate any relationship between accidents and intelligence. But some other researches indicated a relationship between accidents and intelligence. But some other researches indicated a relationship between accident proneness and mental traits. And in these studies it was found that the test scores of intelligence and emotional stability showed more valuable conclusions about accidents than the test scores of emotional stability alone. In another study, the relation between intelligence and accidents was discovered in tests as some professional individual avoided an accident because of his intelligence rather than as a result of his better skill. In a study concerning motor car drivers, it was found that generally individuals with lower intelligence were involved in more accidents than people with more intelligence. But generally it is believed by most people that intelligence is an important factor in avoiding accidents.

4. Sensory and perceptual speed tests In certain tests it was seen that people with greater perceptual speed, meaning people who could rapidly observe even minor differences in perceptible pattern, were less inclined to be involved in accidents. On the other hand, individuals whose perceptual speed was less than their muscular reaction showed a higher degree of accident proneness. In this manner, accident proneness is increased if perceptual speed is less than muscular reaction because such people react faster than they can observe.

5. Tests of visual skills Since the use of the eyes is very important in almost all industries, it is natural that defects of vision result in more accidents. In a study of this kind, it was seen that 63 per cent of people who did not cause accidents passed the eye test while only 33 per cent of the people causing accidents could pass them.[3] Nowadays, in many

---

1. Hersey, R.B., "Emotional Factors in Accidents".
2. Himler, L.E., in *Psychological Factors in Industrial Accidents.*
3. Kephart N.C. and J. Tiffin, "Vision and Accident Experience", *Nat Safety News,* pp. 90-91.

modern industries, efforts are made to find out the minimum level of visual skill which is needed for the successful performance of a particular work. For example, the visual skill of people applying for jobs as signallers in the Indian Railways is tested particularly because if they have some visual defect they may endanger the lives of thousands of people. And the truth of the matter is that as the efficiency of all the sense organs, not only the eyes, increases, accidents decrease in number. They increases when such defects also increase.

Psychologists nowadays emphasize that the difficulties of the accident prone individual should be examined with great care and measures of eliminating them should be evolved and suggested. With the adoption of such an attitude, the rate of accidents of 44 accident prone motor car drivers fell from 1.3 to 0.75 over a distance of one thottsand miles within one year.[1] For a study of this kind, it is necessary to find out and to isolate the particular individual factor which has been responsible for accidents. For example, in connection with motor car drivers it has been seen that about 64 per cent of accidents take place due to a defective aptitude, failure to anticipate the possibility of an accident, incorrect judgement of speed and distance, excessive impulsiveness, irresponsibility and failure to keep attention for a long time, or a combination of these factors. Studies of this kind can help to reduce the accidents in many kinds of jobs but it must also be kept in mind that the analysis of accidents often becomes subjective. Besides, mistakes can be made by an error of human judgement. Again, analysis of this kind cannot take the place of the tests described earlier in establishing a relation between accident proneness and individual traits. But as far as one is concerned with the influence of emotional instability on accidents, such an analysis can be useful.

Causes of Accident Proneness

The major causes of accident proneness can be enumerated on the basis of the above description of the various tests:

1. Low degree of muscular coordination As has been pointed out in the first test of accident proneness, people with a low level of muscular coordination are more prone to accidents.

2. Absence of emotional stability One major cause of accident proneness is lack of emotional stability, as is evident from the earlier description of the second test of accident proneness.

---

1. Viteles, M.S., *Industrial Psychology*, pp. 376-89.

3. Absence of an appropriate mood Generally an unhappy and depressed mood leads to more accidents and lower production than a happy and effervescent mood.

4. Weak intelligence The Traffic Court of Detroit ordered the examination of some drivers for mental hygiene. About one-third of the cases referred were found to be mentally feeble. In this way, feeble-mindedness increases accident proneness.

5. Lack of coordination between perceptual and motor speed In English there is a proverb that 'One should look before leaping'. Obviously, individuals whose speed of jumping is faster than their speed of observing will be involved in accidents. In other words, accident proneness increases when the perceptual speed is less than the motor speed.

6. Visual defects Visual defects are a major cause of accidents in all kinds of work in which vision is to be used extensively and relied upon.

7. Frustration An increase in frustration definitely leads to an increase in the level of accident proneness. For example, aggressiveness with frustration and aggression is a major cause of many accidents.

8. Lack of experience In the modern age only trained individuals are employed to perform complex tasks because lack of experience is another factor causing accidents. Experience leads to an increase in a person's skill with the result that fewer accidents take place.

9. Immature age Generally accident proneness is reduced when age increases because there is an increase in experience, skill, muscular coordination, perceptual speed, emotional stability, intelligence, sensory-motor reaction, with an increase in age. For this reason, certain industries prohibit the employment of individuals below a certain age. Individuals working in coal mines should be between 30 and 39 years of age, while people doing kinds of work below the earth's surface should be between 20 and 29 years. It must be remembered that accident proneness increases not only with immaturity but also if the worker is above the maximum age limit because older people become fatigued more easily and their powers weaken. Yet sometimes the younger people are involved in more accidents than their older counterparts. This is explained not only by their lack of skill but by the desire to work faster and to fake unnecessary risks.

10. Sex Women, in general, are more accident prone than men. Even in a work like motor car driving, in which no physical force is necessary, it was seen that women were responsible for three times as many accidents per mile as men. Nevertheless, in the present situation, it cannot be said definitely that this difference between men and women is based on difference of sex or is caused because women tire more quickly than men.

11. Lack of health It is generally believed that accident proneness increases with ill-health. High blood pressure has been found to be a definite cause of accidents caused by motor car drivers. But accident proneness also increases if a person suffers from mental ill-health. Individuals suffering from nervous and mental disorders or individuals having feeble minds are prone to accidents. The accident rate also increases if the individual is accident prone because it encourages antisocial tendencies.

It is evident from the above description of the causes of accident proneness that psychological means can be used to reduce accidents to a very great extent. If the causes are removed, accidents will definitely decrease. There are certain causes which can be eliminated in all individuals. For example, the lack of experience and training can be eliminated by providing training. But in addition to all these causes of accident proneness, some accidents take place in industry due to human relations. Some people cause accidents because they are completely irresponsible or because they deliberately want to cause damage. In such cases, it is necessary to keep an eye on such individuals so that they can be removed. In this respect, the foreman can play an important part. On the one hand, he can keep an eye on the antisocial elements and thus avert accidents, while on the other hand he can guide each worker in his work and in this way also avoid accidents. Bad behaviour on the part of the foreman leads to frustration and aggressiveness in the workers, with the result, that accidents increase. On the other hand, pleasant and mutually respectful behaviour on the part of the managers generates a happy peaceful atmosphere in the organisation with the result that accidents are kept to minimum. Therefore, the management should assume the role of friend, guide and assistant rather than that of the leader or the judge. This will help to create a group atmosphere in the factory so that the antisocial elements will be suppressed while the other people will cooperate with each other. They will be able to maintain sound mental health so that accidents will not occur so frequently.

QUESTIONS FOR EXERCISE

1. Define accidents. Discuss the environmental causes of industrial accidents.

2. Describe the main causes of industrial accidents.
3. "Accidents do not just happen". Explain this and bring out the major causes of accidents.
4. "Accidents do not happen accidentally." Discuss this remark and say how accidents in industry can be prevented.
5. Analyse the causes of industrial accidents in the light of modern research. Do these support the concept of accident proneness?
6. Attempt an analysis of the phenomenon of accidents in industry.
7. Discuss the main factors causing accidents. Are accidents accidental?
8. Elucidate the question of individual differences in susceptibility to accidents, and show how far the attention to the same has been useful in accident prevention programme in industry.
9. Explain with the aid of factual evidence how far accidents in factories are really accident in the accepted sense of term.
10. Describe various causes of accidents and state the measures that may be taken to prevent them.
11. Write short note on Accident Proneness.
12. Explain the evil consequences of accidents describing researches done on accident proneness.
13. Critically evaluate the theories of accident proneness.
14. What do you understand by accident proneness?
15. What is accident proneness? Are psychological tests useful in identifying accident prone individuals?
16. Describe the psychological factors in accident proneness? What measures should be taken to reduce accident proneness?
17. State the factors associated with accident proneness and discuss their relative importance.
18. Evaluate the concept of accident proneness and show to what extent the individual's liability to accidents may be predicted on the basis of psychological tests.
19. Examine the hypothesis of accident proneness. How will you deal with the human factors with a view to reducing accidents?

25

MALADJUSTED INDUSTRIAL WORKER

KINDS OF MALADJUSTMENT

Workers with a nervous temperament are maladjusted because normalcy of personality is an essential condition of proper adjustment. Before turning to the proper adjustment of the maladjusted worker, it is necessary to understand his main problems. The maladjustment of the worker with a nervous temperament is essentially an emotional maladjustment. It can either be mild or serious. Fisher and Hanna[1] have pointed out six main problems in mild maladjustment and twelve main problems in the more serious manifestations of it.

1. Mild emotional maladjustment In this form, as is evident from the name, the emotional maladjustment is mild and its symptoms are jealousy, self-pity, absence of cheerful cooperation, fault finding, strong instincts, conflict with labour, abnormal desire to attract attention, etc. A worker with this problem is jealous of the other workers over very minor issues and at times believes himself to be a victim of other's enmity. He does not cooperate with others cheerfully and is constantly engaged in finding faults of the management and other colleagues. In attaining his own interests, he pays no attention to the propriety or impropriety of means and fights with others to gain all kinds of advantages. He wants to attract the attention of others towards himself for no reason and is not bothered about the propriety of the means he adopts for this purpose.

2. Serious emotional maladjustment. The main symptoms of this are the following:

---

1. Fisher, V.E., and J.V. Hanna, *The Dissatisfied Worker*, New York, p. 280.

(a) Frequent change of jobs,
(b) Extreme reticence and withdrawal,
(c) Tired feelings,
(d) Spasmodic and irregular application,
(e) Daydreaming,
(f) Deficiency in power of attention,
(g) Extreme irritability,
(h) Indigestion,
(i) Fear,
(j) Feelings of being spied upon,
(k) Hearing voices,
(l) Miscellaneous symptoms.

Workers with serious emotional maladjustments are seen changing jobs frequently. They are not very serious about many things in their minds and experience exhaustion after very little work. Their behaviour does not follow a definite pattern. They are not very practical and are inclined to be lost in the world of imagination. They find it difficult to concentrate their attention in any work. Small things irritate them. They also suffer constantly from indigestion. They are unnecessarily afraid of many things and feel that their friends are making complaints about them. Sometimes they also hear voices which do not actually exist. There is little synthesis between their emotions and feelings. They are victims of self-pity on the one hand and jealousy on the other. They do not turn their attention to their own shortcomings, instead they blame others for their own failure. They try to hide reality but despite this they feel inferior to others.

Explanation of the Causes of Maladjustment

In the opinion of Fisher and Hanna, mild and serious emotional maladjustment is caused by three main factors, as follow:

1. Emotional immaturity,
2. Exaggeration or over-expression of one or more drives,
3. Abnormal expression of emotions.

Maladjustment can also have causes other than these three factors. Many important researches have been conducted on this subject. H.M. Adler[1] examined one hundred patients in 1917 and pointed out the following three causes of professional maladjustment:

---

1. H.M. Adler, "Unemployment and Personality: Study of Psychopathic Causes", *Mental Hygiene*, 1 (1917), pp. 16-24.

1. Paranoid personalities,
1. Inadequate personalities,
2. Emotional instability.

Maladjustment is a common feature in industry. In addition to its adverse effects on the quality of production, it also injures the social environment. According to E. Toulouse, industries have to suffer much damage because of emotional maladjustment. V.E. Fisher and J.V. Hanna[1] have pointed out that in an industry employing five hundred individuals, half the expense lay in selecting and training new employees. Maladjustment is found to be a widespread phenomenon. In one study conducted by M.C. Jarrett[2] half the number of workers suffered from emotional maladjustment but this fact seems to be untrue. The studies of H.W. Stevens[3] appear to be more correct on this subject. Stevens studied four thousand workers working in a store over a period of six months and found that 10 per cent of them had problems of emotional maladjustment. V.V. Anderson[4] examined the twelve hundred employees of the R.H. Massey Company and concluded that 19 per cent of the sales workers and 23 per cent of the other workers suffered from emotional maladjustment. He made a list of the best and worst of the first kind of workers and after testing them demonstrated that 22 per cent of the best had personality defects while 54 per cent of the worst suffered from elementary forms of personality maladjustment while 24 per cent of the worst had acute defects of the personality. In a study of 41 maladjusted wire workers, M. Smith, M. Culpin and E. Farmer found that 31 of them had symptoms of mental diseases like anxiety, manic depression, etc. twenty-six workers suffered from neural defects.

Tests of Maladjustment

While the reports furnished by the authorities are useful, many scientific methods are used to test maladjustment. The more extensively used methods are ergograph test, McDougall-Schuster Dotting Test, Graphic Pursuit Meter, Pressure Test, Medical Examination, finding out the emotional nature and development of the worker by examining his external behaviour, etc. All these methods should be used to discover the maladjusted worker in industry.

---

1. V.F. Fisher and J.V. Hanna, *op. cit.*, pp. 233-34.
2. M.C. Jarrett, "The Mental Hygine in Industry," *Mental Hygiene*, pp. 867-84
3. H.W. Stevens, *The Psychic Aspect of Industrial Disability*, Bulletin: Massachusetts Department of Mental Diseases, pp. 6-7.
4. V.V. Anderson, "The Problem Employee".

CAUSES OF MALADJUSTMENT

Before trying to find out the ways of removing maladjustment, it is necessary to discover the causes. Briefly, the main causes are:

1. Bad health Physical health is directly concerned with mental health, as a result of which the adjustment begins to deteriorate if a person falls ill. As has been pointed out earlier, most of the maladjusted workers suffer from indigestion. Bad health makes a person irritable and he takes offence at the smallest things. Decrease in physical energy has an adverse effect on skill which, in turn, saps him of his self-confidence. All this leads to emotional maladjustment.

2. Marital disorganisation The worker's maladjustment is intimately related with his marital condition. If his marital adjustment is upset then he finds it difficult to be balanced in his behaviour even in the factory. That is why in modern times stress is laid on making his home life happy.

3. Bad condition at home If the worker's domestic condition is not good due to economic imbalance or any other cause, he suffers from anxiety, which is never good for emotional health.

4. Bad conditions of work Broadly speaking, all the working conditions have some or the other effect on the worker's mental health but this, is most susceptible to the effect of the social environment. And in this the foreman's and the manager's behaviour is a very important element. If the social atmosphere of the factory is one of sympathy and cooperation, the worker can maintain a proper mental balance. If it is not of this kind, he immediately succumbs to maladjustment.

5. Wrong methods of work There are many methods of working which tend to increase fatigue, boredom and monotony. They also do not satisfy the worker's desire to complete his work or to learn the results of his work. Besides, he himself feels that he is of no consequence in that particular job and he reduces himself to a cog in the machine. In this way, working conditions of this kind encourage maladjustment.

6. Painful experience of leaving other jobs If a worker has the experience of giving up jobs at a number of places, then this painful experience spoils his mental balance and he cannot adjust himself.

1. Low income Poverty is at the root of all kinds of maladjustment because a poor man finds it difficult to retain balance of mind. Because of low income, the worker continuously lives in a state of anxiety. His needs are not satisfied and hence his emotional adjustment is destroyed.

2. Old age Viteles believes that in addition to the above-mentioned seven causes of maladjustment, old age is another cause. According to

E.D. Smith, in old age an individual cannot change himself according to the conditions of work and for this reason, his power of adjustment is reduced. In the opinion of E.L. Thorndike,[1] the worker's ability to learn is reduced in old age and he cannot adopt the new and more efficient ways of doing work. H.L. Hollingworth[2] opines that, maladjustment in old age is caused not by the inability to learn but by the inability to put the learnt techniques to proper use. Many psychological investigations have indicated that people suffer in old age because they cannot adopt the modern ways of doing things. Their physical vitality is reduced and the desire to learn new things also declines. According to Viteles,[3] in old age the individual cannot adjust with his old fixed habits, ideas and mental attitudes. His balance is disturbed also because his physical and mental vitality is run down. He tends to ramble in his conversation and criticises others for no good reason. Loss of skill also induces loss of self-confidence. Smith points out that in old age, the worker cannot employ the skills and methods he has learnt because more modern methods have come into use by that time, which he is unable to acquire. Hence his adjustment is upset.

READJUSTMENT OF THE MALADJUSTED WORKER

It should not be assumed from the above description of the causes of maladjustment that it cannot be corrected. Not only in the case of maladjustment due to many causes, even maladjustment caused by old age can be remedied. L.J. Martin[4] made use of special experiments to establish proper adjustment in the case of a man of 61 years of age. This worker was the oldest employee of the company and was receiving the highest wages. His production had declined by 39 per cent over a period of five years. On investigation it was found that he was alone at home and he had to cook his own food. When his domestic condition was changed, it was found that his production increased by 10 per cent in the first month, 22 per cent in the second month, fourteen per cent in the third, 19 per cent in the fourth month and by 21 per cent in the fifth month. It is evident from this that adjustment can again be established if some of the causes of maladjustment are removed to some extent. The following measures can be adopted for this purpose:

1. Improvement of health If maladjustment is to be removed, the mental and physical health of the worker should be improved. If necessary,

1. E.L Thorndike, *Adult Learning*, New York (1928), p. 335.
2. H.L. Hollingworth, *Mental Growth and Decline*, New York (1927), p. 396.
3. M.S. Viteles, *Industrial Psychology*, London (1962), p. 602.
4. L.J. Martin and C. de Grochy, *Salvaging Old Age*, New York (1930), p. 173.

arrangements should be made for his medical treatment. If his economic condition is not satisfactory, it should be changed. He should be given proper and nourishing food at the correct time and allowed to rest as long as necessary.

2. Marital adjustment In modern nations personal guidance is offered to the workers to improve their marital adjustment because this helps to improve their general adjustment.

3. Family adjustment Nowadays it is believed that attention should be paid to the family requirements of the worker. If he has a large number of children, the government should provide facilities for free education and medical otherwise long as adjustment cannot be expected.

4. Improvement in the working conditions In every industry, effort should be made to study the working conditions and to improve them wherever necessary. In addition to the working hours, lighting, clean air, water, correct temperature, etc., the industry must provide security of employment, proper wages, security of future, a desirable social climate, sympathetic and cooperative attitude towards the worker, etc. The worker's adjustment is improved if the level of morale is kept high in the industry.

5. Improvements in working methods Sometimes the wrong method of working can lead to maladjustment. This can be certified by corrected examination and improvement of the working methods.

6. Individual care and treatment Many workers suffer from maladjustment which is caused by some individual factors. In such cases each worker should be examined separately and efforts should be made to solve his problems. He may benefit by personal guidance. Some people carry with them bitter experience of past jobs which they have had to give up. Old age is also an individual state. Some people suffer from some physical or mental illness. The problems of some workers have their source in their marital or general family life. If all these problems are to be solved then each worker must be guided individually and helped in his efforts at adjustment. According to E.D. Smith[1], one cause of the worker's maladjustment is that he may be forced to do something he does not wish to do. For this reason the doctors and the organisers should make a study of these workers.

7. Committee for mental hygiene E.E. Southard[2] has suggested the establishment of a committee for mental hygiene to eliminate

---

1. Smith, E.D., "*What are the Psychological Factors of Obsolecence of Worker in Middle Age?*" Assoc. Personnel Series. No. 919, 10, p. 3.
2. Southard, E.E. The Modern Specialist in Unrest.

maladjustment in the worker. This committee should include psychologists, doctors for mental disorders and social reformers in addition to the company organisers. According to H.L. Stevens,[1] the psychiatrist should study each worker and cure symptoms of mental disease if he finds any.

It is evident from the above description of the means of curing maladjustment that in the first place, the individual should be carefully examined so that the causes of his maladjustment can be located. For this it is necessary to win his confidence. Once the causes have been discovered, they can be cured by the cooperation of the organisers, psychologists, the psychiatrists and most of all, the worker himself. It is improper to neglect this problem of maladjustment because this disturbs the adjustment of other people also and creates a social climate directly injurious to work and production. Many serious industrial difficulties are caused by maladjustment nowadays. Hence, if arrangements are made to analyse and cure this problem, the industrialists stand to benefit quite as much as the worker himself.

QUESTIONS FOR EXERCISE

1. Who is a Maladjusted Industrial Worker?
2. What can be the possible problems created by the worker with a nervous temperament? How far is it possible for a psychologist to solve these problems?

---

1. Stevens, H.L. *Psychiatry in Industry,* Monthly Bulletin of the Massachusetts Society for Mental Hygiene, Vol. 6.

26

INDUSTRIAL TRAINING

ADVANTAGES OF INDUSTRIAL TRAINING

It is a matter of common experience that the trained worker takes less time to produce more goods of a better quality than the untrained worker. Where the operation of certain kinds of machinery requires trained personnel, it becomes impossible to do anything without any training. Even in the case of machines which are not so complex, training definitely helps to improve the skill of the worker operating it.

The advantages of training in industry can be briefly summarised as under :

1. **Increase in production** The studies of R.J. Greenly'[1] show that while no progress was seen over a period of six years in the work of changing knives on one machine, a reduction of one-third was noticed after training was imparted. As a result, it became possible to save twenty thousand eight hundred and eighty dollars within one year. C.H. Lawshe[2] conducted a survey of one training programme. Here it was seen that as compared to the untrained employees, the trained employees showed the positive results of their training within eight weeks.

2. **Prevention of breakages** Industrial training leads not only to an increase in production but also to considerable savings in breakages and wastage in other forms. It was discovered by L.G. Lindhahl[3] that a definite reduction in breakages was seen after training had been imparted for twelve weeks. When the quantity of breakages falls, the machines can

---

1. Greenly, R.J. *Job Training, Nat. Assn. Manuf,* Labour Relation Bill.
2. Lawshe, C.H. "Eight ways to check value of a training program".
3. Lindhahl, L.G. "Movement Analysis as an Industrial Training Method".

work for a longer time and raw material can be saved. In this way, training results in very comprehensive advantages and benefits to the company.

1. Prevention of accidents Another advantage of industrial training is that it leads to a prevention of accidents. Although it has not been possible to collect accurate data on this subject through research, it can still be asserted that the trained employees as a rule are less prone to accidents than the untrained workers.

2. Reduction in absenteeism Apart from the more direct advantages of industrial training as outlined above, it also helps to reduce absenteeism. Training makes it easy for the individual to perform even fairly difficult tasks, and because he can produce goods faster and better he wins esteem and sometimes even concrete rewards. This helps to encourage him so that he is less inclined to absent himself. In this manner, training increases morale and job satisfaction in industries.

It is obvious from this brief description of the advantages of industrial training that it promotes the interests of the industrialist. Although no definite conclusions have been arrived at in this sphere despite extensive research, nobody can or does deny that industrial training is really beneficial. In fact, some people believe so implicitly in the advantages of training that they do not think it necessary to investigate it. For example, although teachers have been teaching in colleges for centuries, nobody has ever seen reason to ask whether this teaching has any advantages at all. Neither has it been found necessary to prove the utility of teaching through research. Hence, the importance of training is self-evident.

The Criterion of the Correct Training Method

Having established the importance of training in industry, the next thing to be decided is the method and the time of the actual training imparted to a particular worker in some specific industry. The extent and the method of training vary with the individual differences of the workers and the nature of their functions in a specific industry. The advantages and disadvantages of the various training methods such as the lecture method, or teaching by the use of charts, pictures, sketches and motion pictures, or classroom teaching, etc. have been explained. But before deciding upon a particular training method, it is necessary to determine the objective of that training programme because one method which is good for achieving one objective may prove useless if applied in a training programme with a different objective. While the use of cinema slides, pictures or charts may prove valuable in one particular sphere, it may be better to make use of the discussion or lecture or classroom teaching methods in another sphere. No particular method can be said to be the best for every kind of training programme. So one criterion of the correct training method is the objective to be achieved. Another criterion is the extent of training actually imparted by it, meaning the extent to which the worker has learnt. Some people believe that the importance of training should be evaluated in terms of what has been taught, not by what has been learnt. But this attitude is hardly correct, because the best measure of a training method is the extent of learning absorbed by the trainee. If the trainee has learnt very little, the method cannot be called good, irrespective of the quantity of information which should have been communicated by that particular method. One additional quality of the training method should be that it should teach a trainee only those things which he can easily apply to the job he has to perform. If this cannot be done, he will not benefit very much by the training.

Any training programme will be a failure if the method employed in it does not possess the qualities outlined above. But the failure of the training programme may be caused by many factors such as the wastage of the training time, the futility of the training method used, difference of opinion about the working method between the organiser and the teachers, inaccurate method of testing the training achieved, etc. Sometimes a training programme fails simply because the training is suspended a little earlier than it should have been stopped.

AREAS OF LEARNING IN AN INDUSTRY

Generally, industrial jobs are divided into the skilled and the unskilled. Skilled work is that which normally requires knowledge of some kind and this knowledge is gained through training. Unskilled work, on the other hand, does not require the acquisition of any special skill. So, it is believed that skilled work requires both knowledge and craftmanship, the ability to use one's hands to the best advantage. For example, mere knowledge of the particular trade is not enough to make a man a skilled carpenter, mason or electrician, because he must also possess the ability to efficiently perform the tasks of his trade. No worker can be called skilled unless he possesses this craftmanship. Knowledge of the trade is one thing and craftmanship another. It is for this reason that certain skilled craftsmen produce work which an educated worker can never do, despite all his knowledge. What is this skill? It is a training in the performance of specific movements made in some particular work. Different parts of the body have to make different and specific movements in the performance of different functions. If one can correctly perform the functions required for some particular job, and can also show evidence of coordination of movements, then one is called skilled at that particular work. Hence one objective of industrial training is to impart knowledge about the particular job while the other objective is to create skill in the particular movements required for that job. Industrial training thus requires the following kinds of training:

1. Association In different industries, efficient work requires that there should be association between the various actions which are performed one after the other. If there is association then they can be performed spontaneously and in the correct order. This association works in the memory and also functions as conditioned response.

2. Selection in learning In the actual work situation, it is necessary to pay more attention to certain things than to any other. This involves two kinds of selection — sensory and motor. In sensory selection, the individual must learn to distinguish between different sensations and to recognise the correct ones. For example, among all the other kinds of lights that the car driver sees, he must learn to distinguish the red and the green lights and also to understand the meaning implicit in these two signals. Different motor activities are required in different industrial conditions, and these activities should be performed with economy, while aiming at maximum output. This leads to a reduction in fatigue on one hand and an increase in the total time saved on the other. Time and motion studies can be undertaken in different industries to discover the facts concerning each industry.

3. Sensory discrimination It is necessary for the worker to learn to distinguish between different sensations, as a part of industrial training. Sometimes the worker becomes involved in an accident simply because he cannot discriminate between different sensations. The skilful individual can distinguish between subtle variations in the same thing or between various objects. Some people can recognise the car models at a glance, and therefore it is impossible to deceive them in this respect.

4. Acquisition of skill Workers who work in factories where they have to use their hands in different kinds of work must acquire craftsmanship. What is this manual skill? It is the result of training the muscles of the hand. If he has this kind of training, the worker can tell merely by feeling a thing with his hand how far the work has progressed and whether it is progressing satisfactorily. He needs no more than a glance to distinguish between good and bad work. He continues to do his work only by touching things with hand. The movements of the muscles cannot be measured. Hence, skill of this kind is a matter of practice only. The more skilful tennis players know exactly how much strength to use to throw the ball to a particular spot in the tennis court or how far to bend in order to retrieve a particular ball. All these facts are concerned with the player's skill.

5. Understanding and insight in work Another aspect of industrial training is to instil understanding and insight into work. In the absence of this, simple kinds of functions can be performed but more complex problems cannot be solved. For example, only that engineer can be called skilful who can discover the fault in a machine at a glance and also be able to point out how and why that defect has occurred. The basis of the engineer's skill is his knowledge of the machine's construction and his understanding and insight into technological principles. Hence it is desirable that training should not lead to parrot-like repetition and rote learning but instead to insight into the particular job. If this is done then the workers themselves can evolve the most effective methods of performing their jobs. Although insight and understanding depend, to a large extent, upon the intelligence of the worker, they can be improved to a certain extent by training.

6. Change of attitude As has been indicated earlier, industrial training helps to improve the morale of the worker. A trained worker can easily perform a function which the unskilled worker finds a great burden. Training thus helps to change the worker's attitude to his work because after training he has a more positive attitude to this work.

Nowadays, various methods are used to impart training in the field of industry — lecture method, propaganda through books and pamphlets, the use of audio-visual aids and the exhibition of films, on-the-job training, discussion method, role playing, etc. Now a brief explanation and evaluation of each training method will be given here:

1. The lecture method As is evident from the name itself, in this method, the more learned individuals inform the trainees about their jobs by delivering lectures. Thus it becomes possible to acquaint the trainees with various aspects of the work in a short time. These lectures can be made more objective and concrete by the use of charts and tables. In many industries, lectures by eminent authorities on various subjects are frequently arranged. The lecture method is of eminent value in subjects like industrial organisation but it has the following shortcomings:

(a) ***Inappropriate method*****:** The lecture method is not apt for changing the attitudes of the workers, for establishing simple association, for increasing skills, etc.

(b) *Boring method:* Generally lectures on industrial and technological subjects are not entertaining with the result that the audience cannot concentrate on a lecture for more than 45 minutes at a stretch. And since it is boring, only the discriminating and intelligent listener can benefit by it.

In spite of its above-mentioned shortcomings, many organisations make use of the lecture method for some specific kinds of work. On special occasions, the new employees of the company are acquainted with its policies and its traditions through lectures, so that they know the company. The effectiveness of a lecture can be improved by making it more powerful, which can be done by using forceful words and frequent and violent gestures. It is a common psychological fact that something heard is remembered more than something read. Hence, the importance of the lecture method is obvious.

2. Books and pamphlets Very often books and pamphlets are distributed during exhibition so as to promote know-how about some particular industry. By reading this, people can know where the industry is located and how it is functioning. This method can also be used for spreading information among the workers.

But it is not possible to calculate the effectiveness of this propaganda by counting the number of books and pamphlets distributed or by recording the number of people who receive them. Majority of people accept them because they are attractive and also free. Some people do open the pamphlets but they go no further than glancing at the colourful pictures or bold slogans. Only a very few people take the trouble of actually reading the pamphlet in detail. It has been seen that most of the workers pay no attention to the books and pamphlets distributed to them.

Despite all these shortcomings, this method has certain advantages over others. Once a lecture has been delivered, it cannot be repeated, with the result that if a listener has forgotten something, he has no way of getting that piece of information again. This shortcoming is overcome by the pamphlet since it can be read any number of times and at any time. People can be encouraged to read the pamphlet by making it more attractive by the use of colours. Besides, the very fact that the company gets such pamphlets printed and distributed is proof of the fact that it wants to train its employees. This, in itself, is a fact which has its own significance.

3. Motion pictures Although the exhibition of motion pictures is more expensive than lectures or pamphlets, it has many advantages and for that reason this method is extensively used. While many organisations take the trouble of producing their own films, many companies buy them from the producers. The most important quality of the motion picture is that it can be shown repeatedly and, to a very large audience, simultaneously. Besides, most audiences generally tend to pay attention to what is going on the screen. Motion pictures are the best medium of training and instruction. They can be used to show the various machines and tools employed in a particular industry, and it is also possible to realistically show their actual usage. Motion pictures of this kind are no less effective than a guided tour of a real factory. In fact, they are more useful because they can be seen repeatedly, while it may be difficult to arrange a guided tour more than once. It hardly needs to be pointed out that this method is a fine amalgam of the lecture method and the exhibition method.

In spite of this, there should be no misunderstanding about the value of this method because it also leaves untouched certain aspects of training. While it is possible to show human relations through this medium and also to appeal to the emotions of the viewers, it is impossible to improve skill through it. A worker does not become more skilful merely by viewing a motion picture. The most that can be said is that the motion picture method is an unavoidable part of any training programme.

4. Demonstration and audio-visual aids It is cheaper to collect audio-visual aids than to produce motion picture for training. But it has the same benefits as the motion picture. It helps most obviously in visual training, but it can be most effective if the material used is adapted to the intelligence level of the audience. Hence, the use of such aids is considered a necessary part of industrial training nowadays.

5. On-the-job training The major difficulty in most training methods is that tacts learnt and acquired in artificial circumstances cannot be easily transferred and put into practice in the actual conditions of work. For this reason, on-the-job training is introduced, and it can be imparted easily in all work which is not done at very high speed. In some factories, new employees are trained on the actual machines after normal working hours. In other cases, the employees are trained on simpler machines which gives them practice but minimise the chances of accidents. For example, the telephone operator can be trained in his work by this method. In factories, the functions of the supervisor can be taught by role playing in certain conditions. The major quality of this method is that training is done through actual work. Besides, in this each trainee is trained individually so that he gets a chance to practise and his shortcomings and difficulties are separately attended to. Naturally, this method is more expensive and it is used only in those kinds of work where it is necessary to pay attention to each worker.

6. The case method In this method of industrial training, the managers are employed to give training. In this, the trainees are asked to solve some concrete problem and are required to discuss the means by which it can be solved after understanding the factors involved in the situation. It has the advantages of a group discussion in addition to the practice gained in solving actual problems. But it does not help very much in increasing skill. It only inspires the individual to increase his knowledge of human relations.

7. Discussion method This is another method employed in industrial training and in this many workers get together to discuss some specific problem. Some experts are also present during the discussion. This exchange of ideas improves the worker's understanding and provides practice in problem-solving. This method is of particular use in those subjects where the problem has become complex because of emotions and negative attitudes.

8. Role playing In industrial conditions many workers have to play many kinds of roles. In this method they are given the opportunity of playing a role by which they can improve their ability to perform the task pertaining to that role.

Industrial training makes use of all those principles of learning which are used in training of any other kind. Modern psychologists have found out many means of economizing in the process of learning. These methods of economy are used extensively in industrial training.

FACTORS ASSISTING ASSOCIATION

Formation of many kinds of association is an important aspect of industrial training. Association is helped by the following factors:

1. **Frequent repetition** One common method of making some association firm is the frequent repetition of the subject learnt. This method is particularly useful in the learning acquired through memory. The association between various parts of the subject matter will become more sound as the subject matter is repeated more and more often. Even when something has been learnt by trial and error, repetition can be of some use. This assistance is rendered in two ways — in the first place frequent repetition provides more opportunities of selection while it also helps in forming some association and making it permanent. Works of skill can

be also improved through repetition because the association between the various movements becomes more sound. Repetition also saves time in learning. Nowadays the method of repetition is used in advertisement, propaganda, etc. Advertisements are repeated so frequently that the people who see it remember the subject matter of the advertisement and as soon as the need arises, it is easily remembered. For example, the name Aspro is repeated so often in connection with removing headaches that a person thinks of it automatically as soon as he gets a headache. Hence, repetition is an important method in industrial propaganda. In fact, repetition is sometimes used to propagate some object which is not commonly used.

2. Presence of attention and intention Attention and intention play an important part in learning. If a person is doing something with the intention of learning it, he will inevitably pay more attention to it. Hence, in industrial training, it is of primary importance to generate intention in the trainee. If this is done, he automatically attends to what is being taught to him. And a subject can be easily mastered if one pays attention. In this manner, attention and intention assist each other. In the field of industry, the psychology of attracting attention is used extensively in all kinds of advertisement. If one wants to turn the trainee's periodicity, etc., his motivation should be such that he should be compelled to attend to the training.

3. Spaced repetition It is always better to repeat some object after some interval than to repeat it continuously because if the repetition is continuous, the listener may become exhausted. In this connection, Woodworth has pointed out that interval between repetitions should be of one or two days' duration. In this way, there should be an opportunity to repeat the subject after intervals. The method of spaced repetition is better in all complex subjects because they lead to boredom and inattention if teaching is continued for a long period. This does not imply that continuous repetition is bad in all cases, because in fact sometimes the method of unspaced repetition is better than spaced repetition. For example, the interval should not be introduced so quickly that the individual cannot even warm up to his work. If this is done, then the individual will only be hindered in his learning. On the other hand, the interval should also not be so long that the individual may actually forget all that he has learnt.

Despite the above advantages, these principles are not followed in actual industrial circumstances. For example, an individual who works would not like to be made to work only for one or two hours each day.

Therefore, many other methods are followed. For example, students are imparted training during their period of study itself so that as soon as they have completed their studies, they can quickly acquire the necessary skill. This method is used very much in training bank employees. Another method provides opportunity for training the worker in all aspects of the job, one after the other. In another method, training for some complex function is given while the individual is normally performing a simpler function.

4. Benefits of whole method Generally the whole method proves more useful in teaching than the part method. In the part method of teaching, the entire subject matter is divided into small units, and each unit is taught in a single sitting. On the other hand, in the whole method, the entire subject is learnt at once, the advantages being that some association between the various parts of the subject is created and this assists the trainee in learning the subject. While teaching the use of some machine, it is better to make use of both these methods. In the beginning, the trainee should be told about the operation of the entire machine that followed up by a detailed account of the function of each part he understands it. Hence, industrial training makes use of both the whole and the part methods of teaching. The subject is introduced by the whole method and detailed training is then given through the part method.

5. Active repetition Many experiments have proved that the method of active repetition is more effective than the inactive method. The inactive method implies a condition in which the learner does not pay full attention to what is being taught while in the active method he participates in the teaching with his whole mind. If this is done he derives all the benefits of attention and also intention of learning. Hence, in industrial training, it is desirable to employ a method in which the trainee can take an active part. Otherwise the training will not be really beneficial.

ECONOMIC METHODS OF SELECTION IN LEARNING

In certain types of industrial training, it becomes necessary to pay the greatest attention to some particular aspects. If this is not done, then learning becomes more difficult. Many methods are nowadays employed to help in this kind of selection, for example, reward for proper reaction and punishment for incorrect reaction, positive selection and negative selection, etc. Norman Meyer has suggested that attention be paid to the following things in learning:

1. Use of positive selection Normally, positive selection should be preferred to negative selection. The trainee should be trained both in training and in administration. When there is provision for reward and punishment, the trainee learns to discard one thing and select the other. It is better for the trainee to learn what he has to do rather than what he must avoid doing. That is why the positive method is more beneficial and economic than the negative method. Sometimes mistakes and faults can be rectified if they are repeated consciously and deliberately. Positive selection proves more valuable in removing such defects.

2. Knowledge of results Many experiments have established that if the trainee is aware of the results of his work, he learns better than otherwise. If he is unaware of results he shows no progress in learning because he does not know his good points or the mistakes that he may have made. Hence it is better that the trainee should be informed of his progress.

3. Clarification of cause-effect relationships During training the trainee must be made to understand what happens if something is done. For example, if a trainee is being told about the operation of a particular machine, he must be clearly told of the results of his actions in operating a particular part of the machine. This will help the trainee to understand how far he can use a particular machine to get the desired results.

4. Personal training As a result of individual differences, the same tasks present varying degrees of difficulties to different individuals and they commit all kind of mistakes. Hence, during training, provision should be made for individual guidance and rectification of mistakes.

Discrimination Between Sensations

In industrial work, there are certain functions in which it is necessary to distinguish between various sensations. In training for this kind of work, it is necessary to remember that different individuals have varying powers of distinguishing sensations. Hence, before beginning training of individuals for work of this kind, it is necessary to determine whether the trainees have the requisite ability to distinguish between sensations or not. If they do not have the ability, all the training will probably be wasted. This fact is of extreme importance in the selection of inspectors for various functions.

In the second place, the methods used for teaching how to distinguish between sensations should be favourable to the specific sensory capacity or ability. In every kind of work, one or the other specific sensory ability is required. If vision is the most important factor then it is better to use machines which help vision. Similarly, if the auditory powers are most important then only those instruments should be used which help the power of hearing.

Factors Favourable to the Acquisition of Skills

Most kinds of industrial training concentrate upon giving some special skill to the workers. Psychologists have discovered many methods which help in the acquisition of skills and if these methods are used it becomes much easier to impart these skills. The most important factor in acquiring a skill is the training of muscles because expert craftsmanship requires coordination between the speed of working and sensations. And this is a matter of practice. Only the training of muscles can determine how hard a particular instrument should be pressed. This cannot be learnt only by imitation. The trainee should not only know what the work looks like during the process of doing but he should also experience how it feels. For this it is necessary that he be given the opportunity to do the work himself. Briefly stated, the following things help in the acquisition of skill:

1. Acting through doing The method of acting through doing is the most important in learning skill. Hence the trainee must get an opportunity to do it himself. Less time should be devoted to demonstration. He must also be warned about the dangers of the instrument he is using.

2. Selection of movements Skill means a proper reaction to a specific stimulus. For this reason, the teacher must tell the trainee about the correct movement out of all the movements that he sees or makes. He must also make sure that the student is making the correct movements.

3. Control on guidance In industrial training, many people lay too much stress on the factor of guidance while in fact beyond a certain limit, guidance becomes more a hindrance than a help. It is true that in the beginning, the teacher may hold the trainee's hand to guide him but the sensations he then experiences will not be the same as when he is performing the function without assistance. Consequently, if the trainee is guided too much, he gets into the habit of working only when assisted. Then he cannot acquire the necessary skill, and for this reason, guidance should not be continued beyond a reasonable time.

4. Emphasis on feeling of correct movement The true mark of the skilled craftsman is that he can touch a piece of work and point out if it is correct or wrong. The reason of this is that he has knowledge of the correct movement. Once the trainee develops this feeling of correct movement he will find no difficulty.

5. Control of perception Control of perception plays an important part in the acquisition of skill. If one wants to make use of the telephone directory, it is necessary, first of all, to learn how a name should be seen in order to be recognised. Whether the brush used for painting is a part of the hand or a tool held in the hand, are two different perceptions, and they influence the skill in painting. This fact is also true of other works of manual skill. Accurate perception is necessary for acquiring skill in the different arts. This principle is of particular importance in the teaching of music. A.R. Solem has demonstrated by an experiment that a foreman proved a successful administrator when during a discussion he treated the others not as his subordinates but his equals and his colleagues. In the field of industry, the leaders who treat others as their equals appear to be more kind and cooperative. If the speed in reading is to be improved, it is necessary that the reader must see many words as part of a single group or unit. It is for this reason that it is said that some people read letters, others read words, some read sentences while some read pages.

6. Proper movement in work Knowing the proper movements required for any work of skill is also important. In teaching these, attention should be paid to individual differences. Different individuals will perform the same work at different speeds. Hence the speed of work should be increased according to the individual qualities of the worker.

7. Control on tension The skilled craftsman has one peculiarity in as much as he makes use of only those muscles which are necessary for his work. The other muscles are free from tension. An unskilled worker makes many unnecessary movements because he becomes confused and tries many ways of doing it. Consequently, he gets tired rapidly. In training an individual, it should be stressed that he should not get unnecessarily excited. He should also be taught to use only those muscles which are required for performing some specific action and to let the other muscles relax.

8. Provision of incentives for progress The trainee must be given some incentive for progress if he is to acquire some skill, so that he may be motivated to learn. Roughly speaking, incentives can be financial or non-financial. Financial incentives can take almost innumerable forms such as bonus or additional salary. Non-financial incentives can take the form of improvement in working conditions, praise, social respect, etc. If a study is made of any work curve for any industry, it will be seen that a plateau is reached at one stage or the other if incentives are absent. This plateau can be eliminated by providing incentives, and thus creating motivation.

9. Attention on movements The trainee must pay attention to his movements if he wants to acquire skill. Wrong movements must be eliminated and the right movements established. It is better to draw attention to the right movements and to stress their repetition rather than to point out the wrong movements because if attention is paid to wrong movements they become habits. In work which is done at speed, attention should be paid to rhythm because once the rhythm is established, the work can be performed without hesitation. In this type of work, the various parts of the work must be tied into a single whole because it is not possible to alter attention and focus it on different aspects at a very high speed. In the same way, the movements of muscles are not to be viewed as separate movements but as part of a single movement. The trainee should also concentrate upon the results of his work because in most kinds of work, the movements are made with a view to attaining a particular objective. In all such work, only the correct result is the criterion of good work. Briefly, it is better to learn works of skill as a whole rather than in parts so that all the various functions are seen as part of the whole operation. Here it is necessary that the entire operation should be so divided into units that maximum production should be possible while each unit should also be complete in itself.

Learning through Understanding

There are some functions in industrial work where insight into the work and understanding are more important than manual skill. In these kinds of functions, the following principles are employed for economy:

1. Organisation of material around principles In industries, the worker is faced with many new kinds of work every day. If he is to do all this properly, he must not get lost in the variety of the material. He must have clear understanding of the fundamental principles which govern the material involved in that work. For example, the principles of mathematics help immensely in maintaining accounts. Similarly, the principles of distribution and selling play an important role in all sales work. Hence, whenever the salesman is faced with a new customer, he must keep in mind the principles of selling.

2. Encouragement to discussion Proper training can be imparted only if the trainees are given the freedom to express their opinion and to enter into discussion. Discussion among themselves and the teacher helps to create insight into job and problems can then be solved. Undoubtedly, this is a time consuming process but it helps to focus attention, because it is one method of positive teaching. The intelligent trainer should make use of the correct mode of discussion so that the trainees may develop some insight into their job.

3. Tests of progress If training is to achieve its objectives, it is necessary that the progress of the trainees should be tested from time to time by correct testing procedures. By doing this, the teacher can establish how far the student has progressed. If he is found to be lagging behind others, then the causes of this retarded progress can be discovered and efforts made to eliminate them.

4. Encouragement to use own words If the students are to be given an opportunity to develop insight into their work it is necessary that they be allowed to express the problem in their own words. By doing this they can understand the problem and this helps to improve insight.

METHODS ASSISTING THE TRAINING OF APTITUDES

Sometimes in the course of an industrial training programme, it becomes necessary to pay attention to the trainees' aptitudes because the right aptitude is essential for proper performance of any job. The following means can be employed for this work :

1. Opportunity for discussion Discussion not only allows a trainee to express his own feelings and attitudes but also provides him with an opportunity of knowing the feelings and attitudes of others. In a group discussion, an individual adopts the attitudes of the group because of social pressure. Hence if the teacher himself takes part in the discussion and guides it correctly then the trainees can develop the correct attitude for the work.

2. Opportunity for expression of frustration Some trainees cannot develop the correct attitude at times because of their frustration. In such cases it is best to use methods by which these frustrations can be vented and expressed harmlessly. Unless the condition of frustration is cured, the wrong aptitude cannot be eliminated.

3. Method of role playing One important way of creating correct aptitude is to give the trainee an aptitude to play different roles in different situations. In playing such roles, the trainee gains experience of the problems, aptitudes and feelings implicit in different kinds of work so that he is helped in his understanding of the people who perform this work. For example, if the manager is permitted to work at different posts as foreman, typist, etc., for short times, he will have little difficulty in understanding their problems, aptitudes and viewpoints. Consequently, he will be able to manage the affairs of his organisation much more successfully.

4. Association with pleasant experience It is a commonly accepted psychological principle that people form positive aptitudes for pleasant experiences and negative aptitudes for painful experience. Hence, the worker should have pleasant experience of the work for which he is to form a positive aptitude. If the conditions of work are such that he experiences pain in performing it, then he will develop a negative aptitude for it. This fact must be well understood by supervisors. If their behaviour towards the employees is kind and pleasant and if the general atmosphere in the factory is one of cooperation and friendship, the workers easily generate a positive aptitude for their work.

27

MOTIVATION, INCENTIVES AND METHODS OF PAYMENT

WHAT IS MOTIVATION?

According to Woodworth, "A motive is a state or set of individuals which disposes him for certain behaviour and for seeking certain goal." In this way one finds goal-oriented behaviour in motivation. The aim of this behaviour is to achieve certain specific goals. By analysing motivation, one can find out why man works. No individual can achieve something solely due to motivation when it is beyond his capacity to achieve it. Hence, the power to do something due to motivation is limited by ability or capacity. Motivation is the method of giving expression to an individual's abilities. The condition of motivation has two aspects — the subjective and the objective. In the subjective aspect, this contains that condition of the individual which is called need, desire or drive. And the objective aspect is the incentive or the goal due to which the individual acts. A situation in which the incentive is one for which some need is experienced, is a motivating situation. For example, an individual gets some salary if he works in some industry. Now, if the money received as salary is a means by which an individual can fulfil his desires then he will work in order to get the salary. Obviously, then motivation changes when the incentive and the need both change. Hence, in order to create motivation in activity, it is desirable that the incentive should be concerned with some or the other need of the worker. If, for example, an individual does not need money, then the incentive of money will not form sufficient motivation by which he will be impelled to work. In such a case, non-financial incentives like social prestige, proper utilization of one's time, etc., may form sufficient motives to induce a man to work.

Motivation in Industry

It is apparent from the above description that both an understanding of human wants and a knowledge of industrial incentives are necessary for understanding the importance of motivation in industry. Broadly, human wants are of two kinds — natural or internal, and acquired. The inner needs include hunger, thirst, maternal instinct, sex needs, sleep, etc. The category of acquired needs includes love, sympathy, social prestige and innumerable others which are products of modern culture. Acquired needs change according to past experience and the individual's own qualities. The most important among them are social needs. And one of the major social needs is the desire to maintain one's respect in society and the desire to be a kingpin among other men. In addition to this, human beings have the need to get something with which they can identify themselves and get satisfaction.

Motivation and the Level of Ambition

Different individuals have their own level of ambition and if these are not achieved, the individuals feel frustrated. People who have a high level of ambition make very great efforts to achieve it. In one of the studies conducted by Coch and French, a production level of 60 units was assumed to be the average. The result was that those who were producing less than this, between 55 and 59 units, immediately increased their production and achieved the average, but those who could not achieve it left their jobs. When the level of ambition is low, the individual does not make any effort to exploit his own capabilities to the fullest extent. On the other hand, a person with a high level of ambition often tries to achieve much that is beyond his capabilities.

Motivation and External Circumstances

External circumstances influence the motivation of an individual only when they have some effect on his internal motivation. This internal motivation has its well spring in the individual's egoistic needs. If a person feels respected in his job, he will be motivated to do well in it. If, on the other hand, he feels neglected, he will not be motivated in work. For this reason, group motivation has very great influence.

Internal Motives in Industry

Considering the importance of various motives in the industrial context, T.W. Harrell[1] has laid stress on three motives which he believes to be most important-sex, self-respect and social prestige. But the motives of remaining active, the desire to work and hunger are also important motives. It is a common fact that the majority of people work to earn their bread. By working, most people can earn enough to satisfy the physical needs of the family and can lead a married life. But some individuals continue to work even after these needs have been fulfilled because work gives them social prestige which satisfies their desire for respect in society. And yet some people continue to work even after both these needs have been satisfied. That is because they want to remain active, because activity is the nature of life. It is difficult to spend life in a completely inactive state. Hence, most work is done without any financial or non-financial incentives. It is done only for the sake of working.

Internal Drive

In connection with internal motives, internal drive is mentioned along with needs. Needs include such physical needs as hunger, thirst, sex desire, excretion, respiration and homeostasis, etc. If these needs are not satisfied then the balance of the body is destroyed with the result that mental adjustment is endangered. Drives pertain to more powerful and intense needs, the non-fulfilment of which leads to anxiety. Conditions of such anxiety can be seen in the case of dissatisfaction of the sex instinct. A similar condition can also be seen when hunger and thirst are not satisfied. If these drives are not satisfied, the individual's balance is upset.

Conflict in Motives

Sometimes many motives in an individual come to conflict. In such a condition, work suffers and production falls. In the sphere of industry, care must be taken to avoid such a situation where motives come into conflict. This must be kept in mind while creating motivation. Conflict always leads to mental conflict and the worker cannot decide what to do. Therefore, only those motives should be created which clearly show him the way. In that case, he does not have to think very much and he can continue to work at peace. Nowadays a variety of methods are used to create motivation among the workers. As far as internal motivation is concerned, it is entirely a matter of the individual worker's mental state.

---

1. Harrell, T.W., *Industrial Psychology*.

Only external motives can be provided in an industry, and these are called incentives.

THEORY OF INDIVIDUAL MOTIVATION

McGregor's Theory

McGregor propounded two theories of human behaviour in management philosophy on the theme of dual nature of human being best known as theory 'X' and theory 'Y'. McGregor believes that nearly all management actions flow from these two theories and they (actions) reflect their philosophy. As philosophy controls practice, management assumptions about human behaviour influence the personnel practice decision making, operating practices and even organisation design. McGregor observed that people appear to have a capacity for tenderness, sympathy and love, while they also possess tendencies towards cruelty, callousness, hate and malicious aggression. These two different philosophies are based on two different theories of McGregor, Theory 'X' and Theory 'Y'.

Theory 'X' and its Assumptions

It is the traditional theory of management philosophy. 'Power is supreme' is the main theme of the theory where the people at work-level have no authority to suggest or object anything except to carry out the orders of the supervisor. The line of authority or chain of command traditionally goes direct from the top, down through various layers of organisation with some delegation of authority but full and detailed accountability is up the line. People at work-level have no option except to obey the directives or orders of the authority.

Assumptions of Theory 'X'

1. Most people inherently dislike work and always try to shirk their responsibility.
2. Therefore, people must be cursed, controlled, directed and threatened with punishment, rebuffed or rebuked so as to get them to put forth adequate efforts towards the achievement of organisational goals.
3. The average human being prefers to be directed, wishes to avoid responsibility and puts off the work till it is necessary.
4. Most people at work have little ambition as to the improvement of work. They do not work with interest but wait for direction and act according to it.

5. The average human being wants security and safety above all, hence, he tends to work slowly.
6. Most people have little capacity to contribute something towards solving the organisational problems as their importance in the management is always undermined by the authority and they are treated as an instrument of a machine.
7. Working method of the people is generally traditional and hence, there is little scope for the development and research.
8. People can be motivated at money end. On the basis of financial greed, they can do whatever management wants.

Propositions of Theory 'X'

1. Management is responsible for organising the elements of production — money, material, machine, man and methods — in the interest of economic gain.
2. Management is responsible for directing the efforts of the people, motivating them, controlling their actions and modifying their behaviour to fit the needs of the organisation.
3. People would be passive unless management intervenes. Even they are resistant to organisational needs. They must be persuaded, rewarded punishment and controlled.

Criticism of Theory 'X'

(i) Authoritarian The theory 'X' is quite unwarranted in the modern times. It supports the authoritarian view which is unwarranted in the present-day economy. The man at work is not a machine, he is a human being. He is not only to execute the orders of the top line executives, but, he should also think over the order on its merits before its execution. Management may get results by coercion, or through pressure tactics only in short run till people respond to pressure and controls partly out of fear of consequences of not following the orders of the top line executives. Himself condemning the theory, McGregor says, "The conventional approach of Theory 'X' is based on mistaken notions of what is cause and what is effect. An organisation built upon theory X notions will be one in which there is clear supervision and control of subordinates and high centralisation of authority. Leadership will tend to be autocratic and workers will have very little to say in decisions affecting them.

(ii) Wrong assumptions of human nature The assumptions contained in Theory 'X' do not reveal the true nature of human beings.

Recent behavioural science research does not support the traditional view. It concludes that the most effective way to get better results in an organisation is to work with people rather than through them.

(iii) Against labour welfare In modern times, the governments of most of the countries have stressed that the worker should be given an honourable partnership in management. In this way, the theory has now become out of date.

Theory 'Y'

On the basis of the results of many psychological and social researches, McGregor submits an opposing theory — Theory 'Y' as a more realistic assessment of the capabilities of the people. This theory 'Y' presents an alternative management approach which does not involve abdication of managerial responsibility. Management is still responsible for achieving the organisational objectives, but on different assumptions about human behaviour and motivation. The workers are fully aware of the organisational objectives, which is directly related to the satisfaction of employees' needs. McGregor recognised certain needs that Theory 'X' fails to take into account. For example, self-fulfilment, ego satisfaction and social needs of individual workers. Thus, it pleads for a humanistic and supportive approach to managing people. Management tries to provide an atmosphere of peace and discipline within the organisation, without the oppressive measures. Hence, people work with interest and simultaneously enjoy the benefits of congenial relationship.

Assumptions of Theory 'Y'

1. **Work is natural** The average human being does not dislike work. Work is as natural as play or rest. Work may be a source of satisfaction of punishment depending upon the controllable conditions.
2. **Positive means of motivation** External control and the threat of punishment are not the only means for accomplishing the organisational objectives. Workers are committed to objectives and exercise self-control and self-direction to achieve them. They are fully conscious to their job.
3. **Value of responsibility** The average man works under proper conditions, not only to accept but seek responsibilities. Avoidance of responsibility, lack of ambition and emphasis on security are not

the inherent qualities of the man but they are all consequences of experience.

4. **Reward for work** The reward for the execution of work is that it should be properly recognised. Satisfaction of ego and actualisation needs can be product of efforts directed towards organisational objectives.
5. **Co-operation** The capacity to exercise a relatively high degree of imagination, ingenuity and creativity in the solution of organisational problems is widely distributed in the population, *i.e.*, labour co-operates with the management in solving the problems of the organisation.
6. **Development of abilities** Human abilities and capabilities are not fully developed till now with reference to modern industrial system. Management has ample scope to develop the intellectual potentialities of the average human being.
7. **Democratic theory** The theory is based on democratic principles wherein all persons are given equal chance to develop their skill.

Postulates of Theory

(i) Management is responsible for organising the elements of productive enterprise in the interest of economic and social ends.

(ii) People are not passive but they become so, as a result of experience.

(iii) Motivation, potential for development, capacity for assuming responsibility goal are inherent in the people. It is the responsibility of management to recognise and develop these characteristics.

(iv) The management should arrange for organisational conditions and methods of operations so that workers may achieve their goal through self-direction.

Applicability of Theory 'Y' in India

Thus 'Y' theory establishes co-operation in achieving the objectives of the organisation between the man in authority and the man at work. The fact of interdependence in human organisation is widely recognised. The theory is participative in the sense that supervisors consult their subordinates about proposed course of action before taking any decision. However, management still takes decision for the organisation as a whole.

Development of management in India is slow. Due to the unchanging attitude of employer and employee, relationship of master and servant still persists between them. The development of trade unions is still in its infancy. Organisational behaviour is mainly based on the assumptions of theory 'X'. Recently, some statutory provisions regarding participative management, minimum wages, less hours of work, etc. have been made by the government in order to improve the working conditions and bring about change in the mentality of the employers and the employees. Government has provided training institutes for workers and managers so that they can be conversant with the modern management approaches. Professional Managers have begun to accept the human value for the better management. They repose their faith in workers' participation and profit sharing techniques. But some managements still hesitate to accept the theory is full. Inefficient and uneducated workers are indifferent towards sharing the responsibility. Thus, the assumptions of theory Y have not been fully recognised in India.

Comparison between Theory 'X' and Theory 'Y'

1. Value of work Theory 'X' assumes that the human beings are inherently distasteful to work, whereas Theory 'Y' assumes that for human beings work is as natural as rest or play. They become distasteful to work only as a result of experience.

2. Ambitions and responsibility Theory 'X' assumes that people are unambitious and prefer to be directed and they try to avoid responsibilities in jobs. Theory 'Y', on the other hand, assumes that workers are ambitious, and are capable of directing their own behaviour. They are ready to accept responsibilities if proper working conditions are provided.

3. Creativity and change According to Theory 'X', most people lack capacity for creativity and they always resist change while according to Theory 'Y', the capacity for creativity is widely spread in the population. Most people are creative by nature and they accept every change.

4. Need levels The motivating factors in Theory 'X' are lower level physiological and safety needs. Theory 'Y', on the other hand, recognises both lower level and higher order needs like social esteem and self-actualisation for motivation. However, emphasis is laid on higher order needs.

5. Control and supervision Theory 'X' proposes external control and close supervision to achieve organisational objectives. They lack self-motivation, whereas Theory 'Y' proposes self-direction and self-control.

6. Levels of authority Theory 'X' emphasises scalar chain of command, centralisation of authority and autocratic leadership, whereas theory 'Y' emphasises decentralisation of authority and greater participation in decision-making process.

Criticism of McGregor's Theory

McGregor's theory of motivation helped to crystallise and put into right perspective the findings of the Hawthorne experiments. However, it has been widely criticised on following counts:

(i) Oversimplification It tends to over-generalise and oversimplify people as being one way or the other. People cannot be put on two extremes. No enterprising man belongs either to Theory 'X' or Theory 'Y'.

(ii) Two extremes McGregor's theory squeezes managerial styles and philosophies into two extremes of conduct which is devoid of reality.

(iii) Job and motivation McGregor suggests that job itself is the key to motivation. But all people do not see motivation in the job. The management has to motivate people to work.

(iv) Value of direction and control People who follow theory 'Y' still find that they have to behave in a very directive and controlling manner.

Most people believe Theory 'Y' to be more appropriate but not in all situations. In some routine and formalised situations, Theory 'X' is more suitable. In underdeveloped countries like India, Theory 'X' is more suitable. Neither theory is best in all situations. An amalgam of both the theories may be more useful than either of the two alone as the best approach to motivation is one which is appropriate to the situation.

MASLOW'S NEEDS PRIORITY MODEL

Propositions about Human Behaviour

1. Man is wanting animal Wants of man are innumerable and never ending. As soon as one of his wants is satisfied, another appears in its place. This keeps a man engaged on the work. Human needs are multiple, complex and inter-related.

2. A Satisfied need is no more a motivator As soon as a need is satisfied, it loses its capacity to induce the man to work. Hence only unsatisfied needs or fresh needs can motivate people to work.

3 Needs have hierarchy of importance Maslow is of the opinion that needs are satisfied in an order. As soon as the lower level needs are satisfied, those on the next higher level emerge and demand satisfaction.

Types of Needs

1. Primary needs There are two types of needs — basic or primary or innate or physiological needs and secondary or acquired needs. Primary needs are those needs which are very important for the survival and preservation of life. These needs are universal and are felt by everyone in the universe, but their intensity may differ from man to man or from society to society. Food, water, shelter, sex, air to breathe, sleep, clothing are examples of such needs. This theory has also been supported by McGregor and he states, "Man iss a wanting animal, as soon as one of his needs is satisfied, another appears in its place. This process is unending."

2. Secondary needs These are those needs which are related to mind and spirit rather than physiology. These needs develop as one gets maturity or education. These include rivalry, self-esteem, sense of duty, self-assertion, etc. These are acquired needs.

Man has both these types of needs. A.H. Maslow was the pioneer in contributing a systematic approach to this problem. He arranged the needs of a person in order of priority. Maslow's need-priority model was accepted widely. According to this theory, human needs tend to follow the pattern given below, presented in the sequence in which individuals usually become concerned with them.

Hierarchy of Needs

1. Basic physiological needs The physiological needs include the needs of human body such as food, shelter, clothing, sex, etc. They are basic to preserve human life and are more or less universal. These are at the lowest level in the hierarchy of needs. Therefore, these must be satisfied first of all. These are a powerful motivating force when thwarted. Man lives by bread alone when there is no bread.

2. Safety and security needs These needs are concerned with the physical and financial security. These include job security, physical security, security of income, old age provision, security from risks, etc. Management can influence these needs by providing security against such uncertainties, *i.e.,* by implementing pension scheme, insurance plans, fear of dismissal, etc.

3. Belongingness, social or love needs Being a social animal, man is always interested to live in a society or group which loves him most. He wants to give or receive love. These needs include the needs of conversation, sociability, exchange of feelings and grievances, recognition and belongingness.

4. Esteem and status needs These needs may be : (i) self-esteem or (ii) public esteem. Self-esteem means esteem in the eyes of self, *i.e.,* a feeling that one is doing something worthwhile. Public esteem means esteem or image in the eyes of public such as praise, admiration, public appreciation, etc.

5. Self actualisation or self-realisation needs These are individual's needs for realising his own potentialities, opportunity for creativity and for continuous development of the individual power and skill. Thus, these are, what a person considers to be his mission in life.

Lower-order and Higher-order Needs

Maslow has further classified the five needs into two categories:

(i) Lower-order needs Basic physiological and safety and security needs are labelled by Maslow as lower-level needs. These needs are finite. These are to be satisfied in priority to others because they are the first order needs. A man cannot survive without them and he will be ready to do anything to satisfy these needs. A hungry man can do anything to get the bread. His secondary needs of security and safety get priority as soon as he satisfies his basic needs. Hence a man collects grain for further use or tries to save money for his old age.

(ii) Higher-order needs Belongingness, social or love needs, esteem and status needs and self-actualisation needs are categorised as higher-order needs. They are secondary needs. They relate to the society and are external needs. They are infinite or unlimited. They are satisfied only after lower level needs are satisfied. All the needs under this category should be satisfied in order of priority. Lower-level needs affect the higher order needs and vice versa. Higher order needs are dominant factors in motivating people at higher level in the management.

Appreciation

Maslow's need priority model presenting nature and priority order of needs is a landmark in the field of motivation helping the management in understanding the human behaviour of people at work. It is very simple, direct and practical. Everybody, except few, has some priority of needs, not necessarily in the priority order as described by Maslow. Maslow, himself has admitted that his hierarchy is not rigid.

Criticism

1. Conditional model If the model may not apply at all times, in all places and in all circumstances, it may not follow the sequence as postulated by Maslow. Following are some examples:

(a) ***More self-esteem than love:*** There are some people in whom self-esteem seems to be more important than love. This reversal in hierarchy is possible where a strong or powerful person seeks self-assertion as a means to love.

(b) ***Absence of ambition and initiative*:** In certain people, the level of aspiration may be permanently dead because of prolonged experience of life at a very low level. Such people lack ambition and initiative.

(c) ***Absence of love needs*:** Some people do not have love needs because they have lost love in their early childhood.

2. Other determinants of behaviour There are many determinants of behaviour other than needs and desires such as perceptions, expectations, experience, etc. Thus, the behaviour of a man is not a result of his needs or desires only.

3. Neglect of interaction of needs This approach overlooks the interaction of needs. Motivation is caused by several needs at a time. A person is hardly motivated by a single need.

4. Difference in expectations People differ in their expectations significantly. The same need does not lead to the same response in all individuals. For example, people who have been satisfying their basic needs throughout their lives, may not be very keen to satisfy higher order needs.

5. General impression only Maslow's model gives a general impression. Hierarchical order is not very much rigid as Maslow himself accepted.

While designing a plan for people's motivation, the management must keep in mind the above weaknesses of Maslow's need priority model.

Extent of Application in Organisation

1. Environment The need priority model of Maslow applies to people in general. It does not always apply even to employees working in organisations because people satisfy most of their needs outside their organisations. Needs are conditioned by environment. Importance of different needs is determined by environment or their social system.

2. No general applicability Maslow's model seems to apply to managers and professionals in developed countries. Several studies have tested the model that show that they meet their physiological and security needs and seek higher order needs. Researches show that in some developed countries like Japan and Continental European countries, the model does not apply even to managers. The order in developed countries too differs because of their culture influences.

3. Applicable in underdeveloped countries The model seems to apply even in underdeveloped countries like India, where economic conditions of workers do not seem to be satisfactory. They prefer to satisfy their low-order needs, physiological as well as security needs. A survey of 200 factory workers in India in 1960s showed that they gave top priority to lower-order needs, job security, earnings and personal benefits.

4. Applicable in substantive conditions This model is tightly fit in case of managers and professionals in some of the developed countries and in underdeveloped countries, where men live under substantive conditions. In other cases, the model is unreliable.

HERZBERG'S MOTIVATION — MAINTENANCE MODEL

In the late 1950s, Frederic Herzberg made interesting studies that concentrated heavily on self-esteem and self-actualisation. Out of these studies developed a theory of work-motivation. It has broad implications for management and its efforts towards effective utilisation of human resources. The theory is known as Herzberg Motivation — Maintenance Theory or Motivation Hygiene Theory or Two-Factor Theory of Motivation.

Herzberg's Problem

In his studies, Herzberg tried to understand the motivation problem. He felt that knowledge about human behaviour, nature, motivation and needs could be invaluable to organisations and individuals. In his efforts to uncover the circumstances where a person felt satisfied or dissatisfied with his work, Herzberg conducted a study and interviewed about 200 engineers and accountants from 11 industries in the Pittsburgh area. These engineers and accountants were asked to think of time when they felt especially good about their jobs and the time when they felt particularly bad about it and then to describe the conditions that led to those feelings. Employees named different types of conditions for good and bad feelings. The study revealed that the factors responsible for job satisfaction are different not obverse from the factors that led to dissatisfaction. If a person was satisfied with his job in a particular condition, the absence of such condition would not mean job dissatisfaction but it might be called no job-satisfaction. In this way this theory is based on a two factor hypotheses, *i.e.,* factors leading to job satisfaction and factors leading to job dissatisfaction. These factors were classified into two categories:

(i) Motivational factors and

(ii) Hygienic or Maintenance factors.

1. Motivational Factors Certain factors are related directly to the job itself. Their presence creates a highly motivating situation, though their absence does not cause dissatisfaction. With the presence of such factors, people always respond positively. Herzberg mentions six such motivational factors: (i) achievement, (ii) recognition, (iii) advancement, (iv) work itself, (v) possibility of growth and (vi) responsibility. While achievement and responsibility are related to job itself, others are secured from it. This set of factors has been designated as motivators or satisfiers. They are job-centred factors related to job contents.

2. Maintenance Factors There were other factors, the presence of which did not significantly motivate them but the absence of such factors caused serious dissatisfaction. The presence of such factors prevented dissatisfaction and maintained a certain level of motivation, but any reduction in the availability of these factors was likely to affect motivation and bring down the level of performance. For example, an increase of Rs. 10 in the salary of a person does not mean much but a reduction of Rs. 10 from his salary may upset him and is likely to cause dissatisfaction. Maintenance factors are mostly related to environment outside the job. Herzberg called these factors hygiene or maintenance factors or dissatisfiers because they produce nothing to the worker's capacity but they help maintain or prevent losses to the worker's-performance due to work restriction. Herzberg named 10 maintenance factors as: (i) Company policy and administration, (ii) technical supervision, (iii) interpersonal relations with subordinates, (iv) salary, (v) job security, (vi) personal life, (vii) working conditions, (viii) status, (ix) interpersonal relations with supervisors and (x) interpersonal relations with peers.

Intrinsic and Extrinsic Factors

Intrinsic motivations are internal rewards that occur at the time of performance of work. Due to them, there is a direct motivation to perform work because the act of performance is itself rewarding. The employee is self-motivated in this situation. Extrinsic motivators are external rewards which are not directly related to the performance of work. These occur after or away from the work such as retirement plans, leaves, health, insurance, etc.

Prior to Herzberg's research, organisational managers generally paid attention to extrinsic maintenance factors. Now with better understanding, they insist more on intrinsic motivational factors due to their superior possibilities for the worker's society and organisation.

Implications of Herzberg's Research

Herzberg's findings were in sharp contrast to the existing policies. The management used to emphasize hygienic needs because non- satisfaction of these needs means dissatisfaction among workers and the organisation might have faced the resultant consequences. This, in itself, was not wrong but it was based on wrong assumption that prevention would have positive health and the return of increased productivity, lowered absenteeism, turnover, etc. They did not consider that the effect of improved hygiene lasts only for a short time. In fact, man's avoidance needs are recurrent. They will continue to occupy management's attention. Besides, understanding human needs in totally hygienic terms is fundamentally wrong. It has affected the self-concept of the employee very seriously.

Thus, Herzberg reaches a conclusion on the basis of these factors that people felt motivated if the job is challenging and interesting with the possibility of growth in it; authority to use their discretion; and ability to advance in the profession and receive recognition for the task they did.

1. **Based on opposite points** Herzberg's model is based on two factor theory of motivation, *i.e.,* factors leading to job dissatisfaction and factors; leading to job satisfaction. It suggests job satisfiers and dissatisfiers as two different qualitative factors. This was objected by others on the ground that job satisfaction and dissatisfaction are two opposite points.

2. **Method bound** It is easier to get results favourable to the model by using the Herzberg method, while other methods failed to produce similar results. Thus the model is 'method bound' which limits its applicability for general use.

3. **Neglect of pay, status and relations** This model does not lay sufficient emphasis upon the motivation qualities of pay, status and interpersonal relations. While these are important employee-motivators, the model gives credit primarily to their maintenance capabilities.

4. **Lack of clarity and distinction** The terminology used in this model is confusing. The difference between motivational and maintenance factors is very thin. Items designated as maintenance factors may serve as motivational factors to some and *vice-versa.* There is no absolute distinction among factors, neither factor is wholly unidimensional in its influence.

5. **Limited sample** The theory is based on a small sample of 200 accountants and engineers which cannot be said to be a representative sample. It has not universal application.

In spite of the above criticism, Herzberg's theory is useful in distinguishing factors that motivate people on the job and factors that primarily maintain employees ready to be motivated. The model provides new insights in organisational behaviour.

INCENTIVES IN INDUSTRY

What is Incentive?

Incentives are those goals or objectives which satisfy some needs. For example, food is the incentive of hunger. Water quenches thirst. In the same way, sex activity creates changes in the functioning of internal glands. Curiosity is satisfied by going from one place to another. In this way, incentives are the means of satisfying innate and acquired needs.

Kinds of Incentives

Generally, incentives are divided into two broad classes:

1. Positive incentives These incentives attract people and when they obtain these incentives, they feel satisfied. For example, increase in wages, promotion or bonus are positive incentives. These incentives motivate an individual to work in a particular way. If, for example, it is said that the worker who works an additional hour every day, will get fifty rupees extra, then this statement is an incentive.

2. Negative incentives Negative incentives are those which motivate an individual to abstain from doing something. If, for example, a monetary fine is imposed on causing breakages, then this fine is negative incentive which inspires the individual to avoid breaking things. Sometimes, some reform measures are instituted in industries. These reforms constitute negative incentives and although they are beneficial, they are opposed by many workers.

3. Substitute incentives Sometimes, another class of incentives, the substitute incentives, is also considered. As is evident from the name, this class includes those incentives which are artificial and are replacements of some natural or normal incentives. For example, a worker can be given a rise in pay in lieu of promotion so that he is saved from the frustration of not having been promoted. Evidently, then, the substitute incentive should satisfy the same need which would otherwise have been satisfied by the normal incentive. In the example cited above, the worker satisfies himself with the thought that the actual promotion, too, would only have resulted in a similar improvement of his economic position. It should also be remembered that, in any case, the substitute is not as good or as completely satisfying as the original incentive. To go back to the same example, actual promotion would have resulted not only in an increase in wages but also in the worker getting some additional power and authority. And, in fact, the worker who is satisfied with a rise in salary is only deliberately coming to terms with the situation. He would have been really satisfied only with promotion. And if a worker wants promotion not for economic advantage but for the higher position and the authority accruing with it, he would not be satisfied with an increase in salary. Obviously, then, the substitute incentives cannot satisfy all individuals equally. And the incentive that will satisfy an individual depends upon his individual traits and his condition. For example, a person who does not have a beautiful house will feel satisfied on getting a beautiful house and may even be prepared to give up some post for it, but one who already has such a house will never be willing to give up a post for another good house. Hence, when a substitute motive or incentive is given to a person, it is necessary to keep in mind his individual traits and his needs.

Conflict in Incentives

Sometimes a conflict occurs between incentives. For example, if all the workers in a factory are told that the worker who lives in the quarters provided by the factory will lose are thousand rupees a month while the one who doesn't will get an additional thousand rupees, then there will be a conflict between the incentives of the house and a thousand rupees raise in salary. In such a case, the worker will take sometime to make up his mind. Sometime, positive and negative incentives also come into conflict with each other. There are certain kinds of work, for example, in which the salary is fairly high but the social prestige consequent upon it is not very great. Faced with such a choice, the worker finds it difficult to decide whether he should accept the job with higher pay or the one with greater social prestige. Most industries which take a toll of the worker's health pay more than other industries. The detrimental effect on health is a negative incentive since there is motivation to avoid this kind of work. On the other hand, the higher salary is a positive incentive because it inspires the worker to accept the job. The actual choice made by the worker depends upon his individual needs or his economic condition. Some people would not like to earn money at the expense of their health while others may have such a great need for money, due to their physical or social needs, that they may be willing to endanger their health for the money involved.

Disadvantages of Negative Incentives

In industry, normally positive incentives are offered to motivate the worker to indulge in desirable activity while negative incentives are offered to restrain him from undesirable actions. For example, good work is rewarded with a prize while low production is punished. In certain cases, punishment is given for causing accidents, breakages, destruction of raw materials, etc. There is no doubt that punishment helps as a deterrent and people abstain from such activities, but negative incentives have certain drawbacks, the main ones being the following:

1. Frustration and hostile tendency If a worker takes some punishment to be unjust or improper then he experiences frustration and hostile tendency. This fact assumes greater importance because punishment is often given only to those workers who in the first place are obstinate and non-cooperative. If such a man is punished, these traits are further intensified.

2. Increase of deceit When provision is made for punishment on the performance of some activity then the culprits try to avoid being caught rather than avoid doing it altogether. In this way, punishment also leads to an increase in deceit.

3. Negative suggestion It is believed in psychology that negative suggestion should not be given where it is possible to give a positive suggestion. For example, it is better to say 'Cross this road here' rather than to say 'Do not cross this road here'. In the second case, the pedestrian gets a negative suggestion which does not tell him what to do. The first slogan contains a positive suggestion.

4. Destructive training Apart from the suggestion, the training implicit in the incentive should be constructive. Punishment is intended to deter a worker from doing something, a destructive training, since it creates an obstruction in the satisfaction of some tendency. On the other hand, constructive training tries to find more legitimate and acceptable means for the expression of this destructive urge.

5. Negative attitude Punishment leads to a negative attitude towards the work as well as towards the individual giving the punishment. Individuals who are punished in some factory develop a negative attitude not only towards their work but also against the entire organisation, including the management.

6. Creation of fear The possibility of punishment also creates fear and fear is never a good factor in the working conditions. Hence, instead of creating fear in the worker's mind, it is better to create a positive tendency.

Nowadays many experiments are being conducted in industrial conditions to introduce changes through the medium of positive incentives.

Despite all the above shortcomings, the institution of punishment has been part of industry for a long time because no attention has been paid to the consequences of punishment. In fact, punishment is often given in a state of anger, irrespective of the harm done by it. Besides, few, if any, managers and organisers have the patience to suspend punishment and employ more positive measures. In the third place, the negative method is simpler than the positive method, and it is often adopted because it is more expeditious. On the other hand, the adoption of positive incentives involves considerable thinking about the incentives as well as the methods by which they should be introduced.

Nowadays, two kinds of incentives are employed in industries the financial and the non-financial. The first kind of incentives include all those activities which result in economic benefits. The second category includes all incentives which bestow improvement and benefits other than monetary. Examples of non-financial incentives are praises for work, knowledge of the results of work, encouragement through health competitions, feeling of progress, better work through group motivation, increase in interest in some specific work, reducing boredom, making the job more important, etc.

FINANCIAL INCENTIVES

Money in itself has no value for man but in the context of the existing economic organisation, money has become a means not only of satisfying the physical needs of daily life but also of obtaining social position and power. For this reason, financial incentives have assumed great importance. On getting money man first turns his attention towards the things he needs — food, clothes, house, etc. Then he satisfies the needs of health and education. Once these needs have been satisfied, he tries to obtain more and more luxuries. But some individuals continue to work even after having reached this stage because their social prestige and power increase with their bank balance. Individuals with this lust for money continue their search throughout their life for this search never ends. People who do not feel any specific need for power do not try to earn money once their needs and comforts have been taken care of. In the same way, economic loss has diverse effects. Loss of money deprives the poor man of his bread while the rich man loses his prestige although he does not suffer from hunger. Despite this, the poor man suffers less on account of this loss psychologically because only his body is directly affected. On the other hand, the rich man suffers a blow to his social prestige and his self-respect, which is mental injury. Money has become the means of satisfying many needs because it is the medium of exchange. If social position and power are not based on money in any society, then money will cease to be so powerful an incentive. In communist countries, for example, since the abolition of private property, social respect has been connected with hard work, social service or some other objective, with the result that although there is no possibility of enhancing one's private property, individuals continue to work hard. Money is the most important incentive in a society where a man's success is measured by the money he earns. But where this does not happen money is not a powerful incentive. This analysis will show the importance of financial incentives. Financial incentives are offered in industries in two ways-either in the form of salary increases, or in the form of occasional bonus. Both these financial incentives have the effect of increasing production and inducing the worker to work harder and better.

Method of Wage Payment

The most commonly used financial incentive is the increase in salary. Here we will analyse the advantages and disadvantages of various methods of wage payment to discover the best method which acts as the most powerful motive for the worker to work harder and increase production. Briefly, a description of the methods of wage payment and their respective merits and demerits is given below:

1. Pay according to production In industry, one of the most common methods of wage payment is the payment of salary according to the production achieved by the worker. In most factories, the work is offered on contract and the rate of payment is predetermined. In this contract, the specific wage for a specific amount of work is clearly indicated. This method of wage payment has the following advantages:

(a) ***Stress on individual differences:*** This method of wage payment lays stress on the individual differences of the workers. If one worker is capable of working faster and better than other workers he earns much more money while the comparatively slower and idle worker suffers a proportionate loss.

(b) ***Importance of skill and production:*** The skill and the capacity for production of an individual are shown to be important in this method. Consequently, the worker tries to improve both these qualities. Since lack of skill and idleness lead to less payment, workers try to overcome these handicaps.

(c) ***Importance to uninteresting functions:*** Because of this method of wage payment, the worker tries to do even uninteresting work with equal zeal because he knows what he stands to benefit by taking interest in it and working more.

Despite the above advantages, this method of payment suffers from the following defects:

(a) ***Difference in the standards of life:*** Since payment is made according to the goods produced, different workers doing the same kind of work in the same factory will have different incomes which is reflected in the different standards of living the result of varying incomes. The consequence is that individuals with less income have a lower standard of living than the others, whom they begin to hate. This is one reason why at many places even the more skilful workers do not want to work better than the others because of these social reasons. Even trade unions object to this method of payment because it leads to conflict among the workers and their organisation is disrupted.

(b) ***Absence of respect for age:*** It is a commonly accepted fact that the ability to work decreases as age increases. This fact is particularly true of industrial production. And if wages are paid according to the quantity produced then older people begin to lose their prestige because they earn less. Besides, their entire accumulated experience is also not put to the best use.

(c) ***Practical difficulties:*** The most valid practical difficulty in this method of payment is that it is difficult to determine the value of different kinds of production. For example, it is difficult to compare the production of an engineer with the production of a labourer. This problem can, at best, be solved only by the trial and error method.

(d) ***Undesirable effect on the mobility of workers:*** This method of payment has an adverse effect on the mobility of workers. The more skilful and able workers naturally drift towards factories where wages are determined by production while the comparatively unskilful and less capable workers migrate towards factories where wages are paid according to the time.

(e) ***Conflicts between workers:*** This method of payment creates hatred between the more skilful and the less able workers with the result that the very purpose of giving an incentive is defeated. In fact, since the number of average skilled individuals is far more than the exceptionally skilful individuals in any industry, the better endowed individual is afraid of showing his skill by working better. This fact has been established by many studies.

In spite of the above defects, this method of payment has proved very effective in certain types of work, but generally it is considered better to increase bonus for better work, than to increase wages. Therefore, while evaluating the merits and demerits of this method of payment, it is necessary to keep in mind the economic condition and needs of the worker, etc. It is imperative that the social atmosphere of the factory should not be damaged while the more skilful workers are further encouraged to improve their skill.

2. Payment in terms of time spent Another common method of wage payment adopted in industry is payment in terms of time spent. In this, the worker is paid wages according to the time he spends in work. In this method, the wages are determined in terms of hours, days or weeks. In every case, the wages are determined by the time spent by the worker, not by the quantity of goods produced by him.

This method of wage payment suffers from the following demerits:

(a) ***Absence of motivation to produce:*** Since, in this method, the amount of wages is not influenced by the quantity of production, the worker is inclined to work only so far as his job security is not endangered. Once this level of production has been achieved, the skilful workers are found wasting their time in roaming around. Therefore, this method does not inspire the worker to increase his production. Wherever no means are employed to measure the minimum production of each individual-worker many workers do nothing more than mark time. As a consequence, in many organisations the more skilled workers have to bear the burden of such incompetent individuals.

(b) ***Absence of any stress on individual differences:*** In this method of wage payment, no importance attaches to the individual capabilities, skill and ability of any individual. Old and young people receive equal wages. For this reason, the more skilled workers do not want to work in any organisation where this method of wage payment prevails.

Despite these two defects, this is the most common method of wage payment because it has many advantages, of which the main ones are:

(a) *Respect for old age:* In this case, the earnings do not fall with increase in age although the individual cannot produce as much. In many cases, wages actually increase with age since promotion comes with age. This gives more respect to the older people and since everyone has to grow old some day, this method of wage payment is liked very much.

(b) *Absence of partial behaviour:* Here the managers cannot be partial in their behaviour towards the workers, for they cannot indiscriminately increase the wages of a worker or reduce those of another. This creates more cordial relations among the workers and it becomes difficult to turn them against each other. For this reason, the trade unions are normally in favour of this method.

It is obvious from the above description of the merits and demerits of this method of wage payment that it should be linked with the method of economic advantage in proportion to the production achieved. Wages should be paid according to the time spent but better and more work should be maintained. The major advantage of this method is that there is no difficulty in determining the wages of a worker since time is measured in terms of minutes and hours. Payment in this manner also induces a sense of security in the worker since he is assured that he will not suffer as he grows older and cannot produce as much as he could when young. Besides, he is always aware of the total emoluments he is going to earn and he can therefore plan his expenditure. This helps him to plan his future and to understand the manner in which he can hope to progress.

The Seniority Method of Pay

Industries which pay more attention to experience use the seniority method of pay so that a worker's wages increase with his age and experience. This method has the following advantages:

1. **Importance to experience** In this mode of payment, maximum importance attaches to the experience of the worker with the result that a worker tends to stay at his job with increase in experience. He is not easily tempted to go away.
2. **Security** It is advantageous inasmuch as it induces a sense of security in the worker because he does not stand to lose financially with a decline in output despite his advancing age. In fact, he actually gains because his wages increase as he grows older.

This method is common in many industries because of these advantages. But it also has some demerits, as given below:

In this mode of payment, little or no importance is attached to individual differences, abilities, or skills since the wage is determined only by seniority. One consequence of this is that highly skilled young workers are dissatisfied because they are subordinated to older people. On the other hand, they are not motivated to exploit their capacities to the maximum because they know that their salaries will increase only with age. Secondly, it is not scientific to assume that skill and experience increase with age, since beyond a certain level, experience does not increase and skill begins to decrease. Hence, this mode of wage payment is one-sided. It should be implemented along with some other method which encourages workers to work hard. For this hard work, they should be encouraged by promotion or some other method.

Pay According to Needs

In some industries, the method of pay according to needs has been adopted. This method is very useful for determining the minimum wage because a worker must be paid a sufficient sum of money with which to satisfy his own and his family's basic requirements. And, since some workers have a larger family than others they need a large sum of money to maintain a standard of living similar to that of others. If the worker's needs are not satisfied, he will live in a mood of constant anxiety and dissatisfaction, and, if the needs of his family are not satisfied, then, to that extent, society will have so many more individuals whose normal development is retarded. That is why many modern governments believe that the old age security of its workers is the responsibility of the state. It is also the responsibility of the state to provide free education and medical care for their dependants. In many cases, additional salary is given to those with a larger family.

But if the wages in an industry are to be determined according to the size of the family, the number of children, marital state, etc., then there is great chance of injustice being done because the unmarried young workers will be paid less, irrespective of their skill or efficiency. Hence, wages should not be increased or reduced according to the worker's respective needs, but other arrangements should be made to help them to satisfy their needs. Instead of giving additional salary to meet the educational expenses, it is better to provide free education. In the same way, medical care should be provided free of charge. The government may allow a cut in income-tax rates for an individual with a greater number of dependants. All these measures will help the worker to satisfy his needs, and at the same time, there will be no injustice to the other workers.

It is evident from the above discussion of the various modes of wage payment that no single method can be applied to all circumstances. Each method has its merits and demerits and in order to evolve the most useful method, one will have to take into account the merits of each method. It is necessary to provide security for old age and to meet the needs of the worker's growing family, but it is also no less important to give weightage to the skill and efficiency of the worker. In every case, the method of wage payment should be such that each worker is inspired and encouraged to work more and better. At the same time, it must avoid creating hatred and jealousy, and any sense of injustice to one and partiality to another. Economic and old age security are essential for motivation. Besides, wages should increase with increase in the levels of prices.

Among the various methods, the method of wage payment according to production pays special attention to individual differences. It encourages the worker to produce more. Hence, if the aim is to increase production then this method is the best but if increased production is not an important factor then wages can be paid according to the time spent. If linking wages with total production leads to anxiety and unrest among the workers then those who produce less may be compensated in some other way. Sometimes the more efficient worker is not given additional salary but he is allowed to work for a shorter period. Nowadays old age security is provided through life insurance scheme or pension scheme, in most of the progressive countries. In the same way, the needs of the individual with a large family are kept in view by introducing income tax reduction. In determining the method of payment, it is essential to keep in mind certain technical things. For example, the wages to be paid for a particular level of production in some specific sphere is a relative matter and it needs work analysis. This analysis becomes even more complex in the case of non-productive work, for example, the work of the engineer. Finally, the satisfaction of the worker is also a criterion for the correct method of wage payment. Therefore, the workers and the management should determine the correct level of payment through discussion. It is also necessary in this case to take the views of the trade unions. Putting it briefly, no one method is the best since different methods will meet the requirements in different sets of circumstances.

Non-Financial Incentives

In addition to the financial method of providing motivation, industries make use of many non-financial incentives also. These methods include all those which do not involve the payment of money to the worker. Since work in the industrial sphere is no joke and it must also inevitably lead to boredom at some stage, motivation must be provided. But, this should not be taken to mean that motivation exists only in financial gain. Many people continue to do some work because it is made more pleasant and enjoyable. Hence, many different methods are used to provide motivation, the main ones being the following:

1. Making work pleasant The reason why people enjoy playing but easily become bored with work is that playing is enjoyable, although that does not make it comfortable. Something being enjoyable means simply that it is an outlet for natural instincts. This is possible in the case of work also. Hence, work can also be made enjoyable and pleasant if it is so designed that it allows the worker to express his natural instincts.

2. Use of praise Often children are praised so that they may do some work. This love of praise or the use of praise as an incentive is successful not only in children but also in adults. Human beings in general are amenable to praise and want to do that work which will win them praise. If praise is given then they are inspired to do the work with even greater application. A common mistake made by many employers is that they do not praise good work although they severely criticise all mistakes, a psychologically unsound principle. Studies indicate that praise is a better incentive than criticism. Whether criticism is offered privately or in public, it invariably has some consequences. In the same way, abuse or blunt language is harmful. Very positive results can be obtained, on the other hand, by offering praise in public. Criticism has had consequences because it injures the worker's self-respect. So do abuse and blunt language. Criticism in public is even more harmful than criticism in private because in the former case, the worker also feels insulted and humiliated. Hence, offering criticism in public is the worst method of giving an incentive. Briefly, a worker will be inspired to work better if he is praised in public while the other workers will also be encouraged to work better to win similar acclaim.

3. Knowledge of results Knowledge of results implies simply that the worker is aware of how much work remains to be done, or the consequences of what he has done. Both interest and motivation are influenced by a knowledge of results. No individual likes to play in the dark because then he cannot gauge the results of his play. The value of results has also been established by some experiments. The experiments of S.J. Macpherson, V. Dees and G.C. Grindley[1] have shown that approximately 25 per cent progress in work is seen with a knowledge of results. At the same time the interest in the work is maintained. D.B. Lindsley[2] has demonstrated by his experiments that skill in work deteriorates when there is ignorance about mistakes and progress. In an experiment conducted by W.F. Book and L. Norvelle[3] two groups of students were given mental tasks of reality and the use of speed. One group was asked to put in the maximum effort of which it was capable while the other group was kept informed of

---

1. S.J. Macpherson, V. Dees and G.C. Grindley, "The Effect of Knowledge of Results on Learning and Performance".
2. D.B. Lindsley, Radar Operator Training: Results of Study of CSR 270-271 Operators at Drew Field.
3. W.F. Book and L. Norvelle. *An Experimental Study of Learning Incentives.*

the results and asked to improve upon them. A total of 20 experiments were conducted on these two groups. Finally, it was discovered that the group which was kept informed of results did 16.5 per cent better work than the other group. G.F. Arps[1] conducted an experiment in which the students were asked to raise a weight with one finger and to continue to do so until completely exhausted. This experiment was repeated 11 times with an interval of 48 hours between every two experiments. These students invariably achieved better performance when they were aware of results than when they were kept in the dark about their achievements. In this experiment, self-competition was noticed because each individual wanted to improve upon the grades achieved by him in the earlier experiments. Knowledge of results not only helps to make improvements in the methods of working but also provides inspiration to work harder. The importance of knowing the results in learning has already been established. N.R.F. Maier[2] has given an example to prove the effect of knowledge of results upon motivation. In one telephone industry, the mechanics suggested that they should be sent out to attend to complaints about an instrument rectified by them in the first place. They suggested this because in that case they would be able to gauge how well they had done their work earlier. They argued that just as a doctor wants to find out how far his medicine has helped the patient, in the same way they also wanted to know how well they had worked, and that their plan should be adopted. No such plan had been adopted by the company before this suggestion. And once it was adopted it was seen that cases of repeated complaints fell from 70 per cent to only 4 per cent.

4. Competition Another non-financial means of providing incentive is to organise competitions between different individuals or different group. Sometimes one particular individual may make an effort to improve his earlier performance, which should be an example of self competition. Even if competition does not lead to any economic gain, it has the advantage of giving self-satisfaction to the winner. Hence there should be some advantage attached to the winning of a competition, the advantage, for example, of increased social prestige, winning praise from others, appearing to be ahead of others, etc. But while organising competition among workers, attention must also be paid to the losers because they often suffer from frustration and they may at times also have to face humiliation. Therefore, a competition must be designed in such a way that it should not result in loss of cooperation and lowering

1. G.F. Arps, "Work with knowledge of Results *versus* Work without Knowledge of Results".
2. N.R.F. Maier, *Principles of Human Relations*, pp. 225-28.

of morale. There is normally a healthy competition in games because it is considered unsporting to raise the question of insult or humiliation on losing the competition. If the same spirit can be introduced into industrial context, then competitions can be put to good use. In order to increase the scope of the competition, it is sometimes divided into zones. Prize has a very great importance in competitions and it should normally be clear and obvious. Promotion of sales is done by giving prizes to the best salesmen and competitions are organised for the selection of good salesmen. Competitions have also been organised sometimes to reduce the incidence of accidents. In such a competition, the group involved in the least number of accidents is adjudged to be the best. Because of such a contest, the members of a group prevent each other from causing accidents while themselves taking care to avoid them. But if, as a result of such a competition, the groups try to conceal accidents or if a worker continues to work despite injuries, then these are harmful effects of such contests.

Some industrial trade unions have objected to the use of the competition method as a means of giving incentive since, according to them, this is a means of exploitation used by the employers who follow the policy of divide and rule. Hence in encouraging a spirit of competition, it is necessary to see that the workers are willing to cooperate and that they also understand the objective of such a measure. Competition is rarely introduced artificially because at times it naturally appears among the workers. It may be a competition in doing more and better work or in avoiding work. It also has a favourable impact upon the decision of the group. Factors like regular attendance, punctuality, the quantity and quality of work, safety, avoidance of waste and damage, etc., are amenable to competition and the results can be measured. Yet care must be taken to prevent competition from becoming a burden because in that case, it becomes more frustrating than pleasure giving.

As a result of research, it has been seen that competition between individuals is more effective than between groups because in the latter case ego satisfaction is less since the responsibility is shared. This fact has been established by the experiments of V.M. Sims.[1] In one of his experiments, some college students were given a test of reading. After taking the test, 45 students were divided into three groups having equal ability. They were then tested again. One group was not asked to compete but in comparison to the first test it showed a progress of 8.7 per cent. This was the result of practice. The other two groups were divided into

1. Sims, V.M., "The Relative Influence of two types of Motivation on Improvement".

two equal parts and made to compete, and an improvement of 14.5 per cent was observed. Obviously 8.7 per cent progress was the result of practice while 5.8 per cent was the result of competition. Members of the third group were motivated to individually produce better results than other competitors. This group showed a progress of 34.7 per cent of which 28 per cent was the result of competition alone. Hence it is obvious that individual competition is more productive than group competition. But it is also possible that group competition may be able to raise to a very high level. Team spirit has the effect of putting social pressure so that each member feels more responsible.

5. Experience of progress In many kinds of games, constant notice is taken of the progress achieved. For example, the progress in a foot-ball match is measured by the number of goals scored by a particular team. On the other hand, progress in a card game is measured by the points scored by each individual player. In some other games, progress is measured in more ways than one. In the sphere of industry also, the worker is inspired to work better if he has knowledge of the progress he is making. In that case he works better but the difficulty lies in making an accurate measurement of the progress achieved. This job is done in different ways in different industries. It is measured by the quantity of production, the quality of production, or even by the satisfaction given to the customer. In all these ways, the performance of the worker can be evaluated. As has been pointed out, each individual and each group wants to know how much work it has done. Actually, progress itself is the prize of work since it indicates that the workers' skill is improving. Therefore, each worker wants to feel that he is progressing but as skill continues to increase it becomes more difficult to see this progress clearly. For example, even if safety is increased to extreme limits, accidents can be prevented only up to a certain extent just as the quantity and quality of production can be improved within limits. Describing some experiments on the experience of progress, Viteles has pointed out that motivation improves with a knowledge of results and experience of progress and for this reason, the worker should be told of his progress from time to time. One good way of doing this is to interview him. During this interview, the weekly or terminal report of the worker's performance can be determined by fixing a limit to the work to be done during a day because if he feels that he has completed the day's work, he realizes that he is progressing towards his objective.

6. Social motives In addition to the above-mentioned kinds of non-financial incentives, there are certain motives which act as incentives.

Factors which increase social facilities are among the main social motives. Social facilitation implies an increase in a feeling of co-operation and group formation. Learn spirit is of particular importance in this connection. In an industry, the worker should have the feeling that as a member of a group, he is performing some task of vital importance. Group decision also plays a vital role. Motives which prove an obstacle in progress should be continuously eliminated, examples of which are mutual hatred and jealousy, conflict, unhealthy competition, etc. In order to give motivation, the goal should be made to create a group decision in favour of it. Once the group decision is favourable, the task becomes easier because no individual wants to lag behind the group and become a laughing stock while some individuals want to work more than the others in order to reach a position of command and leadership. The workers should also have the freedom to discuss various aspects of their job because this increases a sense of participation and responsibility, thus leading to more self-satisfaction. For this purpose various committees or groups should be created which can, discuss ways and means of increasing production and of finding new ways of doing the tasks more efficiently.

7. Increasing interest in the work Increase in interest leads to an increase in motivation. Hence, efforts should be made to increase the worker's interest in his job. Human beings naturally take an interest in games because they are chosen by the individual himself and because they provide him with a means of expressing his natural instincts. If the job is also chosen by the worker himself and it also gives him the opportunity of manifesting his natural talents, he will take interest in the job. But sometimes he is compelled to take up a job not preferred by him because of the possibilities of choice, the salaries available in different jobs, his educational ability, etc. Consequently, he finds it difficult to take interest in his job.

In order to create interest, the worker should be made aware of the importance and value of his work because if he feels that he is doing something worthwhile and making a useful contribution to this entire effort, then he will take interest in what he is doing. As F.R. Wickert[1] has demonstrated, a worker's motivation for some work diminishes very rapidly if he does not know why he is doing something or if he does not know the value of his work in relation to the entire work. Hence it is better to explain to the worker the various kinds of work done in the

---

1. Wickert, F.R., "Turnover and Employees Feelings of Ego Involvement in the Day to Day Operation of a Company".

organisation and the part he himself is playing in its success. Motion pictures and meetings can help in doing this, thus increasing the worker's self-respect. In moments of emergency, the level of motivation improves even more because then the worker is aware of his contribution in tiding over a difficult time. It has been seen that in times of emergency in a country, the workers are motivated to work.

Another way of improving interest is to reduce the monotony involved in the work. Fsor this, all those psychological measures can be adopted which are suggested for removing monotony. Monotony itself is the result of low motivation. Therefore, if it is removed, motivation improves. Variety of work and a sense of having completed some task tend to reduce monotony.

8. Consideration of the demands of industrial unions Nowadays it is impossible to do anything by neglecting the industrial unions. These unions take up the task of propagating and ventilating the demands and grievances of the workers. Efforts should be made to increase motivation by keeping these demands in view. It is true that at times these demands are contrary to the well-being of the organisation because these unions promote class-consciousness when they are influenced by political parties. But the industrial unions are the actual representatives of the workers' dissatisfaction and their demands should not be neglected. If these demands can be satisfied, the level of motivation improves automatically.

9. Study of the worker's need Finally, the next important way of improving motivation is to make a detailed study of the demands of the workers. At the same time, his order of preferences out of all the demands should be found out, if he is given the choice to prefer one demand to another. Studies of this kind can help in deciding upon the conditions which must be created for the improvement of morale and motivation. If, for example, the worker places the greatest emphasis upon security of job, the motivation can be improved by making his job secure. If, on the other hand, he grants priority to social prestige then his motivation can be increased by giving him respect. In certain industries, demands for wages or bonus head the list, in which case serious thought should be devoted to increasing them. Therefore, psychologists nowadays pay much attention to the study of the demands.

It is evident from the foregoing account of the financial and non-financial incentives in industry that both kinds of incentives should be used. For effective use of these incentives, there must be cooperation by the employers, workers, trade unions and the government.

QUESTIONS FOR EXERCISE

1. Define motivation and discuss briefly the non-financial methods of motivating workers in industry.
2. Discuss the relating importance of financial and non-financial incentives in industry, giving appropriate examples.
3. Make a critical estimate of the methods commonly used for studying the motivation of industrial workers, and discuss the incentives that generally operate for them. Cite relevant studies.
4. What types of incentives are generally used in industry? Discuss their merits and limitations.
5. Discuss the problem of effective incentives in industry.
6. Discuss the measures that can be adopted to motivate the workers for better work.
7. Discuss the role of financial and non-financial incentives for the promotion of productivity in our country.
8. Comment on the view that an incentive plan to be really effective, must be anchored to the cultural values of the employees.
9. Studies of incentives have borne out the fact that factors other than high pay loom large in the worker's life. Examine.
10. Is it possible to draw up a comprehensive incentive programme by including only the monetary incentives? What are the non-monetary incentives which, according to you, should be considered important?
11. Do you believe that a comprehensive incentive programme in industry could be drawn up based only on monetary incentives? If not, describe in detail the non-monetary incentives which you believe are conducive to individual output.
12. Discuss the problem of inadequancy of financial incentives in industry.
13. Discuss the problem of effective incentives in industry in the light of recent findings.
14. Distinguish between financial and non-financial incentives.
15. How will you distinguish between motive and incentive?
16. Critically examine the merits and demerits of different wage payment.
17. Write a short note on method of payment of wages and their psychological effects.
18. Explain the utility of wage incentive system clarifying the relation of incentive and work.

28

EXECUTIVE DEVELOPMENT

TRAINING AND EDUCATION

Concerned with imparting specific skills for particular purposes, training is the act of increasing the knowledge and skill of an employee for doing a particular job. Education is concerned with increasing general knowledge and understanding of the employee's total environment. For example, teaching a person how to assemble two objects and tighten a nut, means training him to do a specific job but giving him a course in engineering, is education. The distinction between the training and education is like the distinction between pure and applied sciences.

Examples

(a) ***Education*****:** A course in management or human relations is education because no one specific technique or procedure is taught but certain fundamentals common to all business situations are emphasised. A football coach who knows the theory of the game but who is utterly useless as a player is educated, but, not trained.

(b) ***Training*****:** A clerk who an compute the loan value of any insurance policy quickly and accurately is no doubt trained but not necessarily educated because he may be unaware of the actuarial principles upon which the values are determined. A mechanic who repairs an automobile better than an engineer is only trained and not educated for he does not know engineering education and principles.

Distinctions between Training and Education

1. Content and scope The content and scope of training are always specific, narrow and job-related; the content and scope of education are always broad and general.

2. Application and theory Training is always applied and practical; education is usually pure and theoretical.

3. Duration Training is mostly of short duration; education is of long duration.

4. Speed Training gives quick and apparent results; the results of education are not so quick and apparent.

TRAINING AND DEVELOPMENT

The term 'development' includes both training and education. It seeks to improve the overall personality of an individual. It is mostly used in the context of executives. Following are some important distinctions between training and development:

1. Personnel using Training is meant for operatives, while development is meant for executives.

2. Aim While the aim of training is to develop some specific skill in an individual, the aim of development is to develop the total personality of the individual.

3. Periods Training is a one-shot affair, while development is a continuous process.

4. Initiative The initiative for training comes from management while the initiative for development comes from the individual himself. Training is mostly the result of some outside motivation, while development is the result of internal motivation.

5. Process Training is a reactive process, preparation to meet an individual's present needs. Development is a proactive process, a preparation to meet individual's future needs.

PRINCIPLES OF EXECUTIVE TRAINING

1. Knowledge of results Seeking to know what is expected of him and how well he is doing, every employee in a learning situation seeks information, appraisal and guidance about his progress. He is made uneasy by the possibility that he may be making some serious error in his behaviour and not knowing that he is doing so. Knowledge of results provides the trainee the basis for correcting his error. Knowledge of results is mandatory for learning in some tasks as that of a crane operation. It produces motivational effect on the trainee. Once he comes to know what is right, his tendency to repeat it, is strengthened.

2. **Feedback** Researches on feedback have shown that: (i) Positive feedback *i.e.,* telling the trainee what is appropriate has a better effect than negative feedbacks, *i.e.,* telling him that he is not correct. (ii) Delay in feedback is detrimental to learning. (iii) Trainee should not be overburdened with feedback.

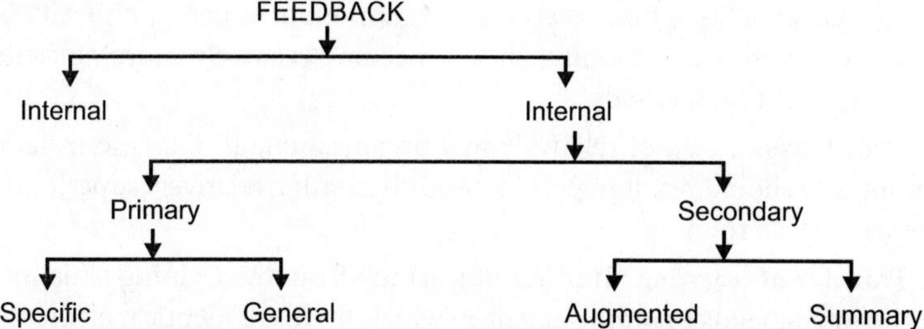

When feedback comes from cues internal to the organism, it is called internal feedback. When it comes from cues external to the organism, it is called external feedback. For example, in target shooting, the feeling that one has shot accurately may either come from cues in the body such as contraction of muscles, etc. or from cues outside the body such as the hole made by the bullet in the target. In the first case, it is internal feedback, in the second it is external feedback. External feedback can be either primary or secondary. It is secondary if someone else has collected it. In our example of target shooting if the learner himself determines his success or failure in hitting the target it is primary feedback. But if he is given feedback by the trainer or someone else, it is secondary feedback. Specific primary feedback pinpoints the error. General feedback does not do so. Secondary feedback can be augmented if it is given simultaneously with the performance, *e.g.,* the trainer exclaiming 'fine' simultaneously with the shooting. It may be summary if it is given some time after the performance.

3. **Motivation** Until the worker has become convinced of the need of training and of the worthwhileness of the returns, the level of motivation will be low and learning will be perfunctory and slow.

4. **Reinforcement** In order to acquire modified and sustained behaviour, it must be rewarded (reinforced). Reward should be distributed cautiously or discreetly as praising an inefficient and poor learner may disappoint the good trainees.

5. **Supporting climate and practice** Practice makes a man perfect. In order not to revert back to the old behaviour, it is essential that the trainee practises the new learning daily. When the internal environment of many

organisations is hostile to this, the trainee is not able to implement in his workplace what he has learned during the training session.

6. Part versus whole learning In a comprehensive literature review, Naylor found that the tasks were seen to differ in complexity and organisation. Naylor suggested the following training principles:

(i) Given a task of relatively high organisation, as task complexity is increased, whole task training should become relatively more efficient than the part task methods.

(ii) Given a task of relatively low organisation, an increase in task complexity should result in part methods becoming relatively superior to the whole task training.

7. Transfer of learning Transfer of learning from the training situation to the job depends upon the extent to which there are identical elements in the two. This means that the trained employee by virtue of his training would display superior "physical fidelity" if the devices and facilities used in training are similar to the devices and facilities used on the job and psychological fidelity where the human elements involved in the training performance on the job. If the physical and psychological fidelities are wanting there would be negative transfer of learning and the trained employee would display inferior performance on the job. Although one can easily ensure physical fidelity in a training programme it is not always easy to ensure psychological fidelity. For example, an employee on return from the training programme to the factory may find that his supervisor is a very different kind of person from the encouraging, understanding training director. The impact of such differences can be controlled to some extent by taking the following steps:

(i) Transfer at least 2 trainees to the same section. The support they can give each other is vital to their morale.

(ii) Let the production supervisor be involved with the training programme and have good relations with the training director.

(iii) On the day of transfer, let the trainer accompany the trainees to their, new section, stay with them a little while and check them at regular intervals for some time subsequently.

EXECUTIVE DEVELOPMENT METHODS

1. Methods for improving the decision-making skills of executives;
2. Methods for improving the inter-personal skills of executives and
3. Methods for improving the executives' knowledge.

1. Methods for Improving the Decision-making Skills of Executives

(i) Case study method A case is a written account seeking to describe an actual situation. A good case brings chunk of reality into the classroom to be discussed over by the class and the instructor. Pioneered by the Harvard Business School, the case study method aims at compelling the student to think actively, to analyse and sift evidence, to see beyond the confines of his speciality and to communicate coherently. The student has the benefit of listening to his companions arriving at different situations using the same data. He learns about himself, his assumptions, talents and limitations. He comes to see that there are many possible good answers to a problem.

There are two types of case study methods — directed and non-directed.

(a) *The directed case study:* In it the students are presented with the case and given a number of questions to answer or decisions to make.

(b) *Non-directed case study:* In this the student is simply presented with the material and is expected to explore the possible outcomes.

(ii) Incident method Developed at the Massachusetts Institute of Technology, it is an outgrowth of dissatisfaction with the case method felt by Paul and Pigors. In the usual case method, the entire problem is presented to the student, whereas in the incident method, only a brief incident is presented to provoke discussion in the class. The group puts questions to the instructor to draw out of him the salient facts and additional information needed to arrive at a reasonable solution or resolution of the case. The method draws the participants into discussion with greater emotional involvement. Its unique advantage over the case method is the procedure of obtaining information by questions, which must take place in actual business situations.

(iii) In-basket method It consists of letters, notes, documents and reports designed to simulate on-the-job reality of the manager's in-basket. The trainee deals with the in-basket materials as he would in his job. Feedback is provided so that he can appraise his results. The advantages of this method are realism, high involvement, and built-in motivation, similar to those of the case method.

(iv) Management games A management game is a dynamic training exercise simulating a real business situation. The participants are divided into various teams placed in competition with each other in resolving some problem, information about which is supplied to all teams. The game tests player's ability to absorb information quickly and make decisions under fire. With the introduction of video and audio, business games are getting more and more into live 'emulations' and away from traditional 'simulations'.

2. Methods for Improving the Inter-personal Skills of Executives

(i) Sensitivity training (or laboratory training) It involves the use of a training-group, in which ten to fifteen persons are put into a face-to-face situation. As the group has no agenda, no established roles, no established norms of performance, it creates tension and anxiety. Group members attempt to relieve it by withdrawing from active participation or by attempting to provide the missing structural elements, assuming leadership, establishing goals, setting up an agenda. These attempts may not meet with unanimous approval but they do reveal the needs of individuals and some of their habitual reactions to stress. Members of the group are told that from continuous observation and analysis of experiences in the group, they can learn much about their own behaviour and that of others and about group behaviour. The trainer does not act as a discussion leader; he helps group members to find ways of utilising their experiences for learning.

A laboratory should develop situations which will induce the individual to examine his incongruities and discrepancies and endeavour to integrate his behaviour, values, need, knowledge and feelings, constituting his inner world with the expectations of his social environment. Thus, the laboratory programme aims at achieving behavioural effectiveness in transactions with one's environment. Conditions for success: (a) There should be exploration of each other's feelings. Without bringing forth one's own feelings and thoughts, and knowing the reactions of others, the individual may not recognise needed changes in his behaviour, (b) In a competitive or hostile atmosphere, exposure of self can lead towards rejection, loss of reputation or ridicule. By encouraging trust among members, laboratory conditions reduce the threats inherent in self-exposure.

(ii) Role playing In the area of "interpersonal relations" discussion of case studies generally remains at an unemotional intellectual level of role-playing has been developed to correct this deficiency. In this method, the instructor assigns parts taken from case materials to group members. Working without a script or memorised lines and improvising as they play the parts, the role players attempt to act their parts as they would behave in a real life situation. The very act of arguing for another view, even if it is purely an exercise, exposes the person to some of its virtues which he had previously denied. A supervisor might play the role of a subordinate, a sales-person the role of a customer and a nurse's aide the role of a hospital patient. The role playing lasts 20-30 minutes, after which data are collected about the performance of each role-play and a discussion takes place. Role playing tends to be enjoyed by participants. It develops empathy and sensitivity in them. It allows for their emotional release in a fairly harmless manner. It promotes insight. It emphasises the importance of acceptability in decision making.

(iii) Transactional analysis A transaction is a social intercourse between two or more people who encounter each other. In every social intercourse, there is a *stimulus* provided by one individual and a response to that stimulus given by another individual. This stimulus-response relationship between two individuals is a transaction. Introduced over two decades ago by Berne and further popularised by Haris and Jongewald, Transactional Analysis (TA) provides an individual with a practical and useful method for analysis and understanding of human behaviour. It is a method of analysing a transaction.

Berne says that every normal individual functions from three ego states — parent, adult and child. An ego state is a system of feelings accompanied by a related set of behaviour patterns. Each ego state can be described as under.

(a) *Parent*: The parent ego is a huge collection of recordings in the brain of an individual of attitudes and behaviours imposed on him in his early years (roughly first five years) from various external sources, primarily his parents. The characteristics of this ego are to be owner protective, officious, distant, dogmatic, etc. Verbal clues that a person is operating from the parent ego state are his use of such words as 'always', 'never', 'should', 'ought', etc. He uses language of threat or tries to resolve conflict by force. There are physical clues also like raised *eyebrows, pointing an accusing finger at* somebody, and so on.

(b) *Child*: The child ego is a collection of recordings of attitudes, behaviours and impulses in the brain of an individual which come to him naturally from his own seeing, hearing, feeling and understanding as a child. Characteristics of a person acting in the child state include being curious, impulsive, sensuous, affectionate, dependent, fearful and depressed. Verbal clues about operating from the child ego state are the use of words like "I wish", "I guess', 'I do not care", and so on. There are physical clues also like temper tantrums, attention seeking, giggling, coyness, silent compliance, etc. The child in us is likely to lead us to behave as dependants, as competitive and to approach conflict resolution through avoidance or smoothing.

(c) *Adult:* Adult ego state includes reality testing, rational behaviour and decision-making or problem-solving analysis. In this state processes, an individual verifies and updates the data which he receives from the other two states. Thus, this state is a shift from the "taught and felt concept" to "tested concepts". Adult data are gathered by the individual's ability to find out for himself the difference between life as it was taught and demonstrated to him (parent), life as he felt, wished or fantasied (child) and life as he figures out by testing now (adult). The adult-ego state does not do away with parent and child data. It examines these data and tries to update them in the reality of the external world. In an individual, the adult shows itself in a variety of ways. The indicators of the adults-ego state in an individual are phrases like "I see", I think", "It is my opinion", words with an emphasis on data collection, *e.g.*, why, where, when, who, how, what, and an emphasis on data processing and problem-solving.

Types of Transactions

When we evoke behaviour from one ego state responded to by the other individual from any one of these three ego states, it gives rise to three types of transactions: complementary, crossed and ulterior.

(a) *Complementary transactions:* It is one in which the stimulus and response ego states are complementary to each other; the communication

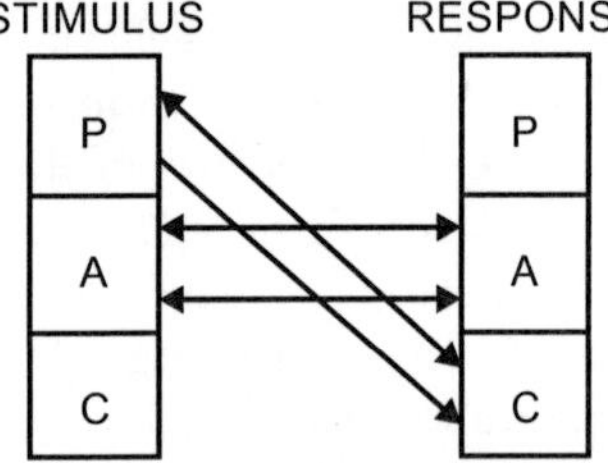

Fig. 28.1 Complementary Transaction

between any two individuals runs along parallel lines between them (Fig. 28.1). Thus, the parent in one individual is responded to by the child in the other as shown and the adult in one is responded to by the adult in the other. Both parties feel satisfied in this type of transaction.

Examples

1.	Workers	:	I cannot do this job myself. Please help me. Will you? (Child-Parent).
	Foreman	:	Sure, I am coming just now. (Parent-Child).

2. Foreman : Have you finished the job? (Adult-Adult).

Worker : Yes, I finished it long back and it has already been delivered to the assembly line. (Adult-Adult).

(b) *Crossed transactions:* When communication runs along crossed lines between individuals, the transactions are crossed. Further transactions stop, in this communication.

Examples

Foreman to Worker : How many pieces have you made by now? (A-A).

Worker to Foreman : Do not disturb me. When I complete the whole work I will let you know (P-C).

(c) *Ulterior transaction*: This type of transaction has double meaning. On the surface level, it is a clear adult message though it also carries a hidden message. For example, husband while sitting on the dining table may find the table dirty. If he writes on the table "I love you" to be read by his wife, he is on the surface using his child ego state but his ulterior motive is to hint her that she has not cleaned the table. Thus, his message is proceeding from the parent state. His wife must respond to it form her child state by cleaning the table.

Thus transaction analysis give an insight into the fundamentals of human psychology and helps to improve interpersonal relations.

(d) *The Johari window*: It is a conceptual model developed by Joseph Left and Harry Ingham; the name Johari combines their first names. It is for increasing personal effectiveness. As shown in Figure 28.2, this model divides an individual's personality into four parts "Arena". The part known to the individual but not to others is called closed. "Blind" is the part which is known to others but not to the individual. The part not known both to the individual and to others is called "Dark".

	Know of self	Not know of self
Know to others	Arena	Blind
Not Know to others	Closed	Dark

Fig. 28.2 Johari Window

In order to make oneself effective in interpersonal relations, should expand one's arena. One must try to reduce the other three areas. "Blind" can be reduced by "receiving feedback from others" "Closed area" can be reduced by self-disclosure.

3. Methods for Improving the Executive's Knowledge

(i) Conferences Mutual problems are the subject of discussion in a conference. In attempting to arrive at improved methods of dealing with these problems, participants pool their ideas and experience for joint exploration.

(ii) Buzz session When a conference group is broken up in several small groups of four-five participants, it is called buzz session. Members of the group come together to teach each other and to learn together. This method is most appropriate for the purpose of presenting new and sometimes complicated material.

(iii) Autonomy training "Autonomy training" is aimed at developing the individual's ability to manage his own training. It leaves the trainee almost on his own. He has first to work out what he would like to learn and then teach himself. This method rests on the concept that with the tremendous speed at which new knowledge is replacing the old one, it is impossible for standardised course to cater for individual training needs. Therefore, the managers must be trained to teach themselves new skills as they go along the situation is kept unstructured. In this training also, as in the sensitivity training, the trainer refuses to direct the programme or give lectures. He merely indicates a vast array of resources such as books, films, articles, management games, psychological tests, etc., from which the participant may choose to build his own programme. Consultants are available for discussion or counselling but only if the participant seeks them out. Participants can also consult with each other.

FACTORS FOR SELECTION OF A TRAINING AND DEVELOPMENT METHOD

1. Training objective It is far more difficult to define the objectives at the managerial level than at the blue-collar level. Experts agree on the form and content of training to be given to a machinist or electrician but they differ widely in case of a junior executive because they do not know why some senior executives are more effective than others or what does a successful manager know better than his less successful colleagues.

From an opinion survey of 200 training directors of large American companies, post training work, it is revealed that:

(i) For acquisition of knowledge, programmed instruction is the best, lectures are the worst.

(ii) For changing trainee's attitudes, sensitivity training is the best, television lectures are the worst.

(iii) For increasing trainees' problem-solving skills, case method is the best, lectures are the worst.

(iv) For increasing trainees' interpersonal skills, sensitivity training is the best, television lectures are the worst.

(v) For increasing trainees' acceptance of the training method, conference (discussion) is the best, television lectures are the worst.

(vi) For trainee's retention of knowledge, programmed instruction is the best, television lectures are the worst.

2. Level of trainees in the organisation's hierarchy At different levels in the organizational hierarchy, training needs of employees differ in the degree to which emphasis is placed on various training inputs. This difference makes certain techniques better for one class of employees than for the other.

3. Method's ability to hold and arouse the interest of trainees during the training period.

4. Availability of competent trainers.

5. Availability of finance.

6. Availability of time.

DIMENSIONS OF EVALUATION

1. Evaluation of contextual factors It involves evaluation of the pre-training and post-training:

(i) ***Pre-training work:*** It includes proper identification of training needs, developing criteria of who should be sent for training, how many at a time and in what sequence, helping people to volunteer for training, building expectations of prospective participants from training, etc.

(ii) ***Post-training work*****:** It includes helping the concerned managers to plan to utilise the participants' training and provide the needed support to them, building linkages between the training section and the line departments and so on.

2. Evaluation of training inputs It involves the evaluation of training curriculum and its sequencing.

3. Evaluation of training process Some of the important elements of the training process which also need to be evaluated are the climate of the training organisation, the relationship between participants and trainers, the general attitudes and approaches of the trainers, training methods, etc.

4. Evaluation of training outcomes The main task of evaluation is measuring the carry home value of a training programme in terms of what has been active and how much. This is a complex technical and professional task. Benefits of a training programme are not always obvious nor are they readily measurable. Pay-offs from training are intangible and slow to become apparent. A central problem is the absence of objective criteria and specific definitions of relevant variables by which to measure the effectiveness either of specific programmes or of results in terms of general employee development or changes in employee behaviour. However, good personnel managers do make an effort to systematically appraise the benefits and result of their programmes.

(i) ***Evaluation in job-related training*** Here the objective is to train people for specific job skills so that their productivity may increase, hence evaluation can be done either according to the direct criterion of increase in output or according to the indirect criteria of decrease in cost, breakage or rejects. Even more indirect are measures that point out changes in absenteeism or turnover.

(ii) ***Evaluation of human relations skills training*** This is given to the supervisors and middle-level managers. Supervisory and managerial training programmes are less amenable to objective review procedures. Since exact standards and criteria are hard to devise, much subjectivity enters into evaluations.

Methods of Evaluation

2. Reaction evaluation Opinion surveys of participants or of people who have seen the participants in action are reaction evaluations. There are following variations of this method:

(i) ***Questionnaire*:** It is given to the participant at the end of the programme which asks him to rate in terms of his personal perceptions what he liked best, what he liked least and any other comments he might have about the programme.

(ii) ***Scalar ratings*:** There are given against every question and the trainee is required to check off the degree of satisfaction which he found in each answer.

(iii) ***Daily ratings*:** Participants are required to give daily ratings for each segment of this programme. It provides an immediate feedback to the manager of the training programme who can use it for the adjustment and improvement of the following day's programme.

(iv) ***In panel questioning* :** Dropping around during a coffee break a management representative may put questions to one or two participants and informally collect information about the success of the training programme. The results may not be always accurate such samplings are not scientifically designed.

(v) *Follow-up opinions:* Sometimes on returning to their organisations, the participants may be asked to send their opinions by mail. It is so because opinions given immediately at the conclusion of the course cannot possibly have the objectivity which is desired in the appraisal of the programme.

2. Outcome evaluation Outcome evaluation may be done at immediate, intermediate and ultimate levels :

(i) *Immediate:* To find out the extent to which positive transfer of learning has taken place from the training to the job situation, this form of evaluation measures, analyses and interprets changes in the knowledge, skills and attitudes of trainees soon after they have returned to their jobs. This evaluation may be done by using behaviourally anchored rating scales or self-reports supplemented by reports of subordinates, peers and supervisors or critical incidents, etc.

(ii) *Intermediate*: Intermediate evaluation measure, analyses and interprets changes in the performance of trainees when they have returned to their jobs. It is based on the assumption that effective training should be reflected in the trainee's increased job proficiency. For example, a training given to salesmen is successful to the extent it increases sales. A training given in cost reduction is successful to the extent it helps people in reducing costs. A training in work simplification is successful to the extent people simplify their jobs. If the trainee is in a supervisory capacity, evaluation may have to be based upon the performance of his subordinates because no objective criteria are available for supervisory personnel. Group standards of performance, group efficiency and group behaviour may become the focal point of study, where the training programme is to be evaluated for its impact on co-operation between the small groups, interpersonal relationships, etc.

There are three basic techniques followed under this method:

(a) Controlled experimentation. It requires the use of two groups of employees, namely, "training" group and a "control" group. Performance is measured of both the groups *before* training is started. The training group is then given the training, while the control group is not. After the first group is trained, performance of both the groups is again measured. A subsequent comparison is made of the improvement in both groups to determine if the training group improves significantly more than the control group. It involves the use of a single training group with performance being measured *before and after* the training.

(b) "Before-and-after" comparison.

(c) After the training study. It involves a single training group but with performance being measured after the training.

Of these controlled experimentation is the most scientific technique that really provides a solid basis for evaluation of the training. Before and after company technique does not provide the basis for knowing how much improvement would have occurred without training. The third technique does not provide any basis for knowing how much improvement actually occurred during training.

Routine appraisal of employees may be used to evaluate the effectiveness and impact of training. For example, if on his annual appraisal, an individual is reported by his boss to be somewhat deficient in human relations, he might be enrolled in a course to correct these defects. It will be appropriate to ask at the conclusion of this course, what his next appraisal showed. If his behaviour did change and the appraisal is better, this is an evidence to show that the training programme had an effect.

(iii) *Ultimate*: Ultimate evaluation measures and analyses changes in the ultimate results achieved by trainees. Sometimes, in the evaluation of management training, instead of attempting atomistics measurements of improvement in an individual, an overall look is taken at the aggregate growth of people in the total organisation. The indexes of productivity, labour turnover, etc., studies of organisational climate and human resources accounting are taken as the ultimate results achieved by trainees.

Principles of Effective Evaluation

1. Planned What is to be evaluated, when, by what means, and by whom, must be determined in advance.

2. Objective It should not be a mere eyewash — an attempt by the trainer to vindicate the programme instead of to verify it.

3. Verifiable Results can be confirmed by the same or different means.

4. Co-operative It must involve all those who are a part of or affected by the training and development programme. It is not a contest between the evaluator and the subject of evaluation.

5. Continuous

6. Specific It should tell about specific strengths and weaknesses and should not make vague generalisations.

7. Quantitative

8. Feasible It must be administratively manageable.

9. Cost Effective The results must be commensurate with the costs incurred.

QUESTIONS FOR EXERCISE

1. Distinguish between:
   (i) Executive Training and Education.
   (ii) Executive Training and Development.
2. Describe the principles of Executive Training.
3. Describe Executive Development methods.
4. How will you select a training and development method? Explain developing of evaluation of training and development.

29

JOB EVALUATION

WHAT IS JOB EVALUATION?

1. Kimball and Kimbal "Job evaluation represents an effort to determine the relative value of every job in a plant and to determine what the fair basic wages for such a job should be."

2. A. Shubin "Job evaluation is a systematic procedure for measuring the relative value and importance of occupation on the basis of their common factor (skill, training effort) for the purpose of determining wage and salary differentials."

3. Bethel, Atwaker, and Smith etc "Job evaluation as a personnel term has both a specific and generic meaning. Specially it means the entire field of wages and salary administration along modern lines."

4. Alford and Beauty "Job evaluation is the application of the job analysis technique to the qualitative measurement of relative job worth, for the purpose of establishing consistent wage rate differentials by objective means. It measures the differences between jobs based on the job requirements and establishes the differential numerically (job rating) so that it can be converted to wage rates after the wage level is determined".

5. Dale Yoder "Job evaluation is a practice which seeks to provide a degree of objectivity in measuring the comparative value of jobs within an organisation and among similar organisations. It is essentially a job rating process, not like the rating of employers."

6. I.L.O. "Job evaluation may be designed as an attempt to determine and compare the demands which the normal performance of particular job makes on normal workers, without taking account of the individual abilities or performance of the workers concerned."

7. Edwin B. Fillippo "The systematic and orderly process of measuring the worth of job within an organisation is called job evaluation."

8. Maurice B. Cuming "Job evaluation is a technique of assessing the worth of each job in comparison with all others throughout an organisation."

9. Wendell L. French Job evaluation is "a process of determining the relative worth of various jobs within the organisation, so that differential wages may be paid to jobs of different worth."

10. Langriser, A and H.G. Zollitsch Job evaluation is "the overall activity of involving an orderly, systematic method and procedure of ranking, grading and weighing of jobs to determine the value of specific job in relation to other jobs."

11. British Institute of Management Job evaluation is "the process of analysing and assessing the content of jobs, in order to place them in an acceptable rank order, which can then be used as a basis for a remuneration system. Job evaluation, therefore, is simply a technique, designed to assist in development of new pay structures by defining relativities between jobs on a consistent and systematic basis."

Thus, job evaluation is a process of determining the relative worth of jobs, ranking and grading them by comparing the duties, responsibilities, requirements like skill, knowledge of a job with other jobs in order to fix compensation payable to the concerned job holder.

OBJECTIVES OF JOB EVALUATION

1. Gathering data To gather data and information relating to job description, job specification and employee specifications of various jobs in an organisation.

2. Comparison To compare the duties, responsibilities and demands of a job with that of other jobs.

3. Determine hierarchy To determine the hierarchy and place of various jobs in an organisation.

4. Determine ranks and grades To determine the ranks or grades of various jobs.

5. Ensure wages To ensure fair and equitable wages on the basis of relative worth or value of jobs. Equal wages are fixed to the jobs of equal worth or value.

6. Minimise discrimination To minimise wage discrimination based on sex, age, caste, region, religion, etc.

Steps in Preparing the Ground for Job Evaluation

1. Appointing job evaluation committee As it is very difficult for a single man to study, review and evaluate all jobs, appointment of a job evaluation committee consisting of technical and non-technical people is more appropriate.

2. Analysing the jobs Analysing the job, job knowledge can be obtained from the job description and job specification records. It can be gathered and collected through interviews, observations, activity sampling, questionnaires, critical incidents, diaries, etc.

3. Identification of compensatory factors This refers to knowledge in respect of education, experience, skill, etc. This ground work is more useful for systematic job evaluation.

Essentials for the Success of Job Evaluation Programme

1. Representative factors Compensable factors should represent all of the major aspects of job content. Compensable factors selected should (a) avoid excessive overlapping or duplication; (b) be definable and measurable; (c) be easily understood by employees and administrators; (d) not cause excessive installation or administrative cost; and (e) be selected with legal considerations in mind.

2. Training Operating managers should be trained in the techniques and programme of job evaluation and fixing and revising the wages based on job evaluation.

3. Information All the employees should be provided with complete information about job evaluation techniques and programme.

4. Coverage All groups and grades of employees should be covered by the job evaluation programme.

5. Facilitation The programme and techniques selected for job evaluation should be easy to understand by all the employees.

6. Unions' support Trade unions' acceptance and support to the programme should be obtained.

JOB EVALUATION METHODS/TECHNIQUES

Jobs are evaluated on the basis of conventional and non-conventional techniques:

(a) ***Conventional techniques*** **:** These are divided into (i) quantitative and (ii) non-quantitative techniques. Non-quantitative techniques include: (i) simple ranking (ii) paired comparison ranking, (iii) job classification and (iv) grading method. Quantitative techniques include points rating and (v) factor comparison method.

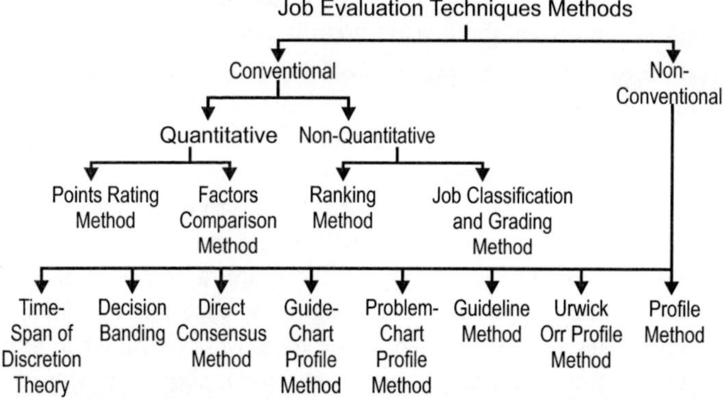

Chart 29.1 Types of Job Evaluation Techniques methods

***(b) Non-conventional methods*:** These consist of (1) time-span of discretion theory, (2) decision-banding, (3) direct consensus method, (4) guide-chart profile method, (5) problem-solving compensable factor, (6) guideline method, (7) Urwick Orr profile method and (8) profile method.

[A] Conventional Techniques/Methods

Non-quantitative conventionally, non-quantitative simple and crude techniques are developed. They are ranking and job classification methods:

1. Ranking Method

(i) *Simple ranking*: This is the simplest and administratively easiest technique. The evaluator compares one job with other jobs about duties, responsibilities and demands made by them on the job incumbent and the degree of importance of the job to the organisation. He ranks all the jobs from the most to the least important. He has to appraise and rank the jobs but not the job incumbents.

(ii) *Ranking the key jobs*: Ranking all the jobs at a stretch under. In order to minimise difficulty, the evaluator identifies the key or representative jobs at the first stage; ranks the key jobs at the second stage; identifies and ranks all other jobs at the third stage.

(iii) *Paired comparison:* As each job cannot be compared with all other jobs for the purpose of ranking, the method of paired comparison is adopted to minimise this problem. Under this method, the evaluator ranks each job against all other jobs to be appraised, so that a series of paired rankings is produced. Compared to the simple ranking method, this method is more comprehensive, logical and reliable.

(iv) ***Simple factor ranking method:*** Ranking method has difficulty of operation of the method, as ranking has to be done on the basis of number of factors. Goldenberg has suggested a single factor ranking scheme which is, the discretionary contents present in each job are related to other jobs. The single most important task to be performed in job is identified and compared within the single most important task to be performed in other jobs. The jobs are to be priced after they are ranked. Money value should be assigned to each job. Key jobs with known monetary values are used as the basis to determine the money value of other jobs. Generally, there is agreement about the rates of key jobs.

Advantages of Ranking

(i) It is the simplest, quickest and least costly from the viewpoint of time and money.
(ii) It is most appropriate in small organisations.
(iii) It is appropriate for ranking the top managerial personnel in large organisations.
(iv) It is useful as a first and basic step of job evaluation.

2. Job classification and grading methods A grade is a group of different jobs of similar difficulty or requiring similar knowledge and skill to perform, while class is a subdivision of a given occupation. In the occupation of Accountant, Assistant Accountant, Senior Accountant and Chief Accountant are the classes. While the jobs within a class have fairly similar tasks to be performed, the jobs within a grade may have more different tasks. As classes and grades are designed for the similar jobs, they receive similar pay. For example, while a grade may consist of jobs like Financial Accountants, Cost Accountants and Management Accountants, a class may consist of Assistant Financial Accountant, Financial Accountant, Senior Financial Accountant and Chief Financial Accountant.

Under grading method, jobs at different levels in the organisational hierarchy are divided into various grades, with a clear-cut definition of each grade. Grades are formulated on the basis of nature of tasks, requirements of skill, knowledge, responsibilities and authority of various jobs.

Steps in Grading Method

(i) Determining the shape and size of organisational structure such as tall or flat organisation, geographical or functional organisation, etc.

(ii) Preparing job descriptions.

(iii Preparing grade descriptions based on various components.

(iv) Establishing a number of job grades and division of the organisation into various grades like Grade-I, Grade-II... Grade VI, as shown in Chart 29.2.

(v) Discussing and negotiating with trade union representatives regarding the number of grades, grade descriptions, getting their consent, finalising the number of grades and grade description and recording them.

(vi) Selecting key jobs and grading them.

(vii) Grading the entire jobs.

(viii) Classifying the jobs of each grade.

(ix) Assigning the money value to the key grades first and then to all other grades.

Advantages of Grading

(i) It is simple and easy to understand and operate.

(ii) It provides an opportunity for a systematic organisation structure.

(iii) Pay grades are better and appropriate for comparison with those of other organisations.

(iv) It is more elaborate than ranking method.

Limitations of Grading Method

(i) It sometimes seems to be arbitrary, though it takes the views of the representatives of the trade unions.

(ii) Writing grade descriptions is not easy in this method.

[B] Conventional Quantitative Techniques

Under conventional quantitative techniques, there are two methods *viz.*, points rating and factor comparison system:

1. Points rating method Introduced by Merill R. Lott, it was one of the earliest approaches for evaluating jobs based on quantitative values. It is analytical in the sense that jobs are broken into components for purposes

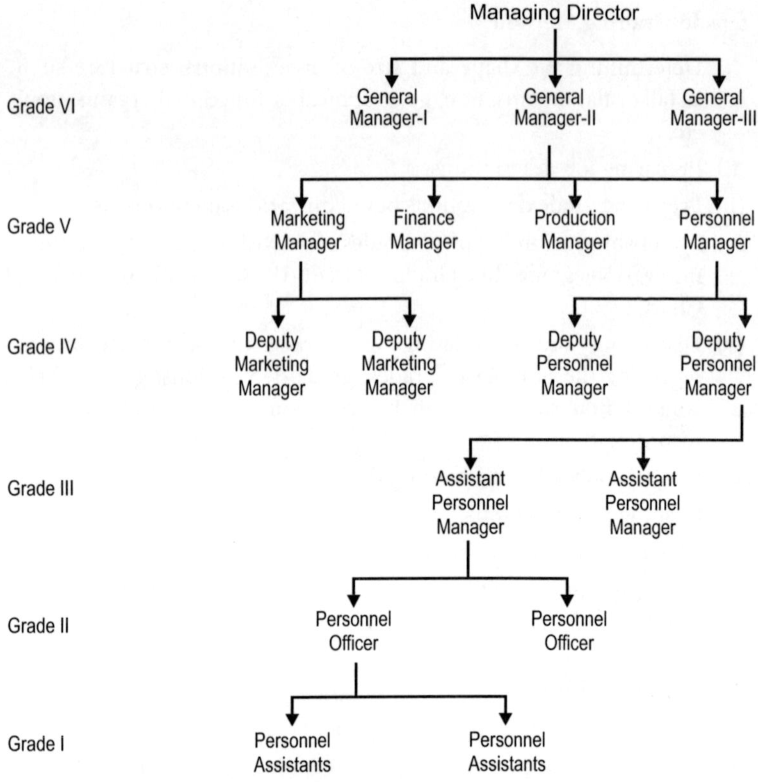

Chart 29.2 Grading the Jobs

of comparison. It is quantitative as each component of the job is assigned a numerical value. The characteristics having a bearing on all jobs in the programme like skill, knowledge, responsibility, working conditions, etc., are selected under this method. Each factor is divided into degrees or levels. Point value is assigned to each level. The total of point values assigned to each factor gives the total point values for each job.

In order to avoid the anomalies, this method of job evaluation should be developed systematically and applied methodically.

Steps in Points Rating Method

(i) ***Committee:*** Constituting a representative committee of members from various departments for job evaluation.

(ii) ***Sample:*** Selecting a sample of jobs and preparing job descriptions, job specifications and employee specifications.

(iii) ***Factors:*** Selecting and defining factors related to all jobs and considered to be most critical in determining the relative degrees of difficulty and responsibility between jobs. Following factors are most desirable:

(a) *Skill*: Education, training, judgement, analysis, mental complexity, mental dexterity, adaptability, etc.

(b) *Effort:* Physical demand, visual effort, concentration, mental effort, alertness etc.

(c) *Responsibility:* For preventing monetary loss, machines, materials, safety policy, etc.

(d) *Job Conditions* : Working conditions, hazards, etc.

(iv) ***Weightage*** **:** Determining the weightage of each factor according to its relative importance. Assigning the percentage value to each factor. The total percentage of all factors is 100.

(v) ***Scope*****:** Defining each factor, specifying the scope and elements of each factor.

(vi) ***Value*****:** Determining relative value of each level within factors. Factors can be divided into point values by arithmetic or geometric progression.

(vii) ***Testing the mechanism*****:** Get the total points with the help of above discussed method for a few sample jobs and compare them with the results obtained through other methods. Proceed further, if the system produces acceptable results.

(viii) ***Appraisal*****:** Appraise all the jobs and arrive at a composite numerical value for each job.

(ix) ***Pricing:*** Price the points in order to arrive at the wage level.

(x) ***Wage structure:*** Establish a wage structure with the help of organisational hierarchy of jobs and salary policy.

Job Factors	**Weights**	**Degrees**				
		1	2	3	4	5
1. Skill	20	4	8	12	16	20
2. Knowledge	15	5	10	15	20	25
3. Training	10	3	6	9	12	15
4. Experience	20	2	4	8	16	32
5. Complexity of duties	10	3	6	9	12	15
6. Contact with others	25	5	10	15	20	25

Total : 100

Factor	Experience
1st degree	up to 6 months
2nd degree	6 months to 1 year
3rd degree	1 year to 2 years
4th degree	2 years—3 years
5th degree	Above 3 years

Chart 29.3. Example of Mechanism of Points Ration Method – Job : Marketing Manager

Regarding factors, sub-factors assigning the weightages, deciding upon degrees and values, there are no hard and fast rules.

Points Rating Method is only a preliminary step is arriving at an equitable pay structure. There are no scientific techniques to guide about assigning money value to the points. But, influence of trade unions, pay structure in comparable industries, financial position of the company, living cost affect the pay level. However, this method may help in arriving at an equitable pay structure. It was important for conversion of point scores into monetary values by assigning a standard unit of money to each point. Money value of various scores can be attained by plotting a graph with points ratings on the X-axis and money value on the Y-axis. There are certain alternatives regarding plotting money on the Y-axis, such as showing current salary rates on Y-axis and the score of the job concerned on X-axis. Trend line through a scatter of points is seen

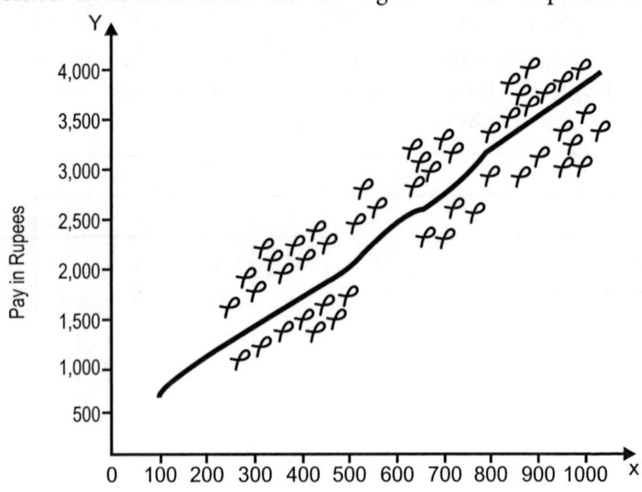

Fig. 29.1. Trend Line through a Scatter of Points

in Fig. 29.1. If point score is divided among various grades of jobs in an organisation, the pay level can be related to the grades as shown in Chart 29.4. While the minimum and maximum pay of each grade are shown in the figures the pay scale of various jobs will be fixed within the minimum and maximum limits of the pay.

Advantages of Point Rating Method

(i) ***Same pay scale:*** As agreement among rates on the same is very close, almost the same pay scale can be arrived at for the same jobs.

(ii) ***Applied definitions:*** Definitions are written in terms applicable to jobs.

(iii) ***Assigning monetary values is very easy.***

(iv) ***Prejudice, bias and error of human judgement are minimised.***

(v) ***Point score or monetary values:*** There cannot be manipulated easily.

(vi) ***Assignment of point score or money values:*** It is consistent and accurate.

(vii) ***The Score:*** Assigned to a particular job, it is long standing.

(viii) ***Wage differentials:*** They are systematic and according to the content of the job under this method.

Disadvantages of Point Rating Method

(i) ***Determination:*** Factor levels and assigned point values are difficult to determine.

(ii) ***Explanation:*** It is difficult to explain the mechanism and operation of this method to employees, supervisors and trade union leaders.

(iii) ***Operation:*** It involves heavy expenditure, spending of much time and clerical work.

However, this technique is superior to the conventional non-quantitative techniques in several respects.

2. The Point factor or factor-comparison method Based both on the principles of points rating and principle of ranking, this method is analytical. Jobs are broken into sub-factors and components. First the components or sub-factors are ranked under various factor headings. Next step is assigned for the monetary values to the components or sub-factors of each job. Thus, each job is ranked a number of times.

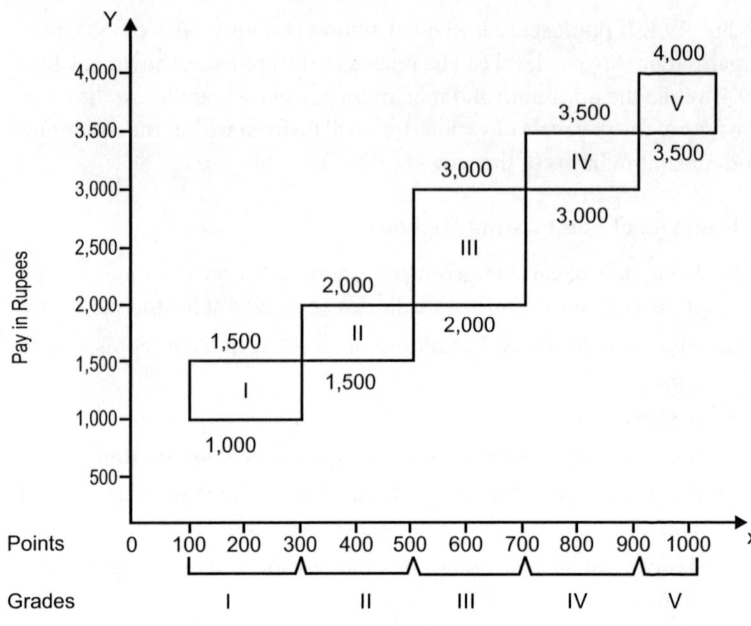

Chart 29.4 Relationship between Pay Level and Job Grades

Points Range	Grade	Pay at the Minimum		Pay at the Maximum
	Grade I Pay Scale	1,000	to	1,500
	Grade II Pay Scale	1,500	to	2,000
	Grade III Pay Scale	2,000	to	3,000
	Grade IV Pay Scale	3,000	to	3,500
	Grade V Pay Scale	3,500	to	4,000

Steps in Factor Comparison Method

1. Development Developing job descriptions, job specifications or job requirements, covering physical requirements, mental requirements, skill requirements, training and experience, responsibility and authority, working conditions, etc.

2. Selection Selecting a number of key jobs is more critical and useful from the point of final evaluation as the other jobs are assigned monetary values based on the fixed wage rates arrived for the key jobs on the basis of negotiations. A key job must be clearly divisible into sub-factors and components. This step also involves dividing the job into sub-factors and components.

3. Ranking. In ranking of key jobs, the sub-factors of each key job are given relative ranks, based on their individual contribution to the total job. Chart 29.5 shows ranking of sub-factors of two key jobs *viz.*, Welder and Mechanical Engineer.

Factor Rank Order	Welder	Mechanical Engineer
1	Physical requirements	Skill requirement
2	Working conditions	Mental requirement
3	Skill requirement	Responsibility
4	Responsibility	Working conditions
5	Mental requirements	Physical requirements

Chart 29.5. Factor Ranking of Two key Jobs

Competitive picture of the ranking of Welder and Mechanical Engineer is shown in a matrix of factor rankings as shown in chart 29.6:

Rank Order	Skill Requirements	Mental Requirements	Physical Requirements	Responsibility	Working Conditions
1.	Mechanical Engineer (25)		Welder (15)		
2.		Mechanical Engineer (20)			Welder (5)
3.	Welder (10)			Mechanical Engineer (15) Welder (4)	
4.					Mechanical Engineer (10)
5.	Welder (5)	Mechanical Engineer (8)			

Chart 29.6. Matrix of Factor Ranking of Welder and Mechanical Engineer

Valuation This involves valuing the sub-factors of each of key jobs. It is also known as factor evaluation. In order to know the total money value (or salary) of each of the key jobs, money worth of each sub-factor of the key jobs in ascertained. Following Chart 29.7 shows factor evaluation or monetary value (per day) of each of the key jobs.

Sub-Factors	Welder (Rs.)	Mechanical Engineer (Rs.)
Mental Requirements	5	20
Skill Requirements	10	25
Physical Requirements	15	8
Responsibility	4	15
Working conditions	5	10
Total	39	10

Chart 29.7. Factor Evaluation or Monetary Value of Key Jobs (per day)

5. Integration This is integrating the monetary value of sub-factors arrived through factors evaluation with those of ranking of factors to find out whether the difference among factors as per the ranking and factor evaluation is one and the same. Cross checking is provided through Chart 29.6 where the money value of each sub-factor is given in brackets.

6. Comparison It is comparing all the jobs (factor by factor) of the same grade or level with the related key job and establishing monetary value to the sub-factors of various jobs based on the monetary value of sub-factors or key jobs.

Advantages of Factor Comparison Method

(i) ***Analytical and Quantitative***

(ii) ***Combination*** : It is a combination of two techniques *i.e.,* ranking and factor comparison.

(iii) ***Easy:*** Its modes operandi is relatively easy to understand. Hence it can be operated and explained to supervisor, employee and trade union leaders.

(iv) ***Reliable*:** It is more reliable and valid, compared to other techniques, as each job is compared with all other jobs from two respects *i.e.,* factor rank order and factor comparison.

(v) ***Objective*:** It assigns money value more or less fairly and objectively. As there is cross checking of money value with rank order.

Limitations of Factor Comparison

(i) ***Costly:*** It is costly and somewhat difficult to operate compared to the conventional non-quantitative techniques.

(ii) *Less objective:* Factor evaluation in this method is not that much objective as that of point-rating technique.

(iii) *Less coverage:* It does not consider all the sub-factors as the operation of the system would be difficult if it considers all the factors.

Non-Conventional Techniques of Job Evaluation

These include: (1) Time-span of discretion theory, (2) Decision-banding, (3) Direct consensus method, (4) Guide-chart profile method, (5) Problem-solving compensable factor, (6) Guideline method and (7) Urwick or profile method, (8) Profile method.

1. Time-span of discretion theory. Based on his investigation into organisational structure, roles relationships at Glacier Metal Company in England, Proferssor Elliott Jaques constructed a different system for determining rates of pay based on psycho-economic considerations. He criticised the conventional techniques of salary determination on the grounds that they are based on relative strengths of the bargaining parties and fixation of salary on subjective judgements and assumptions. The laws of wage fixation are the laws of the jungle. Jaques suggests a technique giving social, psychological and economic satisfaction to the employee. It has an objective and scientific procedure from political and negotiating strengths.

According to Jaques, an employee would be in a state of equilibrium when his capacity to do certain volume of work (C) matches with the actual level of work turned out by the employee in his present role based on job demands (W) for which correct payment is made (P), *i.e.*, C.W.P. Employee feels (i) inequitable treatment when capacity matches work and payment is below par *i.e.*, $C = W < P$, (ii) frustration when capacity matches, with pay and work is below the capacity, *i.e.*, $C = P < W$, (iii) stress when pay is greater than work demanded and it is greater than capacity, *i.e.*, $P < W < C$. Thus according to Jaques, employees "whose capacities are well adjusted to the level of work they do, and where work provides them with a subjectively felt equitable level of payment are said to be in a state of 'psycho-economic' equilibrium." Jaques uses three systems *viz.*, (a) time-span of discretion, (b) equitable work payment scale and (c) Standard Earning-progression:

(a) *Time-span discretion:* The time-span of discretion is "the longest period of time which can elapse in a role before a superior can be sure that his subordinate has not been exercising marginally standard discretion continuously in balancing the pace and quality of his work."

Thus, the time-span is the time in hours (or days) from which an error, for example, wrong discussion or too much material left or too rough a finish by one operator goes until it is detected by the next operator in sequence of work or by the inspector or supervisor:

General and universal pay structure can be introduced and practised when the level of work (W) is measured by 'time-span'. The work is divided into prescribed and discretionary activities. The discretionary activities are those aspects of a work role, about which a subordinate must exercise his own discretion. Prescribed activities are carried out by following the laid down rules and procedures.

(b) ***Equitable work payment scale:*** Jaques relates 'equity payment theory' with the time-span of discretion. He says, "Equitable payment is the common norm, which people in roles of the same time-span, when asked in confidence, indicate, they would consider to be fair pay." Feeling of inequity of pay or dissatisfaction with pay are due not only to comparisons but also from maladjustments in C-W-P relations.

(c) ***Standard earning profession*****:** Standard payment and progression method involves determining the time-span bracket for each job holder and assigning the equitable salary bracket. A person's actual earnings progression over the past years to date are plotted graphically. Based upon his work performance and history Sugesiot makes a potential assessment for the man. Pay adjustments are made in accordance with movements in the countrywide salary index. The immediate superior assesses the performance of the employee and adjusts the pay from time to time. Thus the wages can be fixed on scientific basis of time, span discretion. However, a number of studies conducted during 1960s and 1970s did not confirm this contention. Further, it is difficult to understand and explain the mechanism of this method to workers and union leaders.

2. Decision-Banding According to Paterson, the major weakness of the conventional techniques is subjective measure. This weakness is more apparent when organisations compare dissimilar jobs. Paterson proposed a scheme which uses a single factor, *i.e.*, decision-making. Based on the kind of decisions to be made in performing the job, jobs differ from each other.

Paterson's approach to job evaluation involves four main stages, *viz.*: (i) establishment of job hands according to decision type and structure; (ii) job analysis; (iii) job-grading, sub-grading and ranking of jobs and (iv) job-assessment and assigning money values.

The quality of decision made the significant difference among jobs. Every known job can be compared against the following six basic levels of decision-makings.

(i) ***Band E*****:** Policy-making decisions — made at the top level.

(ii) ***Band D*****:** Programming decisions — made in the execution of the policy.

(iii) ***Band C*****:** Interpretive decisions — made in interpreting the programme.

(iv) ***Band B*****:** Routine decisions — made in execution of interpreted policy.

(v) ***Band A*****:** Automatic decisions — made on the operational aspects of the process such as when, how, where, etc.

(vi) ***Band O*** **:** Defined decisions — decisions permitting very limited discretion.

Each band except 'O' is divided into Upper and Lower Levels.

3. Direct consensus method Developed by Associated Industrial Consultants Ltd., this method can be applied to all types and levels of jobs. The key criteria against which jobs are to be assessed is determined in advance. Key criteria common and relevant to some jobs, are determined by cross-sampling of opinion and statistical analysis. The next step is preparing job descriptions from a representative sample of jobs in the survey. The number of jobs chosen should be 11 and 79. A committee of assessors is to be selected, the number of members must be geared to the number of jobs to be evaluated (for technical reasons) so that assessors ranks an equal percentage of total. The number of paired comparisons number of jobs in the sample. Jobs are ranked on the basis of paired comparisons. If is the number of jobs, the number of comparison is $N\left[\frac{N-1}{2}\right]$. Assigning money value is based on the company policy, negotiation and Market rates.

4. Guide chart profile method Developed by a firm of management consultants Hay-MSL Ltd., it is modification of point method. The concept of accountability of manager's job is a common factor for evaluation. Other important factors necessary for job performance are know-how, problem-solving skill. These three aspects are key elements in any managerial job. Points scales are allocated for know-how and accountability. Problem solving is a percentage of the know-how deployed. Each job is rated under each criterion. Jobs can be plotted on charts to show up the job structures in quantitative terms. Common score is calculated for all the three factors of all the jobs. In order to arrive at the salary figure, money values are assigned to the scores.

5. Problem-solving compensable factor According to A.W. Charles, problem solving skill is a single universal compensable factor. Jobs can be evaluated from the lowest to highest on the basis of degree of the problem solving skill required to perform a job. Wages should be proportional to the responsibility required by the problem solving activities of a job. Wages should be high to those jobs whose responsibility requirements for problem skills are high and vice versa. Charles developed a matrix which permits the measurement of amount of responsibility required of problem solving of a job in comparison with those of other jobs. Charles is confident that this technique overcomes the weakness of point, rating method.

6. Guideline method Richard C. Smith and Matthew J. Murphy used this method consisting of four elements, *viz.,* (i) a guideline scale, (ii) scope data, (iii) market pricing and (iv) horizontal guideline display.

- **(i)** ***The guideline scale*:** A standard scale of salary range indicating minimum, maximum and mid-point, it contends that 5 per cent difference in mid-points between pay grades is ideal. It allows flexibility of moving job up and down.
- **(ii)** ***Scope data*:** In order to identify the salaries paid to these jobs in comparable industries, it helps in identifying, defining and describing key jobs.
- **(iii)** ***Market pricing:*** To find out wages for similar jobs in comparable industries, it involves conducting market survey.
- **(iv)** ***Horizontal guideline displays*:** It involves development of horizontal guideline displays. Its process involves two or more vertical guideline displays for ensuring equitable relationships.

7. Urwick or profile method Developed by management consultants Urwick Orr and Partners Ltd. in 1960, it is more akin to direct consensus method, although it is a combination of points rating and ranking methods at the root level. Because of its adaptability and its participative approach, it is highly accepted in large-scale industries. It involves the following steps:

- **(i)** ***Selecting:*** Key jobs from jobs under consideration.
- **(ii)** ***Rating:*** The jobs based on six sub-factors, *viz.,* responsibility, knowledge, mental demands, social demands, physical demands and work environment. Each sub-factor is scored on a four-point scale, *i.e.,* basic, moderate, high and exceptional. Minor differences in sub-factors are ignored.
- **(iii)** ***Ranking:*** The key jobs according to total score values of sub-factors.
- **(iv)** ***Re-ranking:*** The jobs on a 'Whole' job basis.
- **(v)** ***Comparing and reconciling:*** The ranks based on sub- factors and whole job basis.
- **(vi)** ***Removing discrepancies:*** If any, by reconsidering the weights of sub-factors until a workable and acceptable framework is reached.
- **(vii)** ***Presenting:*** The jobs are a profile and point scores.

Representatives of workers, their unions and management have overall control on the mechanism of this technique.

8. Profile method Similar to guide chart profile method and points system, this method considers smaller number of factors *viz.*, the amount of knowledge of job calls for as shown on the vertical line of Chart 29.8, the experience rating for jobs shown on the horizontal line of Chart 29.8. Degrees are to be assigned to both the factors. A point score for that overall factor is determined on the basis of the points of these two factors where the degrees of these two factors meet. Money values are assigned to the overall points.

Most of these non-conventional techniques have been developed by management consultants for helping their client companies. Based on the variations of the points methods, there techniques are quantitative. To be successful, any scheme should aim at a high degree of reliability and validity. Apart from various theoretical concepts, the adaptability and usage of the job evaluation are increasing. It contributes to the rational wage payment, to building up rational wage structure and helps to stabilise, control and forecast cost of human resources. It is a part of pay fixation machinery along with other concepts like wage theories, seniority, performance, career progression, wage survey and other factors influencing wage determination.

Experience Knowledge	1-2 Years	2-4 Years	4-5 Years	8-12 Years	Over 12 Years
1. Good basic education without specialisation.	10	20	40	80	160
2. Proficiency in a technical subject without a professional qualification.	20	40	80	160	320
3. Professional qualification in a single science or business field.	40	80	160	320	640
4. Highest professional qualification, Expert recognised knowledge in one or more scientific or specialised managerial fields.	80	160	320	640	1280
5. Complete professional knowledge of scientific and/or management function. Recognised authority on L.S. subjects.	160	320	640	1280	2560

Chart 29.8 Profile Method Know-how

Source: G. McBeath and D.N. Rands, Salary, Administration, Business Book Ltd., London, p. 66.

ADVANTAGES OF JOB EVALUATION

1. **Logical and objective** It is a logical and to a certain extent an objective method of ranking and grading the jobs.
2. **Fitting.** It helps to fit the newly created jobs in the existing structure.
3. **Less hrievances** Employee grievances, doubts and complaints would be at the lower ebb, as it is a systematic and objective method of wage fixation.
4. **Eliminates undesirable factors** It eliminates some undesirable factors like it. Equalities in bargaining capacities of employees and employers fluctuations in market rates, etc.
5. **Principles** It satisfies the principles of fair wage, wage equity, uniformity in wages, etc.
6. **Redesigns** It helps to redesign the jobs for minimising wide wage level and wage equity.
7. **Employee satisfaction** It ensures employee satisfaction about wage level and wage equity.
8. **Reallocation** It also helps to redesign the jobs by reallocating the easy and difficult tasks equally among various jobs.

Limitations of Job Evaluation

1. **Less scientific** Job evaluation is not exactly scientific.
2. **Difficult method** *Modus operandi* of most of the techniques is difficult to understand even to the supervisors.
3. **Not exhaustive** The factors taken by the programme are not exhaustive.
4. **Fluctuations** There may be wide fluctuations in compensable factors in view of changes in technology, values and aspirations of employers, etc.
5. **Different perceptions** Employees, trade union leaders, management, and the programme operators may perceive differently in selecting the compensable factors, in giving weightages or degrees, etc.
6. **Unreliable** The results of job evaluation may not exactly coincide with social evaluations, which, in turn, result in employee dissatisfaction.
7. **Only one factor** Job evaluation is only one among several factors in determining wage level. Sometimes other factors like government policy may dominate the job evaluation.

QUESTIONS FOR EXERCISE

1. What is Job Evaluation? Explain the objectives of job evaluation. How do you prepare the ground for evaluating jobs?
2. What are the conventional and non-conventional techniques of job evaluation? What types of technique do you adopt to evaluate the jobs of maintenance, operation marketing and chief engineer in a large machine tools industry?
3. Explain the advantages and limitations of job evaluation as a basis for fixing and removing wages and salaries.

30

QUALITY OF WORK LIFE AND QUALITY CIRCLES

WHAT IS QUALITY OF WORK LIFE?

The term 'Quality of Work Life' (QWL) appeared in research journals and the press in USA in 1970s. It refers to the favourableness or unfavourableness of a job environment for people.

Definitions of QWL

1. Grey Densler Lloy "QWL means different things to different" people.

2. J. Richard and Lloy QWL as, "the degree to which members of a work organization able to satisfy important personal needs through their experience in the organization."

3. Lee M. Ozley and Judith S. Ball Quality of work life improvements are defined as "Any activity which takes place at every level of an organisation, which seeks greater organisational effectiveness through the enhancement of human dignity and growth...a process through which the stakeholders in the organisation — management, unions and employees — learn how to work together better...to determine for themselves what actions, changes and improvements are desirable and workable, in order to achieve the twin and simultaneous goals of an improved quality of life at work for all members of the organisation and greater effectiveness for both the company and unions."

4. Richard E. Walton He explains quality of work life in terms of eight broad conditions of employment that constitute desirable quality of work life (QWL). He proposed the same criteria for measuring QWL.

CRITERIA OF QWL

1. Adequate and fair compensation The Committee on Fair Wages defined fair wage as "...the wage which is above the minimum wage but below the living age."
2. Safe and healthy working conditions Most of the organisations provide safe and healthy working conditions as humanitarian and/or legal requirements. These conditions are a matter of enlightened self-interest.
3. Opportunity to use and develop human capacities QWL is improved "...to the extent that the worker can exercise more control over his or her work, and the degree to which the job embraces an entire meaningful task...." QWL provides opportunities like autonomy in work and participation in planning in order to develop human capabilities.
4. Opportunity for career growth Either due to educational barriers or due to limited openings at the higher level. Opportunities for promotions are limited in case of all categories of employees. By expanding one's capabilities, knowledge and qualification, QWL provides future opportunity for continued growth and security.
5. Social integration in the work force Social integration in the workforce can be established by creating freedom from prejudice, supporting primary work groups, a sense of community and interpersonal openness, egalitarianism and upward mobility.
6. Constitutionalism in the work organisation QWL provides constitutional protection to the employees only to the level of desirability. It hampers workers' satisfaction of doing the job beyond that level. The management's action is challenged in every action and bureaucratic procedures need to be followed at that level. Constitutional protection is provided to employees on such matters as privacy, free speech, equity and due process.
7. Work and quality of life QWL provides for the balanced relationship among work, non-work and family aspects of life. Family life and social life should not be strained by working hours including overtime work, during inconvenient hours, business travel, transfers, vacations, etc.
8. Social relevance of work QWL is concerned about the establishment of social relevance to work in a socially beneficial manner. The workers' self-esteem would be high if his work is useful to the society and *vice versa* is also true.

SPECIFIC ISSUES IN QWL

Klott, Mundick and Schuster suggested 11 major QWL issues as follow:

1. Pay and stability of employment Good pay dominates most of the other factors in employee satisfaction. In view of increase in the cost of living index, increase in levels and rates of income-tax and professional tax, various alternative means for providing wages should be developed. Stability of employment is guaranteed to a certain extent in India. However, stability can be provided by enhancing the facilities for human resources development.

2. Occupational stress According to Keith Davis, stress is a condition of strain on one's emotions, thought process and physical condition determined by the nature of work, working conditions, working hours, pause in the work schedule, worker's abilities and nature and match with the job requirements. Stress is caused due to irritability, hyperxatation or depression, unstable behaviour, fatigue, stuttering, trembling, psychosomatic pains, heavy smoking and drug abuse. It adversely affects employee productivity. In order to minimise the stress, the P.H.R. Manager has to identify, prevent and tackle the problem. He may arrange for the treatment of the problem with the health unit of the company.

3. Organisational health programmes They aim at educating employees about health problems, means of maintaining and improving of health, etc. They cover drinking and smoking cessation, hypertension control, other forms of cardiovascular risk reduction, family planning, etc. Effective implementation of these programmes results in reduction in absenteeism, hospitalisation, disability, excessive job turnover and premature death. This programme should also cover relaxation, physical exercise, diet control, etc.

4. Alternative work schedules As the work schedule offers the individual the leisure time, flexible hours of work are preferred. Alternative work schedules including work at home, flexible working hours, staggered hours, reduced work week, part-time employment may be introduced for the convenience and comfort of the workers.

5. Participative management and control of work Trade unions and workers believe that workers' participation in management and decision-making improve. QWL. Workers feel that they have control over their work. They use their skills and make a real contribution to the job if they are allowed to participate in creative and decision-making process.

6. Recognition Recognising the employee as a human being rather than as a labourer increases the QWL. Some means to recognise the employees are participative management, awarding and rewarding systems, congratulating the employees for their achievement, job enrichment, offering prestigious designations to the jobs, providing well furnished and decent workplaces, offering membership in clubs or associations, providing vehicles, offering vacation trips.

7. Cogenial worker-supervisor relations Harmonious supervisor, worker relations provide the worker a sense of social association, belongingness, achievement of work results, etc. This, in turn, leads to better QWL.

8. Grievance procedure Workers have a sense of fair treatment when the company gives them the opportunity to ventilate their grievances and represent their case succinctly rather than settling the problems arbitrarily.

9. Adequacy of resources Resources should match with stated objectives, otherwise, employees will not be able to attain the objectives. This results in employees, dissatisfaction and lower QWL.

10. Seniority and merit in promotions In case of operating employees, seniority is generally taken as the basis for promotion. For managerial people, merit should be considered as the basis for advancement. Seniority-cum-merit is preferred for promotion of ministerial employees. In order to ensure higher QWL, the promotional policies and activities should be fair and just.

11. Employment on permanent basis While employment of workers on casual, temporary, probationary basis gives them a sense of insecurity, employment on permanent basis gives them security and leads to higher order QWL.

IMPACT ON QWL

1. Fringe benefits P/HR manager has to build and maintain QWL by providing a wide range of fringe benefits. These benefits include medical and health benefits, safety measures, legal and financial services, consumer services, retirement benefits, conveyance, canteen facilities, recreational services, career counselling, employee information reports, etc. They result in improvement in productivity, reduction in absenteeism, turnover, sick leave, alienation, etc.

2. Productivity Improvement over the existing salary, working conditions and benefits cost much but the rate of increase in productivity is higher than that of cost of QWL. Increase in QWL results in increase in productivity. However, continual increase in QWL eventually leads to reduction in productivity due to increase in cost of output because the worker's output does not increase proportionately after a certain level even though QWL increases.

3. Performance Performance is not only physical output but also the behaviour of the worker in helping his colleagues in solving job related problems, accepting orders with enthusiasm, promoting a positive team spirit and accepting temporary unfavourable work conditions without complaint. Improved QWL leads to improved performance.

4. Personnel/human resource management All personnel related activities affect quality of work life. This is as follows:

(i) *Job analysis*: Analyse the job in such a way that human needs like freedom, challenging work, autonomy can be satisfied.

(ii) *Selection*: Select the right man and place him in the right position. This satisfies his needs for reward, interesting work, etc.

(iii) *Job enrichment:* It satisfies higher order needs like pride, ego.

(iv) *Job evaluation:* It leads to equitable wages.

STRATEGIES FOR IMPROVEMENT IN QWL

1. Self-managed work teams Also called autonomous work groups or integrated work teams, these are formed with 10 to 20 employees who plan, co-ordinate and control the activities of the team, with the help of a team leader, who is one among them. Each team performs all activities including selecting their people. Each team has authority to make decisions and regulate the activities. Group, as a whole, is accountable for the success or failure. Salaries are fixed both on the basis of individual and group achievement.

2. Job redesign and enrichment Narrow jobs can be combined into larger units of accomplishment. Jobs are redesigned to enrich them to satisfy higher order human needs.

3. Effective leadership and supervisory behaviour '9-9' style of managerial gird is suitable for effective leadership and supervisory behaviour.

4. Career development Provision should be made for career planning, communicating and counselling the employees about the career opportunities, career path. Education and development and for sound careers.

5. Alternative work schedules Provision should be made for flexible working hours, part-time employments, job sharing and reduced work week.

6. Job security As it tops the employee's list of priorities, it should be adequately taken care of.

7. Administrative or organisational justice The principles of justice, fair play and equity should be taken care of in disciplinary procedure, grievance procedure, promotions, transfers, demotions, work assignment, leave, etc.

8. Participative management Employees should be allowed to participate in management. The most sophisticated participative management is quality circle.

QUALITY CIRCLE (QC)

History of Quality Circles

The credit of developing the concept quality circles has gone to the Union of Japanese Scientists and Engineers along with Kaoru Ishikawa of Tokyo University. Historically 'Gun Mandal' (Quality Circles) have been used in different social, religious, and political settings since the dawn of Indian civilisation to enhance '*Satvic* qualities' *i.e.,* urge for excellence and knowledge, concern for others' interest, trust and confidence, self-actualisation, etc., minimise *rejasic* qualities such as urge for economic resources, authority and power, concern for personal interest, restlessness and tension, craze for ego inflation, etc., and *tamasic* qualities such as prone to err, indolence and wickedness, urge to exploit and damage others, distrust, loss of self-identity, etc. Non-application of the science of Bhagavatgita and Vedas to industrial and business organisations is one of the reasons for dependence of Indian organisations on the techniques developed in foreign countries.

Definition of Quality Circle

According to Edwin B. Flippo, a quality circle is a "self-governing group of workers with or without their supervisors who voluntarily meet regularly to identify, analyse and solve problems of their work field".

Quality circle Vs. Task force Quality circle and task force are not one and the same. Quality circle is not a task force. It is broader than the task force. A task force is a group of most skilled employees selected and appointed by management, engaged in various functions, with an orientation to problem-solving. The QC is a voluntary association of workers engaged in similar work with an orientation of human relations. QCs are formed to attain specific objectives.

Objectives of Quality Circles

1. To develop, enhance and utilise human resources effectively.
2. To improve quality of products/services, productivity and reduce cost of production per unit of output.
3. To satisfy the workers' psychological needs for self-urge, participation, recognition, etc., with a view to motivate them. This will ensure enhancement of employee morale and commitment.

4. To improve various supervisory skills like leadership, problem solving, interpersonal and conflict resolution.
5. To utilise individual imaginative, creative and innovative skills through participation, creating and developing work interest, inculcating problem solving techniques, etc. This requires the use of certain techniques.

Techniques for Quality Circles

Following are the three main techniques used in discussing various problems for quality circles:

1. Brain storming processes This technique is useful to generate as many ideas as possible. Under this technique, completely free environment is created to stimulate creativity. As employees' ideas are free from criticism, they voice all their worthy as well as stupid ideas. These ideas are recorded seriously. Later, the plus and minus points of each idea are discussed, before taking a final decision.

2. Cause and effect Members are asked to find out the causes for the identified problem. They identify one important effect of this cause on the problem. Then they identify other causes and their effects. As charting out of those causes and effects resembles fish-bone diagram, this technique is also called 'fishpond diagram'.

3. Sampling and charting methods Members of the quality circles observe the events and their consequences in the form of positive or negative results. They chart out all their observations either in sequence or in some other relationship, which give clear idea of the problem.

Requirements of Quality Circles

1. Participative management Both employees and management are jointly involved in decision-making process on matters of mutual interest in participative management. The participative management produces better solutions to the problems which benefit all concerned. Participative managers consult their followers and involve them in decision-making so that their group acts as a social unit in work performance. Participating managers are not autocratic or free-rein managers. They are responsible and accountable for the success or failure of their departments.

Participative management satisfies economic, psychological and social needs of employees. It gives them a sense of significance, pride and accomplishment, freedom and opportunity for expression, a feeling of belongingness to the place of work and a sense of creativeness to the employees. It aims at: (i) improving organisational efficiency,

(ii) developing social education for effective solidarity among workers, (iii) attaining industrial peace, (iv) treating the workers as human beings and (v) developing self-management teams in industry. It results in effective management.

2. Group interaction A group is two or more interacting and interdependent individuals who come together to achieve particular objectives. Groups may be formal or informal. Formal groups are defined by organisation structure with clear-cut assignment, responsibility, accountability, rules and norms. Informal groups are the natural formations in the work environment in response to the need for social contact. Both these groups are not structured and determined by the organisation. They satisfy the social needs of their members. The important aspects of group interaction are group goals, participation, leadership norms and cohesiveness.

(i) *Goals*: Group has two types of goals *viz.*, task goal and maintaining the group itself. Task goal is related to the main function for which the group is formed. The other goal is related to dealing with interpersonal conflict, resolving it and maintaining interpersonal relations. Group members' trusting behaviour contributes to increased originality, greater emotional stability, less defensive and improved self-control.

(ii) *Type of participation in group:* Participation in a group may be voluntary, invited or assigned. Members voluntarily join the group.

(a) *Voluntary:* In significant numbers if the group activity is effective. Experts and specialists are invited to join the group as members or advisors. Group as a whole and other members of the group are benefited by the interaction of those special members.

(b) *Assigned:* Participation in group is also assigned. The management forms various groups and assigns the membership including the tasks and responsibilities to various individuals. For example, to suggest measures to minimise absenteeism the personnel manager may form a group with three assistant personnel managers. He assigns three different aspects of the problem like absenteeism among unskilled workers, technical personnel and managerial personnel to the three assistant personnel managers of the group.

(iii) *Leader:* The leader is a must to co-ordinate and control the members as well as activities whether it is a formal group or an informal group. Groups may have two types of leaders *viz.*, tasks leader and unofficial social leader. They achieve two basic objectives, *i.e.*, performing the main task and satisfying members' social needs.

(iv) *Norms:* Group norm is expected behaviour of group members. Norms are normally unwritten in the informal groups. The norm of quality circles is openness which helps to solve the problems better.

(v) *Cohesiveness:* It is the degree of attraction that the group has for its members. It may be in the form of loyalty, sense of belongingness, friendliness, feeling of responsibility for group tasks. It can be increased through stability of membership, similar values of members, providing free communication opportunities, physical isolation from the formal control, small size.

Organisational Structure

Organisational structure of QC consists of four levels, *viz.,* (1) Steering Committee (2) Facilitator, (3) QC Leader (4) QC member.

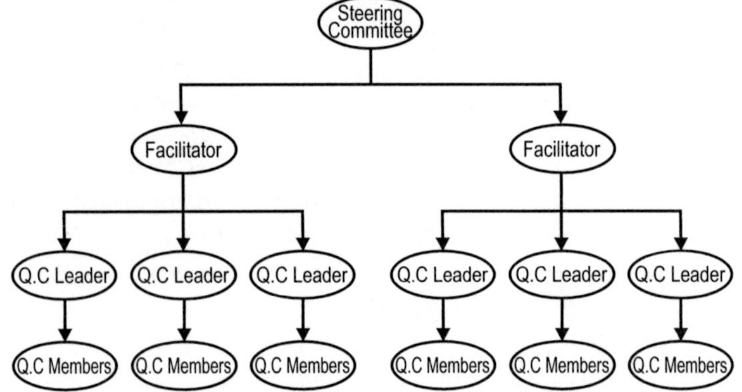

Fig. 30.1. Organisational Structure of Quality Circles

1. Steering committee It consists of representatives of management from different departments at top level and top level representatives of recognised unions/federations of employees.

Functions of Steering Committee (i) Sponsoring QC programme in the entire organisation: This is done by defining overall objectives and operating guidelines relating to the identification of the department where the circles are to be formed, provision of training to leaders and members of QCs, identification of the problems to be discussed, receiving, discussing and finalising the suggestions, action plans, budget, etc.

(ii) Selecting and training the facilitators.

(iii) Providing the resources and moral support to the facilitators.

2. Facilitator An important person between the quality circle and the steering committee, Facilitator (i) acts as a consultant and guide to the QC leaders; (ii) initiates the setting up of QCs by persuading the supervisor, by teaching and training the QC leaders and members; (iii) provides feedback to the steering committee about the proceedings and results of the QCs and (iv) acts as an evaluator and reviewer of QC operations and programmes.

The facilitator maintains sound interpersonal relations in order to function as a social leader. He has to prove himself successful in acting as a co-ordinator, coach, promoter, teacher and innovator. He should be an excellent resource person for training the managers at higher level.

3. QC leader Activities of each circle are co-ordinated and streamlined by its leader who is an elected member of the circle. Manager/supervisor of that particular department/section where the QC is set up, may act as the leader. The leader must have skills in discussion, initiation and promotion of active participation. He should be a trained one in group dynamics, human behaviour and participative leadership styles. The activities of a QC leader are:

Conducting: the meetings, initiating the discussion and motivate the members to participate actively; (i) acting as a link between the members and facilitator; and (ii) training the members in problem identification, discussion and problem-solving techniques.

4. QC members Members of a single work group form a quality circle, joining voluntarily or on invitation. They are free to withdraw from membership. Their activities include: attending meetings, participating actively in problem-identification, contributing ideas in developing solutions to the identified problems and the like.

QC Process

In order to attain the objectives effectively, QCs should follow systematic process. In addition to the sound organisational structure, size of each QC may vary between 6 and 12. QC members and leader are given instructions regarding problem-solving techniques. The QC Members should acquaint themselves about the objectives and role of QCs.

1. Session Each working session of a QC may be for one hour. There should be at least one working session every week, preferably during working hours and in the company premises. If the working session is conducted after the working hours, the members may be paid honorarium for attending the meeting.

2. Problem The members of QC select the problem from the operational problems suggested by management or by the members of the QC. After selecting the problem, the members analyse it by using the various problem-solving techniques. Sometimes the QC leader invites experts to analyse the problem and their effects. The members develop alternative solutions, their effect and consequences on organisation and members, cost-benefit analysis and merits and demerits of each solution.

3. Selection of solution Now, the members select the best solution from among the alternative solutions. Some of then present the selected solution to the management. Management reviews the solution and may or may not accept it but in most cases managers accept the solution.

4. Implementation After the solution is accepted, the members either by themselves and/or with the help of others, implement the solution. Management has to provide of all types of support, including finance, to implement such solutions.

Concepts to make QC Process Effective

According to Edwin B. Floppso, the following concepts make the QC process effective:

1. Acceptance by all, particularly the leader, that there is more than one way to solve a problem successfully.
2. Encouragement of all members to clarify and build on each other's ideas.
3. Periodic summarising of the activities by the leader, or a member to ensure common understanding.
4. Avoidance of heated arguments in favour of one particular position. Vigorous eloquence should not be a substitute for clarity and logic.
5. Avoidance of such techniques as majority vote and conflicting to obtain group agreement.
6. Promotion of constructive disagreements in place of dodging arguments in search of an artificial state of harmony.

QUESTIONS FOR EXERCISE

1. What is quality of work life? Discuss its criteria and items.
2. Explain the impact of fringe benefits, productivity and good human resource management on QWL. Suggest strategies for improvement of QWL.
3. Trace the history of Quality Circle. Give its definitions and objectives and techniques.
4. What are the essential requirements of Quality Circle?
5. Analyse organisational structure of Quality Circle. What concepts make its process effective?

31

EMPLOYEE STRESS

WHAT IS EMPLOYEE STRESS?

Employee stress is a dynamic condition in which an individual is confronted with an opportunity, constraint or demand related to what he or she desires in his working conditions and for which the outcome is perceived to be both uncertain and important.

Typical Symptoms of Stress Employee

1. Adverse strain Employee stress can cause adverse strain on one's emotions, thought processes and physical conditions. When it becomes excessive, employees develop various symptoms of stress that can harm their job performance and health, and even threaten their ability to cope with the environment. Stress is not necessarily bad in and of itself. While stress is typically discussed in negative context, it also has positive value. It is an opportunity when it offers potential gains. Many individuals often use stress positively to rise to the occasion and perform at or near their maximum.

2. Psychological symptoms The individual may become nervous and develop chronic worry. They are easily provoked to anger and are unable to relax. They may be uncooperative or use alcohol or drugs excessively. These conditions are common symptoms of stress.

3. Physical disorders Employee's stress also leads to physical disorders, as the internal body system changes to cope with stress. Some physical disorders are short range such as an upset stomach. Others are long range such as a stomach ulcer. Stress over a prolonged time also leads to degenerative disease of the heart, kidneys, blood vessels, and other parts of the body. Therefore, stress, both on and off the job, should be kept at a level low for most people to tolerate without disorders.

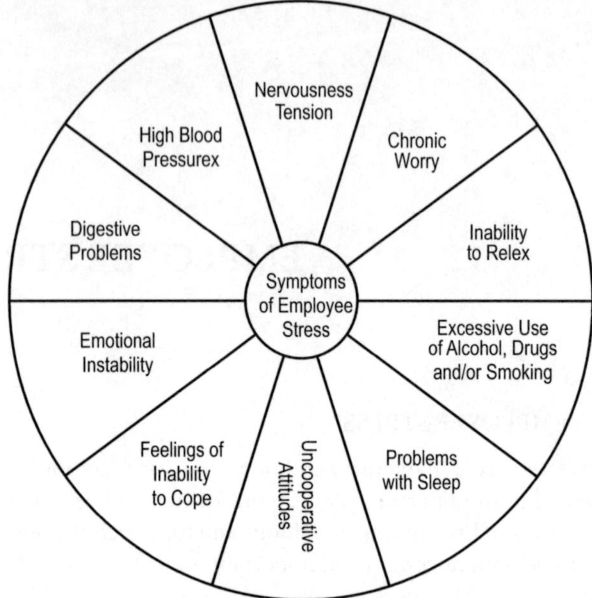

Fig. 31.1. Symptoms of Employee Stress

4. Constraints and demands More typically stress is associated with constraints and demands. The constraints prevent employees from doing what they desire; the demand refers to the loss of something desired.

For potential stress to become actual stress, there must be uncertainty about the outcome and the outcome must be important. Regardless of the conditions, it is only when there is doubt or uncertainty about whether the opportunity will be seized, the constraint removed, or the loss avoided that there is stress. Stress is highest in those individuals who perceive that it is uncertain whether they will win or lose. It is lowest in those individuals who think that winning or losing is an unimportant outcome. If keeping our job or earning promotion doesn't hold any importance for us, we have no reason to feel stress over having to undergo a performance review.

THE POTENTIAL SOURCES OF STRESS

(1) Environmental factors These are as follows:

(i) ***Environmental uncertainty:*** It influences the design of the organisation's structure, which influences stress levels among employees in that organisation.

(ii) *Changes in the business cycle:* These create *economic uncertainties.* When the economy is contracting, people become increasingly anxious about their security.

(iii) *Political uncertainty:* It is also a probable sources of stress. New innovations can make an employee's skill and experience obsolete in a very short period of time.

(iv) *Technological uncertainty:* It is a factor which causes stress.

2. Organisational forces Pressure to avoid errors or complete task in limited time period, work overload, a demanding and insensitive superior and unpleasant co-workers are few examples of organisational forces causing stress.

(i) *Task demands:* These are factors related to a person's job. They include the design of the individual's job (autonomy, task variety, degree of automation), working conditions and the physical work layout. Assembly lines can put pressure on people when their speed is perceived as excessive. Increase in interdependence between a person's tasks and the tasks of others, increase potential stress. On the other hand, autonomy tends to decrease stress. Jobs where temperatures, noise, or other working conditions are dangerous or undesirable can increase anxiety. Working in an overcrowded room or in a visible location where interruptions are constant increases stress.

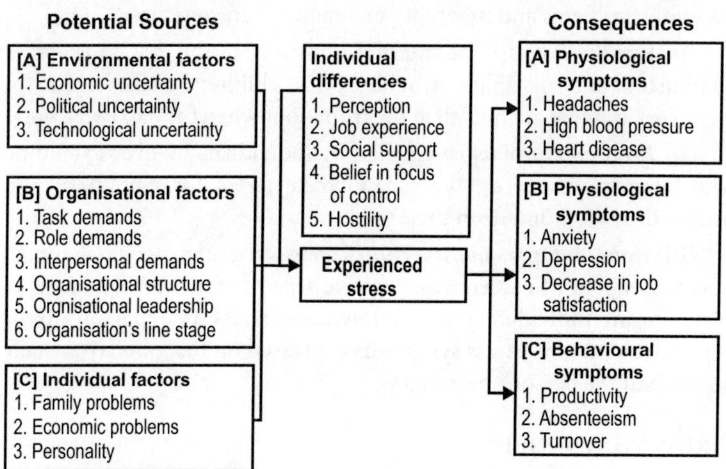

Fig. 31.2. Sources and Consequences of Employee Stress

(ii) *Role demands*: These relate to pressures placed on a person as a function of the particular role he or she plays in the organisation.

(a) *Role conflicts*: These create expectations that may be hard to reconcile or satisfy.

(b) *Role overload*: It is experienced when the employee is expected to do more than time permits.

(c) *Role ambiguity*: It is created when role expectations are not clearly understood and the employee is not sure what he or she is to do.

(iii) *Interpersonal demands:* There are pressures created by other employees. Lack of social support from colleagues and poor interpersonal relationships may cause considerable stress, especially among employees with a high social need.

(iv) *Organisation structure*: It defines the level of differentiation in the organisation, the degree of rules and regulations, and where decisions are made. Excessive rules and lack of participation in decisions that affect an employee are examples of structural variables that might be potential sources of stress.

(v) *Organisational leadership:* It represents the managerial style of the organisation's senior executives. Some chief executive officers create a culture characterised by tension, fear, and anxiety. They create unrealistic pressures to perform in the short run; they impose excessively light controls. They routinely fire employees.

3. Individual factors These factors include family issues. Personal economic problems and inherent personality characteristics:

(i) *Family issues:* The marital difficulties, the breaking off a relationship and discipline troubles with children create stress for employees and that are not left at the front door when they arrive at work.

(ii) *Economic problems:* Created by individuals by over-extending their financial resources, these can create stress for employees and distract their attention from their work.

(iii) *Inherent personality characteristics*: Some people have an inherent tendency to accentuate negative aspects of the world in general. A significant individual factor influencing stress is a person's basic dispositional nature. Stress symptoms expressed on the job may actually originate in the person's personality.

STRESS THRESHOLD

People have different tolerance for stressful situations. This helps to explain variations in employee performance across similar jobs. Stress threshold is the level of stress that one can tolerate before negative feelings of stress occur and performance is adversely affected. Some people are easily upset by the slightest change or disruption in their work routines. Others are cool, calm and collected under the same conditions, because they have confidence in their ability to cope. They have a much higher stress threshold. Their performance does not suffer unless a stress is major or prolonged.

Type A and Type B People (Behaviour)

Type A and Type B persons show different reactions to stress conditions.

1. Type A behaviour It is characterized by feeling a chronic sense of time urgency and by an excessive competitive drive. Type A people are aggressively involved in a chronic incessant struggle to achieve more and more in less time, and against the opposing efforts of other things or other persons. Type A people are:

(i) Always moving, walking and eating rapidly.
(ii) Impatient with the rate at which most events take place.
(iii) Thinking or doing two or more things simultaneously.
(iv) Not coping with leisure time.
(v) Obsessed with numbers, measuring their success in terms of how much of everything they acquire.
(vi) Are more likely to experience stress on or off the job.
(vii) They are at higher risk for heart disease.
(viii) They are chronically angry, suspicious and mistrustful persons.

2. **Type B behaviour** It is the opposite of Type A. Type B are rarely hurried by the desire to obtain a widely increasing number of things or participate in the endless growing series of events in an ever decreasing amount of time. The Type B people:

(i) Never suffer from a sense of time urgency with its accompanying impatience;
(ii) Feel no need to display or discuss their achievements or accomplishments unless such exposure is demanded by the situation;
(iii) Play for fun and relaxation rather than to exhibit their superiority at any cost and
(iv) Can relax without guilt.

STRESS MANAGEMENT STRATEGIES

Some organisations' managements may not be concerned when employees experience low to moderate level of stress, because such levels of stress can be functional and lead to higher employee performance. But high or low levels of stress, sustained over long period of time may lead to reduce employee's performance and this requires stress by management.

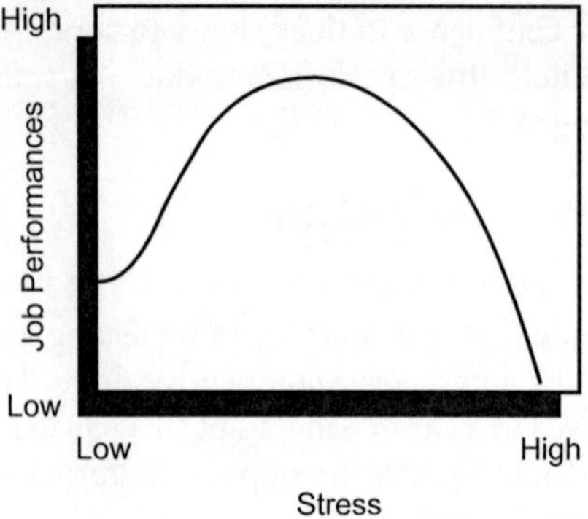

Fig. 31.3. Relation between Stress and Performance

When there is no stress, job challenges are absent and performance tends to be low. As stress increases, performance tends to increase, because stress helps a person call up resources to meet job requirements. Stress is a healthy stimulus that encourages employees to respond to challenges. It reaches a plateau that corresponds approximately with a person's day-to-day performance capability. At this point, additional stress tends to produce no more improvement.

However, if stress becomes too great, performance begins to decline because stress interferes with it. The employee loses ability to cope, becomes unable to make decisions, and is erratic in behaviour. If stress increases to a breaking point, performance becomes zero. The employee has a breakdown; he becomes too ill to work. He is fired, quits, or refuses to come to work to face the stress.

STRESS MANAGEMENT

[A] Individual Approaches to Stress Management

Employees and management have different notions of what constitutes an acceptable level of stress on the job. From the individual's standpoint, even low levels of stress are likely to be perceived as undesirable.

Individual approaches An employee may take personal responsibility for reducing his or her stress level. Through individuals strategies proven effective are:

1. Time management Some people manage the time poorly, though the things they have to accomplish in any given day are not necessarily beyond completion if they manage their time properly. Principles of time management:

(i) Making daily list of activities to be accomplished;
(ii) prioritizing activities by importance and urgency;
(iii) scheduling activities according to the priorities set and
(iv) knowing one's daily cycle and handling the most demanding parts of his/her job during the high part of his/her cycle when he/she is most alert and productive.

2. Physical exercise Physical exercise such as aerobic, jogging, swimming have long been recommended by physicians as a way to deal with excessive stress levels.

3. Relaxation training To reach a state of *deep relaxation,* individuals can teach themselves to relax through techniques such as meditation, hypnosis and biofeedback. When one feels physically relaxed, he is somewhat detached from the body sensations. Deep relaxation of fifteen to twenty minutes a day releases tension and provides a person with a pronounced sense of peacefulness.

(4) Social support Talking to friends, family or work colleagues provide an outlet when stress levels become excessive. Thus, a social support network can considerably reduce the tension.

[B] Organisational Approaches

Management strategies are as follows to control stress:

1. Selection and placement While certain jobs are more stressful than others, individuals also differ in their response to stress situations. The individuals with little experience or an external locus of control are more stress prone. While management cannot have only experienced individuals selection and placement decisions to consider individuals who may adapt to high stress jobs and perform them more effectively.

2. Job redesigning Redesigning jobs to give employees more responsibility, more meaningful work, more autonomy and increased feedback reduces stress, because these factors provide greater control over work activities and lesser dependence on others. As all employees do not want enriched jobs, the right job design for employees with a low need for growth should have less responsibility and increased division of labour.

3. Goal setting Having specific and challenging goals and receiving feedback on how well they are progressing toward these goals, individuals perform better. Thus, goal selling can reduce stress and provide motivation.

Specific goals perceived as attainable clarify performance expectations. Goal feedback reduces uncertainties about actual job performance. This reduces employee frustration, role ambiguity and stress.

4. Organisational communication By lessening role ambiguity and role conflict, increased formal communication with employees reduce uncertainty. Management can use effective communication as a means to shape employee perceptions.

5. Participative decision-making By role stress, employees feel uncertain about goals, expectations, how they will be evaluated and the like. The management can increase employee control and reduce role stress by giving these employees a voice in those decisions that directly affect their job performance.

QUESTIONS FOR EXERCISE

1. What is employee stress? What are its symptoms? Explain its potential sources.
2. What is stress threshold? Analyse A and B behaviour types. How does stress affect job performance?
3. Explain industrial and organisational approaches to stress management strategies.

32

CONSUMER PSYCHOLOGY

ROLE OF NEEDS, GOALS AND SELF-IMAGE

1. Needs Every individual has some innate and acquired needs:

(i) ***Innate needs:*** Innate needs are physiological *(i.e.* biogenic). They include the needs for food, for water, for air, for clothing, for shelter and for sex. As they are needed to sustain biological life, the biogenic needs are considered primary needs or motives.

(ii) ***Acquired needs:*** These needs we earn in response to our culture or environment. These may include needs for self-esteem, for prestige, for affection, for power, and for learning. Acquired needs are generally psychological or psychogenic. They are secondary needs or motives. They result from the individual's subjective psychological state and from relationships with others. For example, as all individuals need shelter from the elements, finding a place to live fulfils an important primary need. However, the kind of residence one rents or buys may be the result of secondary needs. He may seek a place in which he and his wife can entertain large groups of people and fulfil social needs. They may want to live in an exclusive community in order to impress their friends and family and fulfil ego needs. Thus, the house an individual ultimately purchases may serve to fulfil both primary and secondary needs.

2. Goals Goals are the sought-after results of motivated behaviour. All behaviour is goal-oriented. Goals are of many types:

(i) ***Generic goals:*** These are the general classes or categories of goals that consumers select to fulfill their needs. Marketers are even more concerned with consumers.

(ii) ***Product-specific goals*****:** These are the specifically branded or labelled products the individual select to fulfil their needs. For example,

Thomas J. Lipton Company want consumers to view iced tea as a good way to quench summer thirst (*i.e.* as a generic goal). Marketers recognize the importance of promoting both types of goals.

The Selection of Goals

There are many different and appropriate goals for any given need. The goals selected by individuals depend on their personal experiences, physical capacity, prevailing cultural norms and values, and the goal's accessibility in the physical and social environment. For example, an individual may have a strong hunger need. If he is a young college athlete, he may envy a thick sirloin steak as his goal object; if his doctor has advised him to avoid red meat, he may settle for a thick tuna steak instead. If he has a toothache, he may not be able to chew a steak; he may have to select hamburger. If he has never tasted steak, if it is outside his realm of personal experience, he probably would not even think of steak, but instead would select a food that has previously satisfied his hunger.

Finally, the goal object has to be both socially acceptable and physically accessible. If our college athlete was having dinner with his mother, she might frown on his consuming red meat, and insist he eats fish or chicken instead. If he were shipwrecked on an island with no food provisions or living animals, he could not realistically select steak as his goal-object, though he might fantasize about it. If he were in India, where cows are considered sacred, he would not be able to consume steak but select a substitute goal more appropriate to the social environment.

3. Self-Image An individual's own perception of himself or herself serves to influence the specific goals selected. The products a person owns, would like to own, or would not like to own are often perceived in terms of how closely they reflect his self-image. A product that is perceived as matching an individual's self-image has a greater probability of being selected than one that is not. Thus, a man who perceives himself as young and "with it" may drive a Porsche. A woman who perceives herself as rich and conservative may drive a Mercedes. The types of houses people live, the cars they drive, the clothes they wear, the very foods they eat, these specific goal objects are chosen because they symbolically reflect the individual's self-image while they satisfy specific needs.

Interdependence of Needs and Goals

Needs and goals are interdependent; neither exists without the other. However, people are as aware of their needs as they are of their goals. For example, a teenager may not consciously be aware of his social needs but may join a photography club to meet new friends. A local politician may not consciously be aware of a power need but may regularly run for public office.

Among needs, individuals are usually more aware of their physiological needs than of their psychological needs. Most people know when they are hungry or thirsty or cold, and they take appropriate steps to satisfy these needs. They may not be aware of their needs for acceptance, for self-esteem, for status though they may subconsciously engage in behaviour that satisfies these psychological needs.

CONSUMER MOTIVATION

Motivation can be positive or negative. One may feel a driving force towards some object or condition; he may feel a driving force away from some object or condition. For example, a person may be impelled towards a restaurant to fulfil a hunger need and away from motorcycle transportation to fulfil a safety need.

Psychologists refer to positive drives as needs, wants, or desires, and to negative drives as fears or accretions. Thus negative and positive motivational forces seem to differ dramatically in terms of physical and sometimes emotional activity. However, they are basically similar in that both serve to initiate and sustain human behaviour. Therefore, researchers refer to both kinds of drives or motives, needs, wants, and desires. Some theorists distinguish wants from needs, by defining wants as product-specific needs. A person may experience thirst, a need in which she may want Lipton's iced tea as means to alleviate her thirst.

Positive and Negative Goals

A positive goal is one towards which behaviour is directed. It is often referred to as an approach object. A negative goal is one from which behaviour is directed away. It is sometimes referred to as an avoidance object. As both approach and avoidance goals can be considered objects of motivated behaviour, most researchers refer to both simply as goals. A middle-aged woman may have a positive goal of fitness and so join a health club to work out regularly. The house-wife joins a health club to help her achieve her positive goal — health and fitness. Her husband may have a negative goal of getting rid of fat-and so he joins a road runners club to maintain his shape. The husband's action is designed to avoid a negative goal — a bloated figure.

Psychological Reactance

Some people become motivationally aroused by a threat to or elimination of a behavioural freedom such as the freedom to make a product choice without undue influence from a retailer. This motivational state is called psychological reactance. It is usually manifested by a negative consumer response. When the Coca-Cola company changed its traditional formula and introduced "New Coke", many people reacted negatively to the fact that their "freedom to choose" had been taken away. They refused to buy the New Coke. Coca-Cola management responded to this unexpected psychological reaction by reintroducing the original formula as "Classic Coke."

Rational *versus* Emotional Motives

Consumer researchers who subscribe to the positivist perspective tend to view all consumer behaviours as rationally motivated. They try to isolate the causes of such behaviour so that they can predict, and thus influence, future behaviour. Experimentalists are interested in studying the hedonistic pleasures that consumption behaviour requires such as fun, or fantasy, or sensuality. They study consumer behaviour in order to gain insights and understanding of the consumer in his or her unique circumstances. Thus, consumer behaviourists distinguish between so-called rational motives and emotional or non-rational motives. They use the term rationality in the traditional economic sense. It assumes that consumers behave rationally when they carefully consider all alternatives and choose those that give them the greatest utility. In a marketing context, the term rationality implies that consumers select goals based on totally objective criteria, such as size, weight, price, or subjective criteria, *e.g.*, the desire for individuality, pride, fear, affection, status.

The assumption underlying this dissection is that subjective or emotional criteria do not maximize utility or satisfaction. However, it is reasonable to assume that consumers always attempt to select alternatives that, in their view, serve to maximize satisfaction. The assessment of satisfaction is a very personal process. It is based on the individual's own need structure as well as on past behavioural and social or learned experiences. What may appear irrational to an outside observer may be perfectly rational in the context of the consumer's own psychological field. For example, a product purchased to enhance self-image is a perfectly rational form of consumer behaviour. If behaviour does not appear rational to the person at the time it is undertaken, he or she would not do it. Thus the dissection between rational and emotional consumption motives is not always warranted.

THE DYNAMIC NATURE OF MOTIVATION

Constantly Changing Needs and Goals

Motivation is a highly dynamic construct that is constantly changing in reaction to life experiences. Needs and goals are constantly growing and changing in response to an individual's physical condition, environment, interaction with others and experiences. As individuals attain their goals, they develop new ones. If they do not attain their goals, they continue to strive for old goals, or they develop substitute goals.

Reasons of Dynamic Nature

Following are the reasons of the dynamic nature of motivation:

1. Full satisfaction of needs Most human needs are never fully or permanently satisfied. For example, people experience hunger needs at regular intervals. Most people regularly seek companionship and approval from others to satisfy their social needs. Even more complex psychological needs are rarely satisfied, *e.g.*, temporary goal achievement does not fully satisfy the need for power, and the individual keeps striving to satisfy the need more fully. For example, a person may partially or temporarily satisfy a power need by working as assistant to the CEO of a Fortune 500 company, but this small taste of power may not sufficiently satisfy her need, and so she may strive for her own decision-making position in the company.

2. Emergence of new needs Some motivational theorists believe that a hierarchy of needs exists, and that new, higher-order needs emerge as lower-order needs are fulfilled. For example, a man who has largely satisfied his basic psychological needs may turn his efforts to achieving acceptance among his new neighbours by joining their political clubs and supporting their candidates. After achieving acceptance, he may seek recognition by giving lavish parties or making large charitable contributions.

Marketers have to be attuned to changing needs. Car manufacturers stressing the prestige value of their automobiles fail to recognise that many consumers now satisfy needs for prestige eles where — such as through charitable gift-giving or public service. Manufacturers of prestige cars might do better if they stressed other need satisfactions such as family enjoyment or safety as reasons for buying a new model.

Expectations of success or failure in reaching certain goals often influence the nature and persistence of an individual's behaviour. Expectations are often based on past experience. A person who takes good snapshots with an inexpensive camera may be motivated to buy a more sophisticated camera that will enable him to take even better photographs. He may eventually upgrade his camera by several hundred dollars. On the other hand, a person who has not been able to take good photographs is likely to keep the same camera or may even lose all interest in photography.

Effects of success and failure on goal selection have strategy implications for the marketer. Goal should be reasonable. Advertisements should not promise more than the product will deliver. Even a good product will not be approached if it fails to live up to expectations. A consumer is likely to regard a disappointing product with even less satisfaction than its objective performance warrants. Advertisers who create unrealistic expectations for their products may cause dissatisfaction among consumers. The frustration and disappointment resulting from consumer dissatisfaction are the driving force behind consumerism.

3. Substitute Goals When an individual attains a specific goal or the goal that will satisfy certain needs, behaviour may be directed to a substitute goal which may not be satisfactory as the primary goal but is sufficient to dispel uncomfortable tension. Continued deprivation of a primary goal may result in the substitute goal assuming primary-goal status. A man who has stopped drinking whole milk because he is dieting may actually begin to prefer skimmed milk.

4. Frustration Failure to achieve a goal results in feelings of frustration. Everyone has sometimes experienced the frustration that comes from the inability to attain a goal. The barrier that prevents attainment of a goal may be personal to the individual such as physical or financial limitations. It may be an obstacle in the frustrating situations. Some people are adaptive and manage to cope by finding their way around the obstacle or by selecting a substitute goal. An example of adaptive behaviour would be that of the college student who would prefer to own a sports car, but settles for a second-hand sedan. Others are less adaptive and may regard their inability to achieve a goal as a personal failure and experience feelings of anxiety.

5. Defence mechanisms People failing to cope with frustration mentally redesign the frustrating situation to protect their self-image and defend their self-esteem. For example, a young woman may yearn for a mink coat she cannot afford. The coping individual may select a less expensive fur, such as suskrat, or a cloth coat with a fur colour. The person who cannot cope may react with anger towards her boss for not paying her enough money to buy a fur. Alternatively, she may decide that wearing the fur of animals is a barbaric custom in which she will not participate. These last two possibilities are examples respectively of aggression and rationalization. Other defence mechanisms includes regression, withdrawal, projection, autism, identification and repression. People adopt defence mechanisms to protect their egos from feelings of failure when they do not attain their goals:

(i) ***Aggressions:*** Individuals who experience frustration may resort to aggressive behaviour. In attempting to protect their self-esteem being disappointed at their poor showing in a sailing competition, two British Yachtsmen burned their boat and swam ashore. Frustrated consumers have boycotted manufacturers in efforts to improve product quality and boycotted retailers in efforts to have prices lowered.

(ii) ***Rationalization:*** In rationalization, individuals redefine a frustrating situation by inventing plausible reasons for being unable to attain their goals. They may decide that the goal really is not worth pursuing. Rationalizations are not deliberate lies, as the individual is not fully aware of the cognitive distortion that occurs as a result of the frustrating situation. Consumers who cannot quit smoking may convince themselves that they are smoking less if they switch to low-tar cigarettes.

(iii) ***Regression:*** Some people react to frustrating situations with childish or immature behaviour. A shopper attending a bargain sale may fight over merchandise and resort to tearing a garment rather than allow the other person to have it.

(iv) ***Withdrawal*****:** In withdrawal, frustration is often resolved by simply withdrawing from the situation. A person who has officer status in an organization may simply quit it. He may rationalize his resignation by deciding that the organization is not true to its stated ideals and the other members are somewhat shallow. He may decide to use his time more constructively in other activities.

(v) ***Projection:*** By projecting blame for his or her own failures and inabilities on the other objects or persons, an individual may redesign a frustrating situation. For example, the golfer who misses a stroke may blame the caddie or her golf clubs. The driver who has an automobile accident may blame the other driver or the condition of the road.

(vi) ***Autism*****:** Autism means autistic thinking. It refers to thinking that is almost completely dominated by needs and emotions, with little effort made to relate to reality. A person who is shy and lonely, may daydream about a romantic love affair. Daydreaming fantasizing enables the individual to attain imaginary gratification of unfulfilled needs.

(vii) ***Identification*****:** Some people resolve their feelings of frustration by subconsciously identifying with other persons or situations they consider relevant. Marketers have recognized the importance of this defence mechanism and used it as the basis for advertising appeals. Hence slice-of-life commercials and advertisements are so popular. Such advertisements usually portray a stereotypical situation in which an individual experiences a frustration and then overcomes it by using the advertised product. If the viewer can identify with the frustrating situation, he or she may very likely adopt the proposed solution and buy the product advertised. A fellow who has difficulty in attracting dates may decide to use the same mouthwash, shampoo, or clothing that "worked" for the man in the commercial. Use of the product may increase his self-confidence sufficiently to enable him to achieve his goal.

(viii) ***Repression:*** Individuals avoid the tension arising from frustration by repressing the unsatisfied need. Thus, they may "forget" a need. They force the need out of their conscious awareness. Sometimes these repressed needs manifest themselves indirectly. A couple who cannot have children may surround themselves with plants or pets.

(ix) ***Sublimation:*** The manifestation of repressed needs in a socially acceptable form is called sublimation. It is another type of defence mechanism.

(x) ***Other defence mechanisms*****:** People have virtually limitless ways of redefining situations by which they protect their self-esteem from the anxieties resulting from the failure. Based on their early experiences, they tend to develop their own characteristic ways of handling frustration. In their selection of advertising appeals, marketers often consider this fact. A flour manufacturer may try to convince consumers that previous baking failures were caused by the ingredients they used, rather than the ineptness of their efforts.

6. Multiplicity of needs A consumer's behaviour often fulfils more than one need. Specific goals may be selected because they fulfil several needs. We buy clothing for protection and for modesty. Clothing also fulfils an enormous range of personal and social needs. However, there is one overriding need that initiates behaviour. For example, a man may stop smoking because he wants to rid himself of a chronic cough or he may be concerned with cancer or his girlfriend may be "turned off' by the smell of cigarette smoke. If the cumulative amount of the pain produced by each of these reasons is sufficiently strong, he will stop smoking. However, just one of the reasons may also serve as the triggering mechanism. It would be the pre-potent need.

7. Variety of motives One cannot always infer motives from behaviour. People with different needs may seek fulfilment through selection of the same goals. On the contrary, people with the same needs may seek fulfilment through different goals. Five people who are active in a consumer advocacy organization may each belong for a different reason. The first may be genuinely concerned with protecting consumer interests. The second may be concerned about an increase in counterfeit merchandise. The third may seek social contacts from organizational meetings. The fourth may enjoy the status provided by membership in a powerful organization.

Again, five people may be driven by the same need to seek fulfilment indifferent ways. The first may seek advancement and recognition through a professional career. The second may become active in the League of Women voters. The third may join a health club. The fourth may take professional dance lessons. The fifth may seek attention by monopolizing classroom discussions.

AROUSAL OF MOTIVES

Most of the individual's specific needs are dormant much of the time. The arousal of any particular set of needs at a specific point in time may be due to internal stimuli found in the individual's physiological condition, emotional or cognitive processes, or by stimuli in the outside environment. These are as follows:

1. Physiological arousal Physical needs are rooted in an individual's physiological condition at that moment. A drop in blood sugar level or stomach contractions may trigger awareness of a hunger need. Secretion of sex hormones may awaken the sex need. A decrease of body temperature may include shivering. Most of these physiological tensions continue until they are satisfied. A shivering man may turn up the heat in his home to relieve his discomfort; he also may make a mental note to buy flannel pajamas. Television programmes often generate physiological arousal that affects the impact of ensuing commercials.

2. Emotional arousal Thinking or daydreaming may result in the emotional arousal of latent needs. People who are bored or frustrated in attempts to achieve their goals often engage in daydreaming in which they imagine themselves in all sorts of desirable situations. These thoughts tend to arouse dormant needs. These may produce uncomfortable tensions that "push" them into goal-oriented behaviour. A young woman who dreams of becoming a business tycoon may enrol in business school. A young man who dreams of being a writer may sign up for a mail-order writing course.

3. Cognitive arousal Random thoughts or personal achievements may lead to a cognitive awareness of needs. An advertisement that provides reminders of home might trigger instant recognition of the need to speak with one's parents.

4. Environmental arousal The set of needs activated at a particular time are often determined by specific cues in the environment. For example, the six o'clock news, the sight or smell of bakery goods, fast-food commercials on television, the end of the school day — all these may arouse the "need" for food. Thus, modification of the environment may be necessary to reduce the arousal of hunger. A most potent form of situational cue is the goal object itself. A couple may experience an overwhelming need for a new dishwasher when they see their neighbour's new dishwasher. A person may suddenly experience a need for a new car when passing a dealer's display window. Sometimes environmental cue produces a psychological imbalance in the viewer's mind. For example, a man who prides himself on his gardening may see an advertisement for a tractor mower that apparently works more efficiently than his own rotary mower. The ad may make him so unhappy with his old mower that he experiences severe tension until he buys himself a new tractor model.

People living in a complex and highly varied environment experience many opportunities for need arousal. Conversely, fewer needs are activated when their environment is poor or deprived. Therefore, television has such a mixed effect on the lives of the ghetto poor. It exposes them to various lifestyles and expensive products that they would not otherwise see. It awakens wants and desires for which they have little opportunity or even hope of attaining. Thus, while it enriches some lives, it also serves to frustrate people and sometimes results in the adoption of antisocial defence mechanisms such as aggression.

Explanation of Arousal of Motives

There are following two opposing explanations about the arousal of human motives:

1. **The behaviourist** It considers motivation to be a mechanical process. Behaviour is seen as the response to a stimulus. Elements of conscious thoughts are ignored. An extreme example of this stimulus-response theory of motivation is the impulsive buyer who reacts largely to external stimuli in the buying situation. The

consumer's cognitive control is limited or she does not act, but reacts to stimuli in the market-place.

2. **The congestive school** It believes that all behaviours are directed at goal achievement. Needs and past experiences are reasoned, categorized and transformed into attitudes and beliefs that act as predispositions to behaviour. Aimed at helping an individual to satisfy needs, these predispositions determine the direction that he or she takes to achieve this satisfaction.

TYPES AND SYSTEMS OF NEEDS

1. Views of Daniel Starch Most lists of human needs tend to be diverse in content as well as in length. While there is little disagreement about specific physiological needs, there is considerable disagreement about specific psychological or psychogenic needs.

Table 32.1 presents a list of 44 human motives compiled in 1923 by Professor Daniel Starch of the Hayward Business School for use as copy appeals.

2. Views of Henry Murray In 1938, the psychologist Henry Murray prepared a detailed list of 28 psychogenic needs that have served as the basic constructs for a number of widely used personality tests such as the Edwards Personal Preference Schedule. Murray believed that everyone has the same basic set of needs, but individuals differ in their priority ranking of these needs. Murray's basic needs include many motives such as acquisition, achievement, recognition and exhibition that are assumed to play

Table 32.1

MOTIVES IN MALE AND FEMALE ADULTS

Appetite — hunger	Respect for deity
Love of opposing	Sympathy for others
Health	Protection of others
Sex attraction	Domesticity
Parental affection	Social distinction
Ambition	Devotion to others
Pleasure	Hospitality
Bodily comfort	Warmth
Possession	Limitation
Approval of others	Courtesy
Gregariousness	Play-sport

Taste	Managing others
Personal appearance	Coolness
Safety	Fear — caution
Cleanliness	Physical activity
Rest — sleep	Manipulation
Home comfort	Construction
Economy	Style
Curiosity	Humour
Efficiency	Amusement
Competition	Shyness
Co-operation	Teasing

an important role in consumer behaving. These are given in table 32.2.

Table 32.2

MURRAY'S LIST OF PSYCHOGENIC NEEDS

1. **Needs associated with Inanimate Objects**

   Acquisition

   Conservancy

   Order

   Retention

   Constriction

2. **Needs that Reflect Ambition, Power, Accomplishment, and Prestige**

   Superiority

   Achievement

   Recognition

   Exhibition

   Inviolate (inviolate attitude)

   In avoidance (to avoid shame, failure, humiliation, ridicule)
   Defiance (defensive attitude)

   Contraction (constructive attitude)

3. **Needs concerned with Human Power**

   Dominance

   Deference

   Similance (suggestible attitude)

   Autonomy

   Contravene (to act differently from others)

4. **Sado-Masochistic Needs**
   Aggression
   Abasement
5. **Needs concerned with Affection between People**
   Affiliation
   Rejection
   Nurturance (to nourish, aid, or protect the helpless) Succourance (to seek aid, protection, or sympathy) play
6. **Needs concerned with Social Intercourse (the Needs to ask and tell)**
   Cognizance (inquiring attitude)
   Exposition (expositive attitude)

THEORY OF HIERARCHY OF NEEDS

Dr. Abraham Maslow, a clinical psychologist, formulated a widely accepted theory of human motivation. It is based on the notion of a universal hierarchy of human needs. It postulates five basic levels of human needs, which rank in order of importance from lower-level (biogenic) needs to higher-level (psychogenic) needs. It suggests that individuals seek to satisfy lower-level needs before higher-level needs emerge. The lowest level of chronically unsatisfied need that an individual experiences serves to motivate his or her behaviour. A new (and higher) need emerges when that need is fairly well satisfied. When this need is satisfied, a new and still higher need emerges, and so on. However, if a lower-level need experiences some renewed deprivation, it may temporarily become dominant again.

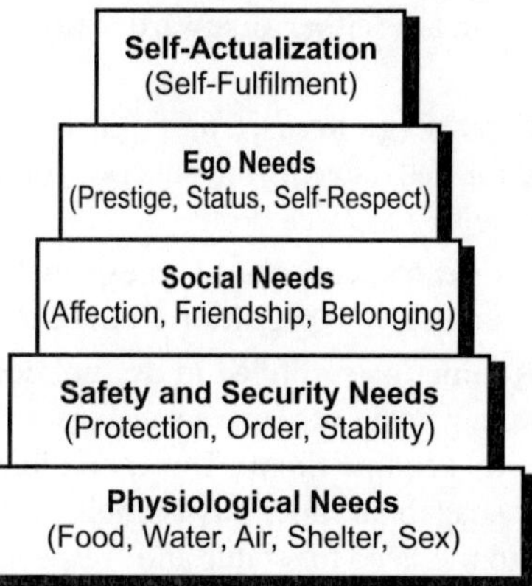

Figure 32.1. Maslow's Hierarchy of Human needs

Figure 32.1 presents Maslow's hierarchy of needs in diagrammatic form. According to the theory, there is some overlap between each level, as no need is ever completely satisfied. Though all levels of need below the dominant level continue to motivate behaviour to some extent, the prime motivator — the major driving force within the individual — is the lowest level of need that remains largely unsatisfied.

1. Physiological needs In the hierarchy-of-needs theory, the first and most basic level of needs is physiological. These needs are required to sustain biological life. These include all the biogenic needs — food, water, air, shelter, clothing, sex.

According to Maslow, physiological needs are dominant when they are chronically unsatisfied. He says, For the man who is extremely and dangerously deprived of food, he thinks about food, he emotes only about food, he perceives only food, and he wants only food." Though the biogenic needs are generally satisfied and the higher-level needs are dominant, yet the lives of a large and growing population of major cities are focused almost entirely on biogenic needs: the needs for food, for clothing, for shelter from the elements in freezing weather.

2. Safety needs Safety and security needs become the driving force behind an individual's behaviour after the first level of needs is satisfied. These needs are concerned with much more than physical safety. They include order, stability, routine, familiarity, control over one's life and environment, and certainty. For example, health is also a safety concern.

3. Social needs These include needs of affection, friendship and belonging.

4. Egoistic needs When the social needs are more or less satisfied, the fourth level of Maslow's hierarchy becomes operative. It is concerned with egoistic needs which can take either an inward or an outward orientation, or both.

(i) *Inwardly-directed ego needs:* These reflect an individual's need for self-acceptance, for self-esteem, for success, for independence, for personal satisfaction with a job well done.

(ii) *Outwardly-directed ego needs*: These include the needs for prestige, reputation, status and recognition from others.

The ego need is sometimes fulfilled in dysfunctional ways. Poverty-stricken youngsters may value expensive sneakers as symbols of status, and steal in order to acquire them. The incredible increase in gun possession among teenagers in inner city schools (in western countries) has been attributed to the need for status and "respect" from their peers. They believe that the bigger the gun, the more respect they command.

5. Need for self-actualization Most people do not satisfy their ego needs sufficiently to ever move to the fifth level — the need for self-actualization (self-fulfilment). This need refers to an individual's desire to fulfil his or her potential to become everything he or she is capable of becoming. In Maslow's words, "What a man can be, he must be." This need is expressed in different ways by different people. A young man may desire to be an Olympic star and work single-mindedly for years to become the best in his sport. An artist may need to express herself on canvas. A research scientist may strive to find a new drug to eradicate disease. The self-actualization need is not necessarily a creative urge. However, in people with some capacity for creativity, it is likely to take that form. Advertisements for art lessons, for banking services, and even for military recruitment often try to appeal to the self- actualization need.

Limitations of the Need Hierarchy Theory

The need hierarchy has received wide acceptance in many social disciplines. It appears to reflect the assumed or inferred motivations of many people. The five levels of need postulated by the hierarchy are sufficiently generic to encompass most lists of individual needs. Some critics, however, maintain that Maslow's concepts are too general. The major problem with the theory is that it cannot be tested empirically; there is no way to measure precisely how satisfied one need must be before the next higher need becomes operative The need hierarchy also appears to be very closely bound to contemporary American culture.

Advantages of Maslow's Theory

1. Tools for understanding consumer behaviour Despite these criticisms, Maslow's hierarchy is a useful tool for understanding consumer motivations. It is readily adaptable for marketing strategy, because consumer goods often serve to satisfy each of the need levels. For example, individuals buy houses, food and clothing to satisfy physiological needs. They buy insurance and radial tires and vocational training to satisfy safety and security needs. Almost all personal care products like cosmetics, mouthwash, shaving cream are bought to satisfy social needs. Luxury products such as furs, or jewels, or big cars are often bought to fulfil ego needs. College training and banking services are sold as ways to achieve self-fulfilment. Maslow's need hierarchy has been called an "emotional trigger" that enables marketers to communicate with their target audiences on a personal, meaningful level that goes beyond product benefits.

The hierarchy theory offers a useful, comprehensive framework for marketers trying to develop appropriate advertising appeals for their products. It enables marketers to focus their advertising appeals on a need level that is likely to be shared by a large segment of the prospective audience. It facilitates product positioning or requisitioning.

2. Segmentation applications The need hierarchy is often used as the basis for market segmentation. Specific advertising appeals are directed to individuals on one or more need levels. For example, soft-drink ads are directed to teenagers stressing a social appeal by showing a group of young people sharing good times as well as the advertised product. Research sponsored by the National Spa and Pool Institute found that men and women had different motivations concerning these products. Women saw the purchase of a pool as an enhancement of family life (the social need), but were concerned about the safety of their small children (the safety need.) Thus, pool advertisement tend to stress the supervision of children, health and family enjoyment. These are targeted primarily to women. As the study found that men were more interested in spas than pools, spa commercials stress a more intimate message relaxation, privacy, time together.

3. Positioning applications The need hierarchy is used for positioning products — that is, deciding how the product should be perceived by prospective consumers. The key to positioning is to find a niche that is not occupied by a competing product or brand. This application of the need hierarchy relies on the notion that no need is ever fully satisfied. It always, continues to be somewhat motivating. Safety, for example, is a continuing need.

Most manufacturers of luxury cars use status appeals ("Impress your friends"), self-actualizing appeals ("You deserve the very best"), or even social appeals ("The whole family can ride in luxurious comfort"). Some automobile companies have used a safety appeal in advertisements directed to well-to-do executives, for example "When your wife is driving the two children home on a dark and stormy night, you can relax if she's driving the Mercedes."

4. Versatility The need hierarchy is useful in designing promotional programmes. Workable appeals for a single product can be developed from each level. For example, the potential promotional appeals for home Nautilus equipment. An appeal to physiological needs would show how the home exercise unit can improve body tone and health; a social appeal might show how much fun it can be to exercise with a friend, or even how a streamlined figure would encourage social encounters. Self-esteem is easily demonstrated through a narcissistic appeal such as "Be proud of your body." Finally, an appeal to self-actualization may suggest to career couples that they deserve the convenience and the luxury of home exercise after a long and challenging work-day.

BUYING MOTIVES

Buying motives induce an ultimate consumer, industrial consumer or user, organisational consumer or merchant buyer to purchase a product. These are controlled by the socio-economic, psychological and other factors. Some of these operate from outside and some from within a person. These imply/stimulate him to realise his need or want; choose a product or service that will satisfy it; select the place from where to purchase it; and decide upon the price he will be willing to pay; and also decide upon the time when he may actually purchase it.

Buying motives range from satisfying hunger to seeking protection against clemencies of weather and attack of wild animals, to gratification of sex urge or that for love, curiosity, prestige, social status, personal advancement, and convenience, etc. Some of these motives may be instinctive, while others are acquired from environment, education, social status, age, etc.

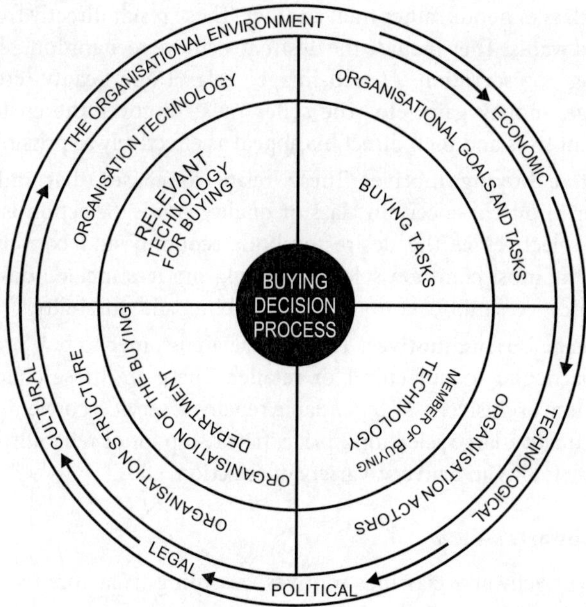

Fig. 32.2. A Model of the Buying Organisation Behaviour

An individual consumer buys goods or services to satisfy his personal or household wants. He is the most important class of buyer and among it, the principal customer is the family. He is located in villages, towns and cities. He purchases product for three important reasons: (i) desire which needs to be satisfied; (ii) urge which induces him to purchase and (iii) reasoning. He is motivated to buy by external and internal forces: external and internal motive.

1. External motives These are outside oneself. A consumer is the product of his environment. His attitudes and behaviour influence his culture and various factors like income, occupation, religion, culture, family and social environment act as motives to buying behaviour.

2. Internal motives These originate in the minds of the people and are both physical and psychological in nature. They are broadly classified into two classes: **(i)** ***Rational:*** These are based on logical reasoning or thinking. (ii) ***Emotional*****:** These are based on personal feelings.

Classification of Buying Motives

The simplest classification is based on primary, selective and patronage motives:

1. Primary buying motives These relate to the reasons why consumers buy one class of goods rather than another. These result directly from the needs and wants. They include the desire to achieve recognition, physical well-being, preservation of self-image, relaxation, beauty creation, knowledge, money gain, etc. The seller must discover the customer's primary motives and then direct his appeal as effectively as possible.

2. Selective buying motives These relate to causes that induce a consumer to purchase certain class or quality goods. Selection is based on such selectives as the desire for both economy and convenience. Some of the most common selective buying motives include desire for convenience, versatility, economy, dependability and durability.

3. Patronage buying motives These cause a customer to buy products from a particular manufacturer or retailer. These are those concerned with fashion, exclusiveness, dependable repairing service, convenience of location, quality, large selections, price, friendship for or reliability of the seller, punctuality in delivery, variety of selection, etc.

David Schwartz's View

Prof. David Schwartz classifies motives according to factors that affect consumer behaviour in following categories :

1. Ego-related motives These include self-interest, desire for a better self-image, desire for status among one's peers.

2. Rational motives Based on a man's reasoning, logic and ability and a consideration of economic consequences, rational motives include the immediate monetary cost, and long-range cost affecting the buyer such as durability, depreciation, length of usage, degree of labour needed and ultimate benefit achieved. Prof. Copeland enumerates following rational motives: handiness; dependability in quality and use; durability; happiness; healthfulness; efficiency in operation and use; reliability of auxiliary service; economy in purchase and use; enhancement of earnings; and enhancing productivity of property.

(i) *The desire for economy:* The purchases that buyers make enable them to gain monetary gain or personal benefits or to acquire better product at a comparatively low cost. Some examples of appeals made are:

"Buy now — only 10 per cent above cost."

"A bumper sale at 15 per cent above cost."

"Shop at ours, get the choicest product at the cheapest price."

(ii) *Efficiency for doing a task:* It provides motive for use of mechanical devices which reduce the physical or mental tiresomeness in completing a task such as electric can-openers, knife sharpeners, blenders, mixers, razors, crushers and grinders in the kitchen and automatic bottlers, sealers, stammers, packaging machines, etc., and in offices, electric typewriters, copiers, pencil sharpeners, and long-distance communication devices. Examples of appeals made are:

"Fabric that never needs ironing."

"Fabrics that never shrink if they have sanforized mark." "Push button control."

(iii) *Dependability motive*: It compels an individual to buy to satisfy his desire to obtain "quality" goods of "reliable" and durable nature. Examples of appeals made are:

"The Firestone tyre rolls at least 3,000 miles".

"This mixer is guaranteed for 2 years".

"It is most dependable for nutrition and purity".

3. Emotional movies Based on personal feelings, emotional buying motives cover a wide range of irrational motives including impulses, instincts, habits and drives and are varied in nature. According to Prof. Copeland, these include: emulation, pride and ambition, economic emulation, social achievement, happy selection of gifts, maintaining and preserving health, satisfaction of appetite, proficiency, expression of artistic taste, ambition, romantic instinct, securing personal comfort, security from danger, securing comfort and obtaining greater leisure, distinctiveness, desire for recreation and entertainment, cleanliness, pride of personal appearance, satisfaction of physical and emotional appetites, alleviation of laborious task; and pleasing sense of taste.

(i) *Attraction for opposite sex*: It works in both young and old and involves pleasing or flattering the opposite sex, or appearing attractive before the other. Men dress in their best to appeal to women; and women put attractive hairdos, jewellery, pleasing perfumes and make-up in a modern style to appeal to men. Appeals to this motive are made in marketing of almost everything- perfumery, cosmetics, lipsticks, deodorants, shampoos, shaving lotions, toiletries, corsets, imitation or real jewellery, birthday presents, sexy books, clothing, automobiles, soft drinks and even cigarettes. The appeals are usually indirect, implying that if you buy a particular product you will be more popular with the opposite sex. Some examples of such appeals are:

"Every woman has a right to look younger than she is".

"Bold, defiant — the male scent".

"It gives your face a sex appeal".

(ii) *Love and affection for others:* It includes a sense of duty, love for family members and society and a desire to see justice done to oneself and others. Baby food, readymade baby suits, toys, children's books and insurance for children; labour saving kitchen appliances, beautiful birthday or marriage anniversary presents of costly jewellery, beauty preparations, fashion goods, perfumes, romantic and sexy novels, costly fruitier and prize bonds for wife are generally purchased to satisfy buyer's affection motive. Examples of its appeals are:

"Don't leave your family helpless".

"Because you love them, protect them".

"Wise parents give their children good education and breeding".

"Wise mothers give their family a nourishing breakfast".

(iii) *Social acceptance motive*: Every individual wants to have respect and information from the group to which he belongs and to escape rejection and loneliness. Taking advantage of this motive, the marketers issue appeals such as the following:

"Your neighbours shop here — you should too".

"It makes you nice to be near all day".

"It's the 'in' thing to do".

(iv) *Recreation and relaxation motive:* Vacations, sports and leisure time activities such as indoor games or going to cinema shows, music concerts, mushairas and Kavi sammelans are activities of the good life desired by most people. Hence people purchase sports and games materials, indoor games, tickets for cinema shows or horse racing, boxing; they buy bathing suits, radios, television sets, record players, light books and magazines. Examples of appeals:

"Quiet heaven for you to spend your holidays-come and stay at Shalimar".

"Relieves all pains and brings safe and restful sleep".

"Enjoy the beauty of nature, warm sunshine, cool breezes on the beach — come and visit once and again".

(v) *Conquering fear motive:* Due to fear, physical or psychological people are induced to buy seat belt, burglar alarms, door locks, lockers in banks, life insurance or general assurance policy, home fire extinguisher, pistol, exercising machines, woollen clothings, medicines and tonics, etc. Example of appeals are:

"Save now for the rainy day".

"Drive slowly, someone is waiting for you at home".

"Safety first, speed next".

(vi) *Curiosity motive:* Adolescent boys and girls and even adults are curious about certain things — such as curios, old paintings, old coins, blue films, cabaret dances, or sex literature. Examples of appeals are:

"For Adults Only".

"Something New has been Added — come and see."

"Be in the know of the Eighth Wonder of the World."

"Everything about Sex and Love Life — Read and enjoy".

(vii) *Satisfaction of pride and vanity motive:* People like to feel important in the society, among friends, in associations and clubs, to achieve status symbols which feed their vanity. Hence, ladies purchase costly costumes, jewellery or join expensive clubs; go to theatres and purchase products of arts; have improvements and expensive home decoration objects. Men purchase television, refrigerators, costly furniture, coolers, scooters and cars, fancy ties, after-shave lotions, perfumes and other variety goods. Appeals are made as the following:

"Be the first to own one".

"Designed exclusively with you in mind".

"It is a limited edition, so buy yours now".

(viii) *Emulate motive*: Some people are motivated to buy what is reported to be used by persons whose opinions matter. Hence, a new company may hire highly respected leaders as corporate directors to entrap the investors to buy its shares. Five-star hotels may say that film artists patronise them. Popular entertainers, athletes, film actors/actresses may give testimonials about the use of a product which are utilised for creating demand for that product.

(ix) *Comfort and convenience motive*: It plays an important part in the sale of luxury articles, labour saving devices, gas cylinders and gas oven; stoves, pressure cookers, electric irons, lounge chairs, sofa set, soft bed, good nourishing and tasty food, some type of conveyance, air conditioners, washing machines, etc. Mortimer gives ten kinds of convenience to be reckoned with in marketing:

(a) *Form*: Products must be available in a wide variety of form. The drug products, for example, may come in liquid, paste, syrup, powder, pill or inhalant form.

(b) *Quantity or units* : Goods must be offered in all sizes, quantities or units desired by the consumer.

(c) *Time:* Products must be available at the time the consumer wants them.

(d) *Place*: Sellers must offer opportunities to consumers for shopping in the most convenient locations possible.

(e) *Packaging*: Packages must be easy to find, open, use and store.

(f) Combination or "Packaging" convenience : It is found in service industries.

(g) *Automation:* Many consumers dream of push-button home.

(h) *Credit*: Instalment and credit purchases of furniture, appliances, radios, and other time, saving devices, where products are purchased now and paid in future.

(i) *Selection* : A seller must offer his products at convenient prices and in an assortment of colours, materials or flavours.

(j) *Readiness:* Everything one purchases must be ready and easy to use.

4. Patronage motives Patronage motives explain why a consumer purchases a product only from one seller rather than another. Following are the key patronage motives:

(i) ***Price:*** As the budget is limited, an individual would like to purchase cheap or at discount. Hence, following "price appeals" attract him:

"Price slashed by 50%".

"Old price Rs. 135/- Today's price Rs. 50/- only. Rush and make a choice before the stock runs short".

"Price right for quick sale".

(ii) ***Location:*** Nearness to one's residence induces people to buy from a particular store which may say:

"Five conveniently located cooperative stores waiting to serve you.

"Come and be satisfied".

"Location in the heart of the city, accessible from all sides".

(iii) ***Quality consciousness*:** It appeals some customers to buy standard quality goods, even if costly. The usual appeals are:

"Our products are priced a bit higher because quality is so much better".

"We guarantee price back, if quality is found inferior".

'The quality goes in before the name goes on".

"We guarantee every product we sell".

(iv) ***Services*:** Services like credit, home delivery, good gift, attractive wrapping, easy returns, guarantees, and free installations, maintenance and technical assistance help in attracting and holding a clientele. Examples of appeals are:

"All this at no extra cost".

"We service what we sell".

"Free home delivery within the town".

(v) ***Integrity of the merchant*:** It attracts buyers, especially of the product as an intangible such as insurance, security or pest control or when post-sale service is likely to be needed as in the case of automobiles.

(vi) ***Variety of goods at one place:*** It saves time and energy in marketing. Hence, appeals like these attract buyers:

"We have the largest selection in town".

"See our complete line of latest fashions in maxis, bikinis and bras".

(vii) ***Likeable and competent personnel:*** Sympathetic and helpful salesmen and clerks do attract customers. Marketers stress that services of trained experts are available. They assure the buyers by saying.

"You are never a stranger when you shop with us".

"The friendliest place in town to shop for you — visit once and be convinced".

According to Carter, buying motives include: money, vanity, acquisitiveness, rivalry, comfort, adornment, cleanliness, companionship, collecting, amusement, sensual gratification, construction, aggrandisement, mental culture, affection, social achievements, ambition, inhibitiveness, reverence, romance, aesthetic tastes, sex, imitation, curiosity, self-preservation, sympathy, gratitude, patriotism and so on.

BARRIERS TO RECOGNISE BUYING MOTIVES

Following barriers may be recognised as rational and emotional buying motives in the costumes:

1. Unawareness The customer may be unaware of his own motives which prevent him from communicating to the seller his desires for wanting certain goods and services. Hence, the salesman must play detective, during his talks with the customer, in order to gain necessary knowledge and insight regarding buying motives of the customers.

2. Unwillingness The customers are sometimes unwilling to disclose their real motives. Hence, it requires a great tact on the part of the marketer to induce them to express their needs.

3. Complexity The actual motives may be so complex or independent that it is very difficult, if not impossible to recognize them.

4. Barriers to Buying

(i) Incompatibility of the product with the self-concept. If a product does not coincide with or support a self-concept or how the costumer really thinks of himself, the customer reacts negatively to sales representation.

(ii) Lack of authority to buy or power to make purchase of a particular product.

(iii) The risk of moving away from one's ideal self-image.

(iv) The feeling of guilt.

Buying Motives of Industrial Consumers or Organisational Market Industrial consumers are business or institutional organisations that buy products and services either to use in making other goods and services or to use in their own business. According to Canfield, following are three types of industrial consumers, *viz.* :

1. Manufacturers These purchase goods for turning them into finished goes such as cotton, pig iron or steel sheets, and all types of raw materials.

2. Manufacturers and service organisations These buy goods for consumption in the operation of their business, such as lighting equipments and furniture and fixtures fitting in a cinema hall.

3. Industrial distributors These buy for resale to industrial consumers. According to R.F. Eider, typical industrial buyers are interested in extractive, processing, construction and transportation industries, public utilities, services and distributive industries, governmental institutions, commercial institutions, specialised service industries (hotels, restaurants, theatres, laundries, dry-cleaners, tailoring and barber shops, etc.).

Items (1)	Ultimate Consumer (2)	Industrial Consumer (3)
1. Product Consideration		
(i) Total volumes of sales market	Smaller than industrial sales market	Larger than ultimate consumer market
(ii) Variety of products offered	Virtually unlimited	Virtually unlimited
(iii) Making of products to buyer's specifications	Uncommon	Very common
(iv) Number of product suppliers	For most products comparatively large.	Comparatively small
(v) Average size of purchase	Small	Very large
(vi) Nature of demand	Sets pace for industrial goods demand	Derived from ultimate consumer demand
2. Promotional Consideration		
(i) Advertising	Extensive use of mass media	More selective — little use of mass media
(ii) Personal selling direct to consumer	Very limited	Very extensive
(iii) Use of trade shows and exhibits	Minor	Major
(iv) Rationality in purchase decision making	Limited	Great
(v) Purchasing skills	Limited	Sophisticated
(vi) Number of people involved in purchasing decision	Two or more	Usually several
(vii) Reason for purchase	Satisfy personal or house hold need	Satisfy business, institutional or governmental need
3. Pricing Consideration		
(i) Price Policy	Usually one price to	Often sell
(ii) Use of discounts	Limited	Very common.

Distinction between Organisational and Consumsers Market

1. **Derived demand** The organisational market has a derived demand, *i.e.,* the demand does not exist as an independent force but is dependent upon the demand for consumer goods and services.
2. **Fewer buyers** It has fewer buyers, as compared to millions of buyers in case of consumer goods.
3. **More concentrated** It is more concentrated than the consumer market, which is usually widely dispersed.
4. **More valuable** It is more valuable to fluctuating demand.
5. **Greater cash flow** It has a greater cash flow than the consumer market.

Comparison between Ultimate and Industrial Consumer Behaviour

According to Stanon, the industrial buyers have two goals: to improve their position in the firm (personal self-interest) and to further their company's position (in profits, competition, acceptance by society). According to Nystorm, the following motives impel industrial consumers to purchase:

1. Efficiency — Performance, practicability and increased capacity.
2. Economy in money, in use or in time.
3. Good quality materials and workmanship.
4. Simplicity in construction, operation and application.
5. Increased saleability of user's product.
6. Ease of operation such as easier handling, greater convenience, handiness or light touch.
7. Space moving, i.e, compactness, ease of storage and holding.
8. Obsolescence which needs improvement, replacement or additions.
9. Safety to employees, clients and customers.
10. Cleanliness in plant, user's product, of workmen.

Schwartz emphasises, "Since industrial consumption is impersonal and for an economic/business reason, it is understandable that industrial users are motivated chiefly by rational or economic factors, the principal being: (i) production quality; (ii) cost; (iii) post-sales service; (iv) efficiency; (v) seller readability, (vi) the terms of sale, (vii) ease and speed of delivery, and (viii) variety. They generally make a conscious and deliberate attempt to 'think rational' and 'do what is best for the company.' However, they are also influenced to some extent by their emotions.

According to Alexander and others, an analysis of the buying motives, practices, and habits in industrial and organisational markets should produce answer to questions such as the following:

1. What functional activities are affected sufficiently by the purchase so that men responsible for these activities have something to say about it?
2. What part in the purchasing procedure does each of these men play?
3. What language do they understand best?
4. What buying appeals are most likely to influence them favourably?
5. What are the most effective and economic ways of transmitting the selling messages to these men?
   (a) If through salesmen, what should their qualification be?
   (b) If through advertising, what media should be employed?
6. How can buying appeals be used in advertising presented to fit peculiarities of the men and the media?
7. How rapid delivery is required?
8. What are the service needs?
   In connection with sale?
   After sale?
9. What are market customs regarding discount structures and credit terms?
10. How important is reciprocal buying?

WHAT DO INDUSTRIAL CONSUMERS BUY?

According to Vergil Reed, Industrial consumers generally by the following wide variety of goods:

1. Building and sites Factories, warehouses, piers, cars, casks, store buildings, office buildings, land, mining properties and drilling rights.

2. Installations and/or major equipments Boilers, generators, rolling mills, conveyers or systems, seamless tube mills, furnaces, kilns, and other items of a stationary or installed nature consisting the major operating equipment and involving usually a high cost per unit.

3. Accessory or secondary equipment Meters, gauges, hand-drills, time systems, hand trucks, slactiers, jacks, and pinion pulleys; office equipment, typewriters, accounting machines, furniture, etc.

4. Supplies Finished goods comprising:

(i) *Operating goods*: Lubricating grease and oil, graphite, grinding or polishing compound, welding wire coal,

(ii) *Maintenance:* Paint, nails, night bulbs, cleaning supplies, *Administrative goods*: Typewriters, ink, pencil, clips, etc.

5. **Fabricated or semi-finished materials** Steel bars, billets, wires; rods, steel sheets, blank stamping, grey cotton piece-goods, wood planks.
6. **Process materials** Dyestuffs, acids, waxes, gums, compositions, alloys and other products of chemical processes or combinations.
7. **Parts** Finished, or about to be assembled, needed for grinding, polishing, fitting and other finishing operation.
8. **Complementary equipments** Finished goods of one manufacturer purchased by another to be supplied with his product at the time of sale and for the purpose of increasing its utility or aiding in its operation, *e.g.*, jacks supplied with coal mining machines and dredges, clam-shell buckets supplied with dredges and careens, tools supplied with trucks and automobiles, tools supplied with milling and grinding machines.
9. **Receptacles and packages** Bottles, jars, cars, cartons, cases, drums, barrels and bags, wrappers, labels and stickers, etc.
10. **Services** Electric power, telephone and telegraph, insurance, banking, advertising, research, legal, medical and dental assistance, employment, credit transportation, warehousing and business consulting.

SOME COMMON BUYING MOTIVES

1. Freedom from fear and danger Fear is a negative but very powerful motive. The most basic instinct of a human being is self-preservation. A person can do almost anything to guarantee his safety. Fear is a very powerful and compelling force in human affairs interlinked with the buying motive. The marketing man must ascertain the possible fear of death, fear of loss and fear for the future. Fear can sell anything like hair-oil through fear of getting bald.

2. Economy Persons desire money to satisfy their other desires. A businessman wants money to make more profits on lower costs. Saving money is a universal desire. Customers spend money to get more money. Dealers who purchase goods to sell to the customers get more money and profit. The manufacturers make purchase of high priced heavy machinery to lower down their cost of production and thereby increase profits. A housewife will go round the shops to save money for other purchases. This is a motive to which everybody would respond.

3. Vanity Women spend much time, thought and money on their personal appearance like cosmetics, hair-do and new styles. Both men and women like to be admired. Hence, vanity is a powerful motive in the hands of the marketing man.

4. Appreciation Everybody desires to be appreciated and complimented and recognised as an important person. He wants to be in a position from where he can issue orders to others. Because of this human trait, it may be useful to follow indirect method in place of direct method that might prove offensive.

5. Fashion Everyone desires to imitate what others are doing. This is imitation motive. Closely linked with pride or desire for importance, every one is motivated by the desire to show oneself superior and to be in fashion with the elite. This motive can be well exploited by the marketer.

6. Possession The instinct of possession or a desire to call things as 'mine' leads persons to hoard and collect things. A miser takes delight in possessing money. Some persons collect postage stamps and old coins. Here the hoarding instinct is at work which can be used in selling even unnecessary things.

7. Sex or romance Fancy clothes, cosmetics, perfumes, etc. are in great demand on account of sex instinct or a desire to attract the opposite sex. Without sex, little interest will remain in styles for men and women. While women spend more on fancy clothes, hair-do and cosmetics to appeal to men, men also do their best to attract women. The sex motive is very powerful; it can sell almost anything. Therefore this instinct is very often used by marketing men.

8. Love of others This motive plays an important part when parents purchase all kinds of things for their children like toys, fancy garments and other presents. They go in for life insurance to make provision for future of the families. The insurance salesmen use this motive to include the prospect to protect his loved ones by purchasing an insurance policy. The young husband purchases all kinds of labour saving devices for his wife. A bachelor going to marry soon will purchase numerous domestic articles. This particular motive is at times described as that of "home building". It is also related to comfort and convenience motive.

9. Health or physical well-being Many people purchase health foods, vitamin tablets and patent medicines to maintain their health and physical well-being.

10. Comfort and convenience Most people like to be easy going and do not exert much. This motive may be well exploited in selling luxury items like motor cars, softest furniture, vacuum cleaners, washing machines, television sets, etc.

USING BUYING MOTIVES IN MARKETING

Human instincts make a person behave differently at different times. The motivation-research is meant to measure the changes of instincts of people. The marketer should plan to make full use of these motives. For the use of low priced, one may suggest approval and quality. If the marketing programme is to be effective and appropriate in terms of product features and advertising strategy, the appropriate motive must be crystallised.

Many people buy their daily requirements from a certain store out of patronage motive. The choice depends on factors such as location, variety of goods stocked, reputation of the store, attitude adopted by the salesmen, the services offered, the general appearance of the store, etc. Advertisement made by the store is to a large extent responsible for the image of the store. Social status plays an important role in the choice of the store and the type of clientele attracted by the store. Some people prefer shopping at glamorous stores while others select economical stores. Thus persons prefer to match with their own values and expectations of the store. The industrial buyer is more objective in purchases on the ground of measurable performance. Thus industrial quality customers are influenced in their patronage motives by factors like product service and price.

QUESTIONS FOR EXERCISE

1. Explain the role of needs, goals and self-image in motivation of consumer behaviour.
2. Distinguish between positive and negative motivation, rational and emotional motives.
3. Discuss the dynamic nature of motivation.
4. Explain different types of arousal of motives.
5. Describe types and systems of needs.
6. Explain and discuss hierarchy of needs.
7. Explain and classify buying motives of the consumer.
8. What are the barrier to recognise buying motives? Explain buying motives of industrial consumers.
9. Describe some common buying motives. How are they used in marketing?

33

PSYCHOLOGY OF ADVERTISEMENT AND SELLING

WHAT IS ADVERTISEMENT?

If you ask a person as to what is the medicine for headache, he will name Aspro even though he may have never used it, because he has heard the name of this patent medicine so many times that it spontaneously comes to the forefront of the mind as soon as headache is mentioned. Not many persons use Dalda in India but how many are there who do not know it? These days, whenever an educated person goes out to purchase cloth, he checks the mark of 'Sanforised' on it. All this is due to advertisement. Advertisement introduces things to persons. It points out to the special characteristics of commodities. In the words of Husband, "Advertisement may be defined as publicity which calls attention to the existence and merits of certain goods and services."[1]

Importance of Advertisement

One finds a lot of competition in the present day in economic field. The problem of selling is not solved by mere manufacturing. To illustrate, suppose a firm manufactures a particular type of soap. Now, unless the buyers come to know about the existence of this particular brand of soap, how can they buy it? Again, even the knowledge of its existence is not sufficient to boost its sale. They should know its peculiarities and qualities. But the problem does not end, here. Even when the buyer is told of the qualities of soap, it is not necessary that he may come to believe

---

1. Husband, R.W., *Applied Psychology,* Harper & Bros, New York.

them. And even if he believes it, still he may have no desire to buy it. This shows the importance of advertisement. These days, advertisement has become a science and even an art. In progressive countries, constant researches are being conducted in the field of advertisement. After a thing is advertised, the results of advertisement are checked. This shows the results of special types of advertisement on the buyers of particular things. Very interesting facts have been discovered by this research. For example, it has been found that advertisement through moving things, animals and human beings are more impressive than through motionless things and animals respectively. In fact, success in the sale of anything depends on success in its advertisement.

AIMS OF ADVERTISEMENT

The following are the main aims of advertisement:

1. Drawing attention The first and foremost aim of advertisement is to draw the attention of the persons towards a particular thing or service. In the cities, on big railway junctions and on busy squares, one finds the word USHA in red light, and at another place there is TATA in moving light. Bare names in capital words are written on very sizeable signboards. These advertisements do not describe the qualities of the objects they advertise. They only introduce these names to the public. Electric bulbs are used to draw attention. Big signboards draw more attention than smaller ones. Figures, colours, headings, form, light, etc., all the different items of advertisement aim at drawing the attention.

2. Creating interest Generally speaking, only that object draws attention which is interesting. Why do you find the pictures of film actresses in the advertisement of Lux toilet soap? Why are pictures of women displayed in posters advertising *bidis?* Have you ever seen the day-by-day of Rexona soap? What is the secret of the success of advertisement? The answer is that it lies in creating interest. The aim of displaying women pictures in the advertisements of things is to create interest in them. Most men take interest in beautiful women. A successful advertiser takes cognigance of the interest of the buyers because interest and attention are closely related.

3. Creating belief As has been pointed out earlier, mere knowledge of the existence of a thing or mere introduction with its qualities is not sufficient for its being sold. The main problem is to create belief among the buyers that it has these particular types of qualities. This can be done in a variety of ways. One way is to seek recommendations from eminent leaders, film actors and actresses, etc. Certificates from eminent physicians are helpful in the advertisement of medicines. Sometimes, the number of commodities sold is advertised to create faith in their quality, *e.g.*, 50,000 copies of such and such book have been sold.

4. Remembering Advertisement should influence memory because a person does not need a thing while he reads its advertisement. The advertisement should be able to recall its name and the name of the firm manufacturing it.

5. Creating a desire to buy In the end, the main purpose of the advertisement is to create a desire among persons to buy it. It is hence, that advertisers check the influence of advertisement on sales. The success of an advertisement is correlated to the success in sales. Though the advertisement is attractive and interesting, this does not constitute its aim. Its main aim is to boost the sales of a commodity. All else is mere means to achieve this end.

Psychological Bases of the Appeal of Advertisement

In the words of Blum, "The core of all advertising is suggestion".[1] Advertisement aims at suggesting buying of a particular thing; advertisement is a science of drawing attention. Some traits attract more attention than others. Much progress has been made in the art of advertisement. In order to understand the importance of attention as the psychological basis of advertisement, it shall be relevant to describe briefly the internal and external determinants of attention.

CONDITIONS OF ATTENTION

As a selective act of the mind, attention depends upon several conditions. These conditions may be of two types — external or objective and internal or subjective. External or objective conditions are related with the environment. In the environment or surroundings of the individual, there are several stimuli, but he does not attend to all of them at the same time, because some stimuli are stronger than others. The factors making these stimuli stronger than others are known as external determinants of attention. Besides, the external conditions, the mental conditions, culture and heredity also influence attention. Owing to these internal conditions some objects attract our attention more than others. These internal factors are internal determinants of attention. The methods of achieving attention are based upon these external and internal determinants of attention.

---

1. Blum, M.I., *Industrial Psychology and Its Social Foundations,* Harper & Bros., New York.

External Determinants of Attention

The following are the most important external determinants of attention:

1. Nature of stimulus Nature of stimulus means its type, *i.e.,* whether it is visual, gustatory, auditory, olfactory or tactual stimulus. It has been found by experiments that in comparison with other sensations, colour and sound attract more attention. Among the pictures, the pictures of human beings attract more attention than those of animals while among human beings, pictures of beautiful women attract more attention. Besides these, the coloured pictures attract more attention than colourless ones. All these factors are important in advertisement. In the auditory stimulus, the melodious voice attracts more attention than other voices.

2. Intensity of the stimulus The intensity of the stimulus is a helpful condition in attention. In comparison with the weak stimuli, the intense stimulus attracts more attention of the organism. High sound, excessive pressure and acute pain attract our attention. In the market, there is always some buzzing sound and yet the pedestrians hear the horn of the motor car, since the sound of the horn is louder than other sounds. But it is not always necessary that one should attend to the intensity of the stimulus. Some times while walking on the road, calling of our name attracts so much attention that we fail to hear even the loud sound of the motor horn. As a matter of fact, the attraction of the attention does not depend on any single factor, but on several factors interconnected with one another. Hence, it can be said that other things being the same, the more intense stimulus will attract more attention.

3. Size of the stimulus In the visual stimuli, the size of the stimulus is also a determinant of attention. As a general rule the bigger size attracts more attention, but a small advertisement on a very wide background also attracts attention. Thus the attraction of an object does not depend upon its size alone, but also on its background. To illustrate, a big black spot on a black face will not attract so much attention as a very small black spot on a white face.

4. Location of the stimulus The location or the stimulus also affects attention. In the visual stimuli, the most effective location is just in front of the eyes. The role of different pages in the newspaper or the magazine and the different places on the same page, is important advertisement. It has been found by experiments that advertisement given on the front page or on the upper half of any page attracts more attention.

5. Contrast of the stimulus The contrast of the stimulus is also an important determinant of attention, *e.g.,* the presence of a woman among men and that of a man among women definitely attracts more attention.

6. Change of the stimulus Attention cannot be concentrated for a long time on some particular object. Hence, the change of the stimulus also affects attention. Attention is sustained by change of the stimulus. The advertisers change their advertisements from time to time lest it may cease to be attractive.

7. Isolation of the stimulus A man sitting alone in some corner of the park, hotel or club attracts more attention than others. A student sitting alone at the far corner of the class is seen first. Thus, isolation is an important external determinant of attention. This fact is based upon the reason that the isolated individual is not mixed with other individuals and hence, seen separately in his own background. By experiments in advertisement, it has been found that only the fact of isolation attracts 30 per cent more attention. In the British journal of *Educational Psychology* of August 1951, D.E. Berlyne pointed out the following principles based upon latest experiments:

(a) In comparison with the unchanged stimulus, the stimulus changed in the near past has more possibility of attracting attention.
(b) The effect of the change goes on diminishing with the passage of time.
(c) Whenever stimuli are changed together and in which one is left unchanged, the effect on change is not noticeable.
(d) If change goes on in the stimuli, the process of attention is rather permanent and strong.

The modes of change also influence the process of attention. If there is a change absolutely, it attracts more attention. While studying one does not hear the sound of the clock or that of electric fan but if either suddenly stops, one cannot fail to attend to it. Man becomes used to regular changes and does not pay much attention to them. But if some irregular change or any sudden change occurs, it at once draws attention.

8. Duration of the stimulus As a general rule, the stimulus having more duration attracts more attention. Thus, duration of the stimulus is an important determinant of attention. But sometimes, the smallest flashing of a movement attracts more attention than the bigger stimuli, *e.g.*, a sudden flash of light for several seconds will attract more attention in a dark night than the continuous burning lamp.

9. Repetition of the stimulus Along with duration, repetition of the stimulus is also an important determinant of attention. It is a commonplace observation that when the teacher has to attract the attention of students towards a particular phenomenon, he repeats it several times. But sometimes, man ceases to attend to a phenomenon simply because it is repeated many times, *e.g.*, if a man says some things about himself, we take interest in it once or twice, but if we find that he always repeats the same thing, we cease to pay attention to it.

10. Movement in the stimulus In comparison with the static, the moving stimuli attract more attention. The position of a stimulus changes due to movements. An object lying in some corner of the room will not attract our attention, but even if there is some illusion of movement in it, we cannot help attending to it. The influence of movement in stimulus is widely used by the shopkeepers and businessmen, who advertise through moving electric lights.

Internal Determinants of Attention

The conditions of attention as described so far are the external determinants of attention. They can also be called external laws of attention. The presence of these conditions in the environment is helpful for attention. Besides these, internal conditions are also helpful in drawing attention. These conditions are related with motives. As a matter of fact, the influence of external conditions depends on these internal conditions to a very great extent. The hungry man will attend to the form and stimuli of the food. A man with full belly will not attend to food, however nice it might appear. In the advertisements, those demonstrating the naked organs of the woman have maximum power of attention. Those interested in cinema look to the advertisements of cinema at first sight. It is difficult to describe all the internal conditions helpful in attention. Hence, only the most important will be ennumerated here:

1. Interest Innate and acquired interests draw the individual's attention to particular objects. Doctors, engineers, professors, all attend to the objects of their own interest. Even among the professors, an object attracting the attention of a professor of Geology need not attract the attention of a processor of Philosophy as well. Thus, the innumerable differences in interests create innumerable determinants of attention in different men. The stimuli influencing innate tendencies attract more attention than those influencing acquired interest.

2. Basic drives The basic drives and impulses of the individual are also important in drawing its attention. The animal attends to particular stimulus when driven by the basic drives of hunger, thirst, sex, etc.; a normal man motivated by sex will naturally attend to the individuals of opposite sex. We all know it by experience that when hungry we may not attend to even a distasteful object, but while our belly is full, we may attend to even the most tasteful food. Among the motives, fear has got definite influence upon attention. All men who fear snake will attend to all things resembling the snakes. Like fear, curiosity also influences attention. We attend to even the smallest details of the object towards which we have curiosity.

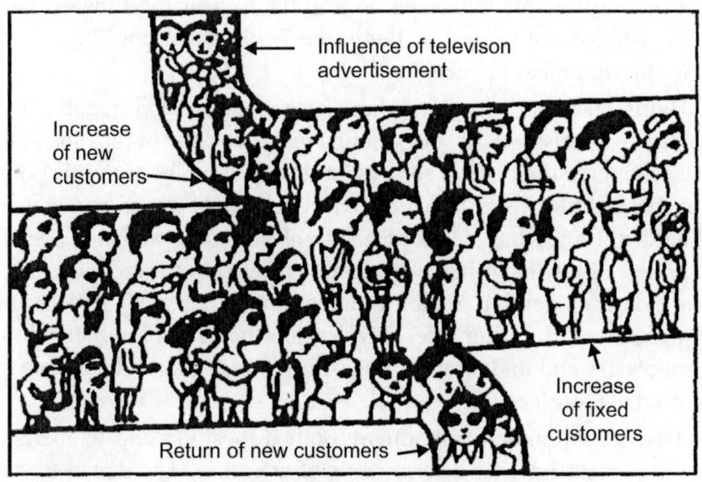

Fig. 33.1. Influence of Television on Advertisement.

Innate need also is very important in attention. The influence of sexual need in attention is very much exploited in advertisements. Normally, the sexual need in human beings can be easily evoked. Hunger, thirst, etc. are felt occasionally and the means to satisfy them are also readily available, but neither the sexual need is ever fully satisfied nor the means of satisfying it, are available to all persons all the time. Hence, most of the advertisements draw attention by stimulating the sexual need in human beings.

3. Mental set Mental set is one of the most important internal determinants of attention. Mental set means the tendency or bent of the whole mind. A man will attend to those objects towards which his mind is set. In the days of examinations, the mental set of the students is generally towards the examination and hence, even the smallest thing concerning the examination will attract their attention.

4. Aim Aim also influences attention. Every man has some immediate and some ultimate aims, *e.g.*, the immediate aim of the student is to pass the examination while the ultimate aim may be to get a job, to earn living or anything else. The man whose aim is not to pass the examination will not be concerned with textbooks or notes, etc., but one who has the aim to pass the examination will at once attend to those.

5. Meaning In comparison with meaningless things, meaningful things and talks attract more attention. A man will not attend to a thing which has no meaning for him. Men do not like to hear meaningless talk. If some persons are talking in Tamil, the Punjabi will not like to hear it since for him it has no meaning.

6. Habit Habit is also an important determinant of attention. If a man is habituated to rising early and winding his clock early in the morning, he must attend to the clock as soon as he gets up. It has been rightly pointed out that man learns as to which object he should attend and which he should not and thus develops habits of attending and not attending to things. Thus, habit has two aspects in relation to attention. On the one side men develop a habit of attending to necessary and desirable things and on the other side, they develop the habit of not attending to unnecessary and undesirable things. Both these kinds of habit help man in his daily routine.

7. Disposition and temperament Both disposition and temperament are important internal determinants of attention, *e.g.,* a man having a religious disposition and spiritual temperament will attend to religious matters, while another person having a sexual disposition and criminal temperament will attend to matters concerning sex or crimes, etc. William James has rightly pointed out that it is our tendency to take interest in particular things. Our innate disposition and mental development determine that which, among the crowd of sensations, should attract our attention.

8. Past experience Past experience also affects attention. If we know it by our past experience that a particular person is sincere to us, we shall pay attention to whatever he advises us. If we know by experience that he is not sincere to us, we shall not attend even to his most serious advice.

9. Emotion Emotion is also an important determinant of attention. It is a matter of everyday experience that we attend to even the smallest fault of a person whom we hate while we do not attend even to the greatest blunder of a person whom we love. A mother seldom finds faults with her child. The lovers find the whole world singing and dancing and immersed in romance.

10. Social motives Social motives are important determinants of attention. In advertisements, the human figures attract more attention than figures of animals and things. The reason is that man is guided by his social motives. News about altruism, bravery and saving others' life by putting oneself in danger, attract our attention because we praise these qualities. Men attend to things concerning their duties for social motives.

Besides the conditions described above, many other factors influence attention. Heredity, education and training have a wide influence on attention. The family, school, club, class and society of which an individual is a member, do have some influence on his attention. The physical condition, desire, purpose of the person concerned also affect his attention. Thus, all the factors influencing the personality of a man affect his attention as well. As a matter of fact, it is difficult to describe all direct and indirect determinants of attention. The description given here, however, includes the most important of such factors.

Advertisement and Memory

Memory has got much importance in the psychological basis of advertisement. The advertisement should be such that those who hear, read or see it may remember it. It is then alone that they will buy it when needed. The thing should be named such as also exhibits its function. This leads to the association of name with function, so that it is recalled whenever that particular function is needed. Examples of some such names are Nahan soap, Sina machine, Sulekha ink, etc. There is much difficulty in the advertisement of things which bear difficult names that cannot be remembered easily. Sometimes, the fact of the relation of advertisement with memory is misused. For example, when a particular trademark becomes famous, some unscrupulous persons give a similar name to their products. Names such as Sunlight and Lifebuoy followed after Sunlight and Lifebuoy soaps became well known.

Advertisement and Suggestion

As has been pointed out earlier, the main psychological basis of advertisement is suggestion. The meaning of suggestion is to motivate a person to do a particular kind of work. Some advertisements directly ask for the purchase of a particular thing. Recommendations of film actors and actresses are used as suggestion in some other advertisements. You must have seen recommendations of many beautiful film actresses for the skin care from Lux soap. Such advertisements involve prestige suggestion. Advertisers of vegetable oil often present certificates of its being harmless. Such advertisements suggest for the purchase of particular things.

Advertisement and Attitude

Attitude is also a very important psychological element in the basis of advertisement. It is a permanent organisation of motivational, emotional, perceptual and cognitive processes in a person towards objects surrounding him. Advertisement cannot be effective unless attitude is favourable. For example, in every free country, one finds pro-nation attitude among people. Hence, things can be advertised in the name of Swadeshi.

Elements of Effective Advertisement

While closing our discussion over the psychological basis of advertisement, it will be relevant to analyse different elements of its psychological appeal. In advertisement consists of illustration, colour, headline, text or copy, trademark or trade name and layout or arrangement of the advertisement. All these must have psychological appeal in order to make advertisement effective. Some important points in this connection will be pointed out here:

1. Illustrations Illustrations in an advertisement should be real and interesting. If they are only real, they will attract less attention. If they are only interesting, they will not motivate purchase.

2. Colour Colour plays an important role in advertisement, but its success depends on right choice of suitable colours. In different seasons, different colours are agreeable. Distinction of age and sex also have considerable bearing on this issue. As a general rule, while blue colour appeals to men, red appeals to women. Again, while dark colours are favoured by the young, the aged favour light colours. In summer, blue and green colours are more agreeable while in winter, red and black may be more useful for advertisement.

3. Headline Generally, every advertisement bears a headline. The headline has two aims — on the one hand, it creates interest in the advertisement and on the other hand, it motivates persons to buy a particular thing. Therefore, firstly, the headline should be such as can be easily remembered. Secondly, it should lead to the desire to read the entire text of the advertisement. Thirdly, it should be brief and attractive. Life Insurance Corporation of India have given many such advertisements.

4. Text of copy An advertisement contains a text or copy to give information regarding the object and its utility. This requires much precaution. Generally, indirect text is more appealing. Sometimes manufacturers of cloth, a rubber and paper advertise the story of cloth, rubber and paper respectively, This is interesting and also advertises the commodity indirectly. Text should be brief. It should tell the truth, create faith and the motive to purchase the things advertised.

5. Trademark or trade name Generally, every manufacturer has a certain trademark or trade name, *e.g.,* Tata, Bata, Lipton, Brook Bond, Kodak, etc. Gradually, these trademarks become popular and things are bought by trade name. Sometimes, however, a trademark becomes so much popular that; it no more represents a particular manufacturer but becomes a synonym for that particular thing. For example, the word Kodak is used for any camera. Some manufacturers only advertise their trade mark.

6. Layout In the end, the above, mentioned items in an advertisement should be organised in a proper layout. In a good layout, sufficient space is left bare. The illustration which has to be emphasised should be very clear. If an advertisement is on the whole page, it need not have any border. If it is less than a page, it may have border. The illustration, colour and background should be sufficiently matching. Generally, plain advertisements are better. If many things are huddled up together, the onlooker may not remember any of them.

While advertising, care should be taken to consider sex, age, class, education and economic level of the persons for whom the advertisement is prepared, for all these factors make difference in the interest, disposition, motivation and attention of the persons concerned. For example, persons belonging to lower and middle income group are more attracted to such advertisements as promise to give things in less expenses, whereas such advertisements will not appeal to rich persons because they do not pay so much attention to price as to quality and novelty of a thing. Arguments may be advanced in the text of the advertisements meant for educated buyers whereas they are useless in the case of uneducated persons. Advertisements for young men and women should be interesting and attractive. Women are more influenced by suggestion and less by reasoning. Thus the effectiveness of advertisement depends on the strength of its appeal to the particular class of persons who are supposed to buy that particular thing. Practical success of an advertisement depends upon the psychological insight of the advertiser.

THE PSYCHOLOGY OF SELLING

In the modern context, psychology plays a vital role in the sphere of buying and selling because it has been established that "buying and selling are based more on psychological than on economic factors". Both buying and selling are modes of behaviour and since all forms of behaviour obey certain rules, it is possible to discover the laws applicable in this case and to control buying and selling. Since he is a human being, the individual is influenced by psychological laws. Hence, if the seller knows what he should do to awaken a specific response is the buyer he can do his job much better. The situation of buying and selling consists of the buyer, the seller and the material to be sold. While it is desirable that the seller's behaviour should be psychologically tenable, it must be kept in mind that it is easy to sell goods which the buyer requires and demands. Therefore, it is better to manufacture goods which satisfy the buyer's demands and fulfil his requirements. Human beings have a variety of psychological and physical needs. Physical needs include hunger, thirst, the need to maintain an even body temperature, sleep, sex desire, etc. Among psychological needs are: ambition, sex instinct and other individual requirements, in addition to more social needs such as the desire to win social prestige or to attract the attention of others towards oneself. Nowadays the manufacturer turns his attention to these needs of his prospective customers and tries to make his products conform to the requirements of the customer. If he succeeds in this, he finds little, if any, difficulty in selling them.

VARIOUS STEPS IN SELLING

The manufacturer's task does not end with the manufacture of an article because the customer must be aware of a particular article that he needs and also of the place where he can procure it. In addition to this, conveying this information to the customer, will not suffice because numerous other similar or even identical products are marketed by many other manufacturers and are available in the market. The customer is attracted to one such product but not towards another. The answer to this lies in advertisement. Advertisement is the science of attracting the attention of the people since it informs the customer about the goods available and the distinctive qualities of each. This is the first stage in selling. In the second stage, the manufacturer aims at interesting the customer in his own product. If interest is lacking, the customer does not buy the product, but if it is present, he can at least be induced to inspect and examine it. Once interest is established, the desire to buy it follows. But the act of buying occurs only after the individual has examined the article. The confidence that the customer would get on first hand examination of the article is created by the manufacturer through advertisement, his own credit and through the gift of the gab, the ability to talk and to convince the customer. If the article is dependable, the customer decides to purchase it. The seller convinces him and removes his doubts, and finally the customer's decision to buy is translated into action. After the actual purchase, if the customer is satisfied with the performance of the article, he talks of it to other people and, if need be, returns to buy it a second time. This mental satisfaction is an essential step in the process of selling.

METHODS OF SALES DIALOGUE

The process of going from the first to the six steps outlined above, in the business of selling, is facilitated by psychological laws. People who pay heed to psychological laws and apply them in practice find it easier to sell their product. People who do not, face considerable difficulty in selling. In order to encourage the customer to move over these five steps, the seller has to talk to him. The method and the nature of this sales interview or sales talk changes with any change in the seller, the customer or the product being sold. For this reason, it is not possible to be a successful salesman merely by reading books. Nevertheless, it is possible to formulate a rudimentary pattern for said dialogues in most conditions. The work has been done very successfully recent years by psychologists. Laboratory experiments have been conduct to determine the validity of the various prevalent methods of sales dialogue. The more prevalent methods of sales dialogue include exhibition through use, verbal description, lengthy inducements to buy, brief inducements of a similar nature, serious lecturing or free and informal approach. A brief description of these methods now follow[1] :

1. Practical demonstration Most people have seen the salesman actually operating a new article in his shop in order to attract the customer. Most manufacturers try to arrange such practical and operational exhibitions of the products in shops, markets and exhibitions. When the customer sees the article in actual use, he is more easily satisfied about its utility and efficiency. But this method cannot be applied to the selling of all objects. For example, it is not possible to display objects of food, medicines, or objects concerned with feelings, in this way. Hence, for such commodities other methods are applied.

2. Verbal description The shopkeeper or the salesman uses the method of verbal description either when a practical demonstration is not possible or when it does not suit him to arrange such a demonstration. In

---

1. Blum, M.L, *Industrial Psychology and Its Social Foundations.*

this method, the salesman describes the article, its qualities and its utility in many ways so that the buyer may be convinced. It is desirable that the description should be psychological. And even if there is an element of deception in this description. It should be mentioned in such a way that the buyer does not suspect it.

3. Entreaty to buy after mentioning facts. In this method, the salesman starts by mentioning facts about the article he wants to sell and then requests, begs or entreats the customer to buy it. This entreaty to buy is made in many ways. Some people talk enthusiastically but seriously about the merits of the article in question. Some salesmen adopt a very rude manner while others assume a friendly manner to win the confidence of the customer. Such salesmen try to convince each customer, that they are concerned only with the customer's welfare and that their aim is not to earn money but to serve the customer by fulfilling his demands. They create the impression that their objective in selling is to provide satisfaction to the customer.

The advantages and disadvantages of each of the above selling methods can be understood by comparing them. One experienced salesman adopted each of these sales techniques so that they could be evaluated by forty students. The results obtained were entertaining. It was seen that the method of practical demonstration was better than verbal description. A factual description was found better than a simple entreaty or request to buy. It was felt that a friendly manner during the sales talk was better than the blunt or rude manner. But the enthusiastic and the very serious and grave descriptions were found to be equally effective.

PSYCHOLOGICAL FACTORS IN SALES AND PURCHASE

In the field of marketing, the psychological importance of motivation, research, analysis of concepts, development of the methods of introducing goods, improvement in questions, evaluation of verbal reactions, consumption, effective advertisement of indirect evidence, the evaluation of its effect, group information, etc., has been discovered. Besides, efforts have been made to discover, through research, the effect produced on consumers by particular forms of behaviour. Considerable data have been collected on this subject by circulating questionnaires through post. Although many researches involve the use of questionnaires it has been found that only those consumers care to reply to the questionnaire who are especially interested in a particular product. But in order to encourage the other consumers, some incentives can also be provided. Sometimes, the consumer's opinion has been obtained through interview in a personal meeting or over a telephone. In research of this kind, it is necessary to keep in mind the fact that many consumers do not provide valid information because every individual does not have a uniform capacity to evaluate things. Some people can arrive at a more objective evaluation than others. Then memory also plays an important part in this. Some people can recall facts heard a long time ago while the majority of people forget them rapidly. Generally, a thing seen can be remembered for a longer time than a thing heard. For this reason, in some cases practical demonstration proves more valuable than a verbal description. Suggestion plays an important part in selling and for that reason it is extensively used in marketing.

The power of suggestion works in the case of fashion also. Certain goods sell because they are fashionable. Sometimes fashion is artificially created, and it can be made so powerful that certain goods and articles come to imply status and become status symbols. In such a case, people are willing to pay a very high price for such things. The sex instinct is exploited frequently in advertisement campaigns. In advertising products to be used by men and women, the advertiser often displays nude and semi-nude figures of beautiful women. In addition to the sales talk of the salesmen, the commodity itself should be useful and attractive. If an article is to remain on the market for a long time, it should have some inherent utility but in order to attract attention the first time, it must also be attractive. For this reason, these days considerable attention is paid to the packing of commodities. The packing should be so attractive that the customer's attention should be diverted towards it, as soon as he enters the shop. He should want to pick it up and touch it. This end is achieved by making bottles of various attractive shapes and by making the containers more colourful. The labels and the words on the outside of boxes and bottles also play an important part in attracting the customer. As far as possible, the description should mention all the qualities of the product besides containing some suggestion for the customer which induces him to buy it. Nowadays the customer is induced to buy things because articles of daily use are offered to him in the form of free gifts along with the things he buys. Most of the successful manufacturers conduct research to find out ways and means of advertising their goods in such a way that they should be able to sell more than their competitors.

QUESTIONS FOR EXERCISE

1. What are the psychological factors working in advertisement? Explain.

2. Why do we advertise? Point out some important methods of advertisement and explain their psychological significance.
3. Pointing out the importance of advertisement in modern times, explain the factors affecting advertisement.
4. How far can psychology be an aid to effective advertising? Give some examples of effective advertising with reasons.
5. Discuss with suitable examples how various psychological principles and concepts are applied in advertising and selling?
6. Describe the methods of measuring the effectiveness of advertising and of the means used for the same.

BIBLIOGRAPHY

Anastasi, A. *Psychological Testing,* Macmillan.

Bell, J.E. *Projective Testing,* Longmans Green.

Bellak, L. *The T.A.T. and C.A.T. in Clinical Use,* New York: Grune and Stratton.

Bhatia, C.M. *Mental Testing and National Reconstruction,* Hind Kitabs.

Blum, M.L. *Industrial Psychology and its Social Foundations.* New York: Harper and Bros.

Blum and Balansky. *Counselling and Psychology,* Prentice Hall.

Ferguson, L.W. *Personality Measurement,* New York: McGraw Hill, Book Co.,

Gardner, B.B. *Human Relations in Industry,* Richard D. Irwin.

Gray, J.S. *Psychology Applied to Human Affairs,* McGraw Hill.

Ghiselli, E.E. and C.W. Brown. *Personnel and Industrial Psychology,* Tokyo.

Harrell, T.W. *Industrial Psychology,* Calcutta.

Heron, A.A. *Why Men Work,* Stanford University Press.

Humphreys, J.A. *Choosing Your Career,* Chicago: S.R.A. Better Living Booklets.

Jones, A.J. *Principles of Guidance,* McGraw Hill, 1951.

Link, N.C. *Employment Psychology.*

Maier, N.R.F. *Psychology in Industry,* Houghton Mifflin.

Moore, B.V. and Hartmann, G.W. *Readings in Industrial Psychology.*

Myers, C.S. *Industrial Psychology.*

Ministry of Education. *Workshop on Vocational Guidance,* Publication No. 83, India.

Ministry of Education. *Workshop on Vocational Guidance,* Publication No. 300, India.

Mundel, H.F. *Motion and Time Study,* Prentice Hall.

Mursell, J.L. *Psychological Testing,* Longmans Green.

Shafer and Shoben, *The Psychology of Adjustment,* Houghton Mifflin. Super. D.E. *Appraising Voc. Fitness,* Harper and Bros.

Smith, M. *Introduction to Industrial Psychology,* New York.

Tiffin, J. *Industrial Psychology,* Prentice Hall.

Vernon, H.M. *Industrial Fatigue and Efficiency,* Dutton.

Vernon, P.E. Recent Trends in Mental Measurement and Statistical Analysis. Published in *Studies in Education,* University of London Press.

Viteles, M.S. *Motivation and Morale in Industry,* Staples Press.

Viteles, M.S. *Industrial Psychology,* Norton.

OBJECTIVE QUESTIONS

1. When giving instruction a leader should keep in mind
    (a) that he does so to coordinate the efforts of others with his
    (b) that his authority and prestige are increased
    (c) that he should not disagree with others as far as possible
    (d) that he is helping others when giving instructions.
2. The only real test of leadership is
    (a) getting blind obedience from the workers
    (b) commanding respect and winning cooperation
    (c) satisfying those in higher positions
    (d) trying to satisfy every wish of the workers.
3. Union organisations are more concerned with the workers's feelings and attitudes than in management.

    True False Do not know
4. Many workers like changes in their job.

    True False Do not know
5. Creative thinking attains its highest level under autocratic leadership.

    True False Do not know
6. High turnover can at times led to low morale although the correlation is low between turnover and morale.

    True False Do not know
7. The relationship between and employee and his supervisor is not very important from the point of view of productivity.

    True False Do not know
8. The interviewer's job is to tell the interviewee about what he does not know.

    True False Do not know

9. Application Blank is the only method for selecting a person in industry.

   True False Do not know

10. Industry is least concerned with psychology.

    True False Do not know

11. A person who is not accepted by others will scarcely be able to accept himself.

    True False Do not know

12. An accurate standard is needed for judging a person's performance.

    True False Do not know

13. Positive incentives always accelerate the drive towards a goal directed activity.

    True False Do not know

14. Occupational status is related to job-satisfaction.

    True False Do not know

15. In Industry people respond to punishment than to praise.

    True False Do not know

16. Accidents do not happen to persons on the basis of equal liability.

    True False Do not know

17. Time studies have not been widely adopted in the United States.

    True False Do not know

18. Non-directive counselling is also known as client-centred counselling.

    True False Do not know

19. In mental abilities, men and women are very similar.

    True False Do not know

20. Job description is the heart of personal selection.

    True False Do not know

21. Mental functions are generally measured by mental tests.

    True False Do not know

22. The subject matter of Industrial Psychology is the scientific study of industrial relations.

    True False Do not know

23. Job-analysis is the method of obtaining the information that makes up a job.

    True False Do not know

24. The atmosphere at an interview should be cordial one.
True False Do not know
25. The lack of a sense of belongingness is felt by all new employees.
True False Do not know
26. A result of a good selection procedure is high production.
True False Do not know
27. Rapport is a very important factor in an interview and should be achieved right in the beginning.
True False Do not know
28. Job analysis is a characteristic procedure in industrial psychology in which nature of work and method for selection work is found out.
True False Do not know
29. The employment interview requires prior preparation.
True False Do not know
30. Good methods of selection reduce the problem of supervision.
True False Do not know
31. Job-analysis is most frequently done by
(a) observing the people at work
(b) having an interview with the employee
(c) reading the literature available on job-description
(d) none of the above
32. Job-description is the heart of
(a) job-satisfaction (b) occupational information
(c) job-evaluation (d) none of the above
33. Regression means behaviour that is
(a) childlike (b) mentally depressed
(c) feeble minded (d) diseased
34. There is a tendency for the bright people to have
(a) low clerical and mechanical aptitude
(b) high clerical and mechanical aptitude
(c) only literary ability
(d) artistic abilities
35. The strong-vocational interest blank is based on:
(a) responses of people from various professions and occupations
(b) initiative judgements

(c) intelligence test scores
(d) objectives assessment of the needs of a profession

36. An important reason for the follow-up of a new employee is
(a) to evaluate his feelings
(b) to evaluate the technique he uses
(c) to evaluate the hours of work he puts in
(d) to evaluate the selection techniques

37. The interviewer in an employment interview must be
(a) well placed in society (b) good looking
(c) well trained (d) highly intelligent

38. A condition in which there is diminished productivity, efficiency or ability to carry on work, because of previous expenditure of energy in doing work is
(a) boredom (b) fatigue
(c) tiredness (d) no interest

39. Hawthorne experiment is the famous study, which is often quoted in the books on
(a) experimental psychology (b) social psychology
(c) educational psychology (d) industrial psychology

40. In order to do a good job of selecting and placing workers an understanding of the functions involved in work is necessary. So it is necessary to know
(a) organisation (b) job description
(c) salaries of workers (d) job environment

41. An important role in the industrial production can be due to
(a) punishment (b) more work hours
(c) incentives (d) atmospheric conditions

42. Individual liability to meet with accidents or accident susceptibility is called accident
(a) circumstances (b) errors
(c) factors (d) proneness

43. Making workers feel responsible and personally worthy contributes to making work
(a) a part of living (b) a difficult task
(c) a pleasant past time (d) a boring business

44. Chronic complainer tend to be
    (a) the most intelligent among the employees
    (b) the muscular type
    (c) maladjusted individuals
    (d) the leas paid of the emplyees
45. Supervision in high producing section tends to be
    (a) self centred (b) production centred
    (c) employee centred
46. The success of an industry requires
    (a) a stress on discipline at all costs
    (b) a stress on cooperation above competition
    (c) a judicious mixture of competition and cooperation
    (d) a stress on competition above cooperation
47. The most basic and important principles in personnel selection and placement is selection and placement
    (a) in terms of least payment of wages
    (b) in terms of the specific requirement of the work to be done
    (c) in terms of attitudes of the worker
    (d) in terms of availability of workers
48. Use of Scientific methods in assessing employee attitudes and feelings is
    (a) superfluous there is personal contact
    (b) a substitute to personal contact
    (c) only a supplement to personal contact
    (d) an unnecessary show
49. Adequate motivation and morale in industry can be achieved only through arranging the industrial environment in such a way that
    (a) employee needs can be satisfied
    (b) no choice be given to employee
    (c) strict discipline can be kept
    (d) higher production is secured
50. One of the important things that should be found out as follow-up of the induction process is
    (a) the amount of sociaising
    (b) the degree of understanding of job responsibilities

(c) the hours of work
(d) the periods of rest

51. A result of systematic training is
(a) increase in a friendly attitude of
(b) increase in a positive attitude to job
(c) increase in a positive attitude to self

52. A direct advantage of definite system of rating is
(a) to know how much an employee can do
(b) to correct the employee
(c) to help and employee with great consistency of accuracy.
(d) to evaluate an employee with great consistency or accuracy.

53. The first step in personnel selection is
(a) interviews (b) application blanks
(c) trade tests (d) letters recommendation

54. Sometimes, fatigue is reflected in decreased.
(a) errors (b) output
(c) motivation (d) problems

55. If a worried employee comes to you, will help him best if you
(a) tell him to stop worrying
(b) let him solve his own worries. Don't do any thing
(c) discover the cause of the worry and help him to get rid
(d) help him to forget what is bothering him.

56. To develop a through understanding of people you should
(a) consider every worker alike
(b) study each worker individually
(c) discover the cause of the worry and help him to get rid of it
(d) allow for their weaknesses

57. If an employee's complaint is not unjustified,
(a) you will carefully explain all the facts to him
(b) tell him he is wrong and should be more careful next time
(c) tell other workers about his mistake
(d) transfer him to another department before he becomes a disturbing influence.

58. If an employee has been emotionally hurt, you should
(a) sympathize with him (b) help him to forget his hurt

(c) help him to stay away form people who have hurt him
(d) help him to get an insight into his hurt

59. Supervisors are taught to
(a) advise employees as to how they can overcome their tensions
(b) to talk employees about how others overcome the same tension
(c) to talk employees feelingly
(d) to express the feelings

60. You can expect to have others follow you
(a) if you are fond of your men
(b) if you have been a supervisor for a long time
(c) if your helpful in satisfying their wants
(d) if you fight up for your men, whether rightly or not.

61. A supervisor's relationship with other supervisors improves if he
(a) meets them often informally and gets like them
(b) cooperates with them fully in conducting the business
(c) is always charming to them
(d) overlooks their actions that conflict with his opinions.

62. If a change in the department is necessary the supervisor should
(a) make the change suddenly so that no one can object
(b) tell the workers about the change that has been planned and why
(c) make the change look an important one so that no one may object
(d) allow the time for the workers to get used to the change.

63. A supervisor should make
(a) all the decision after consulting labourers when necessary
(b) no decision, but leave it to the labourers
(c) important decision after consulting the labourers important
(d) decision after consulting the labourers important

64. The success as a superior as a superior chiefly depends on
(a) how people react to him
(b) the people he meets in his work
(c) how well he performs his duty
(d) how much he instructs the others.

65. What should be the supervisor's per responsibility in respect to company policy?
(a) to adhere to the policies he approves of
(b) to ignore the policies that are unpopular with the workers

(c) to explain all the policies and the reasons for them to the workers so that they all understand

(d) to carry out, somehow all the policies of the company.

66. Who can be most preferred for the vocational guidance?

(a) all the primary teachers

(b) all the secondary teachers

(c) all the educational institutions

(d) all the trained persons who have psychological and occupational informations

67. To measure the leadership traits the most useful method is

(a) application Blank (b) Interview Blank

(c) projective technique (d) group-discussion techniques

68. The concept to Time-motion study was introduced in industry by

(a) A.T. Poffenberger (b) Gilbreth

(c) Tittin (d) Taylor

69. An important cause of accidents realtes to

(a) human errors (b) lack of good ventilation

(c) noise in the factory (d) frustration in the worker

70. Motion study is to be conducted for a good advantage

(a) after time study

(b) before time study

(c) not connected with time study

(d) during time study

71. The most important things in an industry are

(a) increase of production

(b) selection of worker

(c) efficiency of a worker

(d) working conditions

Answers

1. (a)	2. (b)	3. True	4. True	5. False
6. True	7. False	8. False	9. False	10. False
11. True	12. False	13. True	14. True	15. False
16. False	17. True	18. True	19. True	20. True
21. True	22. True	23. True	24. True	25. True
26. True	27. True	28. True	29. True	30. True
31. (a)	32. (b)	33. (a)	34. (a)	35. (a)
36. (a)	37. (c)	38. (c)	39. (d)	40. (a)
41. (c)	42. (d)	43. (a)	44. (c)	45. (c)
46. (c)	47. (b)	48. (c)	49. (a)	50. (b)
51. (b)	52. (d)	53. (b)	54. (c)	55. (b)
56. (b)	57. (a)	58. (d)	59. (a)	60. (c)
61. (b)	62. (d)	63. (d)	64. (a)	65. (c)
66. (d)	67. (d)	68. (d)	69. (d)	70. (d)
71. (d)				